Exploring Raspberry Pi®

Interfacing to the Real World with

Embedded Linux®

Derek Molloy

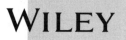

Exploring Raspberry Pi®

Published by
John Wiley & Sons, Inc.
10475 Crosspoint Boulevard
Indianapolis, IN 46256
www.wiley.com

Copyright © 2016 by John Wiley & Sons, Inc., Indianapolis, Indiana

Published simultaneously in Canada

ISBN: 978-1-119-18868-1
ISBN: 978-1-119-18870-4 (ebk)
ISBN: 978-1-119-18869-8 (ebk)

Manufactured in the United States of America

10 9 8 7 6 5 4 3 2

Library of Congress Control Number: 2016933853

To Sally, Daragh, Eoghan, Aidan, and Sarah

(still in order of age, not preference!)

About the Author

Dr. Derek Molloy is a senior lecturer in the School of Electronic Engineering, Faculty of Engineering and Computing, Dublin City University, Ireland. He lectures at undergraduate and postgraduate levels in object-oriented programming with embedded systems, digital and analog electronics, and the Internet of Things. His research contributions have largely been in the fields of computer and machine vision, 3D graphics/visualization, and e-Learning.

Derek produces a popular YouTube video series that has introduced millions of people to embedded Linux and digital electronics topics. In 2013, he launched a personal web/blog site that is visited by thousands of people every day, and which integrates his YouTube videos with support materials, source code, and user discussion. In 2015, he published a book on the BeagleBone platform, *Exploring BeagleBone: Tools and Techniques for Building with Embedded Linux*, which has been very well received.

Derek has received several awards for teaching and learning. He was the winner of the 2012 Irish Learning Technology Association (ILTA) national award for Innovation in Teaching and Learning. The award recognizes his learning-by-doing approach to undergraduate engineering education, which utilizes electronic kits and online video content. In 2012, as a result of fervent nominations from his students and peers, he was also awarded the Dublin City University President's Award for Excellence in Teaching and Learning.

You can learn more about Derek, his work, and his other publications at his personal website: www.derekmolloy.ie.

About the Technical Editor

Dr. Tom Betka came to the world of embedded systems development by way of a previous career in the aviation industry, and then as a physician practicing clinical medicine for well over a decade. During this time his love of computers and software development evolved toward the field of embedded systems, and his training in computer science culminated in a second undergraduate-level degree. After leaving clinical medicine, Dr. Betka began working in the world of software development and has served as a subject-matter expert in both medicine and embedded systems for various companies in the industry. His recent work has included projects at the NASA Kennedy Space Center and the Sierra Nevada Corporation. Tom's first love is the C-family of programming languages and using these languages to program 8-bit microcontrollers. As a Linux user for the past decade, he has also been working with the BeagleBone, BeagleBone Black, and Raspberry Pi devices for the last several years as well. His hobbies include advanced mathematics, aviation, high-powered model rocketry, and robotics. Also, he can often be found building prototype devices in his home-based machine shop. In a previous life, Tom worked for several years as a professional drummer—and was one of the first in his area to embrace the use of electronic percussion devices in live music scenarios.

Credits

Senior Acquisitions Editor
Aaron Black

Project Editor
Adaobi Obi Tulton

Technical Editor
Tom Betka

Production Editor
Barath Kumar Rajasekaran

Copy Editors
Keith Cline
Marylouise Wiack

Production Manager
Kathleen Wisor

**Manager of Content Development
and Assembly**
Mary Beth Wakefield

Marketing Manager
Carrie Sherrill

**Professional Technology &
Strategy Director**
Barry Pruett

Business Manager
Amy Knies

Executive Editor
Jody Lefevere

Project Coordinator, Cover
Brent Savage

Proofreader
Nancy Bell

Indexer
Nancy Guenther

Cover Designer
Wiley

Cover Image
Courtesy of Derek Molloy

Acknowledgments

Many thanks to everyone at Wiley Publishing once again for their outstanding work on this project: to Jim Minatel for encouraging me to take this book concept forward and for yet again supporting the realization of a book that engages in deeper learning; to Aaron Black and Jody Lefevere, for guiding the project forward, and for their support and help throughout the development of this book; to Jennifer Lynn, for keeping me on schedule and for always being available to answer my questions; to Adaobi Obi Tulton, the project editor, for driving this project to completion in the most efficient way possible—it was a real pleasure to work with such an accomplished and adept editor once again; to Keith Cline and Marylouise Wiack the copy editors, for translating this book into readable U.S. English; to Barath Kumar Rajasekaran, the production editor, and Nancy Bell, the proofreader, for bringing everything together to create a final, polished product.

Sincere thanks to Tom Betka, the technical editor, for the incredible amount of work and personal time he selflessly put into ensuring that the content in this book can be utilized seamlessly by readers. Following the publication of my book on the BeagleBone, Tom of this own volition provided valuable comment and feedback via the book website that further strengthened the title. I immediately thought of Tom when I took on this project, and I was delighted when he agreed to take on the role of technical editor. Tom is a scholar, a polymath, and indeed an inspiration, who was always available when I needed to talk through technical issues. This book has benefited hugely from his technical knowledge, world experience, and immense capabilities—I believe there could be no better technical editor for this topic!

Thanks to the thousands of people who take the time to comment on my YouTube videos, blog, and website articles. I truly appreciate all of the feedback, advice, and comments—it has really helped in the development of the topics in my books.

The School of Electronic Engineering, Dublin City University, is a great place to work, largely because of its esprit de corps, and its commitment to rigorous, innovative, and accessible engineering education. Thanks again to all of my colleagues in the School for supporting, encouraging, and tolerating me in the development of this book. Thanks in particular must go to Noel Murphy and Conor Brennan for sharing the workload of the School Executive with me while I was so absorbed in the writing of this book. Thanks again to (my brother) David Molloy for his expert software advice and support. Thanks to Jennifer Bruton for her meticulous and expert review of circuits, software, and content that is used in this book. Thanks also to Martin Collier, Pascal Landais, Michele Pringle, Robert Sadleir, Ronan Scaife, and John Whelan for their ongoing expertise, support, and advice.

The biggest Thank You must of course go to my own family. This book was written over six months, predominantly at night and on weekends. Thanks to my wife Sally and our children Daragh, Eoghan, Aidan, and Sarah for putting up with me (again) while I was writing this book. Thank you Mam, Dad, David, and Catriona for your continued lifelong inspiration, support, and encouragement. Finally, thank you to my extended family for graciously excusing my absence at family events for another six months—I definitely have no excuses now (unless I write another book!).

Contents at a Glance

Contents

Introduction

The core idea behind the Raspberry Pi (RPi) project was the development of a small and affordable computing platform that could be used to stimulate the interest of children in core information and communications technology (ICT) education. The rapid evolution of low-cost system on a chip (SoC) devices for mobile applications made it possible to widely deliver the affordable RPi platform in early 2012. The impact was immediate; by February 2015, more than five million Raspberry Pi boards were sold. Given the proliferation of smartphones, the idea of holding in one hand computers that are capable of performing billions of instructions per second is easy to take for granted, but the fact that you can modify the hardware and software of such small yet powerful devices and adapt them to suit your own needs and create your own inventions is nothing short of amazing. Even better, you can now purchase a Raspberry Pi Zero for as little as $5 (the price of a large cup of coffee)!

The Raspberry Pi boards on their own are too complex to be used by a general audience; it is the ability of the boards to run embedded Linux in particular that makes the resulting platform accessible, adaptable, and powerful. Together, Linux and embedded systems enable ease of development for devices that can meet future challenges in smart buildings, the Internet of Things (IoT), robotics, smart energy, smart cities, human-computer interaction (HCI), cyber-physical systems, 3D printing, advanced vehicular systems, and many, many more applications.

The integration of high-level Linux software and low-level electronics represents a paradigm shift in embedded systems development. It is revolutionary that you can build a low-level electronics circuit and then install a Linux web server, using only a few short commands, so that the circuit can be controlled over the Internet. You can easily use the Raspberry Pi as a general-purpose Linux computer, but it is vastly more challenging and interesting to get underneath the hood and fully interface it to electronic circuits of your own design—and that is where this book comes in!

This book should have widespread appeal for inventors, makers, students, entrepreneurs, hackers, artists, dreamers—in short, anybody who wants to bring the power of embedded Linux to their products, inventions, creations, or projects and truly understand the RPi platform in detail. This is not a recipe book; with few exceptions, everything demonstrated here is explained at a level that will enable you to design, build, and debug your own extensions of the concepts presented. Nor does this book include any grand design project for which you must purchase a prescribed set of components and peripherals to achieve a very specific outcome. Rather, this book is about providing you with enough background knowledge and "under-the-hood" technical details to enable and motivate your own explorations.

I strongly believe in learning by doing, so I present low-cost, widely available hardware examples so that you can follow along. Using these hands-on examples, I describe what each step means in detail, so that when you substitute your own hardware components, modules, and peripherals you will be able to adapt the content in this book to suit your needs. As for that grand design project, that is up to you and your imagination!

In late 2014, I released a well-received book on the BeagleBone platform titled *Exploring BeagleBone: Tools and Techniques for Building with Embedded Linux*. Given the focus of this book on embedded Linux and the emphasis on introducing the core principles, there are some similarities between the introductory content in that book and this book. However, this book has been written from first principles purely for the RPi platform, focusing on its strengths and addressing several of its weaknesses. I also took the opportunity to extend the coverage of the material to cover topics such as Linux kernel development, the Arduino as a service processor, Wi-Fi sensor nodes, XBee communication, MQTT messaging, the Internet of Things (IoT), platform as a service (PaaS), and much more. If you have a copy of *Exploring BeagleBone*, you should visit this book's website (www.exploringrpi.com) to compare the content in both books before you make your purchasing decision.

When writing this book, I had the following aims and objectives:

- To explain embedded Linux and its interaction with electronic circuits—taking you through the topics and challenges on the popular RPi platform.

- To provide in-depth information and instruction on the Linux, electronics, and programming skills that are required to master a pretty wide and comprehensive variety of topics in this domain.

- To create a collection of practical Hello World hardware and software examples on each and every topic in the book, from low-level interfacing, general-purpose input/outputs (GPIOs), buses, bus-attached analog-to-digital converters (ADCs), and universal asynchronous receiver/transmitters (UARTs) to high-level libraries such as OpenCV and the Qt Framework.

The book also covers more advanced topics such as low-level register manipulation and Linux loadable kernel module (LKM) development.

- To enhance and extend the interfacing capability of the RPi platform by developing frameworks for connecting it to circuits (e.g., SPI-based ADCs), to service processors (e.g., Arduino and NodeMCU), and to cloud-based IoT platforms and services.

- To ensure that each circuit and segment of code has a broad pedagogical reach and is specifically designed to work on the Raspberry Pi. Every single circuit and code example in this book was built and tested on the RPi platform (most on multiple board versions).

- To use the Hello World examples to build a library of code that you can use and adapt for your own Raspberry Pi projects.

- To make all the code available on GitHub in an easy-to-use form.

- To support this book with strong digital content, such as the videos on the DerekMolloyDCU YouTube channel, and the www.exploringrpi.com custom website that was developed specifically to support this book.

- To ensure that by the end of this book you have everything you need to imagine, create, and build *advanced* Raspberry Pi projects.

How This Book Is Structured

There is no doubt that some of the topics in this book are quite complex. After all, Raspberry Pi boards are complex devices! However, everything that you need to master them is present in this book within three major parts:

- Part I: Raspberry Pi Basics
- Part II: Interfacing, Controlling, and Communicating
- Part III: Advanced Interfacing and Interaction

In the first part of the book, I introduce the hardware and software of the RPi platforms in Chapters 1 and 2, and subsequently provide three primer chapters:

- Chapter 3, "Exploring Embedded Linux Systems"
- Chapter 4, "Interfacing Electronics"
- Chapter 5, "Programming on the Raspberry Pi"

If you are a Linux expert, electronics wizard, and/or software guru, feel free to skip these primers. However, for everyone else, I have put in place a concise but detailed set of materials to ensure that you gain all the knowledge required to effectively and safely interface to the Raspberry Pi. The remaining chapters refer to these primers often.

The second part of the book, Chapters 6–11, provides detailed information on interfacing to the Raspberry Pi GPIOs, buses (I²C, SPI), UART devices, and USB peripherals. You learn how to configure a cross-compilation environment so that you can build large-scale software applications for the Raspberry Pi. Part II also describes how to combine hardware and software to provide the Raspberry Pi with the capability to interact effectively with its physical environment. In addition, Chapter 11, "Real-Time Interfacing Using the Arduino," shows you how to use the Arduino as a slave processor with the Raspberry Pi, which helps you to overcome some of the real-time constraints of working with embedded Linux.

The third and final part of the book, Chapters 12–16, describes how to use the Raspberry Pi for advanced interfacing and interaction applications such as IoT; wireless communication and control, rich user interfaces; images, video, and audio; and Linux kernel programming. Along the way, you encounter many technologies, including TCP/IP, ThingSpeak, IBM Bluemix, MQTT, Cgicc, Power over Ethernet (PoE), Wi-Fi, NodeMCUs, Bluetooth, NFC/RFID, ZigBee, XBee, cron, Nginx, PHP, e-mail, IFTTT, GPS, VNC, GTK+, Qt, XML, JSON, multithreading, client/server programming, V4L2, video streaming, OpenCV, Boost, USB audio, Bluetooth A2DP, text-to-speech, LKMs, kobjects, and kthreads!

Conventions Used in This Book

This book is filled with source code examples and snippets that you can use to build your own applications. Code and commands are shown as follows:

```
This is what source code looks like.
```

When presenting work performed in a Linux terminal, it is often necessary to display both input and output in a single example. A bold type is used to distinguish the user input from the output. For example:

```
pi@erpi ~ $ ping www.raspberrypi.org
PING lb.raspberrypi.org (93.93.128.211) 56(84) bytes of data.
64 bytes from 93.93.128.211: icmp_seq=1 ttl=53 time=23.1 ms
64 bytes from 93.93.128.211: icmp_seq=2 ttl=53 time=22.6 ms
...
```

The $ prompt indicates that a regular Linux user is executing a command, and a # prompt indicates that a Linux superuser is executing a command. The ellipsis symbol (. . .) is used whenever code or output not vital to understanding a topic has been cut. Editing the output like this enables you to focus on only the most useful information. In addition, an arrow symbol on a line entry indicates that the command spans multiple lines in the book but should be entered on a single line. For example:

```
pi@erpi /tmp $ echo "this is a long command that spans two lines in the →
book but must be entered on a single line" >> test.txt
```

You are encouraged to repeat the steps in this book yourself, whereupon you will see the full output. In addition, the full source code for all examples is provided along with the book using a GitHub repository.

You'll also find some additional styles in the text. For example:

- New terms and important words appear in *italics* when introduced.
- Keyboard strokes appear like this: Ctrl+C.
- All URLs in the book refer to HTTP/S addresses and appear like this: www.exploringrpi.com.
- A URL shortening service is used to create aliases for long URLs that are presented in the book. These aliases have the form tiny.cc/erpi102 (e.g., link two in Chapter 1). Should the link address change after this book is published, the alias will be updated.

There are several features used in this book to identify when content is of particular importance or when additional information is available:

WARNING   This type of feature contains important information that can help you avoid damaging your Raspberry Pi board.

NOTE   This type of feature contains useful additional information, such as links to digital resources and useful tips, which can make it easier to understand the task at hand.

FEATURE TITLE

This type of feature goes into detail about the current topic or a related topic.

EXAMPLE: EXAMPLE TITLE

This type of feature typically provides an example use case, or an important task that you may need to refer to in the future.

What You'll Need

Ideally, you should have a Raspberry Pi board before you begin reading this book so that you can follow along with the numerous examples. If you have not already purchased a Raspberry Pi board, I recommend the Raspberry Pi 3 Model B. Although it is presently the most expensive board ($35–$40), it is also the most powerful. This board has a 64-bit quad-core processor, a wired network adapter, wireless Ethernet, and onboard Bluetooth; therefore, it has all the features required to run any example in this book. You can purchase a Raspberry

Pi board in the United States from online stores such as Adafruit Industries, Digi-Key, SparkFun, and Jameco Electronics. They are available internationally from stores such as Farnell, Radionics, and Watterott.

A full list of recommended and optional accessories for the Raspberry Pi is provided in Chapter 1. If you do not yet have a Raspberry Pi, you should read that chapter before purchasing one. In addition, the first page of each chapter contains a list of the electronics components and modules required if you want to follow along. The book website (www.exploringrpi.com) provides details about how to acquire these components.

I purposefully focus the examples in this book on the lowest-cost and most widely available components, breakout boards, and modules that I could identify that meet the needs of the examples. This should help you follow along with many examples, rather than focusing your budget on a small few. Indicative prices are listed throughout the book to give you a feel for the price of the components before you embark on a project. They are the actual prices for which I purchased the items on websites such as ebay.com, amazon.com, and aliexpress.com.

NOTE No products, vendors, or manufacturers listed in this book are the result of any type of placement deal. I have chosen and purchased all the products myself based on their price, functionality, and worldwide availability. Listed prices are indicative only and are subject to change. Please do your own research before purchasing any item that is listed in this book to ensure that it truly meets your needs.

Errata

We have worked really hard to ensure that this book is error free; however, it is always possible that some were overlooked. A full list of errata is available on each chapter's web page at the companion website (www.exploringrpi.com). If you find any errors in the text or in the source code examples, I would be grateful if you could please use the companion website to send them to me so that I can update the web page errata list and the source code examples in the code repository.

Digital Content and Source Code

The primary companion site for this book is www.exploringrpi.com. It is maintained by the book's author and contains videos, source code examples, and links to further reading. Each chapter has its own web page. In the unlikely event that the website is unavailable, you can find the code at www.wiley.com/go/exploringrpi.

I have provided all the source code through GitHub, which allows you to download the code to your Raspberry Pi with one command. You can also easily view the code online at `tiny.cc/erpi001`. Downloading the source code to your Raspberry Pi is as straightforward as typing the following at the Linux shell prompt:

```
pi@erpi ~ $ git clone https://github.com/derekmolloy/exploringrpi.git
```

If you have never used Git before, don't worry; it is explained in detail in Chapter 3.

Now, on with even more adventures!

Part
I

Raspberry Pi Basics

In This Part

Raspberry Pi Hardware

In this chapter, you are introduced to the Raspberry Pi (RPi) platform hardware. The chapter focuses on recently released Raspberry Pi models and describes the various subsystems and physical inputs/outputs of the boards. In addition, the chapter lists accessories that can prove helpful in developing your own Raspberry Pi–based projects. By the end of this chapter, you should have an appreciation of the power and complexity of this physical-computing platform. You should also be aware of the first steps to take to protect your board from physical damage.

Introduction to the Platform

The RPi models are capable general-purpose computing devices, and for that reason they have found favor for introducing learners to general computing and computer programming. The RPi models, some of which are illustrated in Figure 1-1, are also capable *physical computing* devices that can be used for embedded systems applications—and for Internet-attached embedded applications in particular.

Figure 1-1: Raspberry Pi platform board examples (to relative scale)

Some general characteristics of RPi devices include the following:

- They are low cost, available for as little as $5–$35.
- They are powerful computing devices. For example, the RPi 3 contains a 1.2 GHz ARM Cortex-A53 processor that can perform more than 700 million Whetstone instructions per second (MWIPS).[1]
- They are available in a range of models that are suitable for different applications (e.g., the larger-format RPi 3 for prototyping and the tiny-format RPi Zero or Compute Module for deployment).
- They support many standard interfaces for electronic devices.
- They use little power, running at between approximately 0.5 W (RPi Zero when idle) and approximately 5.5 W (RPi 3 under load).
- They are expandable through the use of Hardware Attached on Top (HAT) daughter boards and USB devices.
- They are supported by a huge community of innovators and enthusiasts, who generously give of their time to help the RPi Foundation with their educational mission.

The RPi platform can run the Linux operating system, which means that you can use many open source software libraries and applications directly

---

[1] www.roylongbottom.org.uk/Raspberry%20Pi%20Benchmarks.htm

with it. Open source software driver availability also enables you to interface devices such as USB cameras, keyboards, and Wi-Fi adapters with your project, without having to source proprietary alternatives. Therefore, you have access to comprehensive libraries of code that have been built by a talented open source community; however, it is important to remember that the code typically comes without any type of warranty or guarantee. If there are problems, you have to rely on the good nature of the community to resolve them. Of course, you could also fix the problems yourself and make the solutions publicly available.

One impressive feature of recent RPi models is that their functionality can be extended with daughter boards, called *HATs* (*Hardware Attached on Top*), that connect to the GPIO header (the 40-pin double-pin connector row on the boards in Figure 1-1). You can design your own HATs and attach them securely to your RPi using this header. In addition, many HATs are available for purchase that can be used to expand the functionality of your RPi platform. Some examples of these are described toward the end of this chapter.

Who Should Use the RPi

Anybody who wants to transform an engineering concept into a real interactive electronics project, prototype, or work of art should consider using the RPi. That said, integrating high-level software and low-level electronics is not an easy task. However, the difficulty involved in an implementation depends on the level of sophistication that the project demands. The RPi community is working hard to ensure that the platform is accessible by everyone who is interested in integrating it into their projects, whether they are students, makers, artists, or hobbyists. For example, the availability of the Scratch visual programming tool on the RPi (`tiny.cc/erpi101`) is an excellent way to engage children with both computer programming and the RPi.

For more advanced users with electronics or computing knowledge, the RPi platform enables additional development and customization to meet specific project needs. Again, such customization is not trivial: You may be an electronics expert, but high-level software programming and/or the Linux operating system might cause you difficulty. Or you may be a programming guru but you have never wired an LED! This book aims to cater to all types of users who are interested in interfacing with the RPi, providing each type of reader with enough Linux, electronics, and software exposure to ensure that you can be productive, regardless of your previous experience level.

When to Use the RPi

The RPi is perfectly placed for the integration of high-level software and low-level electronics in any type of project. Whether you are planning to build an automated home management system, robot, multimedia display, Internet of

Things (IoT) application, vending machine, or Internet-connected work of inter-active art, the RPi has the processing power to do whatever you can imagine of an embedded device.

The major advantage the RPi and other embedded Linux devices have over more traditional embedded systems, such as the Arduino, PIC, and AVR micro-controllers, is apparent when you leverage the Linux OS for your projects. For example, if you build a home automation system using the RPi and you then decide that you want to make certain information available on the Internet, you can simply install the Nginx web server. You could then use server-side scripting or your favorite programming language to interface with your home automa-tion system to capture and share information. Alternatively, your project might require secure remote shell access. In that case, you could install a Secure Shell (SSH) server simply by using the Linux command `sudo apt install sshd` (as covered in Chapter 2). This could potentially save you weeks of development work. In addition, you have the comfort of knowing that the same software is running securely on millions of machines around the world.

Linux also provides you with device driver support for many USB peripherals and adapters, making it possible for you to connect cameras, Wi-Fi adapters, and other low-cost consumer peripherals directly to your platform without the need for complex/expensive software driver development.

The RPi is also an excellent device for playing high-definition video. The RPi has this capability because its Broadcom BCM2835/6/7 processor was designed for multimedia applications, and it has a hardware implementation of H.264/MPG-4 and MPG-2/VC-1 (via additional license) decoders and encoders. The RPi has found popular use for multimedia applications such as running the Kodi home media center[2] (www.kodi.tv) for playing full-HD video content.

When to Not Use the RPi

The Linux OS was not designed for real-time or predictable processing. This would be problematic if, for example, you want to sample a sensor precisely every one millionth of a second. If the precise time arises to take a sample and the kernel is busy with a different task, it cannot be easily interrupted. Therefore, in its default state, the RPi is not an ideal platform for real-time systems applica-tions. Real-time versions of Linux are available, but they are currently targeted at very experienced Linux developers, and there are limits to their real-time capabilities. However, the RPi can be combined with real-time service processors, and the RPi can be used as the "central intelligence." You can interconnect such real-time microcontrollers to the RPi via electrical buses (e.g., I[2]C, UART) and

---

[2] Formerly known as XBMC.

Ethernet, and have the RPi act as the central processor for a distributed control system. This concept is described in Chapters 11, 12, and 13.

The RPi platform is not ideal for project developments that are likely to be commercialized. The Raspberry Pi platform largely utilizes open source software (there are some closed-source blobs used with the GPU), but it is not open source hardware. Schematics are available for RPi boards (e.g., `tiny.cc/erpi102`), but there is a lack of documentation on the hardware used. In addition, the Broadcom bootloader license[3] explicitly states that its redistribution in binary form is only permitted if it will "… *only be used for the purposes of developing for, running or using a Raspberry Pi device.*" It is unlikely that such a license would transfer to a product of your own design.

As described earlier in this chapter, the focus of the RPi Foundation is on education, and product commercialization is far from that brief. If you are planning to build an embedded Linux project that is to be commercialized, you should examine the BeagleBone platform, which is entirely open source and is supported by strong Texas Instruments documentation. In addition, you should of course purchase my book *Exploring BeagleBone* from the same Wiley mini-series.

RPi Documentation

This book integrates my experiences in developing with the RPi platform along with supporting background materials on embedded Linux, software development, and general electronics, to create an in-depth guide to building with this platform. However, it is simply not possible to cover everything in just one book, so I have avoided restating information that is listed in the key documents and websites described in this section. The first starting point for supporting documentation is the following website:

- **The Raspberry Pi Foundation website:** This provides the main support for the RPi platform, with blogs, software guides, community links, and downloads to support your development. See `www.raspberrypi.org`.

A huge amount of documentation is available on the RPi platform, but the most important documents for this book are as follows:

- **The Raspberry Pi Documentation:** This is the official documentation for the RPi that is written by the Raspberry Pi Foundation. It includes guides on getting started, configuration, guides to Linux distributions, and more. See `www.raspberrypi.org/documentation/`.

---

[3] `github.com/raspberrypi/firmware/blob/master/boot/LICENCE.broadcom`

- **Broadcom BCM2835 ARM Peripherals Datasheet:** This is the core document that describes the processor on most RPi models (except the RPi 2/3). It is 200 pages long and provides a technical description of the functionality and capabilities of the processor on the RPi. See `tiny.cc/erpi103`. There is also an important errata document at `tiny.cc/erpi104`.

- **The BCM2836 Document:** This document describes features of the processor on the RPi 2, and related features on the RPi 3. It should be read in association with the previous Broadcom document for the BCM2835. See `tiny.cc/erpi105`.

Key websites are also available to support your learning on this platform, with combinations of tutorials, discussion forums, sample code libraries, Linux distributions, and project ideas to stimulate your creative side. Here is a selection of important websites:

- **The website for this book:** `www.exploringrpi.com`
- **My personal blog site:** `www.derekmolloy.ie`
- **The eLinux.org website:** `www.elinux.org`

Getting started with the RPi platform software is described in Chapter 2. The remainder of this chapter discusses the RPi hardware platform, explaining the functionality that is available, summarizing the technical specifications, and providing some examples of the types of peripherals and HATs that you might like to connect to the RPi.

The RPi Hardware

At their heart, the RPi boards use the Broadcom BCM2835, BCM2836, and BCM2837 system on a chip (SoC). Several different RPi models are currently available, and the content in this book is perfectly applicable to all of them. However, the book focuses on more recent versions of the RPi that have a 40-pin GPIO header (for example, the RPi A+, B+, 2, 3, and Zero). If you have yet to purchase an RPi model, it is recommended that you purchase the RPi 3. It supports wired and wireless networking, and has a multicore processor, which means that it supports the superset of all the concepts described in this book. The RPi A+ and Zero do not have a wired network interface, and the RPi B+ does not have a multicore processor, but the majority of examples in this book also work perfectly well with them. If you are to use the RPi A+ or RPi Zero, it is recommended that you skip forward to the beginning of Chapter 13 so that you can read about configuring a USB wireless network adapter.

Raspberry Pi Versions

Figure 1-2 provides a summary feature comparison of the different RPi models that are presently available. Here is a quick summary of this table:

- If you need an RPi for general-purpose computing, consider the RPi 3. The 1 GB of memory and 1.2 GHz quad-core processor provide the best performance out of all the boards.

- For applications that interface electronics circuits to the Internet on a wired network, consider the RPi 3, RPi 2, or RPi B+, with cost being the deciding factor.

- If you need a small-footprint device with wireless connectivity, consider the RPi Zero. The RPi A+ could be used to develop the initial prototype.

- If you want to design your own PCB that uses the RPi (or multiple RPi boards), investigate the Compute module.

Model	RPi 3	RPi 2	RPi B+	RPi A+	RPi Zero	RPi B	Compute
Characteristics	performance/Wi-Fi Bluetooth/Ethernet	performance/Ethernet	Ethernet	price	price/size	original	integration/eMMC
Price	$35	$35	$25	$20	$5+	$25	$40 ($30 volume)
Processor*	BCM2837 quad core Linux ARMv7	BCM2836 quad core Linux ARMv7	BCM2835 Linux ARMv6	BCM2835 Linux ARMv6	BCM2835 Linux ARMv6	BCM2835 Linux ARMv6	BCM2835 Linux ARMv6
Speed	1.2 GHz	900 MHz	700 MHz	700 MHz	1 GHz	700 MHz	700 MHz
Memory	1 GB	1 GB	512 MB	256 MB	512 MB	512 MB	512 MB
Typical power	2.5 W (up to 6.5 W)	2.5 W (up to 4.1 W)	1 W (up to 1.5 W)	1 W (up to 1.5 W)	1 W (up to 1.5 W)	1 W (up to 1.5 W)	1 W (up to 1.5 W)
USB Ports	4	4	4	1	1 OTG	2	via header
Ethernet	10/100 Mbps, Wi-Fi, and Bluetooth	10/100 Mbps	10/100 Mbps	none	none	10/100 Mbps	none
Storage	micro-SD	micro-SD	micro-SD	micro-SD	micro-SD	SD	4 GB eMMC
Video	HDMI composite	HDMI composite	HDMI composite	HDMI composite	mini-HDMI composite	HDMI RCA video	HDMI via edge TV DAC via edge
Audio	HDMI digital audio and analog stereo via a 3.5 mm jack (where available)						via edge connector
GPU	Dual Core VideoCore IV Multimedia Co-Processor at 250 MHz (24 GFLOPS)						
Camera (CSI)	yes	yes	yes	yes	no	yes	CSI x 2 via edge
Display (DSI)	yes	yes	yes	yes	no	yes	DSI x 2 via edge
GPIO header	40 pins	40 pins	40 pins	40 pins	40 pins	26 pins	48 pins via edge
Usage	General-purpose computing and networking. High-performance interfacing. Video streaming	General-purpose computing. High-performance interfacing. Video streaming	General-purpose computing. Internet-connected host. Video streaming	Low-cost general-purpose computing. Standalone electronics interfacing applications	Low-cost small-profile standalone electronics interfacing projects	General-purpose legacy applications. Internet-connected host	Suitable for plugging into user-created PCBs using a DDR2 SODIMM connector. Open-source breakout board available

Details in this table were gleaned from articles and documents from the RPi Foundation website (www.raspberrypi.org).

* The BCM2835 is an ARM1176JZF-S (ARM11 processor architecture) that has full entitlement to an ARMv6 software architecture. The BCM2836 is a quad-core ARM Cortex-A7 processor that has a NEON Data Engine and full entitlement to an ARMv7 software architecture. The BCM2837 is a 64-bit ARMv8 quad-core ARM Cortex-A53 processor that has a NEON Data Engine and full entitlement to an ARMv7 software architecture.

Figure 1-2: A summary comparison of commonly available RPi models

The Raspberry Pi Hardware

Figure 1-3 and Figure 1-4 detail the core systems of typical RPi models. Figure 1-3(a) illustrates the RPi Zero, and the key systems identified by the callouts 1–11 are described in more detail in Figure 1-4. Similarly, Figure 1-3(b) illustrates the equivalent key systems on the RPi 3, and the callouts 1–15 are described in more detail in Figure 1-4.

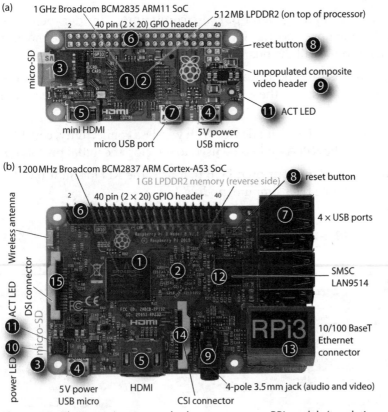

Figure 1-3: The inputs/outputs and subsystems on two RPi models (to relative scale): (a) The RPi Zero; and (b) The RPi 3

Figure 1-4 details the various inputs and outputs that are available on the GPIO header. On recent RPi models (A+, B+, 2, 3, and Zero), there are 40 pins in total on this header (2 × 20); however, not all are available for general-purpose input/outputs (GPIOs). Several of the connections have a fixed configuration:

■ 8 pins are connected to ground.

- 4 pins are allocated to voltage supplies: 3.3 V (up to 50 mA) and to 5 V (up to 300 mA).

- 2 pins are reserved for HATs (discussed later in this chapter) but they can be re-tasked (see Chapter 8).

The remaining 26 connectors are available to be multiplexed to many different functions, several of which are listed in Figure 1-4 (under the GPIOs heading). The function of each of these input/output types is described in detail in Chapter 6 and Chapter 8.

	Function	Physical	Details
❶	Processor	BCM283x (CPU)	The RPi boards use the Broadcom BCM2835/BCM2836/BCM2837 processor. The different boards use slightly different processors that run between 700 MHz and 1.2 GHz and are based on ARMv6, ARMv7, ARMv11, and ARMv8 A53 processor cores.
		Graphics Engine (GPU)	Broadcom VideoCore® IV 3D graphics subsystem with a OpenGL ES 1.1 and 2.0 driver.
❷	Memory	256 MB to 1 GB DDR	The amount of system memory affects performance and the use of the RPi as a general-purpose computing device. Memory is shared between the CPU and GPU.
❸	Storage	micro-SD card	The RPi boards all boot from a micro-SD or SD card, with the exception of the Compute module. It has an on-board eMMC, which is effectively an SD card on a chip. The RPi 3 uses a friction-fit slot, rather than a click-in/click-out slot.
❹	Power	micro-USB connector	A 5 V supply is required that should ideally deliver a current of at least 1.1 A and ideally 2.5 A for the RPi 3. There is over-current protection on this input. Be careful not to confuse the USB hub and USB power inputs on the RPi Zero.
❺	Video Out	HDMI or mini-HDMI connector	Used to connect the RPi boards to a monitor or television. The RPi models support 14 output resolutions, including full-HD (1920 x 1080) and 1920 x 1200.
❻	GPIOs	40 pin (or 26 pin) GPIO header	40 pins that are multiplexed to provide access to the features listed on the following table rows. Not all functionality is available at the same time. These inputs and outputs are described in detail in Chapter 6 and Chapter 8.
		26 x GPIOs	General purpose inputs outputs that are used for reading or writing binary data. The maximum number of GPIOs is 26 on the 40 pin RPi models. All GPIOs are 3.3V tolerant. Using buses and other interfaces reduces the number of available GPIOs.
		2 x I²C bus	I²C is a digital bus that allows you to connect several modules to each of the two-wire buses at the same time. One of these two buses is reserved for HAT support.
		SPI bus	Serial peripheral interface (SPI) provides a synchronous serial data link over short distances. It uses a master/slave configuration and requires 4 wires for communication. The RPi SPI bus has Linux support for two slave select lines.
		UART	Used for serial communication between two devices. The RPi typically (except the RPi 3) has one UART device that is allocated by default to providing a serial console connection.
		PWM	Pulse width modulation (PWM) outputs allow you to send a type of analog output that can be used to control devices (e.g., motors). There is at least one hardware PWM output on all RPi boards, and two on more recent boards.
		GPCLK	General purpose clocks (GPCLK) allow you to establish accurate timing signals.
❼	USB Hub	USB Connectors	There is an internal USB hub on RPi models with varying numbers of inputs. For example, the RPi 2/3 has five internal USB ports – one is connected to the Ethernet port and the other four are available for external connection.
❽	Reset	Unpopulated RUN	Can be used as a reset button for the RPi. This topic is described later in Chapter 1.
❾	Audio and Video	4-pole 3.5 mm jack	This provides composite video and stereo audio on more recent boards.
❿	Power LED	PWR LED	Indicates that the board is powered (not on the RPi Zero).
⓫	Activity LED	ACT LED	Indicates that there is activity on the board (i.e., it flashes on SD card activity).
⓬	USB-to-Ethernet	SMSC LAN9514	This IC provides a USB 2.0 hub and a 10/100 Ethernet Controller. The RPi boards connect to the Internet via USB rather than an on-board Ethernet controller within the SoC.
⓭	Network	RJ-45 Ethernet	10/100 Mbps Ethernet via a RJ45 connector. The RPi 3 has on-board Wi-Fi and Bluetooth using a BCM43438. See the Optional Accessories section in this chapter.
⓮	Camera	CSI	The RPi has a Mobile Industry Processor Interface (MIPI) Camera Serial Interface (CSI), a 15-pin connector that can be connected to a special-purpose camera. See Chapter 15.
⓯	Display	DSI	The Display Serial Interface (DSI) is an interface that is typically used by mobile phone vendors to interface to a screen display. There are few displays available that support this interface – one example is the 7" Raspberry Pi Touchscreen (800 x 480 display).

Figure 1-4: Table of general RPi subsystems and connectors

A RESET BUTTON FOR THE RASPBERRY Pi

The RPi does not have a power or a reset button, which means that if a system lock-up occurs you must unplug and replug the micro-USB power supply. This task can be awkward and can lead to physical damage of the RPi. (On older models, a common issue is that a large 220 μF capacitor is often used for physical leverage when unplugging the USB power input and it tends to fall off!) A low-cost leaded PC power/reset switch, such as that in Figure 1-5(a), can be used to provide a solution. A two-pin male header can be soldered to the unpopulated RUN header on RPi models, as illustrated in Figure 1-5(b), and the switch attached as in Figure 1-5(c). One advantage of the leaded switch is that it can be attached to the outside of a case that contains the RPi.

Figure 1-5: A power/reset button for the RPi: (a) A PC power/reset button; (b) A two-pin male header that is soldered to the board; and (c) Attachment of the PC power/reset button

Should you attach such a button to the RPi, it should not be used to routinely reset the RPi; rather, software commands should be issued, as described in Chapter 2.

Raspberry Pi Accessories

The RPi has minimal external requirements to use the board, typically as follows:

- A USB 2.0 cable (usually a micro-USB plug to USB-A plug) that is used to connect the RPi to a power supply, such as a desktop computer or USB mains supply (e.g., a cell phone charger)

- A micro-SD card that is used to contain the operating system, which is used to boot the board

- A CAT 5 network patch cable to connect your RPi to the network using its RJ-45 10/100 Ethernet connector

The RPi can be connected to a display using a HDMI cable (a mini-HDMI cable for the RPi Zero), but most of the examples in this book assume that the RPi is used in *headless mode*—that is, not connected directly to a display; rather, the RPi is used as a networked device that interfaces to electronic circuits, USB modules, and wireless sensors.

Important Accessories

The following accessories are important for purchase along with your RPi board.

External 5 V Power Supply (for Powering the RPi)

The RPi is best powered using a micro-USB cable that is connected to a good-quality 5 V power supply (±5%) that is rated to deliver a current of at least 1.1 A (1,100 mA) for older boards, and 2.5 A (2,500 mA) for the RPi 3. RPi boards typically require 500 mA–700 mA, but some USB peripherals (e.g., Wi-Fi adapters and webcams) have significant power requirements. The micro-USB input on the RPi boards has a Polyfuse, which limits current input to approximately 1,100 mA (with 700 mA hold current; see Chapter 4) on most RPi models, and 2,500 mA on the RPi 3. You can connect a USB power supply that is capable of supplying current of greater than 2,500 mA, but do not connect one that supplies voltage outside the range 4.75 V–5.25 V (i.e., 5 V ± 5%).

If you are having stability problems such as random reboots, random crashes, or keyboard problems, the power supply is the likely culprit. The power supply may not be able to deliver adequate current or it (or the connecting USB cable) may be of a poor quality and operating outside of tolerance. For example, some poor-quality "generic" 5 V power supplies may be advertised by vendors as suitable for a 1 A current supply (possibly referring to a short-circuit current limit), but their output voltage level may drop to unacceptable levels as the current drawn increases. Should you suspect such a problem, you should measure the voltage level on the RPi. On newer models, you use PP1 or PP2 and GND (or any of the metal shielded components), as illustrated in Figure 1-6(a). On older models use TP1 and TP2.

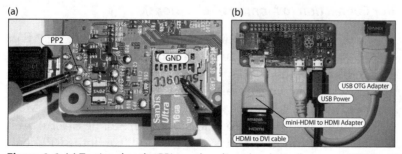

Figure 1-6: (a) Testing that the RPi supply voltage level is in the range 4.75 V to 5.25 V (i.e., 5 V ± 5%); (b) The RPi Zero and its associated connectors

Micro-SD Card (for Booting an Operating System)

Purchase a genuine, branded micro-SD card of at least 8 GB capacity. You may also require a micro-SD-to-SD adapter so that it can be used in your computer's card reader. Older RPi boards (e.g., A, B) require full-size SD cards, and such an adapter can be used with them. Many micro-SD cards are bundled with an adapter, which is a cheaper option than purchasing them separately.

The micro-SD card should be of Class 10 or greater, because the faster read/write speed will save you time in writing images in particular. Ideally, you should use an 8 GB to 32 GB micro-SD card with wear-leveling functionality because it will extend the lifespan of the card, particularly if you format but do not consume the full capacity. Larger micro-SD cards also work, but they may be cost prohibitive. (Alternative approaches to increasing the storage capacity of the RPi using USB storage devices are shortly discussed.)

Ethernet Cable (for Network Connection)

The RPi B/B+/2/3 can be connected to the Internet using a wired network connection. The RPi A/A+/Zero can be connected to the Internet using a USB wireless adapter. If you are connecting an RPi to your wired network, don't forget to purchase a CAT 5 network patch cable to connect your RPi to the network using its RJ-45 10/100 Ethernet connector. If you plan to use more than one RPi simultaneously, you could invest in a low-cost four-port switch, which can be placed close to your desktop computer.

Recommended Accessories

The following accessories are recommended for purchase along with your RPi board. If you are planning to carry out development work with the RPi, you should probably have all of them.

HDMI Cable (for Connection to Monitors/Televisions)

The RPi can be easily connected to a monitor or television that has a HDMI or DVI connector. The majority of RPi models have a full-size HDMI connector. However, the RPi Zero has a mini-HDMI socket (HDMI-C), so be careful to match that to your monitor/television type (usually HDMI-A or DVI-D). The cable that you are likely to need for the RPi Zero is an HDMI-Mini-C plug to HDMI-A male plug. A 1.8 M (6 ft.) cable should cost no more than $10. Be careful with your purchase; an HDMI-D (micro-HDMI) connector will *not* fit the RPi Zero.

Alternatively, you can purchase a low-cost ($3) mini-HDMI (HDMI-C) plug to regular HDMI (HDMI-A) socket adapter or mini-HDMI (HDMI-C) plug to DVI-D socket adapter cable. These enable you to use regular-size HDMI-A or to connect to DVI-D devices, respectively (see Figure 1-6(b)).

RPi ZERO USB ON-THE-GO (OTG)

The RPi Zero uses USB On-The-Go (OTG) to connect to USB peripherals. USB OTG is often used for devices that switch between the roles of USB client and host. For example, USB OTG connectors are often used to allow cell phones or tablet computers to connect to external USB storage devices. The USB OTG connector allows the RPi host to connect to a slave device such as a Wi-Fi or Bluetooth adapter, as illustrated in Figure 1-6(b).

USB to Serial UART TTL 3.3 V (for Finding Problems)

The USB-to-TTL UART serial cable, as illustrated in Figure 1-7(a), is one accessory that proves really useful when there are problems with the Linux installation on your board. It can provide you with a console interface to the RPi without the need for connection to an external display and keyboard.

Ensure that you purchase the *3.3 V level* version and ideally purchase a version with 0.1" female headers pre-attached. This cable contains a chipset and requires that you install drivers on your desktop computer, creating a new COM port. The FTDI TTL-232R-3V3 cable works well and provides a very stable connection (~$20). See `tiny.cc/erpi106` for the datasheet and the VCP link to the software drivers for this adapter cable.

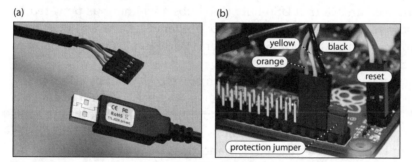

Figure 1-7: (a) The USB-to-TTL 3.3 V serial cable and, (b) its connection to the RPi

The cable connects to the serial UART on the RPi, which is available via the GPIO header. With the RPi powered using a regular USB 5 V supply, connect the cable to the RPi in the following way (as illustrated in Figure 1-7(b)):

- The black ground (GND) wire to Pin 6 on the GPIO header, which is the RPi GND pin
- The yellow receive (RXD) wire to Pin 8 (GPIO14) on the GPIO header, which is the UART transmit pin (TXD0)
- The orange transmit (TXD) wire to Pin 10 (GPIO15) on the GPIO header, which is the UART receive pin (RXD0)

Note that the 40-pin GPIO header is described in detail in Chapter 6. The exact use of this cable is described in Chapters 2, 3, and 8.

This cable is also used to test the UART connection on the RPi in Chapter 8 and to program the Arduino Pro devices in Chapter 11.

> **WARNING**   The RPi is 3.3 V tolerant but makes a 5 V supply available on the GPIO header pins 2 and 4. The easiest way to destroy the RPi is to accidentally connect these pins to a circuit that requires 3.3 V logic levels, or to accidentally short these pins with other pins on the GPIO header. To help prevent accidental contact, you can bridge these pins with an insulated jumper connector, as illustrated in Figure 1-7(b). The plastic cover insulates the pins from contact and prevents you from mistakenly connecting a 5 V supply to your circuit.

Optional Accessories

The following sections describe optional accessories that you may need, depending on the applications that you are developing.

USB Hub (to Connect to Many USB Devices)

Most RPi models have a built-in USB hub that allows several devices to be connected to the RPi simultaneously. If you plan to connect many devices to the RPi, you will need an external USB hub. USB hubs are either bus powered or externally powered. Externally powered hubs are more expensive; however, if you are using several power-hungry adapters (Wi-Fi in particular), you may need a powered hub.

One issue that you have to be aware of with powered USB hubs is that many are back feeding. *Back feeding* (*back powering*) is where a USB hub connected to the RPi hub (not the micro-USB power) supplies power back into the RPi through the RPi hub. It can cause difficulties if you have two separate power supplies competing to power the RPi. In addition, there is no protection on the RPi hub to prevent excessive current from being drawn.

This is not an issue on more-recent RPi models (e.g., the RPi 2/3) because circuitry is present to prevent back powering. However, it can also be useful to use a single power supply for your project. The easy way to do this is to attach a cable from the powered USB hub to the RPi micro-USB power input.

Micro-HDMI to VGA adapters (for VGA Video and Sound)

Several low-cost HDMI-to-VGA adapters are for sale for converting the HDMI output to a VGA output. As well as providing for VGA video output, many of these connectors provide a separate 3.5 mm audio line out, which can be used if you want to play audio using your RPi. There are also USB audio adapters available that can provide high-quality playback and recording functionality. These adapters and their usage is described in Chapter 15. Many RPi models also make composite video and stereo audio available via a four-pole 3.5 mm connector. A standard 3.5 mm four-pole headphone jack (with microphone) can be used for this task. The tip of the jack is connected to the left audio channel, followed by the right audio channel, ground connection, and then the video channel.

Wi-Fi Adapters (for Wireless Networking)

The RPi 3 has on-board Wi-Fi, but this capability can also be added to other RPi models using the many different Wi-Fi adapters that are available, such as those in Figure 1-8(a); however, not all adapters will work on the RPi. The Linux distribution and the chipset inside the adapter will determine the likelihood of success. Wi-Fi configuration and applications are discussed in detail in Chapter 13, which tests a range of different low-cost adapters that are widely available. Be aware that manufacturers can change chipsets within the same product and that buying an adapter from the list in Chapter 13 does not guarantee that it will work. You are more likely to succeed if you can confirm the chipset in the adapter you are planning to purchase and evaluate that against the list. You can use a small low-cost USB current meter, such as the one illustrated in Figure 1-8(c) ($3), which enables you to gain some insight into the power utilization of the RPi and the impact of connecting a Wi-Fi adapter.

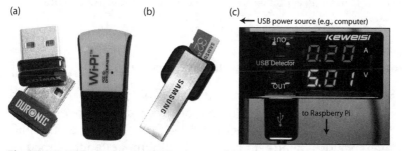

Figure 1-8: USB adapters: (a) Wi-Fi adapters; (b) Memory card reader/writer; and (c) A low-cost USB current and voltage monitor

USB Storage Devices (for Additional Storage)

USB flash drives, USB hard disks, and USB SD card reader/writers can be attached to the RPi for additional storage. The device can be prepared with a Linux file system and mounted under the RPi file system (see Chapter 3). One such device that is particularly useful is a USB card reader/writer, as illustrated in Figure 1-8(b). These devices have similar prices to USB flash drives, and they support "hot swapping" of the micro-SD card. In addition, they prove particularly useful if you need to mount the root file system of one RPi on another RPi for file interchange or to correct a configuration error on the card that is preventing the other RPi from booting (see Chapter 3). In addition, such a device can be utilized on a desktop machine to write a new Linux image to a micro-SD card.

USB Webcam (for Capturing Images and Streaming Video)

Attaching an RPi camera, as illustrated in Figure 1-9(a) and Figure 1-9(b), or a USB webcam, as illustrated in Figure 1-9(c), can be a low-cost way to integrate image and video capture into your RPi projects. In addition, utilizing Linux libraries such as Video 4 Linux and Open Source Computer Vision (OpenCV) enables you to build "seeing" applications. This topic is discussed in detail in Chapter 15.

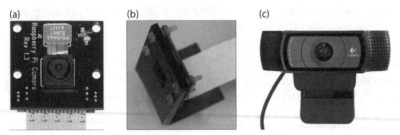

Figure 1-9: (a) RPi NoIR Camera, (b) RPi Camera bracket, and (c) Logitech C920 USB webcam

USB Keyboard and Mouse (for General-Purpose Computing)

It is possible to connect a USB keyboard and mouse to the RPi or to use a 2.4 GHz wireless keyboard and mouse combination. Very small wireless handheld combinations are available, such as the Rii 174 Mini, Rii i10, and ESYNiC mini, all of which include a handheld keyboard with integrated touchpad. A USB Bluetooth adapter is also useful for connecting peripherals to the RPi. A similar Bluetooth keyboard/touchpad is utilized in Chapter 14.

Cases (for Protecting the RPi)

Many different cases are available for protecting your RPi, including the one illustrated in Figure 1-10(a) ($6). Cases are useful for protecting the RPi from accidental short circuits (e.g., placing the RPi on a metal surface), but they do have an impact on the temperature that the RPi operates at (see Chapter 12). Try to ensure that you purchase a case with adequate ventilation, but avoid noisy active-ventilation solutions or ridiculous water-cooled solutions!

HATs

HATs (Hardware Attached on Top) are daughter boards that can be attached to the GPIO expansion header on the RPi. Add-on boards were available for the 26-pin GPIO header on older RPi models, but the RPi had no formal mechanism for identifying which daughter board was attached. HATs were introduced in conjunction with the release of the RPi B+. Some pins on the expanded 40-pin GPIO header (ID_SD and ID_SC) of newer RPi models are utilized to automatically identify which HAT is attached to the RPi. This allows the Linux OS to automatically configure pins on the GPIO header and to load drivers that make working with the HATs very easy.

Figure 1-10(b) illustrates the RPi Sense HAT ($35). It contains an: 8×8 LED matrix display, accelerometer, gyroscope, magnetometer, air pressure sensor, temperature sensor, humidity sensor, and a small joystick. Figure 1-10(d) illustrates a low-cost blank prototyping HAT that can be used to design your own HAT, which includes space on the bottom right for a surface-mounted EEPROM that can be used to identify the HAT to the RPi.

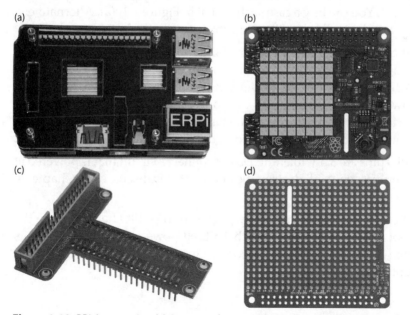

Figure 1-10: RPi Accessories: (a) An example case; (b) The Sense HAT; (c) The T-Cobbler board; and (d) A prototyping HAT

An alternative to designing your own HAT is to use the T-Cobbler board as illustrated in Figure 1-10(c) to break out the RPi GPIO header to a breadboard using a 40-pin ribbon cable, which is available with the T-Cobbler. This sits neatly into a prototyping breadboard (see Chapter 4), providing clear pin labels for all of the RPi GPIO pins.

How to Destroy Your RPi!

RPi boards are complex and delicate devices that are very easily damaged if you do not show due care. If you are moving up from boards like the Arduino to the RPi platform, you have to be especially careful when connecting circuits that you built for that platform to the RPi. Unlike the Arduino Uno, the microprocessor on the RPi cannot be replaced. If you damage the microprocessor SoC, you will have to buy a new board!

Here are some things that you should *never* do:

- Do not shut the RPi down by pulling out the USB power supply. You should shut down the board correctly using a software shutdown procedure (see Chapter 2).

- Do not place a powered RPi on metal surfaces (e.g., aluminum-finish computers) or on worktops with stray/cut-off wire segments, resistors, etc. If you short the pins underneath the GPIO header, you can easily destroy your board. You can buy a case such as that in Figure 1-10(a). Alternatively, you can attach small self-adhesive rubber feet to the bottom of the RPi.

- Do not connect circuits that source/sink other than very low currents from/to the GPIO header. The maximum current that you can source or sink from many of these header pins is approximately 2 mA to 3 mA. The power rail and ground pins can source and sink larger currents. For comparison, some Arduino models allow currents of 40 mA on each input/output. This issue is covered in detail in Chapter 4 and Chapter 6.

- The GPIO pins are 3.3 V tolerant. Do not connect a circuit that is powered at 5 V; otherwise, you will destroy the board. This is discussed in Chapter 4, Chapter 6, and Chapter 8.

- Do not connect circuits that apply power to the GPIO header while the RPi is not powered on. Make sure that all self-powered interfacing circuits are gated by the 3.3 V supply line or using optocouplers. This is covered in Chapter 6.

You should *always* do the following:

■ Carefully check the pin numbers that you are using. There are 40 pins on the GPIO header, and it is very easy to plug into header connector 21 instead of 19. The T-Cobbler board in Figure 1-10(c) is very useful for interconnecting the RPi to a breadboard, and it is highly recommended for prototyping work.

Summary

After completing this chapter, you should be able to do the following:

■ Describe the capability of the Raspberry Pi (RPi) and its suitability for different project types.

■ Describe the major hardware systems and subsystems on the RPi boards.

■ Identify important accessories that you can buy to enhance the capability of your RPi.

■ Have an appreciation of the power and complexity of the RPi as a physical computing platform.

■ Be aware of the first steps to take in protecting your board from physical damage.

Support

The key sources of additional support documentation are listed earlier in this chapter. If you are having difficulty with the RPi platform and the issues are not described in the documentation, visit the Raspberry Pi Community Forums at www.raspberrypi.org/forums/. Please remember that the people on these forums are community members who volunteer their time to respond to questions.

# CHAPTER 2

Raspberry Pi Software

In this chapter, you are introduced to the Linux operating system and software tools that can be used with the Raspberry Pi (RPi). This chapter aims to ensure that you can connect to your board over a network or serial connection and control it using basic Linux commands. RPi-specific configuration tools are examined for customizing and for updating the software on your board. By the end of this chapter, you should be able to control an onboard system LED having followed a step-by-step guide that demonstrates how you can use Linux shell commands in a Linux terminal window. The chapter finishes with a discussion on how to shut down or reset the board safely and correctly.

Equipment Required for This Chapter:

- Raspberry Pi board (ideally RPi 3, RPi 2, or RPi B+)
- USB power cable and power supply
- Micro-SD card (8 GB or greater; ideally class 10+)
- Network infrastructure and cabling, serial cable, or Wi-Fi adapter

Further details on this chapter are available at
www.exploringrpi.com/chapter2/.

Linux on the Raspberry Pi

A *Linux distribution* is a publicly available version of Linux that is packaged with a set of software programs and tools. There are many different Linux distributions, which are typically focused on different applications. For example, high-end server owners might install Red Hat Enterprise, Debian, or OpenSUSE; desktop users might install Ubuntu, Debian, Fedora, or Linux Mint. At the core of all distributions is a common Linux kernel, which was conceived and created by Linus Torvalds in 1991.

In deciding which Linux distribution to use for your embedded system platform, it would be sensible to choose one for which the following apply:

- The distribution is stable and well supported.
- There is a good package manager.
- The distribution is lean and suited to a low storage footprint.
- There is good community support for your particular device.
- There is device driver support for any desired peripherals.

Linux Distributions for the RPi

At their heart, the many different distributions of Linux for embedded system platforms all use the mainline Linux kernel, but each distribution contains different tools and configurations that result in quite different user experiences. The main open source Linux distributions used by the community on the RPi board include Raspbian, Ubuntu, OpenELEC, and Arch Linux.

Raspbian is a version of Debian that is released specifically for the RPi. *Debian* (contraction of *Debbie* and *Ian*) is a community-driven Linux distribution that has an emphasis on open source development. No commercial organization is involved in the development of Debian. Raspbian extends Debian with RPi-specific tools and software packages (e.g., Java, Mathematica, Scratch). Presently, three different versions of Raspbian are available for download from the Raspberry Pi website:

- **Raspbian Jessie:** An image based on Debian Jessie (Debian version 8.x) that has full desktop support. (Image size: approximately 1.3 GB compressed, 4 GB extracted)
- **Raspbian Jessie Lite:** A minimal image that is based on Debian Jessie. It has limited desktop support, but this can be added easily at a later stage. (Image size: approximately 375 MB compressed, 1.4 GB extracted)
- **Raspbian Wheezy:** An older image based on Debian Wheezy (Debian version 7.x) that is available for compatibility with some software packages. You should choose the Jessie image if possible, particularly if you are planning to cross-compile applications.

NOTE Raspbian (Jessie) is used for the practical steps in this book and it is strongly recommended as the distribution of choice. In addition, Debian is used throughout this book as the distribution for the Linux desktop computer because it provides excellent support for cross-platform development through Debian Cross-Toolchains (www.debian.org).

Ubuntu is closely related to Debian. In fact, it is described on the Ubuntu website (www.ubuntu.com) as follows: "Debian is the rock upon which Ubuntu is built." Ubuntu is one of the most popular desktop Linux distributions, mainly because of its focus on making Linux more accessible to new users. It is easy to install, has excellent desktop driver support, and there are binary distributions available for the RPi. The core strength of the Ubuntu distribution is its desktop user experience. If you are using the RPi as a general-purpose computing device (see Chapter 14), you may find that this distribution best suits your needs.

OpenELEC (www.openelec.tv) has a particular focus on multimedia applications and on Kodi (www.kodi.tv) in particular. If you want to use the RPi as a home media center, this distribution may provide the best performance. OpenElec distributions typically use a read-only file system (e.g., squashfs) for performance and reliability. However, such optimizations make prototyping and development work difficult.

Arch Linux (www.archlinuxarm.org) is a lightweight and flexible Linux distribution that aims to "keep it simple," targeting competent Linux users in particular by giving them complete control and responsibility over the system configuration. Prebuilt versions of the Arch Linux distribution are available for the RPi. However, compared to the other distributions, it currently has less support for new Linux users with the RPi platform.

The RPi Foundation developed a Linux installer for new users called *NOOBS*, which contains Raspbian but provides ease of download and installation of other Linux distributions. Many RPi hardware bundles include an SD card that contains NOOBS. However if you have chosen to download and install a Raspbian image, you should download the image directly using the instructions in the next section.

Non-Linux solutions, such as Windows 10 IoT Core and RISC OS, have started to emerge for the RPi. These are interesting and welcome developments. However, they currently have limited device support and quite specific programming requirements when compared to Linux. Because this book focuses on Linux-based solutions, such distributions are best avoided if you want to follow along.

Create a Linux SD Card Image for the RPi

The easiest way to set up an SD card so that it can be used to boot the RPi is to download a Linux distribution image file (.IMG file in a compressed .zip wrapper) from www.raspberrypi.org/downloads and write it to an SD card using an image writer utility. The following image writer tools make this process straightforward.

> **WARNING**   When you write a Linux distribution image file to an SD card, all previous content on the card is lost. Double-check that you are writing the downloaded image to the correct device when using the following tools.

- **Windows:** Use Win32DiskImager (available from `tiny.cc/erpi202`). Insert the SD card *before* you start the application—double-check that you chose the correct drive for your SD card.

- **Mac OS and Linux:** Use the `dd` disk cloning tool (carefully). First identify the device. It should appear as `/dev/mmcblkXp1` or `/dev/sddX` under Linux, or `/dev/rdiskX` under Mac OS, where X is a number. You must be certain that X refers to the SD card to which you want to write the image—for example, check that the available capacity of the device (e.g., use `cat /proc/partitions`) matches the SD card capacity. Then using a terminal window use the `dd` command with root privileges, where `if` is the input file name and `of` is the output device name (a block size `bs` of 1M should work fine):

```
molloyd@desktop:~$ sudo dd bs=1M if=RPi_image_file.img of=/dev/XXX
```

> **NOTE**   The Win32DiskImager and `dd` command create a partition on the SD card that is just big enough for the operating system, regardless of the card's capacity. That issue is addressed later in this chapter.

Transfer the SD card to the RPi, attach the network cable, and insert the 5 V micro-USB power supply. You can further attach a USB keyboard, USB mouse, and HDMI monitor to the RPi to use it as a general-purpose computing device (see Chapter 14), but for electronics interfacing projects the RPi is typically used as a standalone embedded device that communicates via a network. Therefore, the next steps are to connect the RPi to a network and to communicate with it using the network.

Connecting to a Network

There are two main ways to connect to and communicate with the RPi over the network: using *regular Ethernet* or using an *Ethernet crossover cable*. Connecting to the RPi over a network can be a stumbling block for beginners. It is usually straightforward if you are working at home with control of your own network. However, complex networks, such as those in universities, can have multiple subnets for wired and wireless communication. In such complex networks, routing restrictions may make it difficult, if not impossible, to connect to the RPi over regular Ethernet. Both methods are suitable for connecting your RPi to Windows, Macintosh, and Linux desktop machines.

Regular Ethernet

By "regular" Ethernet, I mean connecting the RPi to a network in the same way that you would connect your desktop computer using a wired connection. For the home user and power user, regular Ethernet is probably the best solution for networking and connecting to the RPi. Table 2-1 lists the advantages and disadvantages of using this type of connection. The main issue is the complexity of the network. (If you understand your network configuration and have access to the router settings, this is by far the best configuration.) If your network router is distant from your desktop computer, you could purchase a small network switch ($10–$20) or a wireless access point with integrated multiport router ($25–$35). The latter option is useful for wireless RPi applications involving the use of the RPi 3/Zero/A+ boards and for extending your wireless network's range.

> **NOTE** This discussion is also relevant to wireless networking. If you must use a wireless connection like the RPi Zero, read the section titled "Wi-Fi Communications" at the beginning of Chapter 13 and return to this point. To modify the configuration files for a Wi-Fi adapter, you can use the USB-to-TTL cable (described in the next section). Alternatively, you could mount the micro-SD card for the target RPi under a desktop Linux OS (or a second RPi) and modify the configuration files directly.

Table 2-1: Regular RPi Ethernet Advantages and Disadvantages

ADVANTAGES	DISADVANTAGES
You have full control over IP address settings and dynamic/static IP settings.	You might need administrative control or knowledge of the network infrastructure.
You can connect and interconnect many RPi boards to a single network (including wireless devices).	The RPi needs a source of power, which can be a mains-powered adapter or Power over Ethernet (PoE)(see Chapter 12).
The RPi can connect to the Internet without a desktop computer being powered on.	The setup is more complex for beginners if the network structure is complex.

The first challenge with this configuration is finding your RPi on the network. By default, the RPi is configured to request a *Dynamic Host Configuration Protocol* (DHCP) IP address. In a home network environment, this service is usually provided by a DHCP server that is running on the integrated modem-firewall-router-LAN (or some similar configuration) that connects the home to an Internet service provider (ISP).

DHCP servers issue IP addresses dynamically from a pool of addresses for a fixed time interval, called the *lease time*, which is specified in your DHCP configuration. When this lease expires, your RPi is allocated a different IP address the next time it connects to your network. This change can be frustrating, as you may have to search for your RPi on the network again. (Chapter 13 describes how to set the IP address of your RPi to be *static*, so that it is fixed at the same address each time the board connects.)

You can use any of the following methods to identify the RPi's dynamic IP address:

- **With a web browser:** Use a web browser to access your home router (often address 192.168.1.1, 192.168.0.1, or 10.0.0.1). Log in and look under a menu such as Status for the DHCP Table. You should see an entry that details the allocated IP address, the physical MAC address, and the lease time remaining for a device with hostname raspberrypi. My hostname is erpi, for example:

```
DHCP IP Assignment Table
IP Address      MAC Address Client    Host Name    Leased Time
192.168.1.116   B8-27-EB-F3-0E-C6     erpi         12:39:56
```

- **With a port-scanning tool:** Use a tool like *nmap* under Linux or the *Zenmap* GUI version, available for Windows (see tiny.cc/erpi203). Issue the command nmap -T4 -F 192.168.1.* to scan for devices on a subnet. You are searching for an entry that has an open port 22 for SSH. It should identify itself with the Raspberry Pi Foundation (see Figure 2-1(a)) as a result of the range of MAC addresses allocated to the Foundation. You can then ping test the network connection (see Figure 2-1(b)).

(a)   (b)

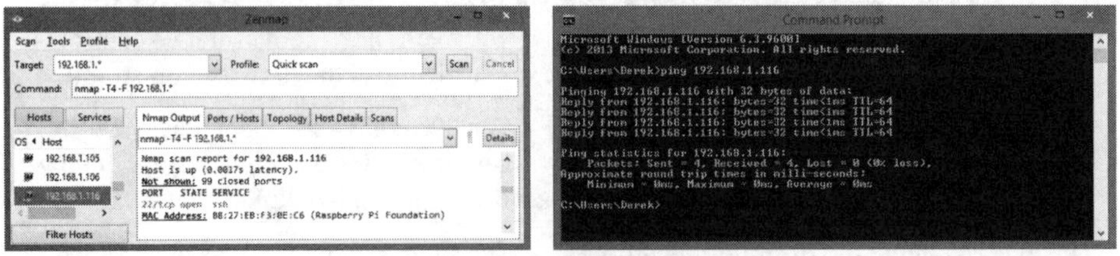

Figure 2-1: (a) Zenmap scan of the network to locate the RPi; (b) A ping test from the desktop machine

- **With zero-configuration networking (Zeroconf):** Zeroconf is a set of tools for hostname resolution, automatic address assignment, and service discovery. By default the RPi Raspbian distribution uses an avahi service to support Zeroconf on your network, which makes the hostname visible. For example, my board's hostname is erpi. It is therefore possible to connect to the RPi by using the string erpi.local:

```
pi@erpi:~$ systemctl status avahi-daemon
● avahi-daemon.service - Avahi mDNS/DNS-SD Stack
    Loaded: loaded (/lib/systemd/system/avahi-daemon.service; enabled)
    Active: active (running) since Thu 2015-12-17 21:53:46 GMT; 8h ago
  Main PID: 385 (avahi-daemon)
    Status: "avahi-daemon 0.6.31 starting up."
    CGroup: /system.slice/avahi-daemon.service
            ├─385 avahi-daemon: running [erpi.local]
            └─419 avahi-daemon: chroot helper
```

NOTE Windows machines do not support Zeroconf by default. You can install the Bonjour Print Services for Windows (or alternatively iTunes) using the link `tiny.cc/ erpi204`. If this is successful, you should be able to perform a ping test (by default the name is raspberrypi.local):

```
C:\Users\Derek> ping erpi.local
Pinging erpi.local [fe80::9005:94c0:109e:9ecd%6] with 32 bytes of data:
Reply from fe80::9005:94c0:109e:9ecd%6: time=1ms ...
```

■ **With a USB-to-TTL serial connection:** A final option is to use a USB-to-TTL serial connection to connect to the RPi and type `ifconfig` to find the IP address. The address is the "inet addr" associated with the `eth0` adapter.

Ethernet Crossover Cable

An Ethernet crossover cable is a cable that has been modified to enable two Ethernet devices to be connected directly without the need for an Ethernet switch. It can be purchased as a cable or as a plug-in adapter. Table 2-2 describes the advantages and disadvantages of this connection type.

Table 2-2: Crossover Cable Network Advantages and Disadvantages

ADVANTAGES	DISADVANTAGES
When you do not have access to network infrastructure hardware, you can still connect to the RPi.	If your desktop machine has only one network adapter, you will lose access to the Internet. It is best used with a device that has multiple adapters.
RPi may have Internet access if the desktop has two network adapters and sharing is enabled.	RPi still needs a source of power (can be a mains-powered adapter).
Provides a reasonably stable network setup.	May require a specialized Ethernet crossover cable or adapter. However, your computer likely has Auto-MDIX.

Most modern desktop machines have an automatic crossover detection function (Auto-MDIX) that enables a regular Ethernet cable to be used. The RPi's network interface also supports Auto-MDIX; therefore, this connection type can be used when you do not have access to network infrastructure. If you have two network adapters on your desktop machine (e.g., a laptop with a wired and wireless network adapter), you can easily share the connection to the Internet with your RPi by bridging both adapters. For example, these are the steps necessary when using the Windows OS:

1. Plug one end of a regular (or crossover) Ethernet cable into the RPi and the other end into a laptop Ethernet socket.

2. Power on the RPi by attaching a micro-USB power supply.

3. Bridge the two network connections. Under Windows, choose Network and Internet ⇨ Network Connections. Select the two network adapters (wired and wireless) at the same time, right-click, and choose Bridge Connections. After some time, the two connections should appear with the status Enabled, Bridged, and a network bridge should appear, as illustrated in Figure 2-2.

4. Reboot the RPi. Ideally, you should use a USB-to-TTL serial cable to do this, or the reset button described in Chapter 1. Once the RPi has rebooted, it should obtain an IP address directly from your network's DHCP server.

You can then communicate with the RPi directly from anywhere on your network (including the laptop itself) using the steps described in the next section. Figure 2-2 provides a configuration example subsequent to the steps in the following section taking place. As illustrated in the figure, the DHCP server allocates the laptop the IP address 192.168.1.111 and the RPi the IP address 192.168.1.115. Therefore, an SSH session from the desktop machine at IP address 192.168.1.4 to the RPi provides the following interaction:

```
molloyd@desktop:~$ ssh pi@192.168.1.115
pi@192.168.1.115's password: raspberry
Debian GNU/Linux comes with ABSOLUTELY NO WARRANTY, to the extent
permitted by applicable law.
pi@erpi ~ $ echo $SSH_CLIENT
192.168.1.4 60898 22
pi@erpi ~ $ ping www.google.com
PING www.google.com (213.233.153.230) 56(84) bytes of data.
64 bytes from www.google.com (213.233.153.230):icmp_seq=1 ttl=61 time=13.6ms
```

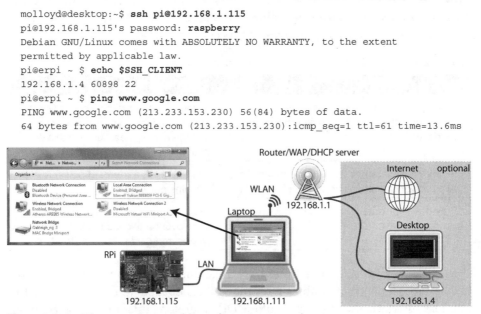

Figure 2-2: An Ethernet crossover cable configuration example

Image icons by GNOME icon artists (GNU GPL CC-BY-SA-3.0)

This connection type is particularly useful inside of complex network infrastructures such as those in universities, because the laptop can connect to the RPi directly. The RPi can also connect to the Internet, as illustrated by its capability to ping the Google web server in this example.

Communicating with the RPi

After you have networked the RPi, the next thing you might want to do is communicate with the RPi. You can connect to the RPi using either a serial connection over USB-to-TTL or a network connection, as described previously. The network connection should be your main focus, because that type of connection provides your RPi with full Internet access. The serial connection is generally used as a fallback connection when problems arise with the network connection. As such, you may skip the next section, but the information is here as a reference for when problems arise.

> **NOTE** The default user account for the Raspbian image is username pi with password raspberry.

Serial Connection with the USB-to-TTL 3.3V Cable

Serial connections are particularly useful when the RPi is close to your desktop computer and connected via a USB-to-TTL cable (as shown previously in Figure 1-7(a) in Chapter 1). It is often a fallback communications method when something goes wrong with the network configuration or software services on the RPi. It can also be used to configure wireless networking on an RPi device that does not have wired network support. You can connect the cable to the RPi (as shown previously in Figure 1-7(b) in Chapter 1).

To connect to the RPi via the serial connection, you need a terminal program. Several Windows-compatible third-party applications are available, including *RealTerm* (tiny.cc/erpi205) and *PuTTY* (www.putty.org). Most distributions of desktop Linux include a terminal program (try Ctrl+Alt+T or Alt+F2 and then type gnome-terminal under Debian). A terminal emulator is included by default under Mac OS X (e.g., use a command such as screen /dev/cu.usbserial-XXX 115200) or by installing Z-Term (see dalverson.com/zterm/).

To connect to the RPi over the USB-to-TTL serial connection, you need the following information:

- **Port number:** To find this, open the Windows Device Manager (or equivalent) and search under the Ports section. Figure 2-3(a) captures an example Device Manager, where the device is listed as COM11 in my case. This differs on different machines.

■ **Connection speed:** By default, you need to enter **115,200** baud to connect to the RPi.

■ **Other information you may need for other terminal applications:** Data bits = 8; Stop bits = 1; Parity = none; and Flow control = XON/XOFF.

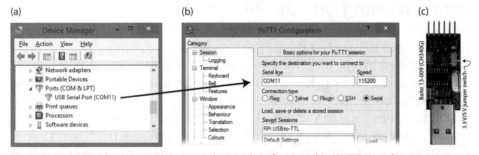

Figure 2-3: (a) Windows Device Manager device identification; (b) a PuTTY serial connection configuration; and (c) a low-cost USB-to-TTL adapter

Save the configuration with a session name (e.g., RPi USB-to-TTL), as illustrated in Figure 2-3(b), so that it is available each time you want to connect. Click Open, and then it is important that you *press Enter when the window displays*. When connecting to Raspbian, you should see the following output:

```
Raspbian GNU/Linux 8 erpi ttyAMA0
erpi login: pi
Password: raspberry
Last login: Fri Dec 18 02:12:32 GMT 2015 from ...
Linux erpi 4.1.13-v7+ #826 SMP PREEMPT Fri Nov 13 20:19:03 GMT 2015 armv7l
Debian GNU/Linux comes with ABSOLUTELY NO WARRANTY, to the extent
permitted by applicable law.
pi@erpi:~$
```

The connection process enables you to log in with username pi and password raspberry. Note that when you reboot the board you will also see the full console output as the RPi boots. This is the ultimate fallback connection because it allows you to see what is happening during the boot process (described in Chapter 3).

NOTE Low-cost alternatives to the USB-to-TTL 3.3V cable, such as the USB device shown in Figure 2-3(c), are available for as little as $1, but generally come without any type of protective casing. Before you purchase the device, however, be sure that it supports 3.3 V TTL logic levels. The one shown in Figure 2-3(c) has a switch that facilitates both 3.3 V and 5 V logic levels. These devices are used in Chapter 9 to extend the number of UART devices that are available on the RPi.

On a Linux desktop computer, you can install the `screen` program and connect to the USB-to-TTL device with these commands:

```
molloyd@debian:~$ sudo apt-get install screen
molloyd@debian:~$ screen /dev/cu.usbserial-XXX/ 115200
```

Connecting through Secure Shell (SSH)

Secure Shell (SSH) is a useful network protocol for secure encrypted communication between network devices. You can use an SSH terminal client to connect to the SSH server that is running on port 22 of the RPi, which allows you to do the following:

- Log in remotely to the RPi and execute commands.
- Transfer files to and from the RPi using the *SSH File Transfer Protocol* (SFTP).
- Forward X11 connections, which allows you to perform virtual network computing.

By default, the RPi Linux distributions run an SSH server (*sshd* under Debian) that is bound to port 22. There are a few advantages in having an SSH server available as the default method by which you log in remotely to the RPi. In particular, you can open port 22 of the RPi to the Internet using the port forwarding functionality of your router. Please ensure that you set a nondefault password for the pi user account before doing so. You can then remotely log in to your RPi from anywhere in the world if you know the RPi's IP address. A service called *dynamic DNS* that is supported on most routers enables your router to register its latest address with an online service. The online service then maps a domain name of your choice to the latest IP address that your ISP has given you. The dynamic DNS service usually has an annual cost, for which it will provide you with an address of the form `dereksRPi.servicename.com`.

Secure Shell Connections Using PuTTY

PuTTY was mentioned previously as a method for connecting to the RPi using a serial connection. PuTTY is a free, open source terminal emulator, serial console, and SSH client that you can also use to connect to the RPi over the network. PuTTY has a few useful features:

- It supports serial and SSH connections.
- It installs an application called psftp that enables you to transfer files to and from the RPi over the network from your desktop computer.
- It supports SSH X11 forwarding (required in Chapter 14).

Figure 2-4 captures the PuTTY configuration settings: Choose SSH as the connection type, enter your RPi's IP address (or Zeroconf name), accept Port

22 (the default), and then save the session with a useful name. Click Open and log in using your username and password. If you see a security alert that warns about man-in-the-middle attacks, which may be a concern on insecure networks, accept the fingerprint and continue. Mac OS X users can run the Terminal application with similar settings (e.g., `ssh -XC pi@192.168.1.116` or `ssh -XC pi@raspberrypi.local`).

Figure 2-4: PuTTY SSH Configuration settings beside an open SSH terminal connection window

You will see the basic commands that can be issued to the RPi later in this chapter, but first it is necessary to examine how you can transfer files to and from the RPi.

Chrome Apps: Secure Shell Client

The Chrome web browser has support for Chrome Apps—applications that behave like locally installed (or native) applications but are written in HTML5, JavaScript, and CSS. Many of these applications use Google's Native Client (NaCl, or Salt!), which is a sandbox for running compiled C/C++ applications directly in the web browser, regardless of the OS. The benefit of NaCl is that applications can achieve near-native performance levels, because they can contain code that uses low-level instructions.

There is a useful "terminal emulator and SSH client" Chrome App available. Open a new tab on the Chrome browser and click the Apps icon. Go to the Chrome Web Store and search the store for "Secure Shell." Once installed, it will appear as the Secure Shell App when you click the Apps icon again. When you start up the Secure Shell App, you will have to set the connection settings as shown in Figure 2-4, and the application will appear as shown in Figure 2-5.

Figure 2-5: The SSH Chrome App

Transferring Files Using PuTTY/psftp over SSH

The PuTTY installation also includes *file transfer protocol (ftp)* support that enables you to transfer files to and from the RPi over your network connection. You can start up the *psftp* (PuTTY secure file transfer protocol) application by typing psftp in the Windows Start command text field.

At the psftp> prompt, type **open pi@raspberrypi.local** (or with the IP address) to connect to the RPi. Your desktop machine is now referred to as the local machine, and the RPi is referred to as the remote machine. When you issue a command, you are typically issuing it on the remote machine. After connecting, you are placed in the home directory of the user account that you used. Therefore, under the RPi Raspbian distribution, if you connect as pi you are placed in the /home/pi/ directory.

To transfer a single file c:\temp\test.txt from the local desktop computer to the RPi, you can use the following steps:

```
psftp: no hostname specified; use "open host.name" to connect
psftp> open pi@erpi.local
Using username "pi".
pi@erpi.local's password: raspberry
Remote working directory is /home/pi
psftp> lcd c:\temp
New local directory is c:\temp
psftp> mkdir test
mkdir /home/pi/test: OK
psftp> cd test
Remote directory is now /home/pi/test
psftp> put test.txt
local:test.txt => remote:/home/pi/test/test.txt
psftp> dir test.*
Listing directory /home/pi/test
-rw-r--r--    1 pi        pi              8 Dec 18 16:45 test.txt
psftp>
```

Commands that contain the l prefix are commands issued for the local machine—for example, lcd (local change directory) or lpwd (local print working directory). To transfer a single file from the local machine to the remote machine, issue the put command. To transfer a file in reverse, use the get command. To "put" or "get" multiple files, use the mput and mget commands. Use help if you forget a command.

If you are using a Linux client machine, you can use the command sftp instead of psftp. Almost everything else remains the same. The sftp client application is also installed on the RPi distribution by default, so you can reverse the order of communication; that is, you can have the RPi act as the client and another machine as the server.

Here are some useful hints and tips to use with the `psftp`/`sftp` commands:

- `mget -r *` performs a recursive get of a directory. This is useful if you want to transfer a folder that has several subfolders. The `-r` option can also be used with `get`, `put`, and `mput` commands.

- `dir *.txt` applies a filter to display only the .txt files in the current directory.

- `mv` moves a file/directory on the remote machine to a new location on the remote machine.

- `reget` resumes a download that was interrupted. The partially downloaded file must exist on the local machine.

The `psftp` command can be issued as a single line or a local script at the command prompt. You could create a file `test.scr` that contains a set of `psftp` commands to be issued. You can then execute `psftp` from the command prompt, passing the password by using `-pw` and the script file by using `-b` (or `-be` to continue on error or `-bc` to display commands as they are run), as follows:

```
c:\temp>more test.scr
lcd c:\temp\down
cd /tmp/down
mget *
quit
c:\temp>psftp pi@erpi.local -pw mypassword -b test.scr
Using username "pi".
Remote working directory is /home/pi ...
```

Controlling the Raspberry Pi

At this point, you should be able to communicate with the RPi using an SSH client application. This section investigates the commands that you can issue to interact with the RPi.

Basic Linux Commands

When you first connect to the RPi with SSH, you are prompted to log in. You can log in with username pi and password raspberry:

```
login as: pi
pi@erpi.local's password: raspberry
Debian GNU/Linux comes with ABSOLUTELY NO WARRANTY, to the extent
permitted by applicable law.
pi@erpi ~ $
```

You are now connected to the RPi, and the Linux terminal is ready for your command. The `$` prompt means that you are logged in as a regular user.

A # prompt means that you are logged in to a superuser account (discusse in Chapter 3). For a new Linux user, this step can be quite daunting because it is not clear what arsenal of commands is at your disposal. This section provides you with sufficient Linux skills to get started. It is written as a reference with examples so that you can come back to it when you need help.

First Steps

The first thing you might do after connecting is determine which version of Linux you are running. This information can prove useful when you are asking a question on a forum:

```
pi@erpi ~ $ uname -a
Linux erpi 4.1.13-v7+ #826 SMP PREEMPT Nov 13 20:19:03 2015 armv7l GNU/Linux
```

In this case, Linux 4.1.13 is being used, which was built for the ARMv7 architecture on the date that is listed.

The Linux kernel version is described by numbers in the form $X.Y.Z$. The X number changes only rarely (version 2.0 was released in 1996, and 4.0 was released in April 2015). The Y value used to change rarely (every 2 years or so), but for the most recent kernel the value has changed quite regularly (for example, 4.1 was released in June 2015). The Z value changes regularly.

Next, you could use the passwd command to set a new password for the pi user account:

```
pi@erpi ~ $ passwd
Changing password for pi.
(current) UNIX password: raspberry
Enter new UNIX password: supersecretpasswordthatImayforget
Retype new UNIX password: supersecretpasswordthatImayforget
```

Table 2-3 lists other useful first-step commands.

Table 2-3: Useful First Commands in Linux

COMMAND	DESCRIPTION
more /etc/issue	Returns the Linux distribution you are using
ps -p $$	Returns the shell you are currently using (e.g., bash)
whoami	Returns who you are currently logged in as
uptime	Returns how long the system has been running
top	Lists all of the processes and programs executing. Press Ctrl+C to close the view.

Finally, you can find out specific information about your RPi using the `host-namectl` application, which can be used to query and change some system settings (e.g., the chassis description and hostname):

```
pi@erpi ~ $ sudo hostnamectl set-chassis server
pi@erpi ~ $ hostnamectl
   Static hostname: erpi
         Icon name: computer-server
           Chassis: server
        Machine ID: 3882d14b5e8d408bb132425829ac6413
           Boot ID: ea403b96c8984e37820b7d1b0b3fbd6d
  Operating System: Raspbian GNU/Linux 8 (jessie)
            Kernel: Linux 4.1.18-v7+
      Architecture: arm
```

Basic File System Commands

This section describes the basic commands that enable you to move around on, and manipulate, a Linux file system. When using Raspbian/Debian and Ubuntu user accounts, you often must prefix certain commands with the word `sudo`. That is because `sudo` is a program that allows users to run programs with the security privileges of the superuser. (User accounts are described in Chapter 3.) Table 2-4 lists the basic file system commands.

Table 2-4: Basic File System Commands

NAME	COMMAND	OPTIONS AND FURTHER INFORMATION	EXAMPLE(S)
List files	ls	-a shows all (including hidden files).	ls -alh
		-l displays long format.	
		-R gives a recursive listing.	
		-r gives a reverse listing.	
		-t sorts last modified.	
		-S sorts by file size.	
		-h gives human readable file sizes.	
Current directory	pwd	Print the working directory.	pwd -P
		-P prints the physical location.	
Change directory	cd	Change directory.	cd /home/pi
		cd then Enter or cd ~/ takes you to the home directory.	cd /
		cd / takes you to the file system root.	
		cd .. takes you up a level.	

NAME	COMMAND	OPTIONS AND FURTHER INFORMATION	EXAMPLE(S)
Make a directory	`mkdir`	Make a directory.	`mkdir test`
Delete a file or directory	`rm`	Delete a file.	`rm bad.txt`
		`-r` recursive delete (use for directories; be careful) .	`rm -r test`
		`-d` remove empty directories.	
Copy a file or directory	`cp`	`-r` recursive copy.	`cp a.txt b.txt`
		`-u` copy only if the source is newer than the destination or the destination is missing.	`cp -r test testa`
		`-v` verbose copy (i.e., show output).	
Move a file or directory	`mv`	`-i` prompts before overwrite.	`mv a.txt c.txt`
		No `-r` for directory. Moving to the same directory performs a renaming.	`mv test testb`
Create an empty file	`touch`	Create an empty file or update the modification date of an existing file.	`touch d.txt`
View content of a file	`more`	View the contents of a file. Use the Space key for the next page.	`more d.txt`
Get the calendar	`cal`	Display a text-based calendar.	`cal 04 2016`

That covers the basics but there is so much more! The next chapter describes file ownership, permissions, searching, I/O redirection, and other topics. The aim of this section is to get you up and running. Table 2-5 describes a few shortcuts that make life easier when working with most Linux shells.

Table 2-5: Some Time-Saving Terminal Keyboard Shortcuts

SHORTCUT	DESCRIPTION
Up arrow (repeat)	Gives you the last command you typed, and then the previous commands on repeated presses.
Tab key	Autocompletes the file name, the directory name, or even the executable command name. For example, to change to the Linux `/tmp` directory, you can type **cd /t** and then press Tab, which autocompletes the command to `cd /tmp/`. If there are many options, press the Tab key again to see all the options as a list.

Continues

Table 2-5 (*continued*)

SHORTCUT	DESCRIPTION
Ctrl+A	Brings you back to the start of the line you are typing.
Ctrl+E	Brings you to the end of the line you are typing.
Ctrl+U	Clears to the start of the line. Ctrl+E and then Ctrl+U clears the line.
Ctrl+L	Clears the screen.
Ctrl+C	Kills whatever process is currently running.
Ctrl+Z	Puts the current process into the background. Typing **bg** then leaves it running in the background, and **fg** then brings it back to the foreground.

Here is an example that uses several of the commands in Table 2-4 to create a directory called `test` in which an empty text file `hello.txt` is created. The entire `test` directory is then copied to the `/tmp/test2` directory, which is off the `/tmp` directory:

```
pi@erpi ~ $ cd /tmp
pi@erpi /tmp $ pwd
/tmp
pi@erpi /tmp $ mkdir test
pi@erpi /tmp $ cd test
pi@erpi /tmp/test $ touch hello.txt
pi@erpi /tmp/test $ ls -l hello.txt
-rw-r--r-- 1 pi pi 0 Dec 17 04:34 hello.txt
pi@erpi /tmp/test $ cd ..
pi@erpi /tmp $ cp -r test /tmp/test2
pi@erpi /tmp $ cd /tmp/test2
pi@erpi /tmp/test2 $ ls -l
total 0
-rw-r--r-- 1 pi pi 0 Dec 17 04:35 hello.txt
```

WARNING   Linux assumes that you know what you are doing! It will gladly allow you to do a recursive deletion of your root directory when you are logged in as root (I won't list the command). *Think before you type when logged in as root!*

NOTE   Sometimes it is possible to recover files that are lost through accidental deletion if you use the `extundelete` command immediately after the deletion. Read the command manual page carefully, and then use steps such as the following:

```
pi@erpi ~ $ sudo apt install extundelete
pi@erpi ~ $ mkdir ~/undelete
pi@erpi ~ $ cd ~/undelete/
pi@erpi ~/undelete $ sudo extundelete --restore-all --restore-directory
 . /dev/mmcblk0p2
pi@erpi ~/undelete $ ls -l
drwxr-xr-x 6 root root 4096 Dec 17 04:39 RECOVERED_FILES
```

```
pi@erpi ~/undelete $ du -sh RECOVERED_FILES/
100M    RECOVERED_FILES/
```

In this example, 100 MB of files were recovered—typically temporary files that were deleted as a result of package installations.

Environment Variables

Environment variables are named values that describe the configuration of your Linux environment, such as the location of the executable files or your default editor. To get an idea of the environment variables that are set on the RPi, issue an env call, which provides a list of the environment variables on your account. Here, env is called on the Raspbian image:

```
pi@erpi ~ $ env
TERM=xterm
SHELL=/bin/bash
SSH_CLIENT=fe80::50b4:eb95:2d00:ac3f%eth0 2599 22
USER=pi
MAIL=/var/mail/pi
PATH=/usr/local/sbin:/usr/local/bin:/usr/sbin:/usr/bin:...
PWD=/home/pi
HOME=/home/pi   ...
```

You can view and modify environment variables according to the following example, which adds the /home/pi directory to the PATH environment variable:

```
pi@erpi ~ $ echo $PATH
/usr/local/sbin:/usr/local/bin:/usr/sbin:/usr/bin:/sbin:/bin
pi@erpi ~ $ export PATH=$PATH:/home/pi
pi@erpi ~ $ echo $PATH
/usr/local/sbin:/usr/local/bin:/usr/sbin:/usr/bin:/sbin:/bin:/home/pi
```

This change will be lost on reboot. Permanently setting environment variables requires modifications to your .profile file when using sh, ksh, or bash shells; and to your .login file when using csh or tcsh shells. To do this, you need to be able to perform file editing in a Linux terminal window.

Basic File Editing

A variety of editors are available, but one of the easiest to use is also one of the most powerful: the *GNU nano editor*. You start the editor by typing **nano** followed by the name of an existing or new filename; for example, typing **nano hello.txt** displays the view captured in Figure 2-6 (after the text has been entered). Typing **nano -c hello.txt** also displays the current line number, which is useful for debugging. You can move freely around the file in the window by using the arrow keys and editing or writing text at the cursor location. You can see some of the nano shortcut keys listed on the bottom bar of the editor window, but there are many more, some of which are presented in Table 2-6.

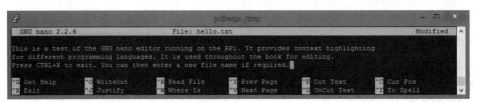

Figure 2-6: The GNU nano editor being used to edit an example file in a PuTTY Linux terminal window

Table 2-6: Nano Shortcut Keys: A Quick Reference

KEYS	COMMAND	KEYS	COMMAND
Ctrl+G	Help	Ctrl+Y	Previous page
Ctrl+C	Find out the current line number	Ctrl+_ or Ctrl+/	Go to line number
Ctrl+X	Exit (prompts save)	Alt+/	Go to end of file
Ctrl+L	Enable long line wrapping	Ctrl+6	Start marking text (then move with arrows to highlight)
Ctrl+O	Save	Ctrl+K or Alt+6	Cut marked text
Arrows	Move around	Ctrl+U	Paste text
Ctrl+A	Go to start of line	Ctrl+R	Insert content of another file (prompts for location of file)
Ctrl+E	Go to end of line	Ctrl+W	Search for a string
Ctrl+Space	Next word	Alt+W	Find next
Alt+Space	Previous word	Ctrl+D	Delete character under cursor
Ctrl+V	Next page	Ctrl+K	Delete entire line

NOTE Ctrl+K appears to delete the entire line but it actually removes the line to a buffer, which can be pasted using Ctrl+U. This is a quick way of repeating multiple lines. Also, Mac users may have to set the meta key in the Terminal application to get the Alt functionality. Select Terminal ⇨ Preferences ⇨ Settings ⇨ Keyboard, and then choose Use option as meta key.

What Time Is It?

A simple question like "What time is it?" causes more difficulty than you can imagine. For example, typing `date` at the shell prompt might produce the following:

```
pi@erpi ~ $ date
Thu 17 Dec 16:26:59 UTC 2015
```

This result happens to be the correct time in this instance because the board is connected to a network. If it is wrong, why did the RPi manufacturer not set the clock time on your board? The answer is that they could not. Unlike a desktop computer, the RPi has no battery backup to ensure that the BIOS settings are retained; in fact, there is no BIOS! That topic is examined in detail in the next chapter, but for the moment, you need a way to set the time, and for that you can use the *Network Time Protocol* (NTP). The NTP is a networking protocol for synchronizing clocks between computers. If your RPi has the correct time, that is only because your RPi is obtaining it from your network using an NTP service that is running the board:

```
pi@erpi ~ $ systemctl status ntp
● ntp.service - LSB: Start NTP daemon
   Loaded: loaded (/etc/init.d/ntp)
   Active: active (running) since Sat 2015-12-19 07:18:04 GMT; 22h ago
  Process: 499 ExecStart=/etc/init.d/ntp start (code=exited, status=0/SUCCESS)
   CGroup: /system.slice/ntp.service
           └─544 /usr/sbin/ntpd -p /var/run/ntpd.pid -g -u 107:112
```

The NTP service is configured using the file `/etc/ntp.conf`, and the lines beginning with the word `server` (hence the ^ in the call to `grep`) identify the servers to which your RPi is communicating to retrieve the current time:

```
pi@erpi ~ $ more /etc/ntp.conf | grep ^server
server 0.debian.pool.ntp.org iburst
server 1.debian.pool.ntp.org iburst
server 2.debian.pool.ntp.org iburst
server 3.debian.pool.ntp.org iburst
```

To be a good NTP citizen, you should adjust these entries to refer to the closest NTP server pool by going to `www.pool.ntp.org` (the closest server to me is `ie.pool.ntp.org` for Ireland) and updating the entries accordingly. If you want to test the settings first, you can install and execute the `ntpdate` command:

```
pi@erpi ~ $ sudo apt install ntpdate
pi@erpi ~ $ sudo ntpdate -b -s -u ie.pool.ntp.org
pi@erpi ~ $ date
Sun 20 Dec 16:02:39 GMT 2015
```

After setting the time, you can set your time zone. Use the following command, which provides a text-based user interface that allows you to choose your location. The RPi is set for Irish standard time (IST) in this example:

```
pi@erpi ~ $ sudo dpkg-reconfigure tzdata
Current default time zone: 'Europe/Dublin'
Local time is now:      Sun Dec 20 16:37:48 GMT 2015.
Universal Time is now:  Sun Dec 20 16:37:48 UTC 2015.
```

> **NOTE** If your RPi is not connected to the Internet, you can manually set the date using the `timedatectl` tool:
>
> ```
> pi@erpi ~ $ sudo timedatectl set-time '2017-1-2 12:13:14'
> pi@erpi ~ $ date
> Mon  2 Jan 12:13:16 GMT 2017
> ```
>
> Unfortunately, this date and time will be lost when the RPi restarts. Chapter 8 describes how a battery-backed real-time clock (RTC) can be connected to the RPi to solve that problem.

Package Management

At the beginning of this chapter, a good package manager was listed as a key feature of a suitable Linux distribution. A *package manager* is a set of software tools that automate the process of installing, configuring, upgrading, and removing software packages from the Linux operating system. Different Linux distributions use different package managers: Ubuntu and Raspbian/Debian use *APT* (Advanced Packaging Tool) over *DPKG* (Debian Package Management System), and Arch Linux uses *Pacman*. Each has its own usage syntax, but their operation is largely similar. Table 2-7 lists some common package management commands.

Table 2-7: Common Package Management Commands (Using nano as an Example Package)

COMMAND	RASPBIAN/DEBIAN/UBUNTU
Install a package.	`sudo apt install nano`
Update the package index.	`sudo apt update`
Upgrade the packages on your system.	`sudo apt upgrade`
Is nano installed?	`dpkg-query -l	grep nano`
Is a package containing the string nano available?	`apt-cache search nano`
Get more information about a package.	`apt-cache show nano`
	`apt-cache policy nano`
Get help.	`apt help`

COMMAND	RASPBIAN/DEBIAN/UBUNTU
Download a package to the current directory.	`apt-get download nano`
Remove a package.	`sudo apt remove nano`
Clean up old packages.	`sudo apt-get autoremove`
	`sudo apt-get clean`

NOTE Over time, the `apt` binary command is slowly integrating the features of the `apt-get` and `apt-cache` commands. This change should reduce the number of tools required to manage packages. However, older Linux distributions may require that you use the `apt-get` command in place of the `apt` command.

Wavemon is a useful tool that you can use in configuring Wi-Fi connections (see Chapter 13). If you execute the following command, you will see that the package is not installed by default:

```
pi@erpi ~ $ wavemon
-bash: wavemon: command not found
```

You can use the platform-specific package manager to install the package, once you determine the package name:

```
pi@erpi ~ $ apt-cache search wavemon
wavemon - Wireless Device Monitoring Application
pi@erpi ~ $ sudo apt install wavemon
Reading package lists... Done
Building dependency tree ...
Setting up wavemon (0.7.6-2) ...
```

The `wavemon` command now executes, but unfortunately it will not do anything until you configure a wireless adapter (see Chapter 13):

```
pi@erpi ~ $ wavemon
wavemon: no supported wireless interfaces found
```

It is also worth noting that packages can be manually downloaded and installed. This method can be useful should you want to retain a specific version or need to distribute a package to multiple devices. For example, the Wavemon package can be removed, manually downloaded as a `.deb` file, and installed:

```
pi@erpi ~ $ sudo apt remove wavemon
pi@erpi ~ $ wavemon
-bash: /usr/bin/wavemon: No such file or directory
pi@erpi ~ $ apt-get download wavemon
pi@erpi ~ $ ls -l wavemon*
-rw-r--r-- 1 pi pi 48248 Mar 28  2014 wavemon_0.7.6-2_armhf.deb
pi@erpi ~ $ sudo dpkg -i wavemon_0.7.6-2_armhf.deb
pi@erpi ~ $ wavemon
wavemon: no supported wireless interfaces found
```

> **NOTE**   Sometimes package installations fail, perhaps because another required package is missing. There are *force options* available with the package commands to override checks. (e.g., `--force-yes` with the `apt-get` command). Try to avoid force options if possible, because having to use them is symptomatic of a different problem. Typing `sudo apt-get autoremove` can be useful when packages fail to install.

Configuring the Raspberry Pi

The RPi community and the Raspberry Pi Foundation have developed RPi-specific tools for configuring your board. These tools simplify some tasks that would otherwise be quite tricky, as you see in the following sections.

The Raspberry Pi Configuration Tool

The Raspberry Pi Configuration Tool, `raspi-config`, is useful for getting started with your RPi. It can be started simply using the following call, whereupon an interface is presented, as shown in Figure 2-7.

```
pi@erpi:~$ sudo raspi-config
```

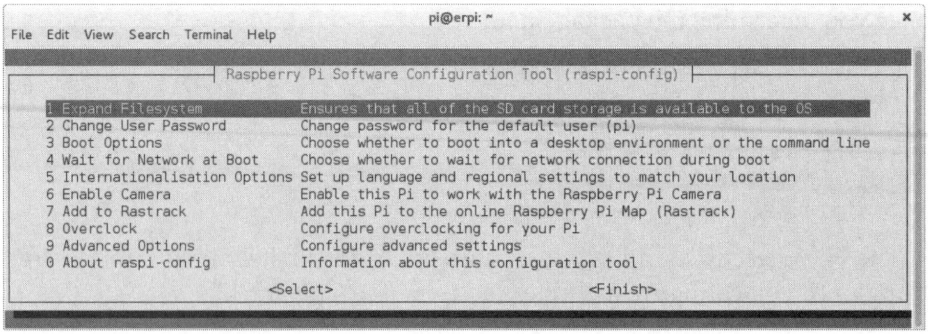

Figure 2-7: The raspi-config tool

The following are tasks that you should perform almost immediately when you boot the RPi from a fresh SD-card image:

- **Expand the root filesystem to fill the SD card:** This is the first option in Figure 2-7. When you write an image to an SD card, it is typically smaller than the capacity of the card. This option allows the root file system to be expanded to use the full capacity of the card. After using this option, you can check the overall capacity as follows:

```
pi@erpi ~ $ df -kh
Filesystem      Size  Used Avail Use% Mounted on
/dev/root        15G  7.7G  6.2G  56% /
...
pi@erpi ~ $ lsblk
```

```
NAME          MAJ:MIN RM  SIZE RO TYPE MOUNTPOINT
mmcblk0       179:0    0 14.9G  0 disk
├─mmcblk0p1 179:1    0   56M  0 part /boot
└─mmcblk0p2 179:2    0 14.8G  0 part /
```

You can see that the SD card now has a capacity of 15 GiB,[1] which is consistent with the capacity of the SD card.

▪ **Enable the camera:** If you have an RPi camera attached to the CSI interface on the RPi, enable the camera. This topic is described in detail in Chapter 15.

▪ **Overclock:** This option allows you to run the processor at a higher clock frequency than was originally intended by the manufacturer. For example, the processor on the RPi 2 can run at 1 GHz instead of the listed maximum of 900 MHz. Note that doing so may reduce the lifespan of your RPi and possibly lead to instabilities. However, many users overclock the processor, without ill effects. This option makes changes to the /boot/config.txt file.

▪ **Overscan (Advanced Options; see Figure 2-8):** Allows you to adjust the video output to the full screen of your television. This option makes changes to the /boot/config.txt file.

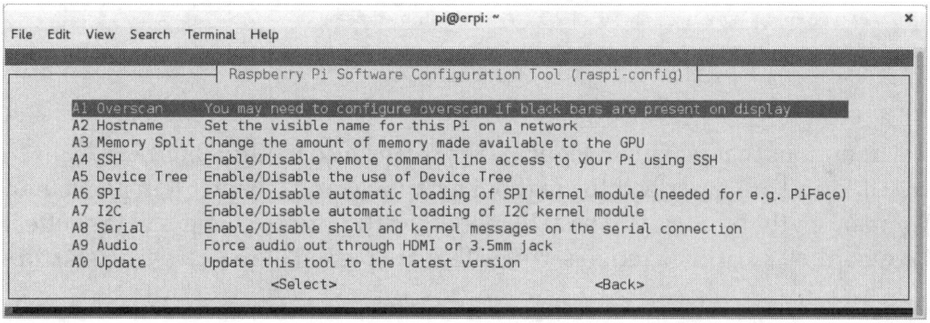

Figure 2-8: The raspi-config tool Advanced Options menu

▪ **Hostname (Advanced Options):** This option allows you to adjust the hostname of the RPi on the network. This option updates the hostname and hosts files and restarts the networking service:

```
pi@erpi ~ $ cat /etc/hostname
erpi
pi@erpi ~ $ cat /etc/hosts
...
127.0.1.1       erpi
```

---

[1] SD cards and hard disks are usually sold where 1 gigabyte (GB) = 1,000,000,000 bytes (i.e., 1000^3 bytes). However, Linux uses gigabyte (technically GiB) to mean 1024^3 bytes. Therefore there is a discrepancy when you format an SD card—a 16 GB card will format to a maximum size of 14.901 GiB (i.e., $16 \times 10^9/1024^3$).

This entry now means that my RPi board is found at the Zeroconf address string `erpi.local`.

- **Memory Split (Advanced Options):** The CPU and graphics processing unit (GPU) on the RPi share the DDR memory on the board. This option allows you to adjust the allocation of memory to the GPU. A good general-purpose memory allocation for a headful display is 64 MB, but this must be increased if you are using the RPi CSI camera (typically to 128 MB; see Chapter 15), or if you are using the GPU for 3D computer graphics. This value is set at boot time (via `/boot/config.txt`) and cannot be altered at runtime.

- **SSH (Advanced Options):** This allows you to enable or disable the SSH server on the RPi. Clearly you should not disable the SSH server if your RPi is in headless mode, especially if you do not have an alternative way of connecting to the board. This option disables the SSH service, which runs on the RPi as follows:

```
pi@erpi ~ $ systemctl status sshd
● ssh.service - OpenBSD Secure Shell server
   Loaded: loaded (/lib/systemd/system/ssh.service; enabled)
   Active: active (running) since Thu 2015-12-17 21:53:47 GMT
  Process: 628 ExecReload=/bin/kill -HUP $MAINPID
 Main PID: 492 (sshd)
   CGroup: /system.slice/ssh.service
           └─492 /usr/sbin/sshd -D
```

The options that remain in Figure 2-8 typically also modify the `/boot/config.txt` file and are described throughout Chapter 6 and Chapter 8 in particular. For many of the options, you have to reboot the RPi for the changes to take effect because they are initialization settings that are passed to the kernel on startup.

Updating the RPi Software

The Raspbian distribution can be updated on the RPi using a few short steps. However, be aware that some of these steps (upgrade in particular) can take quite some time to complete—perhaps even several hours, depending on the currency of your image and the speed of your network connection.

A call to `apt update` downloads the package lists from the Internet locations identified in the file `/etc/apt/sources.list`. This does not install new versions of the software; rather, it updates the lists of packages and their interdependencies:

```
pi@erpi ~ $ sudo apt update
Get:1 http://archive.raspbian.org jessie InRelease [15.0 kB]
Hit http://archive.raspberrypi.org jessie InRelease    ...
Building dependency tree         Reading state information... Done
```

When this update is complete, you can automatically download and install the latest versions of the available software using the `apt upgrade` command. Clearly, you should always perform an `apt update` before an `apt upgrade`:

```
pi@erpi ~ $ sudo apt upgrade
Reading package lists... Done          Building dependency tree
Reading state information... Done       Calculating upgrade... Done ...
After this operation, XXXXX B of additional disk space will be used.
Do you want to continue? [Y/n]
```

There is an additional RPi-specific tool that enables you to update the Linux kernel, driver modules, and libraries on the RPi. The `rpi-update` tool can be called directly with no arguments, but it also has some expert settings, which are described at `github.com/Hexxeh/rpi-update`. For example, these settings permit you to update the firmware without replacing the kernel file:

```
pi@erpi ~ $ sudo apt install rpi-update
pi@erpi ~ $ sudo rpi-update
 *** Raspberry Pi firmware updater by Hexxeh, enhanced by AndrewS and Dom
This update bumps to rpi-4.1.y linux tree ...
 *** Updating firmware
 *** Updating kernel modules
 *** depmod 4.1.15-v7+
 *** Updating VideoCore libraries
 *** Using HardFP libraries ...
 *** A reboot is needed to activate the new firmware
pi@erpi ~ $ sudo reboot
```

After you reboot the board, the current kernel version should be aligned with the newly installed kernel and firmware:

```
molloyd@desktop:~$ ssh pi@erpi.local
pi@erpi ~ $ uname -a
Linux erpi 4.1.15-v7+ #830 SMP Tue Dec 15 17:02:45 GMT 2015 armv7l GNU/Linux
```

Video Output

The RPi video output can be configured using the `tvservice` application (`/opt/vc/bin/tvservice`). You should plug the HDMI monitor cable into the RPi and use the `tvservice` application to list the available modes on the connected CEA (typically televisions) or DMT (typically computer monitors) display:

```
pi@erpi ~ $ tvservice --modes CEA
Group CEA has 0 modes:
pi@erpi ~ $ tvservice --modes DMT
Group DMT has 13 modes:
        ...
          mode 51: 1600x1200 @ 60Hz 4:3,   clock:162MHz progressive
          mode 58: 1680x1050 @ 60Hz 16:10, clock:146MHz progressive
  (prefer) mode 82: 1920x1080 @ 60Hz 16:9,  clock:148MHz progressive
pi@erpi ~ $ tvservice --status
state 0x120006 [DVI DMT(82) RGB full 16:9], 1920x1080 @ 60.00Hz, progressive
```

You can set the RPi output resolution explicitly using the same tool. For example, to update the output resolution to use the DVI 1600 × 1200 mode that is available in the list above:

```
pi@erpi ~ $ tvservice --explicit="DMT 51"
Powering on HDMI with explicit settings (DMT mode 51)
pi@erpi ~ $ tvservice --status
state 0x120006 [DVI DMT (51) RGB full 4:3], 1600x1200 @ 60.00Hz, progressive
pi@erpi ~ $ fbset -depth 8 && fbset -depth 16
```

The last line forces a refresh of the video frame buffer to update the graphics display. After you have tested the new resolution, you can explicitly set the value in the /boot/config.txt file (where hdmi_group=1 sets a CEA mode, and hdmi_group=2 sets a DMT mode):

```
pi@erpi /boot $ more config.txt | grep ^hdmi
hdmi_group=2
hdmi_mode=51
```

If you are not using the HDMI output, you can switch it off entirely, which results in a current saving of approximately 25 mA–30 mA.

```
pi@erpi ~ $ tvservice --off
Powering off HDMI
```

There are additional RPi-specific tools for capturing image and video data that are described in detail in Chapter 15.

Interacting with the Onboard LEDs

This section describes how you can alter the behavior of the RPi onboard user LEDs—the LEDs on the top left corner of the RPi 2 board (see Figure 2-9) and on the bottom left of the RPi 3 board. There are two LEDs on the RPi 2/3 board, where each LED provides information about the board's state:

- The ACT LED (called OK on older models) flashes during micro-SD card activity by default. Within Linux, this LED is called led0.
- The PWR LED lights to indicate that the RPi is powered. Within Linux, this LED is called led1 on some RPi models (e.g., the RPi 2), but is hardwired to the power supply on older models.

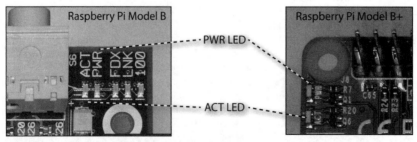

Figure 2-9: The RPi onboard power and activity LEDs

You can change the behavior of these LEDs to suit your own needs, but you will temporarily lose this useful activity and power status information.

> **NOTE**   Note that the RPi Zero has no physical PWR LED (`led1`), despite having Linux file entries to the contrary. You can set the trigger for the ACT LED (`led0`) as described later. Note that the polarity of the LED is inverted. In trigger mode "none," a brightness value of 0 turns on the LED and a brightness value of 1 turns off the LED. This behavior may be adjusted over time.

Sysfs is a virtual file system that is available under recent Linux kernels. It provides you with access to devices and drivers that would otherwise only be accessible within a restricted kernel space. This topic is discussed in detail in Chapter 6. However, at this point, it would be useful to briefly explore the mechanics of how sysfs can be used to alter the behavior of the onboard LEDs.

Using your SSH client, you can connect to the RPi and browse to the directory `/sys/class/leds/`. The output is as follows on the RPi 2:

```
pi@erpi ~ $ cd /sys/class/leds/
pi@erpi /sys/class/leds $ ls
led0   led1
```

> **NOTE**   Sysfs directory locations can vary somewhat under different versions of the Linux kernel and different Linux distributions.

You can see the two LED sysfs mappings: `led0` and `led1`. You can change the directory to alter the properties of one of these LEDs. For example, to alter the behavior of the ACT LED (`led0`):

```
pi@erpi /sys/class/leds $ cd led0
pi@erpi /sys/class/leds/led0 $ ls
brightness   device   max_brightness   subsystem   trigger   uevent
```

Here you see various different file entries that give you further information and access to settings. Note that this section uses some commands that are explained in detail in the next chapter.

You can determine the current status of an LED by typing the following:

```
pi@erpi /sys/class/leds/led0 $ cat trigger
none [mmc0] timer oneshot heartbeat backlight gpio cpu0 cpu1 cpu2
cpu3 default-on input
```

where you can see that the ACT LED is configured to show activity on the mmc0 device—the micro-SD card. You can turn this trigger off by typing the following:

```
pi@erpi /sys/class/leds/led0 $ sudo sh -c "echo none > trigger"
pi@erpi /sys/class/leds/led0 $ cat trigger
[none] mmc0 timer oneshot heartbeat backlight gpio cpu0 cpu1 ...
```

You will then see that the LED stops flashing completely. You can use `cat` `trigger` to see the new state. Now that the LED trigger is off, you can turn the ACT LED fully on or off using:

```
pi@erpi /sys/class/leds/led0 $ sudo sh -c "echo 1 > brightness"
pi@erpi /sys/class/leds/led0 $ sudo sh -c "echo 0 > brightness"
```

You can even set the LED to flash at a time interval of your choosing. If you watch carefully, you will notice the dynamic nature of sysfs. If you perform an `ls` command at this point, the directory will appear as follows, but will shortly change:

```
pi@erpi /sys/class/leds/led0 $ ls
brightness  device  max_brightness  subsystem  trigger  uevent
```

To make the LED flash, you need to set the trigger to timer mode by typing `echo timer > trigger`. You will see the ACT LED flash at a 1-second interval. Notice that there are new `delay_on` and `delay_off` file entries in the `led0` directory, as follows:

```
pi@erpi /sys/class/leds/led0 $ sudo sh -c "echo timer > trigger"
pi@erpi /sys/class/leds/led0 $ ls
brightness  delay_off  delay_on  device  max_brightness  subsystem
trigger  uevent
```

The LED flash timer makes use of these new `delay_on` time and `delay_off` time file entries. You can find out more information about these values by using the concatenate (catenate) command. For example, the following reports the time delay in milliseconds:

```
pi@erpi /sys/class/leds/led0 $ cat delay_on
500
pi@erpi /sys/class/leds/led0 $ cat delay_off
500
```

To make the ACT LED flash at 5 Hz (i.e., on for 100 ms and off for 100 ms), you can use this:

```
pi@erpi /sys/class/leds/led0 $ sudo sh -c "echo 100 > delay_on"
pi@erpi /sys/class/leds/led0 $ sudo sh -c "echo 100 > delay_off"
```

Typing `echo mmc0 > trigger` returns the LED to its default state, which results in the `delay_on` and `delay_off` file entries disappearing:

```
pi@erpi /sys/class/leds/led0 $ sudo sh -c "echo mmc0 > trigger"
pi@erpi /sys/class/leds/led0 $ ls
brightness  device  max_brightness  subsystem  trigger  uevent
```

A HEARTBEAT POWER INDICATOR

When it is available, the power indicator (PWR LED) on the RPi can be configured to display a heartbeat pattern instead of the constantly illuminated indicator. You can test the change using the following:

```
pi@erpi /sys/class/leds/led1 $ ls
brightness  device  max_brightness  subsystem  trigger  uevent
pi@erpi /sys/class/leds/led1 $ sudo sh -c "echo heartbeat > trigger"
```

The PWR LED now flashes in a heartbeat pattern, which is a lively indicator that the board is functioning. The ACT LED flashes on SD card activity by default, but you can also alter its behavior in the same way. Should you want to make this change permanent, you can edit the configuration file /boot/config.txt and add the two lines that are listed here:

```
pi@erpi /boot $ ls -l config.txt
-rwxr-xr-x 1 root root 1705 Dec  5 18:02 config.txt
pi@erpi /boot $ sudo nano config.txt
pi@erpi /boot $ tail -n2 config.txt
dtparam=pwr_led_trigger=heartbeat
dtparam=act_led_trigger=mmc0
pi@erpi /boot $ sudo reboot
```

The tail -n2 command displays the last two lines of the config.txt file, which were added using the nano editor. Once the board reboots, the ACT LED indicates SD card activity, and the PWR LED displays a heartbeat pattern and will continue to do so unless the board should lock up.

Shutdown and Reboot

WARNING Physically disconnecting the power without allowing the Linux kernel to unmount the micro-SD card can cause corruption of your file system.

One final issue to discuss in this chapter is the correct shutdown procedure for your RPi, as improper shutdown can potentially corrupt the ext4 file system and/or lead to increased boot times due to file system checks. Here are some important points on shutting down, rebooting, and starting the RPi:

- Typing sudo shutdown -h now shuts down the board correctly. You can delay this by five minutes by typing sudo shutdown -h +5.
- Typing sudo reboot will reset and reboot the board correctly.

If your project design is enclosed and you need an external soft power down, it is possible to wire an external button to an RPi GPIO input and write a shell script that runs on startup to poll the GPIO for an input. If that input occurs, /sbin/shutdown -h now can be called directly.

Summary

After completing this chapter, you should be able to do the following:

- Communicate with the RPi from your desktop computer using a network connection.
- Communicate with the RPi using a fallback serial connection with a USB-to-TTL 3.3 V cable.
- Interact with and control the RPi using simple Linux commands.
- Perform basic file editing using a Linux shell terminal.
- Manage Linux packages and set the system time.
- Use RPi-specific utilities to further configure the RPi.
- Use Linux sysfs to affect the state of the RPi onboard LEDs.
- Safely shut down and reboot the RPi.

# CHAPTER 3

Exploring Embedded Linux Systems

This chapter exposes you to the core concepts, commands, and tools required to effectively manage the Raspberry Pi embedded Linux system. The first part of the chapter is descriptive; it explains the basics of embedded Linux and the Linux boot process. After that, you learn step by step how to manage Linux systems. For this exercise, you are strongly encouraged to open a terminal connection to your Raspberry Pi or a terminal window on the Raspberry Pi and follow along. Next, the chapter describes the Git source code management system. This topic is an important one because the source code examples in this book are distributed via GitHub. Desktop virtualization is also described; it is useful for cross-platform development in later chapters. The chapter finishes by describing how you can download the source code examples for this book.

Equipment Required for This Chapter:

- Any Raspberry Pi model with a terminal connection (see Chapter 2, "Raspberry Pi Software") or a terminal window, preferably running Raspbian

Further details on this chapter are available at www.exploringrpi.com/chapter3/.

Introducing Embedded Linux

First things first: Even though the term *embedded Linux* is used in this chapter's title, there is no such thing as embedded Linux! There is no special version of the Linux kernel for embedded systems; it is just the mainline Linux kernel running on an embedded system. That said, the term *embedded Linux* has broad and common use; therefore, it is used here instead of "Linux on an embedded system," which is the more accurate phrasing.

The word *embedded* in the term *embedded Linux* is used to convey the presence of an *embedded system*, a concept that can be loosely explained as some type of computing hardware with integrated software that was designed to be used for a specific application. This concept is in contrast to the personal computer (PC), which is a general-purpose computing device designed to be used for many applications, such as web browsing, word processing, and game play. The line is blurring between embedded systems and general-purpose computing devices. For example, the Raspberry Pi (RPi) can be both, and many users will deploy it solely as a capable general-purpose computing device and/or media player. However, embedded systems have some distinctive characteristics:

- They tend to have specific and dedicated applications.
- They often have limited processing power, memory availability, and storage capabilities.
- They are generally part of a larger system that may be linked to external sensors or actuators.
- They often have a role for which reliability is critical (e.g., controls in cars, airplanes, and medical equipment).
- They often work in real time, where their outputs are directly related to present inputs (e.g., control systems).

Embedded systems are present everywhere in everyday life. Examples include vending machines, household appliances, phones/smartphones, manufacturing/assembly lines, TVs, games consoles, cars (e.g., power steering and reversing sensors), network switches, routers, wireless access points, sound systems, medical monitoring equipment, printers, building access controls, parking meters, smart energy/water meters, watches, building tools, digital cameras, monitors, tablets, e-readers, anything robotic, smart card payment/access systems, and more.

The huge proliferation of embedded Linux devices is thanks in part to the rapid evolution of smartphone technology, which has helped drive down the unit price of ARM-based processors. ARM Holdings PLC is a UK company that licenses the intellectual property of the ARMv6 and ARMv7 on the RPi models, for upfront fees and a royalty of about 1% to 2% of the sale price of the processor. Avago Technologies Ltd., the owner of Broadcom Corporation since May 2015, does not currently sell processors to retail customers directly, but processors that are similar to the BCM2835/6/7 are for sale in the $5–$10 price bracket.

Advantages and Disadvantages of Embedded Linux

There are many embedded platform types, each with its own advantages and disadvantages. There are low-cost embedded platforms, with volume prices of less than $1, such as the (8/16-bit) Atmel AVR, Microchip PIC, and TI Stellaris, to high-cost specialized platforms that can cost more than $150, such as multicore digital signal processors (DSPs). These platforms are typically programmed in C and/or assembly language, requiring that you have knowledge of the underlying systems architecture before you can develop useful applications. Embedded Linux offers an alternative to these platforms, in that significant knowledge of the underlying architecture is not required to start building applications. However, if you want to interface with electronic modules or components, some such knowledge is required.

Here are some of the reasons why embedded Linux has seen such growth:

- Linux is an efficient and scalable operating system (OS), running on everything from low-cost consumer-oriented devices to expensive large-scale servers. It has evolved over many years, from when computers were much less powerful than today, but it has retained many of the efficiencies.

- A huge number of open source programs and tools have already been developed that can be readily deployed in an embedded application. If you need a web server for your embedded application, you can install the same one that you might use on a Linux server.

- There is excellent open source support for many different peripherals and devices, from network adapters to displays.

- It is open source and does not require a fee for its use.

- The kernel and application code is running worldwide on so many devices that bugs are infrequent and are detected quickly.

One downside of embedded Linux is that it is not ideal for real-time applications due to the OS overhead. Therefore, for high-precision, fast-response applications, such as analog signal processing, embedded Linux may not be the perfect solution. However, even in real-time applications, it is often used as the "central intelligence" and control interface for a networked array of dedicated real-time sensors (see Chapter 12). In addition, there are constant developments underway in *real-time operating systems* (RTOS) Linux that aim to use Linux in a preemptive way, interrupting the OS whenever required to maintain a real-time process.

Is Linux Open Source and Free?

Linux is released under the *GNU GPL* (General Public License), which grants users the freedom to use and modify its code in any way; so, *free* generally refers to "freedom" rather than to "without cost." In fact, some of the most expensive Linux distributions are those for embedded architectures. You can find a quick guide to the GPLv3 at www.gnu.org that lists the four freedoms that every user should have (Smith, 2013):

The freedom to use the software for any purpose

The freedom to change the software to suit your needs

The freedom to share the software with your friends and neighbors

And, the freedom to share the changes you make

Even if you are using a distribution that you downloaded "for free," it can cost you significant effort to tailor libraries and device drivers to suit the particular components and modules that you want to use in your product development.

Booting the Raspberry Pi

The first thing you should see when you boot a desktop computer is the *Unified Extensible Firmware Interface* (UEFI), which provides legacy support for *BIOS* (Basic Input/Output System) services. The boot screen displays system information and invites you to press a key to alter these settings. UEFI tests the hardware components, such as the memory, and then loads the OS, typically from the solid-state drive (SSD)/hard drive. Therefore, when a desktop computer is powered on, the UEFI/BIOS performs the following steps:

1. Takes control of the computer's processor
2. Initializes and tests the hardware components
3. Loads the OS off the SSD/hard drive

The UEFI/BIOS provides an abstraction layer for the OS to interact with the display and other input/output peripherals, such as the mouse/keyboard and storage devices. Its settings are stored in NAND flash and battery-backed memory—you can see a small coin battery on the PC motherboard that supports the real-time system clock.

The Raspberry Pi Bootloaders

Like most embedded Linux devices, the RPi does not have a BIOS or battery-backed memory by default (A battery-backed real-time clock is added to the

RPi in Chapter 9). Instead, it uses a combination of *bootloaders*. Bootloaders are typically small programs that perform the critical function of linking the specific hardware of your board to the Linux OS:

- They initialize the controllers (memory, graphics, I/O).
- They prepare and allocate the system memory for the OS.
- They locate the OS and provide the facility for loading it.
- They load the OS and pass control to it.

The bootloader for embedded Linux is a custom program that is tailored for each and every board type, including the RPi. There are open source Linux bootloaders available, such as *Das U-Boot* ("The" Universal Bootloader), that can be custom built, given detailed knowledge of the hardware description of the embedded Linux platform, by using board-specific software patches (see `tiny.cc/erpi301`). The RPi uses a different approach: It uses efficient but closed-source bootloaders that were developed specifically for the RPi by Broadcom. These bootloader and configuration files are located in the `/boot` directory of the RPi image:

```
pi@erpi /boot $ ls -l *.bin start.elf *.txt *.img fixup.dat
-rwxr-xr-x 1 root root   17900 Jun 16 01:57 bootcode.bin
-rwxr-xr-x 1 root root     120 May  6 23:23 cmdline.txt
-rwxr-xr-x 1 root root    1581 May 30 14:49 config.txt
-rwxr-xr-x 1 root root    6174 Jun 16 01:57 fixup.dat
-rwxr-xr-x 1 root root     137 May  7 00:31 issue.txt
-rwxr-xr-x 1 root root 3943888 Jun 16 01:57 kernel7.img
-rwxr-xr-x 1 root root 3987132 Jun 16 01:57 kernel.img
-rwxr-xr-x 1 root root 2684312 Jun 16 01:57 start.elf
```

Figure 3-1 illustrates the boot process on the RPi, where each bootloader stage is loaded and invoked by the preceding stage bootloader. The `bootcode.bin` and `start.elf` files are closed source bootloaders that are in binary form and execute on the RPi processor's GPU (graphics processor unit), not its CPU (central processor unit). The license file at `github.com/raspberrypi/firmware/tree/master/boot` indicates that redistribution is permitted "in binary form, without modification" and that it can "only be used for the purposes of developing for, running or using a Raspberry Pi device." You can find the compressed Linux kernel at `/boot/kernel.img`; it is, of course, open source.

The output that follows is a typical boot sequence that was captured using the USB to UART TTL 3V3 serial cable that is introduced in Chapter 1. The cable was attached to pins 6 (GND), 8 (UART_TXD), and 10 (UART_RXD) on the RPi header, and the data was captured at a baud rate of 115,200. Unlike the open source U-boot loaders that execute on the CPU, the early stage RPi bootloaders do not provide output to the console—though they do flash the onboard LEDs with specific patterns should boot problems arise. The following is an extract of the console output as an RPi3 is booting. It displays important system informa-tion, such as memory mappings:

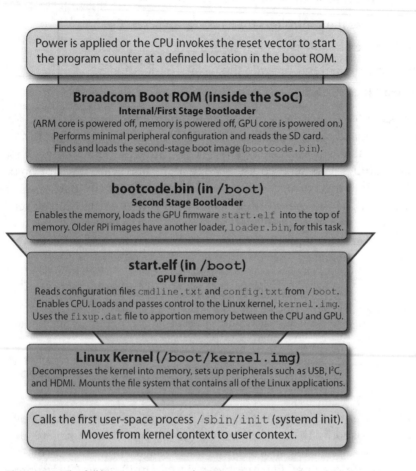

Figure 3-1: The full boot sequence on the RPi

```
Uncompressing Linux... done, booting the kernel.
[    0.000000] Booting Linux on physical CPU 0x0
...
[    0.000000] Linux version 4.1.18-v7+ (dc4@dc4-XPS13-9333) (gcc version
4.9.3 (crosstool-NG crosstool-ng-1.22.0-88-g8460611) ) #846 SMP Thu Feb
25 14:22:53 GMT 2016
[    0.000000] CPU: ARMv7 Processor [410fd034] revision 4 (ARMv7) ...
[    0.000000] Machine model: Raspberry Pi 3 Model B Rev 1.2
[    0.000000] cma: Reserved 8 MiB at 0x36400000 ...
[    0.000000] Kernel command line: 8250.nr_uarts=1 dma.dmachans=0x7f35
bcm2708_fb.fbwidth=656 bcm2708_fb.fbheight=416 bcm2709.boardrev=0xa02082
bcm2709.serial=0xbbbffd b2c smsc95xx.macaddr=B8:27:EB:FF:DB:2C
bcm2708_fb.fbswap=1 bcm2709.uart_clock=48000000 vc_mem.mem_base=0x3dc00000
vc_mem.mem_size=0x3f000000  dwc_otg.lpm_enable=0 console=ttyS0,115200
```

```
root=/dev/mmcblk0p2 rootfstype=ext4 elevator=deadline fsck.repair=yes root-
wait
[    0.000000] Memory: 874456K/901120K available (6024K kernel code, 534K
rwdata, 1660K rodata, 448K init, 757K bss, 18472K reserved, 8192K cma-
reserved)
[    0.000000] Virtual kernel memory layout:
    vector  : 0xffff0000 - 0xffff1000   (   4 kB)
    fixmap  : 0xffc00000 - 0xfff00000   (3072 kB)
    vmalloc : 0xb7800000 - 0xff000000   (1144 MB)
    lowmem  : 0x80000000 - 0xb7000000   ( 880 MB)
    modules : 0x7f000000 - 0x80000000   (  16 MB)
     .text  : 0x80008000 - 0x807895a0   (7686 kB)
     .init  : 0x8078a000 - 0x807fa000   ( 448 kB)
     .data  : 0x807fa000 - 0x8087fac0   ( 535 kB)
      .bss  : 0x80882000 - 0x8093f79c   ( 758 kB)
...


[    0.052103] Brought up 4 CPUs
[    0.052201] SMP: Total of 4 processors activated (153.60 BogoMIPS).
[    0.052231] CPU: All CPU(s) started in HYP mode. ...
[    1.467927] console [ttyS0] enabled
...


[    3.307558] systemd[1]: Detected architecture 'arm'.
[    3.321650] smsc95xx 1-1.1:1.0 eth0: register 'smsc95xx' at
usb-3f980000.usb-1.1, smsc95xx USB 2.0 Ethernet, b8:27:eb:ff:db:2c
[    3.488061] NET: Registered protocol family 10
[    3.498204] systemd[1]: Inserted module 'ipv6'
[    3.510056] systemd[1]: Set hostname to <erpi> ...
[    5.450070] spi spi0.0: setting up native-CS0 as GPIO 8
[    5.450453] spi spi0.1: setting up native-CS1 as GPIO 7 ...
...


Raspbian GNU/Linux 8 erpi ttyS0
erpi login:
```

The same information is available by typing **dmesg|more** in a terminal win-
dow. You can see that the initial hardware state is set, but most entries will
seem quite mysterious for the moment. There are some important points to note
(as highlighted in the preceding output segment):

■ The Linux kernel is uncompressed into memory and then booted. A slightly
   modified kernel image is used for the ARMv7 RPi 2/3, (kernel7.img) than
   for the ARMv6 RPi/RPi B+ (kernel.img).

■ The Linux kernel version is identified (e.g., 4.1.18-v7+).

■ The machine model is identified so that the correct device tree binary
   can be loaded.

■ The default network MAC address (a usually unique hardware address
   that identifies the device on the physical network) is passed as a kernel

command-line argument. The MAC address is automatically set on the RPi using the last 3 bytes of the CPU's serial number, which is set at manufacture. Call `cat /proc/cpuinfo` to display your board's serial number. For this board, the number is `00000000bbffdb2c`, where `ffdb2c` is utilized to provide the unique MAC address.

- Several of the remaining kernel arguments can be user configured by editing the `cmdline.txt` file (e.g., by using `sudo nano cmdline.txt`) as follows:

```
pi@erpi /boot $ more cmdline.txt
dwc_otg.lpm_enable=0 console=serial0,115200 console=tty1 root=/dev/
mmcblk0p2
rootfstype=ext4 elevator=deadline fsck.repair=yes rootwait
```

- The virtual kernel memory layout is presented. The modules entry is particularly important and is utilized in Chapter 8.

The primary configuration file for the RPi is `/boot/config.txt`. Changes that you make using the `raspi-config` tool are reflected in this file. You can manually edit this file (e.g., `sudo nano /boot/config.txt`) to enable/disable bus hardware, overclock the processors, and so on:

```
pi@erpi /boot $ more config.txt
# For more options and information see
# http://www.raspberrypi.org/documentation/configuration/config-txt.md ...
# Uncomment some or all of these to enable the optional hardware interfaces
dtparam=i2c_arm=on
#dtparam=i2s=on
dtparam=spi=on
...
# Additional overlays and parameters are documented /boot/overlays/README
```

The RPi bootloader uses a board configuration file called a *device tree* (also called a *device tree binary*) that contains the board-specific information that the kernel requires to boot the RPi. This file contains all the information needed to describe the memory size, clock speeds, onboard devices, and so on. This device tree binary or DTB (the binary) is created from a DTS (the source) file using the *Device Tree Compiler* (dtc). (This topic is described in detail in Chapter 8.) The `/boot` directory contains the device tree binaries for the different RPi models:

```
pi@erpi /boot $ ls -l *.dtb
-rwxr-xr-x 1 root root 10841 Feb 25 23:22 bcm2708-rpi-b.dtb
-rwxr-xr-x 1 root root 11120 Feb 25 23:22 bcm2708-rpi-b-plus.dtb
-rwxr-xr-x 1 root root 10871 Feb 25 23:22 bcm2708-rpi-cm.dtb
-rwxr-xr-x 1 root root 12108 Feb 25 23:22 bcm2709-rpi-2-b.dtb
-rwxr-xr-x 1 root root 12575 Feb 25 23:22 bcm2710-rpi-3-b.dtb
```

The source code for these DTBs is publicly available in DTS form. Each of the RPi model DTS files has syntax similar to the following extract, which details a hardware description of the two onboard LED pins and one of the two I²C buses on the RPi 2:

```
&i2c1 {
    pinctrl-names = "default";
```

```
        pinctrl-0 = <&i2c1_pins>;
        clock-frequency = <100000>;
};


&leds {
    act_led: act {
        label = "led0";
        linux,default-trigger = "mmc0";
        gpios = <&gpio 47 0>;
    };
    pwr_led: pwr {
        label = "led1";
        linux,default-trigger = "input";
        gpios = <&gpio 35 0>;
    };
};
```

The full source code for the DTS file for the RPi2 (bcm2709-rpi-2-b.dts) is available at: tiny.cc/erpi302. Additional device tree binary files for devices, such as sensors, HATs, and LCD displays, may be attached to the RPi:

```
pi@erpi /boot/overlays $ ls
ads7846-overlay.dtb          i2s-mmap-overlay.dtb       pps-gpio-overlay.dtb
...
hifiberry-amp-overlay.dtb    mcp2515-can0-overlay.dtb   rpi-proto-overlay.dtb
hy28b-overlay.dtb            piscreen-overlay.dtb       w1-gpio-pullup-overlay.dtb
i2c-rtc-overlay.dtb          pitft28-resistive-overlay.dtb
```

The full description for the device tree source for the RPi distribution is available with the source code distribution of this book in the /chp03/dts directory.

EXAMPLE: BUILDING DEVICE TREE BINARIES FOR THE RPi

The device tree source files for the RPi are available in the chp03/dts directory or from tiny.cc/erpi302. It is possible to build the DTB files yourself using the DTS files—it is even possible (but not recommended) to modify the DTS files and build custom DTBs. Please note that changing these files may prevent the RPi from booting, however, so you need a mechanism in place for mounting and editing the file system should a problem arise (see the examples later in this chapter). The device tree compiler (dtc) is first installed and then invoked on the DTS file (all steps take place within /chp03/dts/):

```
pi@erpi …/dts $ sudo apt install device-tree-compiler
pi@erpi …/dts $ dtc -O dtb -o bcm2709-rpi-2-b.dtb -b 0 -@ bcm2709-rpi-2-b.dts
pi@erpi …/dts $ ls -l *.dtb
-rw-r--r-- 1 pi pi 6108 Jun 16 12:30 bcm2709-rpi-2-b.dtb
pi@erpi …/dts $ ls -l /boot/*rpi-2*
-rwxr-xr-x 1 root root 6108 Jun 16 01:57 /boot/bcm2709-rpi-2-b.dtb
```

You can see that the DTB file sizes are consistent with those already on the board.

Kernel Space and User Space

The Linux kernel runs in an area of system memory called the *kernel space*, and regular user applications run in an area of system memory called *user space*. A hard boundary between these two spaces prevents user applications from accessing memory and resources required by the Linux kernel. This helps prevent the Linux kernel from crashing due to badly written user code, and because it prevents applications that belong to one user from interfering with applications and resources that belong to another user, it also provides a degree of security.

The Linux kernel "owns" and has full access to all of the physical memory and resources on the RPi. Therefore, you have to be careful that only the most stable and trusted code is permitted to run in kernel space. You can see the architectures and interfaces illustrated in Figure 3-2, where user applications use the GNU C Library (glibc) to make calls to the kernel's system call interface. The kernel services are then made available to the user space in a controlled way through the use of system calls.

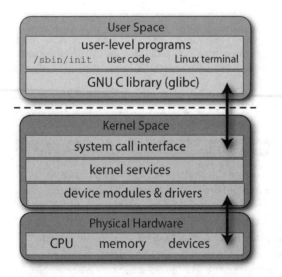

Figure 3-2: The Linux user space and kernel space architectures

A *kernel module* is an object file that contains binary code, which can be loaded and unloaded from the kernel on demand. In many cases, the kernel can even load and unload modules while it is executing, without needing to reboot the RPi. For example, if you plug a USB Wi-Fi adapter into the RPi, it is possible for the kernel to use a loadable kernel module (LKM) to utilize the adapter. Without this modular capability, the Linux kernel would be extremely large, as it would have to support every driver that would ever be needed on the RPi. You would also have to rebuild the kernel every time you wanted to add new hardware. One downside of LKMs is that driver files have to be maintained for each device. (Interaction with LKMs is described throughout the book, and you will see how you can write your own LKMs in Chapter 16.)

As described in Figure 3-1, the bootloader stages pass control to the kernel after it has been decompressed into memory. The kernel then mounts the root file system. The kernel's last step in the boot process is to call `systemd init` (`/sbin/init` on the RPi with Raspbian Jessie), which is the first user-space process that is started, and the next topic that is discussed.

The systemd System and Service Manager

A *system and service manager* starts and stops services (e.g., web servers, Secure Shell [SSH] server) depending on the current state of the RPi (e.g., starting up, shutting down). The *systemd* system and service manager is a recent and somewhat controversial addition to Linux that aims to replace, and remain backward compatible with *System V (SysV) init*. One major drawback of SysV init is that it starts tasks in series, waiting for one task to complete before beginning the next, which can lead to lengthy boot times. The systemd system is enabled by default in Debian 8/Raspbian 8 (Jessie). It starts up system services in parallel, helping to keep boot times short, particularly on multicore processors such as the RPi 2/3. In fact, you can display the boot time using the following:

```
pi@erpi ~ $ systemctl --version
systemd 215 +PAM +AUDIT +SELINUX +IMA +SYSVINIT +LIBCRYPTSETUP +GCRYPT
+ACL +XZ -SECCOMP -APPARMOR
pi@erpi ~ $ systemd-analyze time
Startup finished in 2.230s (kernel) + 6.779s (userspace) = 9.009s
```

WARNING   If you see a "command not found" message at this point, you might be using a Raspbian 7 distribution, which uses SysV init. For more information, check this chapter's web page: www.exploringrpi.com/chapter3/.

As well as being a system and service manager, systemd consists of a software bundle for login management, journal logging, device management, time synchronization, and more. Critics of systemd claim that its development project has suffered from "mission creep," and that it has taken on development work that is outside of its core mission. To some extent, this change in mission has resulted in systemd becoming core to the future of Linux itself, possibly even removing choice from users; however, it is clear that systemd is being widely adopted by many Linux distributions and here to stay.

You can use the `systemctl` command to inspect and control the state of systemd. If called with no arguments, it provides a full list of the services that are running on the RPi (use the spacebar to page, and Q to quit):

```
pi@erpi ~ $ systemctl
networking.service     loaded active exited    LSB: Raise network interfaces
```

```
ntp.service              loaded active running  LSB: Start NTP daemon
serial-getty@ttyAMA0     loaded active running  Serial Getty on ttyAMA0
ssh.service              loaded active running  OpenBSD Secure Shell server
getty.target             loaded active active   Login Prompts  ...
```

systemd uses *service files,* which have a .service extension to configure how the different services should behave on startup, shutdown, reload, and so on; see the /lib/systemd/system directory.

The Network Time Protocol (NTP) service runs by default upon installation. The systemd system can be used to manage such services on the RPi. For example, you can identify the exact service name and get its status using the following steps:

```
pi@erpi:~$ systemctl list-units -t service | grep ntp
ntp.service              loaded active running LSB: Start NTP daemon
pi@erpi:~$ systemctl status ntp.service
● ntp.service - LSB: Start NTP daemon
   Loaded: loaded (/etc/init.d/ntp)
   Active: active (running) since Mon 2016-01-02 13:00:48 GMT; 2h 21min ago
  Process: 502 ExecStart=/etc/init.d/ntp start (code=exited, status=0/ SUCCESS)
   CGroup: /system.slice/ntp.service
           ├─552 /usr/sbin/ntpd -p /var/run/ntpd.pid -g -u 107:112
           └─559 /usr/sbin/ntpd -p /var/run/ntpd.pid -g -u 107:112
```

You can stop the ntp service using the systemctl command, whereupon it will no longer update the clock according to the network time.

```
pi@erpi:~$ sudo systemctl stop ntp
pi@erpi:~$ systemctl status ntp
● ntp.service - LSB: Start NTP daemon
   Loaded: loaded (/etc/init.d/ntp)
   Active: inactive (dead) since Mon 2017-01-02 17:42:26 GMT; 6s ago
  Process: 1031 ExecStop=/etc/init.d/ntp stop (code=exited, status=0/SUCCESS)
  Process: 502 ExecStart=/etc/init.d/ntp start (code=exited, status=0/SUCCESS)
```

The service can then be restarted as follows:

```
pi@erpi ~ $ sudo systemctl start ntp
```

Table 3-1 provides a summary of systemd commands, using the ntp service as a syntax example. Many of these commands require elevation to superuser permissions by the use of the sudo tool, as described in the next section.

Table 3-1: Common systemd Commands

COMMAND	DESCRIPTION
systemctl	List all running services.
systemctl start ntp	Start a service. Does not persist after reboot.

COMMAND	DESCRIPTION
`systemctl stop ntp`	Stop a service. Does not persist after reboot.
`systemctl status ntp`	Display the service status.
`systemctl enable ntp`	Enable a service to start on boot.
`systemctl disable ntp`	Disable a service from starting on boot.
`systemctl is-enabled ssh`	Display if a system service starts on boot.
`systemctl restart ntp`	Restart a service (stop and then start).
`systemctl condrestart ntp`	Restart a service only if it is running.
`systemctl reload ntp`	Reload configuration files for a service without halting it.
`journalctl -f`	Follow the systemd log file. Press Ctrl+C to quit.
`hostnamectl --static set-hostname ERPi`	Change the hostname.
`timedatectl`	Display the time and time zone information.
`systemd-analyze time`	Display the boot time.

The *runlevel* describes the current state of the RPi and can be used to control which processes or services are started by the `init` system. Under SysV, there are different runlevels, identified as 0 (halt), 1 (single-user mode), 2 through 5 (multi-user modes), 6 (reboot), and S (start-up). When the `init` process begins, the runlevel starts at N (none). It then enters runlevel S to initialize the system in single-user mode, and finally enters one of the multi-user runlevels (2 through 5). To determine the current runlevel, type the following:

```
pi@erpi ~ $ who -r
         run-level 5  2016-01-02 03:23
```

In this case, the RPi is running at runlevel 5. You can change the runlevel by typing **init** followed by the level number. For example, you can reboot your RPi by typing the following:

```
pi@erpi ~ $ sudo init 6
```

As demonstrated, systemd retains some backward compatibility with the SysV runlevels and their numbers, as the previous SysV commands work correctly under systemd. However, the use of runlevels in systemd is considered to be dated practice. Instead, systemd uses named *target units*, some of which are listed in Table 3-2, which includes an indicative alignment with SysV runlevels. You can identify the current default target on the RPi:

```
pi@erpi ~ $ systemctl get-default
graphical.target
```

This indicates that the current configuration is for the RPi to have a headful windowing display. You can also see the list of units that the target loads using the following:

```
pi@erpi ~ $ systemctl list-units --type=target
UNIT                    LOAD   ACTIVE SUB    DESCRIPTION
basic.target            loaded active active Basic System
cryptsetup.target       loaded active active Encrypted Volumes
getty.target            loaded active active Login Prompts
graphical.target        loaded active active Graphical Interface
multi-user.target       loaded active active Multi-User System
...
```

Table 3-2: systemd Targets Aligned with SysV Runlevels

TARGET NAMES	SYSV	DESCRIPTION AND EXAMPLE USE
poweroff.target	0	Halt the system: shutdown state for all services
rescue.target	1,S	Single-user mode: for administrative functions such as checking the file system
multi-user.target	2-4	Regular multi-user modes with no windowing display
graphical.target	5	Regular multi-user mode with windowing display
reboot.target	6	Reboot the system: reboot state for all services
emergency.target	—	Emergency shell only on the main console

If you are using the RPi as a network-attached device that does not have a display attached (i.e., headless), it is wasteful of CPU/memory resources to have the windowing services running. You can switch to a headless target using the following call, whereupon the LXDE windowing interface will no longer be present, and the graphical.target entry will no longer appear in the list of units:

```
pi@erpi ~ $ sudo systemctl isolate multi-user.target
pi@erpi ~ $ systemctl list-units --type=target | grep graphical
```

And, you can re-enable the headful graphical display using the following:

```
pi@erpi ~ $ sudo systemctl isolate graphical.target
```

Finally, to set up the RPi so that it uses a different default runlevel on boot (e.g., for a headless display), you can use the following:

```
pi@erpi ~ $ sudo systemctl set-default multi-user.target
Created symlink from /etc/systemd/system/default.target to /lib/systemd/sys
tem/multi-user.target.
pi@erpi ~ $ systemctl get-default
multi-user.target
```

After reboot, the windowing services do not start, and the notional equivalent SysV runlevel is displayed as runlevel 3.

Managing Linux Systems

In this section, you examine the Linux file system in more detail, building on the commands and tools described in Chapter 2, to ensure that you have full administrative control of the RPi.

The Super User

On Linux systems, the system administrator account has the highest level of security access to all commands and files. Typically, this account is referred to as the *root account* or *superuser*. Under Raspbian/Debian, this user account has the user name *root*, but it is typically disabled by default; however, you can enable it by typing **sudo passwd root** from a shell that is logged in with the pi user account (username: **pi**, password: **raspberry**):

```
pi@erpi ~ $ sudo passwd root
Enter new UNIX password: mySuperSecretPassword
Retype new UNIX password: mySuperSecretPassword
passwd: password updated successfully
```

NOTE The naming of the user account as "root" is related to the fact that it is the only user account with permission to alter the top-level root directory (/). For more information, see www.linfo.org/root.htm.

It is recommended when performing general operations on a Linux system that you try to avoid being logged in as the superuser; however, it is important to also remember that when using the RPi you are typically not running a server with thousands of user accounts! In many applications, a single root user account, with a nondefault password, is likely sufficient. However, using a non-superuser account for your development work could protect you from yourself—for example, from accidentally deleting the file system. The pi user account in Raspbian has been carefully configured to simplify the interaction with hardware, enabling it to be used for the majority of tasks that are described in this book. However, it is important to understand how this custom user account is configured and how it works so well.

Under many Linux distributions, including Raspbian, a special tool called *sudo* (*superuser do*) is used whenever you want to perform system administration commands. Typically, the tool prompts you for the administrator password and then authorizes you to perform administrator operations for a short time period, also warning you that "with great power comes great responsibility." The pi user account in Raspbian has been configured so that it does not require you to enter the root password for superuser elevation.

The next section discusses user accounts management, but if you create a new user account and want to enable it to use the sudo tool, the account name must be added to the *sudoers file*, /etc/sudoers, by using the *visudo* tool (type **visudo** while logged in as root, or **sudo visudo** if logged in as pi). The last lines of the /etc/sudoers file provide the configuration for the pi user account, which explains why no password is required for the user pi to execute the sudo tool:

```
#User privilege specification
Root    ALL=(ALL:ALL) ALL
#username hostnames=(users permitted to run commands as) permitted commands
pi      ALL=(ALL)     NOPASSWD: ALL
```

In this configuration, the user pi is granted privileges on all (first ALL) hostnames to execute commands as any user (second ALL) and to execute all commands (third ALL) with no password required. The sudo tool works well; however, it can make the redirection of the output of a command more complex, which is apparent later in this chapter.

There is another command in Linux that enables you to run a shell with a substitute *u*ser: su. Typing **su -** (same as **su - root**) opens a new shell with full superuser access, and it can be used as follows, after you have enabled root login:

```
pi@erpi ~ $ su -
Password: mySuperSecretPassword
root@erpi:~# whoami
root
root@erpi:~# exit
logout
pi@erpi ~ $ whoami
pi
```

The # prompt indicates that you are logged in to the superuser account. To re-disable root login to the RPi, you can type **sudo passwd -l root**.

System Administration

The *Linux file system* is a hierarchy of directories used to organize files on a Linux system. This section examines the ownership of files, the use of symbolic links, and the concept of file system permissions.

The Linux File System

Linux uses data structures, called *inodes*, to represent file system objects such as files and directories. When a Linux *ext*ended file system (e.g., ext3/ext4) is created on a physical disk, an *inode table* is created. This table links to an inode data structure for each file and directory on that physical disk. The inode data structure for each file and directory stores information such as permission attributes, pointers to raw physical disk block locations, time stamps, and link counts. You can see this with an example by performing a listing ls -ail of the root directory, where -i causes ls to display the inode indexes. You will see the following for the /tmp directory entry:

-a show all,   *p. 38*
-l long format

```
pi@erpi ~ $ cd /
pi@erpi / $ ls -ail | grep tmp
    269 drwxrwxrwt   7 root root   4096 Jun 18 01:17 tmp
```

Therefore, 269 is the /tmp directory's *inode index*. If you enter the /tmp directory by using cd, create a temporary file (a.txt), and perform ls -ail, you will see that the current (.) directory has the exact same inode index:

```
pi@erpi / $ cd tmp
pi@erpi /tmp $ touch a.txt
pi@erpi /tmp $ ls -ail
    269 drwxrwxrwt   7 root root 4096 Jun 18 01:41 .
      2 drwxr-xr-x 22 root root 4096 Jun 16 01:57 ..
   4338 -rw-r--r--  1 pi   pi      0 Jun 18 01:41 a.txt
```

You can also see that the root directory (..) has the inode index of 2 and that a text file (a.txt) also has an inode index, 4338. Therefore, you cannot cd directly to an inode index, because the inode index might not refer to a directory.

Figure 3-3 illustrates the Linux directory listing and file permissions that relate to working with files under Linux. The first letter indicates the file type—for example, whether the listing is a (d) directory, (l) link, or (-) regular file. There are also some more obscure file types: (c) character special, (b) block special, (p) fifo, and (s) socket. Directories and regular files do not need further explanation, but links need special attention, as described next.

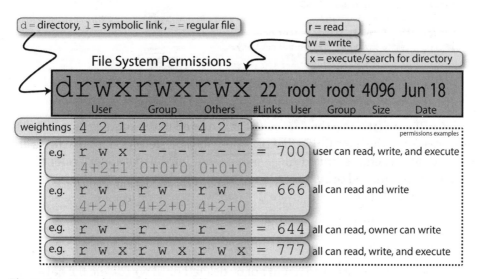

Figure 3-3: Linux directory listing and file permissions

Links to Files and Directories

There are two types of links in Linux: *soft links* and *hard links*. A soft link (or *symbolic link*) is a file that refers to the location of another file or directory. Hard links, conversely, link directly to the inode index, but they cannot be linked to a directory. You create a link using `ln /path/to/file.txt linkname`. You create a symbolic link by adding `-s` to the call. To illustrate the usage, the following example creates a soft link and a hard link to a file `/tmp/test.txt`:

```
pi@erpi ~ $ cd /tmp
pi@erpi /tmp $ touch test.txt
pi@erpi /tmp $ ln -s /tmp/test.txt softlink
pi@erpi /tmp $ ln /tmp/test.txt hardlink
pi@erpi /tmp $ ls -al
total 8
drwxrwxrwt  2 root root 4096 Jun 18 01:55 .
drwxr-xr-x 22 root root 4096 Jun 16 01:57 ..
-rw-r--r--  2 pi   pi      0 Jun 18 01:55 hardlink
lrwxrwxrwx  1 pi   pi     13 Jun 18 01:55 softlink -> /tmp/test.txt
-rw-r--r--  2 pi   pi      0 Jun 18 01:55 test.txt
```

You can see there is a number 2 in front of the file `test.txt` (after the file permissions). This is the number of hard links that are associated with the file. This is a count value that was incremented by 1 when the hard link, called `hardlink`, was created. If you were to delete the hard link (e.g., using `rm hardlink`), this counter would decrement back to 1. To illustrate the difference between soft links and hard links, some text is added to the `test.txt` file:

```
pi@erpi /tmp $ echo "testing links on the RPi" >> test.txt
pi@erpi /tmp $ more hardlink
testing links on the RPi
pi@erpi /tmp $ more softlink
testing links on the RPi
pi@erpi /tmp $ mkdir subdirectory
pi@erpi /tmp $ mv test.txt subdirectory/
pi@erpi /tmp $ more hardlink
testing links on the RPi
pi@erpi /tmp $ more softlink
softlink: No such file or directory
```

You can see that when the `test.txt` file is moved to the subdirectory, the soft link breaks but the hard link still works perfectly. Therefore, symbolic links are not updated when the linked file is moved, but hard links always refer to the source, even if moved or removed. To illustrate the last point, the file `test.txt` can be removed using the following:

```
pi@erpi /tmp $ rm subdirectory/test.txt
pi@erpi /tmp $ more hardlink
testing links on the RPi
```

Yet, the file still exists! And it will not be deleted until you delete the hard link called `hardlink`, thus decrementing the link count to zero. Therefore, if a file has a hard link count of zero, and it is not being used by a process, it will be deleted. In effect, the filename itself, `test.txt`, was just a hard link. Note that you cannot hard link across different file systems, because each file system will have its own inode index table that starts at 1. Therefore, inode 269, which is the inode index of the /tmp directory, is likely describing something quite different on another file system. Type the command **man ln** to see a particularly useful guide on linking.

> **NOTE** You can type `history` to list all previous commands that you have typed. You can also press Ctrl+R to get an interactive search of your history to find a recently used command. Pressing Enter activates the command, and pressing Tab places it on your command line, so that it can be modified.

Users and Groups

Linux is a multi-user OS, which uses the following three distinct classes to manage access permissions:

- **User:** You can create different user accounts on your RPi. This is useful if you want to limit access to processes and areas of the file system. The `root` user account is the superuser of the RPi and has access to every file; so, for example, it may not be safe to run a public web server from this account or the pi user account if the server supports local scripting.

- **Group:** User accounts may be flagged as belonging to one or more groups, whereby each group has different levels of access to different resources (e.g., UART devices, I^2C buses).

- **Others:** All users of the RPi besides the file's owner, or a member of the group listed in the permissions.

You can create users at the Linux terminal. The full list of groups is available by typing **more /etc/group**. The following example demonstrates how you can create a new user account on the RPi and modify the properties of that account to suit your needs.

EXAMPLE: CREATING A NEW USER ACCOUNT ON THE RPi

This example demonstrates how you can create a user account and then retrospectively change its properties, using the following steps:

1. The creation of a new user account called `molloyd` on the RPi

2. The addition of the account to a new group of your own design

3. The addition of the user account to the standard RPi interfacing groups

4. The reset of the password for the new user account

5. Verification that the account is working correctly

Step 1: Create a user molloyd as follows:
```
pi@erpi ~ $ sudo adduser molloyd
Adding user 'molloyd' ...
Adding new group 'molloyd' (1002) ...
Adding new user 'molloyd' (1001) with group 'molloyd' ...
Creating home directory '/home/molloyd' ...
Copying files from '/etc/skel' ...
Enter new UNIX password: ThePassword
Retype new UNIX password: ThePassword
passwd: password updated successfully
Changing the user information for molloyd
Enter the new value, or press ENTER for the default
    Full Name []: Derek Molloy
    Room Number []: Home
    Work Phone []: XXXX
    Home Phone []: XXXX
    Other []: XXXX
Is the information correct? [Y/n] Y
```

Step 2: Add the user to a new group of your design:
```
pi@erpi ~ $ sudo groupadd newgroup
pi@erpi ~ $ sudo adduser molloyd newgroup
Adding user 'molloyd' to group 'newgroup' ...
Adding user molloyd to group newgroup
Done.
pi@erpi ~ $ groups molloyd
molloyd : molloyd newgroup
```

Step 3: Add the user to the standard RPi user and interface groups:
```
pi@erpi ~ $ sudo usermod -a -G pi,adm,dialout,cdrom,sudo,audio,video,
plugdev,users,games,netdev,gpio,i2c,spi,input molloyd
pi@erpi ~ $ groups molloyd
molloyd : molloyd adm dialout cdrom sudo audio video plugdev games users pi
 netdev input spi i2c gpio newgroup
```

Step 4: Reset the password, if required:
```
pi@erpi ~ $ sudo passwd molloyd
Enter new UNIX password: ABetterPassword
Retype new UNIX password: ABetterPassword
passwd: password updated successfully
pi@erpi ~ $ sudo chage -d 0 molloyd
```

You can force the password to expire on login by using sudo chage -d 0 molloyd. For security, the encrypted passwords are stored in the restricted file /etc/shadow, not the public readable /etc/passwd file.

Step 5: Test the account by typing su molloyd from the pi user account and/or log in with a new Linux terminal (using pwd to *print* the *working directory*):
```
pi@erpi ~ $ su molloyd
Password: ABetterPassword
```

```
You are required to change your password immediately (root enforced)
Changing password for molloyd.
(current) UNIX password: ABetterPassword
Enter new UNIX password: MyPrivatePassword
Retype new UNIX password: MyPrivatePassword
molloyd@erpi:/home/pi$ whoami
molloyd
molloyd@erpi:/home/pi$ pwd
/home/pi
molloyd@erpi:/home/pi$ cd /home/molloyd
molloyd@erpi:~$ touch test.txt
molloyd@erpi:~$ ls -l test.txt
-rw-r--r-- 1 molloyd molloyd 0 Jun 18 23:26 test.txt
molloyd@erpi:~$ more /etc/group |grep newgroup
newgroup:x:1003:molloyd
```

The user's home directory for each user account is represented as ~ at the shell prompt. You can see that the test.txt **file is created with the correct user and group ID. Also, note that the** newgroup **group only has one member,** molloyd. **To delete an account, type** sudo deluser --remove-home molloyd, **which removes the user account and its home directory.**

To practice with the topics that are introduced earlier in this chapter, the following examples are performed using the molloyd user account. The first example demonstrates how to change the ownership of a file using the *ch*ange *own*ership chown command and to change the group ownership of the file using the *ch*ange *group* chgrp command.

For the sudo tool to be invoked correctly in the example, the user molloyd must be present in the sudoers file, which is achieved by the pi user account executing the visudo command. The file can be modified to include a molloyd entry, such as the following:

```
pi@erpi ~ $ sudo visudo
pi@erpi ~ $ sudo tail -n 2 /etc/sudoers
pi      ALL=(ALL) NOPASSWD: ALL
molloyd ALL=(ALL) ALL
```

The molloyd user account can now execute the sudo command, but must enter their user password to do so.

EXAMPLE: CHANGING THE OWNERSHIP AND GROUP OF A FILE

SSH to the RPi and log in as the molloyd user. Use superuser access to change a file test.txt **in the** /tmp **directory that is owned by the user** molloyd **with the group** molloyd, **to have owner** root **and group** root:

```
molloyd@erpi:~$ cd /tmp
molloyd@erpi:/tmp$ touch test.txt
```

```
molloyd@erpi:/tmp$ ls -l test.txt
-rw-r--r-- 1 molloyd molloyd 0 Jun 19 00:06 test.txt
molloyd@erpi:/tmp$ sudo chgrp root test.txt
[sudo] password for molloyd: MyPrivatePassword
molloyd@erpi:/tmp$ sudo chown root test.txt
molloyd@erpi:/tmp$ ls -l test.txt
-rw-r--r-- 1 root root 0 Jun 19 00:06 test.txt
```

File System Permissions

The *file system permissions* state what levels of access each of the permissions classes have to a file or directory. The *change mode* command chmod enables a user to change the access permissions for file system objects. You can specify the permissions in a relative way. For example, **chmod a+w test.txt** gives all users write access to a file test.txt but leaves all other permissions the same. You can also apply the permissions in an absolute way. For example, **chmod a=r test.txt** sets all users to only have read access to the file test.txt. The next example demonstrates how to modify the file system permissions of a file using the chmod command.

EXAMPLE: USING THE CHMOD COMMAND IN DIFFERENT FORMS

Change a file test1.txt in the /tmp directory so that users and group members have read and write access, but others only have read access. Perform this task in three different ways:

```
molloyd@erpi:/tmp$ touch test1.txt
molloyd@erpi:/tmp$ ls -l test1.txt
-rw-r--r-- 1 molloyd molloyd 0 Jun 19 00:18 test1.txt
molloyd@erpi:/tmp$ chmod g+w test1.txt
molloyd@erpi:/tmp$ ls -l test1.txt
-rw-rw-r-- 1 molloyd molloyd 0 Jun 19 00:18 test1.txt
molloyd@erpi:/tmp$ chmod 664 test1.txt
molloyd@erpi:/tmp$ ls -l test1.txt
-rw-rw-r-- 1 molloyd molloyd 0 Jun 19 00:18 test1.txt
molloyd@erpi:/tmp$ chmod u=rw,g=rw,o=r test1.txt
molloyd@erpi:/tmp$ ls -l test1.txt
-rw-rw-r-- 1 molloyd molloyd 0 Jun 19 00:18 test1.txt
```

All three calls to chmod have the exact same outcome.

Table 3-3 provides examples of the command structure for chown and chgrp. It also lists some example commands for working with users, groups, and permissions.

Table 3-3: Commands for Working with Users, Groups, and Permissions

COMMAND	DESCRIPTION
chown molloyd a.txt	Change file owner.
chown molloyd:users a.txt	Change owner and group at the same time.
chown -Rh molloyd /tmp/test	Recursively change ownership of /tmp/test. -h affects symbolic links instead of referenced files.
chgrp users a.txt	Change group ownership of the file.
chgrp -Rh users /tmp/test	Recursively change with same -h as chown.
chmod 600 a.txt	Change permissions (as in Figure 3-3) so that the user has read/write access to the file; group or others have no access.
chmod ugo+rw a.txt	Give users, group, and others read/write access to a.txt.
chmod a-w a.txt	Remove write access for all users using a, which describes *all* (the set of users, group, and others).
chmod ugo=rw a.txt	Set the permissions for all to be read/write.
umask umask -S	List the default permissions settings. Using -S displays the umask in a more readable form.
umask 022 umask u=rwx,g=rx,o=rx	Change the default permissions on all newly created files and directories. The two umask commands here are equivalent. If you set this mask value and create a file or directory, it will be: drwxr-xr-x for the directory and -rw-r--r-- for the file. You can set a user-specific umask in the account's .login file.
chmod u+s myexe chmod g+s myexe	Set a special bit called the *setuid bit* (set user ID on execute) and *setgid bit* (set group ID on execute), s, that allows a program to be executed as if by another logged-in user, but with the permissions of the file's owner or group. For example, you could use this to allow a particular program to execute as if the root user account executed it. If the file is not executable, a capital S appears, instead of a lower-case s.
chmod 6750 myexe chmod u=rwxs,g=rxs,o= myexe	Set the setuid bit in an absolute way. Both examples will give myexe the permissions -rwsr-s---, where both the setuid and setgid bits are set (note the space before myexe). For security reasons, the setuid bit cannot be applied to shell scripts.
stat /tmp/test.txt	Provides useful file system status information for a file or directory, such as its physical device and inode information, last access, and modify/change times.

Here is an example of the last entry in Table 3-3, the `stat` command:

```
molloyd@erpi:/tmp$ stat test.txt
  File: 'test.txt'
  Size: 0              Blocks: 0         IO Block: 4096    regular empty file
Device: b302h/45826d   Inode: 6723       Links: 1
Access: (0644/-rw-r--r--)  Uid: (    0/    root)   Gid: (    0/    root)
Access: 2015-06-19 00:06:28.551326384 +0000
Modify: 2015-06-19 00:06:28.551326384 +0000
Change: 2015-06-19 00:07:13.151016841 +0000
 Birth: -
```

Note that each file in Linux retains an access, modify, and change time. You can update the access and modify times artificially using `touch -a text.txt` and `touch -m test.txt`, respectively (the change time is affected in both cases). The change time is also affected by system operations such as `chmod`; the modify time is affected by a write to the file; and the access time is in theory affected by a file read. However, such operational behavior means that reading a file causes a write! This feature of Linux causes significant wear on the RPi's SD card and results in I/O performance deficiencies. Therefore, the file access time feature is typically disabled on the RPi boot SD card using the mount option `noatime` within the `/etc/fstab` configuration file (covered in the next section). Note that there is also a similar `nodiratime` option that can be used to disable access time updates for directories only; however, the `noatime` option disables access time updates for both files and directories.

Just to finish the discussion of Figure 3-3: The example in the figure has `22` hard links to the file. For a directory this represents the number of subdirectories, the parent directory (`..`) and itself (`.`). The entry is owned by root and it is in the root group. The next entry of `4096` is the size required to store the metadata about files contained in that directory (the minimum size is one sector, typically 4,096 bytes).

One final point: If you perform a directory listing `ls -ld` in the root directory you will see a `t` bit in the permissions of the `/tmp` directory. This is called the *sticky bit*, meaning that write permission is not sufficient to delete files. Therefore, in the `/tmp` directory any user can create files, but no user can delete another user's files:

```
molloyd@erpi:/tmp$ cd /
molloyd@erpi:/$ ls -dhl tmp
drwxrwxrwt 7 root root 4.0K Jun 19 00:18 tmp
```

The `ls -dhl` command lists (`d`) directory names (not their contents), with (`h`) human-readable file sizes, in (`l`) long format.

The Linux Root Directory

Exploring the Linux file system can be daunting for new Linux users. If you go to the top-level directory using `cd /` on the RPi and type `ls`, you will get the top-level directory structure, of the following form:

```
molloyd@erpi:/$ ls
bin   boot.bak  etc    lib          media  opt   root  sbin  sys  usr
boot  dev       home   lost+found   mnt    proc  run   srv   tmp  var
```

What does it all mean? Well, each of these directories has a role, and if you understand the roles, you can start to get an idea of where to search for configuration files or the binary files that you need. Table 3-4 briefly describes the content of each top-level Linux subdirectory.

Table 3-4: The Linux Top-Level Directory

DIRECTORY	DESCRIPTION
bin	Contains the binary executables used by all of the users and is present in the PATH environment variable by default. Another directory, /usr/bin, contains executables that are not core to booting or repairing the system.
boot	Contains the files for booting the RPi.
boot.bak	Contains a backup copy of /boot after a system upgrade.
dev	Contains the device nodes (linked to device drivers).
etc	Configuration files for the local system.
home	Contains the user's home directories (/home/pi is the pi user home).
lib	Contains the standard system libraries.
lost+found	After running fsck (file system check and repair) unlinked files display here. The mklost+found command recreates the lost+found directory if it is deleted.
media	Used for mounting removable media, such as micro-SD cards.
mnt	Used typically for mounting temporary file systems.
opt	A good place for installing third-party (non-core Linux) optional software.
proc	A virtual file representation of processes running on the RPi. (For example, if you cd /proc and type cat iomem you can see some memory mapping addresses.)
root	The home directory of root account under the Raspbian and Debian Linux distributions. (This is /home/root on many other distributions.)
run	Provides information about the running system since the last boot.
sbin	Contains executables for root user (superuser) system management.
srv	Stores data related to ftp, web servers, rsync, etc.
sys	Contains a virtual file system that describes the system.
tmp	Contains temporary files.
usr	Contains programs for all of the users, and many subdirectories such as /usr/include (C/C++ header files), /usr/lib (C/C++ library files), /usr/src (Linux kernel source), /usr/bin (user executables), /usr/local (similar to /usr but for local users), and /usr/share (shared files and media between users).
var	Contains variable files such as system logs.

Commands for File Systems

In addition to commands for working with files and directories on file systems, there are commands for working with the file system itself. The first commands you should examine are df (remember as *disk free*) and mount. The df command provides an overview of the file systems on the RPi. Adding -T lists the file system types:

```
pi@erpi / $ df -T
Filesystem      Type        1K-blocks      Used  Available  Use%  Mounted on
/dev/root       ext4         15186900   3353712   11165852   24%  /
devtmpfs        devtmpfs       470400         0     470400    0%  /dev
tmpfs           tmpfs          474688         0     474688    0%  /dev/shm
tmpfs           tmpfs          474688         0     474688    0%  /sys/fs/cgroup
/dev/mmcblk0p1  vfat            57288     19824      37464   35%  /boot
...
```

The df command is useful for determining whether you are running short on disk space; you can see that the root file system /dev/root is 24% used in this case, with 11.2 GB (of a 16 GB SD card) available for additional software installations. Also listed are several temporary file system (tmpfs) entries that actually refer to virtual file systems, which are mapped to the RPi's DDR RAM. (The /sys/fs/* entries are discussed in detail in Chapter 8.) In addition, the /dev/mmcblk0p1 entry has a 57 MB vfat (virtual file allocation table, which was introduced in Windows 95) file system partition on the SD card. A vfat partition is required by the bootloaders and for firmware updates.

> **NOTE**   If you are running out of space on the RPi SD card root file system, check the system logs: /var/log. Excessively large log files are symptomatic of system problems, so review them for any issues. When you have resolved any issues, you can clear the messages log by typing cat /dev/null > /var/log/messages with root permission (also check kern.log, dpkg.log, and syslog). For example, to clear the dpkg.log using the pi account without deleting the file or resetting its file permissions, use the following:
>
> ```
> pi@erpi /var/log $ sudo sh -c "cat /dev/null > dpkg.log"
> ```
>
> The shell sh -c call executes the entire command string in quotations with super user permissions. This is required, because in a call to sudo cat /dev/null > dpkg.log on its own, sudo does not perform the output redirection >, rather it is performed as the pi user and therefore will fail due to insufficient permissions. This is the redirection issue with sudo that is alluded to earlier in the chapter.

The list block devices command lsblk provides you with a concise tree-structure list of the block devices, such as SD cards, USB memory keys, and USB card readers (if any), that are attached to the RPi. As shown in the following output, you can see that mmcblk0 (the boot SD card) is split into two partitions: p1, which is attached to /boot, and p2, which is attached to the root of the file system: /. In this example, there is a USB micro-SD card reader containing a 32 GB card (see Figure 1-8(b)) that is plugged into one of the USB ports. This appears as the block device sda with a single partition sda1, as follows:

```
pi@erpi ~ $ lsblk
NAME           MAJ:MIN RM  SIZE RO TYPE MOUNTPOINT
sda              8:0    1 29.8G  0 disk
└─sda1           8:1    1 29.8G  0 part
mmcblk0        179:0    0 14.9G  0 disk
├─mmcblk0p1 179:1       0   56M  0 part /boot
└─mmcblk0p2 179:2       0 14.8G  0 part /
```

Clearly, the USB ports can be used for additional storage, which is useful if you are capturing video data and there is insufficient capacity on the system SD card. You can test the performance of SD cards to ensure that they meet the needs of your applications using the example that follows.

EXAMPLE: TESTING SD CARD READ PERFORMANCE

You can test the read performance of your SD cards and controllers using the hdparm program. For example, on the RPi 2 (and on the RPi B+):

```
pi@erpi ~ $ sudo apt install hdparm
pi@erpi ~ $ sudo hdparm -tT /dev/mmcblk0 /dev/sda1
/dev/mmcblk0:
  Timing cached reads:    868 MB in  2.00 seconds = 433.95 MB/sec
  Timing buffered disk reads:  56 MB in  3.11 seconds =  18.01 MB/sec
/dev/sda1:
  Timing cached reads:    890 MB in  2.00 seconds = 444.34 MB/sec
  Timing buffered disk reads:  74 MB in  3.09 seconds =  27.24 MB/sec
```

You can see that the SD card in the USB adapter (sda1) performs slightly better than the SD card that is attached to the onboard MMC controller (mmcblk0). Both cards have the same specification (SanDisk Ultra Class 10, 30 MB/sec), so the difference in data read rate appears to be due to the performance of the respective controllers. You can utilize the dd command to test write performance, but be careful, as incorrect usage will result in data loss.

Using the mount command with no arguments provides you with further information about the file system on the RPi.

```
pi@erpi ~ $ mount
/dev/mmcblk0p2 on / type ext4 (rw,noatime,data=ordered)
sysfs on /sys type sysfs (rw,nosuid,nodev,noexec,relatime)
proc on /proc type proc (rw,relatime)   ...
```

As previously discussed, the file system is organized as a single tree that is rooted at the root: /. Typing cd / brings you to the root point. The mount command can be used to attach a file system on a physical disk to this tree. File systems on separate physical devices can all be attached to named points at arbitrary locations on the single tree. Table 3-5 describes some file system commands that you can use to manage your file system, and thereafter follows two examples that demonstrate how to utilize the `mount` command for important RPi system administration tasks.

Table 3-5: Useful Commands for File Systems

COMMAND	DESCRIPTION

`du -h /opt`
 	
`du -hs /opt/*`
 	
`du -hc *.jpg`
	Disk usage: Find out how much space a directory tree uses. Options: (-h) human readable form, (-s) summary, (-c) total. The last command finds the total size of the JPG format files in the current directory.

`df -h`	Display system disk space in (-h) human-readable form.
`lsblk`	List block devices.

`dd if=test.img of=/dev/sdX`
 	
`dd if=/dev/sdX of=test.img`
	`dd` converts and copies a file, where `if` is the input file and `of` is the output file. Use this command under Linux to write an image to an SD card. This is typically used under desktop Linux with the following form:
	
	`sudo dd if=./RPi*.img of=/dev/sdX`
	
	where `/dev/sdX` is the SD card reader/writer device.

`cat /proc/ partitions`	List all registered partitions.
`mkfs /dev/sdX`	Make a Linux file system. Also `mkfs.ext4`, `mkfs.vfat`. This destroys data on the device. Use carefully!
`fdisk -l`	Note that `fdisk` can be used to manage disks, create partitions, delete partitions, etc. `fdisk -l` displays all existing partitions.
`badblocks /dev/ mmcblkX`	Check for bad blocks on the SD card. SD cards have wear leveling controller circuitry. If you get errors, get a new card; don't record them using `fsck`. Run this with root permissions and be aware that it takes some time to run.
`mount /media/ store`	Mount a partition if it is listed in `/etc/fstab`.
`umount /media/ store`	Unmount a partition. You will be informed if a file is open on this partition.

`sudo apt install tree`
 	
`tree ~/ exploringrpi`
	Install the `tree` command and use it to display the code repository for this book as a directory tree structure.

EXAMPLE: FIXING PROBLEMS ON A SD CARD BOOT IMAGE

Occasionally, you make a change to a Linux configuration file on the RPi Linux boot image that prevents the image from booting, or causes the failure of network adapters so that you no longer have access to the device. If you have a RPi-compatible USB card reader (see Figure 1-8(b), shown in Chapter 1), you can use a second "backup" Linux SD card boot image to boot the RPi, whereupon you can mount the "damaged" SD card image as follows:

```
pi@erpi ~ $ lsblk
NAME           MAJ:MIN RM  SIZE RO TYPE MOUNTPOINT
sda              8:0    1 14.7G  0 disk
├─sda1           8:1    1   56M  0 part
└─sda2           8:2    1 14.6G  0 part
mmcblk0        179:0    0 14.9G  0 disk
├─mmcblk0p1    179:1    0   56M  0 part /boot
└─mmcblk0p2    179:2    0 14.8G  0 part /
```

You can create mount points for the vfat and ext4 partitions of the "damaged" SD card that is present in the USB SD card reader as follows:

```
pi@erpi ~ $ sudo mkdir /media/fix_vfat
pi@erpi ~ $ sudo mkdir /media/fix_ext
pi@erpi ~ $ sudo mount /dev/sda1 /media/fix_vfat/
pi@erpi ~ $ sudo mount /dev/sda2 /media/fix_ext/
```

You can then browse the file systems on the "damaged" SD card using your RPi and undo any invalid configuration settings:

```
pi@erpi ~ $ cd /media/fix_vfat/
pi@erpi /media/fix_vfat $ ls
...              issue.txt     start.elf     cmdline.txt    kernel7.img
start_x.elf      config.txt    kernel.img    ...
pi@erpi /media/fix_vfat $ cd ../fix_ext/
pi@erpi /media/fix_ext $ ls
bin   boot.bak  etc   lib           media  opt   root  sbin      srv  tmp  var
boot  dev       home  lost+found    mnt    proc  run   selinux   sys  usr
```

As above, you can edit files on the vfat and ext4 partitions. After completing your changes, remember to unmount the media before physically ejecting the SD card. You can then safely remove the mount points:

```
pi@erpi /media/fix_vfat $ cd ..
pi@erpi /media $ sudo umount /media/fix_vfat
pi@erpi /media $ sudo umount /media/fix_ext
pi@erpi /media $ sudo rmdir fix_vfat fix_ext
```

EXAMPLE: MOUNTING AN SD CARD AS ADDITIONAL STORAGE ON THE RPi

1. Formatting the secondary SD card to have a Linux ext4 file system

2. Mounting the secondary SD card as `/media/store`

3. Mounting the secondary SD card automatically at boot time

4. Configuring the card for user write access and displaying its capacity

In this example, the card is a 32 GB micro-SD card that has been placed in a micro-USB card reader (see Figure 1-8(b), shown in Chapter 1). Ensure that the card is blank, because *this step will destroy its contents*; skip to Step 2 if you want to retain the SD card's contents.

Step 1: Use `lsblk` to identify the device:

```
pi@erpi ~ $ lsblk
NAME          MAJ:MIN RM  SIZE RO TYPE MOUNTPOINT
sda             8:0    1 29.8G  0 disk
└─sda1          8:1    1 29.8G  0 part
mmcblk0       179:0    0 14.9G  0 disk
├─mmcblk0p1   179:1    0   56M  0 part /boot
└─mmcblk0p2   179:2    0 14.8G  0 part /
```

The 32 GB card appears as block device `/sda1` and can be prepared for a file system of choice (Note that using `mmcblk0p1` or `mmcblk0p2` for the next step will destroy the contents of your primary boot SD card.)

Build a file system as follows:

```
pi@erpi ~ $ sudo mkfs.ext4 /dev/sda1
mke2fs 1.42.12 (29-Aug-2014)
/dev/sda1 contains a vfat file system
Proceed anyway? (y,n) y
Creating filesystem with 7814912 4k blocks and 1954064 inodes
Filesystem UUID: e9562aa9-4565-4dfd-b986-4c45d089c7ce
...
Writing superblocks and filesystem accounting information: done
```

Step 2: A mount point can be created, and the secondary card mounted using the `mount` command (`-t` indicates the file type; when omitted, `mount` attempts to auto-detect the file type):

```
pi@erpi ~ $ sudo mkdir /media/store
pi@erpi ~ $ sudo mount -t ext4 /dev/sda1 /media/store
pi@erpi ~ $ cd /media/store
pi@erpi /media/store $ ls
lost+found
pi@erpi /media/store $ lsblk
NAME          MAJ:MIN RM  SIZE RO TYPE MOUNTPOINT
sda             8:0    1 29.8G  0 disk
└─sda1          8:1    1 29.8G  0 part /media/store
...
```

Step 3: To configure this secondary storage device to be mounted automatically at boot time involves adding an entry to the /etc/fstab file. Add an entry to the last line of the file, as follows:

```
pi@erpi ~ $ sudo nano /etc/fstab
pi@erpi ~ $ more /etc/fstab
proc              /proc          proc    defaults           0     0
/dev/mmcblk0p1    /boot          vfat    defaults           0     2
/dev/mmcblk0p2    /              ext4    defaults,noatime   0     1
/dev/sda1         /media/store   ext4    defaults,nofail,user,auto  0   0
pi@erpi ~ $ sudo reboot
```

This entry configures the /dev/sda1 to be mounted at /media/store, identifies the file system as ext4 format and sets the following mount options: defaults (use default settings), nofail (mount the device when present but ignore if absent), user (users have permissions to mount the system), and auto (the card is mounted on start-up, or if the user types mount -a). The 0 0 values are the dump frequency (archive schedule) and pass number (order for file checking at boot) and should both be set to 0 by default. After reboot, you will see that the SD card is mounted correctly at /media/store.

Unfortunately, this approach may not be satisfactory if you have multiple USB SD card readers, as the /sda1 device could refer to a different SD card, depending on the order of device initialization. An alternative approach is to use the UUID (universally unique identifier) of the SD card itself to configure the mounting instruction. The UUID for this 32 GB card is actually displayed toward the end of Step 1, but to identify it explicitly at this point, you can use the following:

```
pi@erpi ~ $ sudo blkid /dev/sda1
/dev/sda1: UUID="e9562aa9-4565-4dfd-b986-4c45d089c7ce" TYPE="ext4"
```

In the /etc/fstab file, you can replace the /dev/sda1 entry with the UUID as follows (it should all appear on a single line in the file):

```
pi@erpi ~ $ more /etc/fstab
...
UUID=e9562aa9-4565-4dfd-b986-4c45d089c7ce  /media/store  ext4   defa →
ults,nofail,user,auto 0 0
```

Again, the RPi boots correctly, regardless of the presence or absence of the micro-SD card. If an alternative micro-SD card is placed in the USB card reader, it will not be mounted at /media/store, but you can use its UUID to configure an additional entry in /etc/fstab. In addition, you can hot swap SD cards, whereupon they will be automatically mounted at their individually defined mount points. Ensure that you execute sudo sync or sudo umount /dev/sda1 before hot swapping any SD cards. For example, to ready the SD card for removal, use umount; to remount it without physical removal and reinsertion, use mount -a:

```
pi@erpi ~ $ sudo umount /dev/sda1
pi@erpi ~ $ sudo mount -a
```

Continues

EXAMPLE: MOUNTING AN SD CARD AS ADDITIONAL (*continued*)

Step 4: The preceding steps result in a mount point that has root user write access only. The mount point can be adapted to give permission so that user accounts who are members of the users group can write to the card:

```
pi@erpi /media $ ls -l
drwxr-xr-x 3 root root 4096 Jun 20 00:58 store
pi@erpi /media $ sudo chgrp users store
pi@erpi /media $ sudo chmod g+w store
pi@erpi /media $ ls -l
drwxrwxr-x 3 root users 4096 Jun 20 00:58 store
pi@erpi /media $ cd store
pi@erpi /media/store $ df -k | grep /media/store
/dev/sda1        30638016   44992  29013660   1% /media/store
pi@erpi /media/store $ touch test.txt
pi@erpi /media/store $ ls
lost+found   test.txt
```

The df command is used to display the available capacity. Also, the mount point permissions changes persist through reboot.

find and whereis

The find command is useful for searching a directory structure for a particular file. It is incredibly comprehensive; type **man find** for a full list of options. For example, use the following call to find the C++ header file iostream somewhere on the RPi file system (using sudo avoids access permission problems):

```
pi@erpi / $ sudo find . -name iostream*
./usr/include/c++/4.9/iostream
./usr/include/c++/4.6/iostream
```

Using -iname instead of -name ignores upper/lowercase letters in the search name.

The following example finds files in /home that were modified in the last 24 hours and prior to the last 24 hours, respectively:

```
pi@erpi ~ $ echo "RPiTest File" >> new.txt
pi@erpi ~ $ sudo find /home -mtime -1
/home/pi
/home/pi/.bash_history
/home/pi/new.txt
pi@erpi ~ $ sudo find /home -mtime +1
/home/pi/.profile
/home/pi/.bashrc      ...
```

Alternatively, you can use access time (-atime), size (-size), owner (-user), group (-group), and permission (-perm).

NOTE Use the grep command to recursively search a directory for files that contain a specific string using, where -r specifies a recursive search, -n displays the location line number in an identified file, and -e is followed by the search pattern:

```
pi@erpi ~ $ sudo grep -rn /home -e "RPiTest"
/home/pi/new.txt:1:RPiTest File
```

For more options use man grep.

The whereis command is different in that it can be used to search for the binary executable, source code, and manual page for a program:

```
pi@erpi ~ $ whereis find
find: /usr/bin/find /usr/share/man/man1/find.1.gz
```

In this case, the binary command is in /usr/bin and the man page is in /usr/share/man/man1 (stored in gzip form to save space).

more or less

The more command has been used several times already, and you have likely gleaned its use. It enables you to view a large file or output stream, one page at a time. Therefore, to view a long file you can type **more filename**. For example, the log file /var/log/dmesg contains all the kernel output messages. You can view this file page by page by typing **more /var/log/dmesg**. However, if you want to keep the display concise, use **-5** to set the page length to be five rows:

```
pi@erpi ~ $ more -5 /var/log/dmesg
[    0.000000] Booting Linux on physical CPU 0xf00
[    0.000000] Initializing cgroup subsys cpu
[    0.000000] Initializing cgroup subsys cpuacct
[    0.000000] Linux version 3.18.11-v7+ (dc4@dc4-XPS13-9333)(gcc version 4.8.3
 20140303 (prerelease)(crosstool-NG linaro-1.13.1+bzr2650-Linaro GCC 2014.03)
--More--(2%)
```

You can use the spacebar to page through the content and the Q key to quit. There is an even more powerful command called less that you can access:

```
pi@erpi ~ $ less /var/log/dmesg
```

The less command gives you a fully interactive view using the keyboard. There are too many options to list here. For example, you can use the arrow keys to move up and down. Or you can page down using the spacebar, search for a string by typing / (e.g., type **/usb** to find messages related to USB devices), and then press the N key to go to the next match (or Shift+N key to go to the previous match).

The Reliability of SD Card File Systems

One of the most likely points of failure of the RPi is its SD card, which is more generally known as a multimedia card (MMC). NAND-based flash memory, such as that in MMCs, has a large capacity and a low cost, but it is prone to wear, which can result in file system errors.

The large capacity of MMCs is largely due to the development of multi-level cell (MLC) memory. Unlike single-level cell (SLC) memory, more than 1 bit can be stored in a single memory cell. The high voltage levels required in the process of deleting a memory cell disturbs adjacent cells, so NAND flash memory is erased in blocks of 1 KB to 4 KB. Over time, the process of writing to the NAND flash memory causes electrons to become trapped, reducing the conductivity difference between the set and erased states. (For a discussion on SLC versus MLC for high-reliability applications, see `tiny.cc/erpi305`.) MLCs use different charge levels and higher voltages to store more states in a single cell. (Commercial MLC products typically offer 4 to 16 states per cell.) Because SLCs only store a single state, they have a reliability advantage (typically 60,000–100,000 erase/write cycles) versus MLC (typically 10,000 cycles). MMCs are perfectly suitable for daily use in applications such as digital photography; 10,000 cycles should last over 27 years at one entire card write per day.

However, embedded Linux devices constantly write to their MMCs for tasks such as logging system events in `/var/log`. If the RPi writes to a log file 20 times per day, the lifespan of the SD card could be as low as 8 months. These are conservative figures, and thanks to *wear leveling algorithms*, the lifespan may be much longer. Wear leveling is employed by MMCs during data writes to ensure that rewrites are evenly distributed over the entire MMC media, thus avoiding system failure of Linux devices due to concentrated modifications, such as changes to log files.

For your RPi, ensure that you purchase a high-quality branded SD card. In addition, the more unused space you have on the SD card, the better, because it further enhances the wear leveling performance. Out of interest, other embedded Linux boards such as the BeagleBone Black use eMMC (embedded MMC) storage—essentially an MMC on a chip. These eMMCs are typically also MLC based and have the same order of reliability as SD cards. However, one advantage is that the board manufacturer has control over the quality and specification of the eMMC device used. Finally, most consumer SSDs are also MLC based, with the more expensive SLC-based SSDs typically reserved for enterprise-class applications.

For RPi applications that require extended reliability, a RAM file system (tmpfs) could be used for the `/tmp` directory, the `/var/cache` directory, and for log files (particularly `/var/log/apt`). You can achieve this by editing the `/etc/fstab` file to mount the desired directories in memory. For example, if you have processes that require file data to be shared between them for the purpose of data interchange, you could use the `/tmp` directory as a RAM file system (`tmpfs`) by editing the `/etc/fstab` file as follows:

```
pi@erpi /etc $ sudo nano fstab
pi@erpi /etc $ more fstab
proc              /proc    proc    defaults             0    0
/dev/mmcblk0p1    /boot    vfat    defaults             0    2
/dev/mmcblk0p2    /        ext4    defaults,noatime     0    1
tempfs            /tmp     tmpfs   size=100M            0    0
```

You can then apply these settings using the `mount` command:

```
pi@erpi /etc $ sudo mount -a
```

And then check that the settings have been applied:

```
pi@erpi /etc $ mount
...
tempfs on /tmp type tmpfs (rw,relatime,size=102400k)
```

The root directory is mounted by default with the `noatime` attribute set, which dramatically reduces the number of writes and increases I/O performance (as described earlier in the chapter). You should apply this attribute when possible to all solid-state storage devices (e.g., USB memory keys), but it is not necessary for RAM-based storage.

Remember that any data written to a `tempfs` will be lost on reboot. Therefore, if you use a tmpfs for `/var/log`, any system errors that caused your board to crash will not be visible on reboot. You can test this fact by creating a file in the `/tmp` directory as configured above and rebooting.

The actual RAM allocation grows and shrinks depending on the file usage on the tmpfs disk; therefore, you can be reasonably generous with the memory allocation. For example, with the 100 MB `/tmp` tmpfs mounted:

```
pi@erpi /tmp $ cat /proc/meminfo | grep MemFree:
MemFree:           824368 kB
pi@erpi /tmp $ fallocate -l 75000000 test.txt
pi@erpi /tmp $ ls -l test.txt
-rw-r--r-- 1 pi pi 75000000 Jul 17 00:04 test.txt
pi@erpi /tmp $ cat /proc/meminfo | grep MemFree:
MemFree:           750788 kB
```

Certain RPi distributions use a read-only file system to improve the lifespan of the SD card and the stability of the file system (e.g., OpenElec with the SquashFS compressed file system), but this requires significant effort and is not suitable for the type of prototype development that takes place in this book. However, keep it in mind for a final project deployment where system stability is crucial.

Linux Commands

When you are working at the Linux terminal and you type commands such as `date`, the output of these commands is sent to the standard output. As a result, the output is displayed in your terminal window.

Output and Input Redirection (>, >>, and <)

It is possible to redirect the output to a file using redirection symbols `>` and `>>`. The `>>` symbol was used previously in this chapter to add text to temporary files. The `>` symbol can be used to send the output to a new file. For example:

```
pi@erpi ~ $ cd /tmp
pi@erpi /tmp $ date > a.txt
pi@erpi /tmp $ more a.txt
Sat 20 Jun 12:59:43 UTC 2015
pi@erpi /tmp $ date > a.txt
pi@erpi /tmp $ more a.txt
Sat 20 Jun 12:59:57 UTC 2015
```

The >> symbol indicates that you want to append to the file. The following example illustrates the use of >> with the new file a.txt:

```
pi@erpi /tmp $ date >> a.txt
pi@erpi /tmp $ more a.txt
Sat 20 Jun 12:59:57 UTC 2015
Sat 20 Jun 13:00:17 UTC 2015
```

Standard input using the < symbol works in much the same way. The inclusion of -e enables parsing of escape characters, such as the return (\n) characters, which places each animal type on a new line:

```
pi@erpi /tmp $ echo -e "dog\ncat\nyak\ncow" > animals.txt
pi@erpi /tmp $ sort < animals.txt
cat
cow
dog
yak
```

You can combine input and output redirection operations. Using the same animals.txt file, you can perform operations such as the following:

```
pi@erpi /tmp $ sort < animals.txt > sorted.txt
pi@erpi /tmp $ more sorted.txt
cat
cow
dog
yak
```

Pipes (| and tee)

Simply put, *pipes* (|) enable you to connect Linux commands. Just as you redirected the output to a file, you can redirect the output of one command into the input of another command. For example, to list the root directory (from anywhere on the system) and send (or "pipe") the output into the sort command, where it is listed in reverse (-r) order, use the following:

```
pi@erpi ~ $ ls / | sort -r
var
usr
...
bin
```

You can identify which user installations in the /opt directory occupy the most disk space: du gives you the disk used. Passing the argument -d1 means only list the sizes of 1 level below the current directory level, and -h means list the values in human-readable form. You can pipe this output into the sort filter command to do a numeric sort in reverse order (largest at the top). Therefore, the command is:

```
pi@erpi ~ $ du -d1 -h /opt | sort -nr
113M    /opt
69M     /opt/sonic-pi
41M     /opt/vc
4.4M    /opt/minecraft-pi
```

Another useful tool, tee, enables you to both redirect an output to a file and pass it on to the next command in the pipe (e.g., store and view). Using the previous example, if you want to send the unsorted output of du to a file but display a sorted output, you could enter the following:

```
pi@erpi ~ $ du -d1 -h /opt | tee /tmp/unsorted.txt | sort -nr
113M    /opt
69M     /opt/sonic-pi
41M     /opt/vc
4.4M    /opt/minecraft-pi
pi@erpi ~ $ more /tmp/unsorted.txt
4.4M    /opt/minecraft-pi
69M     /opt/sonic-pi
41M     /opt/vc
113M    /opt
```

You can also use tee to write the output to several files simultaneously:

```
pi@erpi ~ $ du -d1 -h /opt | tee /tmp/1.txt /tmp/2.txt /tmp/3.txt
```

Filter Commands (from sort to xargs)

Each of the filtering commands provides a useful function:

- sort: This command has several options, including (-r) sorts in reverse; (-f) ignores case; (-d) uses dictionary sorting, ignoring punctuation; (-n) numeric sort; (-b) ignores blank space; (-i) ignores control characters; (-u) displays duplicate lines only once; and (-m) merges multiple inputs into a single output.

- wc (word count): Calculates the number of words, lines, or characters in a stream. For example:

```
pi@erpi /tmp $ wc < animals.txt
  4  4 16
```

This command returns that there are 4 lines, 4 words, and 16 characters. You can select the values independently by using (-l) line count, (-w) word count, (-m) character count, and (-c) prints out the byte count (which would also be 16 in this case).

■ head: Displays the first lines of the input, which is useful if you have a long file or stream of information and want to examine only the first few lines. By default, it displays the first 10 lines. You can specify the number of lines using the -n option. For example, to get the first two lines of output of the dmesg command (display message or driver message), which displays the message buffer of the kernel, use the following:

```
pi@erpi ~ $ dmesg | head -n2
[    0.000000] Booting Linux on physical CPU 0xf00
[    0.000000] Initializing cgroup subsys cpu
```

■ tail: Works like head except that it displays the last lines of a file or stream. Using it in combination with dmesg provides useful output, as shown:

```
pi@erpi ~ $ dmesg | tail -n2
[    8.896654] smsc95xx 1-1.1:1.0 eth0:link up,100Mbps,full-duplex...
[    9.340019] Adding 102396k swap on /var/swap.
```

■ grep: Parses lines using text and regular expressions. You can use this command to filter output with options, including (-i) ignore case; (-m 5) stop after five matches; (-q) silent, will exit with return status 0 if any matches are found; (-e) specify a pattern; (-c) print a count of matches; (-o) print only the matching text; and (-1) list the filename of the file containing the match. For example, the following examines the dmesg output for the first three occurrences of the string usb, using -i to ignore case:

```
pi@erpi ~ $ dmesg | grep -i -m3 usb
[    1.280089] usbcore: registered new interface driver usbfs
[    1.285762] usbcore: registered new interface driver hub
[    1.291220] usbcore: registered new device driver usb
```

You can combine pipes. For example, you get the exact same output by using head and displaying only the first three lines of the grep output:

```
pi@erpi ~ $ dmesg | grep -i usb | head -n3
[    1.280089] usbcore: registered new interface driver usbfs
[    1.285762] usbcore: registered new interface driver hub
[    1.291220] usbcore: registered new device driver usb
```

■ xargs: Enables you to construct an argument list that you use to call another command or tool. In the following example, a text file args.txt that contains three strings is used to create three new files. The output of cat is piped to xargs, where it passes the three strings as arguments to the touch command, creating three new files a.txt, b.txt, and c.txt:

```
pi@erpi /tmp $ echo "a.txt b.txt c.txt" > args.txt
pi@erpi /tmp $ cat args.txt | xargs touch
pi@erpi /tmp $ ls
args.txt  a.txt  b.txt  c.txt
```

Other useful filter commands include awk (to program any type of filter), fmt (to format text), uniq (to find unique lines), and sed (to manipulate a stream). These commands are beyond the scope of this text; for example, awk is a full programming language! Table 3-6 describes useful piped commands to give you some ideas of how to use them.

Table 3-6: Useful Pipe Examples

COMMAND	DESCRIPTION
`apt list --installed |` `grep camera`	List the installed packages and search for one that contains the search string camera. Each command in this table is entered on a single line.
`ls -lt | head`	Display the files in the current directory in order of age.
`cat urls.txt | xargs` `wget`	Download the files, listed in URLs within a text file `urls.txt`.
`dmesg | grep -c usb`	Count the number of times usb is found in the output of dmesg.

`find . -name "*.mp3" |`
`grep -vi "effects" >`
`/tmp/playlist.txt`
	Search your RPi (e.g., run from/with sudo) for mp3 files, ignoring any sound effects files, in order to create a playlist file in /tmp.

echo and cat

The `echo` command simply echoes a string, output of a command, or a value to the standard output. Here are a few examples:

```
pi@erpi /tmp $ echo 'hello'
hello
pi@erpi /tmp $ echo "Today's date is $(date)"
Today's date is Sat 20 Jun 14:31:21 UTC 2015
pi@erpi /tmp $ echo $PATH
/usr/local/sbin:/usr/local/bin:/usr/sbin:/usr/bin:/sbin:/bin
```

In the first case, a simple string is echoed. In the second case, the " " are present as a command is issued within the `echo` call, and in the final case the PATH environment variable is echoed.

The `echo` command also enables you to see the exit status of a command using `$?`. For example:

```
pi@erpi ~ $ ls /tmp
args.txt  a.txt  b.txt  c.txt  playlist  playlist.txt
pi@erpi ~ $ echo $?
0
pi@erpi ~ $ ls /nosuchdirectory
ls: cannot access /nosuchdirectory: No such file or directory
pi@erpi ~ $ echo $?
2
```

Clearly, the exit status for `ls` is 0 for a successful call and 2 for an invalid argument. This can be useful when you are writing scripts and your own programs that return a value from the `main()` function.

The `cat` command (con*cat*enation) facilitates you in joining two files together at the command line. The following example uses `echo` to create two files a.txt and b.txt; cat concatenates the files to create a new file c.txt. You need to use -e if you want to enable the interpretation of escape characters in the string that is passed to echo.

```
pi@erpi ~ $ cd /tmp
pi@erpi /tmp $ echo "hello" > a.txt
pi@erpi /tmp $ echo -e "from\nthe\nRPi" > b.txt
pi@erpi /tmp $ cat a.txt b.txt > c.txt
pi@erpi /tmp $ more c.txt
hello
from
the
RPi
```

diff

The diff command facilitates you in finding the differences between two files. It provides basic output:

```
pi@erpi /tmp $ echo -e "dog\ncat\nbird" > list1.txt
pi@erpi /tmp $ echo -e "dog\ncow\nbird" > list2.txt
pi@erpi /tmp $ diff list1.txt list2.txt
2c2
< cat
---
> cow
```

The value 2c2 in the output indicates that line 2 in the first file changed to line 2 in the second file, and the change is that *cat* changed to *cow*. The character *a* means appended, and *d* means deleted. For a side-by-side comparison, you can use the following:

```
pi@erpi /tmp $ diff -y -W70 list1.txt list2.txt
dog                              dog
cat                            | cow
bird                             bird
```

where -y enables the side-by-side view and -W70 sets the width of the display to 70 character columns.

If you want a more intuitive (but challenging) difference display between two files, you can use the vimdiff command (installed using **sudo apt install vim**), which displays a side-by-side comparison of the files using the vim (Vi IMproved) text editor (type **vimdiff list1.txt list2.txt** and use the VI key sequence: **Escape : q !** twice to quit, or **Escape : w q** to save the changes and quit). Vim requires practice to master the key sequences.

tar

The tar command is an archiving utility that enables you to combine files and directories into a single file (like an uncompressed zip file). This file can then be compressed to save space. To archive and compress a directory of files, such as /tmp, use the following:

```
pi@erpi ~ $ tar cvfz tmp_backup.tar.gz /tmp
```

where (c) means new archive, (v) means verbosely list files, (z) means compress with gzip, and (f) means archive name follows. You might also see .tar.gz represented as .tgz. See Table 3-7 for more examples.

Table 3-7: Useful tar Commands

COMMAND	DESCRIPTION
tar cvfz name.tar.gz /tmp	Compress with gzip form.
tar cvfj name.tar.bz2 /tmp	Compress with bzip2 compression (typically a longer delay, but smaller, file). Enter all commands in this table on a single line.
tar cvfJ name.tar.xz /tmp	Compress with xz file format (used in .deb package files)
tar xvf name.tar.*	Decompress compressed file (x indicates extract). It will auto-detect the compression type (e.g., gzip, bz2).
tar xvf name.tar.* /dir/file	Extract a single file from an archive. Works for a single directory too.
tar rvf name.tar filename	Add another file to the archive.
tar cfz name-$(date +%m%d%y).tar.gz /dir/ filename	Create an archive with the current day's date; useful for scripts and cron job backups. Note that there must be a space between date and +%m%d%y.

md5sum

The md5sum command enables you to check the hash code, to verify that the files have not been corrupted maliciously or accidentally in transit. In the following example, the wavemon tool is downloaded as a .deb package, but not installed. The md5sum command can be used to generate the md5 checksum:

```
pi@erpi ~ $ sudo apt-get download wavemon
Get:1 http://mirrordirector.raspbian.org/raspbian/ jessie/main
wavemon armhf 0.7.6-2 [48.2 kB] Fetched 48.2 kB in 0s (71.4 kB/s)
pi@erpi ~ $ ls -l *.deb
-rw-r--r-- 1 root root 48248 Mar 28  2014 wavemon_0.7.6-2_armhf.deb
pi@erpi ~ $ md5sum wavemon_0.7.6-2_armhf.deb
1dffa011736e25b63a054f1515d18b3e  wavemon_0.7.6-2_armhf.deb
```

You can now check this checksum against the official checksum to ensure you have a valid file. Unfortunately, it can be difficult to find the checksums for

individual packages online. If wavemon is installed, the checksums are in /var/
lib/dpkg/info/wavemon.md5sums. You can install a utility under Debian called
debsums to check the integrity of the file and its constituent parts:

```
pi@erpi ~ $ sudo apt install debsums wavemon
pi@erpi ~ $ debsums wavemon_0.7.6-2_armhf.deb
/usr/bin/wavemon                                    OK
/usr/share/doc/wavemon/AUTHORS                      OK
/usr/share/doc/wavemon/NEWS.gz                      OK
...
```

If you are building your own packages that you want to distribute, it would
be useful to also distribute a checksum file against which users can verify their
downloaded repository. An alternative to md5sum is sha256sum, which can be
used in the same way.

Linux Processes

A process is an instance of a program that is running on the OS. You need to
be able to manage the processes that are running on your RPi, understand
foreground and background processes, and kill a process that becomes locked.

How to Control Linux Processes

The ps command lists the processes currently running on the RPi. Typing **ps**
shows that the following RPi is running two user processes, the bash shell with
process ID (PID) 912 and the ps command itself, which is running with PID
25481. The ps PID is different every time you run it because it runs to completion each time:

```
pi@erpi ~ $ ps
   PID TTY          TIME CMD
   912 pts/0    00:00:05 bash
 25481 pts/0    00:00:00 ps
```

To see all running processes, use **ps ax**. In the following example, it is filtered
to search for the string "ntp" to discover information about the ntp processes
that are running on the RPi:

```
pi@erpi ~ $ ps ax | grep ntp
 1069 ?        Ss   0:00 /usr/sbin/ntpd -p /var/run/ntpd.pid -g -u 107:112
 1077 ?        S    0:00 /usr/sbin/ntpd -p /var/run/ntpd.pid -g -u 107:112
 1132 ttyAMA0 S+   0:00 grep --color=auto ntp
```

It is clear that three different processes are running for the service, enabling
it to handle multiple simultaneous connections. In this example, all threads are
currently waiting for an event to complete (s), PID 1069 is the session leader
(Ss), 1077 is its clones (S), and the 1132 grep process is in the foreground group

(s+). As described earlier, a call to `systemctl status ntp` provides information about the services running on the RPi—if you execute the call, you will see that the process PIDs match those displayed by a call to `ps`.

Foreground and Background Processes

Linux is a multitasking OS that enables you to run processes in the background while using a program that is running in the foreground. This concept is similar to the behavior of a windowing system (e.g., Windows, Mac OS X). For example, the desktop clock continues to update the time while you use a web browser.

The same is true of applications that run in a terminal window. To demonstrate that, here is a small segment of C code to display "Hello World!" every 5 seconds in a Linux terminal. Exactly how this works is covered in Chapter 5, but for the moment, you can enter the code verbatim into a file called `HelloRPiSleep.c` using the nano file editor within the pi user home directory, as follows:

```
pi@erpi ~ $ cd ~/
pi@erpi ~ $ nano HelloRPiSleep.c
pi@erpi ~ $ more HelloRPiSleep.c
#include<unistd.h>
#include<stdio.h>
int main(){
   int x=0;
   do{
      printf("Hello Raspberry Pi!\n");
      sleep(5);
   }while(x++<50);
   return 0;
}
```

The program has 50 iterations, displaying a message and sleeping for 5 seconds on each iteration. After saving the file as `HelloRPiSleep.c`, it can be compiled to an executable by typing the following (`-o` specifies the executable file name):

```
pi@erpi ~ $ gcc HelloRPiSleep.c -o helloRPiSleep
pi@erpi ~ $ ls -l helloRPiSleep
-rwxr-xr-x 1 pi pi 5864 Jun 20 16:40 helloRPiSleep
```

If this works correctly, you will now have the source file and the executable program called `helloRPiSleep` (note that the executable x flag is set). It can then be executed:

```
pi@erpi ~ $ ./helloRPiSleep
Hello Raspberry Pi!
Hello Raspberry Pi! ...
```

It will continue to output this message every 5 seconds; it can be killed using Ctrl+C. However, if you would like to run this in the background, you have two options.

The first way is that, instead of using Ctrl+C to kill the process, use Ctrl+Z, and then at the prompt type the **bg** (*background*) command:

```
pi@erpi ~ $ ./helloRPiSleep
Hello Raspberry Pi!
^Z
[1]+  Stopped                 ./helloRPiSleep
pi@erpi ~ $ bg
[1]+ ./helloRPiSleep &
pi@erpi ~ $ Hello Raspberry Pi!
Hello Raspberry Pi!
Hello Raspberry Pi!
```

When you type Ctrl+Z, the ^z displays in the output. When **bg** is entered, the process is placed in the background and continues to execute. In fact, you can continue to use the terminal but it will be frustrating, because "Hello Raspberry Pi!" displays every 5 seconds. You can bring this process back into the foreground using the **fg** command:

```
pi@erpi ~ $ fg
./helloRPiSleep
Hello Raspberry Pi!
^C
pi@erpi ~ $
```

The application is killed when Ctrl+C is typed (displays as ^c).

The second way to place this application in the background is to execute the application with an **&** symbol after the application name:

```
pi@erpi ~ $ ./helloRPiSleep &
[1] 30965
pi@erpi ~ $ Hello Raspberry Pi!
Hello Raspberry Pi!
```

The process has been placed in the background with PID 30965 in this case. To stop the process, use **ps** to find the PID:

```
pi@erpi ~ $ ps aux|grep hello
pi  30965 0.0 0.0 1612  304 pts/0  S  20:14  0:00 ./helloRPiSleep
pi  30978 0.0 0.1 4208 1828 pts/0  S+ 20:15  0:00 grep hello
```

To kill the process, use the **kill** command:

```
pi@erpi ~ $ kill 30965
[1]+  Terminated              ./helloRPiSleep
```

You can confirm that a process is dead by using ps again. If a process doesn't die, you can use a -9 argument to ensure death! (e.g., kill -9 30965). A separate command, pkill, will kill a process based on its name, so in this case you can kill the process as follows:

```
pi@erpi ~ $ pkill helloRPiSleep
```

One more command worth mentioning is `watch`, which executes a command at a regular interval and shows the outcome full screen on the terminal. For example, to watch the kernel message log, use the following:

```
pi@erpi ~ $ watch dmesg
```

You can specify the time interval between each execution using -n followed by the number of seconds. A good way to understand `watch` is to execute it as follows:

```
pi@erpi ~ $ watch -n 1 ps a
Every 1.0s: ps a                        Sat Jun 20 20:22:39 2015
  PID TTY     STAT    TIME COMMAND
  912 pts/0   Ss      0:06 -bash
31184 pts/0   S+      0:01 watch -n 1 ps a
31257 pts/0   S+      0:00 watch -n 1 ps a
31258 pts/0   S+      0:00 sh -c ps a
31259 pts/0   R+      0:00 ps a
```

You will see the PID of `ps`, `sh`, and `watch` changing every one (1) second, making it clear that `watch` is actually executing the command (`ps`) by passing it to a new shell using `sh -c`. The reason why `watch` appears twice in the list is that it spawns itself temporarily at the exact moment that it executes `ps a`.

Other Linux Topics

At this point of the book, you have covered the core commands for working with Linux on the RPi; however, there is much more to cover on the topic of managing Linux systems. For example, how do you configure a Wi-Fi adapter? How do you use `cron` to schedule jobs with the RPi? These topics and many others are detailed as you work through the book. For example, cron jobs are covered in Chapter 12, in the context of the Internet of Things.

Using Git for Version Control

Simply put, *Git* is a system that enables you to track changes to the content of a software project as it develops. Git, designed by Linus Torvalds, is used today for mainline Linux kernel development. Git is an incredibly useful system to understand for two main reasons: You can use Git when developing your own software, and you can gain an appreciation of how to work with Linux kernel source distributions.

Git is a distributed version control system (DVCS) for source control management. A *version control system* (VCS) tracks and manages changes to documents of any type. Typically, documents that have been changed are marked with revision numbers and time stamps. It is possible to compare revisions and even revert to older versions of the documents. There are two types of VCSs:

- **Centralized (CVCS):** These systems, such as Apache Subversion (SVN), work on the basis that there is a single "master" copy of the project. The workflow is straightforward: You pull down changes from a central server, make your changes, and commit them back to the master copy.

- **Distributed(DVCS):** Using these systems, such as Git and Selenic Mercurial, you do not pull down changes; instead, you clone the entire repository, including its entire history. The clone of the repository is just as complete as the master copy and can even become the master copy if required. Thankfully, by today's standards, text documents and programming source code do not occupy much disk space. Importantly, the DVCS model does not prevent you from having a central master repository that everybody uses; take a look at `git.kernel.org`.

The main advantage of a DVCS over a CVCS is that you can quickly commit and test changes locally, on your own system, without ever having to push them to a master copy; however, changes can be pushed when they reach an appropriate level of quality. The only significant disadvantage is the amount of disk space required to store the project and its entire history, which grows over time.

Git is a DVCS that is focused on programming source control and management. It enables you to create parallel developments that do not affect the original. You can even revert to an older version of one of the source code files, or an older version of the entire project. The project, with its associated files and history, is called a *repository*. This capability is particularly useful in large-scale programming projects for which you may go down a development pathway with the project that is ultimately unsuccessful. The facility for parallel development is also important if you have several people working on the same project.

Git is written in C, and although it originated from the need for version control tools in the development of Linux kernel code, it is used by many other open source developments such as Eclipse and Android.

The easiest way to understand Git is to go through the steps of actually using it. Therefore, the next section is structured as a step-by-step guide. If it is not already, Git is easily installed using `sudo apt install git`, so you should be able to follow the steps, directly at the terminal. *GitHub* is used in this book as the remote repository for providing the source code examples. Except for pushing the source code to the server, you can do everything in this guide without a GitHub account. GitHub provides free public repository accounts, but charges a fee for private repositories, such as those that would be required for retaining intellectual property rights.

NOTE If you are planning to write a large software project and do not want to make it publicly available on www.github.com or pay a subscription fee, you can currently host small-scale private repositories at sites such as bitbucket.org and gitlab .com. With some work, you can even set up GitLab on your own server, as there is an open source version of the platform.

A Practice-Based Introduction

In this guide, I create a repository called "test" on GitHub. Initially, it contains only a README.md file with a short description of the "test" project.

As shown in Figure 3-4, nearly all operations are local operations. A checksum is performed on every file in Git before it is stored. The checksum ensures that Git will be aware if a modification is made outside of Git itself, including file system corruption. Git uses 40-character hash codes for the checksums. This helps Git to keep track of changes between the local repository and remote repository, which enables the range of local operations.

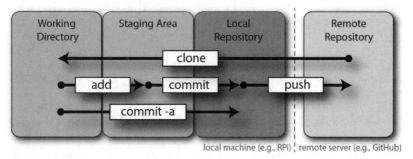

Figure 3-4: The basic Git workflow

Cloning a Repository (git clone)

Cloning a repository means making a copy of all the files in the repository on your local file system, as well as the history of changes to that project. You do this operation only once. To clone the repository, issue the command `git clone` followed by the fully formed repository name:

```
pi@erpi / $ cd ~/
pi@erpi ~ $ git clone https://github.com/derekmolloy/test.git
Cloning into 'test'...
remote: Counting objects: 14, done.
remote: Compressing objects: 100% (5/5), done.
```

```
remote: Total 14 (delta 1), reused 0 (delta 0), pack-reused 9
Unpacking objects: 100% (14/14), done.
Checking connectivity... done.
```

You now have a full copy of the "test" repository in the /test directory. Your repository is just as complete as the version on the GitHub server; if you were to deploy it over a network, file system, other Git server, or even on a different GitHub account, it could assume the role as the main version of this repository. Although there is no need for a central server, it is usually the case, because it enables multiple users to "check in" source code to a known master repository. The repository is created in the /test directory, and it currently contains the following:

```
pi@erpi ~/test $ ls -al
total 20
drwxr-xr-x 3 pi pi 4096 Jun 20 22:00 .
drwxr-xr-x 6 pi pi 4096 Jun 20 22:00 ..
drwxr-xr-x 8 pi pi 4096 Jun 20 22:00 .git
-rw-r--r-- 1 pi pi   59 Jun 20 22:00 README.md
```

You can see the README.md that was created when the project was initialized on GitHub; you can use more to view the contents of this file. The directory also contains a hidden .git subdirectory, which contains the following files and directories:

```
pi@erpi ~/test/.git $ ls
branches   description  hooks  info   objects       refs
config     HEAD         index  logs   packed-refs
```

The hidden .git folder contains all the information about the repository, such as commit messages, logs, and the data objects. For example, the remote repository location is maintained in the config file:

```
pi@erpi ~/test/.git $ more config | grep url
        url = https://github.com/derekmolloy/test.git
```

The "Further Reading" section at the end of this chapter directs you to an excellent book on Git, which is freely available online, that describes the nature of the .git directory structure in detail. Thankfully, in the following discussion, you do not have to make changes in the .git directory structure, because you have Git commands to do that for you.

> **NOTE** This step-by-step guide uses my "test" repository; however, you can easily create your own repository on GitHub. After you set up a free account on GitHub, go to Create New, and then New repository. Give the repository a name and a description, make it publicly available, choose to initialize it with a README, and then choose Create Repository. You can then follow these instructions using your own account, and as a result you will be able to push back from the RPi to your own repository on GitHub.

Getting the Status (git status)

Now that the repository exists, the next step is to add a new text file to the working directory, where it will be it in an untracked state. When you call the command `git status`, you can see a message stating that "untracked files" are present:

```
pi@erpi ~/test $ echo "Just some text" > newfile.txt
pi@erpi ~/test $ git status
On branch master
Your branch is up-to-date with 'origin/master'.
Untracked files:
  (use "git add <file>..." to include in what will be committed)
        newfile.txt
nothing to commit, untracked files present (use "git add" to track)
```

The next step is to add any untracked files to the staging area. However, if you did not want to add a set of files, you could also create a `.gitignore` file to ignore those files. For example, this could be useful if you are building C/C++ projects and you decide that you do not want to add intermediate `.o` files. Here is an example of creating a `.gitignore` file in order to ignore C/C++ `.o` files:

```
pi@erpi ~/test $ echo "*.o" > .gitignore
pi@erpi ~/test $ more .gitignore
*.o
pi@erpi ~/test $ touch testobject.o
pi@erpi ~/test $ git status
On branch master
Your branch is up-to-date with 'origin/master'.
Untracked files:
  (use "git add <file>..." to include in what will be committed)
        .gitignore
        newfile.txt
nothing to commit, untracked files present (use "git add" to track)
```

In this case, two files are untracked, but there is no mention of the `testobject.o` file, as it is being correctly ignored. Note that the `.gitignore` file is itself part of the repository and so will persist when the repository is cloned, along with its revision history and so on.

Adding to the Staging Area (git add)

The files in the working directory can now be added to the staging area by typing `git add .`—this command adds all of the files in the working directory, with the exception of the ignored files. In this example, two files are added from the working directory to the staging area, and the status of the repository can then be displayed using the following:

```
pi@erpi ~/test $ git add .
pi@erpi ~/test $ git status
```

```
On branch master
Your branch is up-to-date with 'origin/master'.
Changes to be committed:
  (use "git reset HEAD <file>..." to unstage)
      new file:   .gitignore
      new file:   newfile.txt
```

To delete (*remove*) a file from the staging area, use `git rm somefile.ext`.

Committing to the Local Repository (git commit)

After you add files to the staging area, you can commit the changes from the staging area to the local Git repository. First, you may want to add your name and e-mail address variables, to identify who is committing the changes:

```
pi@erpi ~/test $ git config --global user.name "Derek Molloy"
pi@erpi ~/test $ git config --global user.email derek@my.email.com
```

These values are set against your Linux user account, so they will persist when you next log in. You can see them by typing `more ~/.gitconfig`.

To permanently commit the file additions to the local Git repository, use the `git commit` command:

```
pi@erpi ~/test $ git commit -m "Testing the repository"
[master 3eea9a2] Testing the repository
 2 files changed, 2 insertions(+)
 create mode 100644 .gitignore
 create mode 100644 newfile.txt
```

The changes are flagged with the username, and a message is also required. If you want to detail the message inline, use -m to set the commit message.

> **NOTE**   The shortcut `git commit -a` commits *modified* files directly to the local repository, without requiring a call to `add`. It does not add new files. Refer back to Figure 3-4, shown earlier in this chapter.

Pushing to the Remote Repository (git push)

To perform this step, you must have your own GitHub account. The `git push` command pushes any code updates to the remote repository. You must be registered to make changes to the remote repository for the changes to be applied. In Git 2.0, a new more conservative approach, called *simple*, has been taken to push to remote repositories. It is chosen by default, but a warning message can be squelched, and the push can be performed as follows (replace the user details and repository name with your own account details):

```
pi@erpi ~/test $ git config --global push.default simple
pi@erpi ~/test $ git push
```

```
Username for 'https://github.com': derekmolloy
Password for 'https://derekmolloy@github.com': mySuperSecretPassword
Counting objects: 4, done.
Delta compression using up to 4 threads.
Compressing objects: 100% (2/2), done.
Writing objects: 100% (4/4), 350 bytes | 0 bytes/s, done.
Total 4 (delta 0), reused 0 (delta 0)
To https://github.com/derekmolloy/test.git
   f5c45f4..3eea9a2  master -> master
```

After the code has been pushed to the remote repository, you can pull changes back to a local repository on any machine by issuing a `git pull` command from within the local repository directory:

```
pi@erpi ~/test $ git pull
Already up-to-date.
```

In this case everything is already up-to-date.

Git Branching

Git supports the concept of branching, which enables you to work on multiple different versions of the set of files within your project. For example, to develop a new feature in your project (version 2) but maintain the code in the current version (version 1), you could create a new branch (version 2). New features and changes that are made to version 2 will not affect the code in version 1. You can then easily switch between branches.

Creating a Branch (git branch)

Suppose, for example, you want to create a new branch called `mybranch`; you can do so using the command `git branch mybranch`, and then you can switch to that branch using `git checkout mybranch`, as shown:

```
pi@erpi ~/test $ git branch mybranch
pi@erpi ~/test $ git checkout mybranch
Switched to branch 'mybranch'
```

Now, to demonstrate how this works, suppose that a temporary file called `testmybranch.txt` is added to the repository. This could be a new code file for your project. You can see that the status of the branch makes it clear that the working directory contains an untracked file:

```
pi@erpi ~/test $ touch testmybranch.txt
pi@erpi ~/test $ ls
newfile.txt  README.md  testmybranch.txt  testobject.o
pi@erpi ~/test $ git status
On branch mybranch
Untracked files:
  (use "git add <file>..." to include in what will be committed)
```

```
        testmybranch.txt
nothing to commit, untracked files present (use "git add" to track)
```

You can then add this new file to the staging area of the branch using the same commands:

```
pi@erpi ~/test $ git add .
pi@erpi ~/test $ git status
On branch mybranch
Changes to be committed:
  (use "git reset HEAD <file>..." to unstage)
        new file:   testmybranch.txt
```

You can commit this change to the mybranch branch of the local repository. This change will affect the mybranch branch but have no impact on the master branch:

```
pi@erpi ~/test $ git commit -m "Test commit to mybranch"
[mybranch d4cabf3] Test commit to mybranch
 1 file changed, 0 insertions(+), 0 deletions(-)
 create mode 100644 testmybranch.txt
pi@erpi ~/test $ git status
On branch mybranch
nothing to commit, working directory clean
pi@erpi ~/test $ ls
newfile.txt  README.md  testmybranch.txt  testobject.o
```

You can see from the preceding output that the file testmybranch.txt is committed to the local repository and you can see the file in the directory.

If you now switch from the branch mybranch to the master branch using the call **git checkout master**, you will see that something interesting happens when you request the directory listing:

```
pi@erpi ~/test $ git checkout master
Switched to branch 'master'
Your branch is up-to-date with 'origin/master'.
pi@erpi ~/test $ ls
newfile.txt  README.md  testobject.o
```

Yes, the file testmybranch.txt has disappeared from the directory! It still exists, but it is in a blob form inside the .git/objects directory. If you return to the branch and list the directory, you will see the following:

```
pi@erpi ~/test $ git checkout mybranch
Switched to branch 'mybranch'
pi@erpi ~/test $ ls
newfile.txt  README.md  testmybranch.txt  testobject.o
```

The file now reappears. Therefore, you can see just how well integrated the branching system is. At this point, you can go back to the master branch and make changes to the original code without the changes in the mybranch branch having any impact on the master code. Even if you change the code in the same file, it has no effect on the original code in the master branch.

Merging a Branch (git merge)

What if you want to apply the changes that you made in the `mybranch` branch to the master project? You can do this by using `git merge`:

```
pi@erpi ~/test $ git checkout master
Switched to branch 'master'
Your branch is up-to-date with 'origin/master'.
pi@erpi ~/test $ git merge mybranch
Updating 3eea9a2..d4cabf3
Fast-forward
 testmybranch.txt | 0
 1 file changed, 0 insertions(+), 0 deletions(-)
 create mode 100644 testmybranch.txt
pi@erpi ~/test $ git status
On branch master
Your branch is ahead of 'origin/master' by 1 commit.
  (use "git push" to publish your local commits)
nothing to commit, working directory clean
pi@erpi ~/test $ ls
newfile.txt  README.md  testmybranch.txt  testobject.o
```

Now the `testmybranch.txt` file is in the master branch and any changes that were made to other documents in the master have been applied. The local repository is now one commit ahead of the remote repository and you can use `git push` to update the remote repository.

Deleting a Branch (git branch -d)

If you want to delete a branch, use the `git branch -d mybranch` command:

```
pi@erpi ~/test $ git branch -d mybranch
Deleted branch mybranch (was d4cabf3).
pi@erpi ~/test $ ls
newfile.txt  README.md  testmybranch.txt  testobject.o
```

In this case the file `testmybranch.txt` is still present in the master project—and it should be, because the branch was merged with the master project. If the branch had been deleted before the merge was performed, the file would have been lost.

Common Git Commands

Table 3-8 provides a summary of the main Git commands. At this point, you have seen the core use of Git. If you are developing code directly on the RPi,

Git can be highly useful, because you can easily push your developments to a remote repository. That capability can be useful in backing up your code and redeploying the code to multiple RPis.

Table 3-8: Summary of the Main Git Commands

OPERATION	DESCRIPTION	OPERATION	DESCRIPTION
git clone	Clone from the remote repository.	git rm	Delete a file or directory from the staging area.
git init	Create a wholly new repository.	git mv	Move or rename a file or folder in the staging area.
git pull	Merge changes from a master repository.	git log	Display a log of commits. The project history.
git fetch	Find what has changed in a master repository without merging.	git tag	Give a commit a name (e.g., version 2).
git status	Show the project's status.	git merge [name]	Merge the branch.
git add	Add a new file or edit an existing file.	git show	Get details about the current or other commit.
git diff	Show the differences that are to be committed.	git branch [name]	Create a new branch. (Use -d to delete.)
git commit	Commit to the repository.	git checkout [name]	Switch to a different branch.
git push	Push changes from the local repository to a remote repository.		

Using Desktop Virtualization

The RPi is a capable general-purpose computing platform, but if you are planning to build a Linux kernel or perform cross-platform development (see Chapter 7), a PC-based Linux installation is highly recommended. You can either use a single/dual boot Linux PC, or if you are a Windows/Mac native, you should investigate desktop virtualization.

Desktop *virtualization* enables a single desktop computer to run multiple OS instances simultaneously. It uses technology called hypervisors, which consist of hardware, firmware, and software elements, to create and run software-emulated machines, known as virtual machines (VMs). If you want to run multiple OS instances on a single computer, VMs provide an alternative to creating a multi-boot configuration.

In virtualization, there are usually two or more distinct OS instances. The *host* OS is the one that was first installed on the physical machine. The hypervisor software is then used to create a *guest* OS within a VM. Figure 3-5 captures a host Windows 8.1 desktop computer running a guest Debian 64-bit Linux Jessie VM within a window. The Debian installation has the Cairo-Dock desktop interface installed.

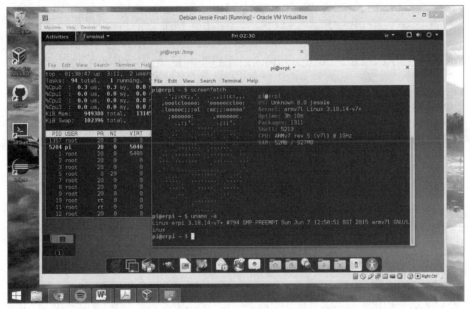

Figure 3-5: VirtualBox running Debian (Jessie) as a guest OS on a Windows host machine

Many virtualization products are available, but most have significant costs, proprietary licenses, and are limited in the type of guest and host OSs that they support. Two of the most popular Linux desktop virtualization products are VMware Player and VirtualBox. VMware Player (www.vmware.com/products/player/) is free for personal use. VirtualBox (www.virtualbox.org) is available under a GNU GPLv2 license (some features are available free under a proprietary license).

Both products use *hosted hypervisors* (Type 2) for virtualization, meaning that they run within a regular OS, enabling you to use both machines simultaneously. VirtualBox is available to run on Windows, Mac OS X, and Linux machines, and it can be used to host guest OSs such as Linux, Windows, and Mac OS X. Currently, VMware Player is not available for Mac OS X host installations; instead, you must purchase a product called VMware Fusion.

Both products are powerful and it is difficult to distinguish between them; however, VirtualBox is released under a GPL, and it supports a useful feature called snapshots. A user interface makes it possible to take a snapshot of the guest OS that can be saved for later use. For example, you could take a snapshot before you make a significant configuration change to your guest OS, enabling you to roll back to that configuration should problems arise. The snapshot stores the VM settings; changes in the contents of the virtual disks; and the memory state of the machine at that point in time. Therefore, when a snapshot is restored, the VM continues running at the exact same point as when the snapshot was taken.

If you install the VirtualBox Guest Additions, you are able to copy and paste text between your guest and host OSs, share directories, and even resize the window dynamically. This chapter's web page (www.exploringrpi.com/chapter3/) provides advice on installing a Linux guest OS under a Windows host OS.

All Linux packages and software in this book are built and tested using a Debian 64-bit desktop distribution that is installed within a VirtualBox VM.

> **NOTE** All Linux packages and software in this book are built and tested using a Debian 64-bit desktop distribution that is installed within a VirtualBox VM.

Code for This Book

Now that you have your Desktop Linux installation up and running under VirtualBox, or you are running a regular Linux desktop installation, you can download all of the source code, scripts, and documentation discussed in this book by opening a Linux terminal session/window and typing the following (on the desktop machine and RPi):

```
pi@erpi ~ $ sudo apt install git
pi@erpi ~ $ git clone https://github.com/derekmolloy/exploringRPi.git
Cloning into 'exploringRPi'...
```

If you want to download the code from within Windows or Mac OS X, a graphical user interface for working with GitHub repositories is available from windows.github.com and mac.github.com.

> **NOTE** If you have your own GitHub account, you can use its web interface to fork this repository to your own account or you can watch the repository for updates and changes. A GitHub account without private repositories is currently free of charge. In addition, students and academics can apply for a free Micro account, which provides for five private repositories for 2 years.

Summary

After completing this chapter, you should be able to do the following:

- Describe the basic concept of an embedded Linux system.
- Describe how an embedded Linux device, such as the RPi, boots the Linux OS.
- Describe important Linux concepts, such as kernel space, user space, and system initialization using systemd.
- Perform Linux system administration tasks on the RPi.
- Use the RPi file system effectively.
- Use a range of Linux commands for file and process management.
- Manage your own software development projects using Git.
- Install a Linux distribution on your desktop computer host OS using desktop virtualization tools, such as VirtualBox.
- Download the source code for this book using Git.

Further Reading

The following texts can help you learn more about embedded Linux, Linux administration, Git, and virtualization:

- Christopher Hallinan's *Embedded Linux Primer: A Practical Real-World Approach, Second Edition* (Upper Saddle River, NJ: Prentice Hall, 2011)
- The Debian Policy Manual: `tiny.cc/erpi303`
- To learn more about Git, start with a call to `man gittutorial` and then if you need detailed information, see Scott Chacon's excellent reference *Pro Git*, at `tiny.cc/erpi304`; also available in paperback (New York: Apress Media, 2009).

Bibliography

- ARM Holdings. (2015, February 11). ARM Holdings PLC Reports Results for the Fourth Quarter and Full Year 2014. Retrieved June 14, 2015, from `www.arm.com/about/newsroom/arm-holdings-plc-reports-results-for-the-fourth-quarter-and-full-year-2014.php`.

- McCracken, J., Sherman, A., & King, I. (2015, May 27). Avago to Buy Broadcom for $37 Billion in Biggest Tech Deal Ever. Bloomberg Business. Retrieved June 14, 2015, from `www.bloomberg.com/news/articles/2015-05-27/avago-said-near-deal-to-buy-wireless-chipmaker-broadcom`.

- Git FAQ. (2013, March 9). Retrieved 2 22, 2014, from Git Wiki: `git.wiki.kernel.org/index.php/GitFaq#Why_the_.27git.27_name.3F`.

- Smith, B. (2013, July 29). A Quick Guide to GPLv3. Retrieved June 14, 2015, from `www.gnu.org/licenses/quick-guide-gplv3.html`.

# CHAPTER 4

Interfacing Electronics

This chapter introduces you to the type of practical electronics that you need to work correctly and effectively in interfacing electronic circuits with the Raspberry Pi (RPi) platform. The chapter begins by describing some equipment that can be very helpful in developing and debugging electronic circuits. It continues with a practical introductory guide to circuit design and analysis, in which you are encouraged to build the circuits and utilize the equipment that is described at the beginning of the chapter. The chapter continues with a discussion on the typical discrete components that can be interfaced to the general-purpose input/outputs (GPIOs) on the RPi, including diodes, capacitors, transistors, optocouplers, switches, and logic gates. Finally, the important principles of analog-to-digital conversion (ADC) are described, as such knowledge is required in Chapter 9 to build circuits that interface the RPi to analog sensors.

Equipment Required for This Chapter:

- Components for this chapter (if following along): The full list is provided at the end of this chapter.
- Digilent Analog Discovery (version 1 or 2) *or* access to a digital multimeter, signal generator, and oscilloscope.

Further details on this chapter are available at www.exploringrpi.com/chapter4/.

NOTE   One chapter cannot be a substitute for full textbooks on digital and analog electronics; however, there are concepts with which you should be comfortable before connecting electronics to the GPIO interface header on the Raspberry Pi, as incorrect configurations can easily destroy the board. Later chapters depend heavily on the electronics concepts that are described in this chapter; however, it is not vital that you assimilate all of the content in this chapter before you move on. Importantly, this chapter is here as a reference for electronics concepts mentioned in later chapters.

Analyzing Your Circuits

When developing electronics circuits for the RPi platform, it is useful to have the following tools so that you can analyze a circuit before you connect it to the RPi inputs/outputs, in order to reduce the chance of damaging your board. In particular, it is useful to have access to a digital multimeter and a mixed-signal oscilloscope.

NOTE   The tools listed here are for your consideration. Be sure to do your homework and seek independent advice before choosing any such product. None of the products I include are the result of any type of product placement agreement or request. All prices are approximate.

Digital Multimeter

A digital multimeter (DMM) is an invaluable tool for measuring the voltage, current, and resistance/continuity of RPi circuits. If you don't already have one, try to purchase one with the following features:

- **Auto power off:** It is easy to waste batteries.
- **Auto range:** It is vital that you can select different measurement ranges. Mid-price meters often have automatic range selection functionality that can reduce the time required to take measurements.
- **Continuity testing:** This feature should provide an audible beep unless there is a break in the conductor (or excessive resistance).
- **True RMS readings:** Most low-cost meters use averaging to calculate AC(~) current/voltage. True RMS meters process the readings using a true root mean square (RMS) calculation, which makes it possible to account for distortions in waveforms when taking readings. This feature is useful for analyzing phase controlled equipment, solid-state devices, motorized devices, etc.

- **Other useful options:** These options are not strictly necessary but are helpful: backlit display, a measurement hold, large digit displays, a greater number of significant digits, PC connectivity (ideally opto-isolated), temperature probe, and diode testing.
- **Case:** Look for a good-quality rubberized plastic case.

Generally, most of the preceding features are available on mid-price DMMs with a good level of accuracy (1% or better), high input impedances (>10 MΩ), and good measurement ranges. High-end multimeters mainly offer faster measurement speed and greater levels of measurement accuracy; some may also offer features such as measuring capacitance, frequency, temperature using an infrared sensor, humidity, and transistor gain. Some of the best known brands are Fluke, Tenma, Agilent, Extech, and Klein Tools.

Oscilloscopes

Standard DMMs provide you with a versatile tool that enables you to measure average voltage, current, and resistance. Oscilloscopes typically only measure voltage, but they enable you to see how the voltage changes with respect to time. Typically, you can simultaneously view two or more voltage waveforms that are captured within a certain bandwidth and number of analog samples (memory). The bandwidth defines the range of signal frequencies that an oscilloscope can measure accurately (typically to the 3 dB point, i.e., the frequency at which a sine wave amplitude is ~30% lower than its true amplitude). To achieve accurate results, the number of analog samples needs to be a multiple of the bandwidth (you will see why later in this chapter when the Nyquist rate is discussed); and for modern oscilloscopes, this value is typically four to five times the bandwidth, so a 25 MHz oscilloscope should have 100 million samples per second or greater. The bandwidth and number of analog samples have the greatest influence on the cost of an oscilloscope.

Several low-cost two-channel oscilloscopes are available, such as those by Owon PDS5022S 25 MHz (~$200), feature-rich Siglent SDS1022DL 25 MHz (~$325), Rigol DS1052 50 MHz (~$325), and Owon SDS6062 60 MHz (~$349). Prices rise considerably as the bandwidth increases, to around $1,500 for a 300 MHz scope. Agilent digital storage (DSOX) and mixed-signal (MSOX) series scopes would be considered to be mid/high range and cost $3,000 (100 MHz) to $16,000 (1 GHz). Mixed-signal scopes also provide you with digital bus analysis tools.

The Digilent Analog Discovery with Waveforms (see Figure 4-1) is used to test all of the circuits in this book. The Analog Discovery (and very similar Analog Discovery 2) is a USB oscilloscope, waveform generator, digital pattern generator, and logic analyzer for the Windows environment. The recently released Waveforms 2015 software now has support for Linux (including ARM) and Mac OS X. The Analog Discovery is generally available for $259–$279. If you are starting out, or refreshing your electronics skills, it is a really great piece of equipment for the price.

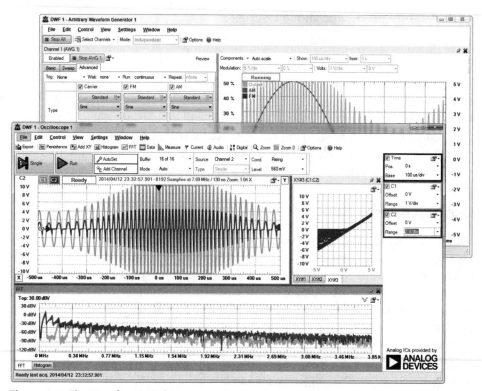

Figure 4-1: The Waveforms application generating a signal and displaying the response from the physical circuit

NOTE   A video I made about the use of the Analog Discovery is available at this chapter's web page: www.exploringrpi.com/chapter4. It demonstrates three different measurement applications of the Analog Discovery: analog analysis of a rectifier diode; using the digital pattern generator and logic analyzer to investigate the behavior of a JK flip-flop; and using the logic analyzer and its I²C interpreter to connect to the BeagleBone Black I²C bus and analyze how it behaves. The analysis performed would be identical on the RPi platform.

The Analog Discovery is used to generate all of the oscilloscope plots that are presented in this book, as all examples have been implemented using real circuits. The scope is limited to two channels at 5 MHz per channel and 50 million samples per second, for both the waveform generator and the differential oscilloscope. As such, the Analog Discovery is mainly focused on students and learners; however, it can also be useful in deciding upon "must-have" features for your next, more expensive, equipment.

There are alternative mixed-signal USB scopes, such as PicoScopes, which range from $160 to $10,000 (www.picotech.com), and the BitScope DSO, from $150 to $1,000 (www.bitscope.com), which has Linux support. However, based on the feature set that is currently available on USB oscilloscopes, it may be the case that a bench scope with a USB logic analyzer (to provide mixed-mode functionality, such as the Saleae logic analyzer, www.saleae.com) provides the best "bang for your buck."

> **NOTE** The BitScope Micro (~$145) is a special version of the BitScope that is built especially for the RPi. Similar to the Analog Discovery, it is a two-channel oscilloscope (20 MHz), logic analyzer (6 channel), and spectrum analyzer. The BitScope Micro is designed to be connected directly to the RPi, and it can be used to create a standalone or network-accessible measurement and data acquisition platform. In addition, it includes software libraries that you can use to build custom acquisition applications. For more information, see bitscope.com/pi/.

Basic Circuit Principles

Electronic circuits contain arrangements of components that can be described as being either passive or active. Active components, such as transistors, are those that can adaptively control the flow of current, whereas passive components cannot (e.g., resistors, capacitors, diodes). The challenge in building circuits is designing a suitable arrangement of appropriate components. Fortunately, there are circuit analysis equations to help you.

Voltage, Current, Resistance, and Ohm's Law

The most important equation that you need to understand is Ohm's law. It is simply stated as follows:

$$V = I \times R$$

where:

- Voltage (V), measured in volts (V), is the difference in potential energy that forces electrical current to flow in the circuit. A water analogy is very useful when thinking of voltage; many houses have a buffer tank of water in the attic that is connected to the taps in the house. Water flows when a tap is turned on, due to the height of the tank and the force of gravity. If the tap were at the same height as the top of the tank of water, no water would flow, because there would be no potential energy. Voltage behaves in much the same way; when a voltage on one side of a component, such as a resistor, is greater than on the other side, electrical current can flow across the component.

- Current (I), measured in amps (A), is the flow of electrical charge. To continue the water analogy, current would be the flow of water from the tank (with a high potential) to the tap (with a lower potential). Remember that the tap still has potential and water will flow out of the drain of the sink, unless it is at ground level (GND). To put the level of current in context, when we build circuits to interface with the RPi's GPIOs, they usually source or sink only about 3 mA, where a milliamp is one thousandth of an amp.

- Resistance (R), measured in ohms (Ω), discourages the flow of charge. A resistor is a component that reduces the flow of current through the dissipation of power. It does this in a linear fashion, where the power dissipated in watts (W), is given by $P = V \times I$ or, alternatively by integrating Ohm's law: $P = I^2 R = V^2/R$. The power is dissipated in the form of heat, and all resistors have a maximum dissipated power rating. Common metal film or carbon resistors typically dissipate 0.125 W to 1 W, and the price increases dramatically if this value has to exceed 3 W. To finish with the water analogy, resistance is the friction between the water and the pipe, which results in a heating effect and a reduction in the flow of water. This resistance can be increased by increasing the surface area over which the water has to pass, while maintaining the pipe's cross-sectional area (e.g., placing small pipes within the main pipe).

As an example, if you had to buy a resistor that limits the flow of current to 100 mA when using a 5 V supply, as illustrated in Figure 4-2(a), which resistor should you buy? The voltage dropped across the resistor, V_R, must be 5 V, as it is the only component in the circuit. Because $V_R = I_R \times R$, it follows that the resistor should have the value $R = V_R/(I_R = 5\,\text{V})/(100\,\text{mA}) = 50\,\Omega$, and the power dissipated by this resistor can be calculated using any of the general equations $P = VI = I^2 R = V^2/R$ as 0.5 W.

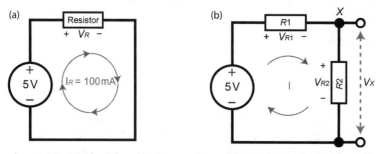

Figure 4-2: (a) Ohm's law circuit example, and (b) a voltage divider example

Buying one through-hole, fixed-value metal-film resistor with a 1% tolerance (accuracy) costs about $0.10 for a 0.33 W resistor and $0.45 for a 1 W power rating. You should be careful with the power rating of the resistors you use in your circuits, as underspecified resistors can blow. A 30 W resistor will cost $2.50 and can get extremely hot—not all resistors are created equally!

WARNING   Why would it be bad practice to connect a voltage supply's positive terminal to the negative terminal without a resistor? This is called a short circuit, and it is the quickest way to damage a sensitive device like the RPi. Connection (hook-up) wire by its nature is a good conductor, and it has a very small resistance. A 100 M (328′) roll of 0.6 mm (0.023″) hook-up wire has a total resistance of about 5 Ω; therefore, connecting a 6″ length of connection wire between a RPi 3.3 V supply and its GND terminal would in theory draw 433 A ($I=V/R=3.3$ V/0.0076 Ω). In practice this will not happen, but the available maximum current would likely damage your RPi! Also, remember that LEDs do not include a fixed internal resistance, so they behave somewhat like a short circuit when forward biased—LEDs nearly always require current-limiting resistors for this reason!

Voltage Division

If the circuit in Figure 4-2(a) is modified to add another resistor in series as illustrated in Figure 4-2(b), what will be the impact on the circuit?

- Because one resistor is after the other (they're in series), the total resistance that the current must pass through to circulate in the circuit is the sum of the two values: $R_T = R1 + R2$.

- The supply voltage must drop across the two resistors, so you can say that $V_{supply} = V_{R1} + V_{R2}$. The voltage that drops across each resistor is inversely proportional to the resistor's value. This circuit is called a voltage divider.

Suppose you want to calculate on paper the voltage value at point X in Figure 4-2(b) if $R1 = 25\,\Omega$ and $R2 = 75\,\Omega$. The total resistance in the circuit is $R_T = 25 + 75 = 100\,\Omega$, and the total voltage drop across the resistors must be 5 V; therefore, by using Ohm's law, the current flowing in the circuit is $I = V/R = 5\,V/100\,\Omega = 50\,mA$. If the resistance of $R1$ is $25\,\Omega$, then the voltage drop across $V_{R1} = I \times R = 0.05\,A \times 25\,\Omega = 1.25\,V$ and the voltage drop across $V_{R2} = I \times R = 0.05\,A \times 75\,\Omega = 3.75\,V$. You can see that the sum of these voltages is 5 V, thus obeying Kirchoff's voltage law, which states that the sum of the voltage drops in a series circuit equals the total voltage applied.

To answer the question fully: In this circuit, 1.25 V is dropped across $R1$ and 3.75 V is dropped across $R2$, so what is the voltage at X? To know that, you have to measure X with respect to some other point! If you measured X with respect to the negative terminal of the supply, the voltage drop is V_X in Figure 4-2(b), and it is the same as the voltage drop across $R2$, so it is 3.75 V. However, it would be equally as valid to ask the question, "What is the voltage at X with respect to the positive terminal of the supply?" In that case, it would be the negative of the voltage drop across $R1$ (as X is at 3.75 V with respect to the negative terminal and the positive terminal is at +5 V with respect to the negative terminal); therefore, the voltage at X with respect to the positive terminal of the supply is –1.25 V.

To calculate the value of V_X in Figure 4-2(b), the voltage divider rule can be generalized to the following:

$$V_X = V \times \frac{R2}{R1+R2}$$

You can use this rule to determine a voltage V_X, but unfortunately this configuration is quite limited in practice, because it is very likely that the circuit to which you connect this voltage supply, V_X, will itself have a resistance (or load). This will alter the characteristic of your voltage divider circuit, changing the voltage V_X. However, most circuits that follow voltage dividers are usually input circuits that have very high input impedances, and therefore the impact on V_X will be minimal.

Figure 4-3(a) captures a variable resistor, or potentiometer (pot), and an associated circuit where it is used as a standalone voltage divider. The resistance between pins 1 and 3 is a fixed value, $10 \text{k}\Omega$ in the case of the multiturn pot; however, the resistance between pins 3 and the wiper pin (pin 2) varies between 0Ω and $10 \text{k}\Omega$. Therefore, if the resistance between pins 2 and 3 is $2 \text{k}\Omega$, then the resistance between pins 1 and 2 will be $10 \text{k}\Omega - 2 \text{k}\Omega = 8 \text{k}\Omega$. In such a case, the output voltage, V_{out}, will be 1 V and it can be varied between 0 V and 5 V by turning the small screw on the pot, using a trim tool or screwdriver.

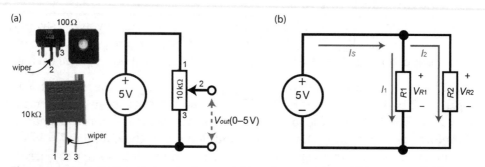

Figure 4-3: (a) Potentiometers and using a variable voltage supply, and (b) a current divider example

Current Division

If the circuit is modified as in Figure 4-3(b) to place the two resistors in parallel, you now have a current divider circuit. Current will follow the path of least resistance, so if $R1 = 100 \Omega$ and $R2 = 200 \Omega$, then a greater proportion of the current will travel through $R1$. So, what is this proportion? In this case the voltage drop across $R1$ and $R2$ is 5 V in both cases. Therefore, the current I_1 will be $I = V/R = 5 \text{V}/100 \Omega = 50 \text{mA}$ and the current I_2 will be $I = 5 \text{V}/200 \Omega = 25 \text{mA}$.

Therefore, twice as much current travels through the $100\,\Omega$ resistor as the $200\,\Omega$ resistor. Clearly, current favors the path of least resistance.

Kirchoff's current law states that the sum of currents entering a junction equals the sum of currents exiting that junction. This means that $I_S = I_1 + I_2 = 25\,\text{mA} + 50\,\text{mA} = 75\,\text{mA}$. The current divider rule can be stated generally as follows:

$$I_1 = I \times \left(\frac{R2}{R1 + R2} \right), \text{ and } I_2 = I \times \left(\frac{R2}{R1 + R2} \right)$$

However, this requires that you know the value of the current I (I_S in this case) that is entering the junction. To calculate I_S directly, you need to calculate the equivalent resistance (R_T) of the two parallel resistors, which is given as follows:

$$\frac{1}{R_T} = \frac{1}{R1} + \frac{1}{R2}, \text{ or } R_T = \frac{R1 \times R2}{R1 + R2},$$

This is $66.66\,\Omega$ in Figure 4-3(b); therefore $I_S = V/R = 5\,\text{V}/66.66\,\Omega = 75\,\text{mA}$, which is consistent with the initial calculations.

The power delivered by the supply: $P = VI = 5\,\text{V} \times 0.075\,\text{A} = 0.375\,\text{W}$. This should be equal to the sum of the power dissipated by $R1 = V^2/R = 5^2/100 = 0.25\,\text{W}$ and, $R2 = V^2/R = 5^2/200 = 0.125\,\text{W}$ giving $0.375\,\text{W}$ total, confirming that the law of conservation of energy applies!

Implementing RPi Circuits on a Breadboard

The breadboard is a great platform for prototyping circuits and it works perfectly with the RPi. Figure 4-4 illustrates a breadboard, describing how you can use the two horizontal power rails for 3.3 V and 5 V power. The RPi GPIO header consists of male header pins, which means that you typically require relatively expensive female jumper connectors for wiring circuits. RPi GPIO extension boards (e.g., the Adafruit Pi T-Cobbler Plus), as illustrated in Figure 4-4, are widely available for interfacing to breadboards. They solve the problem of connecting to the male headers on the RPi using female jumper cables, provide a very stable connection, and allow you to use low-cost hook-up wire for your circuits. Please be especially careful when connecting the RPi end of a GPIO extension board cable to the RPi, as the connector is not polarized and therefore can be connected backward.

A good-quality breadboard like that in Figure 4-4 (830 tie points) costs about $6 to $10. Giant breadboards (3,220 tie points) are available for about $20. Here are some tips for using breadboards:

- Whenever possible, place Pin 1 of your ICs on the bottom left so that you can easily debug your circuits. Always line up the pins carefully with the breadboard holes before applying pressure and "clicking" it home. Also, ICs need power!

- Leaving a wire disconnected is *not* the same as connecting it to GND (discussed later in this chapter).

- Use a flat-head screwdriver to slowly lever ICs out of the breadboard from both ends to avoid bending the IC's legs.

- Be careful not to bridge resistors and other components by placing two of their pins in the same vertical rail. Also, trim resistor leads before placing them in the board, as long resistor leads can accidentally touch and cause circuit debugging headaches.

- Momentary push buttons typically have four legs that are connected in two pairs; make sure that you orient them correctly (use a DMM continuity test).

- Staples make great bridge connections!

- Some boards have a break in the power rails; bridge this where necessary.

- Breadboards typically have 0.1" spacing (lead pitch) between the tie points, which is 2.54 mm metric. Try to buy all components and connectors with that spacing. For ICs, choose the DIP/PDIP (the IC code ends with an N); and for other components, choose the "through-hole" form.

- Use the color of the hook-up wire to mean something—e.g., use red for 5 V and black for GND; it can really help when debugging circuits. Solid-core 22AWG wire serves as perfect hook-up wire and is available with many different insulator colors. Pre-formed jumper wire is available, but long wires lead to messy circuits. A selection of hook-up wire in different colors and a good-quality wire-stripping tool enables the neatest and most stable breadboard layouts.

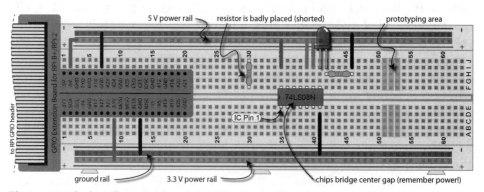

Figure 4-4: The breadboard with an RPi GPIO extension board and a 7408 IC (quad two-input AND gates)

EXAMPLE: MAKING CUSTOM CABLES FOR THE RPI GPIO HEADER

As an alternative to using GPIO expansion boards or pre-crimped female jumper wires, you can make custom cables for the RPi's DuPont PCB interconnector. Custom cables allow for deployable stable connections, custom cable lengths, custom break-out directions, and mixed male/female end connectors. Figure 4-5(a) illustrates a custom-built connector that is attached to the RPi header. Figure 4-5(b) illustrates a typical budget-price crimping tool ($20–$35). A video on this topic is available on the chapter web page and at `tiny.cc/erpi401`.

(a)   (b)

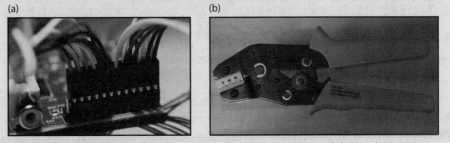

Figure 4-5: (a) The custom-built connector attached to an RPi (model B), and (b) a low-cost crimping tool

Digital Multimeters (DMMs) and Breadboards

Measuring voltage, current and resistance is fairly straightforward once you take a few rules into account (with reference to Figure 4-6):

- *DC voltage (DCV)* is measured in parallel with (i.e., across) the component that experiences the voltage drop. The meter should have the black probe in the COM (common) DMM input.

- *DC current (DCA)* is measured in series, so you will have to "break" the connection in your circuit and wire the DMM as if it were a component in series with the conductor in the circuit in which you are measuring current. Use the black probe lead in COM and the red lead in the μAmA input (or equivalent). Do not use the 10 A unfused input.

- *Resistance* cannot usually be measured in-circuit, because other resistors or components will act as parallel/series loads in your measurement. Isolate the component and place your DMM red probe in the VΩ input and set the meter to measure Ω. The continuity test can be reasonably effectively used in-circuit, provided that it is de-energized.

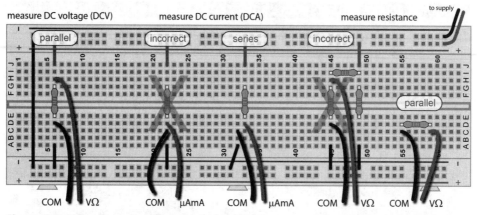

Figure 4-6: Measuring voltage, current, and resistance

If your DMM is refusing to function, you may have blown the internal fuse. Disconnect the DMM probes and open the meter to find the small glass fuse. If you have a second meter you can perform a continuity test to determine whether it has blown. Replace it with a like value (or PTC)—not a mains fuse!

> **WARNING**   Measuring current directly across a voltage supply (even a 9 V battery) with no load is the quickest way to blow the DMM fuse, as most are rated at about 200 mA. Check that the probe is in the VΩ input before measuring voltage.

Example Circuit: Voltage Regulation

Now that you have read the principles, a more complex circuit is discussed in this section, and then the components are examined in detail in the following sections. Do not build the circuit in this section; it is intended as an example to introduce the concept of interconnected components.

A voltage regulator is a complex but easy-to-use device that accepts a varied input voltage and outputs a constant voltage almost regardless of the attached load, at a lower level than the input voltage. The voltage regulator maintains the output voltage within a certain tolerance, preventing voltage variations from damaging downstream electronics devices.

The RPi B+ and RPi 2/3 models have a dual high-efficiency PWM step-down DC-DC converter (PAM2306 on U3, see `tiny.cc/erpi402`) that can supply different fixed voltage levels to on-board devices, along with short-circuit protection. For example, there is a 5 V, 3.3 V, and a 1.8 V output. You can use these 5 V and 3.3 V outputs as supplies on the RPi GPIO header to drive your circuits, but only within certain current supply limits. The RPi can supply up to 200 mA–300 mA on the 5 V pins (Pins 2 and 4), and approximately 50 mA on the 3.3 V pins (Pins 1 and 17).

If you want to draw larger currents for applications like driving motors, you may need to use voltage regulators like that in Figure 4-7. You can build this directly on a breadboard or you can purchase a "breadboard power supply stick 5 V/3.3 V" from SparkFun (www.sparkfun.com) for about $15.

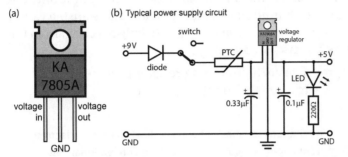

Figure 4-7: The KA7805A/LM7805 voltage regulator and an example regulator circuit

As shown in Figure 4-7, the pin on the left of the regulator is the voltage supply input. When delivering a current of 500 mA, the KA7805/LM7805 voltage regulator will accept an input voltage range of 8 V–20 V, and will output a voltage (on the right) in the range of 4.8 V–5.2 V. The middle pin should be connected to the ground rail. The aluminum plate at the back of the voltage regulator is there to dissipate heat. The hole enables you to bolt on a heat sink, allowing for greater output currents, of up to 1 A.

The minimum input voltage required is about 8 V in order to drive the KA7805/LM7805 voltage regulator. If your supply voltage is lower than that, then you could use a low-dropout (LDO) voltage regulator, which can require a supply as low as 6 V to operate a 5 V regulator. The implementation circuit in Figure 4-7 has the following additional components that enable it to deliver a clean and steady 5 V, 1 A supply:

- The diode ensures that if the supply is erroneously connected with the wrong polarity (e.g., 9 V and GND are accidentally swapped), then the circuit is protected from damage. Diodes like the 1N4001 (1 A supply) are very low cost, but the downside is that there will be a small forward voltage drop (approximately 1 V at 1 A) across the diode in advance of the regulator.

- The switch can be used to power the circuit on or off. A slider switch enables the circuit to remain continuously powered.

- The Positive Temperature Coefficient (PTC) resettable fuse is very useful for preventing damage from overcurrent faults, such as accidental short circuits or component failure. The PTC enables a holding current to pass with only a small resistance (about 0.25 Ω); but once a greater tripping current is exceeded, the resistance increases rapidly, behaving like a circuit breaker. When the power is removed, the PTC will cool (for a few seconds) and it regains its pre-tripped characteristics. In this circuit a 60R110 or equivalent Polyfuse would be appropriate, as it has a holding current of 1.1 A and a trip current of 2.2 A, at a maximum voltage of 60 V DC.

■ The 0.33 µF capacitor is on the supply side of the regulator and the 0.1 µF capacitor is on the output side of the regulator. These are the values recommended in the datasheet to remove noise (ripple rejection) from the supply. Capacitors are discussed shortly.

■ The LED and appropriate current-limiting resistor provide an indicator light that makes it clear when the supply is powered.

> **NOTE** There are two main notations to represent current flow: The first is electron current flow, and it is the flow of negative charge. The second is conventional flow notation, and it is precisely the opposite: It is the flow of positive charge, and it is consistent with all semiconductor symbols. This book uses the conventional flow notation to describe current flow direction.

Discrete Components

The previous example circuit used a number of discrete components to build a standalone power supply circuit. In this section, the types of components that compose the power supply circuit are discussed in more detail. These components can be applied to many different circuit designs, and it is important to discuss them now, as many of them are used in designing circuits that interface to the RPi input/outputs in Chapter 6.

Diodes

Simply put, a diode is a discrete semiconductor component that allows current to pass in one direction but not the other. As the name suggests, a "semi" conductor is neither a conductor nor an insulator. Silicon is a semiconductive material, but it becomes much more interesting when it is doped with an impurity, such as phosphorus. Such a negative (n-type) doping results in a weakly bound electron in the valence band. It can also be positively doped (p-type) to have a hole in the valence band, using impurities such as boron. When you join a small block of p-type and n-type doped silicon together, you get a pn-junction—a diode! The free electrons in the valence band of the n-type silicon flow to the p-type silicon, creating a depletion layer and a voltage potential barrier that must be overcome before current can flow.

When a diode is forward biased it allows current to flow through it; when it is reverse-biased, no current can flow. A diode is forward-biased when the voltage on the anode (+ve) terminal is greater than the voltage on the cathode (−ve) terminal; however, the biasing must also exceed the depletion layer potential barrier (knee voltage) before current can flow, which is typically between 0.5 V and 0.7 V for a silicon diode. If the diode is reverse-biased by applying a greater voltage on the cathode than the anode, then almost no current can flow (maybe 1 nA or so). However, if the reverse-biased voltage is increasingly raised, then eventually the diode will break down and allow current to flow in the reverse direction. If the current is low then this will not damage the diode—in fact, a special diode called a Zener diode is designed to operate in this breakdown region, and it can be configured to behave just like a voltage regulator.

The 1N4001 is a low-cost silicon diode that can be used in a simple circuit (see Figure 4-8) to demonstrate the use and behavior of diodes. The 1N4001 has a peak reverse breakdown voltage of 50 V. In this circuit, a sine wave is applied that alternates from +5 V to −5 V, using the waveform generator of the Analog Discovery. When the V_{in} voltage is positive and exceeds the knee voltage, then current will flow and there will be a voltage drop across the load resistor V_{load}, which is slightly less than V_{in}. There is a small voltage drop across the diode V_d and you can see from the oscilloscope measurements that this is 0.67 V, which is within the expected range for a silicon diode.

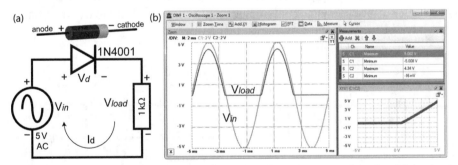

Figure 4-8: Circuit and behavior of a 1N4001 diode with a 5 V AC supply and a 1 kΩ load resistor

The diode is used in the circuit in Figure 4-7 as a reverse polarity protector. It should be clear from the plot in Figure 4-8 why it is effective, as when V_{in} is negative, the V_{load} is zero. This is because current cannot flow through the diode when it is reverse-biased. If the voltage exceeded the breakdown voltage for the diode then current would flow; but since that is 50 V for the 1N4001, it will not occur in this case. Note that the bottom right-hand corner of Figure 4-8 shows an XY-plot of output voltage (y-axis) versus input voltage (x-axis). You can see that for negative input voltage the output voltage is 0, but once the knee voltage is reached (0.67 V), the output voltage increases linearly with the input voltage.

This circuit is called a *half-wave rectifier*. It is possible to connect four diodes in a bridge formation to create a full-wave rectifier.

Light-Emitting Diodes (LEDs)

A light-emitting diode (LED) is a semiconductor-based light source that is often used as a state indication light in all types of devices. Today, high-powered LEDs are being used in car lights, in back lights for televisions, and even in place of filament lights for general-purpose lighting (e.g., home lighting, traffic lights, etc.) mainly due to their longevity and extremely high efficiency in converting electrical power to light output. LEDs provide very useful status and debug information about your circuit, often used to indicate whether a state is true or false.

Like diodes, LEDs are polarized. The symbol for an LED is illustrated in Figure 4-9. To cause an LED to light, the diode needs to be forward biased by connecting the anode (+) to a more positive source than the cathode (–). For example, the anode could be connected to +3.3 V and the cathode to GND; however, also remember that the same effect would be achieved by connecting the anode to 0 V and the cathode to –3.3 V.

Figure 4-9 illustrates an LED that has one leg longer than the other. The longer leg is the anode (+) and the shorter leg is the cathode (–). The plastic LED surround also has a flat edge, which indicates the cathode (–) leg of the LED. This flat edge indication is particularly useful when the LED is in-circuit and the legs have been trimmed.

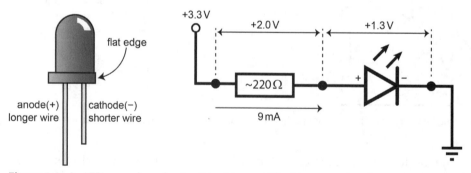

Figure 4-9: An LED example and a circuit to drive an LED with appropriate forward current and voltage levels

LEDs have certain operating requirements, defined by a forward voltage and a forward current. Every LED is different, and you need to reference the datasheet of the LED to determine these values. An LED does not have a significant resistance, so if you were to connect the LED directly across your RPi's 3.3 V supply, the LED would act like a short circuit, and you would drive a very large current through the LED, damaging it—but more important, damaging your RPi! Therefore, to operate an LED within its limits you need a series resistor, called a current-limiting resistor. Choose this value carefully to maximize the light output of the LED and to protect the circuit.

WARNING   Do not connect LEDs directly to the GPIOs on the RPi's GPIO header without using current-limiting resistors and/or transistor switching, as you will likely damage your board. The maximum current that the RPi should source from, or sink to a GPIO pin should be kept at about 2–3 mA.

Referring to Figure 4-9, if you are supplying the LED from the RPi's 3.3 V supply and you want to have a forward voltage drop of 1.3 V across the LED, you need the difference of 2 V to drop across the current-limiting resistor. The LED specifications require you to limit the current to 9 mA, so you need to calculate a current-limiting resistor value as follows:

As $V = IR$, then $R = V/I = 2\,V/0.009\,A = 222\,\Omega$

Therefore, a circuit to light an LED would look like that in Figure 4-9. Here a 220 Ω resistor is placed in series with the LED. The combination of the 3.3 V supply and the resistor drives a current of 9 mA through the forward-biased LED; as with this current the resistor has a 2 V drop across it, then accordingly the LED has a forward voltage drop of 1.3 V across it. Note that this current is fine if you are connecting to the RPi's 3.3 V output, but it is *not* fine for use with the RPi's GPIOs, as the maximum current that the RPi can realistically source from a GPIO pin is about 2 mA–3 mA. You will see a solution for this shortly, and again in Chapter 6.

It is also worth mentioning that you should not dim LEDs by reducing the voltage across the LED. An LED should be thought of as a current-controlled device, where driving a current through the LED causes the forward voltage drop. Therefore, trying to control an LED with a variable voltage will not work as you might expect. To dim an LED you can use a pulse-width modulated (PWM) signal, essentially rapidly switching the LED on and off. For example, if a rapid PWM signal is applied to the LED that is off for half of the time and on for half of the time, then the LED will appear to be only emitting about half of its regular operating condition light level. Our eyes don't see the individual changes if they are fast enough; they average over the light and dark interval to see a constant, but dimmer illumination.

Figure 4-10 illustrates a PWM square wave signal at different duty cycles. The duty cycle is the percentage of time that the signal is high versus the time that the signal is low. In this example, a high is represented by a voltage of 3.3 V and a low by a voltage of 0 V. A duty cycle of 0% means that the signal is constantly low, and a duty cycle of 100% means that the signal is constantly high.

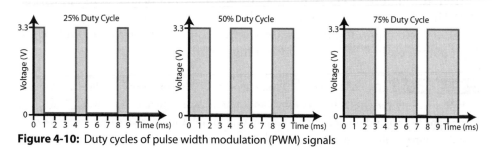

Figure 4-10: Duty cycles of pulse width modulation (PWM) signals

PWM can be used to control the light level of LEDs, but it can also be used to control the speed of DC motors, the position of servo motors, and many more applications. You will see such an example in Chapter 6 when the built-in PWM functionality of the RPi is used.

The period (*T*) of a repeating signal (a periodic signal) is the time it takes to complete a full cycle. In the example in Figure 4-10, the period of the signal in all three cases is 4 ms. The frequency (*f*) of a periodic signal describes how often a signal goes through a full cycle in a given time period. Therefore, for a signal with a period of 4 ms, it will cycle 250 times per second (1/0.004), which is 250 hertz (Hz). We can state that *f* (Hz) = 1/*T* (s) or *T* (s) = 1/*f* (Hz). Some high-end DMMs measure frequency, but generally you use an oscilloscope to measure frequency. PWM signals need to switch at a frequency to suit the device to be controlled; typically, the frequency is in the kHz range for motor control.

Smoothing and Decoupling Capacitors

A capacitor is a passive electrical component that can be used to store electrical energy between two insulated plates when there is a voltage difference between them. The energy is stored in an electric field between the two plates, with positive charge building on one plate and negative charge building on the other plate. When the voltage difference is removed or reduced, then the capacitor discharges its energy to a connected electrical circuit.

For example, if you modified the diode circuit in Figure 4-8 to add a 10 μF smoothing capacitor in parallel with the load resistor, the output voltage would appear as shown in Figure 4-11. When the diode is forward biased there is a potential across the terminals of the capacitor and it quickly charges (while a current also flows through the load resistor in parallel). When the diode is reverse biased, there is no external supply generating a potential across the capacitor/resistor combination, so the potential across the terminals of the capacitor (because of its charge) causes a current to flow through the load resistor, and the capacitor starts to discharge. The impact of this change is that there is now a more stable voltage across the load resistor that varies between 2.758 V and 4.222 V (the ripple voltage is 1.464 V), rather than between 0 V and 4.34 V.

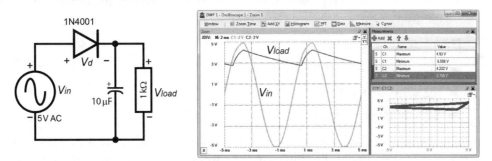

Figure 4-11: Circuit and behavior of a 1N4001 diode with a 5 V AC supply, 1 kΩ load, and parallel 10 µF capacitor

Capacitors use a dielectric material, such as ceramic, glass, paper, or plastic, to insulate the two charged plates. Two common capacitor types are ceramic and electrolytic capacitors. Ceramic capacitors are small and low cost and degrade over time. Electrolytic capacitors can store much larger amounts of energy, but also degrade over time. Glass, mica, and tantalum capacitors tend to be more reliable, but are considerably more expensive.

Figure 4-12 illustrates a 100 nF (0.1 µF) ceramic capacitor and a 47 µF electrolytic capacitor. Note that the electrolytic capacitor is polarized, with the negative lead marked on the capacitor surface with a band; like the LED, the negative lead is shorter than the positive lead.

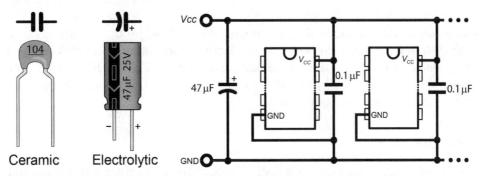

Figure 4-12: Ceramic (non polarized) and electrolytic (polarized) capacitors and an example decoupling circuit

The numbering for capacitors is reasonably straightforward; unfortunately, on ceramic capacitors it can be small and hard to read:

■ The first number is the first digit of the capacitor value.

■ The second number is the second digit of the capacitor value.

- The third number is the number of zeroes, where the capacitor value is in pF (picofarads).

- Additional letters represent the tolerance and voltage rating of the capacitor but can be ignored for the moment.

Therefore, for example:

- 104 = 100<u>000</u> pF = 100 nF = 0.1 µF
- 10<u>2</u> = 1,<u>000</u> pF = 1 nF
- 47<u>2</u> = 4,<u>700</u> pF = 4.7 nF

The voltage regulator circuit presented earlier (refer to Figure 4-7) used two capacitors to smooth out the ripples in the supply by charging and discharging in opposition to those ripples. Capacitors can also be used for a related function known as *decoupling*.

Coupling is often an undesirable relationship that occurs between two parts of a circuit due to the sharing of power supply connections. This relationship means that if there is a sudden high power demand by one part of the circuit, then the supply voltage will drop slightly, affecting the supply voltages of other parts of the circuit. ICs impart a variable load on the power supply lines—in fact, a load that can change very quickly causes a high-frequency voltage variation on the supply lines to other ICs. As the number of ICs in the circuit increases, the problem will be compounded.

Small capacitors, known as decoupling capacitors, can act as a store of energy that removes the noise signals that may be present on your supply lines as a result of these IC load variations. An example circuit is illustrated in Figure 4-12, where the larger 47 µF capacitor filters out lower-frequency variations and the 0.1 µF capacitors filter out higher-frequency noise. Ideally the leads on the 0.1 µF capacitors should be as short as possible to avoid producing undesirable effects (relating to inductance) that will limit it from filtering the highest-level frequencies. Even the surface-mounted capacitors used on the RPi to decouple the ball grid array (BGA) pins on the BCM2835/6/7 SoC produce small inductances (approximately 1 nH – 2 nH).

Transistors

Transistors are one of the core ingredients of the RPi's microprocessor, and indeed almost every other electronic system. Simply put, their function can be to amplify a signal or to turn a signal on or off, whichever is required. The RPi GPIOs can only handle very modest currents, so we need transistors to help us when interfacing them to electronic circuits that require larger currents to operate.

Bipolar junction transistors (BJTs), usually just called transistors, are formed by adding another doped layer to a pn-junction diode to form either a p-n-p or an n-p-n transistor. There are other types of transistors, such as field effect transistors (FETs), which are discussed shortly. The name bipolar comes from the fact that the current is carried by both electrons and holes. They have three terminals, with the third terminal connected to the middle layer in the sandwich, which is very narrow, as illustrated in Figure 4-13.

Figure 4-13 presents quite an amount of information about transistors, including the naming of the terminals as the base (B), collector (C), and emitter (E). Despite there being two main types of BJT transistor (NPN and PNP), the NPN transistor is the most commonly used. In fact, any transistor examples in this chapter use a single BC547 NPN transistor type.

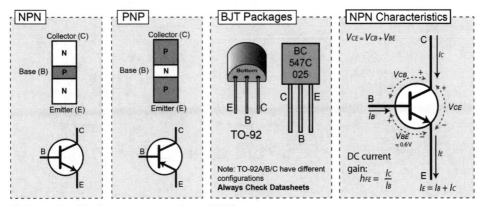

Figure 4-13: Bipolar junction transistors (BJTs)

The BC547 is a 45 V, 100 mA general-purpose transistor that is commonly available, is low cost, and is provided in a leaded TO-92 package. The identification of the legs in the BC547 is provided in Figure 4-13, but please be aware that this order is not consistent with all transistors—always check the datasheet! The maximum V_{CE} (a.k.a. V_{CEO}) is 45 V and the maximum collector current (I_C) is 100 mA for the BC547. It has a typical DC current gain (h_{FE}) of between 180 and 520, depending on the group used (e.g., A, B, C). Those characteristics are explained in the next sections.

Transistors as Switches

> **NOTE**   For the remainder of this book, FETs rather than BJTs are used in the RPi circuits for switching loads. If you become overwhelmed by the detail in this section, please skip ahead to FETs, which are somewhat easier to apply.

Let's examine the characteristics for the NPN transistor as illustrated in Figure 4-13 (on the rightmost diagram). If the base-emitter junction is forward biased and a small current is entering the base (I_B), the behavior of a transistor is such that a proportional but much larger current ($I_C = h_{FE} \times I_B$) will be allowed to flow into the collector terminal, as h_{FE} will be a value of 180 to 520 for a transistor such as the BC547. Because I_B is much smaller than I_C, you can also assume that I_E is approximately equal to I_C.

Figure 4-14 illustrates the example of a BJT being used as a switch. In part (a) the voltage levels have been chosen to match those available on the RPi. The resistor on the base is chosen to have a value of 2.2 kΩ, so that the base current will be small ($I = V/R = (3.3\,V - 0.7\,V)/2200\,Ω$ which is about 1.2 mA). The resistor on the collector is small, so the collector current will be reasonably large ($I = V/R = (5\,V - {\sim}0.2\ V)/100\,Ω = 48\,mA$).

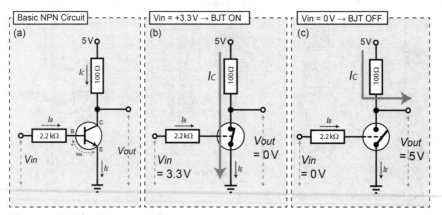

Figure 4-14: The BJT as a switch

Figure 4-14(b) illustrates what happens when an input voltage of 3.3 V is applied to the base terminal. The small base current causes the transistor to behave like a closed switch (with a very low resistance) between the collector and the emitter. This means that the voltage drop across the collector-emitter will be almost zero and all of the voltage is dropped across the 100 Ω load resistor, causing a current to flow directly to ground through the emitter. The transistor is saturated because it cannot pass any further current. Because there is almost no voltage drop across the collector-emitter, the output voltage, V_{out}, will be almost 0 V.

Figure 4-14(c) illustrates what happens when the input voltage $V_{in} = 0\,V$ is applied to the base terminal and there is no base current. The transistor behaves like an open switch (very large resistance). No current can flow through the collector-emitter junction, as this current is always a multiple of the base current and the base current is zero; therefore, almost all of the voltage is dropped across the collector-emitter. In this case the output, V_{out}, can be up to +5 V (though as implied by the illustrated flow of I_C through the output terminal, the exact value of V_{out} depends on the size of I_C, as any current flowing through the 100 Ω resistor will cause a voltage drop across it).

Therefore, the switch behaves somewhat like an inverter. If the input voltage is 0 V, the output voltage is +5 V, and if the input voltage is +3.3 V, the output voltage will be 0 V. You can see the actual measured values of this circuit in Figure 4-15, when the input voltage of 3.3 V is applied to the base terminal. In this case, the Analog Discovery Waveform Generator is used to output a 1 kHz square wave, with an amplitude of 1.65 V and an offset of +1.65 V (forming a 0 V to 3.3 V square wave signal), so it appears like a 3.3 V source turning on and then off, 1,000 times per second. All the measurements in this figure were captured with the input at 3.3 V. The base-emitter junction is forward biased, and just like the diode before, this will have a forward voltage of about 0.7 V. The actual voltage drop across the base-emitter is 0.83 V, so the voltage drop across the base resistor will be 2.440 V. The actual base current is 1.1 mA ($I = V/R = 2.44$ V/2,185 Ω). This current turns on the transistor, placing the transistor in saturation, so the voltage drop across the collector-emitter is very small (measured at 0.2 V). Therefore, the collector current is 49.8 mA ($I = V/R = (4.93$ V − 0.2 V)/96 Ω approx.). To choose an appropriate base resistor to place the BJT deep in saturation, use the following practical formula:

$$R_{Base} = \frac{\left(V_B - V_{BE(sat)}\right)}{\left(2 \times (I_C \div h_{FE(min)})\right)}$$

For the case of a base supply of 3.3 V, with a collector current of 50 mA and a minimum gain $h_{FE(min)}$ of 100, R_{Base} = (3.27 − 0.83)/(2 × (0.05/100)) = 2,440 Ω.

You can find all of these values in the transistor's datasheet. $V_{BE(sat)}$ is typically provided on a plot of V_{BE} versus I_C at room temperature, where we require I_C to be 50 mA. The value of $V_{BE(sat)}$ is between 0.6 V and 0.95 V for the BC547, depending on the collector current and the room temperature. The resistor value is further divided by two to ensure that the transistor is placed deep in the saturation region (maximizing I_C). Therefore, in this case a 2.2 kΩ resistor is used, as it is the closest generally available nominal value.

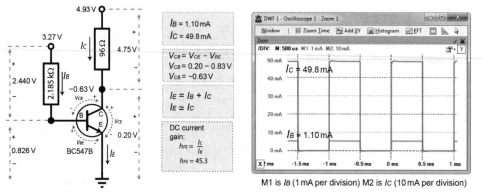

Figure 4-15: Realization of the transistor as a switch (saturation) and confirmation that all relationships hold true[1]

Why should you care about this with the RPi? Well, because the RPi can only source or sink very small currents from its GPIO pins, you can connect the RPi GPIO pin to the base of a transistor so that a very small current entering the base of the transistor can switch on a much larger current, with a much greater voltage range. Remember that in the example in Figure 4-15, a current of 1.1 mA is able to switch on a large current of 49.8 mA (45 times larger, but still lower than the 100 mA limit of the BC547). Using this transistor arrangement with the RPi will allow a 5 mA current at 3.3 V from an RPi GPIO to safely drive a 100 mA current at up to 45 V by choosing suitable resistor values.

One constraint in using transistors to drive a circuit is that they have a maximum switching frequency. If you increase the frequency of the input signal to the circuit in Figure 4-16 to 500 kHz, the output is distorted, though it is still switching from low to high. However, increasing this to 1 MHz means that the controlled circuit never switches off.

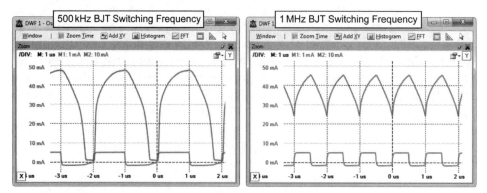

Figure 4-16: Frequency response of the BJT circuit (frequency is 500 kHz and 1 MHz)

---

[1] You can use the Analog Discovery's differential input feature to "measure" current by placing the probes on either side of a resistor (to measure the voltage across it), and then creating a custom math channel that divides the waveform by the resistor's known resistance value. You then set the units to amps in the channel settings.

Field Effect Transistors (FETs) as Switches

A simpler alternative to using BJTs as switches is to use field effect transistors (FETs). FETs are different from BJTs in that the flow of current in the load circuit is controlled by the voltage, rather than the current, on the controlling input. Therefore, it is said that FETs are voltage-controlled devices and BJTs are current-controlled devices. The controlling input for a FET is called the gate (G) and the controlled current flows between the drain (D) and the source (S).

Figure 4-17 illustrates how you can use an n-channel FET as a switch. Unlike the BJT, the resistor on the controlling circuit (1 MΩ) is connected from the input to GND, meaning that a very small current ($I = V/R$) will flow to GND, but the voltage at the gate will be the same as the V_{in} voltage. A significant advantage of FETs is that almost no current flows into the gate control input. However, the voltage on the gate is what turns on and off the controlled current, I_D, which flows from the drain to the source in this example.

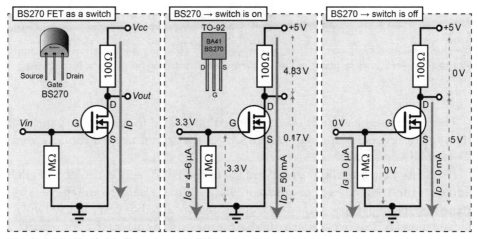

Figure 4-17: The field effect transistor (FET) as a switch

When the input voltage is high (3.3 V), the drain-source current will flow ($I_D = 50$ mA), so the voltage at the output terminal will be 0.17 V, but when the input voltage is low (0 V), no drain-source current will flow. Just like the BJT, if you were to measure the voltage at the drain terminal, the output voltage (V_{out}) would be high when the input voltage is low, and the output voltage would be low when the input voltage is high, though again the actual value of the "high" output voltage depends on the current drawn by the succeeding circuit.

The Fairchild Semiconductor BS270 N-Channel Enhancement Mode FET is a low-cost device (~$0.10) in a TO-92 package that is capable of supplying a continuous drain current (I_D) of up to 400 mA at a drain-source voltage of up to 60 V. However, at a gate voltage (V_G) of 3.3 V the BS270 can switch a maximum drain current of approximately 130 mA. This makes it ideal for use with the RPi, as the GPIO voltages are in range and the current required to switch on the FET is about 3 μA–6 μA depending on the gate resistor chosen. One other feature of using a FET as a switch is that it can cope with much higher switching frequencies, as shown in Figure 4-18. Remember that in Figure 4-16 the BJT switching waveform is very distorted at 1 MHz. It should be clear from Figure 4-18 that the FET circuit is capable of dealing with much higher switching frequencies than the BJT circuit.

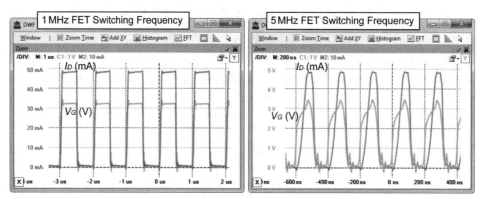

Figure 4-18: Frequency response of the FET circuit as the switching frequency is set at 1 MHz and 5 MHz

The BS270 also has a high-current diode that is used to protect the gate from the type of reverse inductive voltage surges that could arise if the FET were driving a DC motor.

As mentioned, one slight disadvantage of the BS270 is that can only switch a maximum drain current of approximately 130 mA at a gate voltage of 3.3 V. However, the high input impedance of the gate means that you can use two (or indeed more) BS270s in parallel to double the maximum current to approximately 260 mA at the same gate voltage. Also, the BS270 can be used as a gate driver for Power FETs, which can switch much larger currents.

Optocouplers/Opto-isolators

Optocouplers (or opto-isolators) are small, low-cost digital switching devices that are used to isolate two electrical circuits from each other. This can be important for your RPi circuits if you have a concern that a design problem with a connected circuit could possibly source or sink a large current from/to your RPi. They are available in low-cost (~$0.15) four-pin DIP form.

An optocoupler uses an LED emitter that is placed close to a photodetector transistor, separated by an insulating film within a silicone dome. When a current (I_f) flows through the LED emitter legs, the light that falls on the photodetector transistor from the LED allows a separate current (I_c) to flow through the collector-emitter legs of the photo detector transistor (see Figure 4-19). When the LED emitter is off, no light falls on the photo detector transistor, and there will be almost no collector emitter current (I_c). There is no electrical connection between one side of the package and the other, as the signal is transmitted only by light, providing electrical isolation for up to 5,300 V_{RMS} for an optocoupler such as the SFH617A. You can even use PWM with optocouplers, as it is a binary on/off signal.

Figure 4-19 illustrates an example optocoupler circuit and the resulting oscilloscope traces for the resistor and voltage values chosen. These values were chosen to be consistent with those that you might use with the RPi. The resistor value of 470 Ω was chosen to allow the 3.3 V output to drive a forward current I_f of about 4.5 mA through the LED emitter. From Figure 4 in the datasheet[2], this results in a forward voltage of about 1.15 V across the diode); $R = V/I = (3.3\,V - 1.15\,V)/0.0045\,A = 478\,\Omega$. Therefore, the circuit was built using the closest nominal value of 470 Ω.

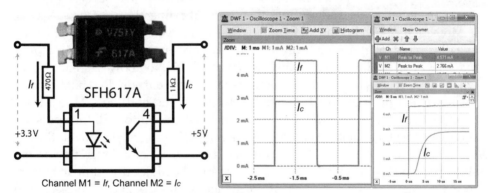

Figure 4-19: Optocoupler (617 A) circuit with the captured input and output characteristics

The oscilloscope is displaying current by using the differential inputs of the Analog Discovery to measure the voltage across the known resistor values, and using two mathematical channels to divide by the resistance values. In Figure 4-19 you can see that I_f is 4.571 mA and that I_c is 2.766 mA. The proportionality of the difference is the current transfer ratio (CTR) and it varies according to the level of I_f and the operating temperature. Therefore, the current transfer at 4.571 mA is 60.5% ($100 \times I_c/I_f$), which is consistent with the datasheet. The rise time and fall time are also consistent with the values in the datasheet of $t_r = 4.6$ μs and $t_f = 15$ μs. These values limit the switching frequency. Also, if it is important to your circuit that you achieve a high CTR, there are optocouplers

---

[2] Vishay Semiconductors (2013, January 14). SFH617A Datasheet. Retrieved April 13, 2014, from Vishay Semiconductors: www.vishay.com/docs/83740/sfh617a.pdf.

with built-in Darlington transistor configurations that result in CTRs of up to 2,000% (e.g., the 6N138 or HCPL2730). Finally, there are high-linearity analog optocouplers available (e.g., the HCNR200 from Avago) that can be used to optically isolate analog signals.

> **NOTE**   In Chapter 6, example circuits are provided for how to use an optocoupler to protect the RPi GPIOs from both an independently powered output circuit (**Figure 6-7**) and an independently-powered input circuit (**Figure 6-8**).

Switches and Buttons

Other components with which you are likely to need to work with are switches and buttons. They come in many different forms: toggle, push button, selector, proximity, joystick, reed, pressure, temperature, etc. However, they all work under the same binary principles of either interrupting the flow of current (open) or enabling the flow of current (closed). Figure 4-20 illustrates several different common switch types and outlines their general connectivity

Momentary push button switches (SPST—single pole, single throw) like the one illustrated in Figure 4-20 are either normally open (NO) or normally closed (NC). NO means that you have to activate the switch to allow current to flow, whereas NC means that when you activate the button, current does not flow. For the particular push button illustrated, both pins 1 and both pins 2 are always connected, and for the duration of time you press the button, all four pins are connected together. Looking at slider switches (SPDT—single pole, double throw), the common connection (COM) is connected to either 1 or 2 depending on the slider position. In the case of microswitches and the high-current push button, the COM pin is connected to NC if the switch is pressed, and is connected to NO if the switch is depressed. Finally, the rocker switch illustrated often has an LED that lights when the switch is closed, connecting the power (VCC) leg to the circuit (CCT) leg.

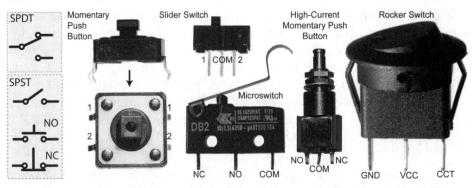

Figure 4-20: Various switches and configurations

All of these switch types suffer from mechanical switch bounce, which can be extremely problematic when interfacing to microprocessors like the RPi. Switches are mechanical devices and when they are pressed, the force of contact causes the switch to repeatedly bounce from the contact on impact. It only bounces for a small duration (typically milliseconds), but the duration is sufficient for the switch to apply a sequence of inputs to a microprocessor.

Figure 4-21 (a) illustrates the problem in action using the rising/falling-edge trigger condition of the Analog Discovery Oscilloscope. A momentary push button is placed in a simple series circuit with a 10 kΩ resistor and the voltage is measured across the resistor. When the switch hits the contact, the output is suddenly high, but the switch then bounces back from the contact and the voltage falls down again. After about 2 ms–3 ms (or longer) it has almost fully settled. Unfortunately, this small bounce can lead to false inputs to a digital circuit. For example, if the threshold were 3 V, this may be read in as 101010101, rather than a more correct value of 000001111.

There are a number of ways to deal with switch bounce in microprocessor interfacing:

- A low-pass filter can be added in the form of a resistor-capacitor circuit as illustrated in Figure 4-21(c) using a 1 μF capacitor. Unfortunately this leads to delay in the input. If you examine the time base, it takes about 2 ms before the input reaches 1 V. Also, bounce conditions can delay this further. These values are chosen using the RC time constant $\tau = R \times C$, so τ (s) $= 1{,}000\,\Omega \times 10^{-6}\,F = 1$ ms, which is the time taken to charge a capacitor to ~63.2% or discharge it to ~36.8%. This value is marked on Figure 4-21(b) at approximately 1.9 V.

- Software may be written so that after a rising edge occurs, it delays a few milliseconds and then reads the "real" state.

- For slider switches (SPDT), an SR-latch can be used.

- For momentary push button switches (SPSTs), a Schmitt trigger (74HC14N), which is discussed in the next section, can be used with an RC low-pass filter as in Figure 4-21(c).

NOTE   There are videos on debouncing SPDT and SPST switches on the web page associated with this chapter: www.exploringrpi.com/chapter4.

Hysteresis

Hysteresis is designed into electronic circuits to avoid rapid switching, which would wear out circuits. A Schmitt trigger exhibits hysteresis, which means that its output is dependent on the present input and the history of previous inputs. This can be explained with an example of an oven baking a cake at 350 degrees Fahrenheit:

- **Without hysteresis:** The element would heat the oven to 350°F. Once 350°F is achieved the element would switch off. It would cool below 350°F and the element would switch on again. Rapid switching!

- **With hysteresis:** The circuit would be designed to heat the oven to 360°F and at that point the element would switch off. The oven would cool, but it is not designed to switch back on until it reaches 340°F. The switching would not be rapid, protecting the oven, but there would be a greater variation in the baking temperature.

With an oven that is designed to have hysteresis, is the element *on* or *off* at 350°F? That depends on the history of inputs—it is *on* if the oven is heating; it is *off* if the oven is cooling.

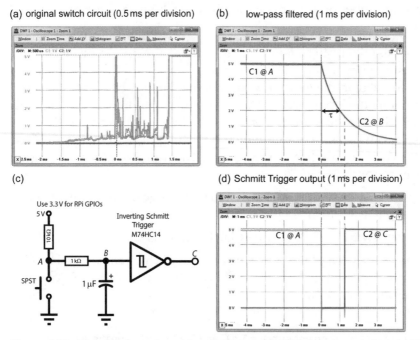

Figure 4-21: (a) Switch bouncing with no components other than the switch and 10 kΩ resistor; (b) low-pass filtered output at point B; (c) a Schmitt trigger circuit; and (d) output of the Schmitt trigger circuit at point C, versus the input at point A

The Schmitt trigger in Figure 4-21(c) exhibits the same type of behavior. The V_{T+} for the M74HC14 Schmitt trigger is 2.9 V and the V_{T-} is 0.93 V when running at a 5 V input, which means that a rising input voltage has to reach 2.9 V before the output changes high, and a falling input voltage has to drop to 0.93 V before the output changes low. Any bounce in the signal within this range is simply ignored. The low-pass filter reduces the possibility of high-frequency bounces. The response is presented in Figure 4-21(d). Note that the time base is 1 ms per division, illustrating how "clean" the output signal is. The configuration uses a pull-up resistor, the need for which is discussed shortly.

Logic Gates

Boolean algebra functions have only two possible outcomes, either true or false, which makes them ideal for developing a framework to describe electronic circuits that are either on or off (high or low). Logic gates perform these Boolean algebra functions and operations, forming the basis of the functionality inside modern microprocessors, such as the BCM2835/6/7 SoC on the RPi. Boolean values are not the same as binary numbers. (Binary numbers are a base 2 representation of whole and fractional numbers, whereas Boolean refers to a data type that has only two possible values, either true or false.)

It is often the case that you will need to interface to different types of logic gates and systems using the RPi's GPIOs to perform an operation such as gating an input or sending data to a shift register. Logic gates fall into two main categories:

- **Combinational logic:** The current output is dependent on the current inputs only (e.g., AND, OR, decoders, multiplexers, etc.).

- **Sequential logic:** The current output is dependent on the current inputs and previous inputs. They can be said to have different states, and what happens with a given input depends on what state they are in (e.g., latches, flip-flops, memory, counters, etc.).

BINARY NUMBERS

Simply put, binary numbers are a system for representing numbers (whole or fractional) within a device whereby the *only* symbols available are 1s and 0s. That is a strong *only*, as when you are implementing binary circuits, you don't have a minus sign or a decimal point (binary point to be precise). Like decimal numbers, you use a place-weighted system to represent numbers of the form:

$$1001_2 = (1 \times 2^3) + (0 \times 2^2) + (0 \times 2^1) + (1 \times 2^0) = 8 + 0 + 0 + 1 = 9_{10}$$

If you only have four bits to represent your numbers, you can only represent $2^4 = 16$ possible decimal numbers in the range 0 to 15. You can add and subtract numbers, just as you can in decimal, but you tend to add the negative value of the right-hand side of the operation, instead of building subtraction circuits. Therefore, to perform 9–5, you would typically perform 9 + (–5).To represent negative numbers, the two's complement form is used. Essentially, this involves inverting the symbols in the

Continues

> **BINARY NUMBERS (continued)**
>
> binary representation of the positive number and adding 1, so −5 would be +5 (0101), inverted to (1010) + 1 = 1011_2. Importantly, you need to know that this number is in two's complement form, otherwise it could be mistaken for 11_{10}. Therefore, to perform 9−5 on a 4-bit computer, perform 9 + −5 = 1001 + (1011) = 10100. The four-bit computer ignores the fifth bit (otherwise it would be a 5-bit computer!), so the answer is 0100, which is 4_{10}. See the video at the chapter web page: www.exploringrpi .com/chapter4.
>
> To multiply by 2, you simply shift the binary digits left (inserting a 0 on the right-most position), e.g., 4_{10} = 0100_2. Shift all the digits left, bringing in a 0 on the right-hand side, giving 1000_2 = 8_{10}. Divide by 2 by shifting to the right.
>
> Finally, understanding binary makes the following infamous joke funny: "There are 10 types of people, those who understand binary and those who don't!"—well, almost funny!

Combinational logic circuits will provide the same output for the same set of inputs, regardless of the order in which the inputs are applied. Figure 4-22 illustrates the core combinational logic gates with their logic symbols, truth tables, and IC numbers. The truth table provides the output that you will get from the gate on applying the listed inputs.

NOTE   You can find a video on wiring an AND gate at the web page associated with this chapter: www.exploringrpi.com/chapter4.

ICs have a number that describes their manufacturer, function, logic family, and package type. For example, the MM74HC08N in Figure 4-23(a) has a manufacturer code of MM (Fairchild Semiconductor), is a 7408 (quad two-input AND gates), is of the HC (CMOS) logic family, and is in an N (plastic dual in-line package) form.

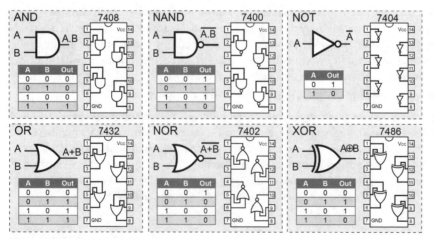

Figure 4-22: General logic gates

ICs are available in different package types. Figure 4-23(a) shows to scale a PDIP (plastic dual in-line package) and a small outline package TSSOP (thin shrink small outline package). There are many types: surface mount, flat package, small outline package, chip-scale package, and ball grid array (BGA). You have to be careful when ordering ICs that you have the capability to use them. DIP/PDIP ICs have perfect forms for prototyping on breadboards as they have a 0.1″ leg spacing. There are adapter boards available for converting small outline packages to 0.1″ leg spacing. Unfortunately, BGA ICs, such as the BCM2835/6/7, require sophisticated equipment for soldering.

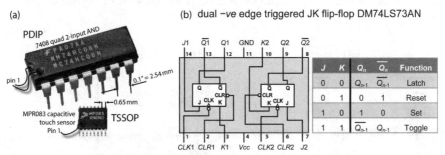

Figure 4-23: (a) IC package examples (to scale), and (b) the JK flip-flop

The family of currently available ICs is usually transistor-transistor logic (TTL) (with Low-power Schottky (LS)) or some form of complementary metal-oxide-semiconductor (CMOS). Table 4-1 compares these two families of 7408 ICs using their respective datasheets. The *propagation delay* is the longest delay between an input changing value and the output changing value for all possible inputs to a logic gate. This delay limits the logic gate's speed of operation.

Table 4-1: Comparison of Two Commercially Available TTL and CMOS ICs for a 7408 Quadruple Two-input AND gates IC

CHARACTERISTIC	SN74LS08N	SN74HC08N
Family	Texas TTL PDIP	Texas CMOS PDIP
	Low-power Schottky (LS)	High-speed CMOS (HC)
V_{CC} supply voltage	4.5 V to 5.5 V (5 V typical)	2 V to 6 V
V_{IH} high-level input voltage	min 2 V	V_{CC} at 5 V min = 3.5 V
V_{IL} low-level input voltage	max 0.8 V	V_{CC} at 5 V max = 1.5 V
Time propagation delay (T_{PD})	Typical 12 ns (↑) 17.5 ns (↓)	Typical 8 ns (↑↓)
Power (at 5 V)	5 mW (max)	0.1 mW (max)

Figure 4-24 illustrates the acceptable input and output voltage levels for both TTL and CMOS logic gates when $V_{DD} = 5$ V. The noise margin is the absolute difference between the output voltage levels and the input voltage levels. This noise margin ensures that if the output of one logic gate is connected to the input of a second logic gate, that noise will not affect the input state. The CMOS logic family input logic levels are dependent on the supply voltage, V_{DD}, where the high-level threshold is $0.7 \times V_{DD}$, and the low-level threshold is $0.3 \times V_{DD}$. It should be clear from Figure 4-24 that there are differences in behavior. For example, if the input voltage were 2.5 V, then the TTL gate would perceive a logic high level, but the CMOS gate (at 5 V) would perceive an undefined level. Also, the output of a CMOS gate, with $V_{DD} = 3.3$ V, would provide sufficient output voltage to trigger a logic high input on a TTL gate, but would not on a CMOS gate with $V_{DD} = 5.0$ V.

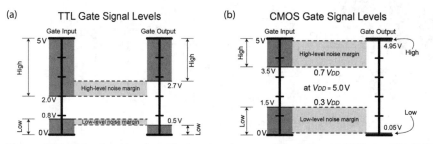

Figure 4-24: Gate signal levels on the input and output of logic gates (a) TTL , and (b) CMOS at 5 V

High-Speed CMOS (HC) can support a wide range of voltage levels, including the RPi 3.3 V input/outputs. The GND label is commonly used to indicate the ground supply voltage, where V_{EE} is often used for BJT-based devices and V_{SS} for FET-based devices. Traditionally, V_{CC} was used as the label for the positive supply voltage on BJT-based devices and V_{DD} for FET-based devices; however, it is now very common to see V_{CC} being used for both.

Figure 4-23(b) illustrates a sequential logic circuit, called a JK flip-flop. JK flip-flops are core building blocks in circuits such as counters. These differ from combinational logic circuits in that the current state is dependent on the current inputs and the previous state. You can see from the truth table that if $J = 0$ and $K = 0$ for the input, then the value of the output Q_n will be the output value that it was at the previous time step (it behaves like a one-bit memory). A time step is defined by the clock input (CLK), which is a square wave synchronizing signal. The same type of timing signal is present on the RPi; it is the clock frequency, and the clock goes through up to 1,200,000,000 square wave cycles per second on the RPi 3!

NOTE The web page associated with this chapter has a video that explains JK flip-flops in detail, and a video on building a 555 timer circuit, which can be used as a low-frequency clock signal for testing logic circuits.

Floating Inputs

One very common mistake when working with digital logic circuits is to leave unused logic gate inputs "floating," or disconnected. The family of the chip has a large impact on the outcome of this mistake. With the TTL logic families these inputs will "float" high and can be reasonably expected to be seen as logic-high inputs. With TTL ICs it is good practice to "tie" (i.e., connect) the inputs to ground or the supply voltage, so that there is absolutely no doubt about the logic level being asserted on the input at all times.

With CMOS circuits the inputs are very sensitive to the high voltages that can result from static electricity and electrical noise and should also never be left floating. Figure 4-25 gives the likely output of an AND gate that is wired as shown in the figure. The correct outcome is displayed in the "Required (A.B)" column.

Unused CMOS inputs that are left floating (between V_{DD} and GND) can gradually charge up due to leakage current, and depending on the IC design could provide false inputs, or waste power by causing a DC current to flow (from V_{DD} to GND). To solve this problem you can use pull-up or pull-down resistors, depending on the desired input state (these are ordinary resistors with suitable values—it's their role that is "pull up" or "pull down"), which are described in the next section.

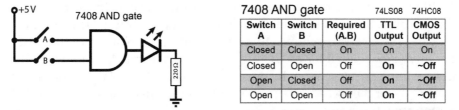

7408 AND gate   74LS08 74HC08

Switch A	Switch B	Required (A.B)	TTL Output	CMOS Output
Closed	Closed	On	On	On
Closed	Open	Off	On	~Off
Open	Closed	Off	On	~Off
Open	Open	Off	On	~Off

Figure 4-25: An AND gate with the inputs accidentally left floating when the switches are open

Pull-Up and Pull-Down Resistors

To avoid floating inputs, you can use pull-up or pull-down resistors as illustrated in Figure 4-26. Pull-down resistors are used if you want to guarantee that the inputs to the gate are low when the switches are open, and pull-up resistors are used if you want to guarantee that the inputs are high when the switches are open.

The resistors are important, because when the switch is closed, the switch would form a short circuit to ground if they were omitted and replaced by lengths of wire. The size of the pull-down/up resistors is also important; their value has to be low enough to solidly pull the input low/high when the switches are open but high enough to prevent too much current flowing when the switches are closed. Ideal logic gates have infinite impedance and any resistor value (short of infinite) would suffice. However, real logic gates leak current and you have to overcome this leakage. To minimize power consumption, you should choose the maximum value that actually pulls the input low/high. A 3.3 kΩ–10 kΩ resistor will usually work perfectly, but 3.3 V will drive 1 mA–0.33 mA through them respectively and dissipate 3.3 mW–1 mW of power respectively when the switch is closed. For power-sensitive applications you could test larger resistors of 50 kΩ or greater.

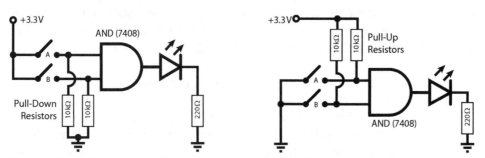

Figure 4-26: Pull-down and pull-up resistors, used to ensure that the switches do not create floating inputs

The RPi has weak internal pull-up and pull-down resistors that can be used for this purpose. This is discussed in Chapter 6. One other issue is that inputs will have some stray capacitance to ground. Adding a resistor to the input creates an RC low-pass filter on the input signal that can delay input signals. That is not important for manually pressed buttons, as the delay will be on the order of 0.1 µs for the preceding example, but it could affect the speed of digital communication bus lines.

Open-Collector and Open-Drain Outputs

To this point in the chapter, all of the ICs have a regular output, where it is driven very close to GND or the supply voltage of the IC (V_{CC}). If you are connecting to another IC or component that uses the same voltage level, then that should be fine. However, if the first IC had a supply voltage of 3.3 V and you needed to drive the output into an IC that had a supply voltage of 5 V, then you may need to perform level shifting.

Many ICs are available in a form with open-collector outputs, which are particularly useful for interfacing between different logic families and for level shifting. This is because the output is not at a specific voltage level, but rather attached to the base input of an NPN transistor that is inside the IC. The output of the IC is the "open" collector of the transistor, and the emitter of the transistor is tied to the IC's GND. It is possible to use a FET (74HC03) instead of a BJT (74LS01) inside the IC, and while the concept is the same it is called an open-drain output. Figure 4-27, illustrates this concept and provides an example circuit using a 74HC03 (quad, two-input NAND gates with open-drain outputs) to drive a 5 V circuit. The advantage of the open-drain configuration is that CMOS ICs support the 3.3 V level available on the RPi's GPIOs. Essentially, the drain resistor that is used in Figure 4-17 is placed outside the IC package, as illustrated in Figure 4-27, it has a value of 10 kΩ in this case.

Interestingly, a NAND gate with one input tied high (or the two inputs tied together) behaves like a NOT gate. In fact, NAND or NOR gates, each on their own, can replicate the functionality of any of the logic gates, and for that reason they are called *universal gates*.

Open-collector outputs are often used to connect multiple devices to a bus. You will see this in Chapter 8 when the RPi's I²C buses are described. When you examine the truth table in the datasheet of an IC, such as the 74HC03, you will see the letter Z used to represent the output (as in Figure 4-27). This means that it is a high-impedance output and the external pull-up resistor can pull the output to the high state.

Interconnecting Gates

To create useful circuits, logic gates are interconnected to other logic gates and components. It is important to understand that there are limits to the interconnect capabilities of gates.

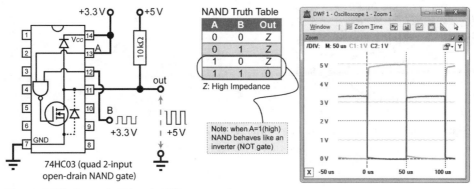

Figure 4-27: Open-drain level-shifting example

The first limit is the ability of the logic gate to source or sink current. When the output of a gate is logic high, it acts as a current source, providing current for connected logic gates or the LEDs shown in Figure 4-26. If the output of the gate is logic low, the gate acts as a current sink, whereby current flows into the output. Figure 4-28(a) demonstrates this by placing a current-limiting resistor and an LED between V_{CC} and the output of the logic gate, with the LED cathode connected to the logic gate output. When the output of the gate is high, there is no potential difference and the LED will be off; but when the output is low, a potential difference is created and current will flow through the LED and be sinked by the output of the logic gate. According to the datasheet of the 74HC08, it has an output current limit (I_O) of ±25 mA, meaning that it can source or sink 25 mA. Exceeding these values will damage the IC.

It is often necessary to connect the output of a single (driving) gate to the input of several other gates. Each of the connected gates will draw a current, thus limiting the total number of connected gates. The fan-out is the number of gates that are connected to the output of the driving gate. As illustrated in Figure 4-28(b), for TTL the maximum fan-out depends on the output (I_O) and input current (I_I) requirement values when the state is low (= $I_{OL(max)}/I_{IL(max)}$) and the state is high (= $I_{OH(max)}/I_{IH(max)}$). Choose the lower value, which is commonly 10 or greater. The fan-in of an IC is the number of inputs that it has. For the 7408 they are two-input AND gates, so they have a fan-in of 2.

CMOS gate inputs have extremely large resistance and draw almost no current, allowing for large fan-out capability (>50); however, each input adds a small capacitance ($C_L \approx 3$–10 pF) that must be charged and discharged by the output of the previous stage. The greater the fan-out, the greater the capacitive load on the driving gate, which lengthens the propagation delay. For example, the 74HC08 has a propagation delay (t_{pd}) of about 11 ns and an input capacitance (C_I) of 3.5 pF (assuming for this example that this leads to $t_{pd} = RC = 3.5$ ns per connection). If one 78HC08 were driving 10 other similar gates, and each added 3.5 ns of delay, then the propagation delay would increase to $11 + (10 \times 3.5) = 46$ ns of delay, reducing the maximum operating frequency from 91 MHz to 22 MHz.

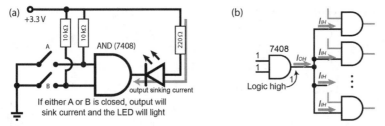

Figure 4-28: (a) Sinking current on the output, and (b) TTL fan-out example

Analog-to-Digital Conversion

Analog-to-digital converters (ADC) can be used to take an analog signal and create a digital representation of this signal. Attaching external ADCs to the RPi (see Chapter 9) enables you to connect to many different types of sensors, such as distance sensors, temperature sensors, light-level sensors, and so on. However, you have to be careful with these inputs, as they should not source or sink current, because the analog outputs of the sensors are likely to be very sensitive to any additional load in parallel with the output. To solve this problem, you need to first look at how operational amplifiers function.

Analog signals are continuous signals that represent the measurement of some physical phenomenon. For example, a microphone is an analog device, generally known as a transducer, which can be used to convert sound waves into an electrical signal that, for example, varies between −5 V and +5 V depending on the amplitude of the sound wave. Analog signals use a continuous range of values to represent information, but if you want to process that signal using your RPi, then you need a discrete digital representation of the signal. This is one that is sampled at discrete instants in time, and subsequently quantized to discrete values of voltage, or current. For example, audio signals will vary over time; so to sample a transducer signal to digitally capture human speech (e.g., speech recognition), you need be cognizant of two factors:

- Sampling rate: Defines how often you are going to sample the signal. Clearly, if you create a discrete digital sample by sampling the voltage every one second, the speech will be indecipherable.

- Sampling resolution: Defines the number of digital representations that you have to represent the voltage at the point in time when the signal is sampled. Clearly, if you had only one bit, you could only capture if the signal were closer to +5 V or −5 V, and again the speech signal would be indecipherable.

Sampling Rate

To represent a continuous signal perfectly in a discrete form requires an infinite amount of digital data. Fortunately (!), there are limits to how well human hearing performs and therefore we can place limits on the amount of data to be discretized. For example, 44.1 kHz and 48 kHz are common digital audio sampling rates for encoding MP3 files, which means that if you use the former, you will have to store 44,100 samples of your transducer voltage every second. The sample rate is generally determined by the need to preserve a certain frequency content of the signal. For example, humans (particularly children) can hear audio signals at frequencies from about 20 Hz up to about 20 kHz. Nyquist's sampling theorem states that the sampling frequency must be at least twice the highest frequency component present in the signal. Therefore, if you want to sample audio signals, you need to use a sampling rate of at least twice 20 kHz, which is 40 kHz, which helps explain the magnitude of the sampling rates used in encoding MP3 audio files (typically 44,100 samples per second—that is, 44.1 kS/s).

Quantization

In Chapter 9, 10-bit and 12-bit ADCs are interfaced to the RPi so that you can sample analog sensors. If you interface a 12-bit ADC that utilizes a voltage reference of 3.3 V, it will sample in the range of 0 V–3.3 V, which means that there are $2^{12} = 4{,}096$ possible discrete representations (numbers) for this sampling resolution. If the voltage is exactly 0 V, we can use the decimal number 0 to represent it. If the voltage is exactly 3.3 V, we can use the number 4,095 to represent it. So, what voltage does the decimal number 1 represent? It is $(1 \times 3.3)/4096 = 0.00080566$ V. Therefore, each decimal number between 0 and 4,095 (4,096 values) represents a step of approximately 0.8 mV.

The preceding audio sampling example also illustrates one of the challenges you face with the RPi. If the sensor outputs a voltage of –5 V to +5 V, or more commonly 0 V to +5 V, you need to alter that range to be between 0 V and 3.3 V to be compatible with the ADC that you have chosen. In Chapter 9, you'll look at how you can solve this problem. A second and more complex problem is that we must not typically source or sink current from/to ADC circuitry, and to solve that we need to briefly introduce a powerful concept that predates the digital computer, called the operational amplifier.

Operational Amplifiers

Operational amplifiers (op-amps) are composed from many BJTs or FETs within the one IC (e.g., the LM741). They can be used to create several very useful circuits, one of which you will need in Chapter 9 to correctly interface to analog sensors.

Ideal Operational Amplifiers

Figure 4-29(a) illustrates an ideal op-amp, placed in a very basic circuit with no feedback (a.k.a. open-loop). The op-amp has two inputs: a noninverting input (+) and an *inverting* input (–), and it produces an output that is proportional to the difference between them, i.e., $V_{out} = G(V_1 - V_2)$, where V_1 and V_2 are the voltage levels on these two inputs, respectively. Some of the characteristics of an ideal op-amp include the following:

- An infinite open-loop gain, G
- An infinite input impedance
- A zero output impedance

No real-world op-amp has an infinite open-loop gain, but voltage gains of 200,000 to 30,000,000 are commonplace. Such a gain can be treated as infinite, which means in theory that even a very small difference between the inputs would lead to a completely impractical output. For example, a difference of 1 V between V_1 and V_2 would lead to a voltage output of at least 200,000 V! If that were really the case, I would now be issuing health warnings on the use of op-amps! The output voltage is of course limited by the supply voltage (V_{CC+} and V_{CC-} in Figure 4-29(a)). Therefore, if you supply $V_{CC+} = +5$ V and $V_{CC-} = 0$ V (GND) to an op-amp using the RPi, the maximum real-world output would be in the range of 0 V to 5 V approximately, depending on the exact op-amp used. Likewise, a real-world op-amp does not have infinite input impedance, but it is in the range of 250 kΩ to 2 MΩ. The term *impedance* is used instead of *resistance*, as the input may be an AC rather than just a DC supply. Likewise, a zero output impedance is not possible, but it will likely be <100 Ω.

The LM358 Dual Operational Amplifier is used for the following circuit configurations (www.ti.com/product/lm358). It is an eight-pin IC in a PDIP that contains two op-amps that have a typical open-loop differential voltage gain of 100 dB, which is 100,000 in voltage gain (*voltage gain in dB = 20 × log (*V_{out}/V_{in}*)*). One advantage of this IC is that it has a wide supply range, in the range of 3 V to 32 V, meaning that you can use the RPi's 3.3 V or 5 V power rails. The LM358 can typically source up to 30 mA or sink up to 20 mA on the output.

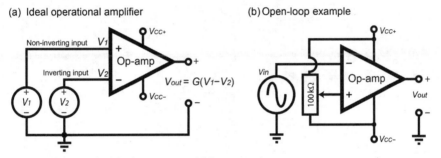

Figure 4-29: (a) The ideal op-amp, and (b) an open-loop comparator example

The behavior of an open-loop op-amp is best explained with an example, which is illustrated in Figure 4-29(b). Note that in this case the input is connected to the inverting input of the op-amp (−*ve*), rather than the noninverting input (+*ve*), which means that V_{out} will be positive when V_{in} is lower than the reference voltage. The circuit was built using the LM358, with a supply of $V_{CC+} = 5$ V and $V_{CC-} = 0$ V (GND). A 100 kΩ potentiometer was used to allow the voltage on the +*ve* input to be varied. This is the voltage that we are effectively comparing the input voltage with, so this circuit is called a comparator. When the voltage on the −*ve* input is greater than the +*ve* input, by even a very small amount, the output will quickly saturate in the negative direction to 0 V. When the voltage on the −*ve* input is less than the voltage on the +*ve* input, the output V_{out} will immediately saturate in the +*ve* direction to the maximum allowable by this configuration with the value of V_{CC} applied.

The actual output of this circuit can be seen in Figure 4-30(a). In this view, the potentiometer is adjusted to give a voltage on the $V+$ input of 1.116 V. When $V-$ is lower than this value, the output V_{out} is saturated to the maximum positive value, in this case it is 3.816 V (LM358 positive saturation voltage). When $V-$ is greater than 1.116 V, then the output V_{out} saturates to the lowest value, which is almost zero (–2 mV). Note the inversion that is taking place.

If everything remains exactly the same but the potentiometer is adjusted to give a different value for $V+$, in this case 0.645 V, the output will be as shown in Figure 4-30(b), where the duty cycle of the output V_{out} will be different. This comparator circuit could also be used to detect low voltage conditions—for example, lighting a warning LED if a battery's voltage output fell below a certain value. The circuit example used in 4-29(b) could be used to generate a PWM signal with a controllable duty cycle, according to the controlling voltage $V+$.

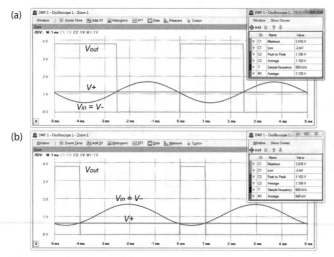

Figure 4-30: Output of the comparator circuit

The very large open-loop gain means that op-amps are generally used with feedback, which is directed to the negative or positive op-amp input. This feedback opens up an enormous range of other applications for the op-amp.

Negative Feedback and Voltage Follower

Negative feedback is formed when you connect the output of an op-amp (V_{out}) back to the inverting input ($V-$). When you apply a voltage (V_{in}) to the noninverting input ($V+$) and increase it slowly, as V_{in} increases, then so would the difference between $V+$ and $V-$; however, the output voltage also increases according to $G(V_1 - V_2)$ and this feeds back into the $V-$ input, causing the output voltage V_{out} to be reduced. Essentially, the op-amp attempts to keep the voltage on the inverting ($V-$) input the same as the noninverting ($V+$) input by adjusting the output. The impact of this action is that the value of V_{out} is stabilized to be the same as the V_{in} voltage on $V+$; the higher the gain of the op-amp, the closer this difference will be to zero.

That action on its own is not very useful to us, except for the fact that the current required to set the voltage on the input is very small, and the op-amp can control much larger currents on the output side. Because the negative feedback keeps the output voltage the same as the input voltage, the configuration as a whole has a gain of 1. This configuration is known as a voltage follower, or unity-gain buffer, and is illustrated in Figure 4-31. This configuration is very important, as it is used in Chapter 9 to protect the ADC circuitry that is attached to the RPi, and it is also used to ensure that the ADC reference voltage is not modified by connecting it to a circuit.

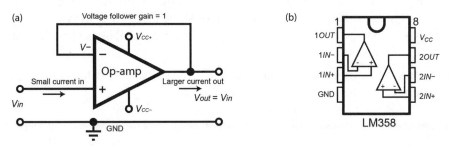

Figure 4-31: The voltage follower op-amp circuit

Positive Feedback

Negative feedback is the most common type of feedback used with op-amps due to its stabilizing impact. An op-amp in a positive feedback configuration is one in which the output is returned to the positive noninverting input of the op-amp. In such a case the feedback signal supports the input signal. For example, positive feedback can be used to add hysteresis to the open-loop op-amp comparator circuit, by connecting V_{out} to $V+$ through a positive feedback resistor. This can be used to reduce the comparator's response to noise on the input signal.

Concluding Advice

There is a lot of material covered in this chapter. So to finish, here is some general advice for working with electrical components and the RPi:

- Never leave inputs floating. Use pull-up/pull-down resistors on all switches. Check if unused IC pins need to be tied high/low.

- Ensure that all of the GNDs in your circuit are connected.

- Remember to power your chips with the correct voltage level.

- Don't assume that a new diode, FET, BJT, or logic gate has the same pin layout as the previous component that you used.

- Just like programming, build a simple circuit first, test it, and then add the next layer of complexity. Never assume something works!

- Don't leave wire joints and croc clip connections hanging where they could touch off each other—the same for resistors on breadboards.

- Use a flat-head screwdriver to remove ICs from breadboards, as it is very easy to bend the IC legs beyond repair.

- CMOS ICs are statically sensitive, so touching them with your fingers may damage them, due to the buildup of static electricity on your body. Touch the back of a computer or some grounding metal object before you touch the ICs.

- Don't assume that components have exact or consistent values—in particular, transistor gains and resistor ranges.

Summary

After completing this chapter, you should hopefully be able to do the following:

- Describe the basic principles of electrical circuit operation, build circuits on breadboards, and measure voltage and current values.

- Use discrete components such as diodes, LEDs, transistors, and capacitors in your own circuit designs.

- Use transistors and FETs as switches to control higher current and voltage signals than would be possible by using the RPi outputs on their own.

- Interconnect and interface to logic gates, being particularly aware of the issues that arise with "floating" inputs.

- Describe the principles of analog-to-digital conversion and design basic operational-amplifier circuits.

- Combine all of these skills to build the type of circuits that are important for safely interfacing to the RPi GPIOs.

Further Reading

Documents and links for further reading have been listed throughout this chapter, but here are some further reference documents:

- T. R. Kuphaldt, "Lessons in Electric Circuits," a free series of textbooks on the subjects of electricity and electronics: `www.ibiblio.org/kuphaldt/electricCircuits/`.

- All About Circuits: `www.allaboutcircuits.com` provides excellent applied examples of many types of electronic circuits.

- The Electronics Club: `www.electronicsclub.info` provides electronics projects for beginners and for reference.

- Neil Storey, *Electronics: A Systems Approach*, 5th ed., New York: Pearson, 2013.

Here is a full list of the components that are used in this chapter:

- Breadboard
- Diodes: 1N4001, general-purpose LED
- Transistors: NPN: BC547, FET: BS270
- Voltage regulator: KA7805/LM7805
- PTC: 60R110
- Button and Switch: General purpose SPST and SPDT
- ICs: 74HC73N, 74HC03N, 74LS08N, 74HC08N, 74HC14, LM358N
- Resistors: 1 MΩ, 2.2 kΩ, 2 x 10 kΩ, 50 kΩ, 100 Ω, 50 Ω, 1 kΩ, 470 Ω, 220 Ω, 100 kΩ POT
- Capacitors: 10 µF, 1 µF, 0.33 µF, 0.1 µF
- Opto-isolator: SFH617A

# CHAPTER 5

Programming on the Raspberry Pi

This chapter describes several different programming options for the Raspberry Pi (RPi), including scripted and compiled languages. An external LED control program is provided in most of the languages so that you can investigate each language's structure and syntax. The advantages and disadvantages of each language type are discussed along with example uses. The chapter then focuses on the C/C++ and Python programming languages, describing their principles, and why object-oriented programming (OOP) is appropriate for the development of scalable embedded systems applications. The chapter details how you can interface directly to the Linux kernel using the GNU C library and finishes with a discussion on how the computational performance of Python code can be greatly improved. A single chapter can only scratch the surface on this topic, so this one focuses on physical programming with the RPi.

Equipment Required for This Chapter:

- A terminal connection to the RPi (see Chapter 2)
- LEDs, resistors, breadboard, hook-up wires, and a FET (BS270) or transistor (BC547) (see Chapter 4)

See `www.exploringrpi.com/chapter5/` for further details on this chapter.

Introduction

As discussed in Chapter 3, embedded Linux is essentially "Linux on an embedded system." If your favorite programming language is available under Linux, it is also likely to be available for the RPi. So, is your favorite language suitable for programming the RPi? That depends on what you intend to do with the board. Are you interfacing to electronics devices/modules? Do you plan to write rich user interfaces? Are you planning to write a device driver for Linux? Is performance very important, or are you developing an early pre-prototype? Each of the answers to these questions will impact your decision regarding which language you should use. In this chapter, you are introduced to several different languages, and the advantages and disadvantages of each category of language are outlined. As you read through the chapter, try to avoid focusing on a favorite language, but instead try to use an appropriate language for the job at hand.

How does programming on embedded systems compare to programming on desktop computers? Here are some points to consider:

- You should always write the clearest and cleanest code that is as maintainable as possible, just as you would on a desktop PC.

- Don't optimize your code until you are certain that it is complete.

- You typically have to be more aware of how you are consuming resources than when programming on the desktop computer. The size of data types matters, and passing data correctly really matters. You have to be concerned with memory availability, file system size, and data communication availability/bandwidth.

- You often have to learn about the underlying hardware platform. How does it handle the connected hardware? What data buses are available? How do you interface with the operating system and low-level libraries? Are there any real-time constraints?

For the upcoming discussion, it is assumed that you are planning to do some type of physical computing—that is, interfacing to the different input or outputs on the RPi. Therefore, the example that is used to describe the structure and syntax of the different languages is a simple interfacing example to control an LED circuit. Before looking at the languages themselves, we will begin with a brief performance evaluation of different languages running on the RPi, to put the following discussions in context.

Performance of Languages on the RPi

Which language performs the best on the RPi? Well, that is an incredibly emotive and difficult question to answer. Different languages perform better on different benchmarks and different tasks. In addition, a program written in a particular language can be optimized for that language to the point that it is barely recognizable as the original code. Nor is speed of execution always an important factor; you may be more concerned with memory usage, the portability of the code, or the ability to quickly apply changes.

However, if you are planning to develop high-speed or real-time number-crunching applications, performance may be a key factor in your choice of programming language. In addition, if you are setting out to learn a new language, and you may possibly be developing algorithmically rich programs in the future, it may be useful to keep performance in mind.

A simple test has been put in place on different RPi models to determine the performance of the languages discussed in this chapter. The test uses the *n*-body benchmark (gravitational interaction of planets) code from `tiny.cc/erpi501`. The code uses the exact same algorithm for all languages and the RPi is running in the same state in all cases. The test uses five million iterations of the algorithm to ensure that the script used for timing does not have to be highly accurate. All of the programs gave the same correct result (i.e., −0.169083134), indicating that they all ran correctly and to completion. The various tests are available in the book's Git repository in the directory `chp05/performance/`.

All the code for the following tests were compiled and executed on the RPi platform. Not all the languages used are available on Raspbian by default, but the test has the added value of giving you confidence that you can utilize these languages on the RPi. Importantly, the code examples that I used in this test contain only typical coding constructs, purposefully avoiding custom optimization libraries. Use the following call to execute the test:

```
pi@erpi ~/exploringrpi/chp05/performance $ ./run
The C/C++ Code Example
-0.169075164
-0.169083134
It took 6544 milliseconds to run the C/C++ test
```

The results of the tests are displayed in Table 5-1. In the third column you can see the results for an RPi 3 (in ARMv7 mode), running at a processor frequency of 1.2 GHz (with default CPU/GPU memory allocation). C/C++ takes 6.5 seconds to complete this number-crunching task, so this time is used as the benchmark and is weighted as 1.00 units. Therefore, Haskell takes 1.16 times longer to complete the same task, Java takes 1.52 times longer, Python 94.1 times longer, and Ruby 147 times longer. The processing durations in seconds are provided in parentheses and the table is ordered with respect to language performance. As you move across the columns, you can see that this performance is relatively consistent, even as the processor frequency is adjusted (discussed in the next section) or a desktop i7 64-bit processor is used.

Table 5-1: Numeric Computation Time for 5,000,000 Iterations of the *n*-Body Algorithm on Raspbian (Jessie Minimal Image)

VALUE	TYPE	RPi 3 at 1.2 GHZ[1]	RPi 2 at 1 GHZ[2]	RPi B+ at 1 GHZ[3]	64-BIT i7 PC[4]
C/C++	Compiled	1.00 × (6.5s)	1.00 × (9.3s)	1.00 × (10.0s)	1.00 × (0.61s)
C++11	Compiled	1.06 × (6.9s)	0.69 × (6.4s)	0.70 × (7.03s)	0.95 × (0.58s)
Haskell	Compiled	1.16 × (7.6s)	1.17 × (10.8s)	1.07 × (10.8s)	1.15 × (0.70s)
Java[5]	JIT	1.52 × (9.94s)	1.45 × (13.4s)	2.29 × (23.0s)	1.36 × (0.83s)
Mono C#	JIT	2.72 × (17.8s)	2.47 × (22.9s)	3.62 × (36.4s)	2.16 × (1.32s)
Cython[6]	Compiled	2.74 × (17.9s)	2.67 × (24.8s)	2.80 × (28.0s)	1.26 × (0.77s)
Node.js[7]	JIT	2.76 × (18.1s)	6.23 × (57.7s)	50.1 × (503s)	6.54 × (3.99s)
Lua	Interpreted	20.2 × (132s)	21.2 × (197s)	25.7 × (258s)	34.3 × (20.9s)
Cython	Compiled	64.2 × (420s)	66.6 × (618s)	163 × (1633s)	58.0 × (34.4s)
Perl	Interpreted	92.6 × (601s)	81.5 × (756s)	171 × (1716s)	82.0 × (50.0s)
Python	Interpreted	94.1 × (616s)	89.9 × (834s)	198 × (1992s)	89.7 × (54.7s)
Ruby	Interpreted	147 × (962s)	140 × (1298s)	265 × (2662s)	47.4 × (28.9s)

[1] RPi 3 running at 1.2 GHz, quad core (only one core utilized), ARMv7 (rev 4 with a 32-bit Linux distribution: Linux 4.1.19-v7+) supports: half thumb fastmult vfp edsp neon vfpv3 tls vfpv4 idiva idivt vfpd32 lpae evtstrm crc32. Please ensure that you use a high-quality power supply that is capable of delivering at least 1.5 A.

[2] RPi 2 overclocked at 1 GHz, quad core (only one core utilized), ARMv7 (rev 5) supports: half thumb fastmult vfp edsp neon vfpv3 tls vfpv4 idiva idivt vfpd32 lpae evtstrm. Note: Overclocking your RPi may reduce its lifespan.

[3] RPi B+ overclocked at 1 GHz, single core, ARMv6 (rev 7 v6) supports: half thumb fastmult vfp edsp java tls.

[4] Windows 8.1 PC running a 64-bit Debian Jessie VirtualBox VM that was allocated 3 threads (of 12) on an Intel i7-5820K @ 3.3 GHz, with the VM allocated 16 GB of RAM. Only one thread is used.

[5] You can use `sudo apt install oracle-java8-jdk` to install the Oracle JDK on the Raspberry Pi platform.

[6] This Cython test involved modifying the Python source code to optimize it. It is not simply the compilation of raw Python code. The second Cython test represents the simple compilation of raw Python source code.

[7] Node.js (`node -v`) is version v5.10.1 and it supports the ARM NEON accelerator processor. NEON is available on the RPi 2/3 (ARMv7) but not on the RPi B+ (ARMv6), which contributes to the poor performance of Node.js on the RPi B+ of 50.1× the baseline. See the feature titled "LAMP and MEAN" in Chapter 12 for instructions on how to install the latest version of Node.js on the RPi.

The code examples have not been optimized for multicore processors, so for example, the C/C++ code only uses a single core of the RPi 3 processor. Albeit, regular Linux threads are automatically offloaded to other cores and the full memory bandwidth is available to the one core. Multicore programming is discussed in the next chapter, where you can see that the performance of the RPi 2/3 can be further improved relative to the RPi B+, which has a single-core processor. All the programs use between 98% and 99% of the CPU while they are executing.

The second column in Table 5-1 indicates the language type, where *compiled* refers to natively compiled languages, *JIT* refers to just-in-time compiled languages, and *interpreted* refers to code that is executed by interpreters. The distinction in these language types is described in detail throughout this chapter and is not quite as clear-cut as presented in the table.

THE 64-BIT RPi 3 BCM2837 SYSTEM ON A CHIP (SOC)

The RPi 3 utilizes a quad-core, Cortex-A53 BCM2837 SoC that supports 64-bit operations. It is clear from the indicative tests at the beginning of this chapter that its performance is impressive, delivering approximately 30% faster performance than the overclocked RPi 2 in the C/C++ test, despite running in 32-bit mode. This performance improvement is mainly due to the faster CPU clock frequency, rather than the 64-bit processor. The move to full Linux support for 64-bit embedded Linux on the RPi 3 will eventually provide advantages (e.g., improved NEON floating-point performance, improved instruction sets). However, Eben Upton from the Raspberry Pi Foundation has indicated that it will take some time before the RPi firmware is updated to support a 64-bit Linux kernel.

It is worth noting that the relative performance of Java is impressive given that code is compiled dynamically ("just-in-time"), which is discussed later in this chapter. Any dynamic compilation latency is included in the timings, because the test script includes the following Bash script code to calculate the execution duration of each program:

```
Duration="5000000"
echo -e "\nThe C/C++ Code Example"
T="$(date +%s%N)"
./n-body $Duration
T="$(($(date +%s%N)-T))"
T=$((T/1000000))
echo "It took ${T} milliseconds to run the C/C++ test"
```

The C++11 code is the version of the C++ programming language that was approved in mid-2011. C++11 requires g++ version 4.7 or greater, and is discussed again in Chapter 7. The binary code has been built using optimizations that do not involve modifications to the binary code (e.g., -O3 for C/C++ and the +AggressiveOpts flag is set for Java).

Despite the "Pi" in Raspberry[8] Pi being derived from "Python," the performance results for the language are particularly poor due to the algorithmic nature of the problem. However, the benchmarks at (debian.org, 2013), indicate that the range will be 9–100 times slower than the optimized C++ code for general processing to algorithm-rich code, respectively. If you are very comfortable with Python and you would like to improve upon its performance, you can investigate *Cython*, a compiler that supports the removal of Python's dynamic typing capability and

---

[8] The RPi brand name continues a global trend of naming devices after fruits (e.g., Apple, BlackBerry)! According to Liz Upton of the Raspberry Pi Foundation, the name is a throwback to Apricot Computers in particular, a 1980s UK company that produced desktop PCs.

facilitates you to generate C code directly from your Python code. Cython and the extension of Python with C/C++ are discussed at the end of this chapter.

The final column provides the results for the same code running on a desktop computer virtual machine. You can see that the relative performance of the applications is broadly in line, but also note that the C++ program runs 10 times faster on a single i7 thread than it does on a single core of the RPi 3. The computational performance of the RPi 3 is very impressive, but it will still struggle with computationally expensive applications like signal processing and computer vision.

As previously discussed, this is only one numerically oriented benchmark test, but it is somewhat indicative of the type of performance you should expect from each language. There have been many studies on the performance of languages. However, a well-specified analysis by Hundt (2011) has found that in terms of performance, "C++ wins out by a large margin. However, it also required the most extensive tuning efforts, many of which were done at a level of sophistication that would not be available to the average programmer" (Hundt, 2011).

RASPBERRY Pi BENCHMARKS

Roy Longbottom's (`roylongbottom.org.uk`) Benchmark Collection is a well-known set of benchmark tests that can be executed on many platforms, including the RPi. As an alternative to the simple tests in this section, you can download and execute these tests on the RPi using the following:

```
pi@erpi:~ $ mkdir perf
pi@erpi:~ $ cd perf/
...~/perf $ wget  http://www.roylongbottom.org.uk/Raspberry_Pi_Benchmarks.zip
...~/perf $ unzip Raspberry_Pi_Benchmarks.zip
...~/perf $ cd Raspberry_Pi_Benchmarks /Source\ Code/
... /Source Code $ gcc whets.c cpuidc.c -lm -O3 -o whets
... /Source Code $ ./whets
Whetstone Single Precision C Benchmark  vfpv4 32 Bit, Mon Apr 11 00:20:12 2016
```

Loop content	Result	MFLOPS	MOPS	Seconds
N1 floating point	-1.12475013732910156	170.579		0.082
N2 floating point	-1.12274742126464844	181.435		0.539
N3 if then else	1.00000000000000000		898.271	0.084
N4 fixed point	12.00000000000000000		748.817	0.306
N5 sin,cos etc.	0.49911010265350342		10.533	5.750
N6 floating point	0.99999982118606567	299.770		1.310
N7 assignments	3.00000000000000000		1198.997	0.112
N8 exp,sqrt etc.	0.75110864639282227		8.721	3.105
MWIPS		644.874		11.289

> The RPi 3 delivers 644.9 million Whetstone instructions per second (MWIPS) in this test. According to the benchmark results at `tiny.cc/erpi507` the RPi Model B delivers 390.6 MWIPS and the RPi 2 (at 1 GHz) delivers 568.4 MWIPS, which is broadly in line with the performance tests described in this section.

Setting the RPi CPU Frequency

In the preceding tests, the clock frequency of the RPi was adjusted dynamically at run time. The RPi has various *governors* that can be used to profile its performance/power usage ratio. For example, if you were building a battery-powered RPi application that has low processing requirements, you could reduce the clock frequency to conserve power. You can find out information about the current state by typing (called on the RPi 2):

```
pi@erpi ~ $ sudo apt install cpufrequtils
pi@erpi ~ $ cpufreq-info
... analyzing CPU 0:
  driver: BCM2835 CPUFreq
  CPUs which run at the same hardware frequency: 0 1 2 3
  CPUs which need to have their frequency coordinated by software: 0 1 2 3
  maximum transition latency: 355 us.
  hardware limits: 600 MHz - 1000 MHz
  available frequency steps: 600 MHz, 1000 MHz
  available cpufreq governors: conservative, ondemand, userspace, powersave,
  performance. current policy: frequency should be within 600 MHz and 1000 MHz.
      The governor "ondemand" may decide which speed to use within this range.
  current CPU frequency is 600 MHz.  ...
```

As listed above, the RPi 2 has four CPU cores (0–3), so each will display an output. In this example, the RPi 2 is overclocked by setting `arm_freq=1000` in `/boot/config.txt`. You can see that different governors are available, with the profile names `conservative`, `ondemand`, `userspace`, `powersave`, and `performance`. To enable one of these governors or to explicitly set the clock frequency, enter the following:

```
pi@erpi ~ $ sudo cpufreq-set -g performance
pi@erpi ~ $ cpufreq-info
... current CPU frequency is 1000 MHz.   ...
pi@erpi ~ $ sudo cpufreq-set -f 600MHz
pi@erpi ~ $ cpufreq-info
... current CPU frequency is 600 MHz.   ...
```

The default governor is `ondemand`, which dynamically switches the CPU frequency. For example, if the CPU frequency is currently 600 MHz and the average CPU usage between governor samplings is above the threshold (called the `up_threshold`) then the CPU frequency will be automatically increased.

You can tweak these and other settings using their sysfs entries. For example, to set the threshold at which the CPU frequency rises to the point at which the CPU load reaches 90% of available capacity, use the following:

```
pi@erpi ~ $ sudo cpufreq-set -g ondemand
pi@erpi ~ $ cd /sys/devices/system/cpu/cpufreq/ondemand/
pi@erpi .../ondemand $ ls
ignore_nice_load  powersave_bias       sampling_rate      up_threshold
io_is_busy        sampling_down_factor  sampling_rate_min
pi@erpi .../ondemand $ cat up_threshold
50
pi@erpi .../ondemand $ sudo sh -c "echo 90 > up_threshold"
pi@erpi .../ondemand $ cat up_threshold
90
```

Finally, if you decide to permanently change the default governor on the RPi to be `performance` rather than `ondemand`, you can edit the `cpufrequtils` file in `/etc/init.d/` as follows:

```
pi@erpi ~ $ cd /etc/init.d/
pi@erpi /etc/init.d $ more cpufrequtils | grep GOVERNOR=
GOVERNOR="ondemand"
pi@erpi /etc/init.d $ sudo nano cpufrequtils
pi@erpi /etc/init.d $ more cpufrequtils | grep GOVERNOR=
GOVERNOR="performance"
pi@erpi /etc/init.d $ sudo reboot
```

A First Circuit for Physical Computing

Figure 5-1 illustrates a circuit that you can connect to the RPi for safely driving an LED using (a) a BS270 FET, and (b) a BC547 NPN transistor. You can use either of these circuits to test the code that is described in this chapter.

As described in Chapter 4, a FET or NPN transistor can be used to switch a load using a very low current. In this example the GPIO pin (GPIO4), which is connected to Pin 7 on the GPIO header, provides the low current required to switch the FET/transistor on or off, depending on whether the GPIO state is high or low. The relatively large current that is required to light the LED (~10 mA–15 mA) is sourced from the 3.3 V supply pin on the RPi using the calculation that is described in Figure 4-9. These circuits are described in more detail in Chapter 6.

> **WARNING**   Be very careful when wiring circuits such as those in Figure 5-1. Incorrect connections or the use of the wrong header pin can destroy your RPi. It is good practice to wire such circuits with the power to the RPi disconnected. Only power the RPi once you have carefully checked the circuit configuration.

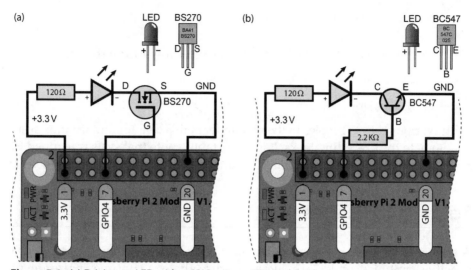

Figure 5-1: (a) Driving an LED with a GPIO using a FET, and (b) driving an LED with a GPIO using an NPN transistor

Once this circuit is wired correctly, you can use Linux sysfs to control the GPIO so that you become familiar with the workflow in the code that follows. The first step is to enable GPIO4 on the RPi using the following steps:

```
pi@erpi ~ $ cd /sys/class/gpio
pi@erpi /sys/class/gpio $ ls
export  gpiochip0  unexport
pi@erpi /sys/class/gpio $ echo 4 > export
pi@erpi /sys/class/gpio $ ls
export  gpio4  gpiochip0  unexport
pi@erpi /sys/class/gpio $ cd gpio4
pi@erpi /sys/class/gpio/gpio4 $ ls
active_low  device  direction  edge  subsystem  uevent  value
```

GPIO4 can now be controlled using the entries in the Linux `gpio4` directory. For example, you can set up the GPIO to be an output, and change its state to be high or low using the following steps:

```
pi@erpi /sys/class/gpio/gpio4 $ echo out > direction
pi@erpi /sys/class/gpio/gpio4 $ echo 1 > value
pi@erpi /sys/class/gpio/gpio4 $ echo 0 > value
```

If the LED circuit in Figure 5-1 is wired correctly, the change in the GPIO state results in the LED switching on and off. You can read the state of the GPIO using the following calls:

```
pi@erpi /sys/class/gpio/gpio4 $ cat direction
out
```

```
pi@erpi /sys/class/gpio/gpio4 $ cat value
0
```

Finally, if you want to redisable the GPIO, you can perform this step:

```
pi@erpi /sys/class/gpio $ echo 4 > unexport
pi@erpi /sys/class/gpio $ ls
export  gpiochip0  unexport
```

The various code examples in the remainder of this chapter utilize Linux sysfs to automate the preceding tasks. It is important to note that sysfs is mapped to memory and that therefore these file operations are actually reasonably efficient.

Scripting Languages

A scripting language is a computer programming language that is used to specify script files, which are *interpreted* directly by a runtime environment to perform tasks. Many scripting languages are available, such as Bash, Perl, Lua, and Python, and these can be used to automate the execution of tasks on the RPi, such as system administration, interaction, and even interfacing to electronic components using sysfs.

Scripting Language Options

Which scripting language should you choose for the RPi? There are many strong opinions and it is a difficult topic, because Linux users tend to have a favorite scripting language. However, you should choose the scripting language with features that suit the task at hand. For example:

- Bash scripting: Is a great choice for short scripts that do not require advanced programming structures. *Bash scripts* are used extensively in this book for small, well-defined tasks, such as the timing code in the previous section. You can use the Linux commands discussed in Chapter 3 in your Bash scripts.

- Lua: Is a fast and lightweight scripting language that can be used for embedded applications because of its very small footprint. *Lua* supports the object-oriented programming (OOP) paradigm (using tables and functions) and dynamic typing, which is discussed shortly. Lua has an important role in Chapter 13 for the programming of NodeMCU Wi-Fi modules.

- Perl: Is a great choice for scripts that parse text documents or process streams of data. It enables you to write straightforward scripts and even supports the OOP paradigm.

- Python: Is great for scripts that need more complex structure and are likely to be built upon or modified in the future. Like Lua, Python supports the OOP paradigm and dynamic typing.

These four scripting languages are available preconfigured on the Raspbian image. It would be very useful to have some knowledge of all of these scripting languages, because you may find third-party tools or libraries that make your current project very straightforward. This section provides a brief overview of each of these languages, including a concise segment of code that performs the same function in each language. It finishes with a discussion about the advantages and disadvantages of scripting languages in general.

NOTE All the code that follows in this chapter is available in the associated GitHub repository in the chp05 directory. If you have not done so already, use git clone https://github.com/derekmolloy/exploringrpi.git in a Linux terminal window to clone this repository.

Bash

Bash scripts are a great choice for short scripts that do not require advanced programming structures, and that is exactly the application that is described here. The first program in Listing 5-1 allows a user to set up a GPIO, turn an LED on or off, get the status of a GPIO, and close the GPIO. Essentially this script automates the steps that are performed using sysfs earlier in this chapter. For example, using this script by calling ./bashLED setup followed by ./bashLED on would light the LED in Figure 5-1.

Listing 5-1: chp05/bashLED/bashLED

```
#!/bin/bash
LED_GPIO=4          # Use a variable -- easy to change GPIO number

# An example Bash functions
function setLED
{                   # $1 is the 1st argument passed to this function
  echo $1 >> "/sys/class/gpio/gpio$LED_GPIO/value"
}

# Start of the program -- start reading from here
if [ $# -ne 1 ]; then          # if there is not exactly one argument
  echo "No command was passed. Usage is: bashLED command,"
  echo "where command is one of: setup, on, off, status and close"
  echo -e " e.g., bashLED setup, followed by bashLED on"
  exit 2           # error that indicates invalid number of arguments
fi
echo "The LED command that was passed is: $1"
if [ "$1" == "setup" ]; then
  echo "Exporting GPIO number $1"
  echo $LED_GPIO >> "/sys/class/gpio/export"
```

```
    sleep 1          # to ensure gpio has been exported before next step
    echo "out" >> "/sys/class/gpio/gpio$LED_GPIO/direction"
elif [ "$1" == "on" ]; then
    echo "Turning the LED on"
    setLED 1         # 1 is received as $1 in the setLED function
elif [ "$1" == "off" ]; then
    echo "Turning the LED off"
    setLED 0         # 0 is received as $1 in the setLED function
elif [ "$1" == "status" ]; then
    state=$(cat "/sys/class/gpio/gpio$LED_GPIO/value")
    echo "The LED state is: $state"
elif [ "$1" == "close" ]; then
    echo "Unexporting GPIO number $LED_GPIO"
    echo $LED_GPIO >> "/sys/class/gpio/unexport"
fi
```

The script is available in the directory /chp05/bashLED/. If you entered the script manually using the nano editor, the file needs to have the executable flag set before it can be executed. (The Git repository retains executable flags.) Therefore, to allow all users to execute this script, use the following call:

/chp05/bashLED$ **chmod ugo+x bashLED**

What is happening within this script? First, all of these command scripts begin with a *sha-bang* #! followed by the name and location of the interpreter to be used, so #!/bin/bash in this case. The file is just a regular text file, but the sha-bang is a *magic-number* code to inform the OS that the file is an executable. Next, the script defines the GPIO number for which you want to change state using the variable LED_GPIO. Using a variable allows the default value to be easily altered should you want to use a different GPIO for this task.

The script contains a function called setLED, mainly to demonstrate how functions are structured within Bash scripting. This function is called later in the script. Each if is terminated by a fi. The ; after the if statement terminates that statement and allows the statement then to be placed on the same line. The elif keyword means else if, which allows you to have multiple comparisons within the one if block. The newline character \n terminates statements.

The first if statement checks if the number of arguments passed to the script ($#) is not equal to 1. The correct way to call this script is in the form **./bashLED on**, where on is the first user argument that is passed ($1) and there is one argument in total. If there were no arguments passed, the correct usage would be displayed and the script would exit with the return code 2. This value is consistent with Linux system commands, where an exit value of 2 indicates incorrect usage. Success is indicated by a return value of 0, so any non-zero return value generally indicates the failure of a script.

If the argument passed is on then the code displays a message and writes the string "1" to the value file in the /gpio4/ directory. The remaining functions modify the GPIO4 state in the same way as described in the last section. You can execute the script as follows:

```
pi@erpi ~/exploringrpi/chp05/bashLED $ ./bashLED
No command was passed. Usage is: bashLED command,
where command is one of: setup, on, off, status and close
 e.g., bashLED setup, followed by bashLED on
pi@erpi ~/exploringrpi/chp05/bashLED $ ./bashLED setup
The LED command that was passed is: setup
Exporting GPIO number setup
pi@erpi ~/exploringrpi/chp05/bashLED $ ./bashLED on
The LED command that was passed is: on
Turning the LED on
pi@erpi ~/exploringrpi/chp05/bashLED $ ./bashLED status
The LED command that was passed is: status
The LED state is: 1
pi@erpi ~/exploringrpi/chp05/bashLED $ ./bashLED close
The LED command that was passed is: close
Unexporting GPIO number 4
```

Interestingly, the script does not have to be prefixed by sudo when it is executed by the pi user under Raspbian. On other Linux distributions this is not the case, because GPIOs are typically owned exclusively by the superuser. However, Raspbian has special udev rules which ensure that the GPIOs are shared within the gpio Linux group, and because the pi user is a member of that group it is permitted access. The user molloyd that is described in Chapter 3 would have to be added to the gpio group to execute the script. This topic is described in more detail in Chapter 6, but for the moment you can confirm group ownership and access permissions as follows:

```
pi@erpi /sys/class/gpio $ groups
pi adm ... gpio i2c spi input
pi@erpi /sys/class/gpio $ ls -ld gpio4
lrwxrwxrwx 1 root gpio 0 Jun 27 12:22 gpio4 -> ...
```

You might ask why the setuid bit could not be used on the bashLED script to give it superuser permissions instead. Well, for security reasons, you cannot use the setuid bit on a script to set it to execute as root. If users had write access to a script that is owned by root and its setuid bit was set, the users could inject any command that they wished into the script and would therefore have *de facto* superuser access to the system.

For a comprehensive online guide to Bash scripting, see Mendel Cooper's "Advanced Bash-Scripting Guide": tiny.cc/erpi502

Lua

Lua is the best performing interpreted language in Table 5-1 by a significant margin. In addition to good performance, Lua has a clean and straightforward syntax that is accessible for beginners. The interpreter for Lua has a small foot-print—on the RPi it is only 130 KB in size (`ls -lh /usr/bin/lua5.1`), which makes it very suitable for low-footprint embedded applications. For example, Lua can be used successfully on the ultra-low-cost ($2–$5) ESP8266 Wi-Fi modules that are described in Chapter 13, despite their modest memory allocations. In fact, once a platform has an ANSI C compiler then the Lua interpreter can be built for it. However, one downside is that the standard library of functions is somewhat limited in comparison to other more general scripting languages, such as Python.

Listing 5-2 provides a Lua script that has the same structure as the Bash script, so it is not necessary to discuss it in detail.

Listing 5-2: chp05/luaLED/luaLED.lua

```lua
#!/usr/bin/lua
local LED4_PATH = "/sys/class/gpio/gpio4/"   -- gpio4 sysfs path
local SYSFS_DIR = "/sys/class/gpio/"         -- gpio sysfs path
local LED_NUMBER = "4"                        -- The GPIO used

-- Example function to write a value to the GPIO
function writeGPIO(directory, filename, value)
    file = io.open(directory..filename, "w") -- append dir and file names
    file:write(value)                        -- write the value to the file
    file:close()
end

print("Starting the Lua LED Program")
if arg[1]==nil then                          -- no argument provided?
    print("This program requires a command")
    print("   usage is: ./luaLED.lua command")
    print("where command is one of setup, on, off, status, or close")
    do return end
end
if arg[1]=="on" then
    print("Turning the LED on")
    writeGPIO(LED4_PATH, "value", "1")
elseif arg[1]=="off" then
    print("Turning the LED off")
    writeGPIO(LED4_PATH, "value", "0")
elseif arg[1]=="setup" then
    print("Setting up the LED GPIO")
    writeGPIO(SYSFS_DIR, "export", LED_NUMBER)
    os.execute("sleep 0.1")         -- ensure the GPIO is exported by Linux
    writeGPIO(LED4_PATH, "direction", "out")
elseif arg[1]=="close" then
    print("Closing down the LED GPIO")
    writeGPIO(SYSFS_DIR, "unexport", LED_NUMBER)
elseif arg[1]=="status" then
    print("Getting the LED status")
    file = io.open(LED4_PATH.."value", "r")
```

```
    print(string.format("The LED state is %s.", file:read()))
    file:close()
else
    print("Invalid command!")
end
print("End of the Lua LED Program")
```

You can execute this script in the same manner as the `bashLED` script (e.g., `./luaLED.lua setup` or by typing `lua luaLED.lua setup` from the `/chp05/luaLED/` directory) and it will result in a comparable output. There are two things to be careful of with Lua in particular: strings are indexed from 1, not 0; and, functions can return multiple values, unlike most languages. Lua has a straightforward interface to C/C++, which means that you can execute compiled C/C++ code from within Lua, or use Lua as an interpreter module within your C/C++ programs. There is an excellent reference manual at `www.lua.org/manual/` and a six page summary of Lua at `tiny.cc/erpi503`.

Perl

Perl is a feature-rich scripting language that provides you with access to a huge library of reusable modules and portability to other OSs (including Windows). Perl is best known for its text processing and regular expressions modules. In the late 1990s it was a very popular language for server-side scripting for the dynamic generation of web pages. Later it was superseded by technologies such as Java servlets, Java Server Pages (JSP), and PHP. The language has evolved since its birth in the 1980s and now includes support for the OOP paradigm. Perl 5 (v20+) is installed by default on the Raspbian image.

A Perl version of the LED program is provided in the `/chp05/perlLED/` directory. Apart from general syntax changes that are described in the comments within the code, very little has actually changed in the translation to Perl. To execute this code, simply type `./perlLED.pl on`, because the sha-bang identifies the Perl interpreter. You could also execute it by typing `perl perlLED.pl status`.

For a good resource about getting started with installing and using Perl 5, see the guide "Learning Perl" at `learn.perl.org`.

Python

Python is a dynamic and strongly typed OOP language that was designed to be easy to learn and understand. *Dynamic typing* means that you do not have to associate a type (e.g., integer, character, string) with a variable; rather, the value of the variable "remembers" its own type. Therefore, if you were to create a variable x=5, the variable x would behave as an integer; but if you subsequently assign it using x="test", it would then behave like a string. *Statically typed* languages such as C/C++ or Java would not allow the re-definition of a variable in this way (within the same scope). *Strongly typed* languages require that the conversion of a variable from one type to another must have an explicit conversion. Unfortunately, dynamic typing has a heavy performance cost, which is apparent from the performance of Python in Table 5-1.

Python is installed by default on the Raspbian image and it is a very popular general-purpose language within the RPi community. The Python3 example to control the GPIO is provided in Listing 5-3. A Python2 example, which has minor modifications, is provided in the same directory.

Listing 5-3: chp05/pythonLED/pythonLED3.py

```python
#!/usr/bin/python3
import sys
from time import sleep
LED4_PATH = "/sys/class/gpio/gpio4/"
SYSFS_DIR = "/sys/class/gpio/"
LED_NUMBER = "4"

def writeLED ( filename, value, path=LED4_PATH ):
   "This function writes the value passed to the file in the path"
   fo = open( path + filename,"w")
   fo.write(value)
   fo.close()
   return

print("Starting the GPIO LED4 Python script")
if len(sys.argv)!=2:
   print("There is an incorrect number of arguments")
   print("   usage is:  pythonLED.py command")
   print("   where command is one of setup, on, off, status, or close")
   sys.exit(2)
if sys.argv[1]=="on":
   print("Turning the LED on")
   writeLED (filename="value", value="1")
elif sys.argv[1]=="off":
   print("Turning the LED off")
   writeLED (filename="value", value="0")
elif sys.argv[1]=="setup":
   print("Setting up the LED GPIO")
   writeLED (filename="export", value=LED_NUMBER, path=SYSFS_DIR)
   sleep(0.1)
   writeLED (filename="direction", value="out")
elif sys.argv[1]=="close":
   print("Closing down the LED GPIO")
   writeLED (filename="unexport", value=LED_NUMBER, path=SYSFS_DIR)
elif sys.argv[1]=="status":
   print("Getting the LED state value")
   fo = open( LED4_PATH + "value", "r")
   print(fo.read())
```

```
    fo.close()
else:
    print("Invalid Command!")
print("End of Python script")
```

The formatting of this code is important; in fact, Python enforces the layout of your code by making indentation a structural element. For example, after the line "if len(sys.argv)!=2:" the next few lines are "tabbed" in. If you did not tab in one of the lines—for example, the sys.exit(2) line—then it would not be part of the conditional if statement and the program would always exit at this point in the code. To execute this example, in the pythonLED directory enter the following:

```
pi@erpi .../chp05/pythonLED $ ./pythonLED3.py setup
Starting the GPIO LED4 Python script
Setting up the LED GPIO
End of Python script
pi@erpi .../chp05/pythonLED $ ./pythonLED3.py on
Starting the GPIO LED4 Python script
Turning the LED on
End of Python script
```

Python is particularly popular on the RPi for very good pedagogical reasons, but as users turn their attention to more advanced applications it is difficult to justify the performance deficit. This chapter concludes with a discussion on how you can use either Cython, or combine Python with C/C++ to dramatically improve the performance of Python. However, the complexity of Cython itself should motivate you to consider using C/C++ directly.

To conclude this discussion of scripting, there are several strong choices for applications on the RPi. Table 5-2 lists some of the key advantages and disadvantages of command scripting on the RPi, when considered in the context of the compiled languages that are discussed shortly.

Table 5-2: Advantages and Disadvantages of Command Scripting on the RPi

ADVANTAGES	DISADVANTAGES
Perfect for automating Linux system administration tasks that require calls to Linux commands.	Performance is poor for complex numeric or algorithmic tasks.
Easy to modify and adapt to changes. Source code is always present and complex toolchains (see Chapter 7) are not required to make modifications. Generally, nano is the only tool that you need.	Generally, relatively poor/slow programming support for data structures, graphical user interfaces, sockets, threads, etc.

Continues

Table 5-12 (*continued*)

ADVANTAGES	DISADVANTAGES
Generally, straightforward programming syntax and structure that is reasonably easy to learn when compared to languages like C++ and Java.	Generally, poor support for complex applications involving multiple, user-developed modules or components.
Generally, quick turnaround in coding solutions by occasional programmers or for prototyping.	Code is in the open. Direct access to view your code can be an intellectual property or a security concern.
	Lack of development tools (e.g., refactoring).

Dynamically Compiled Languages

With the interpreted languages just discussed, the source code text file is "executed" by the user passing it to a runtime interpreter, which then translates and executes each line of code. JavaScript and Java have different life cycles and are quite distinct languages.

JavaScript and Node.js on the RPi

Node.js is JavaScript that is run on the server side. JavaScript is an interpreted language by design. However, thanks to the V8 engine that was developed by Google for their Chrome web browser, Node.js actually compiles JavaScript into native machine instructions as it is loaded by the engine. This is called *just-in-time* (JIT) compilation or *dynamic translation*. As demonstrated at the beginning of this chapter, the performance of Node.js for numeric computation tasks is impressive for a non-compiled language, specifically on the RPi 2/3 due to optimizations for the ARMv7 platform.

Listing 5-4 shows the same LED code example written using JavaScript and executed by passing it to the Node.js interpreter:

Listing 5-4: chp05/nodejsLED/nodejsLED.js

```
// Ignore the first two arguments (nodejs and the program name)
var myArgs = process.argv.slice(2)
var GPIO4_PATH = "/sys/class/gpio/gpio4/"
var GPIO_SYSFS = "/sys/class/gpio/"
var GPIO_NUMBER = 4

function writeGPIO( filename, value, path ){
  var fs = require('fs')
  try {
     fs.writeFileSync(path+filename, value)
  }
  catch (err) {
```

```
        console.log("The Write Failed to the File: " + path+filename)
   }
}

console.log("Starting the RPi LED Node.js Program");
if (myArgs[0]==null){
   console.log("There is an incorrect number of arguments.");
   console.log("  Usage is: nodejs nodejsLED.js command")
   console.log("  where command is: setup, on, off, status, or close.")
   process.exit(2)   //exits with the error code 2 (incorrect usage)
}
switch (myArgs[0]) {
   case 'on':
      console.log("Turning the LED On")
      writeGPIO("value", "1", GPIO4_PATH)
      break
   case 'off':
      console.log("Turning the LED Off")
      writeGPIO("value", "0", GPIO4_PATH)
      break
   case 'setup':
      console.log("Exporting the LED GPIO")
      writeGPIO("export", GPIO_NUMBER, GPIO_SYSFS)
      // need to delay by 100ms or the GPIO will not be exported correctly
      setTimeout(function(){writeGPIO("direction", "out", GPIO4_PATH)},100)
      break
   case 'close':
      console.log("Unexporting the LED GPIO")
      writeGPIO("unexport", GPIO_NUMBER, GPIO_SYSFS)
      break
   case 'status':
```

The code is available in the /chp05/nodejsLED/ directory and it can be executed by typing **nodejs nodejsLED.js setup**, or **node nodejsLED.js setup** for more recent versions of Node.js.

The code has been structured in the same way as the previous examples and there are not too many syntactical differences. However, there is one major difference between Node.js and other languages: *functions are called asynchronously.* Up to this point, all of the languages discussed followed a sequential-execution mode. Therefore, when a function is called, the *program counter* (also known as the *instruction pointer*) enters that function and does not reemerge until the function is complete. Consider, for example, code like this:

```
functionA();
functionB();
```

The functionA() is called and functionB() will not be called until functionA() is fully complete. This is *not* the case in Node.js! In Node.js, functionA() is called first and then Node.js continues executing the subsequent code, including entering functionB(), while the code in functionA() is still being executed.

Node.js permits asynchronous calls because they help ensure that the code is "lively." For example, if you performed a database query, your code may be able to do something else useful while awaiting the result. When the result is available, a *callback function* is executed to process the received data. This asynchronous structure is perfect for Internet-attached applications, where posts and requests are being made of websites and web services, and it is not clear when a response will be received (if at all). Node.js has an *event loop* that manages all the asynchronous calls, creating threads for each call as required, and ensuring that the callback functions are executed when an asynchronous call completes its assigned tasks. Node.js is revisited again in Chapter 12 when the Internet of Things is discussed.

Java on the RPi

Up to this point in the chapter, *interpreted languages* are examined, meaning the source code file (a text file) is executed using an interpreter or dynamic translator at run time. Importantly, the code exists in source code form, right up to the point when it is executed using the interpreter.

With traditional *compiled languages,* the source code (a text file) is translated directly into machine code for a particular platform using a set of tools, which we will call a *compiler* for the moment. The translation happens when the code is being developed; once compiled, the code can be executed without needing any additional runtime tools.

Java is a hybrid language: You write your Java code in a source file, e.g., `example.java`, which is a regular text file. The Java compiler (`javac`) compiles and translates this source code into machine code instructions (called *bytecodes*) for a Java *virtual machine* (VM). Regular compiled code is not portable between hardware architectures, but bytecode files (`.class` files) can be executed on any platform that has an implementation of the Java VM. Originally, the Java VM interpreted the bytecode files at run time. However, more recently, dynamic translation is employed by the VM to convert the bytecodes into native machine instructions at run time.

The key advantage of this life cycle is that the compiled bytecode is portable between platforms; and because it is compiled to a generic machine instruction code, the dynamic translation to "real" machine code is very efficient. The downside of this structure when compared to compiled languages is that the VM adds overhead to the execution of the final executable.

The Oracle Java Development Kit (JDK) and Java Runtime Environment (JRE) are currently installed by default on the RPi Raspbian full image. To install the JDK on the Raspbian Minimal Image, use `sudo apt install oracle-java8-jdk`. Listing 5-5 provides a source code example that is also available in the GitHub repository in bytecode form.

NOTE Large installations such as Oracle Java might cause you to run out of space on your RPi SD card. You can identify the five largest packages that are installed on your distribution using the command `dpkg-query -Wf '${Installed-Size}\ t${Package}\n' | sort -n | tail -n5`. You can then remove large unused packages using `apt remove`. Here are the five largest on the RPi Raspbian image— note that Oracle Java 8 is presently the second largest package.

```
55920    pypy-upstream
65025    sonic-pi
104249   raspberrypi-bootloader
181992   oracle-java8-jdk
448821   wolfram-engine
```

Listing 5-5: chp05/javaLED/LEDExample.java (Segment)

```java
package exploringRPi;
import java.io.*;

public class LEDExample {

  private static String GPIO4_PATH = "/sys/class/gpio/gpio4/";
  private static String GPIO_SYSFS = "/sys/class/gpio/";

  private static void writeSysfs(String filename, String value, String path){
    try{
      BufferedWriter bw = new BufferedWriter(new FileWriter(path+filename));
      bw.write(value);
      bw.close();
    }
    catch(IOException e){
      System.err.println("Failed to access RPi sysfs file: " + filename);
    }
  }

  public static void main(String[] args) {
    System.out.println("Starting the LED Java Application");
    if(args.length!=1) {
      System.out.println("There is an incorrect number of arguments.");
      System.out.println("  Correct usage is: LEDExample command");
      System.out.println("command is: setup, on, off, status, or close");
      System.exit(2);
    }
    if (args[0].equalsIgnoreCase("On") || args[0].equalsIgnoreCase("Off")){
      System.out.println("Turning the LED " + args[0]);
      writeSysfs("value",args[0].equalsIgnoreCase("On")?"1":"0",GPIO4_PATH);
    }
    ...
  }
}
```

The program can be executed using the `run` script that is in the `/chp05/` `javaLED/` directory. You can see that the class is placed in the package directory `exploringRPi`.

Early versions of Java suffered from poor computational performance. However, more recent versions take advantage of dynamic translation at runtime (just-in-time, or JIT, compilation) and, as demonstrated at the start of this chapter, the performance is approximately 50% slower (including dynamic translation) than that of the natively compiled C++ code, with only a minor additional memory overhead. Table 5-3 lists some of the advantages and disadvantages of using Java for development on the RPi.

Table 5-3: Advantages and Disadvantages of Java on the RPi

ADVANTAGES	DISADVANTAGES
Code is portable. Code compiled on the PC can be executed on the RPi or another embedded Linux platform.	Sandboxed applications do not have access to system memory, registers or system calls (except through `/proc`) or JNI (Java Native Interface).
There is a vast and extensive library of code available that can be fully integrated in your project.	Executing as root is slightly difficult due to required environment variables. This is pre-configured for the RPi pi user account.
Well-designed OOP support.	It is not suitable for scripting.
Can be used for user-interface application development on the RPi when it is attached to a display	Computational performance is very respectable, but slower than optimized C/C++ programs. Slightly heavier on memory.
Strong support for multi-threading.	Strictly typed and no unsigned integer types.
Has automatic memory allocation and de-allocation using a garbage collector, removing memory leak concerns.	Royalty payment is required if deployed to a platform that "involves or controls hardware" (Oracle, 2014).

C and C++ on the RPi

C++ was developed by Bjarne Stroustrup at Bell Labs (now AT&T Labs) during 1983–1985. It is based on the C language (named in 1972) that was developed at AT&T for UNIX systems in the early 1970s (1969–1973) by Dennis Ritchie. As well as adding an *object-oriented* (OO) framework (originally called "C with Classes"), C++ also improves the C language by adding features such as better type checking. It quickly gained widespread usage, which was largely due to its similarity to the C programming language syntax, and the fact that it allowed existing C code to be used when possible. C++ is not a pure OO language but rather a hybrid, having the organizational structure of OO languages but retaining the efficiencies of C, such as typed variables and pointers.

Unlike Java, C++ is not "owned" by a single company. In 1998 the ISO (International Organization for Standardization) committee adopted a world-wide uniform language specification that aimed to remove inconsistencies between the various C++ compilers (Stroustrup, 1998). This standardization continues today with C++11 approved by the ISO in 2011 (gcc 4.7+ supports the flag -std=c++11) and more new features appearing in compilers today with the approval of C++14 in August 2014.

Why am I covering C and C++ in more detail than other languages in this book?

- First, I believe that if you can understand the workings of C and C++, you can understand the workings of any language. In fact, most compilers (Java native methods, Java virtual machine, JavaScript, etc.) and interpreters (Bash, Lua, Perl, Python, etc.) are written in C.

- At the beginning of this chapter, a significant performance advantage of C/C++ over other languages was described (yes, it was demonstrated using only one random test!). It is also important to remember that the same code running on the RPi 3 at 1.2 GHz was 10 times slower than the same code running on only one thread (12 total) of an Intel i7-5820K at 3.3 GHz.

- Chapter 16 explains how to develop Linux loadable kernel modules (LKM), which requires a reasonable grasp of the C programming language. Later in this chapter, code is provided that demonstrates how you can communicate directly with Linux kernel space using the GNU C Library (glibc).

- Many of the application examples in this book such as streaming network data and image processing use C++ and a comprehensive library of C++ code called Qt.

Table 5-4 lists some advantages and disadvantages of using C/C++ on the RPi. The next section reviews some of the fundamentals of C and C++ programming, to ensure that you have the skills necessary for the remaining chapters in this book. It is not possible to cover every aspect of C and C++ programming in part of one chapter of one book. The Further Reading section at the end of this chapter directs you to recommended texts.

Table 5-4: Advantages and Disadvantages of C/C++ on the RPi

ADVANTAGES	DISADVANTAGES
You can build code directly on the RPi or you can cross-compile code using professional toolchains. Runtime environments do not need to be installed.	Compiled code is not portable. Code compiled for your x86 desktop will not run on the RPi ARM processor.
C++ has full support for procedural programming, OOP, and support for generics through the use of STL (Standard Template Library).	Many consider the languages to be complex to master. There is a tendency to need to know everything before you can do anything.

Continues

Table 3-12 (*continued*)

ADVANTAGES	DISADVANTAGES
It gives the best computational performance, especially if optimized. However, optimization can be difficult and can reduce the portability of your code.	The use of pointers and the low-level control available makes code prone to memory leaks. With careful coding these can be avoided and can lead to efficiencies over dynamic memory management schemes.
Can be used for high-performance user-interface application development on the RPi using third-party libraries. Libraries such as Qt and Boost provide extensive additional libraries for components, networking, etc.	By default, C and C++ do not support graphical user interfaces, network sockets, etc. Third-party libraries are required.
Offers low-level access to glibc for integrating with the Linux system. Programs can be setuid to root.	Not suitable for scripting (there is a C shell, csh, that does have syntax like C). You can integrated Lua. Not ideal for web development either.
The Linux kernel is written in C and having knowledge of C/C++ can help if you ever have to write device drivers or contribute to Linux kernel development.	C++ attempts to span from low-level to high-level programming tasks, but it can be difficult to write very scalable enterprise or web applications.
The C/C++ languages are ISO standards, not owned by a single company.	

The next section provides a revision of the core principles that have been applied to examples on the RPi. It is intended to serve as an overview and a set of reference examples that you can come back to again and again. It also focuses on topics that cause my students difficulties, pointing out common mistakes. Also, remember that course notes for my object-oriented programming module are publicly available at ee402.eeng.dcu.ie along with further support materials.

C and C++ Language Overview

The following examples can be edited using the nano editor and compiled on the RPi directly using the *gcc* and *g++* compilers, which are installed by default. The code is in the directory chp05/overview.

The first example you should always write in any new language is "Hello World." Listing 5-6 and 5-7 provide C and C++ code respectively, for the purpose of a direct comparison of the two languages.

Listing 5-6: chp05/overview/helloworld.c

```
#include <stdio.h>
int main(int argc, char *argv[]){
   printf("Hello World!\n");
   return 0;
}
```

Listing 5-7: chp05/overview/helloworld.cpp

```cpp
#include<iostream>
int main(int argc, char *argv[]){
   std::cout << "Hello World!" << std::endl;
   return 0;
}
```

The `#include` call is a pre-processor directive that effectively loads the contents of the `stdio.h` file (`/usr/include/stdio.h`) in the C case, and the `iostream` header (`/usr/include/c++/4.X/iostream`) file in the C++ case, and copies and pastes the code in at this exact point in your source code file. These header files contain (or link to) the function prototypes, enabling the compiler to understand the format of functions such as `printf()` in `stdio.h` and streams like `cout` in `iostream`. The actual implementation of these functions is in shared library dependencies. The angular brackets (`< >`) around the include filename means that it is a standard, rather than a user-defined `include` (which would use double quotes).

The `main()` function is the starting point of your application code. There can only be one function called `main()` in your application. The `int` in front of `main()` indicates that the program will return a number back to the shell prompt. As stated before, it is good to use `0` for successful completion, `2` for invalid usage, and any other set of numbers to indicate failure conditions. This value is returned to the shell prompt using the line `return 0;` in this case. The `main()` function will return `0` by default in C++, and an arbitrary value in C. Remember that you can use `echo $?` at the shell prompt to see the last value that was returned.

The *parameters* of the `main()` function are `int argc` and `char *argv[]`. As you saw in the scripting examples, the shell can pass *arguments* to your application, providing the number of arguments (`argc`) and an array of strings (`*argv[]`). In C/C++ the first argument passed is `argv[0]` and it contains the executable name and full path used to execute the application.

The C code line `printf("Hello World!\n");` allows you to write to the Linux shell, with the `\n` representing a new line. The `printf()` function provides you with additional formatting instructions for outputting numbers, strings, etc. Note that every statement is terminated by a semicolon.

The C++ code line `std::cout << "Hello World!" << std::endl;` outputs a string just like the `printf()` function. In this case `cout` represents the output stream; and the function used is actually the `<<`, which is called the *output stream operator*. The syntax is discussed later, but `std::cout` means the output stream in the namespace `std`. The `endl` (end line) representation is similar to `\n`. These programs can be compiled and executed directly on the RPi by typing the following:

```
pi@erpi ~/exploringrpi/chp05/overview $ gcc helloworld.c -o helloworldc
pi@erpi ~/exploringrpi/chp05/overview $ ./helloworldc
Hello World!
pi@erpi ~/exploringrpi/chp05/overview $ g++ helloworld.cpp -o helloworldcpp
pi@erpi ~/exploringrpi/chp05/overview $ ./helloworldcpp
Hello World!
```

The sizes of the C and C++ executables are different from account for the different header files, output functions, and exact compilers that are used:

```
pi@erpi ~/exploringrpi/chp05/overview $ ls -l helloworldc*
-rwxr-xr-x 1 pi pi 5744 Jun 27 23:30 helloworldc
-rwxr-xr-x 1 pi pi 7500 Jun 27 23:30 helloworldcpp
```

Compiling and Linking

You just saw how to build a C or C++ application, but there are a few intermediate steps that are not obvious in the preceding example, because the intermediate stage outputs are not retained by default. Figure 5-2 illustrates the full build process from preprocessing right through to linking.

You can perform the steps in Figure 5-2 yourself by using the `Helloworld` `.cpp` code example. The steps can be performed explicitly as follows, so that you can view the output at each stage:

```
pi@erpi ~/tmp $ ls -l helloworld.cpp
-rw-r--r-- 1 pi pi 114 Jun 28 11:56 helloworld.cpp
pi@erpi ~/tmp $ g++ -E helloworld.cpp > processed.cpp
pi@erpi ~/tmp $ ls -l
total 424
-rw-r--r-- 1 pi pi    114 Jun 28 11:56 helloworld.cpp
-rw-r--r-- 1 pi pi 428379 Jun 28 11:57 processed.cpp
pi@erpi ~/tmp $ g++ -S processed.cpp -o helloworld.s
pi@erpi ~/tmp $ ls
helloworld.cpp  helloworld.s  processed.cpp
pi@erpi ~/tmp $ g++ -c helloworld.s
pi@erpi ~/tmp $ ls
helloworld.cpp  helloworld.o  helloworld.s  processed.cpp
pi@erpi ~/tmp $ g++ helloworld.o -o helloworld
pi@erpi ~/tmp $ ls
helloworld  helloworld.cpp  helloworld.o  helloworld.s  processed.cpp
pi@erpi ~/tmp $ ./helloworld
Hello World!
```

You can see the text file output that results from preprocessing by typing **less processed.cpp**, where the necessary header files are "pasted in" above your code. At the very bottom of this much larger file you will find your code. This file is passed to the C/C++ compiler, which validates the code and generates platform-independent assembler code (`.s`). You can view this code by typing **less helloworld.s**, as illustrated in Figure 5-2.

This `.s` text file is then passed to the assembler, which converts the platform-independent instructions into binary instructions for the RPi platform (the `.o` file). You can see the assembly language code that is generated if you use the `objdump` (object file dump) tool on the RPi by typing **objdump -D helloworld.o**, as illustrated in Figure 5-2.

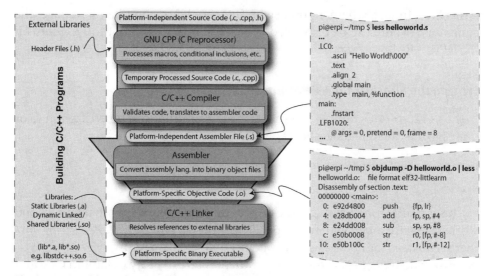

Figure 5-2: Building C/C++ applications on the RPi

Object files contain generalized binary assembly code that does not yet contain sufficient information to be executed on the RPi. However, after linking the final executable code, `helloworld` contains the target-specific assembly language code that has been combined with the libraries, statically and dynamically as required. You can use the `objdump` tool again to disassemble the executable, which results in the following output:

```
pi@erpi ~/tmp $ objdump -d helloworld | more
helloworld:     file format elf32-littlearm
Disassembly of section .init:
00010568 <_init>:
   10568:    e92d4008    push    {r3, lr}
   1056c:    eb00002f    bl      10630 <call_weak_fn>
   10570:    e8bd8008    pop     {r3, pc}...
```

The first column is the memory address, which steps by 4 bytes (32-bits) between each instruction (i.e., `1056c` − `10568` = `4`). The second column is the full 4-byte instruction at that address. The third and fourth columns are the human-readable version of the second column that describes the opcode and operand of the 4-byte instruction. For example, the first instruction at address `10568` is a `push`, which pushes `r3`, which is one of the ARM processor's 16, 32-bit registers (labeled `r0-r15`), followed by `lr` (the link register, `r14`) onto the stack.

Understanding ARM instructions is another book in and of itself (see `infocenter.arm.com`). However, it is useful to appreciate that any natively compiled code, whether it uses the OOP paradigm or not, results in low-level machine code, which does not support dynamic typing, OOP, or any such high-level structures. In fact, whether you use an interpreted or compiled language, the code must eventually be converted to machine code so that it can execute on the RPi's ARM processor.

Writing the Shortest C/C++ Program

Is the HelloWorld example the shortest program that can be written in C or C++? No, Listing 5-8 is the shortest valid C and C++ program.

Listing 5-8: chp05/overview/short.c

```
main(){}
```

This is a fully functional C and C++ program that compiles with no errors and works perfectly, albeit with no output. Therefore, in building a C/C++ program, there is no need for libraries; there is no need to specify a return type for main(), because it defaults to int; the main() function returns 0 by default in C++ and an arbitrary number in C (see echo $? call below); and an empty function is a valid function. This program will compile as a C or C++ program as follows:

```
pi@erpi .../overview $ gcc short.c -o shortc
pi@erpi .../overview $ g++ short.c -o shortcpp
pi@erpi .../overview $ ls -l short*
-rwxr-xr-x 1 pi pi 5580 Jun 28 14:08 shortc
-rw-r--r-- 1 pi pi    9 Jun 16 01:56 short.c
-rwxr-xr-x 1 pi pi 5792 Jun 28 14:09 shortcpp
pi@erpi .../overview $ ./shortc
pi@erpi .../overview $ echo $?
232
pi@erpi .../overview $ ./shortcpp
pi@erpi .../overview $ echo $?
0
```

This is one of the greatest weaknesses of C and C++. There is an assumption that you know everything about the way the language works before you write anything. In fact, aspects of the preceding example might be used by a programmer to demonstrate how clever they are, but they are actually demonstrating poor practice in making their code unreadable by less "expert" programmers. For example, if you rewrite the C++ code in short.cpp to include comments and explicit statements, to create short2.cpp, and then compile both using the -O3 optimization flag, the output will be as follows:

```
pi@erpi .../overview $ g++ --version
g++ (Raspbian 4.9.2-10) 4.9.2
pi@erpi .../overview $ more short.cpp
main(){}
pi@erpi .../overview $ more short2.cpp
// A really useless program, but a program nevertheless
int main(int argc, char *argv[]){
    return 0;
}
```

```
pi@erpi .../overview $ g++ -O3 short.cpp -o short_1
pi@erpi .../overview $ g++ -O3 short2.cpp -o short_2
pi@erpi .../overview $ ls -l short_*
-rwxr-xr-x 1 pi pi 5776 Jun 28 14:15 short_1
-rwxr-xr-x 1 pi pi 5776 Jun 28 14:16 short_2
```

Note that the executable size is exactly the same! Adding the comment, the explicit return statement, the explicit return type, and explicit arguments has had no impact on the size of the final binary application. However, the benefit is that the actual functionality of the code is much more readily understood by a novice programmer.

Static and Dynamic Compilation

You can build a program with the flag -static to statically link the libraries, rather than the default form of linking dynamically with shared libraries. This means that the compiler and linker effectively place all the library routines required by your code directly within the program executable:

```
pi@erpi .../overview $ g++ -O3 short.cpp -static -o short_static
pi@erpi .../overview $ ls -l short_static
-rwxr-xr-x 1 pi pi 581804 Jun 28 14:23 short_static
```

It is clear that the program executable size has grown significantly. One advantage of this form is that the program can be executed by ARM systems on which the C++ standard libraries are not installed; however, unlike dynamic linking, it is not possible to update the linked library code without recompiling.

With dynamic linking, it is useful to note that you can discover which shared library dependencies your compiled code is using, by calling `ldd`:

```
pi@erpi ~/exploringrpi/chp05/overview $ ldd shortcpp
    /usr/lib/arm-linux-gnueabihf/libcofi_rpi.so (0x76efa000)
    libstdc++.so.6 => /usr/lib/arm-linux-gnueabihf/libstdc++.so.6 (0x76de8000)
    libm.so.6 => /lib/arm-linux-gnueabihf/libm.so.6 (0x76d6d000)
    libgcc_s.so.1 => /lib/arm-linux-gnueabihf/libgcc_s.so.1 (0x76d40000)
    libc.so.6 => /lib/arm-linux-gnueabihf/libc.so.6 (0x76c03000)
    /lib/ld-linux-armhf.so.3 (0x76ed8000)
```

You can see that the g++ compiler (and *glibc*) on the Raspbian image for the RPi (all models) has been patched to support the generation of hard floating-point (gnueabihf) instructions. This allows for faster code execution with floating-point numbers than if it used the soft floating-point ABI (application binary interface) to emulate floating-point support in software (gnueabi).

> **NOTE**   The gcc/g++ compilers automatically search certain include and library paths. The include paths are typically /usr/include/, /usr/local/include/, and /usr/include/**target**/ (or /usr/**target**/include/), where **target** in the case of the RPi is typically arm-linux-gnueabihf. The library paths are typically /usr/lib/, /usr/local/lib/, and /usr/lib/**target**/ (or /usr/**target**/lib/). Use g++ -v, or c++ -v for more information, including your target name.

Variables and Operators in C/C++

A variable is a data item stored in a block of memory that has been reserved for it. The type of the variable defines the amount of memory reserved and how it should behave (see Figure 5-3). This figure describes the output of the code example `sizeofvariables.c` in Listing 5-9.

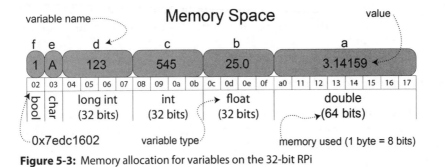

Figure 5-3: Memory allocation for variables on the 32-bit RPi

Listing 5-9 details various variables available in C/C++. When you create a *local variable* c below, it is allocated a box/block of memory on the *stack* (predetermined reserved fast memory) depending on its type. In this case, c is an `int` value; therefore, four bytes (32 bits) of memory are allocated to store the value. Assume that variables in C/C++ are initialized with random values; therefore, in this case c = 545; replaces that initial random value by placing the number 545 in the box. It does not matter if you store the number 0 or 2,147,483,647 in this box; it will still occupy 32 bits of memory! Note that there is no guarantee regarding the ordering of local variable memory—it was fortuitously linear in this particular example.

Listing 5-9: chp05/overview/sizeofvariables.c

```
#include<stdio.h>
#include<stdbool.h>            // required for the C bool typedef

int main(){
    double a = 3.14159;
    float b = 25.0;
    int c = 545;               // note: variables are not = 0 by default!
    long int d = 123;
    char e = 'A';
    bool f = true;             // no need for definition in C++
    printf("a val %.4f & size %d bytes (@addr %p).\n", a, sizeof(a),&a);
    printf("b val %4.2f & size %d bytes (@addr %p).\n", b, sizeof(b),&b);
    printf("c val %d (oct %o, hex %x) & " \
          "size %d bytes (@addr %p).\n", c, c, c, sizeof(c), &c);
    printf("d val %d & size %d bytes (@addr %p).\n", d, sizeof(d), &d);
    printf("e val %c & size %d bytes (@addr %p).\n", e, sizeof(e), &e);
    printf("f val %5d & size %d bytes (@addr %p).\n", f, sizeof(f), &f);
}
```

The `sizeof(c)` operator returns the size of the type of the variable in bytes. In this example, it returns 4 for the size of the `int` type. The `&c` call can be read as the *"address of"* c. This provides the address of the first byte that stores the variable c, in this case returning `0x7edc1608`. The `%.4f` on the first line means display the floating-point number to four decimal places. Executing this program on the RPi gives the following output:

```
pi@erpi ~/exploringrpi/chp05/overview $ ./sizeofvariables
a value 3.1416 and size 8 bytes (@addr 0x7edc1610).
b value 25.00 and size 4 bytes (@addr 0x7edc160c).
c value 545 (oct 1041, hex 221) and size 4 bytes (@addr 0x7edc1608).
d value 123 and size 4 bytes (@addr 0x7edc1604).
e value A and size 1 bytes (@addr 0x7edc1603).
f value      1 and size 1 bytes (@addr 0x7edc1602).
```

On the RPi with a 32-bit Linux image, you typically use four bytes to represent the `int` type. The smallest unit of memory that you can allocate is 1 byte; so, yes, you are representing a Boolean value with 1 byte, which could actually store eight unique Boolean values. You can operate directly on variables using operators. The program `operators.c` in Listing 5-10 contains some points that often cause difficulty in C/C++.

Listing 5-10: chp05/overview/operators.c

```
#include<stdio.h>

int main(){
    int a=1, b=2, c, d, e, g;
    float f=9.9999;
    c = ++a;
    printf("The value of c=%d and a=%d.\n", c, a);
    d = b++;
    printf("The value of d=%d and b=%d.\n", d, b);
    e = (int) f;
    printf("The value of f=%.2f and e=%d.\n", f, e);
    g = 'A';
    printf("The value of g=%d and g=%c.\n", g, g);
    return 0;
}
```

This code will give the following output:

```
pi@erpi ~/exploringrpi/chp05/overview $ ./operators
The value of c=2 and a=2.
The value of d=2 and b=3.
The value of f=10.00 and e=9.
The value of g=65 and g=A.
```

On the line `c=++a;`, the value of a is pre-incremented before the equals assignment to c on the left side. Therefore, a is increased to 2 before assigning the value to c, so this line is equivalent to two statements: `a=a+1; c=a;` However, on the line `d=b++;` the value of b is post-incremented and is equivalent to two statements: d=b; b=b+1; The value of d is assigned the value of b, which is 2, before the value of b is incremented to 3.

On the line e=(int)f; a C-style cast is being used to convert a floating-point number into an integer value. Effectively, when programmers use a cast they are notifying the compiler that they are aware that there will be a loss of precision in the conversion of a floating-point number to an int (and that the compiler will introduce conversion code). The fractional part is truncated, so 9.9999 is converted to e=9, because the .9999 is removed by the truncation. It is worth noting that printf("%.2f",f) displays the floating-point variable to two decimal places, in contrast, rounding the value.

On the line g='A', g is assigned the ASCII equivalent value of capital A, which is 65. The printf("%d %c",g, g); will display either the int value of g if %d is used, or the ASCII character value of g if %c is used.

A const keyword can be used to prevent a variable from being changed. There is also a volatile keyword that is useful for notifying the compiler that a particular variable might be changed outside its control, and that the compiler should not apply any type of optimization to that value. This notification is useful on the RPi if the variable in question is shared with another process or physical input/output.

It is possible to define your own type in C/C++ using the typedef keyword. For example, if you did not want to include the header file stdbool.h in the sizeofvariables.c previous example, it would be possible to define it in this way instead:

```
typedef char bool;
#define true 1
#define false 0
```

Probably the most common and most misunderstood mistake in C/C++ programming is present in the following code segment:

```
if (x=y){    // perform a statement Z  }
```

When will the body statement Z be performed? The answer is whenever y is not equal to 0 (the current value of x is irrelevant!). The mistake is placing a single = (assignment) instead of == (comparison) in the if condition. The assignment operator returns the value on the right side of the operator, which is automatically converted to true if y is not equal to 0. If y is equal to zero, a false value is returned. Java does not allow this error, because it has no implicit conversion between 0 and false, and 1 and true.

Pointers in C/C++

A pointer is a special type of variable that stores the address of another variable in memory—we say that the pointer is "pointing at" that variable. Listing 5-11 is a code example that demonstrates how you can create a pointer p and make it point at the variable y.

Listing 5-11: chp05/overview/pointers.c

```
#include<stdio.h>

int main(){
    int y = 1000;
    int *p;
    p = &y;
    printf("The variable has value %d and the address %p.\n", y, &y);
    printf("The pointer stores %p and points at value %d.\n", p, *p);
    printf("The pointer has address %p and size %d.\n", &p, sizeof(p));
    return 0;
}
```

When this code is compiled and executed, it gives the following output:

```
pi@erpi ~/exploringrpi/chp05/overview $ ./pointers
The variable has value 1000 and the address 0x7e8a0634.
The pointer stores 0x7e8a0634 and points at value 1000.
The pointer has address 0x7e8a0630 and size 4.
```

So, what is happening in this example? Figure 5-4 illustrates the memory locations and the steps involved. In Step 1, the variable y is created and assigned the initial value of 1000. A pointer p is then created with the dereference type of int. In essence, this means that the pointer p is being established to point at int values. In Step 2, the statement p = &y; means "let p equal to the address of y," which sets the value of p to be the 32-bit address 0x7e8a0634. We now say that p is pointing at y. These two steps could have been combined using the call int *p = &y; (i.e., create a pointer p of dereference type int and assign it to store the address of y).

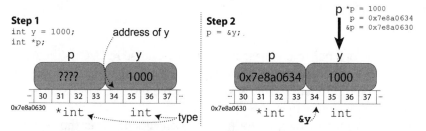

Figure 5-4: Example of pointers in C/C++ on the RPi

Why does a pointer need a dereference type? For one example, if a pointer needs to move to the next element in an array, it needs to know whether it should move by 4 bytes, 8 bytes, etc. Also, in C++ you need to be able to know how to deal with the data at the pointer based on its type. Listing 5-12 is another example of working with pointers that explains how a simple error of intention can cause serious problems.

Listing 5-12: chp05/overview/pointers2.c

```
#include<stdio.h>

int main(){
    int y   = 1000, z;
    int *p = &y;
    printf("The pointer p has the value %d and stores addr: %p\n", *p, p);
    // Let z = 1000 + 5 and the increment p and y to 1001 -- wrong!!!
    z = *p++ + 5;
    printf("The pointer p has the value %d and stores addr: %p\n", *p, p);
    printf("The variable z has the value %d\n", z);
    return 0;
}
```

This code gives the following output:

```
pi@erpi ~/exploringrpi/chp05/overview $ ./pointers2
The pointer  p has the value 1000 and stores addr: 0x7ee5861c
The pointer  p has the value 1005 and stores addr: 0x7ee58620
The variable z has the value 1005
```

In this example, the pointer p is of dereference type int, and it is set to point at the address of y. At this point in the code, the output is as expected, because p has the "value of" 1000 and the "address of" 0x7ee5861c. On the next line, the intention may have been to increase (post-increment) the value of y by 1 to 1001 and assign z a value of 1005 (i.e., before the post-increment takes place). However, perhaps contrary to your intention, p now has the "value of" 1005 and the "address of" 0x7ee58620.

Why has this occurred? Part of the difficulty of using pointers in C/C++ is understanding the order of operations in C/C++, called the *precedence* of the operations. For example, if you write the statement

```
int x = 1 + 2 * 3;
```

what will the value of x be? In this case it will be 7, because in C/C++ the multiplication operator has a higher level of precedence than the addition operator. Similarly, the problem in Listing 5-12 is your possible intention of using *p++ to increment the "value of" p by 1.

In C/C++ the post-increment operator (p++) has precedence over the dereference operator (*p). This means that *p++ actually post-increments the "address of" the pointer p by one int (i.e., 4 bytes), not the dereferenced value *p (as 1000 in this example). Most worrying is the second output line, because it is clear that p is now "pointing at" z, which just happens to be at the next address—it could actually refer to an address outside the program's memory allocation. Such errors of intention are very difficult to debug without using the debugging tools that are described in Chapter 7. To fix the code to suit your intention, simply use (*p)++, which makes it clear that it is the "value of" p that should be post-incremented by 1, resulting in p having the "value of" 1001 and z having the value 1005.

There are approximately 58 operators in C++, with 18 different major precedence levels. Even if you know the precedence table, you should still make it clear for other users what you intend in a statement by using round brackets (()), which effectively groups and overrides operator precedence. Therefore, you should always write the following even if you know that the round brackets are not required:

```
int x = 1 + (2 * 3);
```

Finally, on the topic of C pointers, there is also a *void pointer* that can be declared as void *p;, which effectively states that the pointer p does not have a dereference type and it will have to be assigned at a later stage (see /chp05/overview/void.c) using the following syntax:

```
int a = 5;
void *p = &a;
printf("p points at address %p and value %d\n", p, *((int *)p));
```

When executed, this code gives an output like the following:

```
The pointer p points at address 0xbea546c8 and value 5
```

Therefore, it is possible to cast a pointer from one deference type to another and the void pointer can potentially be used to store a pointer of any dereference type. In Chapter 6 void pointers are used to develop an enhanced GPIO interface.

C-Style Strings

The C language has no built-in string type but rather uses an array of the character type, terminated by the null character (\0), to represent a string. There is a standard C library for strings that can be used as shown in Listing 5-13:

Listing 5-13: chp05/overview/cstrings.c

```
#include<stdio.h>
#include<string.h>
#include<stdlib.h>

int main(){
   char a[20] = "hello ";
   char b[] = {'w','o','r','l','d','!','\0'};      // the \0 is important

   a[0]='H';                     // set the first character to be H
   char *c = strcat(a,b);     // join/concatenate a and b
   printf("The string c is: %s\n", c);
   printf("The length of c is: %d\n", strlen(c));  // call string length
```

```
// find and replace the w with a W
char *p = strchr(c,'w');  // returns pointer to first 'w' char
*p = 'W';
printf("The string c is now: %s\n", c);

if (strcmp("cat", "dog")<=0){      // ==0 would be equal
   printf("cat comes before dog (lexiographically)\n");
}
//insert "to the" into middle of "Hello World!" string - very messy!
char *d = " to the";
char *cd = malloc(strlen(c) + strlen(d));
memcpy(cd, c, 5);
memcpy(cd+5, d, strlen(d));
memcpy(cd+5+strlen(d), c+5, 6);
printf("The cd string is: %s\n", cd);

//tokenize cd string using spaces
p = strtok(cd," ");
while(p!=NULL){
   printf("Token:%s\n", p);
   p = strtok(NULL, " ");
}
return 0;
}
```

The code is explained by the comments within the example. When executed, this code gives the following output:

```
pi@erpi ~/exploringrpi/chp05/overview $ ./cstrings
The string c is: Hello world!
The length of c is: 12
The string c is now: Hello World!
cat comes before dog (lexiographically)
The cd string is: Hello to the World
Token:Hello
Token:to
Token:the
Token:World
```

LED Control in C

Now that you have covered enough C programming to get by, you can look at how to write the external LED control application in C. In Listing 5-14 the same structure as the other examples is retained:

Listing 5-14: chp05/makeLED/makeLED.c

```
#include<stdio.h>
#include<stdlib.h>
#include<string.h>

#define GPIO_NUMBER "4"
#define GPIO4_PATH "/sys/class/gpio/gpio4/"
```

```c
#define GPIO_SYSFS "/sys/class/gpio/"

void writeGPIO(char filename[], char value[]){
   FILE* fp;                              // create a file pointer fp
   fp = fopen(filename, "w+");            // open file for write/update
   fprintf(fp, "%s", value);             // send the value to the file
   fclose(fp);                           // close the file using fp
}

int main(int argc, char* argv[]){
   if(argc!=2){                          // program name is argument 1
      printf("Usage is makeLEDC and one of:\n");
      printf("   setup, on, off, status, or close\n");
      printf(" e.g. makeLEDC on\n");
      return 2;                          // invalid number of arguments
   }
   printf("Starting the makeLED program\n");
   if(strcmp(argv[1],"setup")==0){
      printf("Setting up the LED on the GPIO\n");
      writeGPIO(GPIO_SYSFS "export", GPIO_NUMBER);
      usleep(100000);                    // sleep for 100ms
      writeGPIO(GPIO4_PATH "direction", "out");
   }
   else if(strcmp(argv[1],"close")==0){
      printf("Closing the LED on the GPIO\n");
      writeGPIO(GPIO_SYSFS "unexport", GPIO_NUMBER);
   }
   else if(strcmp(argv[1],"on")==0){
      printf("Turning the LED on\n");
      writeGPIO(GPIO4_PATH "value", "1");
   }
   else if (strcmp(argv[1],"off")==0){
      printf("Turning the LED off\n");
      writeGPIO(GPIO4_PATH "value", "0");
   }
   else if (strcmp(argv[1],"status")==0){
      FILE* fp;          // see writeGPIO function above for description
      char line[80], fullFilename[100];
      sprintf(fullFilename, GPIO4_PATH "/value");
      fp = fopen(fullFilename, "rt");         // reading text this time
      while (fgets(line, 80, fp) != NULL){
         printf("The state of the LED is %s", line);
      }
      fclose(fp);
   }
   else{
      printf("Invalid command!\n");
   }
   printf("Finished the makeLED Program\n");
   return 0;
}
```

Build this program by calling the `./build` script in the /chp05/makeLED/ directory, and execute it using `./makeLEDC setup`, `./makeLEDC on`, etc.

The only topic that you have not seen before is the use of files in C, but the worked example should provide you with the information you need in the `writeLED()` function. The `FILE` pointer `fp` points to a description of the file that identifies the stream, the read/write position, and its state. The file is opened using the `fopen()` function that is defined in `stdio.h`, which returns a FILE pointer. In this case it is being opened for write/update (w+). The alternatives would be as follows: read (r), write (w), append (a), read/update (r+), and append/update (a+). If you are working with binary files, you append a b to the state; for example, "w+b" opens a new binary file for update (write and read). Also, "t" can be used to explicitly state that the file is in text format.

For a full reference of C functions available in the standard libraries, see www.cplusplus.com/reference/.

The C of C++

As discussed previously, the C++ language was built on the C language, adding support for OOP classes. However, a few other differences are immediately apparent when you start working with general C++ programming. Initially, the biggest change that you will notice is the use of input/output streams and the general use of strings.

First Example and Strings in C++

Listing 5-15 is the string example, rewritten to use the C++ string library.

Listing 5-15: chp05/overview/cppstrings.cpp

```
#include<iostream>
#include<sstream>    // to tokenize the string
//#include<cstring>  // how to include the C++ equivalent of a C header
using namespace std;

int main(){
   string a = "hello ";
   char temp[] = {'w','o','r','l','d','!','\0'};  //the \0 is important!
   string b(temp);

   a[0]='H';
   string c = a + b;
   cout << "The string c is: " << c << endl;
   cout << "The length of c is: " << c.length() << endl;

   int loc = c.find_first_of('w');
   c.replace(loc,1,1,'W');
   cout << "The string c is now: " << c << endl;

   if (string("cat")< string("dog")){
      cout << "cat comes before dog (lexiographically)\n";
```

```
  }
  c.insert(5," to the");
  cout << "The c string is now: " << c << endl;

  // tokenize string using spaces - could use Boost.Tokenizer
  // or C++11 to improve syntax. Using stringstream this time.
  stringstream ss;
  ss << c;  // put the c string on the stringstream
  string token;
  while(getline(ss, token, ' ')){
     cout << "Token: " << token << endl;
  }
  return 0;
}
```

Build this code by typing g++ **cppstrings.cpp -o cppstrings**. When executed, this code gives the same output as the cstrings.c example. Some aspects are more straightforward in C++ but there are some points worth mentioning.

The code uses the iostream and sstream header files, which are C++ headers. There is a concept called *namespaces* in C++ that enables a programmer to limit a function or class to a particular scope. In C++, all the standard library functions and classes are limited to the *standard namespace (std)*. You can explicitly identify that you want to use a class from the std namespace by using std::string. However, that is quite verbose. The alternative is to use the statement using namespace std;, which brings the entire namespace into your code. Do *not* do this in one of your C++ header files, because it will pollute the namespace for anyone who uses your header file.

The code uses cout, which is the standard output stream, and the output stream operator (<<) to display strings. There is an equivalent standard input stream (cin) and the input stream operator (>>). The output stream operator "looks to" its right and identifies the type of the data. It will display the data depending on its type, so there is no need for %s, %d, %p, and so on, because you would use in the printf() function. The endl stream manipulation function inserts a newline character and flushes the stream.

The string objects are manipulated in this example using + to append two strings, and < or == to compare two strings. These operators are essentially functions like append() and strcmp(). In C++, you can define what these operators do for your own data types (operator overloading).

Passing by Value, Pointer, and Reference

As you have seen with the code samples, functions enable us to write a section of code that can be called several times, from different locations in our code. There are three key ways of passing a value to a function:

▪ **Pass by value:** This will create a new variable (val in the following code example) and will store a copy of the value of the source variable (a) in this new variable. Any changes to the variable val will not have any impact on the source variable a. Pass by value can be used if you want to prevent the original data from being modified. However, a copy of the data has to be made, and if you are passing a large array of data, such as an image, copying will have a memory and computational cost. An alternative to pass by value is to pass by constant reference. In the following example, a is also passed as the second argument to the function by constant reference and is received as the value cr. The value cr can be read in the function, but it cannot be modified.

- **Pass by pointer:** You can pass a pointer to the source data. Any modifications to the value at the pointer (ptr) will affect the source data. The call to the function must pass an address (&b—the address of b).

- **Pass by reference:** In C++ you can pass a value by reference. The function determines whether an argument is to be passed by value or passed by reference, through the use of the ampersand symbol. In the following example, &ref indicates that the value c is to be passed by reference. Any modifications to ref in the function will affect the value of c.

Here is a function with all four examples (passing.cpp):

```
int afunction(int val, const int &cr, int *ptr, int &ref){
    val+=cr;
// cr+=val; // not allowed because it is constant
    *ptr+=10;
    ref+=10;
    return val;
}

int main(){
    int a=100, b=200, c=300;
    int ret;
    ret = afunction(a, a, &b, c);
    cout << "The value of a = " << a << endl;
    cout << "The value of b = " << b << endl;
    cout << "The value of c = " << c << endl;
    cout << "The return value is = " << ret << endl;
    return 0;
}
```

When executed, this code results in the following output:

```
pi@erpi ~/exploringrpi/chp05/overview $ ./passing
The value of a = 100
The value of b = 210
The value of c = 310
The return value is = 200
```

If you want to pass a value to a function that is to be modified by that function in C++, you can pass it by pointer or by reference. However, unless you are passing a value that could be NULL, or you need to reassign the pointer in the function (e.g., iterate over an array), always use pass by reference. Now you are ready to write the LED code in C++!

Flashing the LEDs Using C++ (non-OO)

The C++ LED flashing code is available in `makeLED.cpp` in the `/chp05/makeLED/` directory. As most of the code is very similar to the C example, it is not repeated here. However, it is worth displaying the following segment, which is used to open the file using the `fstream` file stream class. The output stream operator (`<<`) in this case sends the string to `fstream`, where the `c_str()` method returns a C++ `string` as a C `string`:

```
void writeLED(string filename, string value){
    fstream fs;
    string path(LED3_PATH);
    fs.open((path + filename).c_str(), fstream::out);
    fs << value;
    fs.close();
}
```

Overview of Object-Oriented Programming

The following discussion highlights a few core concepts that you have to understand before you can write object-oriented code. The discussion uses pseudo code as the concepts are relevant to all languages that support the OOP paradigm—including C++, Python, Lua tables, C#, Java, JavaScript, Perl, Ruby, the OOHaskell library, etc.

Classes and Objects

Think about the concept of a television: You do not have to remove the case to use it, because there are controls on the front and on the remote; you can still understand the television, even if it is connected to a games console; it is complete when you purchase it, with well-defined external requirements, such as power supply and signal inputs; and your television should not crash! In many ways that description captures the properties that should be present in a class.

A *class* is a description. It should describe a well-defined interface to your code; represent a clear concept; be complete and well documented; and be robust, with built-in error checking. Class descriptions are built using two building blocks:

- **States (or data):** The state values of the class.
- **Methods (or behavior):** How the class interacts with its data. Method names usually include an action verb (e.g., `setX()`).

For example, here is pseudo-code (i.e., not real C++ code but with similar syntax) for an illustrative `Television` class:

```
class Television{
    int channelNumber;
    bool on;
```

```
    powerOn() { on = true; }
    powerOff(){ on = false;}
    changeChannel(int x) { channelNumber = x; }
};
```

Therefore, the example `Television` class has two states and three methods. The benefit of this structure is that you have tightly bound the states and methods together within a class structure. The `powerOn()` method means nothing outside this class. In fact, you can write a `powerOn()` method in many different classes without worrying about naming collisions.

An *object* is the realization of the class description—an instance of a class. To continue the analogy, the `Television` class is the blueprint that describes how you would build a television, and a `Television` object is the physical realization of those plans into a physical television. In pseudo-code this realization might look like this:

```
void main(){
    Television dereksTV();
    Television johnsTV();
    dereksTV.powerOn();
    dereksTV.changeChannel(52);
    johnsTV.powerOn();
    johnsTV.changeChannel(1);
}
```

Therefore, `dereksTV` and `johnsTV` are instances of the `Television` class. Each has its own independent state, so changing the channel on `dereksTV` has no impact on `johnsTV`. To call a method, it must be prefixed by the object name on which it is to be called (e.g., `johnsTV.powerOn()`). Calling the `changeChannel()` method on `johnsTV` objects does not have any impact on the `dereksTV` object.

In this book, a class name generally begins with a capital letter, e.g., `Television`, and an object generally begins with a lowercase letter, e.g., `dereksTV`. This is consistent with the notation used in many languages, such as Java. Unfortunately, the C++ standard library classes (e.g., `string`, `sstream`) do not follow this naming convention.

Encapsulation

Encapsulation is used to hide the mechanics of an object. In the physical television analogy, encapsulation is provided by the box that protects the inner electronic systems. However, you still have the remote control that will have a direct impact on the way the inner workings function.

In OOP, you can decide what workings are to be hidden (e.g., TV electronics) using an *access specifier* keyword called *private*, and what is to be part of the *interface* (TV remote control) using the access specifier keyword *public*. It is good practice to always set the states of your class to be private, so that you can control how they are modified by public interface methods of your own design. For example, the pseudo-code might become the following:

```
class Television{
   private:
      int channelNumber;
      bool on;
      remodulate_tuner();
   public:
      powerOn() { on = true; }
      powerOff(){ on = false;}
      changeChannel(int x) {
         channelNumber = x;
         remodulate_tuner();
      }
};
```

Now the `Television` class has private state data (`on`, `channelNumber`) that is affected only by the public interface methods (`powerOn()`, `powerOff()`, `changeChannel()`) and a private implementation method `remodulate_tuner()` that cannot be called from outside the class.

There are a number of advantages of this approach: First, users of this class (another programmer) need not understand the inner workings of the `Television` class; they just need to understand the public interface. Second, the author of the `Television` class can modify and/or perfect the inner workings of the class without affecting other programmers' code.

Inheritance

Inheritance is a feature of OOP that enables building class descriptions from other class descriptions. Humans do this all the time; for example, if you were asked, "What is a duck?" you might respond with, "It's a bird that swims, and it has a bill instead of a beak." This description is reasonably accurate, but it assumes that the concept of a bird is also understood. Importantly, the description states that the duck has the *additional behavior* of swimming, but also that it has the *replacement behavior* of having a bill instead of a beak. You could loosely code this with pseudo-code as follows:

```
class Bird{
   public:
      void fly();
      void describe() { cout << "Has a beak and can fly"; }
};

class Duck: public Bird{    // Duck IS-A Bird
      Bill bill;
   public:
      void swim();
      void describe() { cout << "Has a bill and can fly and swim"; }
};
```

In this case, you can create an object of the `Duck` class:

```
int main(){
   Duck d;          // creates the Duck instance object d
```

```
    d.swim();        // specific to the Duck class
    d.fly();         // inherited from the parent Bird class
    d.describe();    // describe() is inherited and over-ridden in Duck
                     // so, "Has a bill and can fly and swim" would appear
}
```

The example here illustrates why inheritance is so important. You can build code by inheriting from, and adding to, a class description (e.g., `swim()`), or inheriting from a parent class and replacing a behavior (e.g., `describe()`) to provide a more specific implementation; this is called *overriding* a method, which is a type of *polymorphism* (multiple forms). Another form of polymorphism is called overloading, which means multiple methods can have the same name, in the same class, disambiguated by the compiler by having different parameter types.

You can check that you have an inheritance relationship by the *is-a* test; for example, a "duck is a bird" is valid, but a "bird is a duck" would be invalid because not all birds are ducks. This contrasts to the *is-a-part-of* relationship; for example, a "bill is a part of a duck." An *is-a-part-of* relationship indicates that the bill is a member/state of the class. Using this simple check can be very useful when the class relationships become complex.

You can also use pointers with objects of a class; for example, to dynamically allocate memory for two `Duck` objects in C++, you can use the following:

```
int main(){
    Duck *a = new Duck();
    Bird *b = new Duck(); // ptr of parent can point to a child object
    b->describe();        // will actually describe a duck (if virtual)
    //b->swim();          // not allowed! Bird does not 'know' swim()
}
```

Interestingly, the `Bird` pointer b is permitted to point at a `Duck` object. As the `Duck` class is a child of a `Bird` class, all the methods that the `Bird` pointer can call are "known" by the `Duck` object. Therefore the `describe()` method can be called. The arrow notation (`b->describe()`) is simply a neater way of writing `(*b).describe()` in C++. In this case, the `Bird` pointer b has the static type `Bird` and the dynamic type `Duck`.

One last point is that an additional access specifier called *protected* can be used through inheritance in C++. If you want to create a method or state in the parent class that you want to be available to the child class but you do not want to make public, use the protected access specifier.

NOTE I have notes publicly available at `ee402.eeng.dcu.ie` on these topics. In particular, Chapters 3 and 4 describe this topic in much greater detail, including material on abstract classes, destructors, multiple inheritance, friend functions, the standard template library (STL).

Object-Oriented LED Control in C++

These OOP concepts can now be applied to a real C++ application on the RPi by restructuring the functionally-oriented C++ code into a class called LED, which consists of states and methods. This code is slightly more verbose. However, the main difference is that the code presented in Listing 5-16 can simultaneously control many GPIOs using multiple objects of the one LED class. To that end, the example assumes that the circuit in Figure 5-1 for GPIO4 (Pin 7) is also replicated for GPIO17 (Pin 11).

Listing 5-16: chp05/makeLEDOOP/makeLEDs.cpp

```cpp
#include<iostream>
#include<fstream>
#include<string>
#include<unistd.h>           // for the microsecond sleep function
using namespace std;
#define GPIO          "/sys/class/gpio/"
#define FLASH_DELAY  50000 // 50 milliseconds

class LED{
    private:                // the following is part of the implementation
        string gpioPath;    // private states
        int     gpioNumber;
        void writeSysfs(string path, string filename, string value);
    public:                 // part of the public interface
        LED(int gpioNumber); // the constructor -- create the object
        virtual void turnOn();
        virtual void turnOff();
        virtual void displayState();
        virtual ~LED();      // the destructor -- called automatically
};

LED::LED(int gpioNumber){  // constructor implementation
    this->gpioNumber = gpioNumber;
    gpioPath = string(GPIO "gpio") + to_string(gpioNumber) + string("/");
    writeSysfs(string(GPIO), "export", to_string(gpioNumber));
    usleep(100000);         // ensure GPIO is exported
    writeSysfs(gpioPath, "direction", "out");
}

// This implementation function is "hidden" from outside the class
void LED::writeSysfs(string path, string filename, string value){
    ofstream fs;
    fs.open((path+filename).c_str());
    fs << value;
```

```
      fs.close();
}

void LED::turnOn(){
    writeSysfs(gpioPath, "value", "1");
}

void LED::turnOff(){
    writeSysfs(gpioPath, "value", "0");
}

void LED::displayState(){
    ifstream fs;
    fs.open((gpioPath + "value").c_str());
    string line;
    cout << "The current LED state is ";
    while(getline(fs,line)) cout << line << endl;
    fs.close();
}

LED::~LED(){   // The destructor unexports the sysfs GPIO entries
    cout << "Destroying the LED with GPIO number " << gpioNumber << endl;
    writeSysfs(string(GPIO), "unexport", to_string(gpioNumber));
}

int main(int argc, char* argv[]){   // the main function start point
    cout << "Starting the makeLEDs program" << endl;
    LED led1(4), led2(17);             // create two LED objects
    cout << "Flashing the LEDs for 5 seconds" << endl;
    for(int i=0; i<50; i++){           // LEDs will alternate
        led1.turnOn();                 // turn GPIO4 on
        led2.turnOff();                // turn GPIO17 off
        usleep(FLASH_DELAY);           // sleep for 50ms
        led1.turnOff();                // turn GPIO4 off
        led2.turnOn();                 // turn GPIO17 on
        usleep(FLASH_DELAY);           // sleep for 50ms
    }
    led1.displayState();               // display final GPIO4 state
    led2.displayState();               // display final GPIO17 state
    cout << "Finished the makeLEDs program" << endl;
    return 0;
}
```

This code uses the `to_string()` function that was introduced in C++11, and therefore the program can be built using the `-std=c++11` flag and executed by typing the following:

```
pi@erpi .../makeLEDOOP $ g++ makeLEDs.cpp -o makeLEDs -std=c++11
pi@erpi .../makeLEDOOP $ ./makeLEDs
Starting the makeLEDs program
Flashing the LEDs for 5 seconds
```

```
The current LED state is 0
The current LED state is 1
Finished the makeLEDs program
Destroying the LED with GPIO number 17
Destroying the LED with GPIO number 4
```

This code results in the LEDs attached to GPIO4 and GPIO17 flashing with alternate state for 5 seconds.

This code is structured as a single LED class with private states for the GPIO path and number, and a private implementation method writeSysfs(). The states and helper method are not accessible outside the class. The public interface methods are turnOn(), turnOff(), and displayState(). There are two more public methods:

- The first is a constructor, which enables you to initialize the state of the object. It is called by LED led(4) to create the object led of the LED class with GPIO number 4. This is similar to the way that you assign initial values to an int, e.g., int x=5;. A constructor must have the exact same name as the class name (LED in this case) and it cannot return anything, not even void.

- The last is a destructor (~LED()). Like a constructor, it must have the exact same name as the class name and is prefixed by the tilde (~) character. This method is called automatically when the object is being destroyed. You can see this happening in the code output as an output message is provided.

You can think of the keyword virtual as "allowing overriding to take place when an object is dynamically bound." It should always be there (except for the constructor), unless you know that there will definitely be no child class. Removing the virtual keyword will result in a slight improvement in the performance of your code.

The syntax void LED::turnOn(){...} is simply used to state that the turnOn() method is the one associated with the LED class. It is possible to have many classes in the one .cpp file, and it would be possible for two classes to have a turnOn() method; therefore, the explicit association allows you to inform the compiler of the correct relationship. I have written this code in a single file, because it is the first example. However, you will see in later examples that it is correct practice to break your code into *header* files (.h or .hpp) and *implementation* files (.cpp), because it allows for separate compilation, which greatly reduces the recompilation times for large-scale C++ projects.

Hopefully the layout of the C++ version of the LED control code is clear at this point. The advantage of this OOP version is that you now have a structure that can be built upon when you want to provide additional functionality. In Chapter 8, you see how you can build similar structures to wrap electronic modules such as accelerometers and temperature sensors, and how to use the encapsulation property of OOP to hide some of the more complex calculations from programmers that interface to the code.

Interfacing to the Linux OS

In Chapter 3, the Linux directory structure is discussed, and one of the directories discussed is the /proc directory—the process information virtual file system. It provides you with information about the runtime state of the kernel and it enables you to send control information to the kernel. In effect, it provides you with a file-based interface from user space to kernel space. There is a Linux kernel guide to the /proc file system at tiny.cc/erpi504. For example, if you type

```
pi@erpi /proc $ cat cpuinfo
processor    : 0
model name   : ARMv7 Processor rev 5 (v7l)
BogoMIPS     : 64.00
Features     : half thumb fastmult vfp edsp neon vfpv3 tls vfpv4
idiva idivt vfpd32 lpae evtstrm ...
Hardware     : BCM2709
Revision     : a01041
Serial       : 00000000ec729acf
```

it provides you with information on the CPU. Try some of the following: **cat uptime, cat interrupts, cat version** in the same directory. The example, chp05/proc/readUptime.cpp, provides an example program to read the system uptime and calculate the percentage of system idle time.

Many /proc entries can be read by programs that execute with regular user accounts, however many entries can only be written to by a program with superuser privileges. For example, entries in /proc/sys/kernel enable you to configure the parameters of a Linux kernel as it is executing.

You have to be careful with the consistency of the files in /proc. The Linux kernel provides for *atomic* operations—instructions that execute without interruption. Certain "files" within /proc (such as /proc/uptime) are totally atomic and cannot be interrupted while they are being read. However, other files such as /proc/net/tcp are only atomic within each row of the file, meaning that the file will change as it is being read, and therefore simply reading the file may not provide a consistent snapshot.

Glibc and Syscall

The Linux GNU C library, *glibc*, provides an extensive set of wrapper functions for system calls. It includes functionality for handling files, signals, mathematics, processes, users, and much more. See tiny.cc/erpi505 for a full description of the GNU C library.

It is much more straightforward to call a glibc function than it is to parse the equivalent /proc entries. Listing 5-17 provides a C++ example that uses the glibc passwd structure to find out information about the current user.

It also uses the `syscall()` function directly to determine the user's ID and to change the access permissions of a file—see the comments in the listing.

Listing 5-17: /exploringrpi/chp05/syscall/glibcTest.cpp

```cpp
#include<gnu/libc-version.h>
#include<sys/syscall.h>
#include<sys/types.h>
#include<pwd.h>
#include<cstdlib>
#include<sys/stat.h>
#include<iostream>
#include<signal.h>
#include<unistd.h>
using namespace std;

int main(){
    // Use helper functions to get system information:
    cout << "The GNU libc version is: " << gnu_get_libc_version() << endl;

    // Use glibc passwd struct to get user information - no error check!:
    struct passwd *pass = getpwuid(getuid());
    cout << "The current user's login is: " << pass->pw_name << endl;
    cout << "-> their full name is: " << pass->pw_gecos << endl;
    cout << "-> their user ID is: " << pass->pw_uid << endl;

    // You can use the getenv() function to get environment variables
    cout << "The user's shell is: " << getenv("SHELL") << endl;
    cout << "The user's path is: "  << getenv("PATH") << endl;

    // An example syscall to call a get the user ID -- see sys/syscall.h
    int uid = syscall(0xc7);
    cout << "Syscall gives their user ID as: " << uid << endl;

    // Call chmod directly -- type "man 2 chmod" for more information
    int ret = chmod("test.txt", 0666);
    // Can use syscall to do the same thing
    ret  = syscall(SYS_chmod, "test.txt", 0666);
    return 0;
}
```

This code can tested as follows, where you can see that the file permissions are altered by the program and the current user's information is displayed:

```
pi@erpi .../chp05/syscall $ ls -l test.txt
-rw-r--r-- 1 pi pi 0 Jun 16 01:56 test.txt
pi@erpi .../chp05/syscall $ sudo usermod -c "Exploring RPi" pi
pi@erpi .../chp05/syscall $ g++ glibcTest.cpp -o glibcTest
pi@erpi .../chp05/syscall $ ./glibcTest
The GNU libc version is: 2.19
The current user's login is: pi
```

```
-> their full name is: Exploring RPi
-> their user ID is: 1000
The user's shell is: /bin/bash
The user's path  is: /usr/local/sbin:/usr/local/bin:/usr/sbin...
Syscall gives their user ID as: 1000
pi@erpi .../chp05/syscall $ ls -l test.txt
-rw-rw-rw- 1 pi pi 0 Jun 16 01:56 test.txt
pi@erpi .../chp05/syscall $ chmod 644 test.txt
```

There are many glibc functions, but the `syscall()` function requires special attention. It performs a generalized system call using the arguments that you pass to the function. The first argument is a system call number, as defined in `sys/syscall.h`.[9] You will have to follow through the header includes files to find the definitions. Alternatively, you can use `syscalls.kernelgrok.com` to search for definitions (e.g., search for `SYS_getuid` and you will see that the register `eax` = `0xc7`, as used in Listing 5-17). Clearly it is better if you use `SYS_getuid` instead.

Improving the Performance of Python

Despite the popularity of Python on the RPi platform, it is clear from Table 5-1 that if you are to use it for certain embedded applications you may need enhanced performance. This section describes two alternative approaches for addressing the performance issue by investigating Cython, and an alternative approach of extending Python with C/C++ code.

Regardless of the approach taken, the first step is to set up your RPi so that you build a C/C++ module. You do this by installing the Python development package for the exact version of Python that you are using. Adapt the instructions in this section to use the library versions that you identify using the following steps:

```
pi@erpi ~ $ sudo apt install python-dev
pi@erpi ~ $ python --version
Python 2.7.9
pi@erpi ~ $ sudo apt install python3-dev
pi@erpi ~ $ python3 --version
Python 3.4.2
pi@erpi ~ $ ls /usr/lib/arm-linux-gnueabihf/libpython*.so
/usr/lib/arm-linux-gnueabihf/libpython2.7.so
/usr/lib/arm-linux-gnueabihf/libpython3.4m.so
```

Cython

Cython is an optimizing compiler for Python and a language that extends Python with C-style functionality. Typically, the Cython compiler uses your Python code

---

[9] This location is typically found underneath the path `/usr/include/arm-linux-gnue-abihf/` and links to other header files such as `asm/unistd.h` and `bits/syscall.h`.

to generate efficient C shared libraries, which you can then import into other Python programs. However, to get the maximum benefit from Cython you must adapt your Python code to use Cython-specific syntax. The top-performing Cython entry in Table 5.1 (i.e., at 2.74×) is available in `chp05/performance/cython_opt/nbody.pyx`). If you inspect the code you will see the use of `cdef` C variable declarations and various variable types (e.g., `double`, `int`), which indicates the removal of dynamic typing from the base Python version (`chp05/performance/n-body.py`).

A concise example is developed here to describe the first steps involved in adapting Python code to create Cython code. The code proves the relationship $\int_0^\pi \sin(x)dx = 2$ by applying a simple numeric integration approach, as provided in Listing 5-18.

Listing 5-18: /chp05/cython/test.py

```
from math import sin
def integrate_sin(a,b,N):
    dx = (b-a)/N
    sum = 0
    for i in range(0,N):
        sum += sin(a+i*dx)
    return sum*dx
```

The code in Listing 5-18 can be executed directly within the Python interpreter as follows (use `exec(open("test.py").read())` under Python3):

```
pi@erpi ~/exploringrpi/chp05/cython $ python
>>> from math import pi
>>> execfile('test.py')
>>> integrate_sin(0,pi,1000)
1.9999983550656624
>>> integrate_sin(0,pi,1000000)
1.9999999999984077
```

And a timer can be introduced to evaluate its performance:

```
>>> import timeit
>>> print(timeit.timeit("integrate_sin(0,3.14159,1000000)",setup="fr →
om __main__ import integrate_sin", number=10))
30.0536530018
>>> quit()
```

The `timeit` module allows you to determine the execution duration of a function call. In this example, the RPi 2 takes 30.0 seconds to evaluate the function 10 times, with N equal to 1,000,000.

It is possible to get a report on computationally costly dynamic Python behavior within your source code using:

```
pi@erpi ~/exploringrpi/chp05/cython $ sudo apt install cython
pi@erpi ~/exploringrpi/chp05/cython $ cython -a test.py
pi@erpi ~/exploringrpi/chp05/cython $ ls -l *.html
-rw-r--r-- 1 pi pi 31421 Jun 30 02:49 test.html
```

You can transfer this file to your desktop machine for viewing. The darker the shade of yellow on a line in the HTML report, the greater the level of dynamic behavior that is taking place on that line.

> **NOTE** If you have both Python2 and Python3 installed you may need to install Cython for Python3 as follows (this appears to hang, but leave it run as it can take longer than 20 minutes to install):
>
> ```
> pi@erpi ~ $ sudo apt install python3-pip
> pi@erpi ~ $ sudo pip3 install cython
> ```

Cython supports static type definitions, which greatly improves the performance of the code. The code can be adapted to test.pyx in Listing 5-19 where the types of the variables and return types are explicitly defined.

Listing 5-19: /chp05/cython/test.pyx

```
cdef extern from "math.h":
    double sin(double x)

cpdef double integrate_sin(double a, double b, int N):
    cdef double dx, s
    cdef int i
    dx = (b-a)/N
    sum = 0
    for i in range(0,N):
        sum += sin(a+i*dx)
    return sum*dx
```

An additional configuration file setup.py is required, as provided in Listing 5-20, so that Cython can compile the module correctly.

Listing 5-20: /chp05/cython/setup.py

```
from distutils.core import setup
from distutils.extension import Extension
from Cython.Distutils import build_ext

ext_modules = [Extension("test", ["test.pyx"])]
setup(
    name = 'random number sum application',
    cmdclass = {'build_ext' : build_ext },
    ext_modules = ext_modules
)
```

Python can use the setup.py configuration file to directly build the test.pyx file into C code (test.c), which is then compiled and linked to create a shared library (test.so). The library code can be executed directly within Python as follows, where the execution duration is 6.42 seconds—a fivefold improvement in performance:

```
pi@erpi .../chp05/cython $ python setup.py build_ext --inplace
running build_ext... cythoning test.pyx to test.c   ...
```

```
pi@erpi ~/exploringrpi/chp05/cython $ ls
build  setup.py  test.c  test.html  test.py  test.pyx  test.so
pi@erpi ~/exploringrpi/chp05/cython $ python
Python 2.7.9 (default, Mar  8 2015, 00:52:26)
>>> import timeit
>>> print(timeit.timeit("test.integrate_sin(0,3.14159,1000000)",setup="imp
ort test",number=10))
6.41986918449
```

It is also worth mentioning that Cython can be used to build a Python program into a standalone executable. Once an execution starting point is added to the Cython file (the equivalent of `main()`) then the following steps can be used to compile the Cython code into a native binary executable:

```
pi@erpi .../chp05/cython_exe $ tail -n 3 test.pyx
if __name__ == '__main__':
   integral = integrate_sin(0, 3.14159, 1000000)
   print("The integral of sin(x) in the range 0..PI is: ", integral)
pi@erpi .../chp05/cython_exe $ cython --embed test.pyx
pi@erpi .../chp05/cython_exe $ gcc test.c -I/usr/include/python3.4/
-lpython3.4m -o test -lutil -ldl -lpthread -lm
pi@erpi ~/exploringrpi/chp05/cython_exe $ ./test
('The integral of sin(x) in the range 0..PI is: ', 1.9999999999906055)
```

Cython goes a long way to addressing performance concerns that you may have in using Python. However, there is a significant learning curve in adapting Python code for efficiency, which has only been touched upon here. An alternative approach is to write custom C/C++ code modules that add to the capability of Python, rather than using Cython at all.

Extending Python with C/C++

It is possible to call compiled C/C++ code directly from within Python programs. This capability enables you to enhance the performance of Python programs using C/C++ code modules that can be called just like regular Python functions.

The Python/C API

This workflow for the Python/C API is reasonably straightforward and is best explained with worked examples. There are examples available for Python2 and Python3 in the `/chp05/python2_C/` and `/chp05/python3_C/` directories, because there were significant changes on module development in the move to Python3.

The difficult step is to develop a C/C++ module that is structured so that it is compatible with Python. Listing 5-21 provides a template example for Python3 that you can use to develop your own modules. It consists of two simple functions `hello()` and `integrate()`. The `hello()` function expects a string argument, for example `Derek`, which it displays in the form `Hello Derek!`. The `integrate()` function has the same form as the `integrate_sin()` function in Listing 5-19. The Python2 example has identical functionality but slightly different syntax.

Listing 5-21: chp05/python3_C/ERPiModule.cpp

```cpp
#include <Python.h>
#include <math.h>

/** A hello() function that can be called from Python3:
 *   @param self A pointer to the calling PyObject
 *   @param args the arguments passed from the Python code
 *   @return All objects types extend PyObject -- return a ptr */
static PyObject* hello(PyObject* self, PyObject* args){
   const char* name;
   if (!PyArg_ParseTuple(args, "s", &name)){
      printf("Failed to parse the string name!\n");
      Py_RETURN_NONE;
   }
   printf("Hello %s!\n", name);
   Py_RETURN_NONE;
}

/** integrate() function to integrate sin(x) over a range a..b*/
static PyObject* integrate(PyObject* self, PyObject* args){
   double a, b, dx, sum=0;
   int N;
   // expecting two doubles and an int from Python
   if (!PyArg_ParseTuple(args, "ddi", &a, &b, &N)){
      printf("Failed to parse the arguments!\n");
      Py_RETURN_NONE;
   }
   dx = (b-a)/N;
   for(int i=0; i<N; i++){
      sum += sin((a+i)*dx);
   }
   return Py_BuildValue("d", sum*dx); // send PyObject back to Python
}

/** An array of structures, where each structure has four fields:
 *   ml_name  (char *)      the name of the function
 *   ml_meth  (PyCFunction) a pointer to the C function above
 *   ml_flags (int)         flag bits - state how call is constructed
 *   ml_doc   (char *)      describes the function
 * hello() and integrate() functions exposed in this example.    */
static PyMethodDef ERPiMethods[] = {
   {"hello", hello, METH_VARARGS, "Displays Hello Derek!"},
   {"integrate", integrate, METH_VARARGS, "Integrates the sin(x) fn."},
   {NULL, NULL, 0, NULL}          // must end with a null structure
};

/** A structure that defines the module structure */
static struct PyModuleDef moduledef = {
    PyModuleDef_HEAD_INIT,     // m_base -- always the same
    "ERPiModule",              // m_name -- module name
    "Module for Exploring RPi", // m_doc -- Docstring for the module
    -1,                        // m_size -- has global state
    ERPiMethods,               // m_methods -- module-level functions
```

```
    NULL,                    // m_reload -- currently unused
    NULL,                    // m_traverse -- function to call GC traversal
    NULL,                    // m_clear -- function to call during GC clearing
    NULL,                    // m_free -- function to call during deallocation
};

/** Initialization function for the module */
PyMODINIT_FUNC PyInit_ERPiModule(void){
    return PyModule_Create(&moduledef);
}
```

The C/C++ code in Listing 5-21 can be built to a shared object file using the following call (the build command is on one line):

```
pi@erpi ~/exploringrpi/chp05/python3_C $ g++ -O3 ERPiModule.cpp -shared
-I/usr/include/python3.4/ -lpython3.4m -o ERPiModule.so
pi@erpi ~/exploringrpi/chp05/python3_C $ ls -l *.so
-rwxr-xr-x 1 pi pi 7168 Jun 29 00:00 ERPiModule.so
```

Once the shared module is in place it can be imported by a Python program and the two functions `hello()` and `integrate()` can be invoked directly. Listing 5-22 provides an example Python3 program that calls the two functions and displays the result of the `integrate()` call.

Listing 5-22: chp05/python3_C/test.py

```
#!/usr/bin/python3
import ERPiModule
print("*** Start of the Python program")
print("--> Calling the C hello() function passing Derek")
ERPiModule.hello("Derek")
print("--> Calling the C integrate() function")
val = ERPiModule.integrate(0, 3.14159, 1000000)
print("*** The result is: ", val)
print("*** End of the Python program")
```

The Python script in Listing 5-22 can be executed as follows:

```
pi@erpi ~/exploringrpi/chp05/python3_C $ ./test.py
*** Start of the Python program
--> Calling the C hello() function passing Derek
Hello Derek!
--> Calling the C integrate() function
*** The result is:  1.9999999999906055
*** End of the Python program
```

Finally, the performance of the code is impressive, taking 3.23 seconds for the C/C++ integration test under both Python2 and Python3:

```
pi@erpi ~/exploringrpi/chp05/python3_C $ python3
>>> import timeit
>>> print(timeit.timeit("ERPiModule.integrate(0,3.14159,1000000)",setup="imp
ort ERPiModule",number=10))
3.2270326350117102
```

Boost.Python

An alternative approach to extending Python with C/C++ is to use a wrapper that binds C/C++ and Python called *Boost.Python*, which essentially wraps the Python/C API. In addition, it simplifies the syntax and provides support for calls to C++ objects. You can search for the latest release and install Boost.Python on your RPi using the following steps (~270 MB):

```
pi@erpi ~ $ apt-cache search libboost-python
libboost-python1.54-dev - Boost.Python Library development files ...
pi@erpi ~ $ sudo apt install libboost-python1.54-dev
```

A C++ program can be developed, as in Listing 5-23, that uses the Boost. Python library and its special `BOOST_PYTHON_MODULE(name)` macro that declares the Python module initialization functions—essentially replacing the verbose syntax that is present in Listing 5-21.

Listing 5-23: /chp05/boostPython/erpi.cpp

```cpp
#include<string>
#include<boost/python.hpp>          // .hpp convention for c++ headers
using namespace std;                // just like cpp for source files

namespace exploringrpi{             // keep the global namespace clean

    string hello(string name) {     // e.g., returns "Hello Derek!"
        return ("Hello " + name + "!");
    }

    double integrate(double a, double b, int n) {     // same as before
        double sum=0, dx = (b-a)/n;
        for(int i=0; i<n; i++){  sum += sin((a+i)*dx);  }
        return sum*dx;
    }
}

BOOST_PYTHON_MODULE(erpi){          // the module is called erpi
    using namespace boost::python;  // require the boost.python namespace
    using namespace exploringrpi;   // bring in custom namespace
    def("hello", hello);            // make hello() visible to Python
    def("integrate", integrate);    // make integrate() also visible
}
```

The code can be built into a shared library as before. Make sure to include the `boost_python` library in the build options:

```
pi@erpi ~/exploringrpi/chp05/boostPython $ g++ -O3 erpi.cpp -shared -I/usr/ →
include/python2.7/ -lpython2.7 -lboost_python -o erpi.so
pi@erpi ~/exploringrpi/chp05/boostPython $ ls -l *.so
-rwxr-xr-x 1 pi pi 27400 Jul 18 18:38 erpi.so
```

The library can then be used by a Python script, such as that in Listing 5-24.

Listing 5-24: /chp05/boostPython/test.py

```
#!/usr/bin/python
# A Python program that calls C program code
import erpi

print "Start of the Python program"
print erpi.hello("Derek")
val = erpi.integrate(0, 3.14159, 1000000)
print "The integral result is: ", val
print "End of the Python program"
```

The script in Listing 5-24 can be executed, resulting in the following output:

```
pi@erpi ~/exploringrpi/chp05/boostPython $ ./test.py
Start of the Python program
Hello Derek!
The integral result is:  1.99999999999
End of the Python program
```

In addition, the `timeit` test results in ~3.225 s, which is consistent with the Python/C API performance. Despite its large footprint, Boost.Python is the recommended approach for integrating C/C++ and Python code due to its performance, simplified syntax, and support for C++ classes. Therefore, Boost.Python is used again in later chapters. See `tiny.cc/erpi506` for further details.

Summary

After completing this chapter, you should be able to do the following:

- Describe the multitude of issues that would impact on your choice of programming languages to use in building physical-computing applications for the RPi.

- Write basic scripting language program code on the RPi that interfaces to an LED, which is attached to an RPi GPIO.

- Compare and contrast scripting, hybrid, and compiled programming languages, and their application to the RPi.

- Write C code examples that interface to the RPi's GPIOs.

- Describe the principles of OOP programming, and write C++ classes that provide program structure for physical-computing applications.

- Write C/C++ code that can interface directly to the Linux OS.

- Write C/C++ modules that can be called directly from Python.

Further Reading

Most of the sections in this chapter contain links to the relevant websites for further reading and reference materials. Here is a list of some books on programming that are relevant to the materials in this chapter:

- Bjarne Stroustrup, *The C++ Programming Language*, 4th ed., Addison-Wesley Professional, 2013, 978-0-321-56384-2.
- Scott Meyers, *Effective Modern C++*, O'Reilly Media, 2014, 978-1-4919-0399-5.
- Bill Lubanovic, *Introducing Python: Modern Computing in Simple Packages*, O'Reilly Media, 2014, 978-1-4493-5936-2.
- Michael Kerrisk, *The Linux Programming Interface*, No Starch Press, 2010, 978-1-59327-220-3.
- Derek Molloy, "EE402: Object-Oriented Programming Module Notes," `ee402.eeng.dcu.ie`.

Bibliography

- debian.org (2013, December 1). The Computer Language Benchmarks Game. Retrieved March 7, 2014, from Debian.org: `benchmarksgame. alioth.debian.org`
- Hundt, R. (2011). Loop Recognition in C++/Java/Go/Scala. Proceedings of Scala Days 2011. Mountain View, CA.: `www.scala-lang.org`.
- Oracle (2014, March 10). Java SE Embedded FAQ. Retrieved March 10, 2014, from Oracle.Com: `www.oracle.com/technetwork/java/embedded/ resources/se-embeddocs/`
- Stroustrup, B. (1998, October 14). International standard for the C++ programming language published. Retrieved March 18, 2014, from stroustrup.com: `www.stroustrup.com/iso_pressrelease2.html`

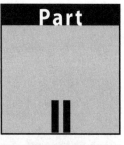

Part

II

Interfacing, Controlling, and Communicating

In This Part

Interfacing to the Raspberry Pi Input/Outputs

This chapter integrates the Linux, programming, and electronics groundwork from earlier chapters to show you how to build circuits and write programs that interface to the Raspberry Pi's single-wire inputs and outputs. In this chapter, you will see practical examples that explain how to use general-purpose input/outputs (GPIOs) to interface to different types of electronic circuits. GPIO interfacing is first performed using sysfs to ensure that you have skills that are transferrable to other embedded Linux devices. Next, memory-mapped approaches are investigated that have impressive performance, but are largely specific to the RPi platform. Finally, the wiringPi library of C functions is discussed in detail. It uses sysfs and memory-mapped approaches to provide a custom GPIO interfacing library for the RPi platform that is very accessible. Examples are provided of how it can be used to communicate with one-wire sensors, to generate pulse-width modulated (PWM) signals, and to generate high-frequency timing signals. Finally, there is a brief discussion on the impact of udev rules and Linux permissions on GPIO interfacing.

Equipment Required for This Chapter:

- Raspberry Pi (ideally an RPi 2/3 for the multicore examples)
- Components from Chapter 4 (e.g., button, LED, optocoupler)
- An Aosong AM230x humidity and temperature sensor
- A generic servo motor (e.g., Hitec HS-422)

Further details on this chapter are available at www.exploringrpi.com/chapter6/.

Introduction

At this point in the book, you have seen how to administer a Linux system, write high-level programming code, and build basic, but realistic, electronic interfacing circuits. It is now time to bring those different concepts together so that you can build software applications that run on Linux to control, or take input from, electronics circuits of your own design.

It is possible to interface electronic circuits and modules to the RPi in several different ways. For example:

- **Using the GPIOs on the RPi's GPIO header:** This provides you with versatility in terms of the type of circuits that you can connect and is the subject of this chapter.

- **Using the buses (e.g., I²C, SPI) or UART on the GPIO header:** Bus connections enable communications to complex modules such as sensors and displays. This topic is the subject of Chapter 8.

- **Connecting USB modules (e.g., keyboards, Wi-Fi):** If Linux drivers are available, many different electronic device types can be connected to the RPi. Examples are provided in later chapters.

- **Communicating through Ethernet/Wi-Fi/Bluetooth to electronics modules:** It is possible to build network-attached sensors that communicate to the RPi using network connections. Chapter 12 first introduces, and Chapter 13 then focuses on, this topic.

The next step in working with the RPi is to connect it to circuits using the GPIO expansion header. The background material of earlier chapters is very important, because this is a surprisingly complex topic that will take some time to get used to, particularly the memory-mapped I/O discussion. However, code and example circuits are provided throughout this chapter that you can use to help you build your own interfacing circuits.

Figure 6-1 provides you with a first view of the functionality of the inputs and outputs on the GPIO header. Many of these pins are multiplexed, meaning they have more functions (or ALT modes) than what is displayed in the figure. This figure illustrates the most commonly used functionality.

		3.3V	1	2	5V		
I2C1 SDA	pull-up	GPIO2	3	4	5V		
I2C1 SCL	pull-up	GPIO3	5	6	GND		
GPCLK0	pull-up	GPIO4	7	8	GPIO14	pull-down	TXD0
		GND	9	10	GPIO15	pull-down	RXD0
	pull-down	GPIO17	11	12	GPIO18	pull-down	PWM0
	pull-down	GPIO27	13	14	GND		
	pull-down	GPIO22	15	16	GPIO23	pull-down	
		3.3V	17	18	GPIO24	pull-down	
SPI0_MOSI	pull-down	GPIO10	19	20	GND		
SPI0_MISO	pull-down	GPIO9	21	22	GPIO25	pull-down	
SPI0_CLK	pull-down	GPIO11	23	24	GPIO8	pull-up	SPI_CE0_N
		GND	25	26	GPIO7	pull-up	SPI_CE1_N
	pull-up	ID_SD	27	28	ID_SC	pull-up	
GPCLK1	pull-up	GPIO5	29	30	GND		
GPCLK2	pull-up	GPIO6	31	32	GPIO12	pull-down	PWM0
PWM1	pull-down	GPIO13	33	34	GND		
	pull-down	GPIO19	35	36	GPIO16	pull-down	
	pull-down	GPIO26	37	38	GPIO20	pull-down	GPCLK0
		GND	39	40	GPIO21	pull-down	GPCLK1

Figure 6-1: The RPi GPIO header (RPi 2/3)

General-Purpose Input/Outputs

This chapter describes how you can interface to the RPi's GPIO header pins in the following ways:

- **Digital output:** How you can use a GPIO to turn an electrical circuit on or off. The example uses an LED, but the principles hold true for any circuit type; for example, you could even use a relay to turn on/off high-powered devices. Circuits are provided to ensure that you do not draw too much current from a GPIO. Code examples are developed to make software interfacing straightforward and efficient.

- **Digital input:** How you can read in a digital output from an electrical circuit into a software application running under Linux. Circuits are provided to ensure that this is performed safely.

- **Analog output:** How you can use PWM to output a proportional signal that can be used as an analog voltage level or as a control signal for certain types of devices, such as servo motors.

- **Analog input:** The RPi does not have a dedicated analog-to-digital converter (ADC). However, this capability can be added using low-cost bus devices, as described in Chapter 9.

This chapter assumes that you have read Chapter 4—in particular, switching circuits using FETs/BJTs and the use of pull-up/down resistors.

> **WARNING**   Be especially careful when working with the GPIO header, because incorrect connections can, and will, destroy your board. Test all new circuits to ensure that their voltage *and* current levels are within range before connecting them to the GPIO header. Also, follow the advice on interfacing circuits using FETs and optocouplers, as described in this chapter. Chapter 8 provides additional advice on interfacing to circuits that use different logic voltage levels.

GPIO Digital Output

The example output configuration illustrated in Figure 6-2(a) uses a GPIO connected to a FET to switch a circuit. As described in Chapter 4, when a voltage is applied to the gate input of a FET, it will close the virtual drain-source "switch," enabling current to flow from the 5 V supply through the 220 Ω current limiting resistor, to GND through a lighting LED. This circuit is different from that in Figure 5-1(a), because a 5 V source is used in place of a 3.3 V source so as to illustrate the switching capability of this circuit configuration. Figure 6-2(b) illustrates an equivalent BJT circuit. Note that both circuits use a larger current limiting resistor (220 Ω versus 120 Ω) to protect the LED.

The advantage of these types of circuit is that they can be applied to many on/off digital output applications, because the BS270 FET datasheet indicates that it can drive a constant current of up to 400 mA (and a pulsed current of up to 2 A) across the drain-source at up to 60 V. However, at a gate voltage of 3.3 V, the BS270 can only switch a maximum drain current of approximately 130 mA. The high input impedance of the gate means that you can use two (or indeed more) BS270s in parallel to double the maximum current to approximately 260 mA at the same gate voltage. Similarly, the BC547 can drive a collector current (I_C) up to 100 mA at a collector-emitter voltage (V_{CE}) of less than 45 V (the total power dissipated, $P \approx V_{CE} \times I_C$, must also be less than 500 mW—i.e., if $V_{CE} = 10$ V then $I_C \leq 50$ mA).

The maximum current is also limited if you are sourcing the supply current from the RPi GPIO header. The 3.3 V header pins (1 and 17) can together supply a maximum of ~50 mA. The 5 V header pins (2 and 4) can together safely supply approximately 200 mA–300 mA. For greater currents, you need an external supply, but you have to be especially careful that your circuit does not apply power to the GPIO pins while the RPi is powered down.

RPi GPIOs are 3.3 V tolerant and you should only source and sink approximately 2 mA–3 mA from or to each pin. Each pin is capable of sourcing/sinking slightly larger currents if GPIO utilization is sparse, but it is best to avoid such a dependency. In Figure 6-2, it is safe to use the 5 V supply to drive the LED, because the drain-source circuit of the FET is never connected to the gate input. You will also notice that, unlike the example in Chapter 4, there is no resistor on the gate of the FET. It is not necessary in this particular case, because an *internal* pull-down resistor is enabled within the RPi by default on this pin. This is discussed shortly.

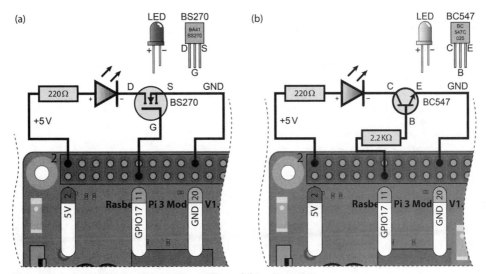

Figure 6-2: A 5 V LED circuit (a) using a FET, and (b) using a BJT

Once the circuit is built and attached to the RPi, you can boot the board and control the LED using a Linux terminal and sysfs as described in Chapter 5. Figure 6-3 displays the actual voltages and currents that are exhibited by the two circuits. You can see that there is a negligible level of current sourced from GPIO17 by the FET circuit in Figure 6-3(a), and the gate voltage is dropped across the gate-source pins of the FET. In Figure 6-3(b) the 2.2 kΩ resistor drives a small current into the base of the transistor, $I_B = (3.3\,V - 0.77\,V) / 2.2\,k\Omega$, that switches on the transistor, thus lighting the LED. The 1.15 mA current is well within tolerance for an RPi GPIO.

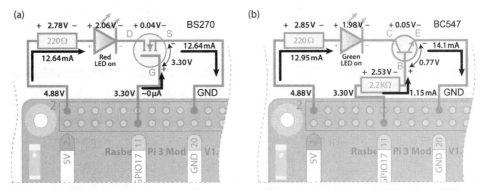

Figure 6-3: The voltage and current characteristics of the circuits in Figure 6-2 (a) using a FET, and (b) using a BJT

To test the performance of this approach, a short bash shell script to toggle the LED as quickly as possible is provided in Listing 6-1. This does not result in a visible "blink," because the LED is flashing faster than a human can observe; however, toggling can be visualized using an oscilloscope.

Listing 6-1: /chp06/flash_script/flash.sh

```bash
#!/bin/bash
#  Short script to toggle a GPIO pin at the highest frequency possible
echo 17 > /sys/class/gpio/export
sleep 0.5
echo "out" > /sys/class/gpio/gpio17/direction
COUNTER=0
while [ $COUNTER -lt 100000 ]; do
    echo 1 > /sys/class/gpio/gpio17/value
    let COUNTER=COUNTER+1
    echo 0 > /sys/class/gpio/gpio17/value
done
echo 17 > /sys/class/gpio/unexport
```

You can see from the oscilloscope trace in Figure 6-4 that the output is cycling every 0.36 ms approximately, equating to a frequency of approximately 2.78 kHz, which is not very high for an embedded controller. The period is reasonably constant, which is largely due to the fact that this Linux kernel utilizes kernel preemption options—as discussed later in this chapter. In addition, the `top` command (executed in another Linux terminal window) indicates that the CPU load for this script is consuming 100% of a single core (on the RPi 2/3 execute **top** and press 1 to see the individual core utilization). You can also see that the current driving the LED is 12 mA–13 mA, which is large enough to damage the RPi if this current were simultaneously sourced from, or sinked to, several GPIOs.

A C++ class is presented in the next section that can be used to control a GPIO using sysfs and it achieves higher switching frequencies, but with similar CPU loads. If you require a high-frequency periodic switching signal, PWM or general-purpose clocks, which are discussed later in this chapter, can be used. PWM can achieve frequencies of 1 MHz or higher, without a significant CPU load. However, many applications require the activation of a switched circuit at low frequencies (e.g., controlling motors, smart home control), and in such cases this configuration is perfectly valid.

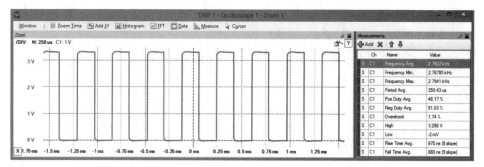

Figure 6-4: Scope display of the GPIO output caused by the flash.sh script

GPIO Digital Input

The next application is to use a GPIO as a *digital input,* which enables software written on the RPi to read the state of a pushbutton or any other logic high/low input. This task is first performed using a Linux terminal, and then it is performed using C/C++ code. The LED circuit should be left connected when building this input circuit because both circuits are reused throughout this chapter.

The circuit shown in Figure 6-5(a) consists of a normally open pushbutton (SPST) that is connected to the RPi Pin 13 (GPIO27). You will notice that, having discussed the need for pull-up or pull-down resistors on pushbutton switches in Chapter 4, none are present in this circuit. This is not accidental, because Pin 13 on the GPIO header is connected by default to GND using an internal pull-down resistor. This is discussed shortly. Use the following steps to read the state of the button (i.e., either 0 or 1) using a Linux terminal:

```
pi@erpi /sys/class/gpio $ echo 27 > export
pi@erpi /sys/class/gpio $ cd gpio27
pi@erpi /sys/class/gpio/gpio27 $ ls
active_low  device  direction  edge  subsystem  uevent  value
pi@erpi /sys/class/gpio/gpio27 $ echo in > direction
pi@erpi /sys/class/gpio/gpio27 $ cat direction
in
pi@erpi /sys/class/gpio/gpio27 $ cat value
0
pi@erpi /sys/class/gpio/gpio27 $ cat value
1
```

Therefore, the value is 1 when the button is pressed and 0 when it is released. GPIO27 sinks approximately 64 µA when the button is pressed. Each time you type cat value, you are *polling* the input to check the value. The downside of this approach is that you will not identify a change in the value of the input unless you constantly poll the value state.

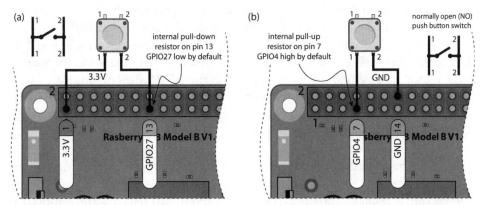

Figure 6-5: Connecting a pushbutton to the RPi (a) internal pull-down resistor, and (b) internal pull-up resistor

Interestingly, if you connect nothing to GPIO4, which is Pin 7, and enter the same sequence of commands, you get a different output:

```
pi@erpi /sys/class/gpio $ echo 4 > export
pi@erpi /sys/class/gpio $ cd gpio4/
pi@erpi /sys/class/gpio/gpio4 $ cat direction
out
pi@erpi /sys/class/gpio/gpio4 $ echo in > direction
pi@erpi /sys/class/gpio/gpio4 $ cat value
1
pi@erpi /sys/class/gpio/gpio4 $ cat value
0
```

With nothing connected to this input, it registers a value of 1. That is because this input is connected via an internal *pull-up* resistor to the 3.3 V line. Figure 6-5(b) illustrates the correct button wiring configuration for such a GPIO. Note that this GPIO input has the opposite polarity to the circuit in Figure 6-5(a); GPIO4 is low when the button is pressed, whereas GPIO27 is high when the button is pressed. It should be clear at this stage that you need to understand the GPIO configuration, including these internal resistors, to use the GPIO pins properly.

Internal Pull-Up and Pull-Down Resistors

The importance of pull-up and pull-down resistors is discussed in some detail in Chapter 4. They ensure that open switches do not allow a GPIO input to float. Such external resistors are typically "strong" pull-up/down resistors in that they "strongly" tie the input to a high/low value using relatively low resistance values (e.g., 5 kΩ–10 kΩ). The RPi has "weak" *internal pull-up* and *internal pull-down* resistors that can be configured using memory-based GPIO control techniques that are described later in this chapter.

You can physically check whether an internal pull-up or pull-down resistor is enabled on a pin by connecting a 100 kΩ resistor between the pin and GND (as shown in Figure 6-6(a), where the shaded area represents functionality that is internal to the RPi's SoC), and then between the pin and the 3.3 V supply (as shown in Figure 6-6(b)). If you connect a 100 kΩ (the one I used had an actual value of 98.5 kΩ) to Pin 16 and measure the voltage across it, you will see that the voltage drop is 0 V when the resistor is connected to GND, and I measured 2.226 V (not 3.3 V) when it was connected to the 3.3 V rail. This indicates that there is an internal pull-down resistor enabled, and the combination of these resistors is behaving like a voltage divider circuit. You can estimate the value of the internal pull-down resistor as in Figure 6-6(b).

Clearly, Pin 16, which is GPIO23, has an internal pull-down resistor enabled, but if you perform the same test on Pin 7, which is GPIO4, you will get a completely different response. When you connect the resistor as shown in Figure 6-6(a) you will get a voltage drop of ~2.213 V across the 100 kΩ resistor, and almost 0 V when you connect it as in Figure 6-6(b). That is because Pin 7 has an internal pull-up resistor enabled. Performing the same calculations gives an internal pull-up resistor value of approximately 48.6 kΩ.

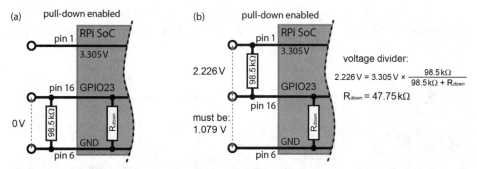

Figure 6-6: Internal pull-down resistor value determination, using a 100 kΩ resistor connected (a) from the GPIO pin to GND, and (b) from the GPIO pin to the 3.3 V supply

You need to factor these resistor values into the behavior of your input/output circuits, and you need to be able to alter the internal resistor configuration in certain circumstances. For example, you may even want to turn them off for certain circuits. Also, note that Pin 3 (GPIO2) and Pin 5 (GPIO3) have two permanent onboard 1.8 kΩ "strong" pull-up resistors attached on the PCB (R23 and R24). This is discussed in Chapter 8.

As well as configuring pins to have either a pull-up or a pull-down resistor configuration, there are also different modes for each pin. This is called the ALT mode for the pin. Later in this chapter, Figure 6-11 provides a full list of alternative modes for each of the GPIO header pins.

Interfacing to Powered DC Circuits

The RPi itself provides the power required for the output and input circuits that are illustrated in Figures 6-2 and 6-5 respectively. The current that can be sourced or sinked by these circuits is limited by the RPi specifications. Therefore, it is often necessary to interface to circuits that are powered by an external supply.

You must be very careful when interfacing the RPi to circuits that have their own power supply (e.g., high-powered LEDs, car alarms, garage openers). For example, you should design the circuit so that it does not attempt to source current from, or sink current to the RPi GPIOs while the board is powered off. In addition, it would be ideal if you could avoid sharing a GND connection between the circuit and the RPi in case something goes wrong with the circuit or its power supply.

A good solution is to utilize low-cost optocouplers, such as those described in Chapter 4 to design circuits in which there is no electrical connection whatsoever between the RPi and the externally powered circuit. Figure 6-7 illustrates an output circuit with an NPN transistor that is placed in a *Darlington pair* arrangement with the optocoupler to switch on or off the externally powered circuit load. A 5 V external power supply is used in this example, but a greater DC supply voltage can be used. In addition, the maximum switching current is limited by the transistor characteristics (e.g., of a BC547), not by the optocoupler's output current I_c level.

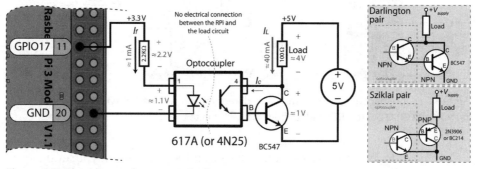

Figure 6-7: The optocoupler output circuit

The 617A optocoupler's current transfer ratio (CTR) of ≈0.5 when $I_f = 1$ mA (i.e., when GPIO17 is high) results in an output current of $I_c = 0.5$ mA, which enters the base of the BC547 transistor. This small current switches on the BC547 transistor, which in turn supplies a current of $I_L = 40$ mA to the resistive load in this example. One downside of this configuration is that the voltage supply to the load is reduced by the V_{CE} of the Darlington pair (≈1 V). An alternative to this arrangement is to use a *Sziklai pair* as illustrated in Figure 6-7, in which a PNP transistor is connected to the optocoupler output. Both arrangements limit the switching frequency capability of your output circuit (typically to the tens of kilohertz range). Unlike the 617A, the 4N25 exposes the base of the optocoupler receiver. This allows for the placement of additional base emitter resistors to improve the circuit's frequency response.

An optocoupler can also be connected to a GPIO to receive an input from an externally powered DC circuit, as illustrated in Figure 6-8. Importantly, this circuit can be adapted for any DC supply voltage and it will not sink any current to the GPIO input when the RPi is powered off. You must choose a resistor value for the input side of the optocoupler to limit the forward current of the diode ($I_{f(max)} < 60$ mA for the 617A/4N25[1]).

GPIO27 is configured with an internal pull-down resistor by default, so it has a low state when the button is not pressed. The RPi GPIO input circuit in Figure 6-5(a) sinks 64 µA to GPIO27 when the button is pressed. Similarly, this is

---

[1] See tiny.cc/erpi603 and tiny.cc/erpi604.

the maximum current that will be sinked by this circuit (when I_f and V_f exceed minimal levels for the optocoupler). This circuit can be adapted to handle a varying DC input voltage (within a range) by using a voltage regulator to maintain a value of I_f that is less than $I_{f(max)}$ for the chosen optocoupler.

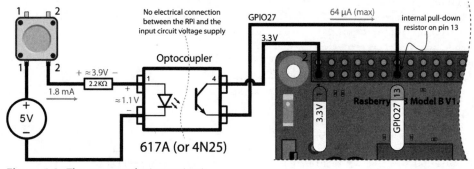

Figure 6-8: The optocoupler input circuit

C++ Control of GPIOs Using sysfs

A C++ class has been written that wraps the sysfs GPIO functionality on the RPi to make it easier to use. The importance of this approach is that it is transferrable to any embedded Linux device. Later in this chapter, memory-mapped approaches are investigated, but they are specific to the RPi.

Listing 6-2 provides the class definition, which lists the available class I/O functionality. The implementation of this functionality is similar to the code in Chapter 5 for the control of an external LED. The full listing is in /chp06/GPIO/GPIO.h and GPIO.cpp.

The C++ code is separated into header (.h) and implementation (.cpp) files, and the process of building applications in this form is called *separate compilation*. Separate compilation makes building large projects much more efficient, but it can be difficult to manage all of the individual files. The next chapter introduces the Eclipse integrated development environment (IDE) for cross-compilation, to make this process seamless.

Listing 6-2: /chp06/GPIO/GPIO.h

```
...
#define GPIO_PATH "/sys/class/gpio/"

namespace exploringRPi {             // all code is within a custom namespace
enum GPIO_DIRECTION{ INPUT, OUTPUT };        // enumerations limit options
enum GPIO_VALUE{ LOW=0, HIGH=1 };
```

```cpp
enum GPIO_EDGE{ NONE, RISING, FALLING, BOTH };

class GPIO {
private:
   int number, debounceTime;
   string name, path;
public:
   GPIO(int number);                              // the constructor exports pin
   virtual int getNumber() { return number; }

   // General Input and Output Settings
   virtual int  setDirection(GPIO_DIRECTION);
   virtual GPIO_DIRECTION getDirection();
   virtual int  setValue(GPIO_VALUE);
   virtual int  toggleOutput();
   virtual GPIO_VALUE getValue();
   virtual int  setActiveLow(bool isLow=true);  // low=1, high=0
   virtual int  setActiveHigh();                // default state
   virtual void setDebounceTime(int time) { this->debounceTime = time; }

   // Advanced output: faster by keeping the stream open (~20x)
   virtual int  streamOpen();
   virtual int  streamWrite(GPIO_VALUE);
   virtual int  streamClose();
   virtual int  toggleOutput(int time); // thread invert output every X ms
   virtual int  toggleOutput(int numberOfTimes, int time);
   virtual void changeToggleTime(int time) { this->togglePeriod = time; }
   virtual void toggleCancel() { this->threadRunning = false; }

   // Advanced input: presented later in this chapter
   virtual int  setEdgeType(GPIO_EDGE);
   virtual GPIO_EDGE getEdgeType();
   virtual int  waitForEdge();          // waits until button is pressed
   virtual int  waitForEdge(CallbackType callback); // threaded callback
   virtual void waitForEdgeCancel() { this->threadRunning = false; }
   virtual ~GPIO();   // destructor unexports the pin

private:
   int write(string path, string filename, string value);
   int write(string path, string filename, int value);
   string read(string path, string filename);
   int exportGPIO();
   int unexportGPIO();
   ofstream stream;
   pthread_t thread;
   CallbackType callbackFunction;
   bool threadRunning;
   int togglePeriod;  // default 100ms
   int toggleNumber;  // default -1 (infinite)
   friend void* threadedPoll(void *value);
```

```
        friend void* threadedToggle(void *value);
};

void* threadedPoll(void *value);        // callback functions for threads
void* threadedToggle(void *value);      // callback functions for threads
} /* namespace exploringRPi */
```

You can extend this C++ class through inheritance to add the functionality that you require, and you can integrate it into your projects without restrictions on its use. Use of this class is demonstrated in Listing 6-3, an example that simultaneously interacts with the LED circuit in Figure 6-2 and the button circuit in Figure 6-5(a).

Listing 6-3: /chp06/GPIO/simple.cpp

```cpp
#include<iostream>
#include<unistd.h>                  // for the usleep() function
#include"GPIO.h"
using namespace exploringRPi;
using namespace std;

int main(){
    GPIO outGPIO(17), inGPIO(27);       // Pin 11 and Pin 13

    outGPIO.setDirection(OUTPUT);       // basic output example
    for (int i=0; i<10; i++){           // flash the LED 10 times
        outGPIO.setValue(HIGH);         // turn the LED on
        usleep(500000);                 // sleep for 0.5 seconds
        outGPIO.setValue(LOW);          // turn the LED off
        usleep(500000);                 // sleep for 0.5 seconds
    }

    inGPIO.setDirection(INPUT);         // basic input example
    cout << "The input state is: "<< inGPIO.getValue() << endl;

    outGPIO.streamOpen();               // fast write example
    for (int i=0; i<1000000; i++){      // write 1 million cycles
        outGPIO.streamWrite(HIGH);      // high
        outGPIO.streamWrite(LOW);       // immediately low, repeat
    }
    outGPIO.streamClose();              // close the stream
    return 0;
}
```

To build and execute Listing 6-3, use the following:

```
pi@erpi .../chp06/GPIO $ g++ simple.cpp GPIO.cpp -o simple -pthread
pi@erpi .../chp06/GPIO $ ./simple
The input state is: 1
```

You must pass both .cpp files to the compiler as the code uses separate compilation. The -pthread flag is required for class functionality that is described later in this chapter. This code example flashes the LED 10 times, reads the state of the button, and then flashes the LED one million times as fast as possible (takes about 8 seconds).

BOOST.PYTHON AND THE GPIO CLASS

As stated toward the end of Chapter 5, it is possible to call C++ class code from within Python by using Boost.Python. There is an example project in the /chp06/ GPIOpython/ directory that provides all of the necessary files. For example, the Python code segment below uses the C++ GPIO class in Listing 6-2 to flash an LED at 5 Hz until a button is pressed. The GPIO.h file contains a BOOST_PYTHON_MODULE() sample that is used to wrap the C++ class.

```
pi@erpi ~/exploringrpi/chp06/GPIOpython $ more simple.py
#!/usr/bin/python
# A Python program that uses the GPIO C++ class
import gpio
from time import sleep
print "Start of the Python Simple GPIO program"
led = gpio.GPIO(17)
button  = gpio.GPIO(27)
led.setDirection(1)
button.setDirection(0)
while button.getValue() == 0:
    led.setValue(1)
    sleep(0.1)
    led.setValue(0)
    sleep(0.1)
print "End of the GPIO program"
```

To test the performance of this code, Figure 6-9 captures the signal output of the LED flashing when the streamWrite() method is used. It is flashing at about 129 kHz. Unfortunately, the C++ application had to run at 100% of CPU usage on a single core to generate these outputs.

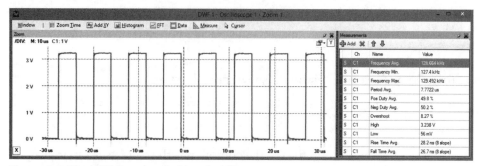

Figure 6-9: The GPIO C++ class flashing the LED

NOTE The load on a Linux device can be determined by identifying the number of processors and by examining the load averages:

```
pi@erpi ~ $ nproc
4
pi@erpi ~ $ uptime
18:53:57 up  7:00,  2 users,  load average: 1.43, 0.73, 0.33
```

The three figures represent the load average for the past 1, 5, and 15 minutes. A figure of 4.00 is the maximum load on a quad-core processor before tasks must be queued. A good rule of thumb is to avoid exceeding an average load of ~70% of this amount (i.e., 2.8 on the RPi 2/3) to provide the processor with the headroom for handling processes efficiently. Available memory is also an important performance consideration: use `cat /proc/meminfo`.

PWM and clocks are described later in this chapter, illustrating how to switch a GPIO using a regular periodic signal, at a fixed frequency, with negligible CPU load. For fast GPIO switching using a nonperiodic signal, one technique that can be used is to switch GPIO states using direct access to system memory. However, such a technique effectively bypasses the operating system and any safeguards that it may have implemented.

THE PREEMPTIBLE LINUX KERNEL

The period and duty cycle of the output in Figure 6-9 is quite regular for an embedded Linux device. This is largely due to the fact that the Raspbian distribution utilizes a preemptive kernel option during kernel build. This option reduces latency delays by making most kernel code preemptible; essentially, the kernel can be interrupted while executing a system call to attend to a higher-priority task. As a result, the code in Listing 6-3 runs with low latency delays, and therefore low signal jitter (period irregularity), despite the fact that the processor is under considerable load.

You can type `uname -a` to determine whether your kernel has the preemption capabilities, but for a more precise description you can check the build options for your kernel by examining the `config.gz` file that is available in the `/proc` directory. For example, you can determine if the kernel was built to support preemption by searching for the `PREEMPT` string within the build options file:

```
pi@erpi /proc $ gunzip -c config.gz | grep PREEMPT
CONFIG_TREE_PREEMPT_RCU=y
CONFIG_PREEMPT_RCU=y
# CONFIG_PREEMPT_NONE is not set
# CONFIG_PREEMPT_VOLUNTARY is not set
CONFIG_PREEMPT=y
CONFIG_PREEMPT_COUNT=y
# CONFIG_DEBUG_PREEMPT is not set
# CONFIG_PREEMPT_TRACER is not set
```

Continues

THE PREEMPTIBLE LINUX KERNEL (*continued*)

You can test the latency of the RPi to a stimulus using the `cyclictest` program, which has a test loop that attempts to sleep for a very precise time period. Immediately after this period, the thread wakes with a high priority. The actual time is determined, the difference in expected versus actual time is calculated, and statistics are collected (e.g., difference, max difference). The loop repeats for a user-defined number of cycles:

```
pi@erpi ~ $ git clone git://git.kernel.org/pub/scm/linux/kernel/git/clrkw →
llms/rt-tests.git
pi@erpi ~ $ cd rt-tests/
pi@erpi ~/rt-tests $ make all
pi@erpi ~/rt-tests $ ./cyclictest --help
cyclictest V 0.92 ...
```

Building `cyclictest` requires the `numactl` and `libnuma-dev` packages, which are installed by default under Raspbian. The test can be performed on the RPi 2 using the following call, where a high run priority is set (e.g., 80):

```
pi@erpi ~/rt-tests $ sudo cpufreq-set -g performance
pi@erpi ~/rt-tests $ sudo ./cyclictest -t 1 -p 80 -n -i 1000 -l 10000 --smp
# /dev/cpu_dma_latency set to 0us
policy: fifo: loadavg: 0.00 0.01 0.15 1/157 8971
T: 0 ( 8966) P:80 I:1000 C:  10000 Min:     9 Act:     9 Avg:    12 Max:    98
T: 1 ( 8967) P:80 I:1500 C:   6671 Min:     8 Act:    12 Avg:    11 Max:    52
T: 2 ( 8968) P:80 I:2000 C:   5003 Min:     9 Act:    12 Avg:    11 Max:    47
T: 3 ( 8969) P:80 I:2500 C:   4002 Min:     9 Act:    12 Avg:    13 Max:    68
```

The results display latency statistics in microseconds for each core on the RPi 2. The same test performed on a multicore Linux desktop machine, which does not have the PREEMPT patch applied gives the following results:

```
molloyd@debian:~/$ sudo ./cyclictest -t 1 -p 80 -n -i 1000 -l 10000 --smp
# /dev/cpu_dma_latency set to 0us
policy: fifo: loadavg: 0.30 0.09 0.06 1/329 3049
T: 0 ( 3047) P:80 I:1000 C:  10000 Min: 17 Act: 1441 Avg:  452 Max: 2581
T: 1 ( 3048) P:80 I:1500 C:   7637 Min: 16 Act:  194 Avg:  412 Max: 2868
T: 2 ( 3049) P:80 I:2000 C:   5774 Min: 19 Act:  102 Avg:  463 Max: 2626
```

To achieve a better understanding of the data, a histogram can be plotted as in Figure 6-10 using steps such as (`-h` and `-p` allow you to specify the histogram latency sample bins (µs) and the task priority respectively):

```
pi@erpi ~/rt-tests $ sudo ./cyclictest -h 100 -p 80 -t 1 -q -n -i 1000 →
 -l 100000 --smp > histogram.dat
pi@erpi ~/rt-tests $ sudo apt install gnuplot
pi@erpi ~/rt-tests $ echo 'set term png; set output "plot.png"; plot →
 "histogram.dat" with linespoints lc rgb "blue";' | gnuplot
```

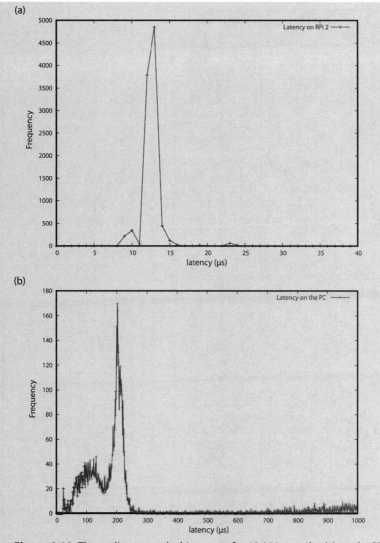

Figure 6-10: The cyclictest results histogram for 10,000 samples (a) on the RPi 2, and (b) on a Linux desktop VM that is under load with no preemption support

The histogram for the RPi 2 has a normal distribution centered on 12μs–13 μs, whereas the test case on the desktop VM with no preemption support has a bimodal distribution with the peaks at approximately 100 μs and 200 μs—it also has long tails, which will lead to considerable jitter problems. Pay particular attention to the difference in the ranges on the *x*-axis of both plots. The low latency results on the RPi 2 with preemption support helps explain the low signal jitter in Figure 6-9. This topic is revisited in Chapter 7.

To view the plot outputs, you can use FTP (see Chapter 3) to transfer the images to your desktop computer, or you can view them remotely on the RPi by using virtual network computing (VNC), which is described at the beginning of Chapter 14.

The RPi GPIO header (note 1)

Model annotations on the ALT function columns: the outer columns are marked **RPi A, B, A+, B+, 2/3** and the inner columns **RPi A+, B+, 2/3 Only**. Pin-number column header: **PI A/B Rev 2 (P1), B+ (J8), PI 2/3 (J8)**.

ALT5	ALT4	ALT3	ALT2	ALT1	ALT0	Pull	WPi	Mode	Pin	Pin	Mode	Pull	WPi	ALT0	ALT1	ALT2	ALT3	ALT4	ALT5
					50mA maximum on 3.3V supply			3.3V	1	2	5V			max current draw ~300mA (cover when not in use)					
		(note 2)	reserved	SA3	I2C1 SDA	up	8	GPIO2	3	4	5V			max current draw ~300mA (cover when not in use)					
		(note 2)	reserved	SA2	I2C1 SCL	up	9	GPIO3	5	6	GND								
ARM_TDI			reserved	SA1	GPCLK0	up	7	GPIO4	7	8	GPIO14	down	15	TXD0	SD6				TXD1
								GND	9	10	GPIO15	down	16	RXD0	SD7				RXD1
RTS1	SPI1_CE1_N	RTS0	reserved	SD9	reserved	down	0	GPIO17	11	12	GPIO18	down	1	PCM_CLK	SD10		BSCSL_SDA/MOSI	SPI1_CE0_N	PWM0
	ARM_TMS	SD1_DAT3	reserved	reserved	reserved	down	2	GPIO27	13	14	GND								
	ARM_TRST	SD1_CLK	reserved	SD14	reserved	down	3	GPIO22	15	16	GPIO23	down	4	reserved	SD15	reserved	SD1_CMD	ARM_RTCK	
					50mA maximum on 3.3V supply			3.3V	17	18	GPIO24	down	5	reserved	SD16	reserved	SD1_DAT0	ARM_TDO	
			reserved	SD2	SPI0_MOSI	down	12	GPIO10	19	20	GND								
			reserved	SD1	SPI0_MISO	down	13	GPIO9	21	22	GPIO25	down	6	reserved	SD17	reserved	SD1_DAT1	ARM_TCK	
			reserved	SD3	SPI0_CLK	down	14	GPIO11	23	24	GPIO8	up	10	SPI CE0_N	SD0	reserved			
								GND	25	26	GPIO7	up	11	SPI CE1_N	SWE_N / SRW_N	reserved			
		Do not use (GPIO0) -- see note 3	reserved	SA5	SDA0	up	30	ID_SD	27	28	ID_SC	up	31	SCL0	SA4	reserved	Do not use (GPIO1) -- see note 3		
ARM_TDO			reserved	SA0	GPCLK1	up	21	GPIO5	29	30	GND								
ARM_RTCK			reserved	SOE_N/SE	GPCLK2	up	22	GPIO6	31	32	GPIO12	down	26	PWM0	SD4	reserved			ARM_TMS
ARM_TCK			reserved	SD5	PWM1	down	23	GPIO13	33	34	GND								
			reserved	SD11	PCM_FS	down	24	GPIO19	35	36	GPIO16	down	27	reserved	SD8	reserved	CTS0	SPI1_CE2_N	CTS1
	ARM_TDI	SD1_DAT2	reserved	reserved	reserved	down	25	GPIO26	37	38	GPIO20	down	28	PCM_DIN	SD12	reserved	BSCSL/MISO	SPI1_MOSI	GPCLK0
								GND	39	40	GPIO21	down	29	PCM_DOUT	SD13	reserved	BSCSL/CE_N	SPI1_SCLK	GPCLK1

Type	Linux DT	Description
GPIO	sysfs	general purpose input/output
SPI	spi	serial peripheral interface
I2C	i2c0/i2c1	I^2C Bus
UART	uart0	UART
PWM	pwm	Pulse Width Modulation
GPCLK	gp_clk	General purpose clock (GPCLK1 is reserved)
PCM	pcm	PCM audio
SA	smi	Secondary Memory Interface
ARM	arm_jtag	ARM JTAG debugger

The data in this table was created from the www.eLinux.org web pages, system information, and datasheets where available.

Note 1: The data in this table was created from the www.eLinux.org web pages, system information, and datasheets where available.

Note 2: On early models of the RPi, Pin 3 is GPIO0 and Pin 5 is GPIO1. Also, these pins have permanent on-board 1.8 KΩ pull-up resistors attached (for the I^2C bus).

Note 3: ID_SD and ID_SC pins are reserved for the ID EEPROM (for different HATs). This is an I^2C interface that is probed at boot time in order to detect attached boards. This allows Linux to load the correct drivers for a HAT. See Chapter 8.

Figure 6-11: The RPi GPIO header

More C++ Programming

To understand some features of the GPIO class, it is necessary to examine some additional programming concepts in C/C++ that are used. These techniques can be applied generally to enhance your programs on the RPi. Callback functions, POSIX threads, and the use of Linux system polling can be used to create an efficient sysfs-based GPIO poll that has negligible CPU overhead and fast response times (i.e., less than 0.15ms). The GPIO class for this chapter supports this functionality so an overview of these programming techniques is all that you require.

> **NOTE** This discussion on C++ programming and the subsequent description of memory-based GPIO control provide important background and context for some advanced concepts on GPIO interfacing. However, at any point you can jump ahead to the practical guide on wiringPi and return here at a later stage.

Callback Functions

In Chapter 5, callback functions are described as they relate to Node.js programs and asynchronous function calls. Essentially, a *callback function* (or *listener function*) is a function that is executed when some type of event occurs. This is vital for asynchronous function calls like those in JavaScript, but it is also useful in C++ applications. For example, in the enhanced GPIO class, this structure is used so that a function can be executed only when a physical pushbutton is pressed. Callback functions are typically implemented in C/C++ using function pointers.

Just like variables, program functions are stored in memory. Therefore, they have a memory address, and this memory address can be passed to another function. *Function pointers* are pointers that store the address of a function. It is possible to pass such a pointer to other functions, which can dereference the function pointer and invoke its associated function. This is best demonstrated with a code example, such as that in Listing 6-4 where the doMath() function is passed a value and a pointer to a function that should be applied to the value.

Listing 6-4: /chp06/callback/callback.cpp

```
#include<iostream>
using namespace std;
typedef int (*CallbackType)(int); // used to tidy up the syntax

int squareCallback(int x){        // callback function that squares
   return x*x;
}

int cubeCallback(int x){          // callback function that cubes
```

```
    return x*x*x;
}

int doMath(int num, CallbackType callback){
    return callback(num);          // call the function that is passed
}

int main() {
    cout << "Math program -- the value of 5: " << endl;
    cout << "->squared is: " << doMath(5, &squareCallback);
    cout << "->cubed is: " << doMath(5, &cubeCallback) << endl;
    return 0;
}
```

Creating a type using `typedef` simply makes it easier to change the type at a later stage and cleans up the syntax somewhat. The address of the `square-Callback()` or `cubeCallback()` function is passed as a pointer to the `doMath()` function. When executed, the output of this code is:

```
pi@erpi ~/exploringrpi/chp06/callback $ ./callback
Math program -- the value of 5:
->squared is: 25  ->cubed is: 125
```

This programming structure is quite common in (and underneath) user-interface programming, where functions can be called when a user interacts with display user-interface components such as buttons and menus. It makes sense to apply the same structure to physical pushbuttons and switches.

> **NOTE** Please edit and build the code examples throughout this book. If something goes wrong, you can use Git to revert to the original file. For example, if you make changes to `callback.cpp` and can no longer get it to work, you can simply delete it and check it out again to get the last version that was added to the staging area (i.e., by `git add callback.cpp`):
>
> ```
> pi@erpi ~/exploringrpi/chp06/callback $ rm callback.cpp
> pi@erpi ~/exploringrpi/chp06/callback $ git checkout callback.cpp
> pi@erpi ~/exploringrpi/chp06/callback $ ls
> callback  callback.cpp
> ```

POSIX Threads

POSIX threads (*Pthreads*) is a set of C functions, types, and constants that provides everything you need to implement threading within your C/C++ applications on the RPi. Adding *threading* to your code can allow parts of your code to execute apparently concurrently (most RPi models have a single-core processor), with each thread receiving a "slice" of processing time. However, the RPi 2/3 has a quad-core processor that enables threads to truly run concurrently, greatly improving the performance of threaded applications.

To use Pthreads in your application you need to include the `pthread.h` header file and use the `-pthread` flag when compiling and linking the code using gcc/g++[2]. All the Pthread functions are prefixed with `pthread_`. Listing 6-5 is an example of using Pthreads on the RPi to create two parallel counters (the comments describe the structure of the code).

Listing 6-5: /chp06/pthreads/pthreads.cpp

```cpp
#include <iostream>
#include <pthread.h>
#include <unistd.h>
using namespace std;

// This is the thread function that executes when the thread is created
//   it passes and receives data by void pointers
void *threadFunction(void *value){
    int *x = (int *)value;      // cast the data passed to an int pointer
    while(*x<5){                 // while the value of x is less than 5
        usleep(10);              // sleep for 10us - encourage main thread
        (*x)++;                  // increment the value of x by 1
    }
    return x;                    // return the pointer x (as a void*)
}

int main() {
    int x=0, y=0;
    pthread_t thread;            // this is our handle to the pthread
    // create the thread, pass the reference, address of the function and data
    // pthread_create() returns 0 on the successful creation of a thread
    if(pthread_create(&thread, NULL, &threadFunction, &x)!=0){
        cout << "Failed to create the thread" << endl;
        return 1;
    }
    // at this point the thread was created successfully
    while(y<5){                  // loop and increment y, displaying values
        cout << "The value of x=" << x << " and y=" << y++ << endl;
        usleep(10);              // encourage the pthread to run
    }
    void* result;                // OPTIONAL: receive data back from pthread
    pthread_join(thread, &result);   // allow the pthread to complete
    int *z = (int *) result;         // cast from void* to int* to get z
    cout << "Final: x=" << x << ", y=" << y << " and z=" << *z << endl;
    return 0;
}
```

Building and executing as follows results in the following output:

---

[2] The Eclipse IDE is used in the next chapter. To use Pthreads in Eclipse, select Project Properties ➪ C/C++ Build Settings ➪ GCC C++ Linker ➪ Miscellaneous ➪ Linker Flags, and add `-pthread`.

```
pi@erpi .../chp06/pthreads $ g++ pthreads.cpp -o threads -pthread
pi@erpi .../chp06/pthreads $ ./threads
The value of x=0 and y=0
The value of x=3 and y=1
The value of x=4 and y=2
The value of x=5 and y=3
The value of x=5 and y=4
Final: x=5, y=5 and z=5
```

However, run it again, and you may get a different output!

```
pi@erpi .../chp06/pthreads $ ./threads
The value of x=1 and y=0
The value of x=3 and y=1
The value of x=5 and y=2
The value of x=5 and y=3
The value of x=5 and y=4
Final: x=5, y=5 and z=5
```

The `usleep()` calls have been introduced to encourage the thread manager to switch to the main thread at that point. The order of the output may change, but the final results will always be consistent due to the `pthread_join()` function call, which blocks execution at this point until the thread has run to completion, regardless if one or more cores are utilized.

Listing 6-6 displays a code outline for a simple performance test on the RPi 2/3 to evaluate the capability of its multicore processor, and to demonstrate how you can use threads to utilize the four cores. Each thread is tasked with generating five million pseudo-random numbers and an evaluation is performed when multicore threading is enabled and effectively disabled.

Listing 6-6: /chp06/multicore/perftest.cpp (Segment)

```
void* thread_function(void*) {         // generate 5M random numbers
   unsigned rand_seed = 0;
   for(int i=0; i<5000000; i++){ rand_r(&rand_seed); }
   return 0;
}

void random_generate_no_threads(int numCalls) {
   for(int i=0; i<numCalls; i++){ thread_function(NULL); }
}

void random_generate_with_threads(int numCalls) {
   pthread_t* threads[numCalls];        // array of thread pointers
   for(int i=0; i<numCalls; i++){ threads[i] = new pthread_t; }
   for(int i=0; i<numCalls; i++){        // create on thread for each call
      pthread_create(threads[i], NULL, thread_function, NULL);
   }                                     // wait for them all to complete
   for(int i=0; i<numCalls; i++){ pthread_join(*threads[i], NULL); }
   for(int i=0; i<numCalls; i++){ delete threads[i]; }
}

int main(int argc, char* argv[]) {      // determine number of cores
```

```
...
    unsigned int numThreads = std::thread::hardware_concurrency();

...
}
```

As the number of calls is increased, you can see the impact of threading on the RPi 2/3 in Figure 6-12. The time measured is *real time*, which is also known as *wall-clock time*—that is, time as we perceive it. This is different from *user time*, which is the amount of CPU time taken by user space code, or *system time*, which is the amount of CPU time taken in kernel space.

The real time required for the multicore RPi 2/3 to calculate 5 M or 20 M pseudo-random numbers is almost the same, because each thread runs in parallel on its own core. When five or more threads are required, the four cores share the additional load; therefore, the slope of the load line is one quarter of that for the single-core implementation. Accurate timing is provided by the C++11 Chrono and the Boost Chrono libraries. See the /chp06/multicore/ directory, where the test can be performed (e.g., for 20 M numbers on the RPi 3) as follows:

```
pi@erpi:~/exploringrpi/chp06/multicore $ ./perftest 4
This hardware supports 4 concurrent threads.
Performing test using 4 thread enabled function calls
Real Time: No threads   646677 us
Real Time: With threads 150989 us
```

All performance tests at the beginning of Chapter 5 are performed using a single core on the RPi 2/3. It is therefore possible to achieve much-improved results on the multicore RPi 2/3 versus other RPi models if the code examples were adapted to parallelize the numeric calculations.

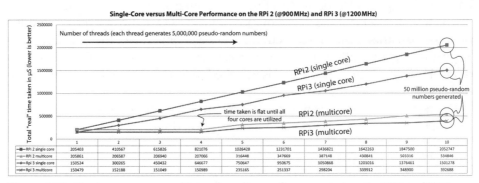

Figure 6-12: Single-core versus multicore threading performance test on the RPi 2 and RPi 3 (measuring real time)

Linux poll (sys/poll.h)

At the beginning of this chapter, code is presented that can be used to detect the state of a button by checking the state of the `value` file. This is a very processor-intensive operation and not really practical. If you listed the contents of the

/sys/class/gpio directory, you may have also noticed a file entry called edge
that up to now has had no relevance:

```
pi@erpi /sys/class/gpio $ echo 4 > export
pi@erpi /sys/class/gpio $ cd gpio4
pi@erpi /sys/class/gpio/gpio4 $ ls
active_low  device  direction  edge  subsystem  uevent  value
pi@erpi /sys/class/gpio/gpio4 $ cat edge
none
```

You can use a system function called poll() from the sys/poll.h header
file, which has the syntax

```
int poll(struct pollfd *ufds, unsigned int nfds, int timeout);
```

where the first argument specifies a pointer to an array of pollfd structures,
each of which identifies a file entry to be monitored and the type of event to
be monitored (e.g., EPOLLIN to read operations, EPOLLET edge triggered, and
EPOLLPRI for urgent data). The next argument, nfds, identifies how many elements are in the first argument array. The final argument identifies a timeout
in milliseconds. If this value is -1, then the kernel will wait forever for the
activity identified in the array. This code has been added to the GPIO class in
the waitForEdge() methods.

An Enhanced GPIO Class

The programming concepts just discussed are complex and may be difficult to
understand if it is your first time seeing them; however, these techniques have
been used to enhance the GPIO class so that it is faster and more efficient; the
code in Listing 6-2 already integrates these changes.

The tests to evaluate the performance of the class are provided as examples
of how to use this class. The test circuit is the combination of the LED circuit in
Figure 6-2 and the button circuit in Figure 6-5(a). Therefore, the LED is attached
to Pin 11 (GPIO17) and the button is attached to Pin 13 (GPIO27). In these tests,
the LED lights when the button is pressed.

Listing 6-7 tests the performance of a synchronous poll that forces the program
to wait for the button to be pressed before proceeding.

Listing 6-7: /chp06/GPIO/tests/test_syspoll.cpp

```cpp
#include<iostream>
#include"GPIO.h"
using namespace exploringRPi;
using namespace std;

int main(){
   GPIO outGPIO(17), inGPIO(27);
   inGPIO.setDirection(INPUT);     //button is an input
```

```
    outGPIO.setDirection(OUTPUT);   //LED is an output
    inGPIO.setEdgeType(RISING);     //wait for rising edge
    outGPIO.streamOpen();           //fast write, ready file
    outGPIO.streamWrite(LOW);       //turn the LED off
    cout << "Press the button:" << endl;
    inGPIO.waitForEdge();           //will wait forever
    outGPIO.streamWrite(HIGH);      //button pressed, light LED
    outGPIO.streamClose();          //close the output stream
    return 0;
}
```

The response time of this code is captured in Figure 6-13(a). This code runs with a ~0% CPU load, because the polling is handled efficiently by the Linux kernel. Using an oscilloscope, the electrical response time is measured between the first rising edge of the button press and the LED turning on. This program responds in ~123 µs, which is well within physical debounce filter times. Using the class's debounce filter will not affect this performance, only the delay between repeated button presses. The downside of this code is that the program cannot perform other operations while awaiting the button press.

The second example, in Listing 6-8, tests the performance of the asynchronous waitForEdge() method, which accepts a function pointer and uses Pthreads to allow the program to continue with other operations. In this example, the main thread counts, but it could be performing other tasks.

Listing 6-8: /chp06/GPIO/tests/test_callback.cpp

```
#include<iostream>
#include<unistd.h>
#include"GPIO.h"
using namespace exploringRPi;
using namespace std;

GPIO *outGPIO, *inGPIO;            // global pointers

int activateLED(int var) {         // the callback function
    outGPIO->streamWrite(HIGH);    // turn on the LED
    cout << "Button Pressed" << endl;
    return 0;
}

int main() {
    inGPIO = new GPIO(27);         // the button GPIO
    outGPIO = new GPIO(17);        // the LED GPIO
    inGPIO->setDirection(INPUT);   // the button is an input
    outGPIO->setDirection(OUTPUT); // the LED is an output
    outGPIO->streamOpen();         // use fast write to LED
    outGPIO->streamWrite(LOW);     // turn the LED off
    inGPIO->setEdgeType(RISING);   // wait for rising edge
    cout << "You have 10 seconds to press the button:" << endl;
    inGPIO->waitForEdge(&activateLED);   // pass the callback function
    cout << "Listening, but also doing something else..." << endl;
```

```
for(int i=0; i<10; i++){
    usleep(1000000);              // sleep for 1 second
    cout << "[sec]" << flush;     // indicates 1 second has elapsed
}
outGPIO->streamWrite(LOW);        // turn off the LED after 10 seconds
outGPIO->streamClose();           // shutdown the stream
return 0;
}
```

The significant change in this code is that when the `setEdgeType()` method is called, a new thread is created within the method and it immediately returns control so that the main thread can continue to perform operations. The main thread simply counts for ten seconds before turning off the LED. If the button is pressed, the `activateLED()` function is called. Whether the pushbutton is pressed or not, the LED will be turned off, and the program will exit after 10 seconds of counting:

```
pi@erpi ~/exploringrpi/chp06/GPIO/tests $ ./test_callback
You have 10 seconds to press the button:
Listening, but also doing something else...
[sec][sec][sec][sec][sec]Button Pressed
[sec][sec][sec]Button Pressed
[sec][sec]
```

(a)   (b)

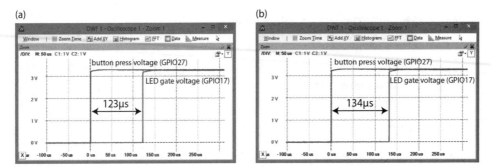

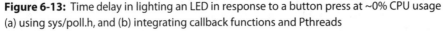

Figure 6-13: Time delay in lighting an LED in response to a button press at ~0% CPU usage (a) using sys/poll.h, and (b) integrating callback functions and Pthreads

The response time of this code is captured in Figure 6-13(b), and it is only marginally slower than the previous code (by ~11 µs), which is the cost of the callback function and the Pthreads code. Again, this code has no noticeable load on the CPU. The full implementation code is available in the GPIO.cpp file, and you can edit it to suit your needs. A more advanced version would use *functors* (function objects) and the C++ Standard Template Library (STL) to remove the requirement for the callback code to be a global function.

Memory-Based GPIO Control

The full datasheet for the Broadcom BCM2835 Peripherals is available from the Raspberry Pi Foundation at `tiny.cc/erpi601`. It is an important document that describes the low-level detail of the SoC, which is used to custom build the Linux kernel for the RPi. However, it is also possible to use such low-level I/O detail to bypass the Linux kernel, using direct memory manipulation to take control of the SoC's inputs and outputs. While this approach can achieve much better I/O performance, you should avoid using it if possible, because your programs will not be portable to other embedded Linux platforms. In addition, since the Linux kernel is unaware of such direct memory manipulations, you could potentially generate resource conflicts.

NOTE This section describes how high-performance GPIO control is achieved on the RPi using memory-mapped techniques, which are specific to the RPi's SoC. This provides context for the impressive performance of the wiringPi library that is described in the next section. Should this material prove difficult, jump to the section on wiringPi and return here at a later stage.

Linux uses a virtual memory system, which means that there is a difference between the physical address used by the hardware and the virtual address that is used to access the hardware. In 32-bit Linux the virtual memory system utilizes the full 32-bit addressing to allocate a virtual space that is much larger than the available physical memory; 32-bit addressing supports 2^{32} addresses (i.e., 4 GB), whereas there is 1 GB of RAM available on the RPi 2/3. The extended address range allows for memory paging and for the mapping of physical devices (e.g., peripherals) into a unified address space. For example, on the RPi 2, you can see that 943 MB[3] of memory is allocated to system RAM:

```
pi@erpi ~/exploringrpi/chp06 $ cat /proc/iomem
 00000000-3affffff : System RAM
 00008000-0075a023 : Kernel code
 007bc000-008de493 : Kernel data
 3f000000-3f000fff : bcm2708_vcio
 3f006000-3f006fff : bcm2708_usb
 3f006000-3f006fff : dwc_otg
 3f200000-3f2000b3 : /soc/gpio
```

---

[3] Note 0x3affffff = 966,655 KB = 943 MB. By default, 64 MB is allocated to the GPU, and vc_mem. mem_size=0x3f000000 (i.e., 1,008 MB) on the current Raspbian image; see the console output of the kernel booting in Chapter 3. Formally speaking, these values should be represented as MiB (mebibytes) and KiB (kibibytes), as 1 MiB = 1,024 KiB is used in these calculations. Linux tends to overlook the IEC notation.

```
...
pi@erpi ~/exploringrpi/chp06 $ cat /proc/meminfo
MemTotal:         949380 kB
MemFree:          730976 kB
...
```

At the bottom of the first list, you can see that the GPIO peripheral base address on the RPi 2/3 of `0x3f200000`. This is `0x20000000` on all other current models of the RPi. You may also notice that the total memory (`MemTotal`) available in the second list is 16 MB short (i.e., 943 MB – 927 MB) of the available System RAM. This is because the kernel allocates a small portion of memory to *reserved memory*, which is mainly used to store the kernel image itself; it has to be stored somewhere!

GPIO Control Using devmem2

You can query the value at a memory address using C code that accesses `/dev/mem` directly. However, to become familiar with the steps, it is best that you build and install Jan-Derk Bakker's `devmem2` program, which is a very useful command-line tool for reading from and writing to memory locations:

```
pi@erpi ~ $ wget http://www.lartmaker.nl/lartware/port/devmem2.c
devmem2.c   100%[=====================>]   3.47K  --.-KB/s   in 0s
2015-07-05 01:13:43 (72.0 MB/s) - 'devmem2.c' saved [3551/3551]
pi@erpi ~ $ gcc devmem2.c -o devmem2
pi@erpi ~ $ ./devmem2
Usage:  ./devmem2 { address } [ type [ data ] ]
    address : memory address to act upon
    type    : access operation type : [b]yte, [h]alfword, [w]ord
    data    : data to be written
```

The registers that are important for GPIO control are described in Figure 6-14. The full list is in Table 6-1 of the *BCM2835 ARM Peripherals* manual.

If the circuit is connected as in Figure 6-2, it is possible to use the `devmem2` program to control the LED circuit. Assuming that the `devmem2` program is currently present in the pi user home directory, you can use it to read the value of the GPLVL0 register on the RPi 2/3 (replace `0x3F20` with `0x2000` for other RPi models):

```
pi@erpi /sys/class/gpio $ echo 17 > export
pi@erpi /sys/class/gpio $ cd gpio17
pi@erpi /sys/class/gpio/gpio17 $ echo out > direction
pi@erpi /sys/class/gpio/gpio17 $ cat value
0
pi@erpi /sys/class/gpio/gpio17 $ sudo ~/devmem2 0x3F200034
/dev/mem opened. Memory mapped at address 0x76f0e000.
Value at address 0x3F200034 (0x76f0e034): 0xB000C1FF
pi@erpi /sys/class/gpio/gpio17 $ echo 1 > value
pi@erpi /sys/class/gpio/gpio17 $ sudo ~/devmem2 0x3F200034
/dev/mem opened. Memory mapped at address 0x76ee3000.
Value at address 0x3F200034 (0x76ee3034): 0xB002C1FF
```

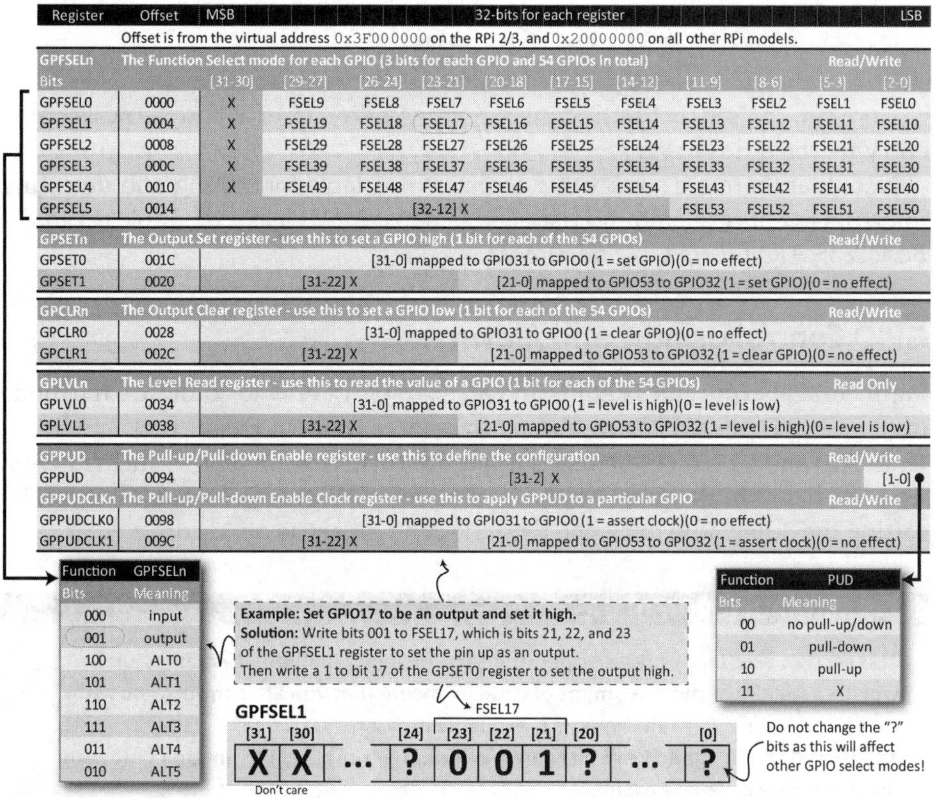

Figure 6-14: Examples of the registers available for memory-mapped GPIO manipulation

Notice that the difference is `0x20000`, which is `10000000000000000` in binary (i.e., `1` followed by 17 zeros, or `1<<17`). GPIO17 is in the first bank of addresses. For GPIO32 to GPIO53, you have to read the GPLVL1 register. The output above indicates that the output is low the first time that the GPLVL0 register is displayed, and high the second time.

You can use the same `devmem2` program to set the LED to be off by setting bit 17 on the GPCLR0 (`0028`) register, and the LED to be on by setting bit 17 on the GPSET0 (`001C`) register:

```
pi@erpi /sys/class/gpio/gpio17 $ cat value
1
pi@erpi /sys/class/gpio/gpio17 $ sudo ~/devmem2 0x3F200028 w 0x20000
/dev/mem opened. Memory mapped at address 0x76f77000.
Value at address 0x3F200028 (0x76f77028): 0x6770696F
Written 0x20000; readback 0x6770696F
pi@erpi /sys/class/gpio/gpio17 $ cat value
0
pi@erpi /sys/class/gpio/gpio17 $ sudo ~/devmem2 0x3F20001C w 0x20000
/dev/mem opened. Memory mapped at address 0x76f7a000.
Value at address 0x3F20001C (0x76f7a01c): 0x6770696F
```

```
Written 0x20000; readback 0x6770696F
pi@erpi /sys/class/gpio/gpio17 $ cat value
1
```

Here you can see that setting these bits has a direct impact on the sysfs value entry for the gpio17 entry.

Note that there are some other registers available for setting and detecting interrupt events (e.g., falling/rising edge detection). Please see Table 6-1 in the *BCM2835 ARM Peripherals* document.

GPIO Control Using C and /dev/mem

Figure 6-14 also provides details and an example of how to configure the mode of a pin. All of the GPIOs can be set to read or write mode, or they can be set to an ALT mode, which are listed in Figure 6-11. The mode is set using a 3-bit value as listed in the table on the bottom left of Figure 6-14. For example, by setting the 3-bit value to be 000 then the pin will act as an input.

BIT MANIPULATION IN C/C++

This section uses many bitwise operations to efficiently manipulate memory. It is worth examining a short segment of code to ensure that you are comfortable with these operations. The full example is available at /chp06/bits/bitsTest.cpp. The uint8_t (unsigned 8-bit integer) type and the display() function below are used to create a concise example:

```cpp
string display(uint8_t a) {
    stringstream ss;    // setw() sets width and bitset formats as binary
    ss << setw(3) << (int)a << "(" << bitset<8>(a) << ")";
    return ss.str();
}

int main(){
    uint8_t a = 25, b = 5;    // 8 bits unsigned is in the range 0 to 255
    cout << "A is " << display(a) << " and B is " << display(b) << endl;
    cout << "A & B  (AND) is " << display(a & b) << endl;
    cout << "A | B  (OR)  is " << display(a | b) << endl;
    cout << "  ~A   (NOT) is " << display(~a) << endl;
    cout << "A ^ B  (XOR) is " << display(a ^ b) << endl;
    cout << "A << 1 (LSL) is " << display(a << 1) << endl;
    cout << "B >> 1 (LSR) is " << display(b >> 1) << endl;
    cout << "1 << 8 (LSL) is " << display(1 << 8) << endl; // warning!
    return 0;
}
```

When this code is compiled and executed it results in the following output:

```
pi@erpi ~/exploringrpi/chp06/bits $ ./bits
A is  25(00011001) and B is   5(00000101)
A & B  (AND) is   1(00000001)
A | B  (OR)  is  29(00011101)
  ~A   (NOT) is 230(11100110)
A ^ B  (XOR) is  28(00011100)
A << 1 (LSL) is  50(00110010)
B >> 1 (LSR) is   2(00000010)
1 << 8 (LSL) is   0(00000000)
```

Note that 1 shifted left 8 times (1<<8) resulted in a value of 0 (and a compiler warning), because overflow has occurred and the 1 has been lost. You can use the limited size of a data type to simplify calculations; this principle is used to simplify a checksum calculation later in this chapter (in Listing 6-14).

The location to which you should write the 3-bit mode is described at the top of Figure 6-14. For example, to set GPIO17 to be an output, you can write 001 to the FSEL17 value, which is bits 21, 22, and 23 in the GPFSEL1 register. Importantly, you need to ensure that you only manipulate those specific 3 bits when you change FSEL17, because to change any other bits will impact on GPIO10–GPIO19, likely changing their pin modes.

Listing 6-9 provides a C code example that sets up GPIO17 as an output and flashes an LED very quickly (at ~1.18 MHz). It also sets up GPIO27 as an input, so that the LED will continue to flash until a pushbutton is pressed. The comments in the code listing describe the bit manipulations that are used.

Listing 6-9: /chp06/memoryGPIO/LEDflash.c

```c
#include <stdio.h>
#include <stdlib.h>
#include <fcntl.h>
#include <errno.h>
#include <sys/mman.h>
#include <stdint.h>   // for uint32_t - 32-bit unsigned integer

// GPIO_BASE is 0x20000000 on RPi models other than the RPi 2/3
#define GPIO_BASE    0x3F200000    // on the RPi 2/3
#define GPSET0       0x1c          // from Figure 6-14
#define GPCLR0       0x28
#define GPLVL0       0x34
static volatile uint32_t *gpio;    // pointer to the gpio (*int)

int main() {
```

```
    int fd, x;
    printf("Start of GPIO memory-manipulation test program.\n");
    if(getuid()!=0) {
        printf("You must run this program as root. Exiting.\n");
        return -EPERM;
    }
    if ((fd = open("/dev/mem", O_RDWR | O_SYNC)) < 0) {
        printf("Unable to open /dev/mem: %s\n", strerror(errno));
        return -EBUSY;
    }
    // get a pointer that points to the peripheral base for the GPIOs
    gpio = (uint32_t *) mmap(0, getpagesize(), PROT_READ|PROT_WRITE,
            MAP_SHARED, fd, GPIO_BASE);
    if ((int32_t) gpio < 0) {
        printf("Memory mapping failed: %s\n", strerror(errno));
        return -EBUSY;
    }
    // Here the gpio pointer points to the GPIO peripheral base address.
    // Set up the LED GPIO FSEL17 mode = 001 at addr GPFSEL1 (0004).
    // Remember that adding one 32-bit value moves the addr by 4 bytes.
    // Writing NOT 7 (i.e., ~111) clears bits 21, 22 and 23.
    *(gpio + 1) = (*(gpio + 1) & ~(7 << 21) | (1 << 21));
    // Set up the button GPIO FSEL27 mode = 000 at addr GPFSEL2 (0008).
    // Both FSEL17 and FSEL27 are 21 bits in, but on different registers.
    *(gpio + 2) = (*(gpio + 2) & ~(7 << 21) | (0 << 21));
    // Writing the 000 is not necessary but is there for clarity.
    do {
        // Turn the LED on using bit 17 on the GPSET0 register
        *(gpio + (GPSET0/4)) = 1 << 17;
//      usleep(10);          // don't use as non-blocking - adds latency!
        for(x=0;x<50;x++){}  // blocking delay hack using a simple loop
        *(gpio + (GPCLR0/4)) = 1 << 17;  // turn the LED off
        for(x=0;x<49;x++){}  // delay hack -- balanced for while()
    }
    while((*(gpio+(GPLVL0/4))&(1<<27))==0); // only true if bit 27 high
    printf("Button was pressed - end of example program.\n");
    close(fd);
    return 0;
}
```

The program can be built and then executed using the sudo tool as follows, where the output appears as in Figure 6-15, which will continue to be displayed until the button is pressed.

```
pi@erpi ~/exploringrpi/chp06/memoryGPIO $ gcc LEDflash.c -o ledflash
pi@erpi ~/exploringrpi/chp06/memoryGPIO $ sudo ./ledflash
Start of GPIO memory-manipulation test program.
Button was pressed - end of example program.
```

Changing the Internal Resistor Configuration

Figure 6-5(b) illustrates the correct way to connect a pushbutton to GPIO4 as it has a pull-up resistor configuration by default. It is remarked earlier that when this circuit is disconnected the GPIO state is high, because the pull-up resistor "pulls up" the disconnected input to the 3.3 V line. This can be observed using sysfs (again, with no circuit connected to GPIO4):

```
pi@erpi /sys/class/gpio $ echo 4 > export
pi@erpi /sys/class/gpio $ cd gpio4
pi@erpi /sys/class/gpio/gpio4 $ echo in > direction
pi@erpi /sys/class/gpio/gpio4 $ cat value
1
```

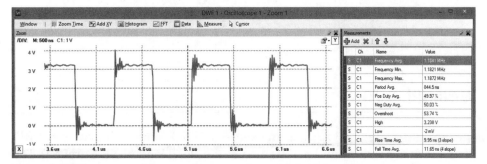

Figure 6-15: The output of the memory-mapped example in Listing 6-9

This GPIO can be adjusted to have a pull-down resistor enabled instead of the pull-up resistor by changing the GPPUD (0094) register in Figure 6-14, where 0x00 = off (i.e., disable), 0x01 = enable pull-down, and 0x02 = enable pull-up. This value is then clocked to the correct output using the GPPUDCLK0 (0098) register—i.e., by setting and removing the clock bit for the specific GPIO. GPIO4 is bit 4, which is 10000 in binary ($0x10_{16}$). So, to set the GPIO to have a pull-down resistor enabled, first set the GPPUD (0094) register to pull-down mode on the RPi 2/3 (use 0x2000 0094 for other RPi models):

```
pi@erpi /sys/class/gpio/gpio4 $ sudo ~/devmem2 0x3F200094 w 0x01
/dev/mem opened. Memory mapped at address 0x76ed3000.
Value at address 0x3F200094 (0x76ed3094): 0x2
Written 0x10; readback 0x0
```

Set bit 4 on the GPPUDCLK0 register, clear the GPPUD register, and then remove the clock control signal from GPPUDCLK0 as follows:

```
pi@erpi /sys/class/gpio/gpio4 $ sudo ~/devmem2 0x3F200098 w 0x10
pi@erpi /sys/class/gpio/gpio4 $ sudo ~/devmem2 0x3F200094 w 0x00
pi@erpi /sys/class/gpio/gpio4 $ sudo ~/devmem2 0x3F200098 w 0x00
```

This process applies the GPPUD register mode solely to GPIO4 because it is the only GPIO identified in the GPPUDCLK0 register.

When the GPIO value is subsequently read (still with no circuit attached), it returns a value of 0, which indicates that a pull-down resistor is now enabled on GPIO4, rather than the previous pull-up resistor:

```
pi@erpi /sys/class/gpio/gpio4 $ cat value
0
```

To set this GPIO back to a pull-up configuration, use the following:

```
pi@erpi /sys/class/gpio/gpio4 $ sudo ~/devmem2 0x3F200094 w 0x02
pi@erpi /sys/class/gpio/gpio4 $ sudo ~/devmem2 0x3F200098 w 0x10
pi@erpi /sys/class/gpio/gpio4 $ sudo ~/devmem2 0x3F200094 w 0x00
pi@erpi /sys/class/gpio/gpio4 $ sudo ~/devmem2 0x3F200098 w 0x00
pi@erpi /sys/class/gpio/gpio4 $ cat value
1
```

WiringPi

WiringPi (www.wiringpi.com) is an extensive GPIO control library for the RPi platform that is written and maintained by Gordon Henderson (@drogon). The library function syntax is similar to that in the Arduino Wiring library, and it is a popular choice among RPi users. The wiringPi library also has third-party bindings for Python, Ruby, and Perl.

WiringPi utilizes the sysfs and memory-mapped techniques described thus far in this chapter to create a highly efficient library and command set that have been custom developed for the RPi platform. It is recommended that you use this library for controlling the GPIOs on the RPi when fast GPIO switching is required; however, be aware that this approach is largely specific to the RPi platform and not to embedded Linux devices in general.

Installing wiringPi

To ensure that you install the latest version of wiringPi, clone its Git repository and build the libraries directly on your RPi, as follows:

```
pi@erpi ~ $ git clone git://git.drogon.net/wiringPi
pi@erpi ~ $ cd wiringPi/
pi@erpi ~/wiringPi $ ls
build          debian  examples  INSTALL  pins       VERSION
COPYING.LESSER devLib  gpio      People   README.TXT wiringPi
pi@erpi ~/wiringPi $ ./build
wiringPi Build script ...
pi@erpi ~/wiringPi $ ls /usr/local/lib/
libwiringPiDev.so        libwiringPi.so       python2.7  python3.4
libwiringPiDev.so.2.25   libwiringPi.so.2.25  python3.2  site_ruby
```

The built libraries are automatically copied to the /usr/local/lib/ directory, and the C header files to /usr/local/include/, which are included by gcc/g++ in the default library and include paths. If you are having difficulties in building wiringPi programs, add `-I/usr/local/include/ -L/usr/local/lib/` as arguments to the gcc/g++ call.

The gpio Command

Installed as part of the wiringPi build, the `gpio` program is a very useful command-line tool for accessing and controlling the GPIOs on the RPi. Figure 6-16 provides a summary of some of the commands that are available, along with some example usage.

For historical reasons wiringPi tends use a different numbering scheme than the physical pin number or GPIO number. These numbers are displayed in the WPi column in Figure 6-11. However, many `gpio` commands can also accept regular GPIO numbering by using a `-g` option. You can use the `gpio` command to write Linux scripts to control the GPIOs. For example:

```
pi@erpi ~ $ gpio -v
gpio version: 2.32
Copyright (c) 2012-2015 Gordon Henderson ...
Raspberry Pi Details:
  Type: Pi 3, Revision: 02, Memory: 1024MB, Maker: Sony ...
pi@erpi ~ $ gpio readall
+-----+-----+---------+------+---+--Pi 3--+---+------+------+-----+-----+
| BCM | wPi |  Name   | Mode | V |Physical| V | Mode | Name | wPi | BCM |
+-----+-----+---------+------+---+---++---+------+------+-----+-----+
|     |     |   3.3v  |      |   | 1 || 2 |   |      | 5v   |     |     |
|  2  |  8  | SDA.1   | ALT0 | 1 | 3 || 4 |   |      | 5V   |     |     |
|  3  |  9  | SCL.1   | ALT0 | 1 | 5 || 6 |   |      | 0v   |     |     |
|  4  |  7  | GPIO.7  | OUT  | 0 | 7 || 8 | 1 | ALT5 | TxD  | 15  | 14  |...
```

Command	Example	Description
gpio read <pin>	gpio read 2	Read a binary value from a WPi numbered pin. Use −g to use GPIO numbers. Example reads button state.
gpio write <pin> <value>	gpio write 0 1	Set a binary value on a WPi numbered pin. Example sets the LED on. <value> is either 1 or 0.
gpio mode <pin> <mode>	gpio mode 1 pwm	Example sets the h/w PWM outputs on (WPi pin 1, GPIO 18). <mode> is one of in, out, pwm, up, down, or tri.
gpio pwm <pin> <value>	gpio pwm 1 256	Set a PWM value on the PWM output pin.
gpio clock <pin> <freq>	gpio mode 7 clock gpio clock 7 2400000	Sets up a clock signal (i.e., 50% duty cycle) on a pin with general purpose clock capabilities. The signal is derived by dividing the 19.2 MHz clock, so integer divisors of this frequency are optimum.
gpio readall	gpio readall	Reads all of the pins and prints a chart of their numbers, modes, and values.
gpio unexportall	gpio unexportall	Unexport all GPIO sysfs entries.
gpio export <gpio> <mode>	gpio export 4 input	Exports a pin using the GPIO numbering. <mode> is either in/input or out/output.
gpio exports	gpio exports	Lists all sysfs exported pins.
gpio unexport <gpio>	gpio unexport 4	Unexport a pin using the GPIO numbering.
gpio edge <pin> <mode>	gpio edge 4 rising	Enables the GPIO pin for edge interrupt triggering. <mode> is one of rising, falling, both, or none.
gpio wfi <pin> <mode>	gpio wfi 2 both	Wait on a state change. <mode> is one of rising, falling, or both.
gpio pwm-bal	gpio pwm-bal	Set the PWM mode to be balanced.
gpio pwm-ms	gpio pwm-ms	Set the PWM mode to be mark-space.
gpio pwmr <range>	gpio pwmr 512	Set the PWM range. <range> is not limited - typically less than 4,095.
gpio pwmc <divider>	gpio pwmc 10	Set the PWM clock divider. PWM frequency = 19.2 MHz / (range × divider).

Figure 6-16: Some gpio command options

To read the pushbutton input value on Pin 13 (GPIO27) from Figure 6-5(a) using the `gpio` command, the WPi number is 2, therefore using either WPi numbering or GPIO numbering gives consistent results:

```
pi@erpi ~ $ gpio mode 2 in
pi@erpi ~ $ gpio read 2
0
pi@erpi ~ $ gpio -g read 27
0
pi@erpi ~ $ gpio read 2
1
pi@erpi ~ $ gpio -g read 27
1
```

Not all `gpio` commands and library calls support the `-g` mode, so the following description retains WPi numbering. To light the LED in Figure 6-2 (GPIO17, Pin 11, WPi number 0) using the `gpio` command:

```
pi@erpi ~ $ gpio mode 0 out
pi@erpi ~ $ gpio write 0 1
pi@erpi ~ $ gpio write 0 0
```

You can also wait for a rising or falling edge on the button press. The first `gpio wfi` command below will not return control until the button is pressed, and the second command awaits the button to be released:

```
pi@erpi ~ $ gpio wfi 2 rising
pi@erpi ~ $ gpio wfi 2 falling
```

The PWM functionality listed in Figure 6-16 is described shortly.

Programming with wiringPi

WiringPi contains a comprehensive library of C functions for controlling RPi GPIOs, regardless of the board model. Listing 6-10 provides a first wiringPi program that displays information about the board that you are using. Again, it is assumed for these examples that the board is connected to the LED and Button circuits as illustrated in Figure 6-2 and Figure 6-5(a).

Listing 6-10: /chp06/wiringPi/info.cpp

```cpp
#include <iostream>
#include <wiringPi.h>
using namespace std;
#define LED_GPIO       17              // this is GPIO17, Pin 11
#define BUTTON_GPIO    27              // this is GPIO27, Pin 13

int main() {                           // must be run as root
   wiringPiSetupGpio();                // use the GPIO numbering form
   pinMode(LED_GPIO, OUTPUT);          // the LED set up as an output
   pinMode(BUTTON_GPIO, INPUT);        // the Button set up as an input
```

```
   int model, rev, mem, maker, overVolted;
   piBoardId(&model, &rev, &mem, &maker, &overVolted);
   cout << "This is an RPi: " << piModelNames[model] << endl;
   cout << " with revision number: " << piRevisionNames[rev] << endl;
   cout << " manufactured by: " << piMakerNames[maker] << endl;
   cout << " it has: " << mem << " RAM and o/v: " << overVolted << endl;
   cout << "Button GPIO has ALT mode: " << getAlt(BUTTON_GPIO);
   cout << "  and value: " << digitalRead(BUTTON_GPIO) << endl;
   cout << "LED GPIO has ALT mode: " << getAlt(LED_GPIO);
   cout << "  and value: " << digitalRead(LED_GPIO) << endl;
   return 0;
}
```

This code can be built using g++ by linking to the wiringPi library (-lwiringPi explicitly links to libwiringPi.so, which is in the /usr/local/lib/ directory). The program must be executed using the sudo tool, because memory-mapping operations require superuser access:

```
pi@erpi ~/exploringrpi/chp06/wiringPi $ g++ info.cpp -o info -lwiringPi
pi@erpi ~/exploringrpi/chp06/wiringPi $ sudo ./info
This is an RPi: Model 2
 with revision number: 1.1
 manufactured by: Sony
 it has: 1024 RAM and o/v: 68956
Button GPIO has ALT mode: 0  and value: 0
LED GPIO has ALT mode: 1  and value: 1
```

Figure 6-17 provides a summary of the C functions that are available in the wiringPi library. The examples that follow describe how you can utilize these wiringPi functions effectively in your own input/output applications.

Toggling an LED Using wiringPi

Listing 6-11 provides a code example for toggling a GPIO at a frequency of ~1.1 MHz on the RPi 2. This is much faster than what is possible using the sysfs approach, and clearly the LED toggle is not visible to humans! However, it is a useful wiringPi performance test. Results are displayed in Figure 6-18(a).

Listing 6-11: /chp06/wiringPi/fasttoggle.cpp

```
// Do not optimize this code using -O3 as it will remove the delay hack
#include <wiringPi.h>
#include <iostream>
using namespace std;
#define LED_GPIO  17                 // this is GPIO17, Pin 11

int main() {
   wiringPiSetupGpio();              // use GPIO, not WPi, labels
   cout << "Starting fast GPIO toggle on GPIO" << LED_GPIO << endl;
   cout << "Press CTRL+C to quit..." << endl;
   pinMode(LED_GPIO, OUTPUT);        // GPIO17 is an output pin
```

```
while(1) {                         // loop forever - await ^C press
    digitalWrite(LED_GPIO, HIGH);  // LED on
    for(int i=0; i<50; i++) { }    // blocking delay hack
    digitalWrite(LED_GPIO, LOW);   // LED off
    for(int i=0; i<49; i++) { }    // shorter delay to balance
}                                  // the duty cycle somewhat
return 0;                          // program will never reach here!
}
```

Return	Function Call	Description
Setup		
int	wiringPiSetup(void)	Initializes wiringPi. Must be used with root privileges. Returns 0 if successful.
int	wiringPiSetupGpio(void)	Same as above. Uses GPIO rather than WPi numbers. Must use root privileges.
int	wiringPiSetupSys(void)	Uses sysfs. Root not required if udev rules in place (see end of chapter). You must manually export pins. Slower, as memory-mapping does not work.
int	wiringPiSetupPhys(void)	Uses the physical pin numbering on the RPi.
int	piBoardRev(void)	Returns the board version (0=n/a, 1=A, 2=B, 3=B+, 4=compute, 5= A+, 6=RPi 2)
GPIO Control		
void	pinMode(int pin, int mode)	Sets the pin to be one of INPUT, OUTPUT, or PWM_OUTPUT (on the hardware PWM pins only). Not available if wiringPiSetupSys() is used.
int	getAlt(int pin)	Get the ALT mode for a pin.
void	pinModeAlt(int pin, int mode)	Set the ALT mode for a pin.
void	digitalWrite(int pin, int value)	Sets the pin to be one of HIGH (1) or LOW (0). The pin mode must be OUTPUT.
void	digitalWriteByte(int value)	Fast parallel write of 8 bits to the first eight GPIO pins.
int	digitalRead(int pin)	Returns the input on a pin and returns either HIGH (1) or LOW (0).
void	pullUpDnControl(int pin, int pud)	Sets the pull-up or pull-down resistor type to be one of PUD_OFF (none), PUD_UP (pull up), or PUD_DOWN (pull down). Not available in sysfs mode.
PWM and Timers		
void	pwmWrite(int pin, int value)	Sets the PWM output for a h/w PWM pin. Not available in sysfs mode.
void	pwmSetMode(int mode)	RPi PWM has two modes PWM_MODE_BAL (balanced) or PWM_MODE_MS (mark-space ratio). MS mode is most commonly used. BAL affects PWM frequency.
void	pwmSetRange(unsigned int range)	Sets the PWM range register. Valid values 2-4,095. Range and divisor affect frequency.
void	pwmSetClock(int divisor)	Sets the PWM clock divisor. PWM frequency = 19.2MHz / (divisor × range)
void	pwmToneWrite(int pin, int freq)	Set the frequency using the hardware PWM pin.
void	gpioClockSet(int pin, int freq)	Sets the frequency on a GPIO clock pin.
Interrupts		
int	waitForInterrupt(int pin,int timeout)	Waits for an interrupt. Timeout is set in ms where -1 is none. You must initialize the pin from outside the program, or using system() and the gpio command.
int	wiringPiISR(int pin, int edgeType, void (*function)(void));	Set a callback function (ISR) to be called on an interrupt event, which is one of INT_EDGE_FALLING, INT_EDGE_RISING, INT_EDGE_BOTH, or INT_EDGE_SETUP.
int	piHiPri(int priority)	Sets the priority of the program (0 to 99) allowing for a reduction in latency. Must be run as root. Returns 0 for success and -1 otherwise.
Helper Functions		
int	wpiPinToGpio(int wPiPin)	Converts WPi numbers into GPIO numbers.
int	physPinToGpio(int physPin)	Converts physical pin numbers to GPIO numbers.
uint32_t	millis(void)	Returns the number of milliseconds since a setup function was called.
uint32_t	micros(void)	Returns the number of microseconds since a setup function was called.
void	delay(unsigned int t_ms)	Delays for t_ms milliseconds. Delay is non-blocking and will exhibit latency.
void	delayMicroseconds(unsigned int t_us)	Delays for a number of microseconds.

Table information gleaned from wiringPi.h and wiringPi.c, which are distributed in the /wiringPi/ directory of the wiringPi repository.

Figure 6-17: Summary of the wiringPi API

On the RPi 2/3, this program utilizes 100% of one core and significant portions of other cores for kernel tasks (such as kworker and ksoftirqd). The for loop is used in place of a sleep call, because it is a simple hack to retain processor control; the usual usleep() alternative is nonblocking and will result in a much larger delay than you might anticipate. This is because the kernel may allocate the core to other tasks, which also results in signal jitter.

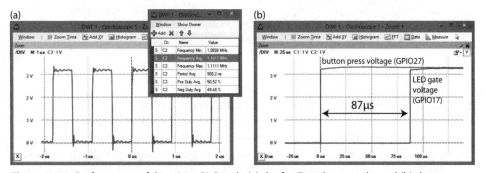

Figure 6-18: Performance of the wiringPi C code (a) the fastToggle example, and (b) the buttonLED example

Button Press—LED Response

Listing 6-12 registers an *interrupt service routine* (ISR) callback function to light the LED once and to count the number of times that the button is pressed. The `wiringPiISR()` function is used to register the callback function with the interrupt, which is triggered on the rising edge of the button circuit input signal. The `lightLED()` function is called whenever the button is pressed (rising edge), but not when it is released (falling edge).

Listing 6-12: /chp06/wiringPi/buttonLED.cpp

```cpp
#include <iostream>
#include <wiringPi.h>
#include <unistd.h>
using namespace std;

#define LED_GPIO      17      // this is GPIO17, Pin 11
#define BUTTON_GPIO   27      // this is GPIO27, Pin 13

// the Interrupt Service Routine (ISR) to light the LED
void lightLED(void) {
   static int x = 1;          // store number of times pressed. Use static
                              // to retain the state on multiple calls
   digitalWrite(LED_GPIO, HIGH);       // turn the LED on
   cout << "Button pressed " << x++ << " times! LED on" << endl;
}

int main() {                           // must be run as root
   wiringPiSetupGpio();                // use the GPIO numbering
   pinMode(LED_GPIO, OUTPUT);          // the LED
   pinMode(BUTTON_GPIO, INPUT);        // the Button
   digitalWrite (LED_GPIO, LOW);       // LED is off
   cout << "Press the button on GPIO " << BUTTON_GPIO << endl;
   // call the lightLED() ISR on the rising edge (i.e., button press)
   wiringPiISR(BUTTON_GPIO, INT_EDGE_RISING, &lightLED);
```

```
for(int i=10; i>0; i--) {              // countdown to program end
   cout << "You have " << i << " seconds remaining..." << endl;
   sleep(1);                           // sleep for 1 second
}
return 0;                              // program ends after 10s
}
```

An example output from this code is displayed below. You can see that the button was pressed soon after the counter started, but that the counter continues to count in parallel. Repeated presses of the button increment the counter and result in multiple messages appearing; however, the LED simply remains lit until the program is restarted. The program ends after 10 seconds; the ISR is no longer active at that point:

```
pi@erpi ~/exploringrpi/chp06/wiringPi $ sudo ./buttonLED
Press the button on GPIO 27
You have 10 seconds remaining...
You have 9 seconds remaining...
Button pressed 1 times! LED on
Button pressed 2 times! LED on
You have 8 seconds remaining...
```

The response time of this circuit is displayed in Figure 6-18(b) and it is impressive for a Linux userspace program. The LED lights ~87 μs after the button is pressed, which is faster than the previous `sys/poll.h` code.

One difficulty with this example is that it is prone to switch bounce. Chapter 4 describes several hardware solutions to overcoming switch bounce using RC circuits and Schmitt triggers, but we can also use software techniques. The `lightLED()` ISR can be modified to include timing code as in Listing 6-13, which ensures that the duration between button presses exceeds a time period (e.g., 200 ms) before registering subsequent presses as valid.

Listing 6-13: /chp06/wiringPi/buttonLEDdebounced.cpp (segment)

```
#define DEBOUNCE_TIME 200                  // debounce time in ms

// the interrupt service routine (ISR) to light the LED - debounced
void lightLED(void){
   static unsigned long lastISRTime = 0, x = 1;
   unsigned long currentISRTime = millis();
   if (currentISRTime - lastISRTime > DEBOUNCE_TIME){
      digitalWrite(LED_GPIO, HIGH);        // turn the LED on
      cout << "Button pressed " << x++ << " times! LED on" << endl;
   }
   lastISRTime = currentISRTime;
}
```

PYTHON AND WIRINGPI

A binding has been developed by Phil Howard (@Gadgetoid) for wiringPi so that you can use it within Python scripts. The package can be installed in Python2 and Python3, respectively, as follows:

```
pi@erpi ~ $ sudo apt install python-dev python-pip
pi@erpi ~ $ sudo pip install wiringpi2
Downloading/unpacking wiringpi2 ...
pi@erpi ~ $ sudo apt install python3-dev python3-pip
pi@erpi ~ $ sudo pip3 install wiringpi2
Downloading/unpacking wiringpi2 ...
```

You can then execute Python with superuser privileges to test that wiringPi is working correctly. The following test controls an LED on GPIO17 (as wired in Figure 6-2) and a pushbutton on GPIO27 (as wired in Figure 6-5(a)):

```
pi@erpi ~ $ sudo python3
Python 3.4.2 (default, Oct 19 2014, 13:31:11) ...
>>> import wiringpi2
>>> wiringpi2.piBoardRev()
2
>>> wiringpi2.wiringPiSetupGpio()
0
>>> wiringpi2.pinMode(17,1)
>>> wiringpi2.digitalWrite(17,1)
>>> wiringpi2.digitalWrite(17,0)
>>> wiringpi2.pinMode(27,0)
>>> wiringpi2.digitalRead(27)
0
>>> wiringpi2.digitalRead(27)
1
```

A Python3 program can be developed using these steps that flashes the LED at 5 Hz until the button is pressed (see /python/ledflash.py):

```
pi@erpi ~/exploringrpi/chp06/python $ more ledflash.py
#!/usr/bin/python3
import wiringpi2 as wpi
from time import sleep
print("Starting the Python wiringPi example")
wpi.wiringPiSetupGpio()
wpi.pinMode(17,1)
wpi.pinMode(27,0)
while wpi.digitalRead(27)==0:
```

Continues

PYTHON AND WIRINGPI (*continued*)

```
    wpi.digitalWrite(17,1)
    sleep(0.1)
    wpi.digitalWrite(17,0)
    sleep(0.1)
print("Button pressed: end of example")


pi@erpi ~/exploringrpi/chp06/python $ chmod ugo+x ledflash.py
pi@erpi ~/exploringrpi/chp06/python $ sudo ./ledflash.py
Starting the Python wiringPi example
Button pressed: end of example
```

NOTE   Once in a while, you might experience unexplainable problems in the behavior of a program that utilizes the RPi GPIOs. If your initial tests do not resolve the problem, reboot the board before further testing. The GPIO registers retain state between GPIO application executions, and it is possible that a previous application GPIO state is interfering with your program.

Communicating to One-Wire Sensors

The Aosong family of temperature and humidity sensors[4] (AM2301, AM2302, and DHT11) can digitally communicate with the RPi using a single GPIO. The GPIO can be set high and low with respect to time to send data bits to the sensor to initiate communication. The same GPIO can then be sampled over time to read the sensor's response. The consistency of the sample time is vital for this application, because the data response is 40 bits long and takes less than 4.3 ms to transfer. Therefore, memory-mapped wiringPi code is used.

Figure 6-19 illustrates how you can connect one of these sensors to the RPi using an arbitrary GPIO pin (e.g., GPIO22). The datasheet for the AM230x sensors recommend that the DATA line is connected to V_{CC} using a strong pull-up resistor, and that a 100 nF decoupling capacitor is used between V_{CC} and GND. Using this configuration, the RPi or the sensor can safely pull the voltage level to GND to communicate bi-directionally.

Communication takes place when the RPi pulls the GPIO low for 18 ms and then releases the line high for a further 20–40 µs. The GPIO switches to read mode and ignores the 80 µs low level and the 80 µs high pulse that follows. The sensor then returns 5 bytes of data (i.e., 40-bits) in most-significant bit (MSB) first form, where the first 2 bytes represent the humidity value, the following 2 bytes represent the temperature, and the final byte is a parity-sum, which can be

---

[4] Datasheets: DHT11 `tiny.cc/erpi605` and DHT22(AM2301/2) `tiny.cc/erpi606`

used to verify that the received data is valid (it is the 8-bit bounded sum of the preceding 4 bytes). The bits are sent by varying the duration of high pulses. A high for 26 µs–28 µs signifies a binary 0, and a high for 70 µs signifies a binary 1.

The top of Figure 6-19 illustrates an actual oscilloscope data capture and worked calculations to explain the process for the AM2301/AM2302 sensors. The DHT11 only sends an MSB for the humidity and the temperature values and therefore does not have fractional precision.

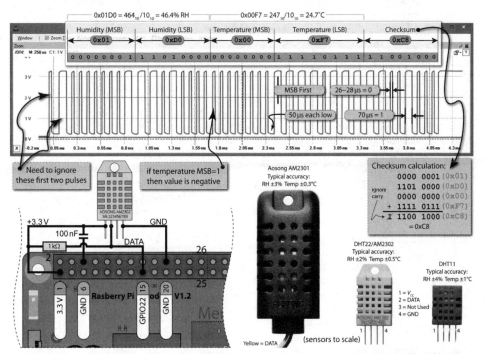

Figure 6-19: Using a one-wire sensor with the RPi and wiringPi (waveform for the AM2301/2302)

Listing 6-14 is a C++ program that can be used to communicate to the AM230x/ DHT family of sensors using the wiringPi library. Note that the count variable represents ~2 µs increments and the LH_THRESHOLD value can be used to adjust the pulse width timing distinction between a 0 and 1.

Listing 6-14: /chp06/dht/dht.cpp

```
#include<iostream>
#include<unistd.h>
#include<wiringPi.h>
#include<iomanip>
using namespace std;

#define USING_DHT11     true    // The DHT11 uses only 8 bits
#define DHT_GPIO        22      // Using GPIO 22 for this example
```

```cpp
#define LH_THRESHOLD    26        // Low=~14, High=~38 - pick avg.

int main(){
    int humid = 0, temp = 0;
    cout << "Starting the one-wire sensor program" << endl;
    wiringPiSetupGpio();
    piHiPri(99);                    // Use a high priority to help timing code
TRYAGAIN:                           // If checksum fails (come back here)
    unsigned char data[5] = {0,0,0,0,0};
    pinMode(DHT_GPIO, OUTPUT);              // gpio starts as output
    digitalWrite(DHT_GPIO, LOW);           // pull the line low
    usleep(18000);                         // wait for 18ms
    digitalWrite(DHT_GPIO, HIGH);          // set the line high
    pinMode(DHT_GPIO, INPUT);              // now gpio is an input

    // need to ignore the first and second high after going low
    do { delayMicroseconds(1); } while(digitalRead(DHT_GPIO)==HIGH);
    do { delayMicroseconds(1); } while(digitalRead(DHT_GPIO)==LOW);
    do { delayMicroseconds(1); } while(digitalRead(DHT_GPIO)==HIGH);
    // Remember the highs, ignore the lows -- a good philosophy!
    for(int d=0; d<5; d++) {        // for each data byte
        // read 8 bits
        for(int i=0; i<8; i++) {    // for each bit of data
            do { delayMicroseconds(1); } while(digitalRead(DHT_GPIO)==LOW);
            int width = 0;          // measure width of each high
            do {
                width++;
                delayMicroseconds(1);
                if(width>1000) break; // missed a pulse -- data invalid!
            } while(digitalRead(DHT_GPIO)==HIGH);    // time it!
            // shift in the data, msb first if width > the threshold
            data[d] = data[d] | ((width > LH_THRESHOLD) << (7-i));
        }
    }
    if (USING_DHT11){
        humid = data[0] * 10;          // one byte - no fractional part
        temp = data[2] * 10;           // multiplying to keep code concise
    }
    else {                             // for DHT22 (AM2302/AM2301)
        humid = (data[0]<<8 | data[1]);  // shift MSBs 8 bits left and OR LSBs
        temp = (data[2]<<8 | data[3]);   // same again for temperature
    }
    unsigned char chk = 0;   // the checksum will overflow automatically
    for(int i=0; i<4; i++){ chk+= data[i]; }
    if(chk==data[4]){
        cout << "The checksum is good" << endl;
        cout << "The temperature is " << (float)temp/10 << "°C" << endl;
        cout << "The humidity is " << (float)humid/10 << "%" << endl;
    }
    else {
```

```
        cout << "Checksum bad - data error - trying again!" << endl;
        usleep(2000000);    // have to delay for 1-2 seconds between readings
        goto TRYAGAIN;      // a GOTO!!! call yourself a C/C++ programmer!
    }
    return 0;
}
```

Set `USING_DHT11` to be `false` if you are using a DHT22 (AM2301/AM2302) sensor and execute it as follows:

```
pi@erpi ~/exploringrpi/chp06/dht $ g++ dht.cpp -o dht -lwiringPi
pi@erpi ~/exploringrpi/chp06/dht $ sudo ./dht
Starting the one-wire sensor program
Checksum is good
The temperature is 24.1°C
The humidity is 47.7%
```

You will not see a fractional output if you are using the DHT11. The Celsius value can be converted to Fahrenheit by multiplying it by 1.8 and then adding 32 (i.e., 24.1°C = 75°F).

The importance of this example is that you can use the same sampling-over-time approach for other one-wire sensors.

PWM and General-Purpose Clocks

The RPi has useful ALT modes for many of its GPIO header pins, as illustrated in Figure 6-11. Several of these ALT modes are described in Chapter 8, but this discussion focuses on the PWM and GPCLK entries.

Pulse-Width Modulation (PWM)

The RPi has pulse-width modulation (PWM) capabilities that can provide digital-to-analog conversion (DAC), or generate control signals for motors and certain types of servos. The number of PWM outputs is very limited on the RPi boards. All RPi models have one PWM (PWM0) output at Pin 12 (GPIO18). On the RPi 2/3 and RPi B+/A+ there is a second PWM (PWM1) output on Pin 33 (GPIO13).

It is possible to use software PWM on the other GPIO pins by toggling the GPIO, but this approach has a high CPU cost and is only suitable for low-frequency PWM signals. Chapter 9 describes circuitry that can be used to add 16–992 hardware PWMs to each I²C bus!

The PWM device on the RPi is clocked at a fixed base-clock frequency of 19.2 MHz, and therefore integer divisor and range values are used to tailor the PWM frequency for your application according to the following expression:

$$\text{PWM frequency} = 19.2\,\text{MHz} / (\text{divisor} \times \text{range}),$$

where the range is subsequently used to adjust the duty cycle of the PWM signal; be careful, though, because a low range value results in poor duty-cycle resolution. RPi PWMs share the same frequency but have independent duty cycles.

The default PWM mode of operation on the RPi is to use balanced PWM (see the MSEN mode in Section 9.4 in the *BCM2835 ARM Peripherals* manual). Balanced PWM means that the frequency will change as the duty cycle is adjusted, therefore to control the frequency you need to use the call pwmSetMode(PWM_MODE_MS) to change the mode to mark-space.[5]

Listing 6-15 provides a first PWM example. It uses both PWMs on the RPi 2/3 to generate two signals with different duty cycles. If you want to use this code on older RPi models, remove all references to PWM1.

Listing 6-15: /chp06/wiringPi/pwm.cpp

```cpp
#include <iostream>
#include <wiringPi.h>
using namespace std;
#define PWM0        12              // this is physical Pin 12
#define PWM1        33              // only on the RPi B+/A+/2/3

int main() {                        // must be run as root
   wiringPiSetupPhys();             // use the physical pin numbers
   pinMode(PWM0, PWM_OUTPUT);       // use the RPi PWM output
   pinMode(PWM1, PWM_OUTPUT);       // only on recent RPis

   // Setting PWM frequency to be 10kHz with a full range of 128 steps
   // PWM frequency = 19.2 MHz / (divisor * range)
   // 10000 = 19200000 / (divisor * 128) => divisor = 15.0 = 15
   pwmSetMode(PWM_MODE_MS);         // use a fixed frequency
   pwmSetRange(128);                // range is 0-128
   pwmSetClock(15);                 // gives a precise 10kHz signal
   cout << "The PWM Output is enabled" << endl;
   pwmWrite(PWM0, 32);              // duty cycle of 25% (32/128)
   pwmWrite(PWM1, 64);              // duty cycle of 50% (64/128)
   return 0;                        // PWM output stays on after exit
}
```

Figure 6-20(a) shows the output results. The base frequency of 19.2 MHz is divided by 15 and a range value of 128, giving a PWM frequency of 10 kHz. At a PWM value of 32 (i.e., 32/128) the signal has a duty cycle of 25% and at 64 it has a duty cycle of 50%. These values are verified in the measurement table that is displayed in Figure 6-20(a).

---

[5] The mark represents the time duration that the PWM waveform is high and the space represents the time duration that the waveform is low. A duty cycle of 50% has a mark-space ratio of 1/1 = 1. A duty cycle of 20% has a mark-space ratio of 1/4 = 0.25.

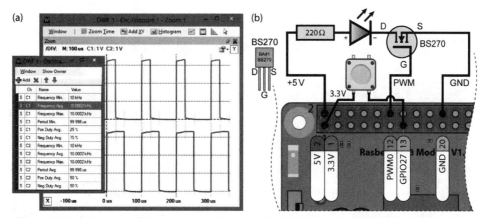

Figure 6-20: (a) Output of the program in Listing 6-15 (b) A button and PWM LED circuit

PWM Application—Fading an LED

Figure 6-20(b) illustrates a circuit that uses a PWM output to control the brightness of an LED. LEDs are current-controlled devices, so PWM is typically employed to provide brightness-level control. This is achieved by flashing the LED faster than can be perceived by a human, where the amount of time that the LED remains on, versus off (i.e., the duty cycle) affects the human-perceived brightness level. Listing 6-16 provides a code example for slowly fading an LED on and off using PWM until a pushbutton is pressed. This example employs an ISR on the button press to ensure that the program ends gracefully, having completed a full fade cycle.

> **NOTE** Instead of fading an LED in and out, you could use PWM to visibly flash an LED with minimal CPU overhead. For example, to flash an LED with a precise 10 Hz frequency and a 50% duty cycle (clock divisor = 1920, range = 1000):
>
> ```
> pi@erpi ~ $ gpio mode 1 pwm
> pi@erpi ~ $ gpio pwm-ms
> pi@erpi ~ $ gpio pwmc 1920
> pi@erpi ~ $ gpio pwmr 1000
> pi@erpi ~ $ gpio pwm 1 500
> ```

Listing 6-16: /chp06/wiringPi/fadeLED.cpp

```cpp
#include <iostream>
#include <wiringPi.h>
#include <unistd.h>
```

```
using namespace std;

#define PWM_LED        18        // this is PWM0, Pin 12
#define BUTTON_GPIO    27        // this is GPIO27, Pin 13
bool running = true;             // fade in/out until button pressed

void buttonPress(void) {         // ISR on button press - not debounced
   cout << "Button was pressed -- start graceful end." << endl;
   running = false;              // the while() loop should end soon
}

int main() {                              // must be run as root
   wiringPiSetupGpio();                   // use the GPIO numbering
   pinMode(PWM_LED, PWM_OUTPUT);          // the PWM LED - PWM0
   pinMode(BUTTON_GPIO, INPUT);           // the button input
   wiringPiISR(BUTTON_GPIO, INT_EDGE_RISING, &buttonPress);

   cout << "Fading the LED in/out until the button is pressed" << endl;
   while(running) {
      for(int i=1; i<=1023; i++) {        // Fade fully on
         pwmWrite(PWM_LED, i);
         usleep(1000);
      }
      for(int i=1022; i>=0; i--) {        // Fade fully off
         pwmWrite(PWM_LED, i);
         usleep(1000);
      }
   }
   cout << "LED Off: Program has finished gracefully!" << endl;
   return 0;
}
```

PWM Application—Controlling a Servo Motor

Servo motors consist of a DC motor that is attached to a potentiometer and a control circuit. The position of the motor shaft can be controlled by sending a PWM signal to the controller.

The Hitec HS-422 is a low-cost (less than $10), good quality, and widely available servo motor that can be supplied using the RPi 5 V supply. It is rated to rotate ±45° from the center. It can rotate in the range ±90°, but the potentiometer does not behave in a perfectly linear way outside of the ±45° range. According to its datasheet, the HS-422 expects a pulse every 20 ms (i.e., 50 Hz) that has duration from 1100 μs (to set the position to −45° from the center position) to 1900 μs (to set the position to +45° from the center position). The center position can be set by passing a pulse of 1500 μs in duration.

Figure 6-21 illustrates the connections and timings for the servo motor that enables it to rotate from −90° using a pulse of 570 μs to +90° using a pulse of 2350 μs. These values and the center point of 1460 μs were manually calibrated, and will vary for each individual servo motor.

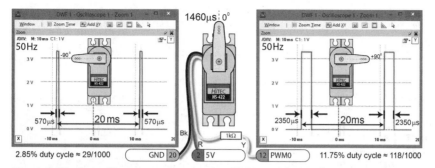

Figure 6-21: Controlling a servo motor using PWM, positioning from −90° to +90° using different pulse widths

The servo motor has three leads: black, red, and yellow. The black lead is connected to the RPi GND (Pin 20); the red lead is connected to the RPi 5 V (Pin 2) supply; and the yellow lead is connected via a 1 kΩ resistor to the RPi PWM0 output (Pin 12). The 1 kΩ resistor limits the current sourced from Pin 12 to about 0.01 mA. C++ code to sweep the servo motor back and forth until a button is pressed is available in Listing 6-17.

CONTROLLING THE SERVO MOTOR USING THE GPIO COMMAND

You can also use the `gpio` command to control the PWM pins. For example, to set up a 50 Hz signal on PWM0 Pin 12 (WPi Pin 1):

```
pi@erpi ~ $ gpio mode 1 pwm
pi@erpi ~ $ gpio pwm-ms
pi@erpi ~ $ gpio pwmc 384
pi@erpi ~ $ gpio pwmr 1000
```

And to control the servo motor in Figure 6-21 using the calculations therein to rotate the servo arm to −90° (29) and then to +90° (118), do the following:

```
pi@erpi ~ $ gpio pwm 1 29
pi@erpi ~ $ gpio pwm 1 118
```

Listing 6-17: /chp06/wiringPi/servo.cpp

```cpp
#include <iostream>
#include <wiringPi.h>
#include <unistd.h>
using namespace std;

#define PWM_SERVO    18      // this is PWM0, Pin 12
#define BUTTON_GPIO  27      // this is GPIO27, Pin 13
#define LEFT         29      // manually calibrated values
#define RIGHT        118     // for the left, right and
```

```cpp
#define CENTER        73        // center servo positions
bool sweeping = true;          // sweep servo until button pressed

void buttonPress(void) {       // ISR on button press - not debounced
    cout << "Button was pressed -- finishing sweep." << endl;
    sweeping = false;          // the while() loop should end soon
}

int main() {                                   // must be run as root
    wiringPiSetupGpio();                        // use the GPIO numbering
    pinMode(PWM_SERVO, PWM_OUTPUT);             // the PWM servo
    pinMode(BUTTON_GPIO, INPUT);                // the button input
    wiringPiISR(BUTTON_GPIO, INT_EDGE_RISING, &buttonPress);
    pwmSetMode(PWM_MODE_MS);                    // use a fixed frequency
    pwmSetRange(1000);                          // 1000 steps
    pwmSetClock(384);                           // gives 50Hz precisely

    cout << "Sweeping the servo until the button is pressed" << endl;
    while(sweeping) {
        for(int i=LEFT; i<RIGHT; i++) {    // rotate to right
            pwmWrite(PWM_SERVO, i);
            usleep(10000);
        }
        for(int i=RIGHT; i>=LEFT; i--) {   // rotate to left
            pwmWrite(PWM_SERVO, i);
            usleep(10000);
        }
    }
    pwmWrite(PWM_SERVO, CENTER);                // rotate to center
    cout << "Program has finished gracefully - servo centred" << endl;
    return 0;
}
```

General-Purpose Clock Signals

WiringPi provides support for the generation of clock signals on the general purpose clock outputs. GPCLK0 (Pin 7 and Pin 38) is available on all RPi models, but GPCLK1 (Pin 29 and Pin 40) and GPCLK2 (Pin 31) are available as in Figure 6-11. GPCLK1 should not be used because it is reserved for internal[6] use. Listing 6-18 provides a short code example that generates a 4.8 MHz clock signal. Figure 6-22 displays an oscilloscope capture of the RPi 2 generating two clock signals simultaneously (a negative DC bias is introduced on the scope for clarity). This capture is at the limit of the capability of the Analog Discovery oscilloscope, which helps explain the "ringing" effects.

Listing 6-18: /chp06/wiringPi/clock.cpp

```cpp
#include <iostream>
#include <wiringPi.h>
```

---

[6] This use appears to involve Ethernet, because GPCLK1 works, but using it instantly terminates your SSH session!

```
using namespace std;
#define GPCLK0        4                  // this is Pin 7 GPIO4
#define GPCLK1        5                  // Pin 29, GPIO5 -- do not use
#define GPCLK2        6                  // Pin 31, GPIO6 -- RPi A+,B+,2/3

int main() {                            // must be run as root
   wiringPiSetupGpio();                 // use the GPIO numbers
   pinMode(GPCLK0, GPIO_CLOCK);         // set up the clock from 19.2MHz base
   gpioClockSet(GPCLK0, 4800000);       // output a clean 4.8MHz clock on GPCLK0
   cout << "The clock output is enabled on GPIO" << GPCLK0 << endl;
   return 0;                            // clock persists after exit
}
```

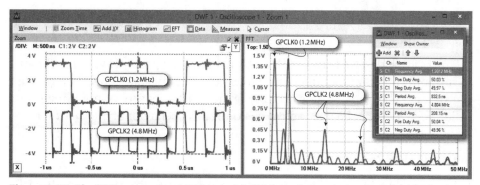

Figure 6-22: The RPi 2 generating 1.2 MHz and 4.8 MHz clock signals simultaneously (FFT also displayed)

HIGH-FREQUENCY CLOCK SIGNALS (ADVANCED)

The pigpio C library (`abyz.co.uk/rpi/pigpio/`) minimal clock access code can be used to set Pin 7 to output a clock frequency of between 4.687 kHz and 500 MHz! The clock can be set to choose different internal clock sources. For example, to output a clock frequency of 10 MHz on GPCLKO (Pin 7) using the PLLD (see Section 6.3 of the *BCM2835 ARM Peripherals* manual):

```
pi@erpi ~ $ wget abyz.co.uk/rpi/pigpio/pigpio.zip
pi@erpi ~ $ unzip pigpio.zip
pi@erpi ~ $ cd PIGPIO/
pi@erpi ~/PIGPIO $ make
pi@erpi ~/PIGPIO $ sudo make install
pi@erpi ~/exploringrpi/chp06/minimal_clk $ gcc minimal_clk.c -o minimal_clk
pi@erpi ~/exploringrpi/chp06/minimal_clk $ sudo ./minimal_clk 10.0m
PLLD:    50    0    10.00 MHz
 OSC:     1 3768 ILLEGAL
HDMI:    21 2457   10.29 MHz
PLLC:   100    0   10.00 MHz
Using PLLD (I=50   F=0    MASH=0)
Press return to exit and disable clock...
```

GPIOs and Permissions

Throughout this chapter, all programs that interface to the GPIOs are executed without using `sudo`. This is not the default behavior under Linux, rather GPIOs are usually only accessible to the superuser. Raspbian has been carefully configured so that GPIO sysfs entries belong to the gpio user group. You can see that this is the case, and that the pi user is a member of the gpio group as follows:

```
pi@erpi /sys/class/gpio $ ls -l
total 0
-rwxrwx--- 1 root gpio 4096 Jul  7 01:17 export
lrwxrwxrwx 1 root gpio    0 Jul  7 01:17 gpiochip0 -> ...
-rwxrwx--- 1 root gpio 4096 Jul  7 01:17 unexport
pi@erpi /sys/class/gpio $ groups
pi adm dialout ... gpio i2c spi input
```

This is a very useful feature of Raspbian, because it prevents you from having to run applications as the superuser, where a coding mistake could damage your file system. This capability is actually an advanced feature of mainline Linux called *udev rules* that enables you to customize the behavior of the *udevd* service.

Writing udev Rules

Udev rules provide you with some userspace control over devices on the RPi, such as renaming devices, changing permissions and executing a script when a device is attached. The first step in understanding this capability is to find out information about the `/sys/class/gpio` directory:

```
pi@erpi ~ $ udevadm info --path=/sys/class/gpio --attribute-walk
...
  looking at device '/class/gpio':
    KERNEL=="gpio"
    SUBSYSTEM=="subsystem"
    DRIVER==""
```

The udev rules are contained in files that are stored in the `/etc/udev/rules.d` and `/lib/udev/rules.d/` directories. The former is for custom rules and the latter is typically used for general system rules. A rule file is a regular text file that is given a name which is prefixed by a *priority number*; the lower the number, the greater the priority of the rules file. The Raspbian configuration uses the `99-com.rules` file, which is provided in Listing 6-19. It has the lowest available priority so that it does not interfere with other rules files in the `/lib/udev/rules.d/` directory.

Listing 6-19: /etc/udev/rules.d/99-com.rules

```
SUBSYSTEM=="gpio*", PROGRAM="/bin/sh -c 'chown -R root:gpio /sys/class/gpio
&& chmod -R 770 /sys/class/gpio; chown -R root:gpio /sys/devices/virtual/gpio
```

```
         && chmod -R 770 /sys/devices/virtual/gpio'"
SUBSYSTEM=="input", GROUP="input", MODE="0660"
SUBSYSTEM=="i2c-dev", GROUP="i2c", MODE="0660"
SUBSYSTEM=="spidev", GROUP="spi", MODE="0660"
```

Essentially, this rules file executes a single line script that uses the `chown` command to change the group of a GPIO device (and all symbolic entries) to be `gpio` when an entry is added. It also contains rules to change the access permissions for input, I²C, and SPI devices (discussed in Chapter 8).

You can edit this file to suit custom user and group requirements. For example, it is possible to replace the user `root:gpio` entry with the user `molloyd:gpio` in Listing 6-19 and test that the rule works as follows:

```
pi@erpi /etc/udev/rules.d $ sudo nano 99-com.rules
pi@erpi /etc/udev/rules.d $ sudo udevadm test --action=add /class/gpio
calling: test  version 215 ...
read rules file: /lib/udev/rules.d/10-local-rpi.rules ...
read rules file: /etc/udev/rules.d/99-com.rules
read rules file: /lib/udev/rules.d/99-systemd.rules  ...
ACTION=add
DEVPATH=/class/gpio
SUBSYSTEM=subsystem
USEC_INITIALIZED=3950621318
```

You can restart the udev service (or reboot) to ensure that your changes to the rules file have been applied. If you then export an entry in the `/sys/class/gpio` directory, the owner of all entries will change and, in this case, the user `molloyd` now owns all GPIO sysfs entries:

```
pi@erpi /sys/class/gpio $ sudo systemctl restart systemd-udevd
pi@erpi /sys/class/gpio $ ls -l
total 0
-rwxrwx--- 1 root gpio 4096 Jul  7 22:03 export
lrwxrwxrwx 1 root gpio    0 Jul  7 01:17 gpiochip0 -> ...
-rwxrwx--- 1 root gpio 4096 Jul  7 01:17 unexport
pi@erpi /sys/class/gpio $ echo 27 > export
pi@erpi /sys/class/gpio $ ls -l
total 0
-rwxrwx--- 1 molloyd gpio 4096 Jul  7 22:05 export
lrwxrwxrwx 1 molloyd gpio    0 Jul  7 22:05 gpio27 -> ...
lrwxrwxrwx 1 molloyd gpio    0 Jul  7 01:17 gpiochip0 -> ...
-rwxrwx--- 1 molloyd gpio 4096 Jul  7 01:17 unexport
```

This is a useful learning exercise, but remember to change the ownership back to `root` before continuing on!

Udev rules are a powerful capability for controlling what happens when devices are attached to the RPi. For example you could create symbolic links when a certain USB webcam or USB flash device is plugged in. For a comprehensive guide on writing udev rules, see `tiny.cc/erpi602`.

Permissions and wiringPi

The wiringPi applications that you wrote often use memory-mapped I/O and require the use of the sudo tool. So, why does the gpio command not require superuser permission, especially given that it is written using the same library? The answer is that it does, and if you examine the executable program you will see how it achieves this permission:

```
pi@erpi /usr/local/bin $ ls -l gpio
-rwsr-xr-x 1 root root 30456 Jul 10 03:38 gpio
```

The gpio executable file is owned by root and the setuid bit, which is described in Chapter 3, is set. This gives the gpio command superuser access, regardless of which user account invokes it. You can use the same permission setting for any of your custom-developed wiringPi programs. For example:

```
pi@erpi ~/exploringrpi/chp06/wiringPi $ ls -l info
-rwxr-xr-x 1 pi pi 9692 Jul 11 14:31 info
pi@erpi ~/exploringrpi/chp06/wiringPi $ ./info
wiringPiSetup: Must be root. (Did you forget sudo?)
pi@erpi ~/exploringrpi/chp06/wiringPi $ sudo chown root info
pi@erpi ~/exploringrpi/chp06/wiringPi $ ls -l info
-rwxr-xr-x 1 root pi 9692 Jul 11 14:31 info
pi@erpi ~/exploringrpi/chp06/wiringPi $ ./info
wiringPiSetup: Must be root. (Did you forget sudo?)
```

Changing the owner to root is insufficient because the program is still executed by the pi user. However, when the setuid bit is set and the file is owned by root then the program is executed as if by root, regardless of the actual user account that executes it:

```
pi@erpi ~/exploringrpi/chp06/wiringPi $ sudo chmod u+s info
pi@erpi ~/exploringrpi/chp06/wiringPi $ ls -l info
-rwsr-xr-x 1 root pi 9692 Jul 11 14:31 info
pi@erpi ~/exploringrpi/chp06/wiringPi $ ./info
This is an RPi: Model 3 ...
```

If you rebuild the executable again then the setuid bit is unset (even if you use sudo on the call to g++). This is for security reasons, because otherwise a user could insert malicious source code into the binary executable:

```
pi@erpi ~/exploringrpi/chp06/wiringPi $ g++ info.cpp -o info -lwiringPi
pi@erpi ~/exploringrpi/chp06/wiringPi $ ls -l info
-rwxr-xr-x 1 pi pi 9692 Jul 11 18:51 info
```

Summary

After completing this chapter, you should be able to do the following:

- Use an RPi GPIO to output a binary signal to a digital circuit, or read in a binary input from a digital circuit.
- Write shell scripts and efficient C/C++ sysfs code to control GPIOs on the RPi.
- Describe the impact of the PREEMPT kernel patch and multiple CPU cores on the performance of GPIO applications.
- Utilize internal pull-up and pull-down resistors for interfacing.
- Manipulate GPIO state using memory-mapped registers on the RPi's SoC using the shell prompt and C/C++ program code.
- Use the wiringPi library of C functions to control the RPi's GPIOs in an efficient and accessible manner.
- Communicate bi-directionally with a sensor using a single GPIO.
- Use PWM on the RPi to fade an LED and drive a servo motor.
- Use general-purpose clocks to output high-frequency clock signals.
- Use Linux udev rules and the setuid bit to improve user-level control of GPIO applications.

# CHAPTER 7

Cross-Compilation and the Eclipse IDE

To this point in the book, all the code is built and executed directly on the RPi. However, for larger projects this can be impractical, because you may need to manage many source files within a single project. In addition, compilation times can be slow on the RPi for building large projects. This chapter first describes how you can use your desktop computer to develop applications that can be deployed directly to the RPi. The Eclipse integrated development environment (IDE) is then introduced, which allows for advanced development capabilities, such as remote debugging. The chapter finishes by outlining how you can build and deploy a custom Linux kernel for the RPi platform.

Equipment Required for This Chapter:

- A Linux (ideally Debian 8+) standalone or virtual machine (VM) desktop instance (see Chapter 3)
- Any RPi board for deployment and debugging

Further details on this chapter are available at
www.exploringrpi.com/chapter7/.

Setting Up a Cross-Compilation Toolchain

This section describes how you can establish a full-featured cross-compilation environment for building code for the RPi using your desktop computer. A typical C/C++ compiler that is executed on a desktop computer (e.g., Intel x86) will build executable machine code for that platform only. Therefore, a *cross-compiler* is required, because it is capable of creating executable code for the RPi ARM platform directly from your desktop computer, even though it has a different hardware architecture. Linux is generally used on the desktop computer for this task, because cross-compiling code that is written under Windows/Mac OS X to run on an ARM Linux device is a challenging process, particularly when integrating third-party libraries. Therefore, if you are using Windows/Mac OS X you can use the VirtualBox configuration that is described in Chapter 3. In fact, a VirtualBox Debian 64-bit VM is used for all the desktop work in this book.

The environment and configuration for cross-platform development is an ever-evolving process. All the steps in this chapter work at the time of this writing, but it is likely that some steps in this chapter will change as updates are performed on the Linux kernel, to the toolchain, and to the Eclipse development environment. Visit the web page associated with this chapter to check for updates: `www.exploringrpi.com/chapter7/`. The primary aim of this chapter is to ensure that you grasp the concepts behind cross-compilation and that you see practical examples of the tools in use.

The first step in cross-compiling Linux applications is the installation of a *Linux toolchain*. A *cross-compilation toolchain* is suitably named as a set of software development tools and libraries (e.g.; gcc, gdb, glibc) that are chained together to enable you to build executable code for an operating system on one type of machine (e.g.; a 64-bit Linux OS on an Intel x86-64 machine), but to execute that code on a different operating system and/or a different architecture, such as a 32-bit Linux or 64-bit Linux OS on an ARM device.

> **NOTE** This chapter assumes that the `sudo` tool is available on your desktop machine. You can enable it as follows:
>
> ```
> molloyd@desktop:~$ su -
> root@desktop:~# apt install sudo
> root@desktop:~# visudo
> root@desktop:~# more /etc/sudoers | grep molloyd
> molloyd ALL=(ALL:ALL) ALL
> root@desktop:~# exit
> ```

To begin, you can discover detailed information about your Linux version by typing the following commands individually or together using `&&`. This information is valuable when deciding which particular toolchain to use:

```
pi@erpi ~ $ uname -a && cat /etc/os-release && cat /proc/version
Linux erpi 4.1.18-v7+ #846 SMP Thu Feb 25 14:22:53 GMT 2016 armv7l GNU/Linux
GNU/Linux PRETTY_NAME="Raspbian GNU/Linux 8 (jessie)" ...
Linux version 4.1.18-v7+ (dc4@dc4-XPS13-9333) (gcc version 4.9.3 ...)
#846 SMP Thu Feb 25 14:22:53 GMT 2016
```

The Linaro Toolchain for Raspbian

Installing a toolchain can be a surprisingly complex task because many different configurations are available. One straightforward approach is to use a prebuilt toolchain from a repository that the RPi Foundation makes available at `github.com/raspberrypi/tools/`. You can clone this repository (~325MB) and used the Linaro[1] toolchain binaries directly as follows on your desktop machine:

```
molloyd@desktop:~$ sudo apt install build-essential git
molloyd@desktop:~$ git clone https://github.com/raspberrypi/tools.git
Receiving objects: 100% (17851/17851), 325.16 MiB | 7.88 MiB/s, done.
```

When the repository is cloned, you can see that the cross-compilation tools are installed on your desktop machine. For example, the `g++` compiler is available in the following directory:

```
molloyd@desktop:~$ cd tools/arm-bcm2708/gcc-linaro-arm-linux-gnueabihf-r →
aspbian-x64/bin/
molloyd@desktop:~/tools/arm-bcm2708/gcc-linaro-arm-linux-gnueabihf-raspb
ian-x64/bin$ ls -l *g++
-rwxr-xr-x 1 molloyd molloyd 739112 Aug  1 12:01 arm-linux-gnueabihf-g++
```

The compiler name is preceded by a triple *X-Y-Z*, where *X* identifies the architecture as *arm*, *Y* identifies the vendor (typically absent for Linux), and *Z* identifies the *application binary interface* (*ABI*) as `linux-gnueabihf`. The *embedded ABI* (*EABI*) defines a standardized machine-code-level interface between compiled programs, compiled libraries, and the OS, which aims to ensure that binary code created with one toolchain can be linked with a project that uses a different toolchain or compiler. Therefore, `linux-gnueabihf` can be read as the GNU EABI for Linux that supports hardware accelerated floating-point operations (i.e., *hard floats*). Hard float operations are much faster than soft float operations as they take advantage of the microprocessor's on-chip *floating-point unit* (*FPU*), rather than having to perform the calculations using software (i.e., *soft floats*).

---

[1] Linaro (`www.linaro.org`) is an organization that aims to support embedded Linux development on the ARM platform by working with industry and the open source community to minimize development fragmentation. It was founded in 2010 by ARM, IBM, Freescale, Samsung, ST-Ericsson, and Texas Instruments.

To test that the toolchain is working correctly you can write a short C++ program that can be built in to binary code using the cross-compiler:

```
molloyd@desktop:~$ nano testrpi.cpp
molloyd@desktop:~$ more testrpi.cpp
#include<iostream>
using namespace std;
int main(){
    cout << "Testing cross compilation for the RPi" << endl;
    return 0;
}
```

Testing the Toolchain

After the toolchain is installed, the program can be compiled by invoking the prebuilt cross-compiler as follows (all on a single line):

```
molloyd@desktop:~$ ~/tools/arm-bcm2708/gcc-linaro-arm-linux-gnueabihf-r →
aspbian-x64/bin/arm-linux-gnueabihf-g++ testrpi.cpp -o testrpi
molloyd@desktop:~$ ls -l testrpi*
-rwxr-xr-x 1 molloyd molloyd 7740 Aug  1 12:03 testrpi
-rw-r--r-- 1 molloyd molloyd  127 Aug  1 12:02 testrpi.cpp
```

Unsurprisingly, when the binary is invoked on the Intel x86 desktop machine, it will not execute, because it contains ARM binary code instructions:

```
molloyd@desktop:~$ ./testrpi
bash: ./testrpi: cannot execute binary file: Exec format error
```

The program can be transferred to RPi using `sftp` as follows:

```
molloyd@desktop:~$ sftp pi@erpi.local
pi@erpi.local's password: raspberry
Connected to erpi.local.
sftp> put testrpi
Uploading testrpi to /home/pi/testrpi
sftp> bye
```

Finally, SSH to the RPi to confirm that the program works correctly:

```
molloyd@desktop:~$ ssh pi@erpi.local
pi@erpi.local's password: raspberry
pi@erpi ~ $ ls -l testrpi
-rwxr-xr-x 1 pi pi 7008 Aug  1 18:34 testrpi
pi@erpi ~ $ ./testrpi
Testing cross compilation for the RPi
```

Success! If you see this output, then you are able to build a binary on the desktop machine that can be executed directly on the RPi. Finally, you can use the `ldd` tool to display the shared library dependencies of the program, which can be useful in debugging dependency problems:

```
pi@erpi ~ $ ldd testrpi
    /usr/lib/arm-linux-gnueabihf/libcofi_rpi.so (0x76f56000)
```

```
libstdc++.so.6 => /usr/lib/arm-linux-gnueabihf/libstdc++.so.6 (0x76e41000)
libm.so.6 => /lib/arm-linux-gnueabihf/libm.so.6 (0x76dc6000)
libgcc_s.so.1 => /lib/arm-linux-gnueabihf/libgcc_s.so.1 (0x76d99000)
libc.so.6 => /lib/arm-linux-gnueabihf/libc.so.6 (0x76c5c000)
/lib/ld-linux-armhf.so.3 (0x76f34000)
```

Updating the PATH Environment Variable

The PATH environment variable can be adjusted so that the call to the compiler is less verbose. This is best performed by editing the `.bashrc` file in the user's home directory so that the bash shell can set the variable on startup:

```
molloyd@desktop:~$ nano .bashrc
molloyd@desktop:~$ tail -1 .bashrc
export PATH=$PATH:~/tools/arm-bcm2708/gcc-linaro-arm-linux-gnueabihf-r
aspbian-x64/bin
```

Rather than reboot on this occasion, you can use the `source` command to apply this change, whereupon the PATH becomes the following:

```
molloyd@desktop:~$ source ~/.bashrc
molloyd@desktop:~$ echo $PATH
/usr/local/bin:/usr/bin:/bin:/usr/local/games:/usr/games:/home/molloyd/
tools/arm-bcm2708/gcc-linaro-arm-linux-gnueabihf-raspbian-x64/bin
```

The compiler can now be executed without requiring its full path:

```
molloyd@desktop:~$ arm-linux-gnueabihf-g++ testrpi.cpp -o testrpi
```

Debian Cross-Toolchains

Recent Debian releases provide support for cross-compilation and a very useful feature called multipackage installations, which greatly reduces the complexity of cross-platform compilation when third-party libraries are required. If you are using a Debian (8+) desktop installation, you can set up a cross-compilation environment using the following steps:

1. Update the sources lists to include the cross-toolchain sources list, which makes a list of cross-compilation packages available:[2]

   ```
   molloyd@desktop:~$ cd /etc/apt/sources.list.d/
   molloyd@desktop:/etc/apt/sources.list.d$ sudo nano crosstools.list
   molloyd@desktop:/etc/apt/sources.list.d$ more crosstools.list
   deb http://emdebian.org/tools/debian jessie main
   ```

---

[2] The Embedded Debian (Emdebian) Project ceased in July 2014, and it is recommended that you use cross-toolchains. For Debian Jessie the armhf cross-toolchain is maintained on the Emdebian repository, but it should be integrated into newer versions of Debian, removing the need for Steps 1 and 2.

2. Use `curl` to download the archive public key and `apt-key` to install it. This allows for the validation of downloaded cross-toolchain packages:

```
molloyd@desktop:/etc/apt/sources.list.d$ sudo apt install curl
molloyd@desktop:/etc/apt/sources.list.d$ curl http://emdebian.org/tools/ →
debian/emdebian-toolchain-archive.key | sudo apt-key add -
molloyd@desktop:/etc/apt/sources.list.d$ cd ~/
```

3. Add armhf as a foreign architecture and update the list of available packages. This step is particularly useful for installing cross-development libraries. You must perform an update at this point:

```
molloyd@desktop:~$ sudo dpkg --add-architecture armhf
molloyd@desktop:~$ dpkg --print-architecture
amd64
molloyd@desktop:~$ dpkg --print-foreign-architectures
armhf
molloyd@desktop:~$ sudo apt update
```

4. You can then install the cross-build toolchain as follows:

```
molloyd@desktop:~$ sudo apt install crossbuild-essential-armhf
... Setting up libyaml-libyaml-perl (0.41-6) ...
Processing triggers for libc-bin (2.19-18) ...
molloyd@desktop:~$ cd /usr/bin
molloyd@desktop:/usr/bin$ ls -l *g++
lrwxrwxrwx 1 root root 27 Jan 16  2015 arm-linux-gnueabihf-g++
-> arm-linux-gnueabihf-g++-4.9
lrwxrwxrwx 1 root root  7 Feb 25 07:13 g++ -> g++-4.9
lrwxrwxrwx 1 root root  7 Feb 25 07:13 x86_64-linux-gnu-g++ -> g++-4.9
```

You can see that the /usr/bin directory now contains a g++ entry for natively compiling x86 code, and an arm-linux-gnueabihi-g++ entry for cross compiling armhf code.

5. The compiler can be tested and its version checked from any location (as /usr/bin is in the default PATH), by using the following:

```
molloyd@desktop:~$ arm-linux-gnueabihf-g++ -v
gcc version 4.9.2 ( 4.9.2-10)
```

6. You can use the code example that is used to test the Linaro toolchain to test this toolchain, and you should obtain the same results. You can install both toolchains on the desktop machine. The cross-toolchains will take precedence as the /usr/bin entry appears first in the PATH environment variable.

NOTE You can use `apt-cache` to search for alternative compiler versions. The RPi with its Raspbian distribution supports hard floats (hf), so use tools with the `hf` suffix when they are available:

```
molloyd@desktop:~$ apt-cache search gnueabihf | grep g++
g++-4.9-arm-linux-gnueabihf - GNU C++ compiler
g++-arm-linux-gnueabihf - GNU C++ cross-compiler for architecture armhf
```

At this point, the binary executable will not execute on your desktop machine because it contains ARM instructions. However, the next section describes how the ARM processor can be emulated on the desktop machine.

Emulating the armhf Architecture

A package called QEMU can be installed on the desktop machine so that it can emulate the RPi's armhf architecture. This is called *user-mode emulation*. QEMU can also perform full *computer-mode emulation*, just like VirtualBox. You can install the QEMU user-mode emulation as follows:

```
molloyd@desktop:~$ sudo apt install qemu-user-static
molloyd@desktop:~$ dpkg --print-foreign-architectures
armhf
```

Now, the armhf instructions can be emulated on the x86 machine (with a performance cost), and the test program can execute on the desktop machine:

```
molloyd@desktop:~$ ./testrpi
Testing the RPi pre-built toolchain
```

Cross-Compilation with Third-Party Libraries (Multiarch)

This section is not necessary to cross-compile C/C++ applications; however, it is likely that you will need to add third-party libraries in the future for tasks such as image and numeric processing. Traditionally, this has been a very difficult topic, but thanks to recent releases in Debian and Ubuntu, this problem has become much more manageable.

At this point, you have a cross-compiler in place, and you should currently be able to cross-compile applications that use the standard C/C++ libraries. However, what if you want to build a C/C++ application that uses a third-party library that contains compiled code? If you install the library on your x86 desktop machine, that library code will contain native x86 instructions. If you want to use the third-party library and deploy it to your RPi, you need to use a library that contains ARM machine code instructions.

Traditionally, developers have used tools like xapt, which converts Debian packages to a cross-platform version on-the-fly (e.g., xapt -a armhf -m libopencv-dev). However, recent releases of Debian (8+) now have strong support for *multiarch*—multi-architecture package installs.

A multiarch-capable package installer can be used to install an RPi armhf library on your desktop machine. The version of dpkg has to be greater than 1.16.2 for multiarch support. Also, if you have not already done so, you should add the armhf target architecture:

```
molloyd@desktop:~$ dpkg --version
Debian `dpkg' package management program version 1.17.26 (amd64).
molloyd@desktop:~$ sudo dpkg --add-architecture armhf
```

Then install a sample third-party library package after performing an update (note the `armhf` after the package name):

```
molloyd@desktop:~$ sudo apt update
molloyd@desktop:~$ sudo apt install libicu-dev:armhf
Reading package lists... Done ...
Setting up libicu-dev:armhf (52.1-8+deb8u2) ...
```

The `libicu-dev` libraries for utilizing Unicode are installed in the `/usr/lib/arm-linux-gnueabihf` directory. This keeps them separate from the x86 libraries that are stored in the `/usr/lib` directory, because otherwise they would overwrite your current x86 libraries, which would be problematic:

```
molloyd@desktop:/usr/lib/arm-linux-gnueabihf$ ls libicu*
libicudata.a        libicui18n.so.52     libicule.a      ...
```

And you are done! If necessary, you can configure your C++ build environment to include the `/usr/lib/arm-linux-gnueabihf` directory. This procedure works well and it is reasonably straightforward; however, it is relatively new to Linux, and interdependency problems currently arise. See `wiki.debian.org/Multiarch/HOWTO` for more information.

Cross-Compilation Using Eclipse

Eclipse is an integrated development environment (IDE) that enables you to manage your code and integrate cross-compilation tools, debuggers, and other plug-ins to create a sophisticated development platform. It can even be extended to provide full remote debugging support for applications that are physically running on your RPi. This is a powerful feature that enables you to debug software applications that are interfacing with the real hardware in your projects, but view the debug values within your desktop Eclipse environment.

Eclipse is written in Java and was initially focused on Java software development. However, Eclipse has excellent support for C/C++ development using the C/C++ Development Tooling (CDT) extension.

Installing Eclipse on Desktop Linux

Using a web browser on your Linux desktop or Linux desktop VM running under Windows (see Chapter 3), download Eclipse from `www.eclipse.org`. There is a version that has CDT (C/C++ Development Tooling) integration (e.g., Eclipse IDE for C/C++ Developers), which you should install. The version of Eclipse that is used in this guide is Mars.2, which was released in February 2016.

After you have downloaded Eclipse, decide whether you want to install it for all users or only for the current user, by extracting the archive in a suitable location. The Iceweasel or Chromium browser will download the file to the user's `~/Downloads` directory. Therefore, use the following steps to install Eclipse in a user's account, and execute it (as a background process using `&`):

```
molloyd@desktop:~/Downloads$ ls eclipse*
eclipse-cpp-mars-R-linux-gtk-x86_64.tar.gz
molloyd@desktop:~/Downloads$ tar -xvf eclipse* -C ..
molloyd@desktop:~/Downloads$ cd ~/eclipse/
molloyd@desktop:~/eclipse$ ./eclipse &
```

At this point, you can use Eclipse to create C++ applications on the desktop machine that are deployed to the desktop machine. However, because the target platform is the RPi, Eclipse must be configured for cross-compilation.

NOTE Instead of executing eclipse using a terminal window, you can execute it directly from your Debian/Ubuntu Linux desktop environment by creating an `eclipse.desktop` file as follows:

```
molloyd@desktop:~/.local/share/applications$ more eclipse.desktop
[Desktop Entry]
Type=Application
Exec=/home/molloyd/eclipse/eclipse
Name=Eclipse
GenericName=An IDE for C/C++ development
Icon=/home/molloyd/eclipse/icon.xpm
Terminal=false
Categories=Development;IDE;C++
MimeType=text/x-c++src;text/x-c++hdr;text/x-xsrc;application/x-designer;
```

An Eclipse icon entry is now available in the Activities window that when double clicked will execute eclipse.

Configuring Eclipse for Cross-Compilation

When Eclipse starts up, you can choose the default Workspace directory, and then you will see a brief guide that describes C/C++ development. You can begin configuration by creating a new project using File ⇨ New ⇨ C++ project. As illustrated in Figure 7-1(a), set the project name to RPiTest, pick the project type Hello World C++ Project, and the Toolchain to be Cross GCC. Repeatedly click Next until you see the Cross GCC Command dialog window, as illustrated in Figure 7-1(b). Enter **arm-linux-gnueabihf-** for the cross-compiler prefix and set its path to `/usr/bin` or to the Linaro toolchain directory. Finally, click Finish.

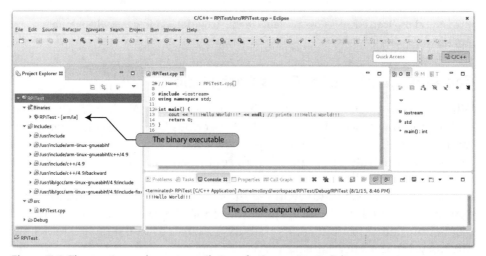

(a)

C++ Project		✕

C++ Project
Create C++ project of selected type

Project name: RPiTest

☑ Use default location

Location: /home/molloyd/workspace/RPiTest [Browse...]

Choose file system: default ▾

Project type: Toolchains:

▸ 🗁 GNU Autotools   Cross GCC
▾ 🗁 Executable   Linux GCC
   ◆ Empty Project
   ◆ Hello World C++ Project
▸ 🗁 Shared Library
▸ 🗁 Static Library

☑ Show project types and toolchains only if they are supported on the platform

⑦   < Back   Next >   Cancel   Finish

(b)

C++ Project		✕

Cross GCC Command
Configure the Cross GCC path and prefix

Cross compiler prefix: arm-linux-gnueabihf-

Cross compiler path: /usr/bin [Browse...]

Use `/home/molloyd/tools/arm-bcm2708/gcc-linaro-arm-linux-gnueabihf-raspbian-x64/bin/` for the Linaro toolchain

⑦   < Back   Next >   Cancel   Finish

Figure 7-1: Creating a new C++ project in Eclipse: (a) the project settings, and (b) the cross-compiler prefix

The Eclipse IDE is now configured for cross-compilation using the cross-compilation toolchain that was set up at the beginning of this chapter. You can choose Project ➪ Build All and then run on the desktop machine by pressing the green arrow or (Run ➪ Run). In Figure 7-2, this results in the message `!!!Hello World!!!` appearing in the Console window. This only appears on the desktop computer if you have installed QEMU, because the executable contains ARM machine code, which is clear from the binary name RPiTest - [arm/le] that is highlighted at the top left of Figure 7-2.

Figure 7-2: The creation and cross-compilation of a C++ project in Eclipse

The preceding steps provide a quick way of configuring the cross-compilation settings within Eclipse Mars or Luna. Older versions of Eclipse (e.g., Kepler) require you to configure the cross-compiler using the project settings. That option is still available within Eclipse Mars; select the project that was just created, and then go to Project ➪ Properties. (If the option is grayed out, it likely means that the project is not selected.) Go to C/C++ Build ➪ Settings and under the Tool Settings tab. You should see the Cross Settings as illustrated in Figure 7-3. Effectively, these settings mean that the `arm-linux-gnueabihf-g++` command is used to compile the project code.

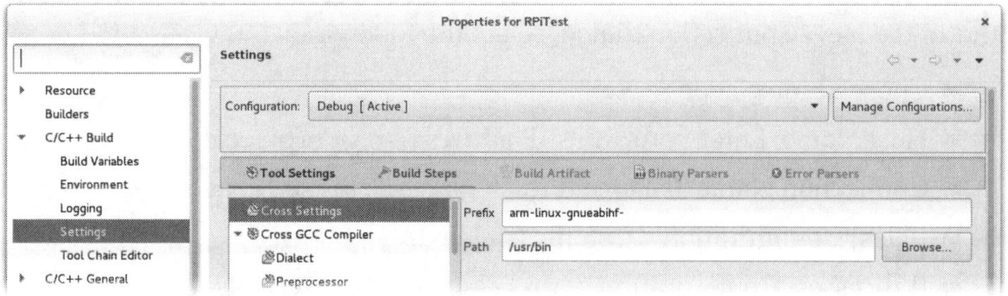

Figure 7-3: Eclipse Mars settings for cross-compilation

It should not be necessary to set the C/C++ includes and library settings explicitly because they are included by default by gcc/g++. However, it might be necessary at a later stage, particularly when using third-party libraries. To do this, go to Project ➪ Properties ➪ C/C++ General ➪ Paths and Symbols, and set the following (the Linaro directories must be set here[3]):

- Includes ➪ GNU C (Include directories) ➪ Add ➪ File System ➪ File System ➪`/usr/include/arm-linux-gnueabihf/` and press OK.

- Includes ➪ GNU C++ (Include directories) ➪ Add ➪ File System ➪ File System ➪`/usr/include/arm-linux-gnueabihf/c++/4.9/` and press OK.

- Library Paths (not Libraries) ➪ Add ➪ File System ➪ File System ➪`/usr/lib/arm-linux-gnueabihf/`.

- Press OK to apply the configuration.

Now you should be able to deploy the binary application directly to the RPi, because it contains ARM machine code instructions. You can transfer the binary application to the RPi using sftp, but it would be better in the longer term if you had a direct link to the RPi from within Eclipse; for this, you can use the Remote System Explorer plug-in.

---

[3] For example, the C++ include directory is currently: ~/tools/arm-bcm2708/gcc-linaro-arm-linux-gnueabihf-raspbian-x64/arm-linux-gnueabihf/include/c++/4.8.3/

Remote System Explorer

The Remote System Explorer (RSE) plug-in enables you to establish a direct connection between your Eclipse environment and the RPi, over a network connection, by using the SSH server on your RPi. You can install the RSE within Eclipse using Help ⇨ Install New Software. Under the "Work with" drop-down menu choose "Mars…" and then select General Purpose Tools ⇨ Remote System Explorer User Actions. Press Next, follow the steps, and then restart Eclipse.

You should now have RSE functionality within Eclipse. Go to Window ⇨ Show View ⇨ Other ⇨ Remote Systems⇨ Remote Systems. In the Remote Systems frame that appears, click the icon for Define a Connection to a Remote System, and in the New Connection dialog, select the following:

- Choose Linux Type ⇨ Next.
- Host Name: Enter your RPi's IP address—e.g., erpi.local.
- Connection Name: Change it to "Raspberry Pi" ⇨ Next.
- [Files] Configuration ⇨ ssh.files ⇨ Next.
- [Processes] Configuration ⇨ processes.shell.linux ⇨ Next.
- [Shells] Configuration ⇨ ssh.shells ⇨ Next.
- Eclipse Luna allows you to install a terminal at this point, but a separate installation is required with Eclipse Mars.

To install the terminal in Eclipse Mars use Help ⇨ Install New Software. Under the "Work with" drop-down menu choose "Mars…" and then search for "terminal." Install TM Terminal and the TM Terminal View RSE add-in.

You can then right-click the Raspberry Pi entry in the Remote Systems tab and choose Connect. You should see the dialog illustrated in Figure 7-4. In this example, the pi user account is used on the RPi as the account into which the executable code is deployed. Usefully, Eclipse uses a master password system to manage passwords for all of your individual connections.

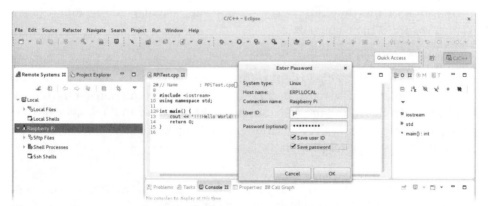

Figure 7-4: Connecting to the RPi for the first time using RSE

Once you are connected to the RPi, you can go to the Project Explorer window, right-click the executable that you just built (RPiTest [arm/le]), and choose Copy. Then go to a directory on the Remote Explorer, such as `testCross` (see Figure 7-5). Right-click it and choose Paste. The file is now on the RPi and can be executed from the Terminal window. Right-click the Raspberry Pi entry in the Remote Systems tab and choose Open Terminal. The output of the test program is illustrated in Figure 7-5. It is necessary to set the RPiTest file to be executable on the first occasion.

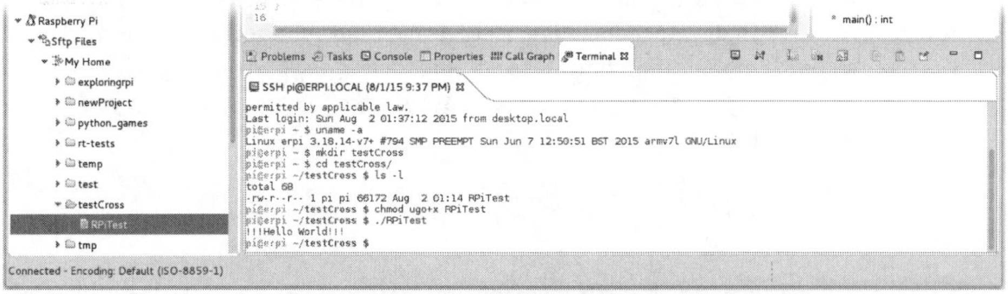

Figure 7-5: The Terminal window, connected to the RPi and executing the cross-compiled RPiTest C++ application

One way to automate the process of copying the files from the desktop computer to the RPi is by using the secure copy command `scp`. You can set up your desktop computer so that it does not need to use a password to `ssh` to the RPi by using the following steps on the desktop computer (when prompted you should leave the passphrase blank):

```
molloyd@desktop:~$ ssh-keygen
molloyd@desktop:~$ ssh-copy-id pi@erpi.local
molloyd@desktop:~$ ssh-add
molloyd@desktop:~$ ssh pi@erpi.local
```

You should now be able to `ssh` to the RPi without requiring a password. You can then configure Eclipse under Project ➪ Properties ➪ C/C++ Build ➪ Settings ➪ Build Steps (tab) ➪ Post-build steps, set the Command to be `scp RPiTest pi@erpi.local:/home/pi/testCross/`

SECURE COPY (SCP) AND RSYNC

The *secure copy* program, *scp*, provides a mechanism for transferring files between two hosts using the Secure Shell (SSH) protocol. For example, to transfer a file `test1.txt` from a Linux desktop machine to the RPi, you can use the following (all commands are executed on the desktop machine):

```
molloyd@desktop:~/test$ echo "Testing SCP" >> test1.txt
molloyd@desktop:~/test$ scp test1.txt pi@erpi.local:/tmp
test1.txt                    100%   12    0.0KB/s   00:00
```

Continues

SECURE COPY (SCP) AND RSYNC (*continued*)

To copy a file from the RPi back to the Linux desktop machine, you can use the following:

```
molloyd@desktop:~/test$ scp pi@erpi.local:/tmp/test1.txt test2.txt
test1.txt                     100%  12    0.0KB/s   00:00
molloyd@desktop:~/test$ more test2.txt
Testing SCP
```

Use -v to see full, *v*erbose output of the transfer. Using -C will automatically *c*ompress and decompress the files to speed up the data transfer. Using -r allows for the *r*ecursive copy of a directory, including all of its files and subdirectories. Using -p will *p*reserve the modification times, access times, and modes of the original files. Therefore, to copy the entire desktop test directory to the RPi /tmp directory, you could use the following:

```
molloyd@desktop:~$ scp -Cvrp test pi@erpi.local:/tmp
... Transferred: sent 3664, received 2180 bytes, in 0.1 seconds
```

Just like scp, the *rsync* utility can copy files; however, it can also be used to synchronize files and directories across multiple locations, where only the differences are transferred (*delta encoding*). For example, to perform the same operation using rsync, you can use the following:

```
molloyd@desktop:~$ rsync -avze ssh test pi@erpi.local:/tmp/test
sending incremental file list
test/
test/test1.txt
test/test2.txt
sent 231 bytes  received 58 bytes  578.00 bytes/sec
total size is 24  speedup is 0.08
```

Using -a requests *a*rchive mode (like -p for scp), -v requests *v*erbose output, -z requests the compression of data (like -C for scp), and -e ssh requests rsync to use the SSH protocol. To test rsync, create an additional file in the test directory and perform the same command again using the following:

```
molloyd@desktop:~$ rsync -avze ssh test pi@erpi.local:/tmp/test
sending incremental file list
test/
test/test3.txt
sent 180 bytes  received 39 bytes  438.00 bytes/sec
total size is 24  speedup is 0.11
```

Importantly, you can see that only one file has been transferred in this case. The rsync utility can delete files after transfer (using -delete), which you should only use after performing a dry run (using -dry-run).

Integrating GitHub into Eclipse

A very useful plug-in can be installed into Eclipse that allows for full GitHub integration, enabling you to link to your own GitHub repositories or to get easy access to the example code and resources for this book. To install it, open Help ➪ Install New Software, and choose Mars... in the Work with section. Then, under the tree item Collaboration, choose Eclipse GitHub integration with task focused interface.

Once this plug-in is installed, you can open Window ➪ Show View ➪ Other ➪ Git, and there are several options, such as Git Interactive Rebase, Git Reflog, Git Repositories, Git Staging, and Git Tree Compare. If you choose Git Repositories, select the options Clone a Git repository ➪ GitHub, and you can search for "Derek Molloy." You should find the repository derekmolloy/exploringRPi.

If not, you can go back to the Clone URI option and add the repository directly using `git://github.com/DerekMolloy/ExploringRPi.git`. You will then have full access to the source code in this book directly from within the Eclipse IDE, as captured in Figure 7-6. Because there are so many projects in this repository, the easiest way to use this code repository is to copy the files that you need into a new project.

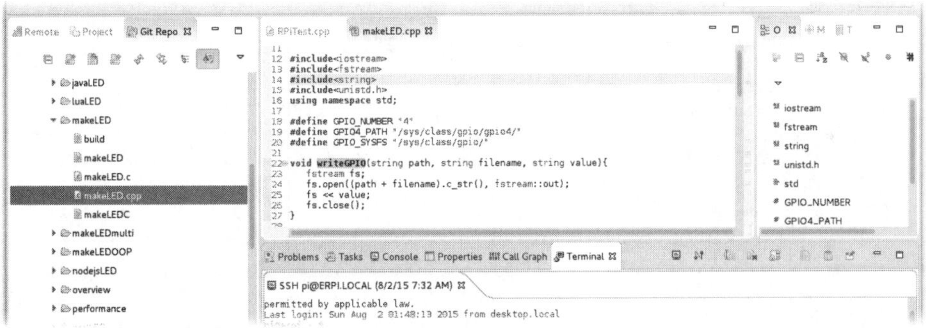

Figure 7-6: Eclipse GitHub integration, displaying the exploringRPi repository

Remote Debugging

Remote debugging is the next step in developing a full-featured, cross-development platform configuration. Because you are likely planning to interact with hardware modules that are physically connected to the RPi, it would be ideal if you could debug your code live on the RPi. Remote debugging with Eclipse enables you to control the execution steps, and even view debug messages and memory values directly from within Eclipse on your desktop machine.

A short program in Listing 7-1 is used to test that remote debugging is working correctly. This program can be used directly within the `/chp07/` repository directory to check that you have local command-line debugging and remote debugging working correctly.

Listing 7-1: /chp07/test.cpp

```cpp
#include<iostream>
using namespace std;

int main(){
    int x = 5;
    x++;
    cout << "The value of x is " << x << endl;
    return 0;
}
```

COMMAND-LINE DEBUGGING

It is possible to use the GNU debugger, gdb directly at the command line. For example, if you want to debug the code in Listing 7-1 directly on the RPi, you could perform the following steps (-g ensures that symbolic debugging information is included in the executable):

```
pi@erpi ~/exploringrpi/chp07 $ g++ -g test.cpp -o test
pi@erpi ~/exploringrpi/chp07 $ gdb test
This GDB was configured as "arm-linux-gnueabihf" ...
Reading symbols from test...done.
(gdb) break main
Breakpoint 1 at 0x1075c: file test.cpp, line 5.
(gdb) info break
Num     Type           Disp Enb Address    What
1       breakpoint     keep y   0x0001075c in main() at test.cpp:5
(gdb) run
Starting program: /home/pi/exploringrpi/chp07/test
Breakpoint 1, main () at test.cpp:5
5       int x = 5;
(gdb) display x
1: x = 0
(gdb) step
6       x++;
1: x = 5
(gdb) step
7       cout << "The value of x is " << x << endl;
1: x = 6
(gdb) continue
Continuing.
The value of x is 6
[Inferior 1 (process 15870) exited normally]
(gdb) quit
```

The Eclipse IDE executes tools such as gdb from your chosen toolchain and interprets their outputs, providing a fully integrated interactive display.

You need the debug server gdbserver to run on the RPi for the Eclipse desktop installation to connect to the debugger. This tool is installed by default on the Raspbian image, but you can install or update it using the following command:

```
pi@erpi ~ $ sudo apt install gdbserver
```

The gdb server executes on the RPi and is controlled by the Eclipse IDE on the desktop machine. The built executable is still transferred to the RPi using the RSE configuration described earlier.

The Linux desktop machine requires an ARM-compatible debugger that can connect to the gdb server on RPi. There are two ways to do this: You can install the GNU multi-architecture debugger, or you can use `arm-linux-gnueabihf-gdb` from the Linaro toolchain that is described at the beginning of this chapter. The GNU multi-architecture debugger can be installed on the desktop machine as follows:

```
molloyd@desktop:~$ sudo apt install gdb-multiarch
```

To complete this configuration, you may need to create a file called `.gdbinit` in the project folder that defines the remote architecture as `arm`:

```
molloyd@desktop:~/workspace/RPiTest$ echo "set architecture arm" >> .gdbinit
molloyd@desktop:~/workspace/RPiTest$ more .gdbinit
set architecture arm
```

Check that your version of `gdb-multiarch` is not 7.7.x, because there is a known problem in using it to remotely debug ARM code. If you have difficulties, use the Linaro `arm-linux-gnueabihf-gdb`.

COMMAND-LINE REMOTE DEBUGGING

If you are experiencing difficulties with the Eclipse setup, you can use command-line remote debugging to familiarize yourself with the underlying tools and to test your configuration. The code in Listing 7-1 is once again used for this example. The first step is to execute the gdb server on the RPi and request that it listens to TCP port (e.g., 12345), as follows:

```
pi@erpi ~/exploringrpi/chp07 $ gdbserver --multi localhost:12345
Listening on port 12345
```

The use of `--multi` means that the server has not yet started to debug a target program, and therefore a target must be identified by the desktop machine.

The Linaro debugger can then be used to connect to the gdb server from the desktop machine as follows (where `-q test` requests a quiet mode and for the symbols to be read from the `test` binary in the current directory):

```
molloyd@desktop:~/exploringrpi/chp07$ arm-linux-gnueabihf-gdb -q test
Reading symbols from /home/molloyd/exploringrpi/chp07/test...done.
(gdb) target extended erpi.local:12345
Remote debugging using erpi.local:12345
(gdb) set remote exec-file test
(gdb) break main
Breakpoint 1 at 0x1075c: file test.cpp, line 5.
(gdb) run
Starting program: /home/molloyd/exploringrpi/chp07/test
Breakpoint 1, main () at test.cpp:5
5            int x = 5;
(gdb) display x
1: x = 0
(gdb) step
```

Continues

COMMAND-LINE REMOTE DEBUGGING (*continued*)

```
6           x++;
1: x = 5
(gdb) continue
Continuing.
[Inferior 1 (process 18125) exited normally]
```

The final output of the gdb server on the RPi is as follows:

```
pi@erpi ~/exploringrpi/chp07 $ gdbserver --multi localhost:12345
Listening on port 12345
Remote debugging from host 192.168.1.107
Process test created; pid = 18125
The value of x is 6

Child exited with status 0
```

Just to reiterate, the `test` **program is executed on the RPi, but the debugger is controlled on the desktop machine by passing commands over the network.**

Eclipse must be configured so that it can connect to the RPi's gdb server. Go to Run ⇨ Debug Configurations ⇨ Debugger, and delete any current debug configurations. Select C/C++ Remote Applications on the left side and right-click it to create a new configuration. In this example, the configuration is called RPiTest, as illustrated in Figure 7-7. The Connection entry can be set to the Raspberry Pi connection (as described in the Remote System Explorer section), and you should be able to browse to the remote path (i.e., on the RPi) for the C/C++ application, as illustrated in the same figure.

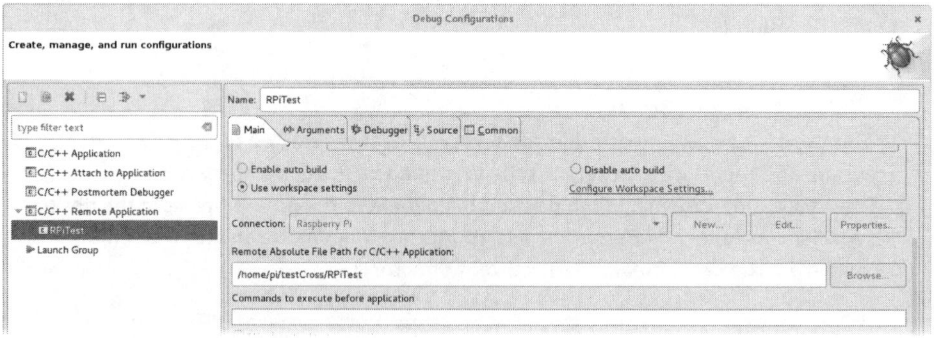

Figure 7-7: Setting the debug configuration

Change the GDB debugger from `gdb` to `gdb-multiarch` or `arm-linux-gnue-abihf-gdb`, as illustrated in Figure 7-8. You should also identify the `.gdbinit` file that was just created. Press the Browse button to the right of "GDB command file:" and locate your workspace directory. You may have to right-click the File Explorer window and choose Show Hidden Files to find the hidden file `.gdbinit`. That configuration file can be used to set many more configuration options. For example, it can be used to further configure the remote server and to identify different default breakpoints.

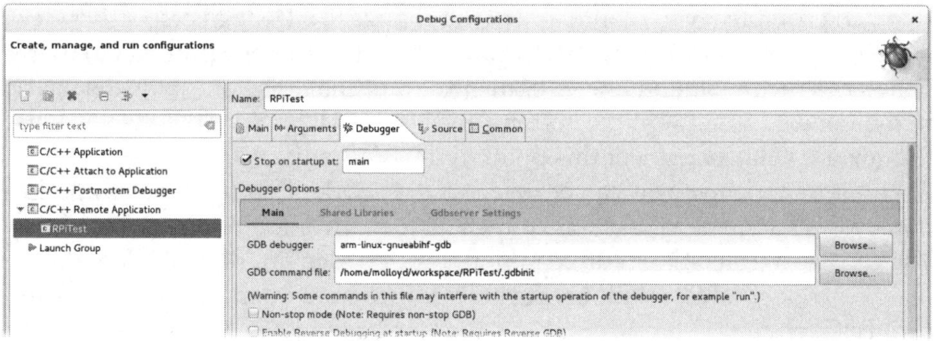

Figure 7-8: Setting up the remote debugger

Any program arguments can be added to the Arguments tab in Figure 7-8. Finally, under the Gdbserver Settings tab (see Figure 7-9), set the executable path and an arbitrary port number for the `gdbserver` command. This allows the desktop computer to remotely invoke the `gdbserver` command on the RPi and to connect to it over TCP/IP using its port number.

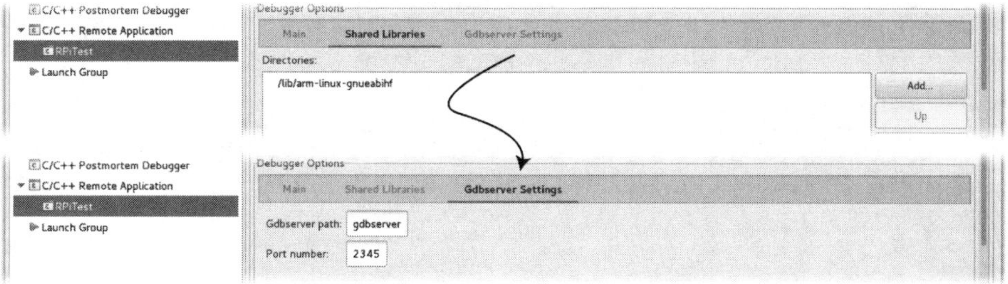

Figure 7-9: Setting the RPi gdb server port

You can enable this debug configuration to be added to the debugger "bug" menu on the main window (see Figure 7-11) by using the Common tab. Finally, you can start debugging by clicking the Debug button on the bottom right of Figure 7-10.

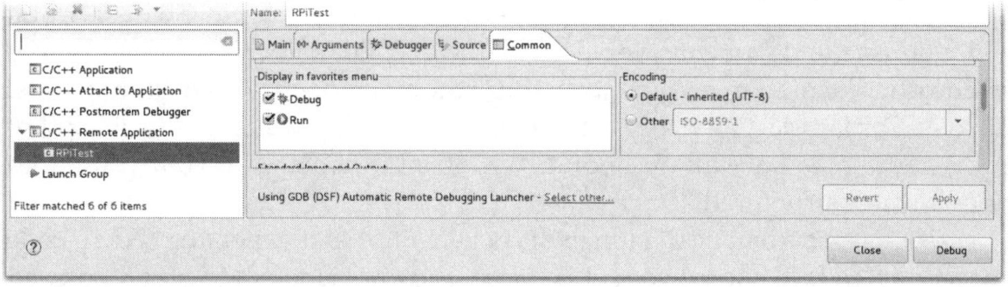

Figure 7-10: Adding to the "bug" menu

When prompted, you should accept the change to a Debug Perspective view, which appears as in Figure 7-11. You can see that the program is currently halted at a breakpoint on line 15 of the program code. The output is displayed in the Console window at the bottom, and the Variables window displays that the current value of x is 6 at this point in the program.

This type of debug view can be invaluable when developing complex applications, especially when the RPi is connected to electronic circuits and modules. You can use the Step Over button to step through each line of your code, watching the variable values, while seeing how the program interacts with physically connected circuits.

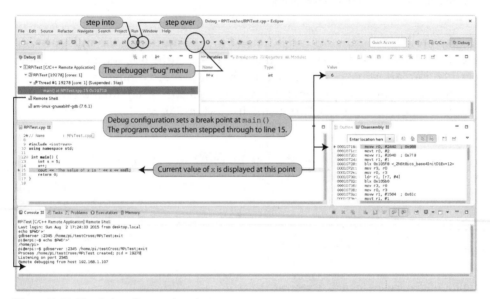

Figure 7-11: The Debug Perspective view

Automatic Documentation (Doxygen)

As your RPi projects grow in capability and complexity, it will become especially important that your code is self-documenting. If you follow good programming practice when naming variables and methods, as discussed in Chapter 5, you will not have to document every single line of code. Rather, you should write inline documentation comments, using automatic documentation tools like Doxygen or Javadoc, for every class, method, and state. This will enable other programmers to have an immediate understanding of what your code does and how it is structured.

Javadoc is an automatic documentation generator that generates HTML code directly from Java source code. Likewise, *Doxygen* is a tool that can be used for generating documentation from annotated C/C++ source files in HTML, LaTeX, and other formats. Doxygen can also generate documentation for the other programming languages that are discussed in Chapter 5, but the following discussion focuses on how it can be used for C++ documentation and how it can be integrated with the Eclipse IDE. An output example, which documents the C++ GPIO class from Chapter 6, is displayed in Figure 7-12.

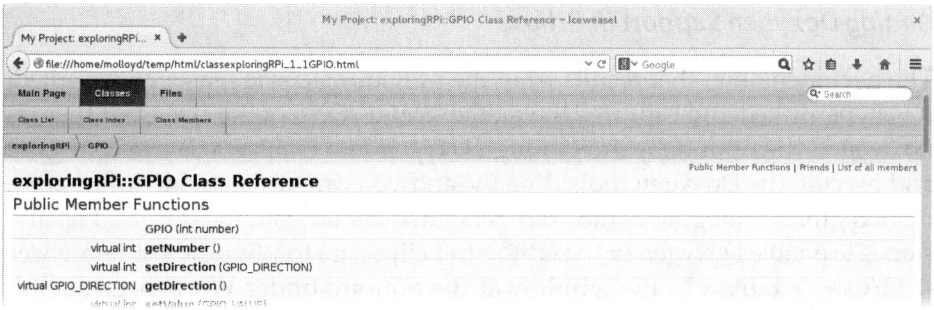

Figure 7-12: Example Doxygen HTML output

First, you need to install Doxygen on the Linux desktop machine using the following command:

```
molloyd@desktop:~$ sudo apt install doxygen
```

Once installed, you can immediately begin generating documentation for your project. For example, copy the GPIO.h and GPIO.cpp files from the chp06/ GPIO/ directory into a temporary directory such as ~/temp and then build the documentation as follows:

```
molloyd@desktop:~/temp$ ls
GPIO.cpp   GPIO.h
molloyd@desktop:~/temp$ doxygen  -g
Configuration file `Doxyfile' created ...
molloyd@desktop:~/temp$ ls
Doxyfile  GPIO.cpp  GPIO.h
molloyd@desktop:~/temp$ doxygen -w html header.html footer.html stylesheet.css
molloyd@desktop:~/temp$ ls
Doxyfile  footer.html  GPIO.cpp  GPIO.h  header.html  stylesheet.css
```

This automatically generates HTML files that you can customize for your project, adding headers, footers, and style sheets to suit your needs. Next, call the doxygen command on the Doxyfile configuration:

```
molloyd@desktop:~/temp$ doxygen Doxyfile
molloyd@desktop:~/temp$ ls
Doxyfile       doxygen_sqlite3.db  footer.html  GPIO.cpp      GPIO.h
header.html    html                latex        stylesheet.css
```

You can see that there are `html` and `latex` folders containing the automatically generated documentation. You can view the output by browsing (e.g., in Chromium/Iceweasel, type `file://` and press Enter in the address bar) to the `~/temp/html/` directory and opening the `index.html` file. There is a comprehensive manual on the features of Doxygen at www .doxygen.org.

Adding Doxygen Support in Eclipse

The documentation that results from the previous steps is reasonably limited. It is hyperlinked and captures the methods and states of the class, but there is no deeper description. By integrating Doxygen into Eclipse, you can configure and execute the Doxygen tools directly, and you can also provide inline commentary that is integrated into your generated documentation output. The first step is to enable Doxygen in the editor. In Eclipse, go to Window ⇨ Preferences ⇨ C/C++ ⇨ Editor. In the window at the bottom, under Workspace default select Doxygen. Apply the settings, and then in the editor type /** followed by the Return key above any method, and the IDE will automatically generate a comment as follows:

```
/**
 * @param number
 */
GPIO::GPIO(int number) {
```

You can then add a description of what the method does, as shown in the following example:

```
/**
 * Constructor for the General Purpose Input/Output (GPIO) class. It
 * will export the GPIO automatically.
 * @param number The GPIO number for the RPi pin
 */
GPIO::GPIO(int number) {
```

To complete the installation, you can install the *Eclox plug-in* for Eclipse by going to Help ⇨ Install New Software, and add a new site http://download .gna.org/eclox/update/ to install the Eclox plug-in.

After Eclipse restarts, you will see a blue @ symbol in the top bar of Eclipse. Press this button to add a `Doxyfile` to your project. You can then open the `Doxyfile` to set the Doxygen configuration for your project, as illustrated in Figure 7-13. You can then press on the blue @ symbol again to generate the documentation for your project, whereupon `html` and `latex` directories will appear in your project. You can browse to these directories and open the documentation files directly within Eclipse.

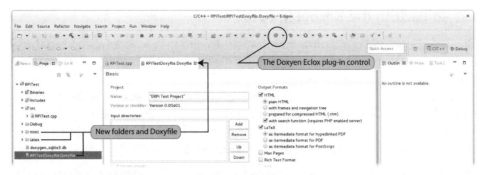

Figure 7-13: Doxygen Eclox plug-in running within Eclipse Mars

At this point, you have everything you need to cross-compile applications for your RPi. The next part of this chapter outlines how you can cross-compile Linux itself and deploy it to an RPi board.

Building Linux

The Linux kernel is essentially a large C program that forms the central core of the Linux OS. Together with loadable kernel modules (LKMs), it is responsible for managing almost everything that occurs on a Linux-based RPi. The kernel is custom built for each architecture type, which means that there is a different kernel required for the ARMv7 RPi2/3 than other ARMv6 RPi models. The custom-built kernel for ARM devices utilizes device tree binary (DTB) files, which provide a standardized description of the device to reduce the amount of custom code required for each device model.

The Raspbian image contains a full Linux distribution that includes a kernel; however, advanced users may want to replace the kernel with a very recent or user-configured kernel. Typically, this involves building the kernel from source code, which can be performed directly on the RPi, but it can take quite some time. Alternatively, the cross-compilation tools that are described in this chapter can be used, which can greatly reduce compilation time by leveraging the resources of a capable Linux desktop machine.

The following description is written with the assumption that you have installed a cross-compilation toolchain, as described at the beginning of this chapter. The steps involved in this process are constantly undergoing change, so updates are maintained on the chapter web page at `www.exploringrpi` `.com/chapter7`.

Downloading the Kernel Source

The Raspberry Pi Foundation maintains the code that is required to build the kernel for the RPi on a GitHub repository. This reduces the complexity of the build process in comparison to cloning the "vanilla" repository from www.kernel .org, because the GitHub repository contains helpful configuration files. You can clone the entire GitHub repository, but you should typically use a *shallow clone*, which greatly reduces the download time because the development history is truncated (~143MB versus the full repository size of ~1.25GB):

```
molloyd@desktop:~$ git clone --depth=1 git://github.com/raspberrypi/linux.git
Cloning into 'linux'...
molloyd@desktop:~$ cd linux/
molloyd@desktop:~/linux$ ls
arch            CREDITS       drivers  include   Kbuild   lib        mm
REPORTING-BUGS  security      usr      block     crypto   firmware   init
Kconfig         MAINTAINERS   net      samples   sound    virt       COPYING
fs              ipc           kernel   Makefile  README   scripts    tools
```

If you would like to build a different kernel version than the current master version, you can clone the full repository and check out a particular development branch:

```
molloyd@desktop:~/linux$ git branch -a
* rpi-4.1.y
  remotes/origin/HEAD -> origin/rpi-4.1.y
  remotes/origin/linux_stable
  remotes/origin/master
  remotes/origin/rpi-3.10.y   ...
  remotes/origin/rpi-3.18.y   ...
molloyd@desktop:~/linux$ git checkout rpi-3.18.y
Branch rpi-3.18.y set up to track remote branch rpi-3.18.y from origin.
Switched to a new branch 'rpi-3.18.y'
molloyd@desktop:~/linux$ git branch -a
* rpi-3.18.y
  rpi-4.1.y  ...
```

If you need to verify the exact version of Linux that you are about to build (including the sublevel):

```
molloyd@desktop:~/linux$ git checkout linux_stable
molloyd@desktop:~/linux$ head -3 Makefile
VERSION = 3
PATCHLEVEL = 18
SUBLEVEL = 14
```

Typically, if you need to check out a different sublevel version, you can use git tag -l and then perform a checkout of that branch (e.g., git checkout -b v3.18.12), but the tags in the GitHub repository are not aligned with the "vanilla" kernel, and you might not be able to check out a desired release.

As an alternative to cloning the full repository, you can obtain a full list of the remote references, and then clone a specific branch as follows:

```
molloyd@desktop:~$ git ls-remote --heads git://github.com/raspberrypi/linux →
.git
51af817611f2c0987030d024f24fc7ea95dd33e6    refs/heads/linux_stable
645fd9b0c0b3c1f79f71f92dac79bd2f87010444    refs/heads/master
1b49b450222df26e4abf7abb6d9302f72b2ed386    refs/heads/rpi-3.10.y
8f768c5f2a3314e4eacce8d667c787f8dadfda74    refs/heads/rpi-3.11.y  ...
6db93ee810fe7c58b02f71e76c8efef49e701084    refs/heads/rpi-4.5.y ...
molloyd@desktop:~ $ git clone -b rpi-3.11.y --depth=1 --single-branch →
git://github.com/raspberrypi/linux.git
molloyd@desktop:~ $ cd linux/
molloyd@desktop:~/linux$ git branch -a
* rpi-3.11.y
  remotes/origin/rpi-3.11.y   ...
```

Building the Linux Kernel

The core tools and configuration files that are required to build the kernel should already be installed on your desktop machine.[4] Therefore, to build the kernel, you begin by choosing your target RPi model:

■ For the RPi2/3 (ARMv7), type the following (from 3.18.y on):

```
molloyd@desktop:~/linux$ export CC=arm-linux-gnueabihf-
molloyd@desktop:~/linux$ make ARCH=arm CROSS_COMPILE=${CC} →
bcm2709_defconfig
```

■ Or, for other RPi models (ARMv6):

```
molloyd@desktop:~/linux$ export CC=arm-linux-gnueabihf-
molloyd@desktop:~/linux$ make ARCH=arm CROSS_COMPILE=${CC} →
bcmrpi_defconfig
```

This step identifies that you are building for the ARM architecture, and it identifies a prefix for the cross-compilation tools. It results in the creation of a configuration file (.config) in the current directory.

You can further customize the kernel configuration by installing the ncurses-dev package and calling make menuconfig, as follows:

```
molloyd@desktop:~/linux$ sudo apt install ncurses-dev
molloyd@desktop:~/linux$ make ARCH=arm CROSS_COMPILE=${CC} menuconfig
```

This step displays the Kernel Configuration tool, as illustrated in Figure 7-14. Effectively, this tool enables you to modify the .config file in a structured manner, where available options are presented in menu form.

---

[4] You may need to install build-essential, git, ncurses-dev, and crossbuild-essential-armhf.

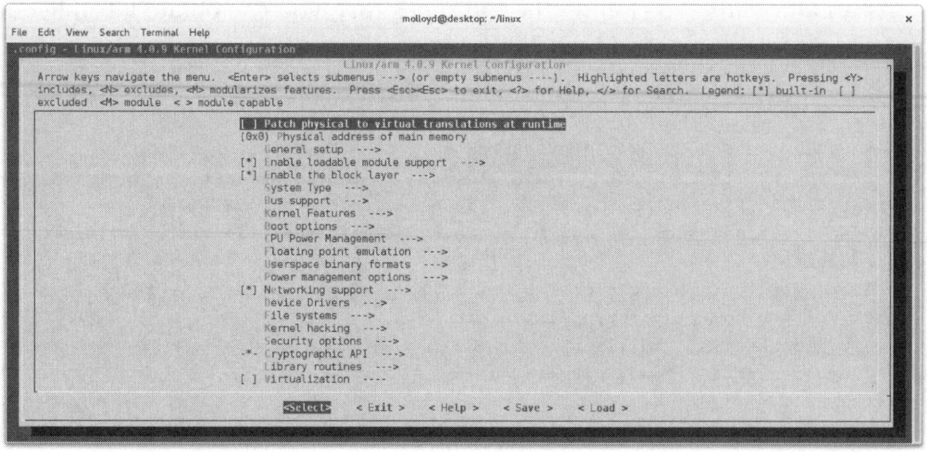

Figure 7-14: The Kernel Configuration tool for Linux 4.0.9

You should browse the configuration menu to see some entries that may be of interest in relation to the RPi platform:

- Under System Type, you can see that there are options for the BCM2709 platform. For example under Broadcom BCM2709 Implementations, you can see that device tree support and GPIO support are enabled by default.

- In the Kernel Features menu, you can see that the number of CPUs is set at 4 for the RPi2/3. You can alter the Preemption Model in the same menu (see Figure 7-15(a)).

- In the Boot options menu, you can see the Default kernel command string, which begins "console=ttyAMA0, 115200 …" (see the boot log in Chapter 3).

- Under CPU Power Management, you can use the CPU Frequency scaling menu to enable/disable the various governors. You can also change the default governor from "powersave" to one of the other governors if you so want.

- In the Floating point emulation menu, you can see that the configuration includes Advanced SIMD (NEON) Extension support for the RPi2/3 platform.

- The Device Drivers menu provides options for configuring I²C, SPI, USB devices, and much more.

The configuration is saved in the .config file when you exit this tool. You are then ready to build the kernel, its associated LKMs, and DTBs. You can do so by calling this command:

```
... ~/linux$ make -j 6 ARCH=arm CROSS_COMPILE=${CC} zImage modules dtbs
```

The argument `-j 6` enables parallel execution, allowing the `make` command to execute several jobs simultaneously. My VM has six CPU threads in this case. This option dramatically improves compilation time; in fact, it took approximately 8 minutes to build the kernel on my VM. Note that you might have to perform a `make clean` between subsequent kernel builds.

THE FULLY PREEMPTIBLE KERNEL (RT) PATCH

You can also apply patches to the kernel that you are building. For example, you can download the PREEMPT_RT patch from `www.kernel.org/pub/linux/kernel/projects/rt/` as a `.gz` file for the *exact kernel version* that you are building. Unfortunately, the patch is not available for all kernel versions, so some research is required to ensure that you choose a kernel for which a patch has been released. You can open the URL above in a web browser to identify available options. You can apply the patch to your kernel source as follows:

```
molloyd@desktop:~/linux$ git checkout rpi-3.18.y
molloyd@desktop:~/linux$ wget https://www.kernel.org/pub/linux/ker →
nel/projects/rt/3.18/older/patch-3.18.16-rt13.patch.gz
molloyd@desktop:~/linux$ gunzip patch-3.18.16-rt13.patch.gz
molloyd@desktop:~/linux$ cat patch-3.18.16-rt13.patch | patch -p1
```

If the patch does not apply correctly, you can reverse it by using the following:

```
molloyd@desktop:~/linux$ cat patch-3.18.16-rt13.patch | patch -R -p1
```

In Figure 7-15(a), the RT patch has been applied, which results in a new option for a fully preemptible kernel in the `menuconfig` tool.

(a)   (b)

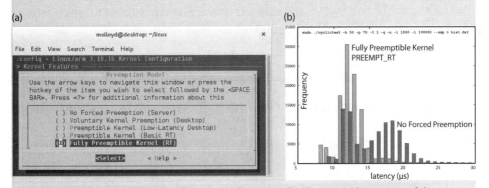

Figure 7-15: (a) The PREEMPT_RT menuconfig option (b) The results histogram of the cyclictest under load

The patched kernel can be deployed using the steps that follow in this section. On reboot, `uname -a` should display a message that includes RT. Figure 7-15(b) illustrates the cyclictest results histogram of the fully preemptible kernel in comparison to a kernel with no forced preemption. These kernels were tested under load by using the

Continues

THE FULLY PREEMPTIBLE KERNEL (RT) PATCH (*continued*)

performance tests from Chapter 5 to create the load. The RT results on the RPi2 are as follows:

```
pi@erpi ~ $ uname -a
Linux erpi 3.18.16-rt13-v7+ #1 SMP PREEMPT RT Aug 6 12:41:42 EDT
2015 armv7l GNU/Linux
pi@erpi ~/rt-tests $ sudo ./cyclictest -t 1 -p 70 -n -i 1000 -l 100000 --smp
policy: fifo: loadavg: 0.87 0.34 0.15 2/175 1150
T: 0 ( 1238) P:70 I:1000 C: 100000 Min:    8 Act:  13 Avg:  11 Max:    87
T: 1 ( 1239) P:70 I:1500 C:  66669 Min:    8 Act:  23 Avg:  12 Max:    64
T: 2 ( 1240) P:70 I:2000 C:  50001 Min:    8 Act:  17 Avg:  12 Max:    48
T: 3 ( 1241) P:70 I:2500 C:  40001 Min:    8 Act:  15 Avg:  12 Max:    54
```

The same kernel built with the No Forced Preemption model does not perform as well when tested under load. The maximum latency is higher, and the average latency is somewhat higher:

```
pi@erpi ~/rt-tests $ uname -a
Linux erpi 3.18.16-rt13-v7+ #2 SMP Aug 6 19:14:58 EDT 2015 armv7l GNU/Linux
pi@erpi ~/rt-tests $ sudo ./cyclictest -t 1 -p 70 -n -i 1000 -l 100000 --smp
policy: fifo: loadavg: 0.90 0.40 0.19 4/153 932
T: 0 (  874) P:70 I:1000 C: 100000 Min:    7 Act:  11 Avg:  17 Max:   466
T: 1 (  875) P:70 I:1500 C:  66668 Min:    8 Act:  12 Avg:  15 Max:   206
T: 2 (  876) P:70 I:2000 C:  50001 Min:    7 Act:  13 Avg:  14 Max:   488
T: 3 (  877) P:70 I:2500 C:  40000 Min:    7 Act:  11 Avg:  15 Max:   188
```

The new Linux kernel image appears in the `/arch/arm/boot/` directory in uncompressed form (`Image`), and in a self-extracting compressed form (`zImage`). The latter should be used, as it reduces boot times:[5]

```
molloyd@desktop:~/linux/arch/arm/boot$ ls -l *Image
-rwxr-xr-x 1 molloyd molloyd 8743476 Aug  3 09:06 Image
-rwxr-xr-x 1 molloyd molloyd 4000616 Aug  3 09:06 zImage
```

The new DTB files are stored in the `dts/` and `dts/overlays/` directories, as follows:

```
molloyd@desktop:~/linux/arch/arm/boot/dts$ ls -l *.dtb
-rw-r--r-- 1 molloyd molloyd 9900 Aug  2 17:02 bcm2709-rpi-2-b.dtb
molloyd@desktop:~/linux/arch/arm/boot/dts/overlays$ ls *.dtb
ads7846-overlay.dtb            iqaudio-dac-overlay.dtb
rpi-proto-overlay.dtb          ...
```

The final build step is to package the LKMs so that they can be deployed to the RPi. A temporary directory `temp_modules/` is used for this task, and you can view the resulting structure using the `tree` command:

```
molloyd@desktop:~/linux$ make ARCH=arm CROSS_COMPILE=arm-linux-gnueabihf- →
INSTALL_MOD_PATH=temp_modules/ modules_install
```

---

[5] A zImage or bzImage (big zImage) file contains executable decompression code and the Linux kernel, which is compressed in gzip format by default (see the kernel compression mode in the kernel configuration tool as illustrated in Figure 7-14).

```
molloyd@desktop:~/linux/temp_modules$ sudo apt install tree
molloyd@desktop:~/linux/temp_modules$ tree . | more
└── lib
    ├── firmware
    │   ├── cpia2
    │   │   └── stv0672_vp4.bin
    ...
    └── modules
        └── 4.0.9-v7+
            ├── build -> /home/molloyd/linux
            ├── kernel
            │   ├── arch
            │   │   └── arm
            │   │       ├── crypto
            │   │       │   ├── aes-arm-bs.ko
    ...
```

Deploying the Linux Kernel

You can test the new kernel using an existing Raspbian image to which you can copy the kernel image, DTBs, and the LKMs for the new kernel. You can do this by mounting the SD card from your offline RPi onto your Linux desktop machine. More information on this approach is available at tiny .cc/erpi701.

An online approach is used here, where the files are copied to a live Raspberry Pi over the network. Regardless of the approach that you take, you should back up the live RPi's existing kernel configuration (e.g., in /boot/backup/) using the following steps:

```
pi@erpi /boot $ sudo mkdir backup
pi@erpi /boot $ sudo cp kernel*.img backup/
pi@erpi /boot $ sudo cp -r overlays backup/
pi@erpi /boot $ sudo cp -a /lib/firmware/ /boot/backup/
```

Also, if you are replacing a kernel with the exact same version number, you should also back up its /lib/modules/X.X.X-X directory.

ENABLING SSH ROOT LOGIN WITH RASPBIAN

To transfer files to certain directories on the RPi using scp or rsync, you may need to enable SSH root login. The first step is to enable root login (as described in Chapter 5) using the following:

```
pi@erpi ~ $ sudo passwd root
Enter new UNIX password: secretpassword
...
```

Continues

ENABLING SSH ROOT LOGIN WITH RASPBIAN (*continued*)

Then edit the sshd configuration file (`sshd_config`) to permit root login by changing the `PermitRootLogin` value to `yes`. Then restart the service:

```
pi@erpi /etc/ssh $ sudo nano sshd_config
pi@erpi /etc/ssh $ more sshd_config | grep RootLogin
PermitRootLogin yes
pi@erpi /etc/ssh $ sudo systemctl restart sshd
```

To reverse this configuration, set the `PermitRootLogin` value back to `without-password` and disable root login using `sudo passwd -l root`.

You may need to enable SSH root login on your RPi to copy the files to the board. Then use `scp` or `rsync` to transfer the files as follows:

```
molloyd@desktop:~/linux/arch/arm/boot$ scp zImage root@erpi.local:/boot/ker →
nel7_erpi.img
root@erpi.local's password:
zImage                    100% 3907KB   3.8MB/s   00:00
molloyd@desktop:~/linux/arch/arm/boot$ scp dts/*.dtb root@erpi.local:/boot/
molloyd@desktop:~/linux/arch/arm/boot$ scp dts/overlays/*.dtb root@erpi.loc →
al:/boot/overlays/
molloyd@desktop:~/linux/arch/arm/boot$ cd ~/linux/temp_modules/
```

Unfortunately, the `lib/modules/` directory contains symbolic links that cannot be easily ignored by `scp`. You can delete them and use `scp`, or you can use the `rsync` command for the last file copy step:

```
molloyd@desktop:~/linux/temp_modules$ rsync -avhe ssh lib/ root@erpi.local:/
```

The files are now in place on the RPi. You should then edit the `/boot/config.txt` file to select your new kernel (`kernel7_erpi.img`) rather than overwriting the current `kernel.img` or `kernel7.img` files:

```
pi@erpi /boot $ sudo nano config.txt
pi@erpi /boot $ more config.txt | grep kernel
kernel=kernel7_erpi.img
```

Finally, you can reboot the RPi and verify the new kernel version:

```
pi@erpi /boot $ sudo reboot
...
pi@erpi ~ $ uname -a
Linux erpi 4.0.9-v7+ #1 SMP PREEMPT Aug 2 17:06:27 EDT 2015 armv7l GNU/Linux
```

NOTE The RPi firmware is also available on a separate GitHub repository: `github.com/raspberrypi/firmware.git`. However, it is a very large repository (4GB+). In the repository, you will find the latest prebuilt kernels, versions of the boot files (e.g., `bootcode.bin`, `start.elf`), and the latest VideoCoreIV userspace libraries. The firmware files are updated relatively infrequently, and an `apt update` followed by an `apt upgrade` is the easiest way to keep your RPi image and firmware up to date.

Building a Linux Distribution (Advanced)

In the previous section, a new Linux kernel was deployed to an existing Raspbian image distribution. It is also possible to build a custom Linux distribution for the RPi using open source projects such as *OpenWRT* (www.openwrt.org), *Buildroot* (buildroot.uclibc.org), and the *Yocto Project* (www.yoctoproject.org). These projects aim to create tools, templates and processes to support you in building custom embedded Linux distributions.

Poky (www.pokylinux.org) is an open source build tool from the Yocto Project that can be used to build customized Linux images for more complex embedded systems, such as the RPi. The Poky platform builder, which is derived from *OpenEmbedded*, can be used to build ready-to-install Linux file system images, by automatically downloading and building all the Linux applications (e.g., SSH servers, gcc, X11 applications), and configuring and installing them within a root file system. The alternative approach to using a build system such as Poky is that you would have to configure each Linux application by hand, matching dependency versions—a difficult task that would have to be repeated for each system type.

Poky uses the *BitBake* build tool to perform tasks such as downloading, compiling and installing software packages and file system images. The instructions as to which tasks BitBake should perform are contained in metadata *recipe* (.bb) files. There is a full "Poky Handbook" that is co-authored by Richard Purdie of the Linux Foundation at tiny.cc/erpi702.

Here is a short guide that works through the steps that are currently required to build a minimal Linux distribution for the RPi. This is intended as a learning exercise that aims to give you a flavor of what to expect; there are full books written on this topic! Depending on the specification of your PC, these steps can take several hours to complete:

1. Clone the Poky repository (~113MB), and within the repository download the RPi recipes (~350KB), which are placed in the poky/meta-raspberrypi directory:

```
molloyd@desktop:~$ git clone git://git.yoctoproject.org/poky.git
Cloning into 'poky'...
molloyd@desktop:~$ cd poky/
molloyd@desktop:~/poky$ git clone git://git.yoctoproject.org/meta-raspberrypi
Cloning into 'meta-raspberrypi'...
```

2. Configure the build environment and create the build directory and the configuration files that you can use to configure the build:

```
molloyd@desktop:~/poky$ source oe-init-build-env erpi
### Shell environment set up for builds. ###
You can now run 'bitbake <target>'
Common targets are: core-image-minimal ...
molloyd@desktop:~/poky/erpi$ cd conf
```

```
molloyd@desktop:~/poky/erpi/conf$ ls
bblayers.conf   local.conf   templateconf.cfg
```

3. Add the `meta-raspberrypi` recipes directory to the `BBLAYERS` entry in the `bblayers.conf` file:

```
molloyd@desktop:~/poky/erpi/conf$ more bblayers.conf
...
BBLAYERS ?= " \
  /home/molloyd/poky/meta \
  /home/molloyd/poky/meta-yocto \
  /home/molloyd/poky/meta-yocto-bsp \
  /home/molloyd/poky/meta-raspberrypi \
  " ...
```

4. You can configure the build by adding entries to the configuration files. Note that the README file in the `poky/meta-raspberrypi` directory contains a guide to the available RPi options. Edit the `local.conf` file to replace `qemux86` with `raspberrypi` (or `raspberrypi2`), enable the camera, and set the GPU memory size. So, for example:

```
molloyd@desktop:~/poky/erpi/conf$ more local.conf
...
MACHINE ??= "raspberrypi2"
GPU_MEM = "16"
VIDEO_CAMERA = "1"
...
```

5. Set the cross-compiler variables and you are ready to build an RPi image (use either rpi-hwup-image or rpi-basic-image). The basic image includes SSH support and so is used here:

```
molloyd@desktop:~/poky/erpi$ CC=arm-linux-gnueabihf-gcc
molloyd@desktop:~/poky/erpi$ LD=arm-linux-gnueabihf-ld
molloyd@desktop:~/poky/erpi$ bitbake rpi-basic-image
Parsing recipes: 100% |###################################| Time: 00:00:38
Parsing of 904 .bb files complete (0 cached, 904 parsed). 1318 targets, 61
skipped, 0 masked, 0 errors ...
```

You may have to run this step several times until you have resolved missing dependencies. For example, I had to install the following:

```
molloyd@desktop:~/poky/erpi$ sudo apt install diffstat chrpath →
libsdl-dev
```

At this point the build should begin; it takes approximately 45 minutes on a VM that has an allocation of six i7 threads.

6. You can then write the final image to an SD card using the steps described in Chapter 2. The SD image file is located at

```
molloyd@desktop:~/poky/erpi/tmp/deploy/images/raspberrypi2$ ls -l →
*.rpi-sdimg
-rw-r--r-- 1 molloyd molloyd 130023424 Aug 8 17:44 rpi-basic-image-
raspberrypi2-20150810205912.rootfs.rpi-sdimg
```

After the RPi has been booted with the new distribution, you can connect to it using its IP address (see Chapter 2), and you can log in as root with no password required:

```
molloyd@desktop:~$ ssh root@192.168.1.116
root@raspberrypi2:~# uname -a
Linux raspberrypi2 3.18.11 #2 SMP PREEMPT Aug 8 8:38:21 EDT 2015 armv7l ...
root@raspberrypi2:~# df -h
Filesystem            Size      Used Available Use% Mounted on
/dev/root            73.5M     58.3M     11.1M  84% /
devtmpfs            427.6M         0    427.6M   0% /dev
tmpfs               431.8M    156.0K    431.6M   0% /run
tmpfs               431.8M     52.0K    431.7M   0% /var/volatile
```

The ext4 partition on this minimal image is ~58MB in size, so you do not have access to anything like the same range of tools as within the Raspbian image. Typically, packages are added to the distribution at the build stage, but it is possible to add a package manager such as deb/apt.[6] However, adding typical package management capabilities to your custom build involves pointing /etc/apt/sources.list on the RPi at your own web server, which contains packages that are custom built for your distribution (e.g., from /poky/erpi/tmp/deploy/).

At this stage, you can adjust the configuration files, and BitBake will only rebuild packages that are affected by your changes. For example, it is possible to configure kernel settings using the menuconfig tool (as in Figure 7-14) at this stage and rebuild the SD image within a matter of minutes:

```
molloyd@desktop:~/poky/erpi$ bitbake virtual/kernel -c menuconfig
molloyd@desktop:~/poky/erpi$ bitbake virtual/kernel -c compile -f
molloyd@desktop:~/poky/erpi$ bitbake virtual/kernel
molloyd@desktop:~/poky/erpi$ bitbake rpi-basic-image
```

One key strength of the Poky build tool is that there is strong community support; see pokylinux.org/support/.

Summary

After completing this chapter, you should be able to do the following:

- Install a cross-compilation toolchain on desktop Linux that can be used to build applications for the RPi using your desktop PC.

- Use a package manager to install multi-architecture third-party libraries that may be required for cross-compilation.

- Emulate the ARM architecture on the desktop PC using QEMU.

---

[6] Add three line entries for IMAGE_FEATURES += "package-management", +PACKAGE_CLASSES ?= "package_deb", and CORE_IMAGE_EXTRA_INSTALL += "apt" to the local.conf file.

- Install and configure the Eclipse integrated development environment (IDE) for cross-compilation to build RPi applications.
- Configure Eclipse for remote deployment of applications, remote debugging, GitHub integration, and automated documentation.
- Build a custom Linux kernel and deploy it to the RPi.

Further Reading

The steps in this chapter are prone to changes of the Linux distribution, the Eclipse version, and the kernel configuration. If you are experiencing difficulties with this configuration or want to contribute information that will make it easier for others to do the same tasks that are presented in this chapter, visit `www.exploringrpi.com/chapter7/`.

CHAPTER

8

Interfacing to the Raspberry Pi Buses

This chapter describes bus communication in detail, explaining and comparing the different bus types that are available on the Raspberry Pi. It describes how you can configure them for use, and how you can communicate with and control I²C, SPI, and UART devices, using both Linux tools and custom-developed C/C++ code. Practical examples are provided using different low-cost bus devices, such as a real-time clock, an accelerometer, a serial shift register with a seven-segment display, a USB-to-TTL 3.3 V cable, and a GPS receiver. After reading this chapter, you should have the skills necessary to begin interfacing almost any type of bus device to the Raspberry Pi.

Equipment Required for This Chapter:

- Raspberry Pi (ideally an RPi 2/3)
- A real-time clock on a breakout board (e.g., the DS3231)
- ADXL345 accelerometer on an I²C/SPI breakout board
- 74HC595 shift register, seven-segment display, and resistors
- A USB-to-TTL 3.3 V cable (see Chapter 1 and Chapter 2)
- A low-cost UART GPS receiver (e.g., the GY-GPS6MV2)

Further details on this equipment and chapter are available at
`www.exploringrpi.com/chapter8`.

Introduction to Bus Communication

In Chapter 6, the use of general-purpose input/outputs (GPIOs) is discussed in detail, which makes it clear how you can connect the RPi to standalone components, including one-wire sensors that have custom communications protocols. This chapter examines more complex communications that can be performed using the bus interfaces that are available on the RPi. *Bus communication* is a mechanism that enables data to be transferred between the high-level components of an embedded platform, using standardized communications protocols. The two most commonly used embedded system buses are available on the RPi, and they are the subject of this chapter: *Inter-Integrated Circuit* (I^2C) and *Serial Peripheral Interface (SPI)*. In addition, *Universal Asynchronous Receiver/Transmitter (UART)* devices are discussed. These are computer hardware devices that can be configured and used to send and receive serial data. When combined with appropriate driver interfaces, UARTs can implement standard serial communication protocols, such as RS-232, RS-422, or RS-485.

Understanding the behavior and use of bus communication protocols and devices enables the possibility of building advanced RPi electronic systems. There are a huge number of complex sensors, actuators, input devices, I/O expanders, and other microcontrollers that conform to these communication protocols, and the RPi is capable of communicating with them all. Several such devices are used in Chapter 9 to enhance the interfacing capabilities of the RPi, and in Chapter 10 to interface the RPi to the physical environment using sensors and actuators. In addition, Chapter 11 describes how you can use the popular Arduino microcontroller to build your own advanced bus devices, which can be interfaced directly to the RPi using these buses.

The topics discussed in this chapter are all demonstrated using practical examples with devices that were largely chosen based on their wide availability and low cost. However, the focus of this chapter is on imparting an understanding of the techniques employed in using the RPi's buses, rather than just describing the specific bus devices used. To this end, the chapter provides generic communications code that you can use in order to apply the principles described to any device of your choosing.

I^2C

Inter-Integrated Circuit (IIC or I^2C) is a two-wire bus that was designed by Philips in the 1980s to interface microprocessors or microcontrollers to low-speed peripheral devices. A *master* device, such as the RPi, controls the bus, and many addressable *slave* devices can be attached to the same two wires. It has remained popular over the years, mainly due to its relative simplicity and breadth of adoption. It is currently used in smartphones, most microcontrollers, and even environmental management applications in large-scale server farms. Here are some general features of the I²C bus:

- Only two signal lines are required for communication, the *Serial Data (SDA)* line for the bidirectional transmission of data, and the *Serial Clock (SCL)* line, which is used to synchronize the data transfer. Because the bus uses this synchronizing clock signal, the data transfer is said to be *synchronous*. The transmission is said to be *bidirectional* because the same SDA wire can be used for sending and receiving data.

- Each device on the bus can act as a master or a slave. The *master device* is the one that initiates communication and the *slave device* is the one that responds. Designated slave devices cannot initiate communication with the master device.

- Each slave device attached to the bus is pre-assigned a unique address, which is in either 7-bit or 10-bit form. In the following examples, 7-bit addressing is used, i.e., 0x00 to 0x7F ($2^7 = 128_{10} = 0x80$).

- It has true *multi-master bus facilities*, including collision detection and arbitration if two or more master devices activate at once.

- On-chip noise filtering is built in as standard.

I²C Hardware

Figure 8-1(a) illustrates the interconnection of multiple slave devices to the I²C bus. All output connections to the SDA and SCL lines are in open-drain configuration (discussed in Chapter 4), whereby all devices share a common ground connection. This means that devices with different logic families can be intermixed on the bus, and that a large number of devices can be added to a single bus. In theory, up to 128 devices could be attached to a single bus, but doing so would greatly increase the capacitance of the interconnecting lines. The bus is designed to work over short distances, as long bus lines are prone to electrical interference and *capacitance effects* (e.g., a pair of 22 AWG shielded wires has a capacitance of about 15 pF/ft).

Transmission line capacitance has a huge impact on data transmission rates. In Chapter 4 (see Figure 4-11), when a 10 µF capacitor is connected in parallel with a resistive load and an AC voltage supply is applied, the capacitor had a very clear smoothing effect on the voltage across the load. This smoothing effect is unwelcome in the transmission of digital data; for example, if a random binary signal (0 V–3.3 V) switches at a high frequency, then severe smoothing could result in a constant 1.65 V signal, which carries no binary information at all. Typically, the longer the bus length and the more I²C devices that are attached to it, the slower the speed of data transmission. There are I²C repeaters available that act as current amplifiers to help solve the problems associated with long lines. Further documentation on the I²C bus is available from NXP directly at tiny.cc/erpi801.

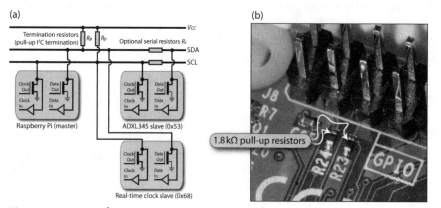

Figure 8-1: (a) The I²C bus configuration, and (b) the built-in pull-up resistors on the I2C1 bus

I²C on the RPi

I²C on the RPi is implemented using the Broadcom Serial Controller (BSC), which supports 7-bit/10-bit addressing and bus frequencies of up to 400 kHz (see Chapter 3 of the *BCM2835 ARM Peripherals* document). NXP (formerly Philips) has newer I²C Fast-mode Plus (Fm+) devices that can communicate at up to 1 MHz[1], but this capability is not available on the RPi.

The I²C bus requires pull-up resistors (R_p) on both the SDA and SCL lines, as illustrated in Figure 8-1(a). These are called *termination resistors* and they usually have a value of between 1 kΩ and 10 kΩ. Their role is to pull the SDA and SCL lines up to V_{CC} when no I²C device is pulling them down to GND. This pull-up configuration enables multiple master devices to take control of the bus, and for the slave device to "stretch" the clock signal (i.e., hold SCL low). *Clock stretching* can be used by the slave device to slow down data transfer until it has finished processing and is ready to transmit. These termination resistors (R23 and R24) are physically attached to the RPi's I2C1 bus (Pins 3 and 5), as illustrated in Figure 8-1(b). Termination resistors are often also present on the

---

[1] In 2012 NXP released Ultra Fast-mode (UFm) I²C, which offers a 5 MHz mode. However, it is quite different from other I²C modes as it is unidirectional and there is only a single master. It is currently not widely adopted.

breakout board that is associated with an I²C device. This can be a useful feature, but their equivalent parallel resistance should be factored into your design if you are using several boards on the same bus.

The optional *serial resistors* (R_S) shown in Figure 8-1(a) usually have low values (e.g., 250 Ω), and can help protect against overcurrent conditions. The I²C devices are typically attached to the SDA and SCL lines using built-in Schmitt trigger inputs (see Chapter 4) to reduce the impact of signal noise by building in a degree of switching hysteresis.

WARNING   The I²C bus on the RPi is 3.3 V tolerant; consequently, you may need logic-level translation circuitry if you want to connect 5 V powered I²C devices to it. That topic is discussed at the end of this chapter.

Enabling the I²C bus on the RPi

The primary I²C bus is not enabled by default on the RPi. You can enable it using the `raspi-config` tool (see Chapter 2) using the "Advanced Options" menu. However, the change does not always apply correctly and it is useful to understand the system changes that the tool makes. Essentially, the tool adds an entry to the `/boot/config.txt` and the `/etc/modules` files. You can make these changes manually by adding an `i2c_arm` entry line to the boot configuration file:

```
pi@erpi /boot $ more config.txt | grep i2c_arm
dtparam=i2c_arm=on
```

Save the configuration file and reboot; at this point, the bus is not yet available. The I²C bus implementation on the RPi uses loadable kernel modules (LKMs). Therefore, at this point you can manually load the LKMs using the `modprobe` command, as follows:

```
pi@erpi /dev $ sudo modprobe i2c-bcm2708
pi@erpi /dev $ sudo modprobe i2c-dev
pi@erpi /dev $ lsmod | grep i2c
Module              Size  Used by
i2c_dev             6027  0
i2c_bcm2708         4990  0
```

These modules are loaded from the modules directory for your kernel version. For example:

```
pi@erpi:/lib/modules/4.1.19-v7+/kernel/drivers/i2c $ ls -l i2c-dev.ko
-rw-r--r-- 1 root root 15576 Mar 14 15:39 i2c-dev.ko
```

A new `i2c-1` device is then available in the `/dev` directory:

```
pi@erpi /dev $ ls -l i2c*
crw-rw---T 1 root i2c 89, 1 Mar 26 16:33 i2c-1
```

Instead of loading the modules manually, you can edit the `/etc/modules` file and add the module names to the file. The I²C LKMs are then automatically loaded on boot.

```
pi@erpi /etc $ cat modules
snd-bcm2835
i2c-bcm2708
i2c-dev
```

NOTE If you are having difficulties with these steps, check that any required modules are not listed in a blacklist file within `/etc/modprobe.d/`, and ensure that you are using the latest firmware by using `sudo rpi-update`. You should also check the chapter web page for updates.

Enabling a Second I²C Bus

There is a second I²C bus (see Table 8-1) on recent RPi models that is reserved for the automatic configuration of HATs that are attached to the board. If you are not using HATs, then you can use this bus for your own applications. To do this, you must edit the kernel command line arguments in `/boot/cmdline .txt` to include the text, "bcm2708.vc_i2c_override=1" (the entire command must be on a single line):

```
pi@erpi /boot $ sudo nano cmdline.txt
pi@erpi /boot $ more cmdline.txt
dwc_otg.lpm_enable=0 console=ttyAMA0,115200 console=tty1 root=/dev/mmcbl →
k0p2 rootfstype=ext4 elevator=deadline rootwait bcm2708.vc_i2c_override=1
```

You must also add an entry to `/boot/config.txt` as follows:

```
pi@erpi /boot $ tail -1 config.txt
dtparam=i2c_vc=on
```

After reboot, you should now have two I²C devices.

```
pi@erpi ~ $ ls /dev/i2c*
/dev/i2c-0  /dev/i2c-1
```

WARNING The second I²C bus does not have onboard pull-up resistors. You will have to add them to your circuit or it will not work correctly. Standard resistor values of 1.8 kΩ, 2.2 kΩ, and 4.7 kΩ should work well in most applications. Use a larger value if possible, as each time you add a device with on-board pull-up resistors to the bus, the combined parallel resistance is further reduced and a larger current will flow.

Table 8-1: I²C Buses on the RPi[2]

H/W BUS	S/W DEVICE	SDA PIN	SCL PIN	DESCRIPTION
I2C1	`/dev/i2c-1`	Pin 3	Pin 5	General I²C bus. This is disabled by default.
I2C0	`/dev/i2c-0`	Pin 27	Pin 28	Reserved I²C bus for HAT management. This is not available on the older RPi A/B boards.

CHANGING THE I²C BAUD RATE

The current I²C clock frequency can be determined from the sysfs LKM parameters:

```
pi@erpi ~ $ sudo cat /sys/module/i2c_bcm2708/parameters/baudrate
100000
```

On some Linux image releases, it is possible to adjust the baud rate for the I²C buses on reboot using device tree parameters. You can edit the `/boot/config.txt` file and add a line that contains `dtparam=i2c_baudrate=400000` to change the frequency to 400 kHz. The updated baud rate is set on reboot.

```
pi@erpi ~ $ sudo cat /sys/module/i2c_bcm2708/parameters/baudrate
400000
```

On other Linux image releases and configurations, it is possible to reload the LKM with a custom argument at run time, for example:

```
pi@erpi:~ $ sudo modprobe -r i2c_bcm2708
pi@erpi:~ $ sudo modprobe i2c_bcm2708 baudrate=400000
pi@erpi:~ $ sudo cat /sys/module/i2c_bcm2708/parameters/baudrate
400000
```

This change can be made to persist on reboot by creating a file named `i2c_bcm2708.conf` in the `/etc/modprobe.d/` directory that contains the following:

```
pi@erpi:/etc/modprobe.d $ more bcm_2708.conf
options i2c_bcm2708 baudrate=400000
```

An I²C Test Circuit

There are many I²C devices available that can be connected to the RPi, and two different types are described in this section—a real-time clock and an

---

[2] There is a third 5 V I²C bus available via the HDMI connector. It is possible to use it from Linux user space but you must use kernel patches. Also, the primary I²C bus on early RPi versions is `i2c-0`, not `i2c-1` as on later versions.

accelerometer. These particular devices have been chosen because they have a low cost, are widely available, are useful, and have high-quality datasheets.

A Real-Time Clock

Unlike a desktop computer, the RPi does not have an onboard battery-backed clock. This means that the clock time is lost on each occasion that the board reboots; however, a network-attached RPi can retrieve the current time from the network using the Network Time Protocol (NTP). If you are using an RPi that cannot remain connected to a stable network, then a battery-backed real-time clock (RTC) can be a valuable addition.

Devices synchronize time with an RTC only occasionally, so RTCs are typically attached to an I²C bus. If you are purchasing a module, then you should ensure that it is supported by an LKM for your kernel. This allows for full OS integration of the RTC, which is discussed shortly.

```
pi@erpi /lib/modules/4.1.5-v7+/kernel/drivers/rtc $ ls
rtc-bq32k.ko   rtc-ds3234.ko   rtc-m41t93.ko   rtc-pcf8563.ko   rtc-rx8025.ko
rtc-ds1305.ko rtc-em3027.ko    rtc-m41t94.ko   rtc-pcf8583.ko   rtc-rx8581.ko
rtc-ds1307.ko rtc-fm3130.ko    rtc-max6900.ko rtc-r9701.ko      rtc-s35390a.ko
rtc-ds1374.ko rtc-isl12022.ko rtc-max6902.ko rtc-rs5c348.ko     rtc-x1205.ko
rtc-ds1390.ko rtc-isl12057.ko rtc-pcf2123.ko rtc-rs5c372.ko
rtc-ds1672.ko rtc-isl1208.ko   rtc-pcf2127.ko rtc-rv3029c2.ko
rtc-ds3232.ko rtc-m41t80.ko    rtc-pcf8523.ko rtc-rx4581.ko
```

The DS3231 has been chosen for this chapter, as it is a high-accuracy RTC that keeps time to ±63 seconds per year (i.e., ±2ppm[3] at 0°C–50°C), and it is widely available in module form at very low cost (even less than $1). The DS3231 is compatible with the DS1307 LKM (`rtc-ds1307.ko`).

The ADXL345 Accelerometer

The Analog Devices ADXL345 is a small, low-cost *accelerometer* that can measure angular position with respect to the direction of Earth's gravitational force. For example, a single-axis accelerometer at rest on the surface of the Earth, with the sensitive axis parallel to Earth's gravity, will measure an acceleration of 1*g* (9.81 m/s²) straight upward. While accelerometers provide absolute orientation measurement, they suffer from high-frequency noise, so they are often paired with gyroscopes for accurate measurement of change in orientation (e.g., in game controllers)—a process known as *sensor fusion*. However, accelerometers have excellent characteristics for applications in which low-frequency absolute rotation is to be measured. For simplicity, an accelerometer is used on its own in the following discussions, because the main aim is to impart an understanding of the I²C bus.

---

[3] Two parts per million evaluates to (31,536,000 seconds per year × ±2)/1,000,000 = ±63.072 seconds.

The ADXL345 can be set to measure values with a fixed 10-bit resolution, or using a 13-bit resolution at up to ±16g. The ADXL335 analog accelerometer is utilized in Chapter 10—it provides voltages on its outputs that are proportional to its orientation. Digital accelerometers such as the ADXL345 include analog-to-digital conversion circuitry along with real-time filtering capabilities—they are more complex devices with many configurable options, but it is actually easier to attach them to the RPi than their analog equivalents. The ADXL345 can be interfaced to the RPi using an I²C or SPI bus, which makes it an ideal sensor to use in this chapter as an example for both bus types. The chapter web page identifies suppliers from whom you can purchase this particular sensor.

The I²C slave address is determined by the slave device itself. For example, the ADXL345 breakout board has the address 0x53, which is determined at manufacture. Many devices, including the ADXL345, have selection inputs that allow you to alter this value within a defined range[4]. If the device does not have address selection inputs, then you cannot connect two of them to the same bus, as their addresses will conflict. However, there are I²C multiplexers available that would enable you to overcome this problem.

The data sheet for the ADXL345 is an important document that should be read along with this chapter. It is available at www.analog.com/ADXL345 or tiny .cc/erpi802.

Wiring the Test Circuit

Figure 8-2 illustrates a test circuit that can be used to evaluate the function of I²C devices that are attached to the RPi. In this circuit an ADXL345 and a DS3231 breakout board are connected to the same I2C1 bus. The ADXL345 has the address 0x53 and the DS3231 has the address 0x68, so there will not be a conflict. The CS input of the ADXL345 breakout board is set high to place the module in I²C mode.

Even if you do not have these particular sensors, the following discussion is fully representative of the steps required to connect any type of I²C sensor to the RPi.

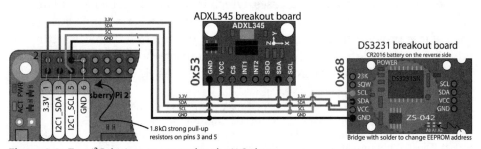

Figure 8-2: Two I²C devices connected to the I2C1 bus

---

[4] The ADXL345's alternative address pin ALT is tied to GND on this particular breakout board, fixing the device at I²C address 0x53, despite the capability of the device itself to be configured for an alternative address.

Using Linux I2C-Tools

Linux provides a set of tools, called *i2c-tools*, for interfacing to I²C bus devices; it includes a bus probing tool, a chip dumper, and register-level access helpers. You can install these tools using the following command:

```
pi@erpi ~ $ sudo apt install i2c-tools
```

i2cdetect

The first step is to detect that the devices are present on the bus. When both I²C buses are enabled, the `i2cdetect` command displays:

```
pi@erpi ~ $ i2cdetect -l
i2c-0    i2c    3f205000.i2c                I2C adapter
i2c-1    i2c    3f804000.i2c                I2C adapter
```

If the circuit is wired as in Figure 8-2 with an ADXL345 and a DS3231 break-out board attached to the /dev/i2c-1 bus, then it can be probed for connected devices, which will result in the following output:

```
pi@erpi ~ $ i2cdetect -y -r 1
     0  1  2  3  4  5  6  7  8  9  a  b  c  d  e  f
00:          -- -- -- -- -- -- -- -- -- -- -- --
10: -- -- -- -- -- -- -- -- -- -- -- -- -- -- -- --
20: -- -- -- -- -- -- -- -- -- -- -- -- -- -- -- --
30: -- -- -- -- -- -- -- -- -- -- -- -- -- -- -- --
40: -- -- -- -- -- -- -- -- -- -- -- -- -- -- -- --
50: -- -- -- 53 -- -- -- 57 -- -- -- -- -- -- -- --
60: -- -- -- -- -- -- -- -- 68 -- -- -- -- -- -- --
70: -- -- -- -- -- -- -- --
```

Hexadecimal addresses 0x03 to 0x77 are displayed by default. Using -a will display the full range 0x00 to 0x7F. When -- is displayed, the address was probed but no device responded. If UU is displayed, then probing was skipped, as the address is already in use by a driver.

The ADXL345 breakout board occupies address 0x53 and the DS3231 ZS-042 breakout board occupies addresses 0x68 and 0x57[5]. Each of the attached break-out boards defines its own addresses, which means that problems will arise if two slave devices with the same address are connected to a single bus. Many I²C devices provide an address selection option that often involves setting an additional input high/low, which is typically implemented on breakout boards by jumper connections or contact points that can be bridged with solder.

---

[5] There is a 32Kb AT24C32 Serial EEPROM on the DS3231 ZS-042 breakout board. The A0, A1, and A2 pins on the breakout board can be used to adjust its address. Also, the SQW pin on the board can be used for an interrupt alarm signal or a square-wave output (1Hz, 1KHz, 4KHz, or 8KHz). The 32K pin provides a 32KHz clock signal.

i2cdump

The i2cdump command can be used to read in the values of the registers of the device attached to an I²C bus and display them in a hexadecimal block form. You should not use this command without consulting the datasheet for the slave device, as in certain modes the i2cdump command will write to the device. The argument -y ignores a related warning. The devices in Figure 8-2 can be safely used, and when the address 0x68 is probed on the i2c-1 bus in byte mode (b), it results in the following output:

```
pi@erpi ~ $ i2cdump -y 1 0x68 b
     0  1  2  3  4  5  6  7  8  9  a  b  c  d  e  f    0123456789abcdef
00: 37 45 02 03 03 01 00 00 00 00 01 00 00 00 1c 88    7E????....?...??
10: 00 17 00 XX XX XX XX XX XX XX XX XX XX XX XX XX    .?.XXXXXXXXXXXXX
```

If the device is probed again in quick succession, then a similar output results, but in this example the register value for address 0x00 changes from 37 to 43. This value actually represents the number of clock seconds (in decimal form) on the RTC module. Therefore, six seconds had elapsed between these two calls to the i2cdump command:

```
pi@erpi ~ $ i2cdump -y 1 0x68 b
     0  1  2  3  4  5  6  7  8  9  a  b  c  d  e  f    0123456789abcdef
00: 43 45 02 03 03 01 00 00 00 00 01 00 00 00 1c 88    CE????....?...??
10: 00 17 00 XX XX XX XX XX XX XX XX XX XX XX XX XX    .?.XXXXXXXXXXXXX
```

To understand the meaning of such registers, you need to read the datasheet for the device. The datasheet for the DS3231 is available at tiny.cc/erpi803 and the most important registers are illustrated in Figure 8-3. In this figure, the hwclock function (see the feature on Utilizing Linux Hardware RTC Devices that follows) is used to display the time value from the RTC module. The i2cdump command is called (a few seconds later) to display the registers, allowing their meaning to be verified. Note that the Irish Standard Time (IST) time zone results in a shift of plus one hour from UTC/GMT.

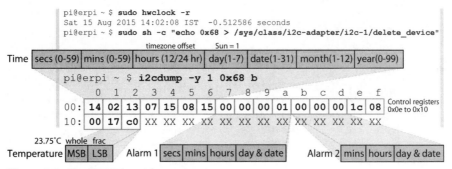

Figure 8-3: The DS3231 registers summary

UTILIZING LINUX HARDWARE RTC DEVICES

Linux supports the use of RTCs directly within the OS using LKMs. If a compatible LKM is available for your chosen RTC, then the RTC can be used to maintain the current time on the RPi without requiring you to write software. The first step is to associate the I²C device with a compatible LKM. The DS3231 is compatible with the `rtc-ds1307.ko` LKM (see `tiny.cc/erpi812`), and can be associated with the bus device at address 0x68 using the following:

```
pi@erpi ~ $ ls /lib/modules/4.1.5-v7+/kernel/drivers/rtc/*1307*
/lib/modules/4.1.5-v7+/kernel/drivers/rtc/rtc-ds1307.ko
pi@erpi ~ $ sudo modprobe rtc-ds1307
pi@erpi ~ $ lsmod|grep rtc
rtc_ds1307             9690  0
pi@erpi ~ $ sudo sh -c "echo ds1307 0x68 > /sys/class/i2c-adapt →
er/i2c-1/new_device"
pi@erpi ~ $ dmesg|tail -1
[23895.440259] i2c i2c-1: new_device: Instantiated device ds1307 at 0x68
pi@erpi ~ $ ls -l /dev/rtc*
crw------- 1 root root 254, 0 Aug 15 01:08 /dev/rtc0
```

A new RTC device is now present in `/dev`. Note that a call to `i2cdetect` now displays `UU` instead of `68` for the RTC device, which indicates that probing is skipped for the address as it is in use by a driver.

```
pi@erpi ~ $ i2cdetect -y -r 1
     0  1  2  3  4  5  6  7  8  9  a  b  c  d  e  f ...
60: -- -- -- -- -- -- -- -- UU -- -- -- -- -- -- --   ...
```

The RTC device also contains a sysfs entry that you can use to display the time, as follows:

```
pi@erpi ~ $ cd /sys/class/rtc/rtc0/
pi@erpi /sys/class/rtc/rtc0 $ ls
date  dev  device  hctosys  max_user_freq  name  since_epoch
subsystem  time  uevent
pi@erpi /sys/class/rtc/rtc0 $ cat time
01:12:01
```

If necessary, you can delete the device using sysfs:

```
pi@erpi /sys/class/i2c-adapter/i2c-1 $ sudo sh -c "echo 0x68 > →
delete_device"
pi@erpi /sys/class/i2c-adapter/i2c-1 $ ls
delete_device  device  i2c-dev  name  new_device  of_node subsystem uevent
pi@erpi /sys/class/i2c-adapter/i2c-1 $ ls /dev/rtc*
ls: cannot access /dev/rtc*: No such file or directory
```

The hwclock utility can be used to read (-r) time from or write (-w) time to the RTC device. It can also use the RTC to set (-s) the system clock. For example:

```
pi@erpi ~ $ date
Sat 15 Aug 01:10:50 GMT 2015
pi@erpi ~ $ sudo hwclock -r
Mon 03 Jan 2000 09:11:53 UTC   -0.845753 seconds
pi@erpi ~ $ sudo hwclock -w
pi@erpi ~ $ sudo hwclock -r
Sat 15 Aug 2015 01:11:24 UTC   -0.113358 seconds
pi@erpi ~ $ sudo hwclock --set --date="2000-01-01 00:00:00"
pi@erpi ~ $ sudo hwclock -r
Sat 01 Jan 2000 00:00:04 UTC   -0.238222 seconds
pi@erpi ~ $ sudo hwclock -s
pi@erpi ~ $ date
Sat  1 Jan 00:02:38 GMT 2000
```

You can automate the process of using the RTC to set the system time on boot, by writing a systemd service and adding the LKM to the /etc/modules file. An example systemd service file is listed in the following code and in the directory chp08/i2c/systemd/.

```
pi@erpi ~ $ tail -1 /etc/modules
rtc-ds1307

pi@erpi ~ $ more /lib/systemd/system/erpi_hwclock.service
[Unit]
Description=ERPI RTC Service
Before=getty.target

[Service]
Type=oneshot
ExecStartPre=/bin/sh -c "/bin/echo ds1307 0x68 > /sys/class/i2c-ada →
pter/i2c-1/new_device"
ExecStart=/sbin/hwclock -s
RemainAfterExit=yes

[Install]
WantedBy=multi-user.target
```

Next, this custom service must be enabled and the current network time protocol (NTP) service disabled from starting on boot:

```
pi@erpi /lib/systemd/system $ sudo systemctl enable erpi_hwclock
pi@erpi /lib/systemd/system $ sudo systemctl disable ntp
pi@erpi /lib/systemd/system $ sudo reboot
```

Continues

UTILIZING LINUX HARDWARE RTC DEVICES (*continued*)

On reboot you can check the service status, and you should see that the date and time are set according to the RTC module.

```
pi@erpi ~ $ sudo systemctl status erpi_hwclock.service
● erpi_hwclock.service - ERPI RTC Service
   Loaded: loaded (/lib/systemd/system/erpi_hwclock.service; enabled)
   Active: active (exited) since Sat 2000-01-01 00:09:30 GMT; 1min 3s ago
  Process: 661 ExecStart=/sbin/hwclock -s (code=exited, status=0/SUCCESS)
...
pi@erpi ~ $ date
Sat  1 Jan 00:10:45 GMT 2000
```

To return the system to the way it was before this feature discussion, simply disable the custom RTC service, enable the NTP service, and reboot.

```
pi@erpi ~ $ sudo systemctl disable erpi_hwclock
pi@erpi ~ $ sudo systemctl enable ntp
pi@erpi ~ $ sudo reboot
```

---

i2cget

The `i2cget` command can be used to read the value of a register in order to test the device, or as an input for Linux shell scripts. For example, to read the number of seconds on the clock, you can use the following:

```
pi@erpi ~ $ i2cget -y 1 0x68 0x00
0x30
```

The Analog Discovery digital Logic Analyzer functionality can be used to analyze the physical I²C bus in order to view the interaction of the SDA and SCL signals as data is written to and read from the I²C bus. The Logic Analyzer functionality has interpreters for I²C buses, SPI buses, and UART communication, which can display the numerical equivalent values of the serial data carried on the bus. Figure 8-4 captures the signal transitions of the `i2cget` command used in the preceding example. Here, you can see that the clock is running at *I²C standard data transfer mode* (i.e., 100 kHz).

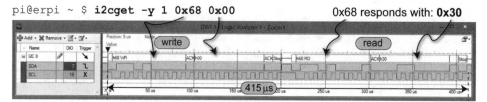

Figure 8-4: Using `i2cget` to read the number of seconds on the RTC from register 0x00

WARNING   A Logic Analyzer is used throughout this chapter to gain a deeper understanding of communication over I²C, SPI, and serial connections. Remember that you *should use a common ground connection* for the Logic Analyzer and the RPi in all cases. It is easy to forget to do this but it can result in inconsistent readings, which may cause hours of frustration and confusion!

The ADXL345 accelerometer can be accessed in the same way as the RTC module. Figure 8-5 illustrates the important registers that are utilized in this chapter. To test that the ADXL345 is correctly connected to the bus, read the DEVID of the attached device, which should be returned as 0xE5:

```
pi@erpi ~ $ i2cget -y 1 0x53 0x00
0xe5
```

You can see that the first value at address 0x00 is 0xE5, and this value corresponds to the DEVID entry in Figure 8-5—successful communication has been verified.

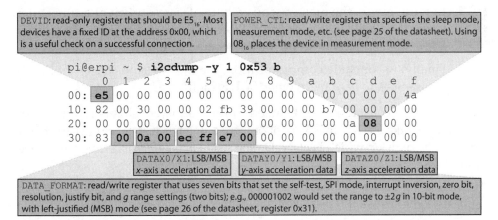

Figure 8-5: Important ADXL345 registers

i2cset

As previously stated, the datasheet for the ADXL345 from Analog Devices is available at www.analog.com/ADXL345. It is a comprehensive and well-written datasheet that details every feature of the device. In fact, the real challenge in working with new bus devices is in decoding the datasheet and the intricacies of the device's behavior. The ADXL345 has 30 public registers and Figure 8-5 illustrates those that are accessed in this chapter. Other registers enable you to set power save inactivity periods, orientation offsets, and interrupt settings for free-fall, tap, and double-tap detection.

The *x*-, *y*-, and *z*-axis acceleration values are stored using a 10-bit or 13-bit resolution; therefore, two bytes are required for each reading. Also, the data is in 16-bit two's complement form (see Chapter 4). To sample at 13 bits, the ADXL345 must be set to the ±16 *g* range. Figure 8-6 (based on the ADXL345 datasheet) describes the signal sequences required to read and write to the device. For example, to write a single byte to a device register, the master/slave access pattern in the first row is used as follows:

1. The master sends a *start bit* (i.e., it pulls SDA low, while SCL is high).

2. While the clock toggles, the 7-bit slave address is transmitted one bit at a time.

3. A read bit (1) or write bit (0) is sent, depending on whether the master wants to read or write to/from a slave register.

4. The slave responds with an *acknowledge bit* (ACK = 0).

5. In write mode, the master sends a byte of data one bit at a time, after which the slave sends back an ACK bit. To write to a register, the register address is sent, followed by the data value to be written.

6. Finally, to conclude communication, the master sends a *stop bit* (i.e., it allows SDA to float high, while SCL is high).

The `i2cset` command can be used to set a register. This is required, for example, to take the ADXL345 out of power-saving mode, by writing 0x08 to the `POWER_CTL` register, which is at 0x2D. The value is written and then confirmed as follows:

```
pi@erpi ~ $ i2cset -y 1 0x53 0x2D 0x08
pi@erpi ~ $ i2cget -y 1 0x53 0x2D
0x08
```

The call to `i2cset` and `i2cget` invokes the handshaking sequences that are described in the ADXL345 datasheet and illustrated in Figure 8-6, which also identifies these numbered steps.

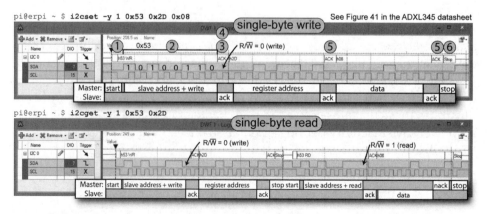

Figure 8-6: Capture and timings required for communication with the ADXL345 device

When the i2cdump command is subsequently used, the registers 0x32 through 0x37 (as identified in Figure 8-5) display the acceleration values, which change as the sensor is physically rotated and the i2cdump command is repeatedly called. The next step is to write program code that can interpret the values contained in the DS3231 and the ADXL345 registers.

I²C Communication in C

The first C program example, in Listing 8-1, reads in all of the DS3231 RTC registers and displays the current time and temperature. The time is contained in binary coded decimal (BCD) form in registers 0x00 (seconds), 0x01 (minutes), and 0x02 (hours). The temperature is in hexadecimal form in registers 0x11 (whole number temperature) and in the two most-significant bits of 0x12 (the fractional part—i.e., $00_2=0$, $01_2=\frac{1}{4}$, $10_2=\frac{1}{2}$, and $11_2=\frac{3}{4}$).

This is a useful first example because it is self-contained, will work on all generic embedded Linux platforms, and can be adapted for other I²C devices.

Listing 8-1: exploringrpi/chp08/i2c/test/testDS3231.c

```
#include<stdio.h>
#include<fcntl.h>
#include<sys/ioctl.h>
#include<linux/i2c.h>
#include<linux/i2c-dev.h>
#define BUFFER_SIZE 19        //0x00 to 0x13

// the time is in the registers in encoded decimal form
int bcdToDec(char b) { return (b/16)*10 + (b%16); }

int main(){
   int file;
   printf("Starting the DS3231 test application\n");
   if((file=open("/dev/i2c-1", O_RDWR)) < 0){
      perror("failed to open the bus\n");
      return 1;
   }
   if(ioctl(file, I2C_SLAVE, 0x68) < 0){
      perror("Failed to connect to the sensor\n");
      return 1;
   }
   char writeBuffer[1] = {0x00};
   if(write(file, writeBuffer, 1)!=1){
      perror("Failed to reset the read address\n");
      return 1;
   }
   char buf[BUFFER_SIZE];
   if(read(file, buf, BUFFER_SIZE)!=BUFFER_SIZE){
      perror("Failed to read in the buffer\n");
      return 1;
   }
   printf("The RTC time is %02d:%02d:%02d\n", bcdToDec(buf[2]),
```

```
        bcdToDec(buf[1]), bcdToDec(buf[0]));
    // note that 0x11 = 17 decimal and 0x12 = 18 decimal
    float temperature = buf[0x11] + ((buf[0x12]>>6)*0.25);
    printf("The temperature is %f°C\n", temperature);
    close(file);
    return 0;
}
```

The code can be built and executed as follows:

```
pi@erpi ~/exploringrpi/chp08/i2c/test $ gcc testDS3231.c -o testDS3231
pi@erpi ~/exploringrpi/chp08/i2c/test $ ./testDS3231
Starting the DS3231 test application
The RTC time is 11:55:59
The temperature is 25.25°C
```

The temperature functionality is used to improve this RTC's accuracy by modeling the impact of environmental temperature on time keeping—it is updated every 64 seconds and it is only accurate to ±3°C.

The ADXL345 digital accelerometer measures acceleration in three axes using analog sensors, which are internally sampled and filtered according to the settings that are placed in its registers. The acceleration values are then available for you to read from these registers. Therefore, the sensor performs timing-critical signal processing that would otherwise have to be performed by the RPi. However, further numerical processing is still required in converting the 16-bit two's complement values stored in its registers into values that describe angular pitch and roll. As such, C/C++ is a good choice for this type of numerical processing.

To display all the registers and to process the accelerometer values, a new program (`chp08/i2c/test/ADXL345.cpp`) is written that breaks the calls into functions, such as the `readRegisters()` function:

```
int readRegisters(int file){    // read all 64(0x40) registers to a buffer
    writeRegister(file, 0x00, 0x00);  // set address to 0x00 for block read
    if(read(file, dataBuffer, BUFFER_SIZE)!=BUFFER_SIZE){
        cout << "Failed to read in the full buffer." << endl;
        return 1;
    }
    if(dataBuffer[DEVID]!=0xE5){
        cout << "Problem detected! Device ID is wrong" << endl;
        return 1;
    }
    return 0;
}
```

This code writes the address 0x00 to the device, causing it to send back the full 64 (0x40) registers (`BUFFER_SIZE`). In order to process the two raw 8-bit acceleration registers, code to combine two bytes into a single 16-bit value is written as follows:

```
short combineValues(unsigned char upper, unsigned char lower){
    //shift the MSB left by 8 bits and OR with the LSB
    return ((short)upper<<8)|(short)lower;
}
```

The types of the data are vital in this function, as the register data is returned in two's complement form. If an int type (of size 32 bits, int32_t) were used instead of short 16-bit integral data (int16_t), then the sign bit would be located in the incorrect bit position (i.e., not at the MSB, bit 31). This function shifts the upper byte left (multiply) by eight places (equivalent to a multiplication by $2^8 = 256$) and ORs the result with the lower byte, which replaces the lower byte with eight zeroes that are introduced by the shift. This results in a 16-bit signed value (int16_t) that has been created from two separate 8-bit values (uint8_t). When executed, the ADXL345.cpp application will give the following output, with the program updating the acceleration data on the same terminal shell line:

```
pi@erpi ~/exploringrpi/chp08/i2c/test $ ./ADXL345
Starting the ADXL345 sensor application
The Device ID is: e5
The POWER_CTL mode is: 08
The DATA_FORMAT is: 00
X=11 Y=2 Z=233 sample=22
```

Additional code is required to convert these values into pitch and roll form. This is added to the C++ class in the next section. For your information, the Logic Analyzer indicates that it takes 4.19 ms to read in the full set of 64 registers at a bus speed of 100 kHz.

I²C AND WIRINGPi

The wiringPi library that is installed in Chapter 6 has a library of C functions for interacting with I²C bus devices. This short code example reads the first three registers from the DS3231 RTC and displays the current time:

```
pi@erpi ~/exploringrpi/chp08/i2c/wiringPi $ more DS3231.c
#include<wiringPiI2C.h>
#include<stdio.h>
int main(){
    int fd    = wiringPiI2CSetup(0x68);
    int secs  = wiringPiI2CReadReg8(fd, 0x00);
    int mins  = wiringPiI2CReadReg8(fd, 0x01);
    int hours = wiringPiI2CReadReg8(fd, 0x02);
    printf("The RTC time is %2d:%02d:%02d\n", hours, mins, secs);
    return 0;
}
pi@erpi ~/exploringrpi/chp08/i2c/wiringPi $ gcc DS3231.c -o rtc -lwiringPi
pi@erpi ~/exploringrpi/chp08/i2c/wiringPi $ ./rtc
The RTC time is 10:08:83
```

There is more information on this library at tiny.cc/erpi804. Be aware that this library is written specifically for the RPi platform; it will not work on other embedded Linux devices that do not contain the same SoC.

Wrapping I²C Devices with C++ Classes

Object-oriented programming is described in Chapter 5 as a suitable framework for developing code for embedded systems. A specific C++ class can be written to wrap the functionality of the ADXL345 accelerometer; because it is likely that you will need to write code to control several different types of I²C devices, it would be useful if the general I²C code could be extracted and placed in a parent class. To this end, a class has been written for this chapter called I2CDevice that captures the general functionality you would associate with an I²C bus device. You can extend this code to control any type of I²C device. It can be found in the I2CDevice.cpp and I2CDevice.h files in the chp08/i2c/cpp/ directory. The class has the structure described in Listing 8-2.

Listing 8-2: /exploringrpi/chp08/i2c/cpp/I2CDevice.h

```
class I2CDevice {
private:
   unsigned int bus, device;
   int file;
public:
   I2CDevice(unsigned int bus, unsigned int device);
   virtual int open();
   virtual int write(unsigned char value);
   virtual unsigned char readRegister(unsigned int registerAddress);
   virtual unsigned char* readRegisters(unsigned int number,
                                  unsigned int fromAddress=0);
   virtual int writeRegister(unsigned int registerAddress, unsigned char value);
   virtual void debugDumpRegisters(unsigned int number);
   virtual void close();
   virtual ~I2CDevice();
};
```

The implementation code is available in the chp08/i2c/cpp/ directory. This class can be extended to control any type of I²C device, and in this case it is used as the parent of a specific device implementation class called ADXL345. Therefore, you can say that ADXL345 *is an* I2CDevice. This inheritance relationship means that any methods available in the I2CDevice class are now available in the ADXL345 class in Listing 8-3 (e.g., readRegister()).

Listing 8-3: /exploringrpi/chp08/i2c/cpp/ADXL345.h

```
class ADXL345:protected I2CDevice{
   //  protected inheritance means that the public I2C methods are no
   //  longer publicly accessible by an object of the ADXL345 class
public:
```

```
    enum RANGE {          // enumerations are used to limit the options
       PLUSMINUS_2_G = 0,
       PLUSMINUS_4_G = 1,
       PLUSMINUS_8_G = 2,
       PLUSMINUS_16_G = 3
    };
    enum RESOLUTION { NORMAL = 0, HIGH = 1 };

private:
    unsigned int I2CBus, I2CAddress;
    unsigned char *registers;
    ADXL345::RANGE range;
    ADXL345::RESOLUTION resolution;
    short accelerationX, accelerationY, accelerationZ;
    float pitch, roll;   // in degrees
    short combineRegisters(unsigned char msb, unsigned char lsb);
    void calculatePitchAndRoll();
    virtual int updateRegisters();

public:
    ADXL345(unsigned int I2CBus, unsigned int I2CAddress=0x53);
    virtual int readSensorState();
    virtual void setRange(ADXL345::RANGE range);
    virtual ADXL345::RANGE getRange() { return this->range; }
    virtual void setResolution(ADXL345::RESOLUTION resolution);
    virtual ADXL345::RESOLUTION getResolution() {return this->resolution;}
    virtual short getAccelerationX() { return accelerationX; }
    virtual short getAccelerationY() { return accelerationY; }
    virtual short getAccelerationZ() { return accelerationZ; }
    virtual float getPitch() { return pitch; }
    virtual float getRoll() { return roll; }
    virtual void displayPitchAndRoll(int iterations = 600);
    virtual ~ADXL345();
};
```

The enumerations are used to constrain the range and resolution selections to contain only valid options. A short example (application.cpp) can be used to test this structure, as follows:

```
int main(){
    ADXL345 sensor(1,0x53);         // sensor is on bus 1 at the address 0x53
    sensor.setResolution(ADXL345::NORMAL);       //using 10-bit resolution
    sensor.setRange(ADXL345::PLUSMINUS_4_G);     //range is +/-4g
    sensor.displayPitchAndRoll();            // put the sensor in display mode
    return 0;
}
```

This code can be built and executed as follows, where the pitch and roll are angular values that each vary between ±90°:

```
/chp08/i2c/cpp $ g++ application.cpp I2CDevice.cpp ADXL345.cpp -o ADXL345
/chp08/i2c/cpp $ ./ADXL345
Pitch:2.48021 Roll:-4.96507
```

You can use this approach to build wrapper classes for any type of I²C sensor on any type of embedded Linux device.

SPI

The *Serial Peripheral Interface (SPI)* bus is a fast, full-duplex synchronous serial data link that enables devices such as the RPi to communicate with other devices over short distances. Therefore, like I²C the SPI bus is synchronous, but unlike the I²C bus the SPI bus is *full duplex*. This means that it can transmit and receive data at the same time, by using separate lines for both sending data and receiving data.

In this section, the SPI bus is introduced, and two separate applications are developed. The first uses the SPI bus to drive a seven-segment LED display using the ubiquitous 74HC595 8-bit shift register. The second application interfaces to the ADXL345 accelerometer again, this time using its SPI bus instead of the I²C bus used previously.

SPI Hardware

SPI communication takes place between a single master device and one or more slave devices. Figure 8-7(a) illustrates a single slave example, where four signal lines are connected between the master and slave devices. To communicate with the slave device, the following steps take place:

1. The *SPI master* defines the clock frequency at which to synchronize the data communication channels.

2. The SPI master pulls the *chip select (CS)* line low, which activates the client device—it is therefore said to be *active low*. This line is also known as *slave select (SS)*.

3. After a short delay, the SPI master issues clock cycles, sending data out on the *master out - slave in (MOSI)* line and receiving data on the *master in - slave out (MISO)* line. The *SPI slave* device reads data from the MOSI line and transmits data on the MISO line. One bit is sent and one bit is received on each clock cycle. The data is usually sent in 1-byte (8-bit) chunks.

4. When complete, the SPI master stops sending a clock signal and then pulls the CS line high, deactivating the SPI slave device.

Unlike I²C, the SPI bus does not require pull-up resistors on the communication lines, so connections are very straightforward. A summary comparison of I²C versus SPI is provided in Table 8-2.

Table 8-2: Comparison of I²C versus SPI on the RPi

	I²C	SPI
Connectivity	Two wires, to which up to 128 addressable devices can be attached.	Typically four wires, and requires additional logic for more than one slave device.
Data rate	I²C fast mode is 400 kHz. It uses half-duplex communication.	Faster performance (~32 MHz) on the RPi. It uses full duplex (except the three-wire variant).
Hardware	Pull-up resistors required.	No pull-up resistors required.
RPi support	Fully supported with two external buses (plus one HDMI).	Fully supported with one bus.[6] There are two slave selection pins on all boards.
Features	Can have multiple masters. Slaves have addresses, acknowledge transfer, and can control the flow of data.	Simple and fast, but only one master device, no addressing, and no slave control of data flow.
Application	Intermittently accessed devices, e.g., RTCs, EEPROMs.	For devices that provide data streams, e.g., ADCs.

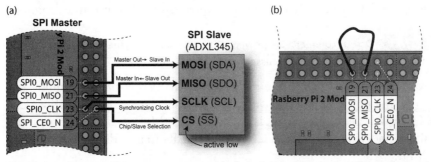

Figure 8-7: (a) Using SPI to connect to one slave device; and (b) testing SPI using a loopback configuration

The SPI bus operates using one of four different modes, which are chosen according to the specification defined in the SPI device's datasheet. Data is synchronized using the clock signal, and one of the *SPI communication modes* listed in Table 8-3 is set to describe how the synchronization is performed. The *clock polarity* defines whether the clock is low or high when it is idle (i.e., when CS is

---

[6] There is an auxiliary SPI bus on the RPi (B+, A+, 2, and 3), but it does not currently have Linux kernel support.

high). The *clock phase* defines whether the data on the MOSI and MISO lines is captured on the rising edge or falling edge of the clock signal. When a clock's polarity is 1, the clock signal is equivalent to an inverted version of the same signal with a polarity of 0. Therefore, a rising edge on one form of clock signal polarity is the equivalent of a falling edge on the other. You need to examine the datasheet for the slave device in order to determine the correct SPI mode to use.

Table 8-3: SPI Communication Modes

MODE	CLOCK POLARITY (CPOL)	CLOCK PHASE (CPHA)
0	**0** (low at idle)	**0** (data captured on the rising edge of the clock signal)
1	**0** (low at idle)	**1** (data captured on the falling edge of the clock signal)
2	**1** (high at idle)	**0** (data captured on the falling edge of the clock signal)
3	**1** (high at idle)	**1** (data captured on the rising edge of the clock signal)

The SPI protocol itself does not define a maximum data rate, flow control, or communication acknowledgment. Therefore, implementations vary from device to device, so it is very important to study the datasheet of each type of SPI slave device. There are some three-wire SPI variants that use a single bidirectional MISO/MOSI line instead of two individual lines. For example, the ADXL345 sensor supports I²C, and both *four-wire* and *three-wire SPI* communication.

> **WARNING**   Do not connect a 5 V-powered SPI slave device to the MISO input on the RPi. Logic-level translation is discussed at the end of this chapter.

According to Section 10.5 of the *BCM2835 ARM Peripherals* document, the SPI CLK register permits the *serial clock* rate to be set according to SCLK = Core Clock / CDIV, where the core clock is nominally 250 MHz and the divisor must be a multiple[7] of two. Therefore, a CDIV of 8 results in an SPI clock frequency of 31.25 MHz.

SPI on the RPi

The GPIO header layout in Figure 6-11 of Chapter 6 identifies that the SPI bus is accessible from this header. Figure 8-7(a) illustrates the pins that are used for SPI on the RPi. The bus is disabled by default on the Raspbian image. To enable the bus, you must perform similar steps to those described earlier in this chapter

---

[7] The datasheet states that it must be a "power of 2"; however, that appears to be a typographic error as other rates work correctly, and the datasheet also states that "odd numbers are rounded down."

for enabling the I²C bus. Add an entry to the `/boot/config.txt` and to the `/etc/modules` files as follows:

```
pi@erpi /boot $ cat config.txt | grep spi
dtparam=spi=on
pi@erpi /etc $ cat modules | grep spi
spi-bcm2708
pi@erpi /etc $ sudo reboot
...
pi@erpi /dev $ ls spi*
spidev0.0  spidev0.1
```

Despite the fact that there are two entries in `/dev`, there exists only one SPI device, `spidev0`, which has two different enable modes (0 and 1).

Testing the SPI Bus

To test the SPI bus, you can use a program called `spidev_test.c` that is available from `www.kernel.org`. However, the latest version at the time of writing has added support for dual and quad data-wire SPI transfers, which are not supported on the RPi. An older version of this code has been placed in `/chp08/spi/spidev_test/` and can be built using the following:

```
~/exploringrpi/chp08/spi/spidev_test$ gcc spidev_test.c -o spidev_test
```

Because the pins have been enabled in pull-down mode, the output displayed by the `spidev_test` program should be 0x00 when nothing is connected to the bus and the test program is executed:

```
pi@erpi ~/exploringrpi/chp08/spi/spidev_test $ ./spidev_test
spi mode: 0
bits per word: 8
max speed: 500000 Hz (500 KHz)
00 00 00 00 00 00
00 00 00 00 00 00
00 00 00 00 00 00
00 00 00 00 00 00
00 00 00 00 00 00
00 00 00 00 00 00
00 00
```

Connect the SPI0_MOSI (Pin 19) and SPI0_MISO (Pin 21) pins together, as shown in Figure 8-7(b). When the test program is executed again, the output should be as follows:

```
pi@erpi ~/exploringrpi/chp08/spi/spidev_test $ ./spidev_test
spi mode: 0
bits per word: 8
max speed: 500000 Hz (500 KHz)
FF FF FF FF FF FF
40 00 00 00 00 95
```

```
FF FF FF FF FF FF
FF FF FF FF FF FF
FF FF FF FF FF FF
DE AD BE EF BA AD
F0 0D
```

This is the exact block of data that is defined in the `tx[]` array inside the `spidev_test.c` code. Therefore, in this case, the block of data has been successfully transmitted from SPI0_MOSI (Pin 19) and received by SPI0_MISO (Pin 21). You can see the same stream of data captured using the Logic Analyzer in Figure 8-8. The clock frequency of SCLK is 500 kHz. Interestingly, you can determine a maximum SCLK by increasing the frequency within the `spidev_test.c` code until you get an inconsistent block of data. I was able to increase the frequency to 62 MHz on the RPi 2 (at 1 GHz) with no errors, but it is widely reported that the maximum practical frequency is ~32 MHz and therefore you should not exceed that level.

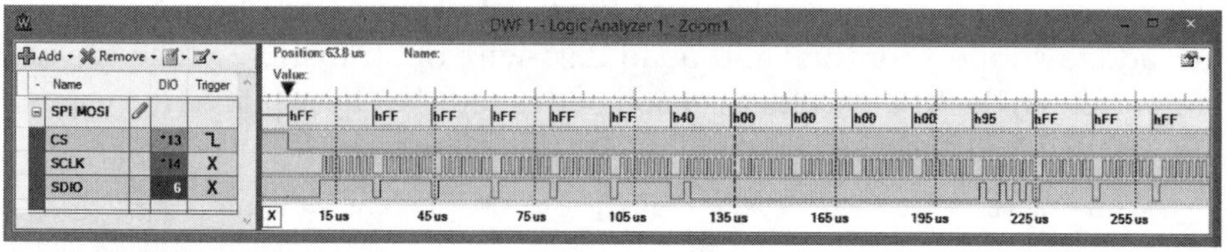

Figure 8-8: The SPI loopback test

A First SPI Application (74HC595)

The first circuit application to test the SPI bus is illustrated in Figure 8-9. It uses a 74HC595, which is an 8-bit shift register with latched outputs that can be supplied at 3.3 V logic levels. The 74HC595 can typically be used at frequencies of 20 MHz or greater, depending on the supply voltage V_{CC}. The circuit in Figure 8-9 uses a seven-segment display and resistors to create a circuit that can display seven-segment symbols.

Seven-segment displays typically consist of eight LEDs that can be used to display decimal or hexadecimal numerals with a "decimal" point. They are available in a range of sizes and colors and are described as being either *common cathode* or *common anode* displays. This means that the cathodes or anodes of the array of LEDs that make up the display are connected together as on the top right of Figure 8-9. You should not limit the current passing through the display by placing a single resistor on the common anode or the common cathode connection, as the limited current will be shared among the segments that are lighting. This results in an uneven light level, the intensity of which depends on the number of segments that are lit. Therefore, eight current-limiting resistors (or a resistor network) are required for each seven-segment display.

It is possible to drive these displays using eight GPIO pins per seven-segment module, but using serial shift registers and the SPI interface has the advantage of requiring only three SPI pins, regardless of the number of segments that are daisy chained together.

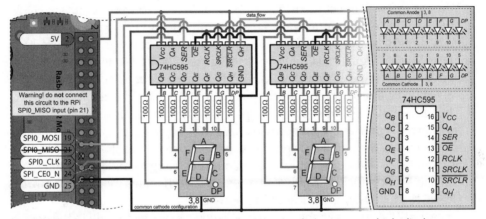

Figure 8-9: The 74HC595 seven-segment display SPI example (supports multiple display modules)

> **NOTE** For a video on serial-to-parallel conversion that explains the concept of output latching by comparing the 74HC164 to the 74HC595, see the chapter web page
> `www.exploringrpi.com/chapter8`.

Wiring the 74HC595 Circuit

The 74HC595 is connected to the RPi using three of the four SPI lines, as a MISO response from the 74HC595 is not required. In addition to the 5 V and GND inputs, the SPI connections are as follows:

- SPI0_CLK is connected to the Serial Clock input (Pin 11) of the 74HC595. This line is used to synchronize the transfer of SPI data on the MOSI line.

- SPI0_MOSI is the MOSI line and is used to transfer the data from the RPi to the 74HC595 Serial Input (Pin 14). This will send one byte at a time, which is the full capacity of the 74HC595.

- SPI_CE0_N is connected to the Serial Register Clock input, which is used to latch the 74HC595 state to the output pins, thus lighting the LEDs.

As previously discussed, the 3.3 V supply rail on the RPi is capable of delivering ~50 mA. Depending on the specification of the seven-segment display modules, 50 mA is likely insufficient to power several modules—remember to allow for the fact that all LED segments could be on! To avoid the need for an external power supply, this circuit is powered using the RPi's 5 V supply. However, this means that the circuit is now using 5 V logic levels and *it would damage your RPi if you were to connect any of the 74HC595 outputs (e.g., Q_H) back to the RPi.*

You can safely connect the RPi's MOSI line directly to the circuit, as a 3.3 V output can be safely connected to a 5 V input. However, strictly speaking, 3.3 V is slightly below the threshold of 3.5 V (i.e., 30% below 5 V) required for an input to a 5 V logic-level CMOS IC (see Figure 4-24 in Chapter 4). In practice, the circuit works fine; however, a 74LS595 (at $V_{CC} = 5$ V) or a 74LVC595 (at $V_{CC} = 3.3$ V) would be more appropriate, despite their high cost and lack of availability.

The LEDs on the seven-segment display will light according to the byte that is transferred. For example, sending 0xAA should light every second LED segment (including the dot) if the setup is working correctly, as $0xAA = 10101010_2$. This circuit is useful for controlling eight outputs using a single serial data line and it can be extended to further seven-segment displays by daisy chaining 74HC595 ICs together, as indicated in Figure 8-9.

Once the SPI device is enabled on the RPi, you can write directly to the device as follows to light *most* of the LEDs (-n suppresses the newline character, -e enables escape character interpretation, and \x escapes the subsequent value as hexadecimal):

```
pi@erpi /dev $ echo -ne "\xFF" > /dev/spidev0.0
```

The following will turn *most* of the LEDs off:

```
pi@erpi /dev $ echo -ne "\x00" > /dev/spidev0.0
```

This may not work exactly as expected, as the current SPI communication mode does not align by default with the operation of the 74HC595, as wired in Figure 8-9. However, it is a useful test to confirm that there is some level of response from the circuit. The transfer mode issue is resolved within the code example in the next section.

SPI Communication Using C

A C program can be written to control the seven-segment display. Basic open() and close() operations on the /dev/spidevX.Y devices work, but if you need to alter the low-level SPI transfer parameters, then a more sophisticated interface is required.

The following program uses the Linux user space SPI API, which supports reading and writing to SPI slave devices. It is accessed using Linux ioctl() requests, which support SPI through the sys/ioctl.h and linux/spi/spidev.h header files. A full guide on the use of this API is available at www.kernel.org/doc/Documentation/spi/.

The program in Listing 8-4 counts in hexadecimal (i.e., 0 to F) on a single seven-segment display using the encoded value for each digit. For example, 0 is obtained by lighting only the segments *A*, *B*, *C*, *D*, *E*, and *F* in Figure 8-10—this value is encoded as 0b00111111 in Listing 8-4, where *A* is the LSB (on the right) and *H* (the dot) is the MSB (on the left) of the encoded value. The transfer() function is the most important part of the code example, as it transfers each encoded value to the 74HC595 IC.

Listing 8-4: /exploringrpi/chp08/spi/spi595Example/spi595.c

```
#include<stdio.h>
#include<fcntl.h>
#include<unistd.h>
#include<sys/ioctl.h>
#include<stdint.h>
#include<linux/spi/spidev.h>
#define SPI_PATH "/dev/spidev0.0"

// The binary data that describes the LED state for each symbol
// A(top)        B(top right) C(bottom right)  D(bottom)
// E(bottom left) F(top left)  G(middle)       H(dot)
const unsigned char symbols[16] = {      //(msb) HGFEDCBA (lsb)
     0b00111111, 0b00000110, 0b01011011, 0b01001111,   // 0123
     0b01100110, 0b01101101, 0b01111101, 0b00000111,   // 4567
     0b01111111, 0b01100111, 0b01110111, 0b01111100,   // 89Ab
     0b00111001, 0b01011110, 0b01111001, 0b01110001    // CdEF
};

int transfer(int fd, unsigned char send[], unsigned char rec[], int len){
    struct spi_ioc_transfer transfer;         // transfer structure
    transfer.tx_buf = (unsigned long) send;   // buffer for sending data
    transfer.rx_buf = (unsigned long) rec;    // buffer for receiving data
    transfer.len = len;                       // length of buffer
    transfer.speed_hz = 1000000;              // speed in Hz
    transfer.bits_per_word = 8;               // bits per word
    transfer.delay_usecs = 0;                 // delay in us
    // transfer.cs_change = 0;        // affects chip select after transfer[8]
    // transfer.tx_nbits = 0;         // no. bits for writing (default 0)
    // transfer.rx_nbits = 0;         // no. bits for reading (default 0)
    // transfer.pad = 0;              // interbyte delay - check version
    // send the SPI message (all of the above fields, inc. buffers)
    int status = ioctl(fd, SPI_IOC_MESSAGE(1), &transfer);
    if (status < 0) {
```

---

[8] There is an unusual quirk with the RPi SPI software implementation in that you often have to explicitly set values for many of the kernel-version-specific fields of the spi_ioc_transfer struct fields, even if you want to use default values. If you see the error, "Transfer SPI_IOC_MESSAGE Failed: Invalid argument," check the spidev.h for the kernel version that you are using at lxr.free-electrons.com and explicitly set the default values for each of the fields in your program code.

```
        perror("SPI: SPI_IOC_MESSAGE Failed");
        return -1;
    }
    return status;
}

int main(){
    unsigned int fd, i;                     // file handle and loop counter
    unsigned char null=0x00;                // sending only a single char
    uint8_t mode = 3;                       // SPI mode 3

    // The following calls set up the SPI bus properties
    if ((fd = open(SPI_PATH, O_RDWR))<0) {
        perror("SPI Error: Can't open device.");
        return -1;
    }
    if (ioctl(fd, SPI_IOC_WR_MODE, &mode)==-1) {
        perror("SPI: Can't set SPI mode.");
        return -1;
    }
    if (ioctl(fd, SPI_IOC_RD_MODE, &mode)==-1) {
        perror("SPI: Can't get SPI mode.");
        return -1;
    }
    printf("SPI Mode is: %d\n", mode);
    printf("Counting in hexadecimal from 0 to F now:\n");
    for (i=0; i<=15; i++) {
        // This function can send and receive data, just sending now
        if (transfer(fd, (unsigned char*) &symbols[i], &null, 1)==-1){
            perror("Failed to update the display");
            return -1;
        }
        printf("%4d\r", i);    // print the number in the terminal window
        fflush(stdout);        // need to flush the output, no \n
        usleep(500000);        // sleep for 500ms each loop
    }
    close(fd);                 // close the file
    return 0;
}
```

The `main()` function sets the SPI control parameters. These are `ioctl()` requests that allow you to override the device's current settings for parameters such as the following, where xx is both RD (read) and RW (write):

- `SPI_IOC_xx_MODE`: The SPI transfer mode (0–3)

- `SPI_IOC_xx_BITS_PER_WORD`: The number of bits in each word

- `SPI_IOC_xx_LSB_FIRST`: 0 is MSB first, 1 is LSB first

- `SPI_IOC_xx_MAX_SPEED_HZ`: The maximum transfer rate in Hz

The current Linux implementation provides for synchronous transfers only. When executed, this code results in the following output, where the count value continually increases (0 to F) on the one line of the terminal window:

```
pi@erpi ~/exploringrpi/chp08/spi/spi595Example $ ./spi595
SPI Mode is: 3
Counting in hexadecimal from 0 to F now:
  4
```

At the same time, this code is sending signals to the 74HC595 as captured using the SPI interpreter of the Logic Analyzer in Figure 8-10, in which the symbol 0 is being displayed by the seven-segment display (i.e., 0b00111111). During this time period, the CS (SPI_CE0_N) line is pulled low, while the SCLK clock (SPI0_CLK) that is "high at idle" is toggled by the SPI master after a short delay. The data is then sent on the SDIO (MOSI) line, MSB first, to the 74HC595, and it is transferred on the rising edge of the clock signal. This confirms that the SPI transfer is taking place in mode 3, as described in Table 8-3.

The total transfer takes less than 18 µs (the data transfer takes ~9 µs). If the channel were held open, it would be capable of transferring a maximum of ~111 kB/s (~0.9 Mb/s) at a clock rate of 1 MHz.

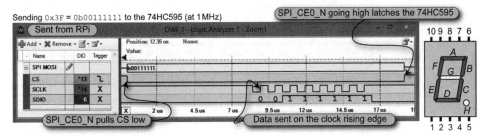

Figure 8-10: The 74HC595 SPI signal and output

Bidirectional SPI Communication in C/C++

The 74HC595 example only sends data from the RPi to the 74HC595, and as such is a unidirectional communication example. In this section a bidirectional communication example is developed that involves using the registers on the ADXL345 sensor. As discussed previously, the ADXL345 has both an I²C and an SPI communications interface. This makes it a useful device with which to examine bidirectional SPI communication, as the register structure is already described in detail earlier in this chapter.

> **NOTE** For reference, the main guide for writing user space code for bidirectional SPI communication under Linux is available at `www.kernel.org/doc/Documentation/spi/spidev`.

The ADXL345 SPI Interface

SPI is not a formal standard with a standards body controlling its implementation, and therefore it is vital that you study the datasheet for the device that you want to attach to the RPi. In particular, the SPI communication timing diagram should be studied in detail. This is presented for the ADXL345 in Figure 8-11.

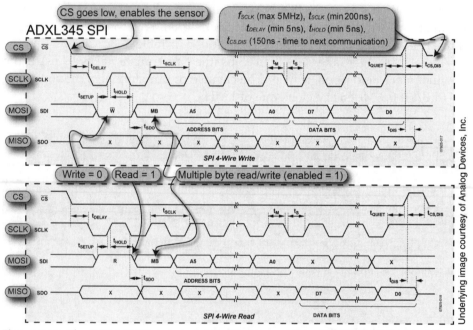

Figure 8-11: The ADXL345 SPI communication timing chart (from the ADXL345 datasheet)

Note the following very important points, which can be observed directly from the datasheet figure, as summarized in Figure 8-11:

- To write to an address, the first bit on the SDI line must be low. To read from an address, the first bit on the SDI line must be high.

- The second bit is called MB. From further analysis of the datasheet, this bit enables multiple byte reading/writing of the registers (i.e., send the first address and data will be continuously read from that register forward).

This leaves six bits in the first byte for the address ($2^6 = 64_{10} = 40_{16}$), which is sufficient to cover the available registers.

- As shown in the figure, the SCLK line is high at rest and data is transferred on the rising edge of the clock signal. Therefore, the ADXL345 device must be used in communications mode 3 (refer to Table 8-3).

- When writing (top figure), the address (with a leading 0) is written to SDI, followed by the byte value to be written to the address.

- When reading (bottom figure), the address (with a leading 1) is written to SDI. A second byte is written to SDI and will be ignored. While the second (ignored) byte is being written to SDI, the response will be returned on SDO detailing the value stored at the register address.

Connecting the ADXL345 to the RPi

The ADXL345 breakout board can be connected to the SPI bus as illustrated in Figure 8-12(a), where MOSI on the RPi is connected to SDA and MISO is connected to SDO. The clock lines and the slave select lines are also interconnected.

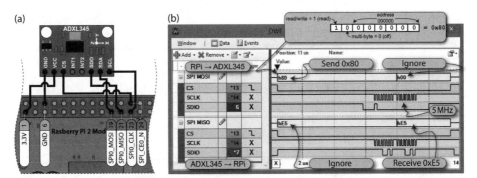

Figure 8-12: (a) SPI connection to the ADXL345; and (b) a capture of the communications required to read register 0x00

You may notice that the value that was sent was 0x80 and not 0x00. This is because (as detailed in Figure 8-12) the leading bit must be a 1 to read and a 0 to write from/to an address. Sending 0x00 is a write request to address 0x00 (which is not possible), and sending 0x80 (i.e., **1**0000000 + 00**000000**) is a request to read the value at address 0x00. The second bit is 0 in both cases, thus disabling multiple-byte read functionality for this example.

The code in Listing 8-4 is adapted in `/spi/spiADXL345/spiADXL345.c` so that it reads the first register (0x00) of the ADXL345, which should return the DEVID, as illustrated in Figure 8-5. This value should be $E5_{16}$, which is 229_{10}.

The maximum recommended SPI clock speed for the ADXL345 is 5 MHz, so this value is used in the program code.

```
pi@erpi ~/exploringrpi/chp08/spi/spiADXL345 $ gcc spiADXL345.c -o spiADXL345
pi@erpi ~/exploringrpi/chp08/spi/spiADXL345 $ ./spiADXL345
SPI mode: 3
Bits per word: 8
Speed: 5000000 Hz
Return value: 229
```

The Logic Analyzer can be used to capture the bus communication that takes place when this program is executed, resulting in an output as illustrated in Figure 8-12(b).

Wrapping SPI Devices with C++ Classes

A C++ class is available in Listing 8-5 that wraps the software interface to the SPI bus, using the OOP techniques that are described in Chapter 5. This class is quite similar to the I2CDevice class that is described in Listing 8-2.

Listing 8-5: /chp08/spi/spiADXL345_cpp/SPIDevice.h

```cpp
class SPIDevice {
public:
    enum SPIMODE{    //!< The SPI Mode
        MODE0 = 0,   //!< Low at idle,   capture on rising clock edge
        MODE1 = 1,   //!< Low at idle,   capture on falling clock edge
        MODE2 = 2,   //!< High at idle, capture on falling clock edge
        MODE3 = 3    //!< High at idle, capture on rising clock edge
    };
public:
    SPIDevice(unsigned int bus, unsigned int device);
    virtual int open();
    virtual unsigned char readRegister(unsigned int registerAddress);
    virtual unsigned char* readRegisters(unsigned int number,
                                    unsigned int fromAddress=0);
    virtual int writeRegister(unsigned int registerAddress, unsigned char value);
    virtual void debugDumpRegisters(unsigned int number = 0xff);
    virtual int write(unsigned char value);
    virtual int write(unsigned char value[], int length);
    virtual int setSpeed(uint32_t speed);
    virtual int setMode(SPIDevice::SPIMODE mode);
    virtual int setBitsPerWord(uint8_t bits);
    virtual void close();
    virtual ~SPIDevice();
    virtual int transfer(unsigned char read[], unsigned char write[],
                         int length);
private:
    std::string filename; //!< The precise filename for the SPI device
    int file;             //!< The file handle to the device
```

```
    SPIMODE mode;           //!< The SPI mode as per the SPIMODE enumeration
    uint8_t bits;           //!< The number of bits per word
    uint32_t speed;         //!< The speed of transfer in Hz
    uint16_t delay;         //!< The transfer delay in usecs
};
```

The SPI class in Listing 8-5 can be used in a standalone form for any SPI device type. For example, Listing 8-6 demonstrates how to probe the ADXL345 device.

Listing 8-6: /chp08/spi/spiADXL345_cpp/SPITest.cpp

```cpp
#include <iostream>
#include <sstream>
#include "SPIDevice.h"
#include "ADXL345.h"
using namespace std;
using namespace exploringRPi;

int main(){
    SPIDevice spi(0,0);
    spi.setSpeed(5000000);
    cout << "The device ID is: " << (int)spi.readRegister(0x00) << endl;
    spi.setMode(SPIDevice::MODE3);
    spi.writeRegister(0x2D, 0x08);
    spi.debugDumpRegisters(0x40);
}
```

This will give the following output when built and executed ($0xE5 = 229_{10}$):

```
.../chp08/spi/spiADXL345_cpp $ g++ SPITest.cpp SPIDevice.cpp -o SPITest
.../chp08/spi/spiADXL345_cpp $ ./SPITest
The device ID is: 229
SPI Mode: 3
Bits per word: 8
Max speed: 5000000
Dumping Registers for Debug Purposes:
e5 00 00 00 00 00 00 00 00 00 00 00 00 00 00 4a
82 00 30 00 00 00 ff 07 00 00 00 b7 00 00 00 00
00 00 00 00 00 00 00 00 00 00 00 00 0a 08 00 00
02 0b 0a 00 ff ff e9 00 00 00 00 00 00 00 00 00
```

The same SPIDevice class can be used as the basis for modifying the ADXL345 class in Listing 8-3 to support the SPI bus rather than the I²C bus. Listing 8-7 provides a segment of the class that is complete in the /chp08/spi/spiADXL345_ cpp/ directory.

Listing 8-7: /chp08/spi/spiADXL345_cpp/ADXL345.h (Segment)

```cpp
class ADXL345{
public:
    enum RANGE {    ...    };
    enum RESOLUTION {    ...    };
private:
```

```
    SPIDevice *device;
    unsigned char *registers;
    ...
public:
    ADXL345(SPIDevice *busDevice);
    virtual int readSensorState();
    ...
    virtual void displayPitchAndRoll(int iterations = 600);
    virtual ~ADXL345();
};
```

The full class from Listing 8-7 can be used to build an example as in Listing 8-8. This example helps demonstrate how an embedded device that is attached to one of the buses can be wrapped with a high-level OOP class.

Listing 8-8: /chp08/spi/spiADXL345_cpp/testADXL345.cpp

```
#include <iostream>
#include <sstream>
#include "SPIDevice.h"
#include "ADXL345.h"
using namespace std;
using namespace exploringRPi;

int main(){
    cout << "Starting RPi ADXL345 SPI Test" << endl;
    SPIDevice *spiDevice = new SPIDevice(0,0);
    spiDevice->setSpeed(500000);
    spiDevice->setMode(SPIDevice::MODE3);
    ADXL345 acc(spiDevice);
    acc.displayPitchAndRoll(100);
    cout << "End of RPi ADXL345 SPI Test" << endl;
}
```

When this program is executed, it displays the current accelerometer pitch and roll values on a single line of the terminal window:

```
pi@erpi ~/exploringrpi/chp08/spi/spiADXL345_cpp $ ./testADXL345
Starting RPi ADXL345 SPI Test
Pitch:2.75709 Roll:79.8124
```

Three-Wire SPI Communication

The ADXL345 supports a *three-wire SPI* (*half duplex*) mode. In this mode the data is read and transmitted on the same SDIO line. To enable this mode on the ADXL345, the value 0x40 must be written to the 0x31 (DATA_FORMAT) register and a $10\,k\Omega$ resistor should be placed between SD0 and V_{CC} on the ADXL345. There is a draft project in place in the chp08/spi/spiADXL345/3-wire directory, but at the time of writing, there is a lack of support for this mode in current RPi Linux distributions.

SPI AND WIRINGPi

The wiringPi library that is installed in Chapter 6 also has a basic set of C functions for interacting with SPI bus devices. This short code example reads and displays the full set of registers from the ADXL345 sensor:

```
pi@erpi ~/exploringrpi/chp08/spi/wiringPi $ more ADXL345.c
#include<wiringPiSPI.h>
#include<stdio.h>
#include<string.h>              // for memset and memmove calls

int main(){
   unsigned char data[0x41];     // a buffer to store the write/read data
   int i;                        // need 0x41 to read the last value back
   memset(data, 0x00, 0x41);     // clear the full memory buffer
   data[0]=0xC0;                         // continuous read of the data
   wiringPiSPISetupMode(0, 1000000, 3);  // SPI channel, speed, mode
   wiringPiSPIDataRW(0, data, 0x40);     // write & read all 0x40 registers
         // Shift the data back by one for the ADXL345 (e.g., 0x01->0x00)
   memmove(data, data+1, 0x40);
   printf("The DEVID is %d\n", data[0x00]); // display register 0x00
   printf("The full set of 0x40 registers are:\n");
   for(i=0; i<0x40; i++){                 // display all 0x40 registers
      printf("%02X ", data[i]);           // display value in hexadecmial
      if(i%16==15) printf("\n");          // place \n after each 15th value
   }
   return 0;
}
.../chp08/spi/wiringPi $ gcc ADXL345.c -o ADXL345 -lwiringPi
.../chp08/spi/wiringPi $ ./ADXL345
The DEVID is 229
The full set of 0x40 registers are:
E5 00 00 00 00 00 00 00 00 00 00 00 00 00 00 4A
82 00 30 00 00 02 01 3B 00 00 00 B7 00 00 00 00
00 00 00 00 00 00 00 00 00 00 00 00 0A 08 00 00
02 00 0B 00 04 00 ED 00 00 00 00 00 00 00 00 00
```

A memory shift operation is required in this example because the wiringPiSPI-DataRW() function performs an SPI write and read in a single call. The response from the ADXL345 in the example code is currently stored in the array index that follows the request. For example, if the request to read the device ID (0x80) is stored in data[0], then the ADXL345's response to that request (i.e., 0xE5) is stored in data[1]. The memmove() function shifts all returned values back by one address (e.g., data[1] is moved to data[0]). There is more information on this library at tiny.cc/erpi806.

Multiple SPI Slave Devices on the RPi

To this point in the chapter, only one SPI device is attached to the bus, which is quite a limited bus! The SPI bus can be shared with *multiple slave devices*, provided that only one slave device is active when communication takes place. The RPi Raspbian image has kernel support for two slave selection pins on the SPI bus: SPI_CE0_N (Pin 24) and SPI_CE1_N (Pin 26). This is the reason for the two SPI device entries in the /dev directory.

```
pi@erpi /dev $ ls -l spi*
crw-rw---T 1 root spi 153, 0 Jan  1  1970 spidev0.0
crw-rw---T 1 root spi 153, 1 Jan  1  1970 spidev0.1
```

The first device spidev0.0 is associated with the SPI_CE0_N (Pin 24) enable output, and the second device spidev0.1 is associated with the SPI_CE1_N (Pin 26) enable output. For example, if you want to attach two sensors to the same bus, you could use the wiring configuration illustrated in Figure 8-13(a). Your program code would then open either the spidev0.0 or spidev0.1 device, depending on which ADXL345 is to be accessed.

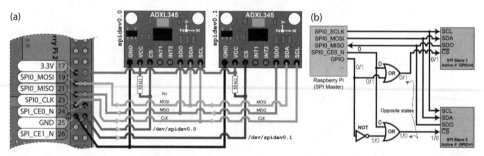

Figure 8-13: (a) Using two ADXL345 accelerometers on a single SPI bus; and (b) control of more than one slave device using GPIO pins and additional logic

If you need to connect more than two devices to the same bus, then you will not have the same level of kernel support, but you can introduce GPIOs and logic gates (or decoders) to build a custom solution. For example, if you want to allow the Linux SPI interface library code to retain control of the slave selection functionality, then a wiring configuration like that in Figure 8-13(b) could be used. This configuration uses OR gates and an inverter to ensure that only one slave device CS input is pulled low at a single time. In Figure 8-13(b), the first slave device is active when CS = 0 and GPIO = 0, and the second slave device is active when CS = 0 and GPIO = 1.

> **NOTE** It is good practice to place a pull-up resistor on each of the CS lines, as it can prevent two devices that share the SPI bus from being simultaneously active, should an unused CS line "float" low. For illustration, you can see two 10 kΩ resistors on the CS lines in Figure 8-13(a). However, Pin 24 and Pin 26 on the RPi already have internal pull-up resistors enabled by default, so it is not necessary to add resistors for this application in the RPi's default state.

Depending on the particular slave devices being used, the GPIO output combined with a single inverter may be sufficient, as you could "permanently" pull the CS line low on the slave device, ignoring the CS output of the master. However, this would not work for the 74HC595 example, as the RPi's CS line is used to latch the data to the output LEDs.

For more than two slave devices, a 3-to-8 line decoder, such as the 74HC138, would be a good solution. It has inverted outputs, which means that only one of its eight outputs is low at a single point in time. This device could be controlled using three of the RPi's GPIOs and it could enable one of eight slave devices ($2^3 = 8$). There are also 4-to-16 line decoders with inverting outputs, such as the 74HC4515, which would enable you to control 16 slave devices with only four GPIOs ($2^4 = 16$). For both of these devices, one of the RPi's CS outputs could be connected to their active-low *E* enable input(s).

UART

A *Universal Asynchronous Receiver/Transmitter* (*UART*) is a microprocessor peripheral device used for the serial transfer of data, one bit at a time, between two electronic devices. UARTs were originally standalone ICs, but now are often integrated with the host microprocessor/microcontroller. A UART is not, strictly speaking, a bus, but its capacity to implement serial data communications overlaps with similar capacities of the I²C and SPI buses described earlier. A UART is described as *asynchronous* because the sender does not have to send a clock signal to the recipient in order to synchronize the transmission; rather, a communication structure is agreed upon that uses start and stop bits to synchronize the transmission of data. Because no clock is required, the data is typically sent using only two signal lines. Just like a regular telephone line, the *transmit data connection* (*TXD*) from one end is connected to the *receive data connection* (*RXD*) on the other end of the connection, and vice versa.

Traditionally, UARTs have been used with level converters/line drivers to implement interfaces such as RS-232 or RS-485, but for short-distance communications, it is possible to use the original logic level for the UART outputs and inputs to enable two UARTs to communicate with each other. Note that this is a perfectly possible but nonstandardized use of UARTs.

The number of symbols per second is known as the *baud rate* or modulation rate. With certain encoding schemes, a symbol could be used to represent two bits (i.e., four states, for example, by using quadrature phase-shift keying [QPSK]). Then the *bit rate* would be twice the baud rate. However, for a simple bi-level UART connection, the baud rate is the same as the bit rate.

The transmitter and receiver agree upon a bit rate before communication begins. The *byte rate* is somewhat lower than 1/8th of the bit rate, as there are overhead bits associated with the serial transmission of data. Transmission begins when the transmitter sends a *start bit* (logic low), as shown in Figure 8-14. On the receiver's end, the falling edge of the start bit is detected and then after 1.5 bit periods, the first bit value is sampled. Every subsequent bit is sampled after 1.0 bit periods, until the agreed-upon number of bits is transferred (typically seven or eight). The *parity bit* is optional (though both devices must be configured to either use it or not); if used, it can identify whether a transmission error has occurred. It would be high or low, depending on whether odd or even *parity checking* is employed. Finally, one *stop bit* is sent (or optionally two stop bits), which is always a logic high value. The examples that follow in this section all use a standard *8N1* form, which means that eight bits are sent in each frame, with no parity bits and one stop bit.

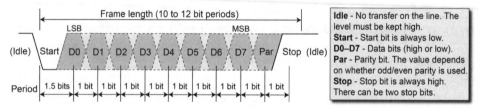

Figure 8-14: UART transmission format for a typical one-byte transfer

WARNING   Again, it is important that you do not connect a 5 V UART device to the UART RXD input of the RPi or you will damage the RPi. A solution to this problem is provided at the end of this chapter.

The RPi UART

The RPi has one full UART that is accessible via the GPIO header:

- **TXD0 (Pin 8):** Output that transmits data to a receiver
- **RXD0 (Pin 10):** Input that receives data from a transmitter

Chapter 9 describes how you can add additional UARTs to the RPi using USB devices, but this chapter focuses on the built-in full UART. The first test is to connect these two pins together as in Figure 8-15 (a), so that the RPi UART is literally "talking to itself."

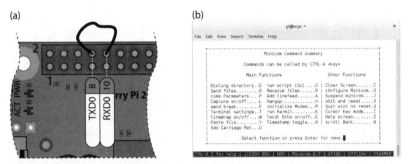

Figure 8-15: (a) Loopback testing the UART; and (b) configuring the minicom program settings

The /dev directory includes an entry for ttyAMA0. This is the "teletype" (terminal) device, which is a software interface that enables you to send and receive data via the on-board UART. First, check that the terminal device is listed:

```
pi@erpi /dev $ ls -l ttyAMA0
crw-rw---- 1 root tty 204, 64 Aug 16 00:31 ttyAMA0
```

UART DEVICES ON THE RPi 3

The RPi boards typically support two UART devices, a mini UART (UART1, with TXD1/RXD1 on mode ALT5 of Pin 8/10), and a full UART (UART0, with TXD0/RXD0 on mode ALT0 of Pin 8/10). See Figure 6-11 in Chapter 6 and page 175 in the *BCM2835 ARM Peripherals* guide. The mini UART is typically not used on earlier RPi models, but the RPi 3 utilizes both UARTs: The full UART is required for onboard Bluetooth (a feature that is not present on earlier RPi models), and the mini UART is used for the serial console function. The use of the mini UART results in the serial console being mapped to the device /dev/ttyS0 instead of the usual /dev/ttyAMA0. The mini UART does not have parity support and its baud rate is derived from the system clock, rather than being programmable.

At the time of writing, to communicate between the RPi 3 and a desktop machine using the mini UART (/dev/ttyS0) device, you have to ensure that the CPU frequency does not change during communication—for example, as a result of a CPU governor state. You may also have to set the core frequency to 250 MHz to improve communication stability. This latter setting can reduce communication glitches, but it also impacts upon the performance of the RPi GPU. You can set explicit CPU and core frequency values by editing the /boot/config.txt file as follows:

```
pi@erpi:/boot $ tail -n 3 config.txt
force_turbo=1
```

Continues

UART DEVICES ON THE RPi 3 (*continued*)

```
arm_freq=1200
core_freq=250
```

After reboot, you can check the CPU frequency:

```
pi@erpi:~ $ sudo apt install cpufrequtils
pi@erpi:~ $ cpufreq-info
...   cpufreq stats: 1.20 GHz:100.00%
```

The serial console should work correctly and you should have bidirectional communication.

Several of the examples in this chapter require that you terminate the serial console service. As the serial console on the RPi 3 is mapped to /dev/ttyS0 by default, you can shut down the console service as follows (remember to also set the device to the value /dev/ttyS0 in the code examples):

```
pi@erpi ~ $  sudo systemctl stop serial-getty@ttyS0
```

If you have difficulties in your applications with the simple UART on the RPi 3, you should examine the low-cost (~$1) USB UART devices that are described towards the end of Chapter 9.

Finally, it is also possible to disable the UART1 and enable UART0 on Pins 8/10 (i.e., GPIO14/15) on the RPi 3 by using a device tree overlay:

```
pi@erpi:/boot/overlays $ ls -l pi3-mini*
-rwxr-xr-x 1 root root 1250 Mar 13 17:04 pi3-miniuart-bt-overlay.dtb
```

Edit the /boot/config.txt file and add the following line:

```
dtoverlay=pi3-miniuart-bt
```

The serial console reverts to /dev/ttyAMA0 after reboot, but Bluetooth functionality is now disabled on the RPi 3:

```
Raspbian GNU/Linux 8 erpi ttyAMA0
erpi login:
```

The source code for this overlay is available at tiny.cc/erpi814.

By default, this terminal device is set up as a Linux console for the RPi. As described in Chapter 2, you can connect to the Linux console using a USB-to-TTL 3.3 V cable and open a terminal connection using the *getty* ("get teletype") service. However, to perform the loopback test in Figure 8-15(a), you need to detach the serial-getty service from the UART device. You can do this under SysVinit or systemd as follows:

▪ Under SysVinit you can disable the console by rebooting after editing /etc/inittab to comment out the line that begins with T0:23 using a # character:

```
pi@erpi /etc $ tail -2 inittab
#Spawn a getty on Raspberry Pi serial line
#T0:23:respawn:/sbin/getty -L ttyAMA0 115200 vt100
```

■ Under systemd the device is currently attached to the `serial-getty` service. It can be stopped using the following:

```
pi@erpi ~ $ systemctl|grep ttyAMA0
serial-getty@ttyAMA0.service loaded active running  Serial Getty on ttyAMA0
pi@erpi ~ $ sudo systemctl stop serial-getty@ttyAMA0
```

NOTE The first human-computer interface was the teletypewriter, also known as the teletype or TTY, an electromechanical typewriter that can be used to send and receive messages. This terminology is still in use today!

Once you have disabled the terminal service, you can test the device using the `agetty` (*alternative getty*) command or the `minicom` terminal emulator, both of which enable you to send and receive data on the `ttyAMA0` device. The `minicom` program enables you to dynamically change the serial settings while it is executing (e.g., number of bits in a frame, number of stop bits, parity settings) by pressing Ctrl+A followed by Z, as illustrated in Figure 8-15(b). Install and execute `minicom` using the following commands:

```
pi@erpi ~ $ sudo apt install minicom
pi@erpi ~ $ sudo minicom -b 115200 -o -D /dev/ttyAMA0
Welcome to minicom 2.7
OPTIONS: I18n
Compiled on Jan 12 2014, 05:42:53.
Port /dev/ttyAMA0, 18:28:58
Press CTRL-A Z for help on special keys
```

At this point, you should press Ctrl+A followed by Z and then E to turn on local Echo. Now when the RPi is wired as in Figure 8-15(a), and you press a key, you should see the following output when you type letters:

```
hheelllloo  RRaassppbbeerrrrryy  PPii
```

Whichever key you press is transmitted in binary form (as in Figure 8-14) from the TXD output, and is also echoed on the console. When the character is received on the RXD input, it is then displayed on the terminal. Therefore, if you can see the characters appearing twice for the keys that you are pressing, then the simple UART test is working correctly. You can verify this by briefly disconnecting one end of the TXD-RXD loopback wire in Figure 8-15(a), whereupon the key presses will only appear once.

The Analog Discovery has an interpreter that can be used for analyzing serial data communication. The Logic Analyzer can be connected in parallel to the TXD and RXD lines in order to analyze the transfer of data from the RPi to another device. An example of the resulting signals is displayed in Figure 8-16 for the loopback test in Figure 8-15(a) when only the letter "h" is being transmitted. The start and stop bits can be observed, along with the eight-bit data as it is sent, LSB first, from the TXD pin to the RXD pin, with a sample bit-period of 8.7 µs. At a baud rate of 115,200, the effective byte rate will be somewhat lower, due to the overhead of transmitting start, stop, and parity bits.

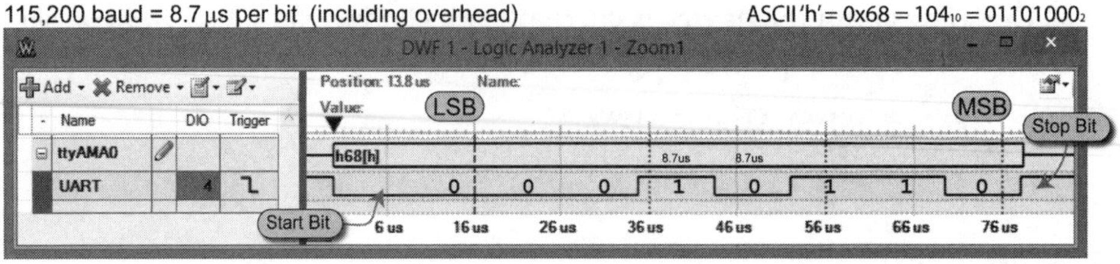

115,200 baud = 8.7 µs per bit (including overhead)   ASCII 'h' = 0x68 = 104₁₀ = 01101000₂

Figure 8-16: Logic Analyzer display of the loopback serial transmission of the letter "h"

Chapter 6 describes the use of GPIO one-wire communication (*bit-banging*), and this chapter describes SPI and I²C communication. However, using a UART connection is probably the most straightforward approach, and it has the additional advantage that there can be some degree of physical distance between the two controllers. Table 8-4 lists some advantages and disadvantages of using a UART in comparison to using I²C or SPI.

Table 8-4: Advantages and Disadvantages of UART Communication

ADVANTAGES	DISADVANTAGES
Simple, single-wire transmission and single-wire reception of data with error checking.	The typical maximum data rate is low compared to SPI (typically 460.8 kb/sec).
Easy interface for interconnecting embedded devices and desktop computers, etc., especially when that communication is external to the device and/or over a significant distance— some tens of feet. I²C and SPI are not suited for external/distance communication.	Because it is asynchronous, the clock on both devices must be accurate, particularly at higher baud rates. You should investigate Controller Area Network (CAN) buses for high-speed external asynchronous data transfer.
Can be directly interfaced to popular RS-232 physical interfaces, enabling long-distance communication (15 meters or greater). The longer the cable, the lower the speed. RS-422/485 allows for 100-meter runs at greater than 1 Mb/s.	UART settings need to be known in advance of the transfer, such as the baud rate, data size, and parity checking type.

UART Examples in C

The next step is to write C code on the RPi that can communicate with the desktop computer using the USB-to-TTL 3.3 V cable (see Chapter 2).

RPi Serial Client

The C program in Listing 8-9 sends a string to a desktop machine (or any other device) that is listening to the other end of the connection. It uses the Linux *termios* library, which provides a general terminal interface that can control asynchronous communication ports.

Listing 8-9: exploringrpi/chp08/uart/uartC/uart.c

```
#include<stdio.h>
#include<fcntl.h>
#include<unistd.h>
#include<termios.h>
#include<string.h>

int main(int argc, char *argv[]){
    int file, count;
    if(argc!=2){
        printf("Please pass a string to the program, exiting!\n");
        return -2;
    }
    if ((file = open("/dev/ttyAMA0", O_RDWR | O_NOCTTY | O_NDELAY))<0){
        perror("UART: Failed to open the device.\n");
        return -1;
    }
    struct termios options;
    tcgetattr(file, &options);
    options.c_cflag = B115200 | CS8 | CREAD | CLOCAL;
    options.c_iflag = IGNPAR | ICRNL;
    tcflush(file, TCIFLUSH);
    tcsetattr(file, TCSANOW, &options);
    if ((count = write(file, argv[1], strlen(argv[1])))<0){
        perror("UART: Failed to write to the output\n");
        return -1;
    }
    write(file, "\n\r", 2);          // new line and carriage return
    close(file);
    return 0;
}
```

This code uses the `termios` structure, setting flags to define the type of communication that should take place. The `termios` structure has the following members:

- `tcflag_t c_iflag`: Sets the input modes
- `tcflag_t c_oflag`: Sets the output modes
- `tcflag_t c_cflag`: Sets the control modes
- `tcflag_t c_lflag`: Sets the local modes
- `cc_t c_cc[NCCS]`: Used for special characters

A full description of the `termios` functionality and flag settings is available by typing **man termios** at the RPi shell prompt.

```
pi@erpi ~/exploringrpi/chp08/uart/uartC $ gcc uart.c -o uart
```

```
.../chp08/uart/uartC $ sudo ./uart "Hello desktop!"
.../chp08/uart/uartC $ sudo ./uart "Greetings from the Raspberry Pi..."
.../chp08/uart/uartC $ sudo sh -c "echo hello >> /dev/ttyAMA0"
.../chp08/uart/uartC $ sudo sh -c "echo hello >> /dev/ttyAMA0"
```

The output appears on the desktop PC as in Figure 8-17 when PuTTY is set to listen to the correct serial port (e.g., COM11). The C program functionality is very similar to a simple echo to the terminal device; however, it does have access to set low-level modes such as the baud rate, parity types, etc.

Figure 8-17: A PuTTY desktop COM terminal that is listening for messages from the Raspberry Pi

RPi LED Serial Server

For some applications it can be useful to allow a desktop computer master to take control of an RPi slave. In this section a serial server runs on the RPi, and awaits commands from a desktop serial terminal. Once again, the USB-to-TTL 3.3 V cable is used; however, it is important to note that a similar setup could be developed with wireless technologies, such as Bluetooth, infrared transmitter/receivers, and serial ZigBee (see Chapter 13).

In this example, the RPi is connected to a simple LED circuit and the USB-to-TTL cable, as illustrated in Figure 8-18(a). When the PuTTY client on the desktop computer issues simple string commands such as LED on and LED off, as illustrated in Figure 8-18(b), the hardware LED that is attached to the RPi performs a corresponding action. Importantly, this program permits safe remote control of the RPi, as it does not allow the serial client access to any other functionality on the RPi—in effect, the serial server behaves like a shell that only has three commands!

(a)   (b)

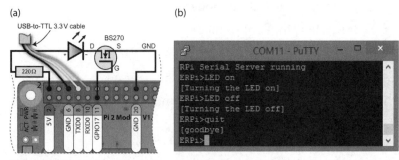

Figure 8-18: (a) The LED serial server circuit, and (b) PuTTY on the PC communicating to the RPi LED serial server

The source code for the serial server is provided in Listing 8-10. The example uses wiringPi to control the LED circuit (see Chapter 6). Ensure that you remember to shut down the `serial-getty` service on the RPi before running this program. If you have rebooted the RPi, then the service will have restarted. On execution, the server displays the following output:

```
pi@erpi .../chp08/uart/server $ gcc server.c -o server -lwiringPi
pi@erpi .../chp08/uart/server $ sudo ./server
RPi Serial Server running
LED on
Server>>>[Turning the LED on]
LED off
Server>>>[Turning the LED off]
quit
Server>>>[goodbye]
```

It is possible to disable the `serial-getty` service permanently on the RPi using `systemctrl disable`. You can then add a new service entry for the server code in this section so that it starts on boot. If your intention is to run this program as a service, then you should, of course, remove the client-controlled "quit" functionality!

Listing 8-10: /exploringrpi/chp08/uart/server/server.c

```c
#include<stdio.h>
#include<fcntl.h>
#include<unistd.h>
#include<termios.h>
#include<string.h>
#include<stdlib.h>
#include<wiringPi.h>
#define  LED_GPIO    17

// Sends a message to the client and displays the message on the console
int message(int client, char *message){
   int size = strlen(message);
   printf("Server>>>%s\n", (message+1));    // print message with new line
   if (write(client, message, size)<0){
      perror("Error: Failed to write to the client\n");
      return -1;
   }
   write(client, "\n\rERPi>", 7);           // display a simple prompt
   return 0;                                // \r for a carriage return
}

// Checks to see if the command is one that is understood by the server
int processCommand(int client, char *command){
   int val = -1;
   if (strcmp(command, "LED on")==0) {
      val = message(client, "\r[Turning the LED on]");
      digitalWrite(LED_GPIO, HIGH);         // turn the physical LED on
   }
   else if(strcmp(command, "LED off")==0) {
```

```c
        val = message(client, "\r[Turning the LED off]");
        digitalWrite(LED_GPIO, LOW);          // turn the physical LED off
    }
    else if(strcmp(command, "quit")==0) {   // shutting down server!
        val = message(client, "\r[goodbye]");
    }
    else { val = message(client, "\r[Unknown command]"); }
    return val;
}

int main(int argc, char *argv[]) {
    int client, count=0;
    unsigned char c;
    char *command = malloc(255);
    wiringPiSetupGpio();                      // initialize wiringPi
    pinMode(LED_GPIO, OUTPUT);                // the LED is an output
    if ((client = open("/dev/ttyAMA0", O_RDWR | O_NOCTTY | O_NDELAY))<0){
        perror("UART: Failed to open the file.\n");
        return -1;
    }
    struct termios options;
    tcgetattr(client, &options);
    options.c_cflag = B115200 | CS8 | CREAD | CLOCAL;
    options.c_iflag = IGNPAR | ICRNL;
    tcflush(client, TCIFLUSH);
    fcntl(STDIN_FILENO, F_SETFL, O_NONBLOCK);  // make reads non-blocking
    tcsetattr(client, TCSANOW, &options);
    if (message(client, "\n\rRPi Serial Server running")<0) {
        perror("UART: Failed to start server.\n");
        return -1;
    }
    // Loop forever until the quit command is sent from the client or
    //  Ctrl-C is pressed in the server's terminal window
    do {
        if(read(client,&c,1)>0) {
            write(STDOUT_FILENO,&c,1);
            command[count++]=c;
            if(c=='\n') {
                command[count-1]='\0';  // replace \n with \0
                processCommand(client, command);
                count=0;                // reset the command string
            }
        }
        if(read(STDIN_FILENO,&c,1)>0) { // can send from stdin to client
            write(client,&c,1);
        }
    } while(strcmp(command,"quit")!=0);
    close(client);
    return 0;
}
```

UART Applications - GPS

A low-cost *Global Positioning System* (*GPS*) module has been chosen as an example device to demonstrate interconnection to RPi UART devices. The GY-GPS6MV2 breakout board (~$10) uses the u-blox NEO-6M series GPS module (tiny.cc/erpi807). It can be powered at 3.3 V and therefore can be connected directly to the RPi's UART pins.

Figure 8-19 illustrates the RPi UART connection to the GPS module. As with all UART connections, ensure that you connect the transmit pin of the RPi to the receive pin of the device, and the receive pin of the RPi to the transmit pin of the device.

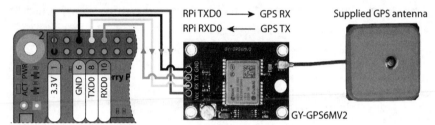

RPi TXD0 ⟶ GPS RX
RPi RXD0 ⟵ GPS TX
Supplied GPS antenna
GY-GPS6MV2

Figure 8-19: RPi UART connection to the GPS module

The GPS module is set for 9600 baud by default, so to connect to the module you can use the following (remember to ensure that the serial-getty service is not running):

```
pi@erpi ~ $ sudo minicom -b 9600 -o -D /dev/ttyAMA0
Welcome to minicom 2.7
OPTIONS: I18n
Compiled on Jan 12 2014, 05:42:53.
Port /dev/ttyAMA0, 23:31:46
Press CTRL-A Z for help on special keys
$GPRMC,133809.00,A,5323.12995,N,00615.36410,W,1.015,,190815,,,A*60
$GPVTG,,T,,M,1.015,N,1.879,K,A*21
$GPGGA,133809.00,5323.12995,N,00615.36410,W,1,08,1.21,80.2,M,52.9,M,,*73
$GPGSA,A,3,21,16,18,19,26,22,07,27,,,,,2.72,1.21,2.44*06
$GPGSV,4,1,14,04,07,227,17,07,24,306,16,08,33,278,09,13,05,018,*7A
$GPGSV,4,2,14,15,04,048,08,16,61,174,25,18,39,096,31,19,35,275,21*78
$GPGSV,4,3,14,20,12,034,08,21,36,061,23,22,29,142,21,26,32,159,12*71
$GPGSV,4,4,14,27,75,286,26,30,10,334,*75
$GPGLL,5323.12995,N,00615.36410,W,133809.00,A,A*78
```

The GPS module outputs NEMA 0183 sentences, which can be decoded to provide information about the sensor's position, direction, velocity, etc. There is a lot of work involved in decoding the sentences, so it is best to use a client application to test the performance of your sensor. For example:

```
pi@erpi ~ $ sudo apt install gpsd-clients
pi@erpi ~ $ sudo gpsmon /dev/ttyAMA0
```

This results in the output shown in Figure 8-20 that provides an intuitive display of the NEMA 0183 sentences. An LED on the module flashes at a rate of 1 PPS (pulse per second) when it is capturing valid data. This pulse is extremely accurate and can therefore be used as a calibration method for other applications. The gpsmon application was executed in my office, which overlooks a courtyard, so I was surprised that the low-cost sensor achieved line of sight with 11 satellites.

Walter Dal Mut (@walterdalmut) has made a C library available for interfacing to GPS sensors. The library can be easily integrated within your project to utilize GPS, as follows:

```
pi@erpi ~ $ git clone git://github.com/wdalmut/libgps
pi@erpi ~ $ cd libgps/
pi@erpi ~/libgps $ make
pi@erpi ~/libgps $ sudo make install
pi@erpi ~/libgps $ ls /usr/lib/libgps*
/usr/lib/libgps.a
```

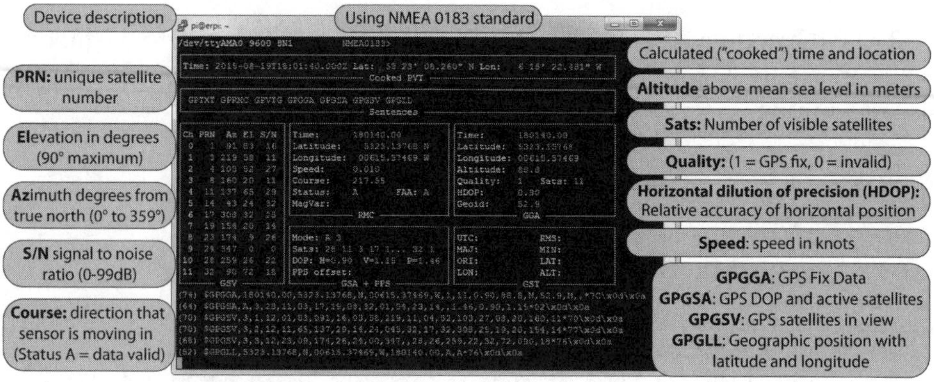

Figure 8-20: The gpsmon output display

Once the library has been installed, you can use a straightforward C program to identify the RPi's GPS information, as in Listing 8-11.

Listing 8-11: /chp08/uart/gps/gps_test.c

```c
#include<stdio.h>
#include<stdlib.h>
#include<gps.h>

int main() {
    gps_init();                      // initialize the device
```

```
    loc_t gps;                          // a location structure
    gps_location(&gps);                 // determine the location data
    printf("The RPi location is (%lf,%lf)\n", gps.latitude, gps.longitude);
    printf("Altitude: %lf m. Speed: %lf knots\n", gps.altitude, gps.speed);
    return 0;
}
```

You can build and execute the code as follows:

```
.../chp08/uart/gps $ gcc gps_test.c -o gps_test -lgps -lm
.../chp08/uart/gps $ sudo ./gps_test
The RPi location is (53.385511,-6.256224)
Altitude: 85.900000 m. Speed: 0.060000 knots
```

You can enter the co-ordinate pair in `maps.google.com` to find my office at Dublin City University (`tiny.cc/erpi813`)!

Logic-Level Translation

As noted throughout this chapter, it is important that you are cognizant of the voltage levels used in communicating with the RPi. If you connect a device that uses 5 V logic levels, then when the device is sending a high state to the RPi, it will apply a voltage of 5 V to the RPi's input pins. This would likely permanently damage the RPi. Many embedded systems have overvoltage-tolerant inputs, but the RPi does not. Therefore, *logic-level translation* circuitry is required if you want to connect the buses to 5 V or 1.8 V logic-level circuits.

For *unidirectional data buses*, like four-wire SPI, logic-level translation can be achieved using a combination of diodes (using their ~0.6 V forward-voltage drop characteristic) combined with resistors, or transistors. However, *bidirectional data buses* like the I²C bus are more complex because the level must be translated in both directions on a single line. This requires circuits that use devices such as N-channel MOSFETs (e.g., the BSS138). They are available in surface-mounted packages and, unfortunately, there are very few through-hole alternatives. Fortunately, this is a common problem and there are straightforward unidirectional and bidirectional breakout board solutions available from several suppliers, including the following:

- SparkFun Bi-directional Logic Level Converter (BOB-12009), which uses the BSS138 MOSFET (~$3)

- Adafruit Four-Channel Bi-directional Level Shifter (ID:757), which uses the BSS138 MOSFET (1.8 V to 10 V shifting) (~$4)

- Adafruit Eight-Channel Bi-directional Logic Level Converter (ID:395; ~$8), which uses the TI TXB0108 Voltage-Level Translator that automatically senses direction (1.2–3.6 V or 1.65–5.5 V translation). Note that it does not work well with I²C due to the pull-up resistors required. However, it can switch at frequencies greater than 10 MHz.

■ Watterott Four-Channel Level Shifter (20110451), which uses the BSS138 MOSFET (~$2)

Some of these products are displayed in Figure 8-21. With the exception of the Adafruit eight-channel converter, they all use BSS138 MOSFETs. A small test was performed to check the switching frequency of these devices, as displayed in Figure 8-22, and it is clear from the oscilloscope traces that there are data-switching performance limitations when using these devices that you must factor into your circuit design. In this test, the 3.3 V input is switching a 5 V level output using a square wave, and it is clear that the output signal is distorted at higher frequencies. For example, when switching at 1MHz, the distortion means that the output signal does not actually reach a 5 V level.

Figure 8-21: Adafruit four-channel, Adafruit eight-channel, and Watterott four-channel logic-level translators

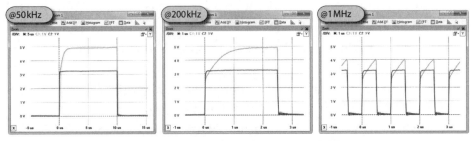

Figure 8-22: Switching BSS138-based translators from 3.3 V to 5 V logic levels at 50 kHz, 200 kHz, and 1 MHz

For further information on logic-level shifting techniques in I²C-bus design, see the application notes from NXP (AN97055), which are linked on the chapter web page and also available at `tiny.cc/erpi808`.

Summary

After completing this chapter, you should be able to do the following:

- Describe the most commonly used buses or interfaces that are available on the RPi, and choose the correct bus to use for your application.
- Configure the RPi to enable I²C, SPI, and UART capabilities.
- Attach circuits to the RPi that interface to its I²C bus, and use the Linux I2C-tools to communicate with those circuits.
- Build circuits that interface to the SPI bus using shift registers, and write C code that controls low-level SPI communication.
- Write C/C++ code that interfaces to and "wraps" the functionality of devices attached to the I²C and SPI buses.
- Communicate between UART devices using both Linux tools and custom C code.
- Build a basic distributed system that uses UART connections to the RPi to allow it to be controlled from a desktop PC.
- Interface to a low-cost GPS sensor using a UART connection.
- Add logic-level translation circuitry to your circuits in order to communicate between devices with different logic-level voltages.

Further Reading

Documents and links for further reading have been listed throughout this chapter, but here are some further reference documents:

- *The I²C Manual*, Jean-Marc Irazabal and Steve Blozis, Philips Semiconductors, TecForum at DesignCon 2003 in San Jose, CA, on January 27, 2003, at `tiny.cc/erpi809`.
- *The Linux I²C Subsystem*, at `i2c.wiki.kernel.org`.
- *Serial Programming Guide for POSIX Operating Systems*, 5th ed., Michael R. Sweet, 1994–1999, at `tiny.cc/erpi810`.
- *Serial Programming HOWTO*, Gary Frerking, Revision 1.01, at `tiny.cc/erpi811`.

# CHAPTER 9

Enhancing the Input/Output Interfaces on the RPi

This chapter describes how the input/output interface capabilities of the Raspberry Pi (RPi) can be enhanced and extended using low-cost modules, integrated circuits (ICs), and USB devices. The RPi is a competent interfacing and physical computing device, but analog interfacing functionality is absent, and other input/output capabilities may need to be expanded for your applications. This chapter begins by describing how you can utilize the RPi's buses to add analog-to-digital and digital-to-analog conversion capabilities to the RPi. The chapter then describes how you can expand the number of available pulse-width modulation (PWM) outputs and general-purpose inputs/outputs (GPIOs) on the RPi. The chapter finishes with a discussion on the use of USB-to-TTL devices, which can be used to expand the number of available serial UART devices. This chapter also provides you with further experience of interfacing to SPI and I²C bus devices.

Equipment Required for This Chapter:

- Raspberry Pi (ideally an RPi 2/3)
- Analog-to-digital converter ICs (e.g., the MCP3208)
- Digital-to-analog converter ICs (e.g., the MCP4725, MCP4921/2)
- PWM expander module (e.g., the Adafruit PCA9685)
- GPIO expander ICs (MCP23017, MCP23S17)
- USB UART device (e.g., CP2102 or CH340G compatible)

Further details on this equipment and chapter are available at www.exploringrpi .com/chapter9/.

Introduction

The onboard input/output capabilities of the RPi are described in detail in Chapters 6 and 8, where it is made clear that certain functionality is multiplexed—for example, enabling the SPI bus or I²C bus reduces the number of available GPIOs. In addition, the RPi does not have onboard analog-to-digital conversion (ADC) or digital-to-analog conversion (DAC) capabilities. This is a weakness of the RPi in comparison to other SBCs such as the BeagleBone Black, which has multiplexed onboard support for 7 × ADC channels, 4 × UART devices, 65 × GPIOs, and 8 × PWM outputs. This chapter aims to address this weakness using low-cost, widely available modules, ICs, and USB devices.

An alternative way to address this weakness is to use input/output expansion HATs (Hardware Attached on Top). The *Gertboard* ($60–$65), which is illustrated in Figure 9-1, is a popular choice. It has 12 × buffered input/outputs, 6 × open-collector drivers, an 18 V 2 A motor controller, an Arduino microcontroller, a two-channel DAC, and a two-channel ADC. See tiny.cc/erpi901 for the full manual. Alternatives to the Gertboard include the PiFace Digital (www.piface .org.uk) and the GrovePi (www.dexterindustries.com/GrovePi/).

Expansion HATs are useful for prototyping work, and their functionality is described in detail by their manuals. Therefore, expansion HATs are not investigated in this book; rather, this chapter focuses on using discrete components and modules to provide the required expanded input/output functionality. This approach is typically more complex, but it has advantages in terms of cost, availability, and implementation footprint. It is also an important learning exercise that reinforces the bus interfacing techniques, which are described in Chapter 8.

Analog-to-Digital Conversion

The concept of *analog-to-digital conversion* (ADC) is introduced in Chapter 4, even though the RPi does not have onboard ADC capabilities. This section describes how you can add an external ADC to your RPi using multichannel SPI ADCs that retail from $1 to $3. Adding ADC capabilities to the RPi means that it can then interface directly to thousands of types of analog sensors, some examples of which are described in this chapter and in Chapter 10.

Several other SBCs, including the BeagleBone, have internal ADC circuitry that can be easily damaged by incorrect usage (e.g., sourcing/sinking excessive current). Therefore, replaceable external ADCs are a good choice for prototyping work, even when an internal ADC is available.

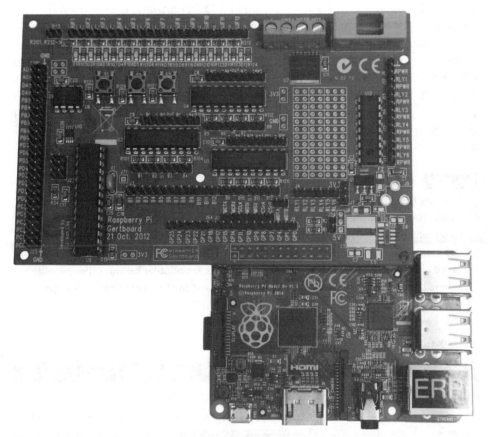

Figure 9-1: The Gertboard attached to the RPi GPIO header

SPI Analog-to-Digital Converters (ADCs)

There are ADCs available that can be used with the I²C bus (e.g., the ADS1015), but the SPI bus is preferable for this application, especially for sampling a sensor output at moderately high data rates. This section focuses on two families of SPI ADCs that are produced by Microchip, the MCP300x 10-bit and the MCP320x 12-bit families. Each of these families has discrete ICs with different numbers of input channels—for example, the MCP320x has one-channel (MCP3201), two-channel (MCP3202), four-channel (MCP3204), and eight-channel (MCP3208) variants.

The MCP3208 SPI ADC

The MCP3208 is the most capable device in the two families of ADCs, as it supports eight 12-bit *successive approximation* ADC channels. It is chosen for this discussion for that reason and the fact that it is a low-cost (~$3) device that is widely available in PDIP form. It is suitable for interfacing to the RPi because it can be powered at 3.3 V and has an SPI interface. It is capable of sampling at ~75 thousand samples per second (kSPS) and has a differential nonlinearity of ±1 LSB. By default, the MCP3208 supports eight single-ended inputs, but it can be programmed to provide four pseudo-differential input pairs.[1] Table 9-1 describes the input/output pins of the 16-pin IC. The full datasheet is available at `tiny.cc/erpi902`.

> **NOTE** A successive approximation ADC uses an analog voltage comparator to compare the analog input voltage to an estimated digital value that is passed through a DAC. The result of the analog comparison is used to update the estimated digital value, which is stored in a successive approximation register (SAR). The process continues iteratively until all the bits (12 in the case of a 12-bit ADC) are weighted and compared to the input. Successive approximation ADCs are popular because they provide a good balance of speed, accuracy, and cost; however, the higher the resolution, the slower the ADC performance.

Table 9-1: Input/Output Pins for the MCP3208

IC PINS	PIN TITLE	DESCRIPTION
Pins 1-8	CH0-CH7	The eight ADC input channels.
Pin 9	DGND	Digital ground—connected to the internal digital ground. Can be connected to the RPi GND.
Pin 10	CS/SHDN	Chip Select/Shutdown—used to initiate communication with the device when pulled low. When pulled high it ends the conversation. Must be pulled high between conversions.
Pin 11	D_{IN} (MOSI)	Used to configure the ADC by selecting the input to use, and whether to use single-ended or differential inputs.
Pin 12	D_{OUT} (MISO)	The data output sends the results of the ADC back to the RPi. The data bit changes on the falling edge of the clock cycle.

[1] Single-ended ADC inputs share a common reference ground. Differential inputs are applied to the ADC in pairs (IN+, IN−), which are compared against each other to determine the ADC value. This is particularly beneficial for the common-mode rejection of coupled noise, which could cause single-ended inputs to exceed their range. Note that there is also a MCP330x family of 13-bit differential input SPI ADCs that can also be used in the way that is described in this section.

IC PINS	PIN TITLE	DESCRIPTION
Pin 13	CLK	The SPI clock is used to synchronize communication. A clock rate of greater than 10 KHz should be maintained to avoid introducing linearity errors.
Pin 14	AGND	Analog ground—connected to the internal analog circuit GND.
Pin 15	V_{REF}	Reference voltage input.
Pin 16	V_{DD}	Voltage Supply (2.7 V–5.5 V). Can be connected directly to the RPi 3.3 V supply rail, but not to the 5 V supply without adding logic-level translation circuitry to the D_{OUT} pin.

Wiring the MCP3208 to the RPi

Figure 9-2 illustrates how the MCP3208 can be connected directly to the RPi using its SPI bus. The figure also includes an ADC input example that is used to test the circuit.

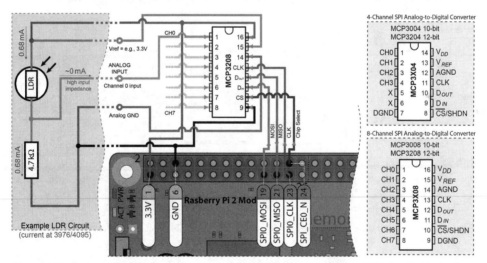

Figure 9-2: A general SPI ADC configuration for the RPi with an example LDR circuit attached to Channel 0 of the MCP3208 IC

Communicating with the MCP3208

The ADC functionality is controlled by the RPi using the MOSI line to the D_{IN} pin and the resulting sample data is returned on the MISO line from the D_{OUT} pin. Figure 9-2 illustrates the bits that must be written to and read from the MCP320x and MCP300x ADCs to complete a transaction. Essentially, the RPi must identify which channel (0–7) it wants to read, and whether the circuit is configured for single-ended or differential inputs:

- The channel is selected using a three-bit identifier ($2^3 = 8$), as illustrated on the right side of Figure 9-3.

- The example circuits in this section utilize single-ended inputs, so the Single/Diff bit is 1. However, by setting the bit to 0 you can use the inputs as four differential pairs (CH0/CH1, CH2/CH3, CH4/CH5, and CH6/CH7). For example, 000 sets CH0 as IN+ and CH1 is IN−, 001 sets CH1 as IN+ and CH0 as IN−, and 010 sets CH2 as IN+ and CH3 as IN−, etc.

The data transaction takes 24 serial clock (SCLK) cycles. The RPi writes low bits followed by a start bit (high), the SGL/Diff bit (high for a single-ended configuration), and the three channel-select bits. The write takes place on the rising edge of the clock signal. The MCP320x then sends 12 bits of data back to the RPi on the falling edge of the clock signal (delayed by 3.5 clock cycles). The signal patterns required for the MCP300x are also identified at the bottom of Figure 9-3. They are almost the same, but because 10 bits are returned rather than 12 bits, there are two fewer leading lows on the MOSI (D_{IN}) line.

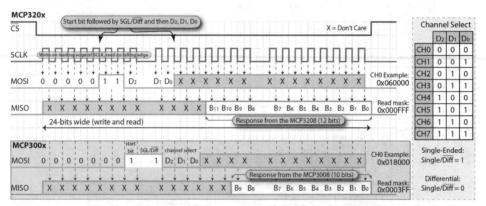

Figure 9-3: Reading data from the 12-bit MCP320x and the 10-bit MCP300x families of SPI ADCs

ADC Application: An Analog Light Meter

Figure 9-2 includes an example *light-dependent resistor* (LDR) circuit, which demonstrates how you can connect an analog sensor to the MCP3208. LDRs have a resistance that is dependent on the ambient light level; the brighter the room, the lower the resistance and vice versa. This circuit is designed in a voltage divider configuration, where a low resistance value on the LDR will cause a greater proportion of the supply voltage (3.3 V) to drop across the paired resistor (the 4.7 kΩ resistor in Figure 9-2), resulting in a higher voltage level at

CH0 of the MCP3208. Therefore, if the room is bright then a high ADC digital value is expected.

To achieve a full range (i.e., from ~0 V to ~3.3 V) on CH0, it is essential that a suitable pairing resistor value R is chosen. For a typical LDR voltage divider circuit, a good rule of thumb is to use the equation $R = \sqrt{R_{MIN} \times R_{MAX}}$, where R_{MAX} (maximum resistance) is the measured resistance of the LDR when it is covered (e.g., with your finger) and R_{MIN} (minimum resistance) is the measured resistance of the LDR when a light source (e.g., cellphone torch app) is close to its surface. In this example, the resistance of the LDR was 98 kΩ when covered and 220 Ω when the light source was close. The preceding formula thus gives a value for R of 4,643 Ω, so a 4.7 kΩ resistor provides a suitable pairing.

Listing 9-1 provides a code example that uses the MCP3208 circuit as illustrated in Figure 9-2. The LDR circuit is connected to CH0 and is sampled using a single-ended configuration.

Listing 9-1: /exploringrpi/chp09/ldr/ldrExample.cpp

```cpp
#include <iostream>
#include "bus/SPIDevice.h"
using namespace exploringRPi;

int main(){
    std::cout << "Starting the RPi LDR ADC Example" << std::endl;
    SPIDevice *busDevice = new SPIDevice(0,0);
    busDevice->setSpeed(5000000);
    busDevice->setMode(SPIDevice::MODE0);
    unsigned char send[3], receive[3];
    send[0] = 0b00000110;           // Start bit=1, SGL/Diff=1 and D2=0
    send[1] = 0b00000000;           // MSB 00 is D1=0, D0=0 for channel 0
    busDevice->transfer(send, receive, 3);
    // MCP320X: use full second byte and the four LSBs of the first byte
    int value = ((receive[1]&0b00001111)<<8)|receive[2];
    std::cout << "LDR value is " << value << " out of 4095." << std::endl;
    return 0;
}
```

The code in Listing 9-1 uses the SPIDevice class that is described in Chapter 8 to send a request on the MOSI line and to read the response on the MISO line. The program can be built and executed as follows:

```
pi@erpi ~/exploringrpi/chp09/ldr $ g++ -o ldrExample ldrExample.cpp →
 bus/SPIDevice.cpp bus/BusDevice.cpp
pi@erpi ~/exploringrpi/chp09/ldr $ ./ldrExample
Starting the RPi LDR ADC Example
LDR value is 3952 out of 4095.
pi@erpi ~/exploringrpi/chp09/ldr $ ./ldrExample
Starting the RPi LDR ADC Example
LDR value is 207 out of 4095.
```

The light source was close to the LDR when the program was first executed, and the LDR was covered on the second occasion.

The circuit configuration in Figure 9-2 can be used for resistance-based sensors, where a voltage/current is required for sensor excitation, and the resistance of the sensor varies in proportion to the quantity under measurement. Some such sensors include: resistance thermometers, strain gages, moisture sensors, pressure sensors, light sensors, displacement sensors, etc.

This code in Listing 9-1 can be easily adapted to read from all eight of the channels by altering the three channel select bits, as described in Figure 9-3. For example, if the LDR circuit was connected to CH7 (`111`), then the send bytes would be `send[0]=0b00000111` and `send[1]=0b11000000` for the MCP3208.

Testing the SPI ADC Performance

The previous ADC example clearly works well for applications where occasional sampling is required; however, it is important to be aware of the limitations of this circuit under embedded Linux.

According to its datasheet (`tiny.cc/erpi902`), the MCP3208 is capable of sampling at a rate of 100 kSPS at $V_{DD} = 5$ V and 50 kSPS at $V_{DD} = 2.7$ V, which is interpolated to ~63 kSPS at $V_{DD} = 3.3$ V. However, to achieve this rate would require the RPi to write/read 63,000 requests to the MCP3208 every second (and a SCLK rate of at least 24 bits × 63,000 = 1.5 MHz). Essentially, a request would have to be sent every 16 µs, and the requests would have to be perfectly spaced in time, because otherwise the captured data would suffer from sample-clock jitter. This is a particular problem for embedded Linux applications, because the kernel has to balance the requests for analog sampling along with other processes that are running on the board; this can cause the sample-clock to deviate from a truly periodic signal (i.e., jitter). This topic is described in some detail in Chapter 6 and Chapter 7 when testing is performed on the preemption performance of the RPi. The histogram plot in Figure 6-10(a) is indicative of the sample-clock jitter problems that you can expect.

To test the performance of this configuration, a known input signal can be applied to one of the input channels, whereupon the captured sample data can be compared against the known input signal. You can use the Analog Discovery Waveform Generator for this simple test. It can generate a sinusoidal input signal and the sampled output can be inspected visually.

Listing 9-2 provides a short program that captures 200 ADC samples as quickly as possible, and then outputs the results to the terminal window. The output of the program can be piped into the Gnuplot tool so that the sampled data can be plotted.

GNUPLOT

Gnuplot is a powerful command-line graphing tool that can be used to graph functions and plot data directly on the RPi. It can be configured to display on-screen custom plots, or to save the output plot to a file. You can display the plot using virtual network connections (VNCs) or headful displays, which are described in Chapter 14. However, this short feature describes how you can save the plot to a file, which can be transferred to a desktop machine.

Using the following steps you can ensure that Gnuplot is installed on the RPi, and then use it to output a plot of *sin(x)* in both vector-mapped postscript (PS) file and bit-mapped PNG image form:

```
pi@erpi ~ $ sudo apt install gnuplot
pi@erpi ~/tmp $ gnuplot
   G N U P L O T   Version 4.6 patchlevel 6 ...
gnuplot> set term postscript
Terminal type set to 'postscript' ...
gnuplot> set output "sinx.ps"
gnuplot> plot [-pi: pi] sin(x)
gnuplot> set term png
Terminal type set to 'png'  ...
gnuplot> set output "sinx.png"
gnuplot> plot [-2*pi:2*pi] sin(x)
gnuplot> exit
pi@erpi ~/tmp $ ls
sinx.png  sinx.ps
pi@erpi ~/tmp $ ps2pdf sinx.ps sinx.pdf
pi@erpi ~/tmp $ ls
sinx.pdf  sinx.png  sinx.ps
```

These plots are available in the /chp09/gnuplot/ directory. You can view the results of these calls directly on the book's Github repository at tiny.cc/erpi903.

Gnuplot is used in Chapter 5 to display histogram plots and in this section it is used to visually inspect the data that is captured by the ADC circuit. Gnuplot can be called using scripts, which is demonstrated in the example that follows in this section (Listing 9-3). For detailed information on the use of Gnuplot, see: www.gnuplot.info and www.gnuplot.info/docs_4.0/gpcard.pdf.

Listing 9-2: /chp09/spiADC/ADCmulti.cpp

```cpp
#include <iostream>
#include "bus/SPIDevice.h"
#define SAMPLES 200
using namespace exploringRPi;
```

```
int main(){
    short data[SAMPLES];       // output preceeded by # ignored by gnuplot
    std::cout << "# Starting RPi SPI ADC Example" << std::endl;
    SPIDevice *busDevice = new SPIDevice(0,0);
    busDevice->setSpeed(5000000);
    busDevice->setMode(SPIDevice::MODE0);
    unsigned char send[3], receive[3];
    send[0] = 0b00000110;      // Reading single-ended input from channel 0
    send[1] = 0b00000000;
    for(int i=0; i<SAMPLES; i++) {
        busDevice->transfer(send, receive, 3);
        data[i] = ((receive[1]&0b00001111)<<8)|receive[2];
    }
    for(int i=0; i<SAMPLES; i++) {      // print after data captured
        std::cout << i << " " << data[i] << std::endl;
    }
    busDevice->close();
    std::cout << "# End of RPi SPI ADC Example" << std::endl;
    return 0;
}
```

The program in Listing 9-2 is not called directly; instead, it is called by the short script in Listing 9-3, which plots the resulting sample data to a PDF format file, so that it can be easily viewed.

Listing 9-3: /exploringrpi/chp09/spiADC_MCP3208/plot

```
#!/bin/bash
echo "Capturing 200 samples from the memory and dumping to capture.dat"
./ADCmulti > capture.dat
echo "Plotting the data to a PS file"
gnuplot <<_EOF_
set term postscript enhanced color
set output 'plot.ps'
set title 'Exploring RPi Plot'
plot 'capture.dat' with linespoints lc rgb 'blue'
_EOF_
echo "Converting the PS file to a PDF file"
ps2pdf plot.ps plot.pdf
```

If the current CPU frequency profile is set to be adaptive (e.g., the ondemand governor), problems would arise with this test. The test has a significant CPU load that would cause the governor to increase the CPU frequency, which would alter the ADC sample-clock rate as the test is taking place. Therefore, it is important to first set the governor to use a profile that fixes the CPU frequency, regardless of the CPU load:

```
pi@erpi ~ $ sudo cpufreq-set -g performance
pi@erpi ~ $ cpufreq-info | grep "current CPU frequency"
  current CPU frequency is 1000MHz ...
pi@erpi ~ $ cd ~/exploringrpi/chp09/spiADC
```

```
pi@erpi ~/exploringrpi/chp09/spiADC $ ./plot
Capturing 200 samples from the memory and dumping to capture.dat
Plotting the data to a PS file
Converting the PS file to a PDF file
pi@erpi ~/exploringrpi/chp09/spiADC $ ls -l *.dat *.pdf
-rw-r--r-- 1 pi pi 1294 Aug 23 21:29 capture.dat
-rw-r--r-- 1 pi pi 6514 Aug 23 21:29 plot.pdf
```

The results are available in the plot.pdf file. The test can then be repeated for different input frequencies, providing results such as those in Figure 9-4. You can also view these plots from the chp09/spiADC/results folder.

At 1 GHz the overclocked RPi 2 displays impressive results, as illustrated in Figure 9-4(a). The plot displays 200 samples of a 500 Hz sinusoidal input signal, which took 0.00525 seconds to capture. This means that each sample took 26.25 μs—a sample rate of 39.1kSPS. Unfortunately, this approach suffers from occasional jitter (as illustrated in Figure 9-4(b)), which is difficult to overcome at high sample rates. At lower rates (e.g., 5kSPS) the signal could be *oversampled* and the results averaged. Finally, Figure 9-4(c) illustrates the problems that arise if the sample clock rate is insufficient to properly sample an input signal.

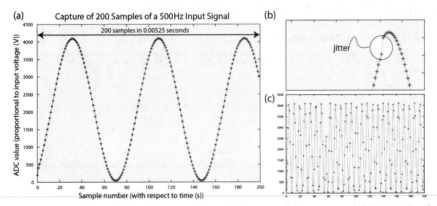

Figure 9-4: (a) Plot of a data capture of a 500 Hz sinusoidal input signal; (b) example of sample-clock jitter; (c) data capture of a 5 kHz sinusoidal input signal

The C Library for BCM2835 (Advanced)

There is an alternative library to wiringPi that provides strong memory-mapped support for RPi SPI devices. As discussed in Chapter 6, memory-mapped code is specific to the RPi platform only, whereas the earlier code in this chapter can be generally applied to all embedded Linux devices. The advantage of bypassing the Linux OS and accessing the registers on the RPi directly is that greater I/O performance can be achieved, which improves the quality of the sampled data.

The C Library for BCM2835[2] is written by Mike McCauley and is available at (`tiny.cc/erpi904`). You should identify the most recent version of the library by visiting the website, and then you can download, build, and install it using the following steps:

```
pi@erpi ~ $ wget http://www.airspayce.com/mikem/bcm2835/bcm2835-1.45.tar.gz
pi@erpi ~ $ ls -l *.gz
-rw-r--r-- 1 pi pi 251081 Aug  5 04:40 bcm2835-1.45.tar.gz
pi@erpi ~ $ tar zxvf bcm2835-1.45.tar.gz
pi@erpi ~ $ cd bcm2835-1.45/
pi@erpi ~/bcm2835-1.45 $ ./configure
pi@erpi ~/bcm2835-1.45 $ make
pi@erpi ~/bcm2835-1.45 $ sudo make check
pi@erpi ~/bcm2835-1.45 $ sudo make install
pi@erpi ~/bcm2835-1.45 $ ls -l /usr/local/lib/*bcm*
-rw-r--r-- 1 root staff 47982 Aug 24 01:47 /usr/local/lib/libbcm2835.a
```

The code in Listing 9-4 demonstrates how Listing 9-2 can be adapted to utilize the BCM2835 C Library. In addition, the code is adapted to use the maximum system priority, and memory paging is disabled for the memory associated with the resulting binary executable. Memory paging is a common cause of latency, which is expressed in the output as lost samples or noise.

Listing 9-4: /chp09/bcm2835/adc_bcm2835.cpp

```
/** Based on the spi.c example at www.airspayce.com/mikem/bcm2835/ **/
#include <bcm2835.h>
#include <iostream>
#include <string.h>
#include <sys/mman.h>
#define SAMPLES 2000
using namespace std;

int main() {
   short data[SAMPLES];
   if (!bcm2835_init()) {
      cout << "Failed to intialize the bcm2835 module" << endl;;
      return 1;
   }
   // Set the maximum possible priority and switch from regular Linux
   // round-robin scheduling to FIFO fixed-priority scheduling
   struct sched_param sp;
   sp.sched_priority = sched_get_priority_max(SCHED_FIFO);
   if (sched_setscheduler(0, SCHED_FIFO, &sp)<0) { // change scheduling
      cout << "Failed to switch from SCHED_RR to SCHED_FIFO" << endl;
      return 1;
   }
   // lock the process' memory into RAM, preventing page swapping
   if (mlockall(MCL_CURRENT|MCL_FUTURE)<0) { // lock cur & future pages
```

---

[2] Despite the name, this library also works with the BCM2836 and BCM2837 SoCs on the RPi 2 and RPi 3.

```
    std::cout << "Failed to lock the memory." << std::endl;
    return 1;
}
bcm2835_spi_begin();
bcm2835_spi_setBitOrder(BCM2835_SPI_BIT_ORDER_MSBFIRST);
bcm2835_spi_setDataMode(BCM2835_SPI_MODE3);
bcm2835_spi_setClockDivider(BCM2835_SPI_CLOCK_DIVIDER_64); // limit!
bcm2835_spi_chipSelect(BCM2835_SPI_CS0);
bcm2835_spi_setChipSelectPolarity(BCM2835_SPI_CS0, LOW);
for(int i=0; i<SAMPLES; i++) {
    char msg[3] = { 0b00000110, 0x00, 0x00 };
    for(int x=0; x<700; x++) { };    // hacked delay - do not optimize
    bcm2835_spi_transfern(msg, 3);
    data[i]=((msg[1]&0b00001111)<<8)|msg[2];
}
for(int i=0; i<SAMPLES; i++) {
    cout << i << " " << data[i] << endl;
}
bcm2835_spi_end();       // clean up SPI
bcm2835_close();         // close the driver
munlockall();            // unlock the process memory
return 0;
}
```

The code in Listing 9-4 can be built and executed as follows:

```
pi@erpi .../chp09/bcm2835 $ g++ adc_bcm2835.cpp -o adc -lbcm2835
pi@erpi .../chp09/bcm2835 $ sudo ./adc
```

The output is displayed in Figure 9-5, where the results are impressive for an embedded Linux device. Figure 9-5(a) shows minimal jitter and Figure 9-5(b) demonstrates that sampling can take place over an extended period of at least one million samples, without suffering from noticeable latency problems. Note that the plot in Figure 9-5(b) consists of 1 million discrete points; the fineness of the resulting plot lines indicates a good quality sampling result.

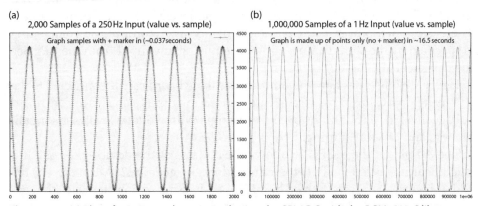

Figure 9-5: (a) Plot of 2,000 samples captured using the SPI ADC with the BCM2835 C library; (b) plot of 1 million samples using the same library

Clearly, the BCM2835 C library improves the overall sampling performance, albeit using RPi-specific code.

One significant limitation of using an SPI ADC as described in this section is that the sample rate is difficult to determine, and it is dependent on the CPU frequency of the RPi. In this example, the sample rate is set by altering the number of iterations in the empty `for` loop, which creates a blocking delay. An external sample clock is required to resolve this limitation. One such option is to use the RTC module that is described in Chapter 8, which has a configurable clock output. Alternatively, a clock generator from Chapter 6 could be used. Once the clock is attached to a GPIO, you can replace the empty `for` loop with code that reads the GPIO and waits for it to change state (i.e., on a rising or a falling edge). The data can be sampled on the GPIO state transition, and the cycle would repeat for the next sample. This proposed circuit configuration would result in a more precise sampling-clock period.

Digital-to-Analog Conversion

Digital-to-analog conversion (DAC) enables a digital device to output an analog voltage level, which is specified using a digital value; this is the opposite of ADC. In this section, DAC capabilities are added to the RPi using both the I²C and the SPI buses. The SPI approach is more suitable for signal generation, but the I²C approach is useful in particular for the generation of a software-controlled DC voltage level.

An I²C Digital-to-Analog Converter

The MCP4725 is a single-channel 12-bit DAC with built-in EEPROM memory. It is a surface mounted device (SOT-23) so a breakout board, such as the one that is available from Adafruit ($5), is required for prototyping work. The built-in EEPROM memory allows the desired output level to be permanently stored. Therefore, when power is applied to the device it will output the voltage that is specified by the stored value, without requiring any input from the RPi. See the datasheet at `tiny.cc/erpi905`.

Figure 9-6 illustrates how the Adafruit breakout board can be connected to the RPi using an I²C bus. This circuit can be used to output a software-controlled voltage level for applications such as setting a point-voltage level, sensor calibration, and offset trimming.

The A0 pin on the MCP4725 allows the address of the device to be set. If it is left floating or tied to GND then the address is set at 0x62. Alternatively, the address is 0x63 if the input is tied high. This addressing option facilitates the connection of two such devices to the same I²C bus.

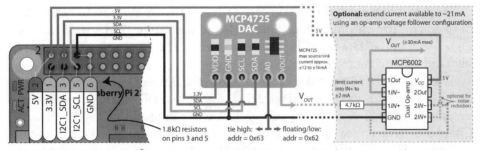

Figure 9-6: The MCP4725 I²C DAC with an optional op-amp circuit that improves the output current range

To set the analog output level you simply send the digital value to the device in a hexadecimal format. It is a 12-bit DAC, therefore there are 4,096 steps between 0 V and 3.3 V—0_{10} to 4095_{10}, which is 0x0000 to 0x0FFF in hexadecimal form. For example, to output a voltage level of 1 V, you must set a decimal value of $(1 \times 4096) \div 3.3\,V = 1241_{10} = 0x04D9$ in hexadecimal. Similarly, 2 V→0x09B0 and 3 V→0x0E8B. You must then write both bytes, MSB first, to the device. For example, to set the DAC output voltage to be 1V, 2V, 3V, and then 3.3V, use the following steps respectively:

```
pi@erpi ~ $ i2cset -y 1 0x62 0x04 0xD8
pi@erpi ~ $ i2cset -y 1 0x62 0x09 0xB0
pi@erpi ~ $ i2cset -y 1 0x62 0x0E 0x8B
pi@erpi ~ $ i2cset -y 1 0x62 0x0F 0xFF
```

The I2CDevice class from Chapter 8 can be used to build a DACDriver class, as defined in Listing 9-5. This class wraps the functionality of the MCP4725 device with methods for setting the output level, and for defining the DC output impedance as either 1Ω (DISABLE), 1kΩ, 100kΩ, or 500kΩ.

Listing 9-5: /exploringrpi/chp09/i2cDAC/DACDriver.h

```
class DACDriver:protected I2CDevice{
public:   // the power-down mode
   enum PD_MODE { DISABLE, GND_1K, GND_100K, GND_500K };
private:
   unsigned int I2CBus, I2CAddress;
   unsigned int lastValue;
   int setOutput(unsigned int value, DACDriver::PD_MODE mode);
public:
   DACDriver(unsigned int I2CBus=1, unsigned int I2CAddress=0x62);
   virtual int powerDown(DACDriver::PD_MODE mode = GND_500K);
   virtual int wake();
   virtual int setOutput(unsigned int value);
   virtual int setOutput(float percentage);
   virtual int setOutput(unsigned int waveform[], int size, int loops=1);
   virtual unsigned int getLastValue() { return lastValue; }
   virtual ~DACDriver();
};
```

The maximum current that you can source or sink to the output of the DAC depends on the output voltage, but varies in the range 12 mA to 16 mA (see Figure 2-16 in the datasheet). However, you must also be cognizant of the total demand for current from the RPi's 3.3 V supply.

An optional circuit extension is provided on the right side of Figure 9-6, which describes the addition of a MCP6002 dual op-amp in DIP form. One of the two op-amps in this IC is used in a voltage-follower configuration (as described in Chapter 4), which means that the output voltage of the op-amp (*1Out*) mirrors the input voltage (*1IN+*) that is set by the DAC. Importantly, the current on the output is supplied by the MCP6002, and not by the DAC. At room temperature, the MCP6002 can source or sink a maximum of 21.5 mA with a power supply of 5 V (see Figure 2-13 in the MCP6002 datasheet). Alternative op-amp devices can further extend this range.

Listing 9-6 provides a short code example that can be used to output a 50% voltage level on the output (i.e., 1.65 V in this example). The program then turns off the output until a key is pressed. The DAC maintains its output voltage level even after the program terminates, or even if the RPi is restarted.

Listing 9-6: /chp09/i2cDAC/dacTestApp.cpp (segment)

```
int main() {
    DACDriver *driver = new DACDriver(1,0x62);
    driver->setOutput(50.0f);                      // 50% (i.e., 2048)
    cout << "The output is " << driver->getLastValue() << endl;
    cout << "Press ENTER to sleep the DAC..." << endl;
    getchar();
    driver->powerDown(DACDriver::GND_100K);     // leave blank for 500K
    cout << "Press ENTER to wake the DAC..." << endl;
    getchar();
    driver->wake();
    cout << "DAC is on and maintains value on exit" << endl;
    return 0;
}
```

Listing 9-6 can be built and executed as follows:

```
pi@erpi ~/exploringrpi/chp09/i2cDAC $ ./build
pi@erpi ~/exploringrpi/chp09/i2cDAC $ ./dactest
The output is 2048
Press ENTER to sleep the DAC...
Press ENTER to wake the DAC...
DAC is on and maintains value on exit
```

A separate example is provided in the same directory (dacSignalTest.cpp) that demonstrates how to use the I²C DAC to output a sine wave signal. The application generates a sine wave of ~30 Hz for a sine wave period that consists of 100 discrete samples. The output is limited by the speed of the I²C bus; a similar example is presented for an SPI DAC, which can achieve much greater output frequencies.

An SPI Digital-to-Analog Converter

The MCP4921 is a low-cost ($2) single-channel 12-bit SPI DAC that is available in DIP form (see `tiny.cc/erpi906`). It is part of a family of Microchip SPI DACs that also contains an 8-bit (MCP4901) and a 10-bit (MCP4911) variant. The family of DACs supports 2.7 V to 5.5 V supply operation with rail-to-rail outputs (i.e., from GND to V_{DD}), and an SPI data clock frequency of up to 20 MHz.

Figure 9-7(a) illustrates how the MCP4921 can be connected to the SPI bus on the RPi. The DAC does not send data back to the RPi, so there is no MISO connection required. Once again, you could use the "optional" circuit that is illustrated in Figure 9-6 to extend the output current range; however, choosing an SPI device means that you are less likely to be using the device as a voltage source, and more likely to be using it as a signal/waveform generator.

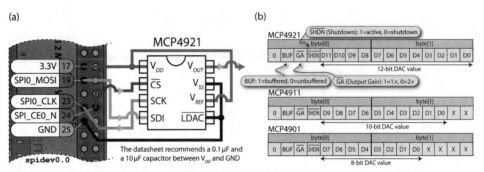

Figure 9-7: (a) Connecting to the MCP4921 SPI DAC; (b) the SPI message format for the MCP4921/11/01

The SPI message format for the full family of devices is illustrated in Figure 9-7(b). There is a leading `0`, followed by three configuration bits, and then the data value that describes the desired DAC output—the value varies in bit length according to the DAC that is used. The three configuration bits are:

- **The Buffer bit:** Identifies whether the output should be buffered (`1`) or unbuffered (`0`). The active-low LDAC input can be used to transfer the input value that is stored in a latch register to the output. By tying this pin to GND, the output is automatically set on the rising edge of the SPI_CE0_N chip-select (CS) signal and the Buffer bit should be set to `0`.

- **The Output Gain bit:** A selectable gain control (`1` = 1 × V_{REF} or `0` = 2 × V_{REF}). The output voltage cannot exceed the supply voltage V_{DD}, and because $V_{REF} = V_{DD}$ in this example, this bit is set to `1`.

- **The Shutdown bit:** A bit that allows the DAC to be shut down using software (e.g., to conserve power). `0` = shutdown, `1` = on.

The datasheet for this device provides excellent additional advice and sample circuits on how it can be used effectively (see `tiny.cc/erpi906`)

A code example is provided in Listing 9-7 that generates a sine wave using 100 samples per period. The sine wave is biased by +2,047 so that it oscillates between 0 and 4,095, rather than being centered on zero. This code is written for the MCP4921 but it can be adapted for the other DACs in the family by changing the gain, bias, and by shifting the DAC value left by two bits for the MCP4911, or by four bits for the MCP4901.

Listing 9-7: /chp09/spiDAC/DACTest.cpp

```cpp
#include <iostream>
#include <math.h>
#include "bus/SPIDevice.h"
using namespace exploringRPi;

int main() {                        // mask = (MSB) 0 (BUF) 0 (GA) 1 (SHDN) 1
   unsigned char mask = 0b00110000;
   std::cout << "Starting RPi SPI DAC Example" << std::endl;
   SPIDevice *busDevice = new SPIDevice(0,0);
   busDevice->setSpeed(20000000);        // max for MCP49xx family
   busDevice->setMode(SPIDevice::MODE0); // using SPI mode 0

   // calculate a 12-bit sine wave function using 100 samples per period
   unsigned short fn[100];              // using 16-bit data
   float gain  = 2047.0f;              // gain of 1.65V
   float phase = 0.0f;                 // phase not important here
   float bias  = 2048.0f;              // center on 1.65V
   float freq  = 2.0f * 3.14159f / 100.0f;  // 2*Pi/period (real pi!)
   for (int i=0; i<100; i++) {          // calculate sine waveform
      fn[i] = (unsigned short)(bias + (gain * sin((i * freq) + phase)));
   }
   unsigned char send[2];               // sending 16-bits in total
   for(int x=0; x<10000; x++) {         // send 10,000 periods
      for(int i=0; i<100; i++) {        // 100 samples per period
         send[0] = mask | fn[i]>>8;     // first 4 bits as above
         send[1] = fn[i] & 0x00FF;      // remaining 8 lsbs of sample
         busDevice->transfer(send, NULL, 2);// send the data
      }
   }
   busDevice->close();
   std::cout << "End of RPi SPI DAC Example" << std::endl;
   return 0;
}
```

On execution this results in the output as illustrated in Figure 9-8(a), which is captured using an oscilloscope that is attached to the V_{OUT} pin of the MCP4921. The DAC is outputting a sine wave of 269.5 Hz, where each cycle is made up of 100 samples. Therefore, the DAC is processing 26,950 samples per second (SPS).

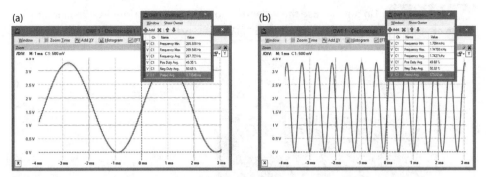

Figure 9-8: (a) The SPI DAC output signal; (b) the SPI DAC output using the C Library for BCM2835

A further code example is provided in the `chp09/spiDAC/bcm2835/` directory that utilizes the BCM2835 C Library to send the samples to the SPI DAC. The output of this code is displayed in Figure 9-8(b), where you can see that the frequency of the sine wave is 1.75 kHz, which means that the DAC is processing 175,000 SPS when a memory-mapped approach is used that is specific to the RPi.

Adding PWM Outputs to the RPi

The concept of pulse-width modulation (PWM) is introduced in Chapter 4, and its use with the RPi is described in detail in Chapter 6. PWM outputs can be used to control the brightness of LEDs or to control servo motors (as described in Chapter 6), by adjusting the duty cycle of a control signal. Unfortunately, the number of onboard hardware PWM outputs on the RPi is limited, which may constrain your development projects. However, you can add PWM outputs to the RPi using I²C PWM controllers.

There are many types of PWM controllers available, such as the popular TLC5940, but such devices often require external oscillators and timers, greatly increasing the complexity of an implementation for the RPi. The PCA9685 does not require any external timing circuitry as it has a 25 MHz internal oscillator, therefore it is chosen as the focus of this discussion. It is a 16-channel 12-bit PWM controller that interfaces to an I²C bus. It can output a signal frequency of between 24 Hz and 1,526 Hz, where each of the 16 outputs can be adjusted to have an individual duty cycle (0%–100%). It is packaged as a surface-mounted TSSOP28, which has 0.65 mm between each of the 28 pins. For prototyping work you must either purchase it on a ready-made module from suppliers such as Adafruit (~$15), or you can purchase a 0.65 mm to 0.1" adapter board. The Adafruit module is used in this discussion as it is well designed and it can be easily interfaced to the RPi, as illustrated in Figure 9-9.

> **WARNING**   Do not confuse the V_{CC} and V+ inputs on the Adafruit PCA9685 module or you could damage your RPi. V_{CC} is a 3.3 V logic-level supply and V+ is the motor supply voltage (e.g., often 5 V).

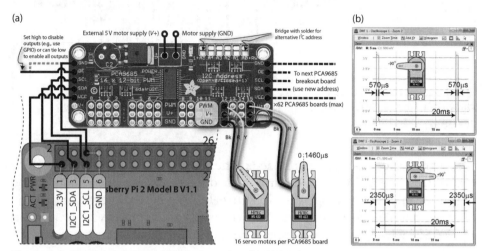

Figure 9-9: The Adafruit PCA9685 16-channel 12-bit PWM driver

The top of the Adafruit module has terminal block connectors with reverse-polarity protection that facilitate the connection of an external motor power supply. The motor power supply should not exceed 5.5 V. (At that voltage level, it can be safely controlled using 3.3 V logic levels.) Ideally, the module should be powered using an external power supply, because servo motors can cause significant noise on the RPi supply line. However, if you are only connecting one servo motor to the board, you should be able to use the RPi 5 V supply. There is a space on the Adafruit module for an electrolytic smoothing capacitor (e.g., 470 μF) that can be sized according to the number and total requirement of the attached servo motors. Each of the 16 outputs has an onboard 220 Ω resistor, which simplifies its use in driving LEDs and servo motors. In addition to typical I²C bus connections, there is an Output Enable (OE) input. If this value is set high, the PWM outputs are disabled.

It is possible to attach 62 of these modules to a single I²C bus, because each board can be assigned an address by bridging the six Alternative Address (A5–A0) contact points with solder.[3] Attaching 62 of these boards to the same bus gives you

---

[3] Six solder bridges provides $2^6 = 64$ possible addresses; however, the chip has a special feature that allows you to reset all outputs by using a different I²C address called Software Reset (0x06) and to control all outputs using an I²C address called LED All Call (enabled by default at I²C address 0x70). Therefore, these two addresses are not available for use and so the total is reduced from 64 to 62. Do not solder bridge to select address 0x70.

the possibility of controlling up to 992 servo motors using a single bus on the RPi! Figure 9-10 captures the output that results from a call to `i2cdump` on the device address, which is at I²C bus address 0x40 by default.

Figure 9-10 also illustrates the registers that can be used to control the output of the PCA9685. There are two mode registers (0x00 and 0x01) that control the behavior of the device, using bit patterns that are described at the bottom of Figure 9-10. The mode registers are followed by four address registers (0x02–0x05), which if enabled by Mode1 allow multiple PCA9685 modules to respond to a single "virtual" I²C address, because if they were a single device. For example, you could potentially control all the servos that are attached to Channel0 on multiple modules using a single call to a single sub-address that is enabled on each of the boards. Writing to the All Call I²C address (0x70) affects all the modules on the bus unless they have set the Mode1 bit so as to ignore write requests to the All Call address.

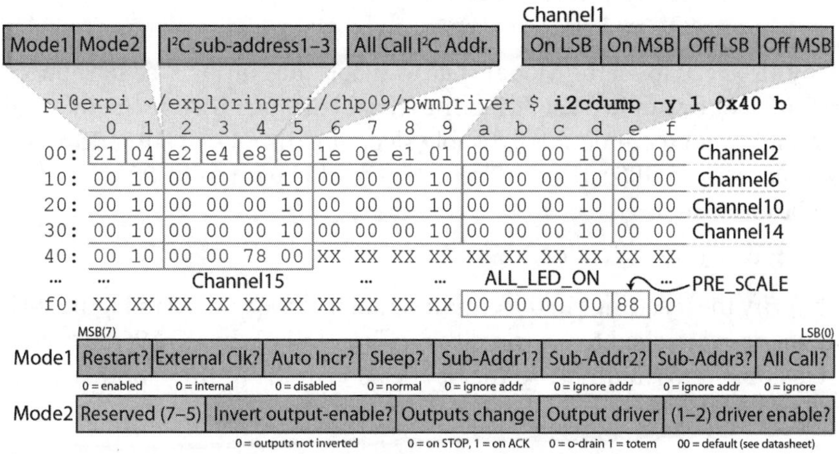

Figure 9-10: Registers for the PCA9685 16-channel 12-bit PWM controller

The address registers are followed by 16 quadruples of addresses—one quadruple for each of the output channels. For example, Channel0 occupies the four addresses 0x06 to 0x09, where the first two addresses are used to store the 12-bit "on time" value and the last two addresses are used to store the 12-bit "off time." Both 12-bit values are stored in Little Endian byte order. The "on time" is the time after which the signal goes high and the "off time" is the time after which the signal goes low. These values do not represent the time for which the output is high and the output is low. The advantage of the PCA9685 timing format is that a phase shift can be introduced into the output signal.

For example, to use the Linux i2c-tools to set up two PWM signals, as illustrated in Figure 9-11:

1. The first has a 20% duty cycle and a phase shift of 25% on Channel0: the "turn on" time is 0.25 × 4,096 = 1,024 (0x0400) and the "turn off" time is 0.45 × 4,096 = 1,843 (0x0733). Therefore, these values must be written to the registers (0x06 to 0x09) as follows:

```
pi@erpi ~ $ i2cset -y 1 0x40 0x06 0x00
pi@erpi ~ $ i2cset -y 1 0x40 0x07 0x04
pi@erpi ~ $ i2cset -y 1 0x40 0x08 0x33
pi@erpi ~ $ i2cset -y 1 0x40 0x09 0x07
```

2. The second has a duty cycle of 33% and a phase shift of 0% on Channel1: the "turn on" time is therefore 0 (0x0000) and the "turn off" time is 0.33 × 4,096 = 1,352 (0x0548). Therefore, these values must be written to the registers (0x0a to 0x0d) as follows:

```
pi@erpi ~ $ i2cset -y 1 0x40 0x0a 0x00
pi@erpi ~ $ i2cset -y 1 0x40 0x0b 0x00
pi@erpi ~ $ i2cset -y 1 0x40 0x0c 0x48
pi@erpi ~ $ i2cset -y 1 0x40 0x0d 0x05
```

You many also need to set the Mode1 state to enable the outputs (see the bottom of Figure 9-10). For example, to set Mode1 to disable restart (1), use the internal clock (0), enable auto increment (1), disable sleep (0), disable all sub-addresses (000), and enable All Call (1), the 0x00 register should be set to 10100001, which is 0xA1 in hexadecimal:

```
pi@erpi ~ $ i2cset -y 1 0x40 0x00 0xA1
```

You can verify these settings in the output signal that is captured in Figure 9-11, where the scope is attached to Channel0 and Channel1 of the PCA9685. A voltage offset is applied to Channel1 so that it is visible in the figure—both signals vary between 0 V and 3.3 V.

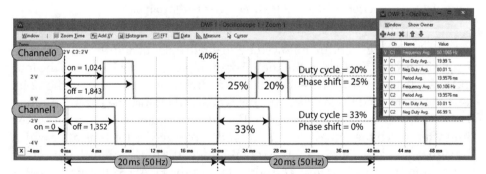

Figure 9-11: Example PWM output of Channel0 and Channel1 of the PCA9685

Code is provided in the /chp09/pwmDriver/ directory as an example of how you can wrap the PCA9685 module with a class. Listing 9-8 provides a description of the methods that are available in the class and the code implementation is in the pwmDriver.cpp file. This class utilizes the I2CDevice class that is described in Chapter 8.

In particular, it is worth noting the code that is used to set the PWM channel output values (from PWMDriver::setOutput()):

```
writeRegister((LED0_ON_L  + (4*outputNumber)), (timeOn  &  0xFF));
writeRegister((LED0_ON_H  + (4*outputNumber)), (timeOn  >> 8));
writeRegister((LED0_OFF_L + (4*outputNumber)), (timeOff &  0xFF));
writeRegister((LED0_OFF_H + (4*outputNumber)), (timeOff >> 8));
```

This code performs the same function as was just performed manually using the Linux i2c-tools calls. Rather than maintain a full list of registers, the code offsets the address by four times the desired output number. For example, to set the "turn on" LSB for Channel5, the calculation is LED0_ON_L + (5 × 4) = 0x06 + 20_{10} = 0x1A. You can confirm this result in Figure 9-10 by locating the first register address of Channel5.

Listing 9-8: /chp09/pwmDriver/pwmDriver.h (segment)

```
class PWMDriver:protected I2CDevice{
private:
    unsigned int I2CBus, I2CAddress;
public:
    PWMDriver(unsigned int I2CBus=1, unsigned int I2CAddress=0x40);
    virtual int reset();
    virtual int sleep();
    virtual int wake() { reset(); }
    virtual int setOutput(unsigned int outputNumber, float dutyCycle,
                          float phaseOffset=0.0f);  // 0-15, 0.0-100, 0.0f
    virtual int setOutputFullyOn(unsigned int outputNumber) {
                 setOutput(outputNumber, 100.0f); }
    virtual int setOutputFullyOff(unsigned int outputNumber) {
                 setOutput(outputNumber, 0.0f);   }
    virtual int setFrequency(float frequency);  // between 24 and 1526Hz
    virtual float getFrequency();
    virtual ~PWMDriver();
};
```

Listing 9-8 also contains code to adjust the frequency of the PWM signal, which is common to all outputs. The PRE_SCALE register (0xFE, see the PCA9685 datasheet 7.3.5) defines the frequency at which all the outputs modulate.

This is determined by the formula: *pre-scale value = round* ($25\,\text{MHz} \div (4{,}096 \times$ *frequency*)) − 1. The code in Listing 9-8 contains a function that performs this calculation for the desired frequency.

Listing 9-9 provides an example program that uses the `PWMDriver` class to set the PWM frequency and output a signal on Channel0 and Channel1.

Listing 9-9: chp09/pwmDriver/pwmTestApp.cpp (segment)

```
int main() {
    PWMDriver driver(1, 0x40);
    driver.reset();
    driver.setFrequency(100.0f);
    float frequency = driver.getFrequency();
    cout << "The frequency is currently: " << frequency << endl;
    driver.setOutput(0, 12.5);          // channel, duty cycle
    driver.setOutput(1, 25.0, 12.5); // channel, duty cycle, phase shift
    cout << "Press Enter to sleep the outputs..." << endl;
    getchar();
    driver.sleep();
    cout << "The outputs are now off" << endl;
    cout << "Press Enter to wake the outputs..." << endl;
    getchar();
    driver.wake();
    cout << "The outputs are now on" << endl;
    return 0;
}
```

The program in Listing 9-9 can be built and executed as follows, and results in the output in Figure 9-12. Importantly, this output signal continues even after the `pwmtest` program terminates.

```
pi@erpi ~/exploringrpi/chp09/pwmDriver $ ./build
pi@erpi ~/exploringrpi/chp09/pwmDriver $ ./pwmtest
The frequency is currently: 99.3896
Press Enter to sleep the outputs...
The outputs are now off
Press Enter to wake the outputs...
The outputs are now on
```

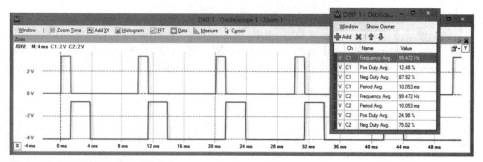

Figure 9-12: Output of Listing 9-9

This section finishes with a `Servo` class that uses the `PWMDriver` class to simplify the use of servo motors with the PCA9685 module. The class in Listing 9-10 contains a calibration method, which allows the output to be tailored specifically for each individual motor.

Listing 9-10: chp09/pwmDriver/Servo.h (segment)

```
class Servo {
private:
    PWMDriver *pwmDriver;                  // pointer to the PCA9685 driver
    int outputNumber;                      // the output on the PCA9685 breakout
    float minDutyCycle, maxDutyCycle, zeroDutyCycle;  // duty cycles
    float plusMinusRange;                             // servo range (+/-)
    float angleStepSize;                              // calculated
public:
    Servo(PWMDriver *pwmDriver, int outputNum, float plusMinusRange=90.0f);
    virtual int calibrate(float minDutyCycle, float maxDutyCycle);
    virtual int setAngle(float angle);
    virtual ~Servo();
};
```

The code in Listing 9-11 uses the class in Listing 9-10 to sweep a servo motor (with range ±90°) on Channel15 to −90° and then back to +90°.

Listing 9-11: chp09/pwmDriver/servoTestApp.cpp (segment)

```
int main() {
    PWMDriver *driver = new PWMDriver(1, 0x40);  // bus 1, device 0x40
    driver->reset();                             // remove prev state
    driver->setFrequency(50.0f);                 // freq for all PWMs
    Servo *servo = new Servo(driver, 15, 90.0);  // channel 15, ±90°
    servo->calibrate(2.85, 11.75);               // manual calculation
    for(int i=-90; i<90; i+=2){                  // from left to right
        servo->setAngle(i);                      // in degrees
        usleep(10000);                           // 10ms sleep per step
    }
    for(int i=90; i>-90; i-=2){                  // from right to left
        servo->setAngle(i);
        usleep(10000);
    }
    driver->sleep();                             // remove holding torque
    return 0;
}
```

Extending the RPi GPIOs

The use of the RPi GPIOs is described in detail in Chapter 6, where it is discussed that there is a maximum of 26 GPIOs accessible via the GPIO header on the RPi 3/2/B+/A+, and 17 on earlier models. The number of available GPIOs reduces significantly if you require the I²C bus, SPI bus, or UART devices. Fortunately, it is possible to use low-cost I/O expanders, such as the Microchip 16-bit MCP23017 I²C I/O Expander and the 16-bit MCP23S17 SPI Expander, which are both available in PDIP form for $1–$2.

Figure 9-13(a) illustrates the connection of the MCP23017 to the I²C bus, and Figure 9-13(b) illustrates the connection of the MCP23S17 to the SPI bus. These are different physical devices, but their pin layouts are consistent, which assists with design for possible bus interchange. In fact, both devices are described by a single datasheet: `tiny.cc/erpi907`.

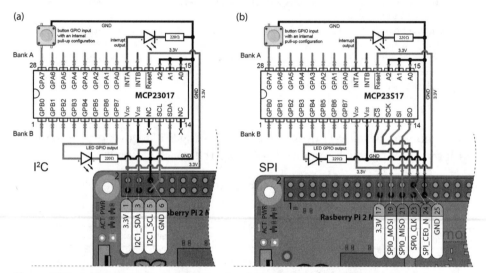

Figure 9-13: Adding GPIOs to the RPi using the: (a) MCP23017 I²C GPIO expander, and (b) MCP23S17 SPI GPIO expander

There are some physical features of each device that should be noted:

- The MCP23017 has three address pins (A0–A2) that allow up to eight ICs to be connected to a single I²C bus, which facilitates the addition of up to 128 GPIOs to each I²C bus. The device supports 100 kHz, 400 kHz, and 1.7 MHz bus speeds.

- The MCP23S17 also has three address pins (A0–A2) that are used to address separate devices which have been daisy chained together as a single SPI device (discussed shortly). This facilitates the addition of up to 256 GPIOs to the single SPI bus on the RPi by using both chip select pins. The MCP23S17 supports SPI bus speeds of up to 10 MHz.

It is worth noting up front that these are capable devices that are surprisingly complex. For example: the GPIO pins can be configured as inputs/outputs, internal pull-up/pull-down resistor configuration is possible, input polarity is selectable, and different types of interrupt conditions can be configured. This is all useful functionality that can greatly improve the I/O capabilities of the RPi (and of other embedded devices), so it is worth the effort involved in becoming familiar with their configuration and use.

The internal register configuration of both devices is consistent. They have two banks of registers (A and B), each associated with eight configurable GPIOs. In addition, the devices have two interrupt pins (INTA and INTB) that can be configured to react to a programmable set of input conditions.

The illustrations in Figure 9-13 each include three test circuits that are used in this section to help explain the capability of these devices:

- A pushbutton circuit is connected to GPA7, which is configured shortly to have an internal pull-up resistor enabled.

- An LED circuit is connected to GPB7, which is configured to be an output. The LED lights when GPB7 is high.

- An LED circuit is connected to the interrupt pin, INTA, which is used to test the interrupt capabilities of the devices.

The I²C device is investigated first, because the Linux i2c-tools (see Chapter 8) are very useful for familiarizing yourself with the registers on a new device.

The MCP23017 and the I²C Bus

The MCP23017 appears on the bus at address 0x20 by default. You can alter this address by tying A0, A1, and A2 high or low. For example, if A0 and A1 are tied to the 3.3 V line, then the device address becomes 0x23. In the default configuration, as in Figure 9-13(a) you can verify the device address:

```
pi@erpi ~ $ i2cdetect -y 1
     0  1  2  3  4  5  6  7  8  9  a  b  c  d  e  f
00:          -- -- -- -- -- -- -- -- -- -- -- --
10: -- -- -- -- -- -- -- -- -- -- -- -- -- -- -- --
20: 20 -- -- -- -- -- -- -- -- -- -- -- -- -- -- ...
```

The registers can then be displayed as in Figure 9-14 using the i2cdump command. This figure identifies the name and role of each of the registers, which are organized into pairs so as to align against the two 8-bit ports (Port A and Port B) on the devices.

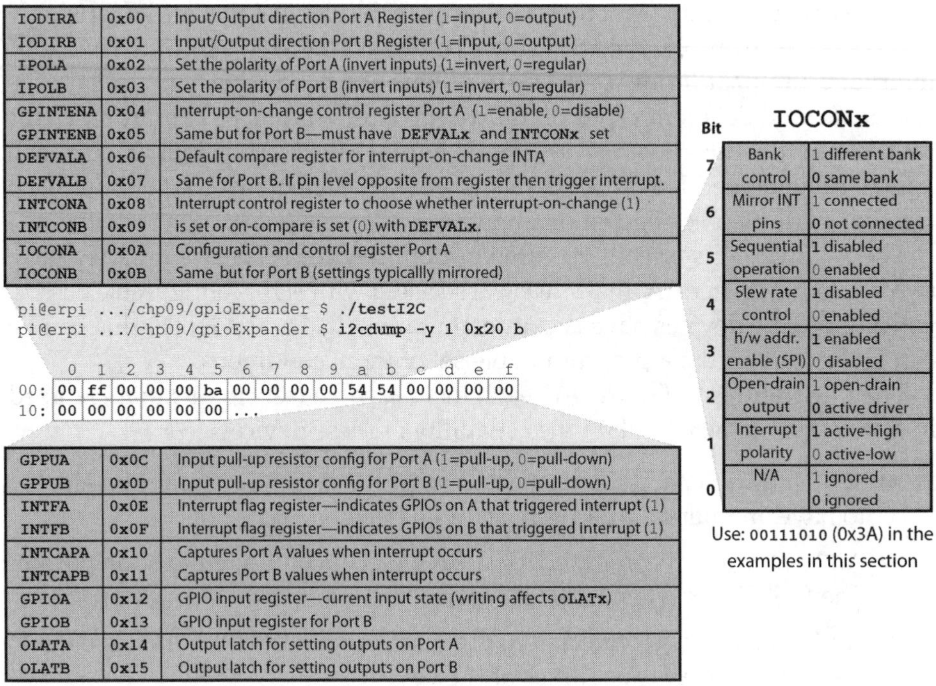

IODIRA	0x00	Input/Output direction Port A Register (1=input, 0=output)
IODIRB	0x01	Input/Output direction Port B Register (1=input, 0=output)
IPOLA	0x02	Set the polarity of Port A (invert inputs) (1=invert, 0=regular)
IPOLB	0x03	Set the polarity of Port B (invert inputs) (1=invert, 0=regular)
GPINTENA	0x04	Interrupt-on-change control register Port A (1=enable, 0=disable)
GPINTENB	0x05	Same but for Port B—must have DEFVALx and INTCONx set
DEFVALA	0x06	Default compare register for interrupt-on-change INTA
DEFVALB	0x07	Same for Port B. If pin level opposite from register then trigger interrupt.
INTCONA	0x08	Interrupt control register to choose whether interrupt-on-change (1)
INTCONB	0x09	is set or on-compare is set (0) with DEFVALx.
IOCONA	0x0A	Configuration and control register Port A
IOCONB	0x0B	Same but for Port B (settings typicallly mirrored)

Bit	IOCONx		
7	Bank control	1 different bank
		0 same bank
6	Mirror INT pins	1 connected
		0 not connected
5	Sequential operation	1 disabled
		0 enabled
4	Slew rate control	1 disabled
		0 enabled
3	h/w addr. enable (SPI)	1 enabled
		0 disabled
2	Open-drain output	1 open-drain
		0 active driver
1	Interrupt polarity	1 active-high
		0 active-low
0	N/A	1 ignored
		0 ignored

```
pi@erpi .../chp09/gpioExpander $ ./testI2C
pi@erpi .../chp09/gpioExpander $ i2cdump -y 1 0x20 b

     0  1  2  3  4  5  6  7  8  9  a  b  c  d  e  f
00: 00 ff 00 00 00 ba 00 00 00 00 00 54 54 00 00 00 00
10: 00 00 00 00 00 00 ...
```

GPPUA	0x0C	Input pull-up resistor config for Port A (1=pull-up, 0=pull-down)
GPPUB	0x0D	Input pull-up resistor config for Port B (1=pull-up, 0=pull-down)
INTFA	0x0E	Interrupt flag register—indicates GPIOs on A that triggered interrupt (1)
INTFB	0x0F	Interrupt flag register—indicates GPIOs on B that triggered interrupt (1)
INTCAPA	0x10	Captures Port A values when interrupt occurs
INTCAPB	0x11	Captures Port B values when interrupt occurs
GPIOA	0x12	GPIO input register—current input state (writing affects OLATx)
GPIOB	0x13	GPIO input register for Port B
OLATA	0x14	Output latch for setting outputs on Port A
OLATB	0x15	Output latch for setting outputs on Port B

Use: 00111010 (0x3A) in the examples in this section

Figure 9-14: The MCP23x17 registers

To become familiar with the use of these devices a good starting point is to use the i2cset and i2cget commands to control the LED circuit and the push-button circuit, both of which are illustrated in Figure 9-13(a).

Controlling the GPIO LED Circuit

The output LED is attached to Port B Pin 7 (GPB7) as in Figure 9-13(a). To set the state of the LED, you first need to perform the following steps:

- Set the IOCONB configuration and control register state (0x0B) to be 0x3A, as determined on the right side of Figure 9-14:

  ```
  pi@erpi ~ $ i2cset -y 1 0x20 0x0B 0x3A
  ```

- Set GPB7 in the IODIRB (0x01) direction register to be in output mode by setting bit 7 to be low (note that the following call will set all eight GPB pins to be outputs):

  ```
  pi@erpi ~ $ i2cset -y 1 0x20 0x01 0x00
  ```

- To light the LED that is attached to GPB7 you can set bit 7 on the OLATB output latch register (0x15) high. You can then read the current Port B state using the GPIOB register (0x13) as follows:

```
pi@erpi ~ $ i2cset -y 1 0x20 0x15 0x80
pi@erpi ~ $ i2cget -y 1 0x20 0x13
0x80
```

■ At this point the LED is lighting and the GPIO bit 7 (0b10000000 = 0x80) is set. The LED can be turned off by setting bit 7 low:

```
pi@erpi ~ $ i2cset -y 1 0x20 0x15 0x00
pi@erpi ~ $ i2cget -y 1 0x20 0x13
0x00
```

Note that all the operations above affect all the GPB input/outputs. For example, turning the LED off by writing the value 0x00 also sets GPB0–GPB6 low. To solve this problem you can read in the current state of the outputs using the GPIOB registers (0x13), modify the value of the desired bit, and then write it back to the OLATB register (0x15). For example, if a read of GPIOB returned 0x03, then GPB0 and GPB1 are high. To retain this state and to set GPB7 high you should OR the two values together (i.e., 0x03 | 0x80), which results in a value of 0x83. If this value is written to OLATB, all three pins are now set high (GPB0, GPB1, and GPB7).

Reading the GPIO Button State

To read the pushbutton state that is attached to Bank A pin 7 (GPA7) you can use a similar method:

■ Set the IOCONA control register to be 0x3A, as illustrated on the right side of Figure 9-14:

```
pi@erpi ~ $ i2cset -y 1 0x20 0x0A 0x3A
```

■ Set GPA7 to be an input using the IODIRA register (0x00):

```
pi@erpi ~ $ i2cset -y 1 0x20 0x00 0x80
```

■ Set GPA7 to be in a pull-up mode using the GPPUA input pull-up configuration register (0x0C):

```
pi@erpi ~ $ i2cset -y 1 0x20 0x0C 0x80
```

■ Read the Port A state using the GPIOA input register (0x12):

```
pi@erpi ~ $ i2cget -y 1 0x20 0x12
0x80
pi@erpi ~ $ i2cget -y 1 0x20 0x12
0x00
```

When the button is not pressed the state is 0b10000000 (0x80) and when the button is pressed the state is 0b00000000 (0x00), indicating that the button circuit is working correctly and that it has a pull-up configuration.

An Interrupt Configuration Example (Advanced)

The devices can be programmed to activate an interrupt output (INTA or INTB) when one of two configurable conditions arises:

1. The input state changes from its current state, where a mask can be set using the GPINTENx register to check or ignore individual bits.

2. The input state differs from a defined value, which is set using the DEFVALx register.

The INTA and INTB output pins can be configured to activate individually or they can be programmed to both activate if either port causes the interrupt.

The use of interrupts is best explained with an example, which is once again illustrated in Figure 9-13(a). In this example, the device is configured so that if the pushbutton that is attached to GPA7 is pressed (or released), the LED attached to the INTA pin will light.

- Set up the pushbutton to be input, as described in the previous example. Remember that the button is in a pull-up configuration, so that when the button is not pressed that the output is as follows:

```
pi@erpi ~ $ i2cget -y 1 0x20 0x12
0x80
```

- Set the GPINTENA interrupt-on-change control register (0x04) to enable GPB7. The DEFVALA default interrupt-on-change compare value (0x06) should be set to 0x80, and the INTCONA interrupt control register (0x08) should also be set to 0x80:

```
pi@erpi ~ $ i2cset -y 1 0x20 0x04 0x80
pi@erpi ~ $ i2cset -y 1 0x20 0x06 0x80
pi@erpi ~ $ i2cset -y 1 0x20 0x08 0x80
```

- Reading the output clears the interrupt. If the INTA LED is currently lighting then displaying the Port A state using the GPIOA input register (0x12) should cause it to turn off:

```
pi@erpi ~ $ i2cget -y 1 0x20 0x12
0x80
```

- Pressing the button at this point should trigger the interrupt and cause the INTA LED to light. You can then use the INTFA interrupt flag register (0x0E) to identify which input caused the interrupt, and you can use the INTCAPA capture register (0x10) to determine the Port A state when the interrupt occurred:

```
pi@erpi ~ $ i2cget -y 1 0x20 0x0E
0x80
```

```
pi@erpi ~ $ i2cget -y 1 0x20 0x10
0x00
```

■ Reading the value of INTCAPA clears the interrupt. So, it is once again ready to trigger an interrupt when the button is pressed.

Clearly you do not need such a complex arrangement to trigger an LED when a button is pressed! However, it is possible to configure the device so that a particular bit pattern on all the Port A and Port B pins is used to trigger the interrupt. My tests indicate that in this example the LED lights 190 ns after the button is pressed, which is extremely fast in comparison to the response times reported for the RPi GPIOs in Chapter 6. Clearly, it is possible to build a hardware circuit using logic gates that can react to a bit pattern even more quickly, but it is important to remember that this behavior is software configurable and can be changed dynamically at run time.

A code example is introduced shortly to facilitate the structured use of these devices.

The MCP23S17 and the SPI Bus

The MCP23S17 SPI version of the MCP23017 I²C device has the same register configuration and therefore the input/output circuits that are illustrated in Figure 9-13(a) and Figure 9-13(b) are identical.

The registers on the SPI device are accessed using the same techniques as described in Chapter 8. However, there is one important difference in the way that this device operates in comparison to other SPI bus devices examined to this point—it implements a custom internal device addressing architecture. Figure 9-15 illustrates how up to eight MCP23S17 devices can be attached to a single SPI bus as a single SPI device. The address lines A0–A2 are used to assign each device a unique 3-bit hardware address, which each device uses to decide whether it should act upon or ignore messages on the bus.

As illustrated in Figure 9-15 all the devices share the same MOSI, MISO, CLK, and CS lines, which means that all data read/write requests are simultaneously sent to all the daisy-chained devices. Each device must identify which requests it should act upon and which requests it should ignore based on its hardware-defined address (A0–A2), and addressing information that is contained within the SPI data message. Therefore, the structure of the SPI message is different than those that are described in Chapter 8. For example, each write request must contain the device address, the register address, and the data to write to the register address. Figure 9-16 illustrates an example data write transaction taking place, which has the form: "on device 000 set the IOCONA control register (0x0A) to have the value 0x3A."

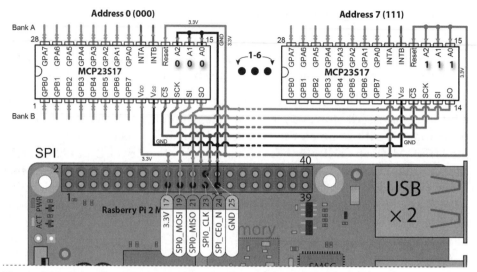

Figure 9-15: Daisy chaining up to eight MCP23S17s as a single SPI bus device

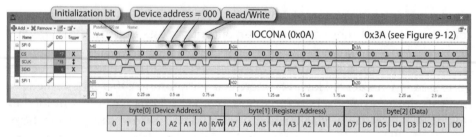

Figure 9-16: An SPI write request to the MCP23S17 at device address 000 to set the IOCONA register to 0x3A

A C++ Class for the MCP23x17 Devices

A C++ class that simplifies the use of the MCP23x17 devices is provided in Listing 9-12, and is available in the /chp09/gpioExpander/ directory. The class wraps the register functionality that is illustrated in Figure 9-14 and provides a framework for accessing the general functionality and interrupt functionality of the MCP23017 and MCP23S17 devices.

Listing 9-12: /chp09/gpioExpander/gpioExpander.h (segment)

```cpp
class GPIOExpander {
private:
    I2CDevice *i2cDevice;
    SPIDevice *spiDevice;
```

```
        bool isSPIDevice;
        unsigned char spiAddress; configRegister;

public:
        enum PORT { PORTA=0, PORTB=1 };
        int writeDevice(unsigned char address, unsigned char value);
        unsigned char readDevice(unsigned char address);
        GPIOExpander(I2CDevice *i2cDevice);
        GPIOExpander(SPIDevice *spiDevice, unsigned char address=0x00);

        // 16-bit -- PORTA is LSB (8-bits), PORTB is MSB (8-bits)
        virtual int setGPIODirections(PORT port, unsigned char value);
        virtual int setGPIODirections(unsigned short value);

        virtual unsigned char getOutputValues(PORT port);
        virtual unsigned short getOutputValues();
        virtual std::string getOutputValuesStr();
        virtual int setOutputValues(PORT port, unsigned char value);
        virtual int setOutputValues(unsigned short value);

        virtual unsigned char getInputValues(PORT port);
        virtual unsigned short getInputValues();
        virtual std::string getInputValuesStr();
        virtual int setInputPolarity(PORT port, unsigned char value);
        virtual int setInputPolarity(unsigned short value);

        // Pull-up resistors for the input ports -- 100k Ohm value
        virtual int setGPIOPullUps(PORT port, unsigned char value);
        virtual int setGPIOPullUps(unsigned short value);
        virtual int updateConfigRegister(unsigned char value);
        virtual int setInterruptOnChange(PORT port, unsigned char value);
        virtual int setInterruptOnChange(unsigned short value);

        // Get the value on the port when interrupt occurs
        virtual unsigned char getInterruptCaptureState(PORT port);
        virtual unsigned short getInterruptCaptureState();
        virtual std::string getInterruptCaptureStateStr();

        // Sets if the interrupt is configured on change or on comparison
        virtual int setInterruptControl(PORT port, unsigned char value);
        virtual int setInterruptControl(unsigned short value);

        // Sets the default comparison register
        virtual int setDefaultCompareValue(PORT port, unsigned char value);
        virtual int setDefaultCompareValue(unsigned short value);

        // Get the interrupt flag register
        virtual unsigned char getInterruptFlagState(PORT port);
        virtual unsigned short getInterruptFlagState();
        virtual std::string getInterruptFlagStateStr();
        virtual void dumpRegisters();  ...
};
```

An example is provided in Listing 9-13 that uses the `GPIOExpander` class to perform the same test operations as described with the Linux i2c-tools, to control the circuit that is illustrated in Figure 9-13.

Listing 9-13: /chp09/gpioExpander/example.cpp

```
int main(){
    cout << "Starting the GPIO Expander Example" << endl;
    SPIDevice *spiDevice = new SPIDevice(0,0);
    spiDevice->setSpeed(10000000);                    // MCP23S17 bus speed
    spiDevice->setMode(SPIDevice::MODE0);

//  I2CDevice *i2cDevice = new I2CDevice(1, 0x20);  // for an I2C device
//  GPIOExpander gpio(i2cDevice);                     // for an I2C device
    GPIOExpander gpio(spiDevice, 0x00);              // SPI dev. addr. 000
    cout << "The GPIO Expander was set up successfully" << endl;

    // PORTA are inputs and PORTB are outputs -- can mix bits
    gpio.setGPIODirections(GPIOExpander::PORTA, 0b11111111); // input=1
    gpio.setGPIODirections(GPIOExpander::PORTB, 0b00000000); // output=0
    gpio.setGPIOPullUps(GPIOExpander::PORTA, 0b10000000);    // pullup GPA7
    gpio.setInputPolarity(GPIOExpander::PORTA, 0b00000000);  // non-inverted

    // Example: get the values of PORTA and set PORTB accordingly
    unsigned char inputValues = gpio.getInputValues(GPIOExpander::PORTA);
    cout << "The values are in the form [B7,..,B0,A7,..,A0]" << endl;
    cout << "The PORTA values are: [" << gpio.getInputValuesStr() << "]\n";
    cout << "Setting PORTB to be " << (int)inputValues << endl;
    gpio.setOutputValues(GPIOExpander::PORTB, inputValues);

    // Example: attach on-change interrupt to GPIOA GPA7
    cout << "Interrupt flags[" << gpio.getInterruptFlagStateStr() << "]\n";
    cout << "Capture state[" << gpio.getInterruptCaptureStateStr() << "]\n";
    gpio.setInterruptControl(GPIOExpander::PORTA, 0b00000000);  // on change
    gpio.setInterruptOnChange(GPIOExpander::PORTA, 0b10000000); // to GPA7
    gpio.dumpRegisters();                           // display the registers
    cout << "End of the GPIO Expander Example" << endl;
}
```

The code example reads the state of the Port A inputs and sets Port B accordingly (remember that GPA7 is in a pull-up configuration, so it is high when the button is not pressed). In addition, an interrupt-on-change configuration is set for INTA, which lights the LED that is attached to INTA when the button is pressed:

```
pi@erpi ~/exploringrpi/chp09/gpioExpander $ ./example
Starting the GPIO Expander Example
The GPIO Expander was set up successfully
The values are in the form [B7,..,B0,A7,..,A0]
The PORTA values are: [1000000010000000]
Setting PORTB to be 128
Interrupt flags[0000000000000000]
Capture state[0000000000000000]
Register Dump:
Register IODIRA  :    255  B: 0
```

```
Register IPOLA    :      0  B: 0
Register GPINTENA:     128  B: 0
Register DEFVALA :      0  B: 0
Register INTCONA :      0  B: 0
Register IOCONA  :     58  B: 58
Register GPPUA   :     128  B: 0
Register INTFA   :      0  B: 0
Register INTAPA  :      0  B: 0
Register GPIOA   :     128  B: 128
Register OLATA   :      0  B: 128
End of the GPIO Expander Example
pi@erpi ~/exploringrpi/chp09/gpioExpander $
```

At this point, the program has run to completion, but it is important to note that the interrupt will still trigger at any future point. The MCP23x17 is programmed to handle the interrupt independently of the RPi.

If the button is pressed, the interrupt is triggered and a call to the display program in the same directory displays the register states. In this example, the interrupt flag register (INTFA) indicates that GPA7 caused the interrupt (i.e., $128_{10} = 0b10000000$):

```
pi@erpi ~/exploringrpi/chp09/gpioExpander $ ./display
Starting the SPI GPIO Expander Example
Register Dump:
Register IODIRA  :    255  B: 0
Register IPOLA   :      0  B: 0
Register GPINTENA:    128  B: 0
Register DEFVALA :      0  B: 0
Register INTCONA :      0  B: 0
Register IOCONA  :     58  B: 58
Register GPPUA   :    128  B: 0
Register INTFA   :    128  B: 0
Register INTAPA  :      0  B: 0
Register GPIOA   :    128  B: 128
Register OLATA   :      0  B: 128
End of the GPIO Expander Example
```

The display program reads the GPIOx registers, so the interrupt is once again primed, even without executing the example program again. Also, if you hold the pushbutton and simultaneously execute the display program, then the interrupt is triggered when you release the button, which demonstrates that an interrupt-on-change condition is configured.

Adding UARTs to the RPi

As described in Chapter 8, UART devices provide a mechanism for serial communication to discrete modules such as GPS units, microprocessors, microcontrollers, sensor modules, actuator modules, and much more. In addition, UARTs can be combined with line driver hardware, such as RS-485 modules, to communicate over long distances—RS-485 supports a network of up to

32 devices communicating at distances of up to 4,000 ft (1,200 m) using a single pair of twisted-pair wires and a common ground connection[4].

Unfortunately, there is only one full onboard UART on the RPi, which is accessible via the GPIO header. In addition, it is typically configured as a serial console, which is a very useful function. It is possible to use the SPI or I²C bus to add UART devices to the RPi. For example, the SparkFun SC16IS750 module ($15) supports high-speed (up to 921,600 baud) communication using the NXP chip of the same name. You can interface this device to the RPi using approaches similar to those described in this chapter. However, a much easier solution is to use the USB ports on the RPi and USB-to-TTL converters, which have Linux driver support.

There are several low-cost USB-to-TTL converters available, many of which have stable Linux driver support. Figure 9-17(a) illustrates three such devices that are available from as little as $1–$2. They can be attached directly to the RPi USB ports as in Figure 9-17(b); however, be careful to ensure that the pins from one adapter do not touch the pins or the tracks on the base of the adapter that is inserted into an adjacent USB slot.

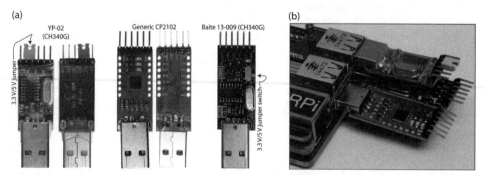

Figure 9-17: (a) Three low-cost USB-to-TTL converters, and (b) three such devices attached to the RPi

Modern Linux kernels support *USB hot plugging*, which allows USB devices to be plugged in to the RPi after it has booted. The kernel then loads the correct LKM for the device. You can use the `dmesg` command to display system-level driver messages, which can help you in diagnosing any device driver problems. For example, when the YP-02 USB-to-TTL module is plugged into the RPi, the following messages are displayed:

```
pi@erpi ~ $ uname -a
Linux erpi 4.1.5-v7+ #809 SMP PREEMPT Thu Aug 13 00:50:56 BST 2015 armv7l
pi@erpi ~ $ dmesg
[97660.915863] usb 1-1.5:new full-speed USB device number 4 using dwc_otg
```

---

[4] See tiny.cc/erpi908 for further details.

```
[97661.019017] usb 1-1.5:New USB device found,idVendor=1a86,idProduct=7523
[97661.019044] usb 1-1.5:New USB device strings: Mfr=0,Product=2,SerNum=0
[97661.019062] usb 1-1.5:Product: USB2.0-Serial
[97661.055002] usbcore:registered new interface driver usbserial
[97661.056961] usbcore:registered new interface driver usbserial_generic
[97661.057231] usbserial:USB Serial support registered for generic
[97661.060665] usbcore:registered new interface driver ch341
[97661.061478] usbserial:USB Serial support registered for ch341-uart
[97661.061600] ch341 1-1.5:1.0:ch341-uart converter detected
[97661.067149] usb 1-1.5:ch341-uart converter now attached to ttyUSB0
```

You can then list the attached USB devices using the `lsusb` command, where-upon a new device is displayed:

```
pi@erpi ~ $ lsusb
...
Bus 001 Device 004:ID 1a86:7523 QinHeng Elec HL-340 USB-Serial adapter
```

There are also new LKMs loaded that are associated with this device:

```
pi@erpi ~ $ lsmod | grep ch34
ch341                  4921  0
usbserial             22429  1 ch341
```

The process results in a new "teletype" terminal device in the `/dev/` directory. You can see below that the dialout group has read/write access to this device, and you can confirm the current user's membership of this group using the `id` command:

```
pi@erpi ~ $ ls -l /dev/ttyUSB*
crw-rw---T 1 root dialout 188, 0 Aug 30 15:40 /dev/ttyUSB0
pi@erpi ~ $ id
uid=1000(pi) gid=1000(pi) groups=1000(pi), 4(adm), 20(dialout), 24(cdrom),
 27(sudo), 29(audio), 44(video), 46(plugdev), 60(games), 100(users),
 106(netdev), 996(gpio), 997(i2c), 998(spi), 999(input)
```

With three devices plugged into the RPi, as in Figure 9-17(b), each USB device has its own device entry in the `/dev/` directory:

```
pi@erpi ~ $ lsusb
Bus 001 Device 004: ID 1a86:7523 QinHeng Elec HL-340 USB-Serial adapter
Bus 001 Device 006: ID 1a86:7523 QinHeng Elec HL-340 USB-Serial adapter
Bus 001 Device 005: ID 10c4:ea60 Cygnal Integrated Products, CP210x UART ...
pi@erpi ~ $ ls -l /dev/ttyUSB*
crw-rw---T 1 root dialout 188, 0 Aug 30 15:40 /dev/ttyUSB0
crw-rw---T 1 root dialout 188, 1 Aug 30 15:44 /dev/ttyUSB1
crw-rw---T 1 root dialout 188, 2 Aug 30 15:44 /dev/ttyUSB2
```

Several of the available USB devices have built-in logic-level translation circuitry, which is very useful for interfacing to both 3.3 V and 5 V tolerant devices. For, example the YP-02 has a jumper that you can move to bridge its VCC and 5 V pins, or the VCC and 3 V3 pins, as illustrated in Figure 9-18(a). The Baite module has a slider selector switch on its side that can be used to select either logic level.

USB DEVICES AND UDEV RULES

When you plug out the USB device that is associated with `/dev/ttyUSB0`, then the other device names will be updated to close any numbering "gaps":

```
pi@erpi ~ $ ls -l /dev/ttyUSB*
crw-rw---T 1 root dialout 188, 0 Aug 30 15:40 /dev/ttyUSB0
crw-rw---T 1 root dialout 188, 1 Aug 30 16:49 /dev/ttyUSB1
```

This can cause difficulty for your software applications, because they will not be aware of the update (e.g., a serial motor controller could become connected to a serial sensor module). You can solve this problem using udev rules. Each USB device has a vendor and a product ID, and sometimes a unique serial number. This information can be used to construct a rule that associates the USB adapter with a custom device name. You can find the adapter's details using `lsusb` (as above) and/or by using the `udevadm` command:

```
pi@erpi ~ $ sudo udevadm info -a -n /dev/ttyUSB1 | grep idVendor
    ATTRS{idVendor}=="10c4" ...
pi@erpi ~ $ sudo udevadm info -a -n /dev/ttyUSB1 | grep idProduct
    ATTRS{idProduct}=="ea60" ...
pi@erpi ~ $ sudo udevadm info -a -n /dev/ttyUSB1 | grep serial
    ATTRS{serial}=="0001" ...
```

You can then write a rule to create a custom device entry when the USB adapter is plugged in. For example, if a motor was attached to the CP210x device (ID 10c4:ea60) you could write the following rule to create a custom device entry (note that `==` is for comparison, and `=` is for assignment):

```
pi@erpi /etc/udev/rules.d $ sudo nano 98-erpi.rules
pi@erpi /etc/udev/rules.d $ more 98-erpi.rules
SUBSYSTEM=="tty", ATTRS{idVendor}=="10c4", ATTRS{idProduct}=="ea60", →
ATTRS{serial}=="0001", SYMLINK+="erpi_motor"
```

On reboot a new device appears in `/dev/` that is automatically linked to the correct `ttyUSBx` device whenever the CP210x device is plugged in:

```
pi@erpi ~ $ ls -l /dev/er*
lrwxrwxrwx 1 root root 7 Jan  1  1970 /dev/erpi_motor -> ttyUSB1
```

The symbolic link is automatically removed if the device is plugged out and will appear again if the device is reinserted (hot plugged). Clearly, you should use the `/dev/erpi_motor` symbolic link within your code.

The serial number can usually be used to distinguish between two identical devices. Unfortunately, these low-cost adapters often do not have unique serial numbers. There are tools available to write serial numbers onto USB devices, but they can destroy the devices. An alternative solution is to use the physical USB slot to identify the device, but it is not straightforward. Please see: `tiny.cc/erpi909` for more information on writing udev rules. If your device does not have a definite serial number, or you cannot seem to get the udev rule to work correctly when adding the apparent serial number for your device, try to remove that portion from the udev rules file. For example, for the YP-02 adapter in Figure 9-17(a), use:

```
SUBSYSTEM=="tty", ATTRS{idVendor}=="1a86", ATTRS{idProduct}=="7523", →
SYMLINK+="erpi_serial"
```

With two devices attached to the RPi, you can test them by opening two terminal windows to the RPi and connecting the TXD output of one module to the RXD input of the other module and vice versa, as illustrated in Figure 9-18(a). There is no need to connect the GND connections, as they are both plugged into the same device in this example. Start a minicom session in each terminal window, each connecting to the alternate `ttyUSB` device. Remember to turn on local echo (Ctrl+A Z E). These devices often support high baud rates—for example, the following test is performed at 921,600 baud. In the first terminal window type:

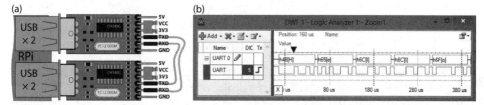

Figure 9-18: (a) The UART device loopback test, and (b) The UART output displaying "Hello" at 115,200 baud

```
pi@erpi ~ $ minicom -b 921600 -o -D /dev/ttyUSB0
Welcome to minicom 2.7
OPTIONS: I18n
Compiled on Jan 12 2014, 05:42:53.
Port /dev/ttyUSB0, 15:40:38
Press CTRL-A Z for help on special keys
Hello from the first minicom session
Hello from the second minicom session
```

And, simultaneously in a second terminal window:

```
pi@erpi ~ $ minicom -b 921600 -o -D /dev/ttyUSB1
Welcome to minicom 2.7
```

```
OPTIONS: I18n
Compiled on Jan 12 2014, 05:42:53.
Port /dev/ttyUSB1, 16:49:18
Press CTRL-A Z for help on special keys
Hello from the first minicom session
Hello from the second minicom session
```

This test performed correctly at the supported baud rates of: 115.2kbps, 230.4kbps, 460.8kbps, 500kbps, 576kbps, 921.6kbps, 1Mbps, 1.152Mbps, 1.5Mbps, 2Mbps, 2.5Mbps, 3Mbps, and 4Mbps. The interconnector length was less than 6 inches, but still the devices performed very well.

THE DEFAULT TERMINAL LINE SETTINGS

It is possible to define a default baud rate for a terminal device using the set terminal line settings command, `stty`. For example, you can get the current device baud rate and then set it to be 115,200 using the following steps:

```
pi@erpi ~ $ stty < /dev/ttyUSB0
speed 4000000 baud; line = 0;
min = 1; time = 5; ignbrk -brkint -icrnl -imaxbel -opost -onlcr
-isig -icanon -iexten -echo -echoe -echok -echoctl -echoke
pi@erpi ~ $ stty -F /dev/ttyUSB0 115200
pi@erpi ~ $ stty < /dev/ttyUSB0
speed 115200 baud; line = 0;
min = 1; time = 5; ignbrk -brkint -icrnl -imaxbel -opost -onlcr
-isig -icanon -iexten -echo -echoe -echok -echoctl -echoke
```

After you have configured the device with the new baud rate, you can write to and read from the devices directly by using the device entry. For example, this command will listen for incoming traffic from the /dev/ttyUSB1 device:

```
pi@erpi ~ $ cat /dev/ttyUSB1
Hello from the second terminal
```

This output results from the following commands that are entered in a second terminal window:

```
pi@erpi ~ $ stty -F /dev/ttyUSB1 115200
pi@erpi ~ $ echo "Hello from the second terminal" > /dev/ttyUSB0
```

Note that the string was sent to the ttyUSB0 device but it is displayed after it is received by the ttyUSB1 device. The logic analyzer displays this communication taking place in Figure 9-18(b). Note that if the baud rates are mismatched, you will not get a valid transfer of information between the two devices.

Summary

After completing this chapter, you should be able to do the following:

- Extend the input/output capability of the RPi to include analog inputs by using SPI ADCs.
- Interface simple resistance-based sensors, where a voltage/current is required for sensor excitation.
- Extend the input/output capability of the RPi to include analog outputs using both I²C and SPI DACs.
- Expand the number of PWMs available on the RPi using a low-cost SPI module.
- Increase the number of available GPIOs on the RPi using both I²C and SPI GPIO expanders, and utilize the interrupt functionality that is available on such devices.
- Increase the number of available serial UART devices on the RPi using low-cost USB-to-TTL devices.

# CHAPTER 10

Interacting with the Physical Environment

In this chapter, you learn how to build on your knowledge of general-purpose input/output (GPIO) and bus interfacing. In particular, you can combine hardware and software to provide the Raspberry Pi (RPi) with the ability to interact with its physical environment in the following three ways: First, by controlling actuators such as motors, the RPi can affect its environment, which is very important for applications such as robotics and home automation. Second, the RPi can gather information about its physical environment by communicating with sensors. Third, by interfacing to display modules, the RPi can present information. This chapter explains how each of these interactions can be performed. Physical interaction hardware and software provides you with the capability to build advanced projects (for example, to build a robotic platform that can sense and interact with its environment). The chapter finishes with a discussion on how you can create your own C/C++ code libraries and utilize them to build highly scalable projects.

Equipment Required for This Chapter:

- Raspberry Pi, DMM, and oscilloscope
- DC motor and H-bridge interface board (e.g., DRV8835)
- Stepper motor, EasyDriver interface board, and a 5 V relay
- MCP3208 SPI ADC, op-amp (MCP6002/4), diodes, and resistors

- TMP36 temperature sensor and Sharp infrared distance sensor
- ADXL335 three-axis analog accelerometer
- 74HC595 serial shift registers
- LCD character display module, MAX7219 seven-segment display module, SSD1306 OLED dot-matrix module

Further details on this chapter are available at www.exploringrpi.com/chapter10/.

Interfacing to Actuators

Electric motors can be controlled by the RPi to make physical devices move or operate. They convert electrical energy into mechanical energy that can be used by devices to act upon their surroundings. A device that converts energy into motion is generally referred to as an *actuator*. Interfacing the RPi to actuators provides a myriad of application possibilities, including robotic control, home automation (watering plants, controlling blinds), camera control, unmanned aerial vehicles (UAVs), 3D printer control, and many more.

Electric motors typically provide rotary motion around a fixed axis, which can be used to drive wheels, pumps, belts, electric valves, tracks, turrets, robotic arms, and so on. In contrast to this, *linear actuators* create movement in a straight line, which can be very useful for position control in computer numerical control (CNC) machines and 3D printers. In some cases, they convert rotary motion into linear motion using a screw shaft that translates a threaded nut along its length as it rotates. In other cases, a solenoid moves a shaft linearly through the magnetic effects of an electric current.

Three main types of motors are commonly used with the RPi: servo motors, DC motors, and stepper motors. A summary comparison of these motor types is provided in Table 10-1. Interfacing to servo motors (a.k.a *precision actuators*) through the use of PWM outputs is discussed in Chapter 6, so this section focuses on interfacing to DC motors and stepper motors.

Table 10-1: Summary Comparison of Common Motor Types

	SERVO MOTOR	DC MOTOR	STEPPER MOTOR
Typical application	When high torque, accurate rotation is required.	When fast, continuous rotation is required.	When slow and accurate rotation is required.
Control hardware	Position is controlled through pulse width modulation (PWM). No controller required. May require PWM tuning.	Speed is often controlled through PWM. Additional circuitry required to manage power requirements.	Typically requires a controller to energize stepper coils. The RPi can perform this role, but an external controller is preferable and safer.

	SERVO MOTOR	DC MOTOR	STEPPER MOTOR
Control type	Closed-loop, using a built-in controller.	Typically closed-loop using feedback from optical encoders.	Typically open-loop, because movement is precise and steps can be counted.
Features	Known absolute position. Typically, limited angle of rotation.	Can drive very large loads. Often geared to provide very high torque.	Full torque at standstill. Can rotate a large load at very low speeds. Tendency to vibrate.
Example applications	Steering controllers, camera control, and small robotic arms.	Mobile robot movement, fans, water pumps, and electric cars.	CNC machines, 3D printers, scanners, linear actuators, and camera lenses.

High-current inductive loads are challenging to interface with the RPi; they invariably require more current than the RPi can supply, and they generate voltage spikes that can be extremely harmful to the interfacing circuitry. The applications discussed in this section often require a secondary power supply, which could be an external battery pack in the case of a mobile platform or a high-current supply for powerful motors. The RPi needs to be isolated from these supplies; as a result, generic motor controller boards are described here for interfacing to DC motors and stepper motors. Circuitry is also carefully designed for interfacing to relay devices.

DC Motors

DC motors are used in many applications, from toys to advanced robotics. They are ideal motors to use when continuous rotation is required, such as in the wheels of an electric vehicle. Typically, they have only two electrical terminals to which a voltage is applied. The speed of rotation and the direction of rotation can be controlled by varying this voltage. The tendency of a force to rotate an object about its axis is called *torque*, and for a DC motor, torque is generally proportional to the current applied.

The higher the gear ratio, the slower the rotation speed, and the higher the stall torque. For example, the DC motor in Figure 10-1(a) has a no-load speed of 80 *revolutions per minute* (rpm) and a stall torque of 250 oz·in (18 kg·cm).[1] Similarly, if a 70:1 gear ratio is used, the rotation speed becomes 150 rpm, but the stall torque

---

[1] DC motor datasheets often do not use SI units, which would be newton-meters (N·m) in this case. It is therefore important to understand the meaning of 250 oz·in: Imagine that you fixed a 1-inch metal bar to the motor shaft at 90 degrees to the direction of rotation, and rotated the shaft until the bar is horizontal to the surface of the Earth. Should you attach a weight of greater than 250 ounces to the end of the 1-inch bar, this motor would not be able to rotate its shaft; this is called its stall torque limit. Because 250 ounces = 7.08738 kg and 1 inch = 2.54 cm, the conversion to metric units is $7.08738 \times 2.54 = 18.002$ kg·cm (i.e., the torque effect of 18 kg at the end of a 1cm bar is equivalent to 7.08738 kg at the end of a 1-inch bar—the law of the lever). Also note that 70×150 rpm = 131.25×80 rpm = $10,500$ rpm (the 1:1 rotation speed of the motor). See tiny.cc/erpi1002.

reduces to 200 oz·in (14.4 kg·cm). The DC motor in Figure 10-1(a) has a free-run current of 300 mA at 12 V, but it has a stall current of 5 A—a large current that must be factored into the circuit design.

Most DC motors require more current than the RPi can supply; therefore, you might be tempted to drive them from the RPi by simply using a transistor or FET. Unfortunately, this will not work well, due to a phenomenon known as *inductive kickback*, which results in a large voltage spike that is caused by the inertia of current flowing through an inductor (i.e., the motor's coil windings) being suddenly switched off. Even for modest motor power supplies, this large voltage could exceed 1 kV for a very short period of time. The FETs discussed in Chapter 4 cannot have a drain-source voltage of greater than 60 V and will therefore be damaged by such large voltage spikes.

(a)   (b)

Figure 10-1: (a) A 12 V DC motor with an integrated 131¼:1 gearbox ($40), and (b) an integrated counts per revolution (CPR) Hall Effect sensor shaft encoder

One solution is to place a Zener diode across the drain-source terminals of the FET (or collector-emitter of a transistor). The Zener diode limits the voltage across the drain-source terminals to that of its reverse breakdown voltage. The downside of this configuration is that the ground supply has to sink a large current spike, which could lead to the type of noise in the circuit that is discussed in Chapter 4. With either of these types of protection in place, it is possible to use an RPi PWM output to control the speed of the DC motor. With a PWM duty cycle of 50%, the motor will rotate at half the speed that it would if directly connected to the motor supply voltage.

The DC motor in Figure 10-1 has a 64 counts per revolution (CPR) quadrature encoder that is attached to the motor shaft, which means that there are 64 × 131.25 = 8,400 counts for each revolution of the geared motor shaft. Shaft encoders are often used with DC motors to determine the position and speed of the motor. For example, the encoder has an output as illustrated in Figure 10-2(a) when rotating clockwise and Figure 10-2(b) when rotating counterclockwise. The frequency of the pulses is proportional to the speed of the motor, and the order of the rising edges in the two output signals describes the direction of rotation. Note that the Hall Effect sensor must be powered, so four of the six motor wires are for the encoder: *A* output (yellow), *B* output (white), encoder power supply (blue), GND (green). The remaining two wires are for the motor power supply (red and black).

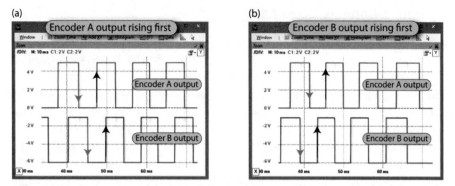

Figure 10-2: The output from the shaft encoder in Figure 10-1(b) when rotating: (a) clockwise, and (b) counterclockwise

For *bidirectional motor control*, a circuit configuration called an *H-bridge* can be used, which has a circuit layout in the shape of the letter *H*, as illustrated in Figure 10-3. Notice that it has Zener diodes to protect the four FETs. To drive the motor in a forward (assumed to be clockwise) direction, the top-left and bottom-right FETs can be switched on. This causes a current to flow from the positive to the negative terminal of the DC motor. When the opposing pair of FETs is switched on, current flows from the negative terminal to the positive terminal of the motor and the motor reverses (turns counterclockwise). The motor does not rotate if two opposing FETs are switched off (open circuit).

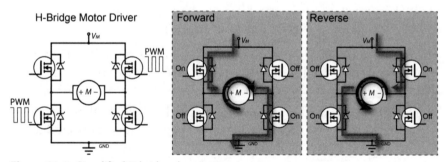

Figure 10-3: Simplified H-bridge description

This circuit could be combined with the PCA9685 PWM board that is described in Chapter 9, so that four of its outputs could be connected to the H-bridge circuit. Particular care would have to be taken to ensure that the two FETs on the left side or the right side of the circuit are not turned on at the same time, because this would result in a large current (*shoot-through current*)—the motor supply would effectively be shorted (V_M to GND). Because high-current capable power supplies are often used for the motor power supply, this is very dangerous, because it could even cause a power supply or a battery to explode! An easier and safer approach is to use an H-bridge driver that has already been packaged in an IC, such as the SN754410, a quadruple high-current half-H driver, which can drive 1 A at 4.5 V to 36 V per driver (see tiny.cc/erpi1001).

Driving Small DC Motors (up to 1.5 A)

There are many more recently introduced drivers that can drive even larger currents using smaller package sizes than the SN754410. In this example, a DRV8835 dual low-voltage motor driver carrier on a breakout board ($4) from www.pololu.com is used, as illustrated in Figure 10-4. The DRV8835 itself is only 2 mm × 3 mm in dimension and can drive 1.5 A (max) per H-bridge at a motor supply voltage up to 11 V. It can be driven with logic levels of 2 V to 7 V, which enables it to be used directly with the RPi. Note that you will need a more recent RPi to drive two motors from this board as you require two PWM channels. For older RPi models or for more than two motors, you can integrate the PCA9685 PWM board that is described in Chapter 9.

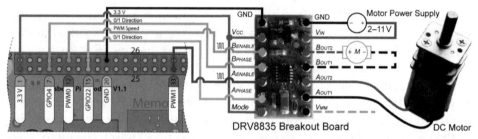

Figure 10-4: Driving a DC motor using an example H-bridge driver breakout board

The DRV8835 breakout board can be connected to the RPi as illustrated in Figure 10-4. This circuit uses four pins from the RPi:

- The PWM0 and PWM1 pins provide PWM outputs from the RPi that can be used to control the rotation speed of each of the two motors, because they are connected to the A_{ENABLE} and B_{ENABLE} inputs on the DRV8835.

- The GPIO22 and GPIO4 outputs can be used to set whether the motor is rotating clockwise or counterclockwise, because it is connected to the A_{PHASE} and B_{PHASE} inputs of the DRV8835.

The motor power supply voltage is set according to the specification of the DC motor that is chosen. By tying the *Mode* pin high, the DRV8835 is placed in PHASE/ENABLE mode, which means that one input is used for direction and the other is used for determining the rotation speed.

WARNING   The DRV8835 IC can get hot enough to burn, even while operating within its normal operating parameters. This is a common characteristic of motor driver ICs—so be careful! Heat sinks can be added to dissipate heat, and they have the added advantage of extending the constant run time, because thermal protection circuitry will shut motor driver ICs down to prevent them from overheating when driving large loads.

Listing 10-1 provides a source code example that uses the wiringPi library to control the DC motor circuit in Figure 10-4. This program rotates Motor *A* in a notional forward direction at 50% of the available maximum speed for 5 seconds. It then reverses the motor at full speed for 5 seconds. The program then rotates Motor *B* forward at 75% of the available maximum speed for 5 seconds and then backward at 25% for 5 seconds.

Listing 10-1: /chp10/drv8835/motor.cpp

```cpp
#include <iostream>
#include <unistd.h>
#include <wiringPi.h>
using namespace std;
#define APHASE          15          // physical pin for GPIO22
#define AENABLE_PWM1    33          // physical pin for PWM1
#define BPHASE           7          // physical pin for GPIO4
#define BENABLE_PWM0    12          // physical pin for PWM0

int main() {                        // must be run as root
   wiringPiSetupPhys();             // use the physical pin numbers
   pinMode(APHASE, OUTPUT);         // controls direction
   pinMode(AENABLE_PWM1, PWM_OUTPUT); // speed - only on RPi B+/A+/2
   pinMode(BPHASE, OUTPUT);         // controls direction
   pinMode(BENABLE_PWM0, PWM_OUTPUT); // PWM output used for speed
   pwmSetMode(PWM_MODE_MS);         // use a fixed frequency
   pwmSetRange(128);                // range is 0-128
   pwmSetClock(15);                 // gives a precise 10kHz signal
   cout << "Motor A: Rotate forward at 50% for 5 seconds" << endl;
   digitalWrite(APHASE, LOW);       // notional foward
   pwmWrite(AENABLE_PWM1, 64);      // duty cycle of 50% (64/128)
   usleep(5000000);
   cout << "Motor A: Rotate backward at 100% for 5 seconds" << endl;
   digitalWrite(APHASE, HIGH);      // notional backward
   pwmWrite(AENABLE_PWM1, 128);     // duty cycle of 100% (64/128)
   usleep(5000000);
   pwmWrite(AENABLE_PWM1, 0);       // Motor A off - duty cycle of 0%
   cout << "Motor B: Rotate forward at 75% for 5 seconds" << endl;
   digitalWrite(BPHASE, LOW);       // notional foward
   pwmWrite(BENABLE_PWM0, 96);      // duty cycle of 75% (96/128)
   usleep(5000000);
   cout << "Motor B: Rotate Backward at 25% for 5 seconds" << endl;
   digitalWrite(BPHASE, HIGH);      // notional backward
   pwmWrite(BENABLE_PWM0, 32);      // duty cycle of 25% (35/128)
   usleep(5000000);
   cout << "End of Program turn off both motors" << endl;
   pwmWrite(BENABLE_PWM0, 0);       // Motor B off - duty cycle of 0%
   return 0;                        // would keep going after exit
}
```

The code in Listing 10-1 can be built and executed as follows:

```
pi@erpi:~/exploringrpi/chp10/drv8835 $ g++ motor.cpp -o motor -lwiringPi
pi@erpi ~/exploringrpi/chp10/drv8835 $ sudo ./motor
```

```
Motor A: Rotate forward at 50% for 5 seconds
Motor A: Rotate backward at 100% for 5 seconds
Motor B: Rotate forward at 75% for 5 seconds
Motor B: Rotate Backward at 25% for 5 seconds
End of Program turn off both motors
```

Driving Larger DC Motors (greater than 1.5 A)

The Pololu *Simple Motor Controller* family ($30–$55), illustrated in Figure 10-5(a), supports powerful brushed DC motors with continuous currents of up to 23 A and maximum voltages of 34 V. It supports USB, TTL serial, analog, and hobby radio-control (RC) PWM interfaces. The controller uses 3.3 V logic levels, but it is also 5 V tolerant.

Despite its name, this is an advanced controller that can be configured with settings such as maximum acceleration/deceleration, adjustable starting speed, electronic braking, over-temperature threshold/response, etc., which makes it a good choice for larger-scale robotic applications. The controller can be configured using a Windows GUI application, as illustrated in Figure 10-5(b), or by using a Linux command-line user interface. The Windows configuration tool can also be used to monitor motor temperature and voltage conditions and control the speed settings, braking, PWM, communications settings, and so on over USB, even while the motor is connected to the RPi with a TTL serial interface.

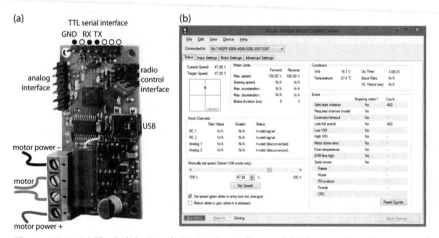

Figure 10-5: (a) The Pololu Simple Motor Controller, and (b) the associated motor configuration tool

The 3.3 V TTL serial interface is likely the best option for embedded applications, as it can be used directly with a UART device. A low-cost USB UART device can be utilized for communication, as described in Chapter 8.

```
pi@erpi ~ $ lsusb
Bus 001 Device 004: ID 1a86:7523 QinHeng Ele. HL-340 USB-Serial adapter
pi@erpi ~ $ ls -l /dev/ttyUSB0
crw-rw---T 1 root dialout 188, 0 Jan  1  1970 /dev/ttyUSB0
```

> **NOTE** Connect a power supply to the Simple Motor Controller board before attempting serial communication. The power supply must be sufficient for the controller board, or the red LED will flash to indicate an error state. Also, configure the controller using a Windows machine before connecting it to the RPi and choose a fixed baud rate of 115,200, rather than choosing the auto-negotiate option.

The Simple Motor Controller can be configured to be in a serial ASCII mode, whereupon it can be controlled using a UART device from the RPi with minicom. For example, with ASCII mode enabled and a fixed baud rate of 115,200 (8N1) set in the Input Settings tab (see Figure 10-5(b)), the RPi can connect directly to the motor controller and issue text-based commands to control the motor, such as V (version), F (forward), B (brake), R (reverse), GO (exit safe-start mode), X (stop), etc. See the comprehensive manual for the full list of commands (tiny .cc/erpi1003):

```
pi@erpi ~ $ sudo minicom -b 115200 -o -D /dev/ttyUSB0
V
!161 01.04
GO
.
F 50%
.
B
?
GO
.
R 25%
.
```

The Simple Motor Controller can also be controlled directly using the C/C++ UART communications code that is described in Chapter 8. The configuration tool can be used to set the serial TTL mode to be Binary mode with a baud rate of 115,200. Assuming the motor controller is attached to /dev/ttyUSB0 (as above), the motor.c code example in the /chp10/simple/ directory can be used to control the motor directly:

```
pi@erpi ~/exploringrpi/chp10/simple $ gcc motor.c -o motor
pi@erpi ~/exploringrpi/chp10/simple $ sudo ./motor
Starting the motor controller example
Error status: 0x0000
Current Target Speed is 0.
Setting Target Speed to 3200.
```

Stepper Motors

Unlike DC motors, which rotate continuously when a DC voltage is applied, *stepper motors* normally rotate in discrete fixed-angle steps. For example, the stepper motor that is used in this chapter rotates with 200 *steps per revolution*, and therefore has a *step angle* of 1.8°. The motor steps each time a pulse is applied to its input, so the speed of rotation is proportional to the rate at which pulses are applied.

Stepper motors can be positioned very accurately, because they typically have a positioning error of less than 5% of a step (i.e., typically ±0.1°). The error does not accumulate over multiple steps, so stepper motors can be controlled in an open-loop form, without the need for feedback. Unlike servo motors, but like DC motors, the absolute position of the shaft is not known without the addition of devices like rotary encoders, which often include an absolute position reference that can be located by performing a single shaft rotation.

Stepper motors, as illustrated in Figure 10-6(a), have toothed permanent magnets that are fixed to a rotating shaft, called *the rotor*. The rotor is surrounded by coils (grouped into *phases*) that are fixed to the stationary body of the motor (*the stator*). The coils are electromagnets that, when energized, attract the toothed shaft teeth in a clockwise or counterclockwise direction, depending on the order in which the coils are activated, as illustrated in Figure 10-6(b) for full-step drive:

- **Full step:** Two phases always on (max torque).

- **Half step:** Double the step resolution. Alternates between two phases on and a single phase on (torque at about 3/4 max).

- **Microstep:** Uses sine and cosine waveforms for the phase currents to step the motor rather than the on/off currents illustrated in Figure 10-6(b) and thus allows for higher step resolutions (though the torque is significantly reduced).

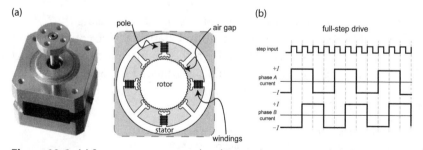

Figure 10-6: (a) Stepper motor external and internal structure, and (b) full- and half-step drive signals

The EasyDriver Stepper Motor Driver

An easy way to generate the stepper motor pulse signals is to use a stepper-motor driver board. The EasyDriver board (illustrated in Figure 10-7) is a low-cost (~$15) open-hardware stepper motor driver board that is widely available. It can be used to drive four-, six- and eight-wire stepper motors, as illustrated in Figure 10-8. The board has an output drive capability of between 7 V and 30 V at ±750 mA per phase. The board uses the Allegro A3967 Microstepping Driver with Translator, which allows for full, half, quarter, and one-eighth step microstepping modes. In addition, the board can be driven with 5 V or 3.3 V logic levels, which makes it an ideal board for the RPi. For 3.3 V logic control levels, there is a jumper (SJ2) that has to be bridged with solder.

WARNING   Do not disconnect a motor from the EasyDriver board while it is powered, because it may destroy the board.

Figure 10-7: Driving a stepper motor using the open-hardware EasyDriver board

The merit in examining this board is that many boards can be used for higher-powered stepper motors that have a very similar design.

NOTE   If you don't have access to a datasheet for a stepper motor (e.g., you rescued it from an old printer), you can determine the connections to the coils by shorting pairs of wires and rotating the motor. If there is noticeable resistance to rotation for a particular shorted pairing, you have identified the connections to a coil. You cannot determine the coils using the colors of the wires alone, because there is no standard format.

An RPi Stepper Motor Driver Circuit

The EasyDriver board can be connected to the RPi, as illustrated in Figure 10-8, using GPIOs for each of the control signals. The pins are described in Figure 10-7, and a table is provided in the figure for the MS1/MS2 inputs. A C++ class called `StepperMotor` is available that accepts alternative GPIO numbers.

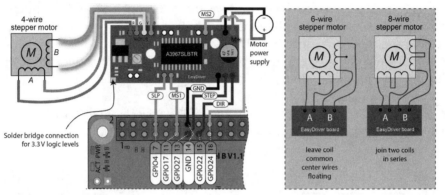

Figure 10-8: Driving a stepper motor using the RPi and the EasyDriver interface board

Controlling a Stepper Motor Using C++

Listing 10-2 presents the description of a class that can be used to control the EasyDriver driver board using five RPi GPIO pins. This code can be adapted to drive most types of stepper driver boards.

Listing 10-2: /chp10/stepper/motor/StepperMotor.h (Segment)

```
class StepperMotor {
public:
    enum STEP_MODE { STEP_FULL, STEP_HALF, STEP_QUARTER, STEP_EIGHT };
    enum DIRECTION { CLOCKWISE, COUNTERCLOCKWISE };
private:
    // The GPIO pins MS1, MS2 (microstep options), STEP (low->high step)
    // SLP (sleep - active low) and DIR (direction)
    GPIO *gpio_MS1, *gpio_MS2, *gpio_STEP, *gpio_SLP, *gpio_DIR;
    ...
public:
    StepperMotor(GPIO *ms1, GPIO *ms2, GPIO *step, GPIO *sleep,
                 GPIO *dir, int speedRPM = 60, int stepsPerRev=200);
    StepperMotor(int ms1, int ms2, int step, int sleep,
                 int dir, int speedRPM = 60, int stepsPerRev=200);
    virtual void  step();
    virtual void  step(int numberOfSteps);
```

```
virtual int    threadedStepForDuration(int numOfSteps, int dur_ms);
virtual void   threadedStepCancel() { this->threadRunning=false; }
virtual void   rotate(float degrees);
virtual void   setDirection(DIRECTION direction);
virtual DIRECTION getDirection() { return this->direction; }
virtual void   reverseDirection();
virtual void   setStepMode(STEP_MODE mode);
virtual STEP_MODE getStepMode() { return stepMode; }
virtual void   setSpeed(float rpm);
virtual float  getSpeed() { return speed; }
virtual void   setStepsPerRevolution(int steps) { stepsPerRev=steps; }
virtual int    getStepsPerRevolution() { return stepsPerRev; }
virtual void   sleep();
virtual void   wake();
virtual bool   isAsleep() { return asleep; }
   ...
};
```

The library code is used in Listing 10-3 to create a `StepperMotor` object, and rotate the motor counterclockwise 10 times at full-step resolution. It then uses a threaded step function to microstep the stepper motor clockwise for one full revolution over five seconds at one-eighth step resolution.

Listing 10-3: /chp10/stepper/stepper.cpp

```cpp
#include <iostream>
#include <unistd.h>
#include "motor/StepperMotor.h"
using namespace std;
using namespace exploringRPi;

int main(){
   cout << "Starting RPi Stepper Motor Example:" << endl;
   // using 5 GPIOs, RPM=60 and 200 steps per revolution
   // MS1=17, MS2=24, STEP=27, SLP=4, DIR=22
   StepperMotor m(17,24,27,4,22,60,200);
   m.setDirection(StepperMotor::COUNTERCLOCKWISE);
   m.setStepMode(StepperMotor::STEP_FULL);
   m.setSpeed(100);   //rpm
   cout << "Rotating 10 times 100 rpm co-clockwise, full step" << endl;
   m.rotate(3600.0f);   //in degrees
   cout << "Finished regular (non-threaded) rotation)" << endl;
   m.setDirection(StepperMotor::CLOCKWISE);
   cout << "Performing 1 threaded rev in 5s using micro-step:" << endl;
   m.setStepMode(StepperMotor::STEP_EIGHT);
   if(m.threadedStepForDuration(1600, 5000)<0){
      cout << "Failed to start the Stepper Thread" << endl;
   }
   cout << "Thread should now be running..." << endl;
      for(int i=0; i<10; i++){ // sleep for 10 seconds.
      usleep(1000000);
```

```
            cout << i+1 << " seconds has passed..." << endl;
    }
    m.sleep();    // cut power to the stepper motor
    cout << "End of Stepper Motor Example" << endl;
}
```

After calling the associated build script, the program can be executed and should result in the following output:

```
pi@erpi ~/exploringrpi/chp10/stepper $ sudo ./stepper
Starting RPi Stepper Motor Example:
Rotating 10 times 100 rpm co-clockwise, full step
Finished regular (non-threaded) rotation)
Performing 1 threaded rev in 5s using micro-step:
Thread should now be running...
1 seconds has passed...
2 seconds has passed...
...
10 seconds has passed...
End of Stepper Motor Example
```

It is important to note that the threaded revolution completes the revolution after five seconds. The counter continues for a further 5 seconds, during which time a holding torque is applied. The final call to m.sleep() removes power from the stepper motor coils, thus removing holding torque.

It is possible to further reduce the number of pins that are used in this motor controller example by using 74HC595 ICs and the SPI bus. That topic is discussed in the section "Interfacing to Display Modules," later in this chapter.

Relays

Traditional relays are electromechanical switches that are typically used to control a high-voltage/high-current signal using a low-voltage/low-current signal. They are constructed to enable a low-powered circuit to apply a magnetic force to an internal movable switch. The internal switch can turn on or turn off a second circuit that often contains a high-powered DC or AC load. The relay itself is chosen according to the power requirements; whether the circuit is designed so that the high-powered circuit is normally powered or normally disabled; and the number of circuits being switched in parallel.

Electromechanical relays (EMRs) are prone to switch bounce and mechanical fatigue, so they have a limited life span, particularly if they are switched constantly at frequencies of more than a few times per minute. Rapid switching of EMRs can also cause them to overheat. More recent, solid-state relays (SSRs) are electronic switches that consist of FETs, thyristors, and opto-couplers. They have no moving parts and therefore have longer life spans and higher maximum switching frequencies (about 1 kHz). The downside is that SSRs are more expensive, and they are prone to failure (often in the switched "on" state) due to overloading or improper wiring. They are typically installed with heat sinks and fast-blow fuses on the load circuit.

EMRs and SSRs are available that can switch very high currents and voltages. That makes them particularly useful for applications like smart home installations, for the control of mains-powered devices, motor vehicle applications for switching high-current DC loads, and powering high-current inductive loads in robotic applications. **Importantly, wiring mains applications are for expert users only, because even low currents coupled with high voltages can be fatal. Seek local professional advice if dealing in any way with high currents or high voltages, including, but not limited to, AC mains voltages.**

WARNING   The circuit in Figure 10-9 is intended for connection to low-voltage supplies only (e.g., 12 V supplies). High voltages can be extremely dangerous to human health, and only suitably trained individuals with appropriate safety equipment and taking professional precautions should wire mains-powered devices. Suitable insulation, protective enclosures, or additional protective devices such as fuses or circuit breakers (possibly including both current-limiting circuit breakers and earth-leakage circuit breakers) may be required to prevent creating either a shock or a fire hazard. Seek advice from a qualified electrician before installing mains-powered home automation circuitry.

Figure 10-9(a) illustrates the type of circuit that can be used to interface the RPi to a relay. It is important that the relay chosen is capable of being switched at 5 V and that, like the motor circuit, a flyback diode is placed in parallel to the relay's inductive load to protect the FET from damage. Pololu (www.pololu .com) sells a small SPDT relay kit (~$4), as illustrated in Figure 10-9(b), that can be used to switch 8 A currents at 30 V DC using an Omron G5LE power relay. The breakout board contains a BSS138 FET, the flyback diode, and LEDs that indicate when the relay is switched to enable—that is, close the circuit connected to the normally open (NO) output. Figure 10-9(b) also illustrates a low-cost four relay breakout board.

The relays on both boards can be connected to a regular GPIO for control. For example, if the relay were connected as shown in Figure 10-9(a), to GPIO 4, it can be switched using the following steps:

```
pi@erpi /sys/class/gpio $ echo 4 > export
pi@erpi /sys/class/gpio $ cd gpio4
pi@erpi /sys/class/gpio/gpio4 $ echo out > direction
pi@erpi /sys/class/gpio/gpio4 $ cat value
0
pi@erpi /sys/class/gpio/gpio4 $ echo 1 > value
pi@erpi /sys/class/gpio/gpio4 $ echo 0 > value
```

NOTE   Occasionally, changes to the udev rules on your board can mean that the GPIOs are no longer owned by the pi user, but by the root user. You can fix the udev rules files, but it is useful to note that you can use the sudo tool to direct an output to root. For example, to perform the last command above where the entries are owned by root, you can use the following call:

```
pi@erpi /sys/class/gpio/gpio4 $ ls -l value
-rw-r--r-- 1 root root 4096 Sep 16 00:16 value
pi@erpi /sys/class/gpio/gpio4 $ sudo sh -c "echo 0 > value"
```

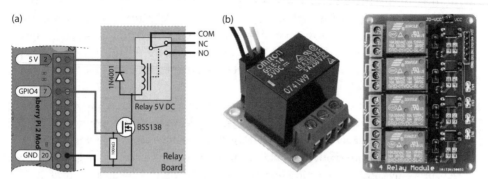

Figure 10-9: (a) Controlling a relay using the RPi, and (b) example relay breakout boards

Interfacing to Analog Sensors

A *transducer* is a device that converts variations in one form of energy into proportional variations in another form of energy. For example, a microphone is an acoustic transducer that converts variations in sound waves into proportional variations in an electrical signal. In fact, actuators are also transducers, because they convert electrical energy into mechanical energy.

Transducers, the main role of which is to convert information about the physical environment into electrical signals (voltages or currents), are called *sensors*. Sensors may contain additional circuitry to further condition the electrical signal (e.g., by filtering out noise or averaging values over time), and this combination is often referred to as an *instrument*. The terms *sensor, transducer,* and *instrument* are in fact often used interchangeably, so too much should not be read into the distinctions between them. Interfacing to sensors enables you to build an incredibly versatile range of project types using the RPi, some of which are described in Table 10-2.

Table 10-2: Example Analog Sensor Types and Applications

MEASURE	APPLICATIONS	EXAMPLE SENSORS
Temperature	Smart home, weather monitoring	TMP36 temperature sensor. MAX6605 low-power temperature sensor
Light Level	Home automation, display contrast adjustment	Mini photocell/photodetector (PDV-P8001)
Distance	Robotic navigation, reversing sensing	Sharp infrared proximity sensors (e.g., GP2D12)

MEASURE	APPLICATIONS	EXAMPLE SENSORS
Touch	User interfaces, proximity detection	Capacitive touch
Acceleration	Determine orientation, impact detection	Accelerometer (ADXL335). Gyroscope (LPR530) detects change in orientation
Sound	Speech recording and recognition, UV meters	Electret microphone (MAX9814), MEMS microphone (ADMP401)
Magnetic Fields	Noncontact current measurement, home security, noncontact switches	100 A Non-invasive current sensor (SCT-013-000). Hall effect and reed switches. Linear magnetic field sensor (AD22151)
Motion detection	Home security, wildlife photography	PIR Motion Sensor (SE-10)

The ADXL345 I^{2}C/SPI digital accelerometer is discussed in Chapter 8, and Table 10-2 identifies another accelerometer, the ADXL335, which is an analog accelerometer. Essentially, the ADXL345 digital accelerometer is an analog sensor that also contains filtering circuitry, analog-to-digital conversion, and input/output circuitry. It is quite often the case that both analog and digital sensors are available that can perform similar tasks. Table 10-3 provides a summary comparison of digital versus analog sensors.

Table 10-3: Comparison of Typical Digital and Analog Sensor Devices

DIGITAL SENSORS	ANALOG SENSORS
ADC is handled by the sensor, freeing up limited microcontroller ADC inputs	Provide continuous voltage output and capability for very fast sampling rates
The real-time issues surrounding embedded Linux, such as variable sampling periods, are not as significant	Typically less expensive, but may require external components to configure the sensor parameters
Often contain advanced filters that can be configured and controlled via registers	Output is generally easy to understand without the need for complex datasheets
Bus interfaces allow for the connection of many sensor devices	Relatively easy to interface
Less susceptible to noise	

Digital sensors typically have more advanced features (e.g., the ADXL345 has double-tap and free-fall detection), but at a greater cost and level of complexity. Many sensors are not available in a digital package, so it is very important to understand how to connect analog sensors to the RPi using the SPI ADC circuit that is described in Chapter 9. Ideally, the analog sensor that you connect should not have to be sampled at a rate of thousands of times per second, or it will add significant CPU overhead.

Linear Analog Sensors

In Chapter 9, a first example is provided of using the MCP3208 SPI ADC to interface to a light-dependent resistor (LDR). The LDR is a resistance-based sensor, where a voltage/current is required for sensor excitation, and the resistance of the sensor varies in proportion to the quantity under measurement.

The TMP36 (tiny.cc/erpi1004) is a low-cost precision analog temperature sensor that provides a voltage output which is linearly proportional to the temperature. The TMP36 has a range of −40°C to +125°C, and a typical accuracy of ±1°C at +25°C. It can be powered at between 2.7 V and 5.5 V and is available in a three-pin TO-92 package, which makes it suitable for prototyping work.

Analog sensors with configurable linear voltage outputs can be easily attached to the RPi SPI ADC combination. The TMP36 provides an output of 750 mV at 25°C. It has a linear output, where the output scale factor is 10mV/°C. This means that the minimum output voltage is 0.75 V − (65 × 0.01 V) = 0.1 V and the maximum output voltage is 0.75 V + (100 × 0.01 V) = 1.75 V. The sensor output current will be between 0 µA and 50 µA, depending on the input impedance of the device to which it is attached. The high input impedance of the MCP3208 ADC means that current supplied is only a few nanoamps.

The C/C++ code required to convert the ADC value to a temperature in degrees Celsius is expressed in C code as follows:

```
float getTemperature(int adc_value) {              // from the datasheet
    float cur_voltage = adc_value * (3.30f/4096.0f); // Vcc = 3.3V, 12-bit
    float diff_degreesC = (cur_voltage-0.75f)/0.01f; // how many 0.1V steps?
    return (25.0f + diff_degreesC);
}
```

The TMP36 datasheet provides details on how the sensor can be wired using twisted-pair cable to be physically distant from the RPi itself. Such a configuration would allow the sensor to be used for external temperature monitoring applications. It is also important to note that analog sensors such as the TMP36 can be combined with op-amp circuits to build analog differential thermometers (e.g., to measure the difference in temperature between two locations) or to create an over/under-temperature interrupt signal—you do not have to write code for every application! Such circuits are described in the TMP36 datasheet (tiny.cc/erpi1004).

Figure 10-10 illustrates the circuit that can be used to connect the TMP36 to the RPi via the MCP3208 family of SPI ADCs. You can use a 10-bit MCP3008 ADC, but you will have to change the value in the temperature calculation code above from 4,096 (i.e., 2^{12}) to 1,024 (i.e., 2^{10}), and adjust the send[0] and send[1] bytes as described in Chapter 9. The full code example is available in Listing 10-4. This code uses the SPIDevice C++ class that is described in Chapter 8.

Listing 10-4: /chp10/tmp36/tmp36.cpp

```
#include <iostream>
#include "bus/SPIDevice.h"
using namespace exploringRPi;
```

```
using namespace std;

float getTemperature(int adc_value) {      // from the TMP36 datasheet
   float cur_voltage = adc_value * (3.30f/4096.0f); // Vcc = 3.3V, 12-bit
   float diff_degreesC = (cur_voltage-0.75f)/0.01f;
   return (25.0f + diff_degreesC);
}

int main(){
   cout << "Starting the RPi TMP36 example" << endl;
   SPIDevice *busDevice = new SPIDevice(0,0);
   busDevice->setSpeed(5000000);
   busDevice->setMode(SPIDevice::MODE0);
   unsigned char send[3], receive[3];
   send[0] = 0b00000110;      // Reading single-ended input from channel 0
   send[1] = 0b00000000;      // Use 0b00000001 and 0b10000000 for MCP3008
   busDevice->transfer(send, receive, 3);
   float temp = getTemperature(((receive[1]&0b00001111)<<8)|receive[2]);
   float fahr = 32 + ((temp * 9)/5);    // convert deg. C to deg. F
   cout << "Temperature is " << temp << "°C (" << fahr << "°F)" << endl;
   busDevice->close();
   return 0;
}
```

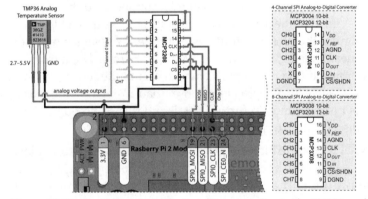

Figure 10-10: The RPi SPI ADC circuit and its connection to the TMP36 analog temperature sensor

This code can be built and executed as follows:

```
pi@erpi ~/exploringrpi/chp10/tmp36 $ ./build
pi@erpi ~/exploringrpi/chp10/tmp36 $ ./tmp36
Starting the RPi TMP36 example
Temperature is 23.1543°C (73.6777°F)
```

Nonlinear Analog Sensors

Sharp infrared distance measurement sensors are very useful for robotic navigation applications (e.g., object detection and line following) and proximity switches (e.g., automatic faucets and energy-saving switches). These sensors can also be attached to servo motors and used to calculate range maps (e.g., on the front of a mobile platform). They work well in indoor environments but have limited use in direct sunlight. They have a response time of ~39 ms, so at 25–26 readings per second, they will not provide dense range images. Figure 10-11(a) shows two aspect views of a low-cost sensor, the Sharp GP2D12 (`tiny.cc/erpi1005`).

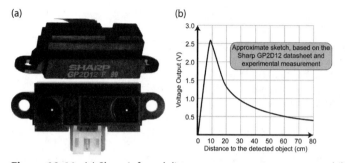

Figure 10-11: (a) Sharp infrared distance measurement sensor, and (b) its analog output response

This is a good analog sensor integration example because three problems need to be resolved, which occur generally with other sensors:

1. The sensor response in Figure 10-11(b) is highly nonlinear, so that two different distances can give the same sensor output. Thus you need to find a way to disambiguate the sensor output. For example, if the sensor output is 1.5 V, it could mean that the detected object is either 5 cm or 17 cm from the sensor. A common solution to this problem is to mount the sensor so that it is physically impossible for an object to be closer than 10 cm from the sensor. This problem is not examined in further detail and it is assumed here that the detected object cannot be closer than 10 cm from the sensor.

2. The output signal is prone to high-frequency noise. A simple first-order low-pass RC averaging filter can be designed to solve this problem. Alternatively, you could simply digitally average the sample values over time in your program code.

3. Even for the assumed distances of 10 cm or greater, the relationship between distance and voltage output is still nonlinear. A curve-fitting process can be employed to solve this problem if a linear relationship is required (e.g., threshold applications do not require a linear relationship—just a set value).

Despite the fact that the sensor is powered using a 5 V supply, the output voltage range from 0 V to 2.6 V is well within range for the SPI ADC when the voltage reference is 3.3 V. If it were outside the 0 V to 3.3 V range, a fixed-value voltage divider could be designed to limit the output voltage.

To solve the second problem, the circuit in Figure 10-12(a) includes a simple single-order low-pass RC filter to remove high-frequency signal noise. An RC pair needs to be created to suit the equation $RC = 1/(2\pi \times f_c)$, where the cutoff sampling frequency, f_c, which has been experimentally determined as ~52 Hz in this case[2]. A capacitor value of 1 µF is chosen and the resistor value is determined to be approximately 3.3 kΩ, using the RC equation, as illustrated in Figure 10-12(a).

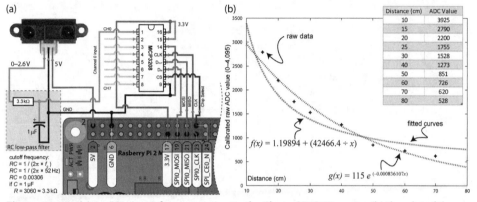

Figure 10-12: (a) An RPi circuit for connecting to the Sharp GP2D12 sensor; (b) the plot of the gnuplot fitted functions

To solve the final problem, a small test rig can be set up to calibrate the distance sensor. A measuring tape can be placed at the front of the sensor and a large object can be positioned at varying distances from the sensor, between 10 cm and 80 cm. In my case, this provided the raw data for the table in Figure 10-12(b), which is plotted on the graph with the + markers.

This raw data is not sufficiently fine to determine the distance value represented by an ADC measurement intermediate between the values corresponding to the + markers. Therefore, curve fitting can be employed to provide an expression that can be implemented in program code. The data can be supplied to the curve fitting tools that are freely available on the Wolfram Alpha website at www.wolframalpha.com. Using the command string

```
exponential fit {3925,10}, {2790,15}, {2200,20}, {1755,25}, {1528,30}, →
{1273,40}, {851,50}, {726,60}, {620,70}, {528,80}
```

results in the expression $distance = 115.804e^{-0.000843107v}$ (see tiny.cc/erpi1006). The following feature describes how you can perform the same task using gnuplot, the results of which are captured in Figure 10-12(b).

---

[2] The sample rate is a maximum of 25 to 26 readings per second for this sensor. A simple passive first-order low-pass filter allows frequency signals from 0 Hz to the cut-off frequency f_c to pass, while greatly attenuating higher-frequency signals (including noise). The Nyquist sampling theorem states that the *sampling frequency should be at least twice the highest frequency contained in the signal* ($f_s \geq 2 \times f_c$). However, you cannot just set the cutoff frequency to be half of the sample rate, as it will not perform well for such applications. For an excellent article entitled "What Nyquist Didn't Say, and What to Do About It," by Tim Wescott, please see www.wescottdesign .com/articles/Sampling/sampling.pdf.

FITTING DATA TO A CURVE USING GNUPLOT

In addition to plotting data, gnuplot can also be used to fit data to a curve using the nonlinear least-squares (NLLS) Marquardt-Levenberg algorithm. For example, the data in Figure 10-12(b) can be fitted to a function of the form $1/x$ using the following steps:

```
pi@erpi ~/exploringrpi/chp10/sharp $ more data
9925 10
2790 15
...
pi@erpi ~/exploringrpi/chp10/sharp $ gnuplot
    G N U P L O T
    Version 4.6 patchlevel 6    ...
gnuplot> f(x) = a + b/x
gnuplot> fit f(x) "data" using 1:2 via a,b
...
Final set of parameters            Asymptotic Standard Error
a             = 1.19894            +/- 1.415           (118%)
b             = 42466.4            +/- 1335            (3.144%)
...
```

The best fit function is therefore: $f(x) = 1.19894 + (42466.4/x)$, where x is the captured ADC input value. The plot of the fitted function with respect to the calibration data is available in Figure 10-12(b).

You can also use gnuplot to fit the data against a function with the form of an exponential decay by continuing on from the previous steps. Providing an initial estimate of the c and d values can help the NLLS algorithm converge on a valid solution. For this, you can use the values that are identified by the output of Wolfram Alpha, or appropriate estimate values:

```
gnuplot> g(x) = c * exp(-x * d)
gnuplot> c = 115
gnuplot> d = 0.0008
gnuplot> fit g(x) "data" using 1:2 via c,d
...
Final set of parameters            Asymptotic Standard Error
c             = 115                +/- 7.632           (6.637%)
d             = 0.000836107        +/- 7.244e-05       (8.664%)
...
gnuplot> set term postscript
gnuplot> set output "fittings.ps"
gnuplot> plot "data" using 1:2, f(x), g(x)
gnuplot> exit
pi@erpi ~/exploringrpi/chp10/sharp $ ps2pdf fittings.ps
pi@erpi ~/exploringrpi/chp10/sharp $ ls fittings*
fittings.pdf  fittings.ps
```

The best fit function is therefore: $g(x) = 115e^{-0.000836107x}$, where x is the captured ADC input value The standard error values in this case are lower and Figure 10-12(b) indicates that the exponential decay function provides a slightly better fit, particularly at close distances.

Note that this process can be used for many analog sensor types to provide an expression that can be used to interpolate between the measured sensor values. What type of fitting curve best fits the data will vary according to the underlying physical process of the sensor. For example, you could use a linear fit to derive an expression for the LDR described in Chapter 9. A C++ code example can be written to read in the ADC value and convert it into a distance as shown in Listing 10-5, where an exponential fix expression is coded on a single line.

Listing 10-5: /chp10/sharp/sharp.cpp (Segment)

```cpp
...
int main(){
    cout << "Starting the RPi GP2D12 sensor example" << endl;
    SPIDevice *busDevice = new SPIDevice(0,0);
    busDevice->setSpeed(5000000);
    busDevice->setMode(SPIDevice::MODE0);
    for(int i=0; i<1000; i++) {
        unsigned char send[3], receive[3];
        send[0] = 0b00000110;      // Reading single-ended input from channel 0
        send[1] = 0b00000000;
        busDevice->transfer(send, receive, 3);
        int raw = ((receive[1]&0b00001111)<<8)|receive[2];
        float distance = 115.804f * exp(-0.000843107f * (float)raw);
        cout << "The distance is: " << distance << " cm" << '\r' << flush;
        usleep(100000);
    }
    busDevice->close();
    return 0;
}
```

When the code example is executed, it continues to output the distance of a detected object in centimeters, for about 100 seconds:

```
pi@erpi ~/exploringrpi/chp10/sharp $ ./build
pi@erpi ~/exploringrpi/chp10/sharp $ ./sharp
Starting the RPi GP2D12 sensor example
The distance is: 16.117 cm
```

Listing 10-6 is a segment of code that performs the distance calculation using the three different curve-fitted approximations.

Listing 10-6: /chp10/sharp/sharpfit.cpp (Segment)

```cpp
...
    cout << "Raw value is " << (int)raw << endl;
    float distance = 115.804f * exp(-0.000843107f * (float)raw);
    cout << "Estimate 1 (Wolfram): " << distance << " cm" << endl;
    distance = 1.19894f + (42466.4f / (float)raw);
    cout << "Estimate 2 (1/x)    : " << distance << " cm" << endl;
    distance = 115.0f * exp(-0.000836107f * (float)raw);
    cout << "Estimate 3 (exp dec): " << distance << " cm" << endl;
...
```

The program gives the following output:

```
pi@erpi ~/exploringrpi/chp10/sharp $ ./sharpfit
Starting the RPi GP2D12 sensor example
Raw value is 1462
Estimate 1 (Wolfram): 33.76 cm
Estimate 2 (1/x)    : 30.2457 cm
Estimate 3 (exp dec): 33.8705 cm
```

This result aligns with the plot in Figure 10-12(b), where the second estimate ($f(x)$) is lower than the third estimate ($g(x)$) for an ADC input value of 1,462.

If the speed of execution of such code is vital in the application, then it is preferable to populate a lookup table (LUT) with the converted values. This means that each value is calculated once, either at the initialization stage of the program, or perhaps during code development, rather than every time a reading is made and has to be converted. When the program is in use, the subsequent memory accesses (for reading the LUT) are much more efficient than the corresponding floating-point calculations. This is possible because a 12-bit ADC can only output 4,096 unique values, and it is not unreasonable to store an array of the 4,096 possible outcomes in the memory associated with the program.

DISTANCE SENSING AND THE RASPBERRY PI

Two low-cost distance sensors are described in detail in this book: The Sharp infra-red distance measurement sensor is described in this chapter, and the HC-SR04 ultrasonic distance sensor is described in Chapter 11. Both of these sensors have quite limited precision and sample rates. Infrared sensors have a narrow beam, but are prone to sunlight interference. Ultrasonic sensors perform well in sunlight but do not work well with sound-absorbing materials and are prone to ghost echo (e.g., sound reflections that hit more than one surface). These low-cost sensors perform well for obstacle avoidance applications, but for precision applications such as spatial mapping you could investigate *LiDAR* (*light detection and ranging*) sensors. The laser-based LIDAR-Lite v2 ($115) sensor from www.pulsedlight3d.com has a 40 meter range capability, 1 cm resolution, ±2.5 cm accuracy, and is capable of 500 readings per second. It can be interfaced to the RPi using its I²C bus.

Analog Sensor Signal Conditioning

One of the problems with analog sensors is that they may have output signal voltage levels quite different from those required by the RPi. *Signal conditioning* is the term used to describe the manipulation of an analog signal so that it is suitable for the next stage of processing. To condition a sensor output as an input to the RPi SPI ADC, this often means ensuring that the signal's range is typically between 0 V and 3.3 V.

Scaling Using Voltage Division

The voltage divider circuit in Figure 10-13(a) can be used to condition a sensor output voltage. If the output voltage from the sensor is greater than 3.3 V but not less than 0 V, a voltage divider circuit can be used to linearly reduce the voltage to remain within a 0 V to 3.3 V range, which is then passed into the SPI ADC device.

A voltage divider circuit will load the sensor output impedance and it may be necessary to use a unity-gain buffer (for example a MCP6002 op-amp in a voltage follower configuration, as illustrated in Figure 10-13(b)). The MCP6002 will act as a buffer that prevents the sensor circuit from exceeding the maximum input impedance of the ADC. (Remember that ideal voltage follower circuits have infinite input impedance and zero output impedance.) Remember also that resistors have a manufacturing tolerance (often 5%–10% of the resistance value), which will affect the scaling accuracy of the voltage division circuit. You may need to experiment with combinations or use a potentiometer to adjust the resistance ratio. With multi-op-amp packages, unused inputs should be connected as shown in Figure 10-13(b) (in light gray) to avoid random switching noise.

This circuit works well for linearly scaling down an input signal, but it would not work for a zero-centered or negatively biased input signal. For that, a more general and slightly more complex op-amp circuit is required.

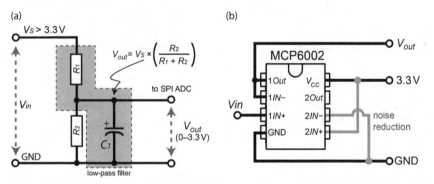

Figure 10-13: (a) A voltage divider with a low-pass filter, and (b) the MCP6002 dual op-amp in a voltage-follower configuration

Signal Offsetting and Scaling

Figure 10-14(a) provides a general op-amp circuit that can be used to set the gain and offset of an input signal. It is designed as an adjustable prototyping circuit to use in conjunction with an oscilloscope to design a fixed-signal conditioning circuit for your particular application. Some notes on this circuit:

- The *Vcc–* input of the op-amp is tied to GND, which is representative of the type of circuit that is built using the RPi, as a –5 V rail is not readily available.

- The 3.3 V level can be provided by the analog voltage reference on the SPI ADC.

- A 100 nF decoupling capacitor can be used on the V_{IN} input to remove the DC component of the incoming sensor signal. However, for many sensor circuits the DC component of the sensor signal is important and should not be removed.

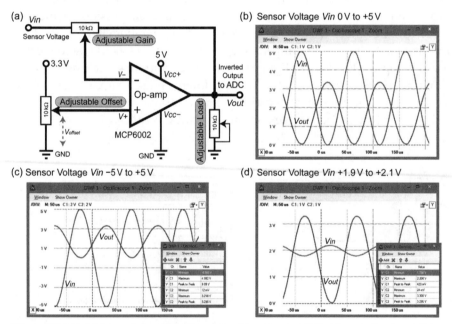

Figure 10-14: (a) A general op-amp signal conditioning circuit that inverts the input, (b) conditioned output when V_{in} is 0 V to 5 V, (c) conditioned output when V_{in} is –5 V to +5 V, and (d) conditioned and amplified output when the input signal is 1.9 V to 2.1 V

The circuit in Figure 10-14(a) amplifies (or attenuates), offsets, and inverts the input signal according to the settings of the potentiometers:

- The gain is set using the adjustable gain potentiometer, where $V_- = G \times V_{IN}$.

- The offset is set using the adjustable offset potentiometer. This can be used to center the output signal at 1.65 V if desired.

- The output voltage is approximately. $V_{out} = V_+ - V_- = offset - (G \times V_{IN})$ As such, the output is an inverted and scaled version of the input signal.

- The inversion of the signal (you can see that the output is at a maximum when the input is at a minimum) is a consequence of the circuit used. Noninverting circuits are possible, but they are more difficult to configure. The inversion can easily be corrected in software by subtracting the received ADC input value from 4,095.

In Figure 10-14(b), (c), and (d) the offset voltage is set to 1.65 V and the gain is adjusted to maximize the output signal (between 0 V and 3.3 V) without clipping the signal. In Figure 10-14(b) the gain and offset are adjusted to map a 0 V to +5 V signal to a 3.3 V to 0 V inverted output signal. In Figure 10-14(c) a −5 V to +5 V signal is mapped to a 3.3 V to 0 V signal. Finally, in Figure 10-14(d) a 1.9 V to 2.1 V input signal is mapped to a 3.3 V to 0 V output. The last case is applied to an example application in the next section.

The MCP6002 is a dual op-amp package, and it is used because the MCP6001 is not readily available in a DIP package. You could use the MCP6002 to condition two separate sensor signals.

Interfacing to an Analog Accelerometer

Similar to the ADXL345 digital accelerometer, the ADXL335 is a three-axis *analog* accelerometer that can use the static acceleration of gravity to measure tilt, or the dynamic acceleration of movement to measure vibration, motion, or impact. Unlike the ADXL345, the ADXL335 has three analog outputs, one for each axis, which can be configured using capacitors to define the bandwidth of the device. You will typically purchase this device on a breakout board that will define this bandwidth at manufacture. The module can be powered with a 1.8 V to 3.6 V supply. The datasheet is available at tiny.cc/erpi1007.

When measuring tilt, the *x*-axis output provides ~1.30 V at 0°, ~1.64 V at 90°, and ~1.98 V at 180°. This means that the output signal of the breakout board is centered on 1.64 V and has a variation of ±0.34 V. A circuit can be designed as shown in Figure 10-15 to map the center point to 1.65 V and to extend the variation over the full 3.3 V range of the MCP3208. This is not strictly necessary, but it is a useful task for experimenting with analog signal conditioning.

Unfortunately, there are output impedance problems with this particular ADXL335 breakout board, and the voltage divider circuit in the conditioning circuit will not function correctly. A buffer circuit is therefore required, and an op-amp in voltage follower configuration can be used. The MCP6002 is perfect for this application, because one of its op-amps can be used as a unity-gain buffer and the second can be used for the purpose of signal conditioning.

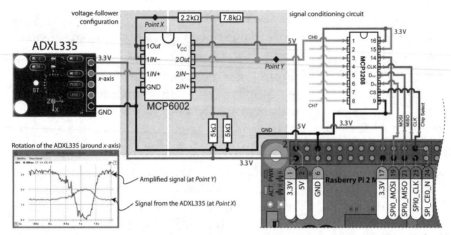

Figure 10-15: The ADXL335 analog accelerometer and its connection to the RPi with further signal conditioning

This overall circuit is a little complex and it may be overkill, because the amplification of a signal does not necessarily improve the information content of that signal—noise is amplified along with the signal. It is quite possible that the 12-bit ADC performs just as well over a linearly scaled 1.3 V to 1.98 V range as it does over the full 0 V to 3.3 V range for this particular sensor. However, it is important that you are exposed to the process of offsetting and scaling a signal using op-amps, because it is required for many sensor types, particularly those that are centered on 0 V, such as microphone audio signals. You can see the amplified signal on the bottom left side of Figure 10-15. It is important to note that the signal conditioning circuit used results in an inverted output, which is corrected easily using software.

The adxl335 program can be used to print out the digitized x-axis acceleration value. In my case, the program prints out the raw ADC value 2,272 at rest ($+90°$), 568 at $0°$, and 3,973 at $+180°$. More values could be used to improve the quality of the fit. A simple linear interpolation is therefore used in the code example so that it provides the output in degrees:

```
pi@erpi ~/exploringrpi/chp10/adxl335 $ more data
# Simple calibration data
568    0
2272   90
3973   180
pi@erpi ~/exploringrpi/chp10/adxl335 $ gnuplot
        G N U P L O T ...
gnuplot> y(x) = m*x + c
gnuplot> fit y(x) "data" using 1:2 via m,c
...
Final set of parameters          Asymptotic Standard Error
m              = 0.0528634       +/- 2.689e-05    (0.05087%)
c              = -30.0528        +/- 0.0716       (0.2382%) ...
```

The equation of a line, *y(x)* = *mx* + *c*, can then be used in the source code to convert the raw ADC value into the acceleration value that it represents:

```
float angle = (0.0528634 * raw) - 30.0528;
cout << "The tilt angle is " << angle << " degrees" << endl;
```

The full source code example is available in the `chp10/adxl335` directory, and it is executed as follows:

```
pi@erpi ~/exploringrpi/chp10/adxl335 $ ./adxl335
Starting the RPi ADXL335 example
The raw value is: 2263
The tilt angle is 89.5771 degrees
```

The circuit in Figure 10-15 can be extended using an MCP6004 quad op-amp package to support the *y*-axis and *z*-axis acceleration values, and the software can be extended to read these values from the CH1 and CH2 inputs on the MCP3204 SPI ADC.

Interfacing to Local Displays

The RPi can be attached to computer monitors and digital televisions using the HDMI output connector. In addition, LCD HATs can be attached to the RPi GPIO header connector. The downsides of such displays are that they may not be practical or they may be overly expensive for certain applications. When a small amount of information needs to be relayed to a user, a simple LED can be used; for example, the RPi onboard power and activity LEDs are useful indicators that the board continues to function. For more complex information, two possibilities are to interface to low-cost LED displays and low-cost character LCD modules.

In Chapter 8, an example is provided for driving seven-segment displays using SPI and 74HC595 serial shift register ICs. That is a useful educational exercise, but the wiring can quickly become impractical for multiple digits. In the following sections more advanced solutions are described for adding low-cost onboard display to the RPi.

MAX7219 Display Modules

The Maxim Integrated MAX7219 is a serially interfaced 8-digit LED display driver that is widely available and built in to very low-cost multi-seven-segment display modules. The module in Figure 10-16(a) ($2–$3) is a 5 V 8-digit red LED display that contains the MAX7219 IC, which can be interfaced using SPI. The datasheet for the IC is available at `tiny.cc/erpi1008`.

The module can be connected to the RPi using its SPI bus, which in this case is connected to the SPI_CE1_N enable pin, as illustrated in Figure 10-16(a). This allows the character LCD module in the next section to be simultaneously connected to the same bus. Note that the module is powered using the 5 V line, but is controlled using 3.3 V logic levels. Do not connect the *DOUT* line on the module directly back to the RPi MISO input!

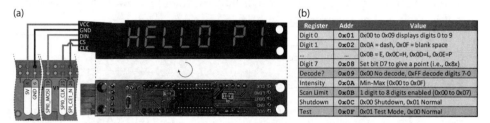

(a)

(b)

Register	Addr	Value
Digit 0	0x01	0x00 to 0x09 displays digits 0 to 9
Digit 1	0x02	0x0A = dash, 0x0F = blank space
...		0x0B = E, 0x0C=H, 0x0D=L, 0x0E=P
Digit 7	0x08	Set bit D7 to give a point (i.e., 0x8x)
Decode?	0x09	0x00 No decode, 0xFF decode digits 7-0
Intensity	0x0A	Min-Max (0x00 to 0x0F)
Scan Limit	0x0B	1 digit to 8 digits enabled (0x00 to 0x07)
Shutdown	0x0C	0x00 Shutdown, 0x01 Normal
Test	0x0F	0x01 Test Mode, 0x00 Normal

Figure 10-16: (a) The MAX7219 8-digit 7-segment display module, and (b) a summary register table for the MAX7219

In decode mode the module can display eight digits consisting of the numeric values 0–9 (with a point), the letters *H, E, L, P*, a space, and a dash. The decode mode can also be disabled, permitting each of the seven segments to be controlled directly. For example, the following steps that use the summary list of registers in Figure 10-16(b) can be used to test that the module is configured correctly by sending pairs of bytes to the device—the register address and data value to write:

1. Turn on the module and then place the module in test mode (i.e., all segments on):[3]

```
pi@erpi ~ $ echo -ne "\x0C\x01" > /dev/spidev0.1
pi@erpi ~ $ echo -ne "\x0F\x01" > /dev/spidev0.1
```

2. Take the module out of test mode (return to its previous state):

```
pi@erpi ~ $ echo -ne "\x0F\x00" > /dev/spidev0.1
```

3. Change to 8 segment mode, and display the number 6.5 using the last two digits (i.e., on the RHS):

```
pi@erpi ~ $ echo -ne "\x09\xFF" > /dev/spidev0.1
pi@erpi ~ $ echo -ne "\x01\x05" > /dev/spidev0.1
pi@erpi ~ $ echo -ne "\x02\x86" > /dev/spidev0.1
```

4. Display the words "Hello Pi" (as in Figure 10-16(a)):

```
pi@erpi ~ $ echo -ne "\x08\x0C" > /dev/spidev0.1
pi@erpi ~ $ echo -ne "\x07\x0B" > /dev/spidev0.1
pi@erpi ~ $ echo -ne "\x06\x0D" > /dev/spidev0.1
pi@erpi ~ $ echo -ne "\x05\x0D" > /dev/spidev0.1
```

---

[3] As discussed with the echo command: -n means do not output a trailing newline character, -e means enable interpretation of backslash escape sequences, and \xHH means a byte with a hexadecimal value HH. Writing to /dev/spidev0.1 uses the SPI_CE1_N rather than the SPI_CE0_N enable pin on the RPi.

```
pi@erpi ~ $ echo -ne "\x04\x00" > /dev/spidev0.1
pi@erpi ~ $ echo -ne "\x03\x0F" > /dev/spidev0.1
pi@erpi ~ $ echo -ne "\x02\x0E" > /dev/spidev0.1
pi@erpi ~ $ echo -ne "\x01\x01" > /dev/spidev0.1
```

5. Adjust the LED intensity to its darkest and to its brightest:

```
pi@erpi ~ $ echo -ne "\x0A\x00" > /dev/spidev0.1
pi@erpi ~ $ echo -ne "\x0A\x0F" > /dev/spidev0.1
```

6. Turn off the module:

```
pi@erpi ~ $ echo -ne "\x0C\x00" > /dev/spidev0.1
```

The code in Listing 10-7 uses the SPIDevice class from Chapter 8 to create a high-speed counter. The display module is very responsive at an SPI bus speed of 10 MHz, updating the display 1,000,000 times in approximately 18 seconds. The output of the program in Listing 10-7 is displayed in Figure 10-17. The display is counting quickly, so the blurred digits on the right-hand side are caused by the update speed of the count relative to the camera shutter speed.

Listing 10-7: chp10/max7219/max7219.cpp

```cpp
#include <iostream>
#include "bus/SPIDevice.h"
using namespace exploringRPi;
using namespace std;

int main(){
   cout << "Starting the RPi MAX7219 example" << endl;
   SPIDevice *max = new SPIDevice(0,1);
   max->setSpeed(10000000);              // max speed is 10MHz
   max->setMode(SPIDevice::MODE0);

   // turn on the display and disable test mode -- just in case:
   max->writeRegister(0x0C, 0x01);       // turn on the display
   max->writeRegister(0x0F, 0x00);       // disable test mode
   max->writeRegister(0x0B, 0x07);       // set 8-digit mode
   max->writeRegister(0x09, 0xFF);       // set decode mode on

   for(int i=1; i<9; i++){           // clear all digits to be dashes
      max->writeRegister((unsigned int)i, 0x0A);
   }
   for(int i=0; i<=100000; i++){     // count to 100,000
      int val = i;                   // need to display each digit
      unsigned int place = 1;        // the current decimal place
      while(val>0){                  // repeatedly divide and get remainder
        max->writeRegister( place++, (unsigned char) val%10);
        val = val/10;
      }
   }
   max->close();
   cout << "End of the RPi MAX7219 example" << endl;
   return 0;
}
```

Figure 10-17: The MAX7219 eight-digit seven-segment display counting due to Listing 10-7

Character LCD Modules

Character LCD modules are LCD dot-matrix displays that feature preprogrammed font tables so that they can be used to display simple text messages without the need for complex display software. They are available in a range of character rows and columns (commonly 2 × 8, 2 × 16, 2 × 20, and 4 × 20) and usually contain an LED backlight, which is available in a range of colors. Recently, *OLED* (organic LED) versions and *E-paper* (e-ink) versions have been released that provide for greater levels of display contrast.

To understand the use of a character LCD module, you should study its datasheet. While most character LCD modules have common interfaces (often using a Hitachi HD44780 controller), the display modules from Newhaven have some of the best datasheets. The datasheet for a typical Newhaven display module is available at `tiny.cc/erpi1009`. It is recommended that the datasheet be read in conjunction with this discussion. The datasheet for the HD44780 controller is available at `tiny.cc/erpi1010`. The following code works for all character LCD modules that are based on this controller.

Character LCD modules are available with integrated I²C and SPI interfaces, but the majority of modules are available with an 8-bit and 4-bit parallel interface. By adding a 74HC595 serial-shift register to the circuit, it is possible to develop a custom SPI interface, which provides greater flexibility in the choice of modules. A generic character LCD module can be attached to the RPi using the wiring configuration illustrated in Figure 10-18.

You can interface to character LCD modules using either an 8-bit or a 4-bit mode, but there is no difference in the functionality available with either mode. The 4-bit interface requires fewer interface connections, but each 8-bit value has to be written in two steps—the lower 4 bits (*lower nibble*) followed by the higher 4 bits (*upper nibble*).

To write to the character LCD module, two lines are required: the RS line (register select signal) and the E line (operational enable signal). The circuit in Figure 10-18 is designed to use a 4-bit interface, because it requires only 6 lines, rather than the 10 lines that are required with the 8-bit interface. This means that a single 8-bit 74HC595 can be used to interface to the module when it is in 4-bit mode. The downside is that the software is slightly more complex to write, because each byte must be written in two nibbles. The 4-bit interface uses the inputs DB4–DB7, whereas the 8-bit interface requires the use of DB0–DB7.

WARNING   Do not attempt to read data from this display module directly into the RPi, because it uses 5 V logic levels.

It is possible to read data values from the display, but it is not required in this application; therefore, the R/W (read/write select signal) is tied to GND to place the display in write mode. The power is supplied using VCC (5 V) and VSS (GND). VEE sets the display contrast level and must be at a level between VSS and VCC. A 10 kΩ multi-turn potentiometer can be used to provide precise control over the display contrast. Finally, the LED+ and LED− connections supply the LED backlight power.

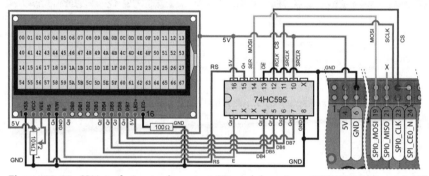

Figure 10-18: SPI interfacing to character LCD modules using a 74HC595 8-bit serial shift register

The display character address codes are illustrated on the module in Figure 10-18. Using *commands* (on pg. 6 of the datasheet), *data* values can be sent to these addresses. For example, to display the letter *A* in the top-left corner, the following procedure can be used with the 4-bit interface:

- Clear the display by sending the value 00000001 to D4-D7. This value should be sent in two parts: the lower nibble (0001), followed by the higher nibble (0000). The E line is set high then low after each nibble is sent. A delay of 1.52 ms (datasheet pg. 6) is required. The module expects a *command* to be sent when the RS line is low. After sending this command, the cursor is placed in the top left corner.

- Write data $01000001 = 65_{10} = A$ (datasheet pg. 9) with the lower nibble sent first, followed by the upper nibble. The E line is set high followed by low after each nibble is sent. The module expects *data* to be sent when the RS line is set high.

A C++ class is available for you to use in interfacing the RPi to display modules using SPI. The class assumes that the 74HC595 lines are connected as shown in Figure 10-18 and the data is represented as in Table 10-4. The code does not use bits 2 (Q_D) and 3 (Q_C) on the 74HC595, so it is possible for you to repurpose these for your own application. For example, one pin could be connected to the gate of a FET and used to switch the backlight on and off. The class definition is provided in Listing 10-8 and the implementation is in the associated `LCDCharacterDisplay.cpp` file.

Table 10-4: Mapping of the 74HC595 Data Bits to the Character LCD Module Inputs, as Required for the C++ LCDCharacterDisplay Class

	BIT 7 MSB	BIT 6	BIT 5	BIT 4	BIT 3	BIT 2	BIT 1	BIT 0 LSB
Character LCD module	D7	D6	D5	D4	Not used	Not used	E	RS
74HC595 pins	Q_H	Q_G	Q_F	Q_E	Q_D	Q_C	Q_B	Q_A

Listing 10-8: /chp10/character/display/LCDCharacterDisplay.h

```
class LCDCharacterDisplay {
private:
    SPIDevice *device;
    int width, height;
    ...
public:
    LCDCharacterDisplay(SPIDevice *device, int width, int height);
    virtual void write(char c);
    virtual void print(std::string message);
    virtual void clear();
    virtual void home();
    virtual int  setCursorPosition(int row, int column);
    virtual void setDisplayOff(bool displayOff);
    virtual void setCursorOff(bool cursorOff);
    virtual void setCursorBlink(bool isBlink);
    virtual void setCursorMoveOff(bool cursorMoveOff);
    virtual void setCursorMoveLeft(bool cursorMoveLeft);
    virtual void setAutoscroll(bool isAutoscroll);
    virtual void setScrollDisplayLeft(bool scrollLeft);
    virtual ~LCDCharacterDisplay();
};
```

The constructor requires an `SPIDevice` object and details about the width and height of the character display module (in characters). The constructor provides functionality to position the cursor on the display and to describe how the cursor should behave (e.g., blinking or moving to the left/right). This class can be used as shown in Listing 10-9 to create an `LCDCharacterDisplay` object, display a string, and display a count from 0 to 10,000 on the module.

Listing 10-9: /chp10/character/character.cpp

```cpp
#include <iostream>
#include <sstream>
#include "display/LCDCharacterDisplay.h"
using namespace std;
using namespace exploringRPi;

int main(){
    cout << "Starting LCD Character Display Example" << endl;
    SPIDevice *busDevice = new SPIDevice(0,0);
    busDevice->setSpeed(1000000);       // access to SPI Device object
    ostringstream s;                    // using to combine text and ints
    LCDCharacterDisplay display(busDevice, 20, 4); // a 20x4 display
    display.clear();                    // Clear the character LCD module
    display.home();                     // Move to the (0,0) position
    display.print("   Exploring RPi");
    display.setCursorPosition(1,3);
    display.print("by Derek Molloy");
    display.setCursorPosition(2,0);
    display.print("www.exploringrpi.com");
    for(int x=0; x<=10000; x++){        // Do this 10,000 times
       s.str("");                       // clear the ostringstream object
       display.setCursorPosition(3,7);  // move the cursor to second row
       s << "X=" << x;                  // construct a string with an int
       display.print(s.str());          // print the string X=***
    }
    cout << "End of LCD Character Display Example" << endl;
    return 0;
}
```

The code example in Listing 10-9 can be built and executed using the following steps:

```
pi@erpi ~/exploringrpi/chp10/character $ ./build
pi@erpi ~/exploringrpi/chp10/character $ ./character
Starting LCD Character Display Example
End of LCD Character Display Example
```

The count incrementally updates on the display and finishes with the output illustrated in Figure 10-19.

It takes 22 seconds to display a count that runs from 0 to 10,000, which is approximately 455 localized screen updates per second. This means that you could potentially connect many display modules to a single SPI bus and still achieve reasonable screen refresh rates. At its maximum refresh rate, the top command gives the following output:

```
  PID USER      PR  NI  VIRT  RES  SHR S  %CPU %MEM    TIME+   COMMAND
  309 root      20   0     0    0    0 S  32.8  0.0  1:02.55 spi0
 4120 pi        20   0  3304  784  688 D  32.8  0.1  0:05.72 character
```

This indicates that the `character` program and its associated `spi0` device are utilizing 65.6% of the available CPU time at this extreme module display refresh rate of 455 updates per second. To be clear, the display maintains its current display state without any RPi overhead, and refresh is only required to change the display contents.

Figure 10-19: Output from Listing 10-9 on a 4 × 20 and a 2 × 16 inverted RGB character display module[4]

OLED Dot-Matrix Display

Organic LED (OLED) dot-matrix displays are one other popular type of graphic displays that can be easily connected to the RPi. In particular, displays that utilize the Solomon Systech SSD1306 driver can be interfaced directly to an I²C or SPI bus. Figure 10-20 illustrates two such display modules: the first is a 1.3" SPI/I²C module from Adafruit ($24) and the second is a generic 0.96" I²C only module ($4). In both case, the screens have a display resolution of 128 × 64 pixels. See `tiny.cc/erpi1011` for the SSD1306 datasheet.

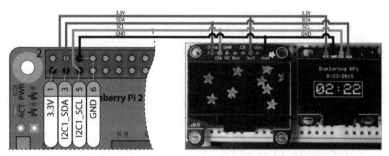

Figure 10-20: Connection to two OLED dot-matrix displays using the I²C bus

---

[4] Note that the JHD204A module has a built-in fixed-value resistor to set the contrast, therefore a connection to VEE is not required. The RGB character display module (NHD-0216K1Z-NS(RGB)) has three separate LED backlight connections for red, green, and blue. Pay particular attention to the voltage levels specified in the datasheet for these three channels.

As other display examples in this chapter all use SPI, this section utilizes the I²C bus. However, the code that follows can be tailored for either I²C or SPI devices. The two example modules can be connected to the I²C bus as illustrated in Figure 10-20. Note that the Adafruit module requires that SJ1 and SJ2 on the back of the board are bridged with solder to select the I²C interface mode. The Adafruit board appears at the I²C address 0x3d and the generic board appears at the I²C address 0x3c. Note that different versions of the Adafruit board appear interchangeably at 0x3c and 0x3d. With the circuit wired as in Figure 10-20, a call to i2cdetect gives the following output:

```
pi@erpi ~ $ i2cdetect -y -r 1
    0  1  2  3  4  5  6  7  8  9  a  b  c  d  e  f  ...
30: -- -- -- -- -- -- -- -- -- -- -- -- 3c 3d -- --  ...
```

These devices have advanced controllers and therefore the easiest way to use them is to install a library—the Adafruit SSD1306 OLED display driver for Raspberry Pi by Charles-Henri Hallard (www.hallard.me). The repository includes the Adafruit graphics library, which can be used to draw shapes on the display (e.g., the box surrounding the time in Figure 10-20, and the bitmap Adafruit star logos). The library can be installed as follows:

```
pi@erpi ~ $ git clone https://github.com/hallard/ArduiPi_OLED
pi@erpi ~ $ cd ArduiPi_OLED/
pi@erpi ~/ArduiPi_OLED $ ls
Adafruit_GFX.cpp     autogen.sh   hwplatform           README.mono.md
Adafruit_GFX.h       bcm2835.c    Makefile             Wrapper.cpp
ArduiPi_OLED.cpp     bcm2835.h    mono
ArduiPi_OLED.h       examples     README.bananapi.md
ArduiPi_OLED_lib.h   glcdfont.c   README.md
```

To build the library, you must install the libi2c-dev package as follows:

```
pi@erpi ~/ArduiPi_OLED $ sudo apt install libi2c-dev i2c-tools
```

WARNING   Note that the libi2c-dev package will conflict with the existing i2c headers that are used to develop other code in this book. You can remove this package at any stage using `sudo apt remove libi2c-dev`. It would be best if you remove this package after you build the ArduiPi_OLED library and have tested that it is working.

The library can then be built and deployed using a call to make:

```
pi@erpi ~/ArduiPi_OLED $ sudo make
g++ -Wall -fPIC -fno-rtti -Ofast -mfpu=vfp -mfloat-abi=hard ...
[Install Library]
[Install Headers]
pi@erpi ~/ArduiPi_OLED $ ls /usr/local/lib/libAr*
/usr/local/lib/libArduiPi_OLED.so     /usr/local/lib/libArduiPi_OLED.so.1.0
/usr/local/lib/libArduiPi_OLED.so.1
```

You can then test that it is working by building and running the demonstration programs that are included:

```
pi@erpi ~/ArduiPi_OLED $ cd examples/
pi@erpi ~/ArduiPi_OLED/examples $ ls
Makefile  oled_demo.cpp  teleinfo-oled.cpp
pi@erpi ~/ArduiPi_OLED/examples $ make
...
pi@erpi ~/ArduiPi_OLED/examples $ sudo ./oled_demo --verbose --oled 3
oled_demo v1.1
-- OLED params --
Oled is    : Adafruit I2C 128x64
```

This demonstration provides multiple examples, including the stars display in Figure 10-20. To run the demonstration and to use this library on the Adafruit device at the I²C address 0x3d, you must edit the `ArduiPi_OLED_lib.h` file and alter the value of `ADAFRUIT_I2C_ADDRESS` to 0x3d. Then rebuild the library.

Listing 10-10 provides the code for the clock display in Figure 10-20. The generic display module that is illustrated in Figure 10-20 displays the text "Exploring RPi" in yellow, and the clock date and time in a blue color. This is not a true multi-color display; rather, the pixels have a single fixed color with a yellow band at the top and the remainder of the display in blue—the color of the individual pixels cannot be changed.

Listing 10-10: /chp10/oled/oledTest.cpp

```cpp
#include "ArduiPi_OLED_lib.h"
#include "ArduiPi_OLED.h"
#include "Adafruit_GFX.h"
#include <stdio.h>
#include <ctime>

int main(){
   ArduiPi_OLED display;
   if(!display.init(OLED_I2C_RESET, OLED_ADAFRUIT_I2C_128x64)){
      perror("Failed to set up the display\n");
      return -1;
   }
   printf("Setting up the I2C Display output\n");
   display.begin();
   display.clearDisplay();
   display.setTextSize(1);
   display.setTextColor(WHITE);
   display.setCursor(27,5);
   display.print("Exploring RPi");
   time_t t = time(0);
   struct tm *now = localtime(&t);
   display.setCursor(35,18);
   display.printf("%2d/%2d/%2d", now->tm_mon, now->tm_mday,
                  (now->tm_year+1900));
```

```
display.setCursor(21,37);
display.setTextSize(3);
display.printf("%02d:%02d", now->tm_hour, now->tm_min );
display.drawRect(16, 32, 96, 32, WHITE);
display.display();
display.close();
printf("End of the I2C Display program\n");
return 0;
}
```

This code can be built and executed as follows:

```
pi@erpi .../chp10/oled $ g++ oledTest.cpp -o oledTest -lArduiPi_OLED
pi@erpi .../chp10/oled $ sudo ./oledTest
Setting up the I2C Display output
End of the I2C Display program
```

The ArduiPi OLED library uses the *C Library for BCM2835* that is described in Chapter 9. This library is not compatible with the WiringPi library and it is difficult to use these libraries together in the same project. It is possible to use the C Library for BCM2835 to perform much the same tasks as the WiringPi library. To illustrate this, a further example is available in the code repository (`oledDHT.cpp`) that uses the C Library for BCM2835 to communicate with the Aosong AM2302 single-wire temperature and humidity sensor that is described in Chapter 6.

The circuit in Figure 10-21(a) can be used to connect both the Aosong AM230x (and DHT) sensors to the RPi along with an OLED dot-matrix display. The program code is available in the `/chp10/oled/` directory and when executed it will result in the display as in Figure 10-21(b). The display alternates between the current room humidity value and the current room temperature value. It continues until the program is stopped by using Ctrl C.

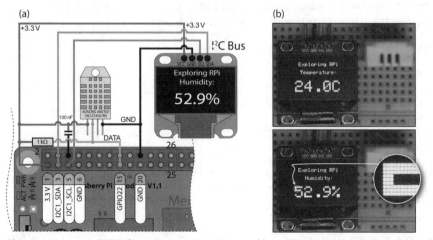

Figure 10-21: An OLED dot-matrix temperature and humidity sensing and display example

Building C/C++ Libraries

In this chapter, a number of different actuators, sensors, and display devices are interfaced to the RPi using standalone code examples. Should you embark upon a grand design project, it will quickly become necessary to combine such code examples together into a single software project. In addition, it would not be ideal if you had to recompile every line of code in the project each time that you made a change. To solve this problem, you can build your own libraries of C/C++ code, and to assist you in this task, you can use *makefiles*, and better still, *CMake*.

Makefiles

As the complexity of your C/C++ projects grows, an IDE such as Eclipse can be used to manage compiler options and program code interdependencies. However, there are occasions when command-line compilation is required; and when projects are complex, a structured approach to managing the build process is necessary. A good solution is to use the `make` program and *makefiles*.

The process is best explained by using an example. To compile a `hello.cpp` and a `test.cpp` program within a single project without makefiles, the build script can be as follows:

```
pi@erpi ~/exploringrpi/chp10/makefiles $ more build
#!/bin/bash
g++ -o3 hello.cpp -o hello
g++ -o3 test.cpp -o test
```

The script works perfectly fine; however, if the project's complexity necessitated separate compilation, then this approach lacks structure. Following is a simple `Makefile` that could be used instead (it is very important to use the Tab key to indent the lines with the `<Tab>` marker below):

```
pi@erpi ~/exploringrpi/chp10/makefiles $ more Makefile
all: hello test

hello:
<Tab> g++ -o3 hello.cpp -o hello

test:
<Tab> g++ -o3 test.cpp -o test

pi@erpi ~/exploringrpi/chp10/makefiles $ rm hello test
pi@erpi ~/exploringrpi/chp10/makefiles $ make
g++ -o3 hello.cpp -o hello
g++ -o3 test.cpp -o test
```

If the `make` command is issued in this directory, the `Makefile` file is detected and a call to "make all" will automatically be invoked. That will execute the commands under the `hello:` and `test:` labels, which build the two programs. However, this `Makefile` does not add much in the way of structure, so a more complete version is required, such as this:

```
pi@erpi ~/exploringrpi/chp10/makefiles2 $ more Makefile
CC      = g++
CFLAGS  = -c -o3 -Wall
LDFLAGS =

all: hello test

hello: hello.o
<Tab> $(CC) $< -o $@

hello.o: hello.cpp
<Tab> $(CC) $(CFLAGS) $< -o $@

test: test.o
<Tab> $(CC) $(LDFLAGS) $< -o $@

test.o: test.cpp
<Tab> $(CC) $(CFLAGS) $< -o $@

clean:
<Tab> rm -rf *.o hello test
```

In this version, the compiler choice, compiler options, and linker options are defined at the top of the `Makefile`. This enables the options to be easily altered for all files in the project. In addition, the object files (.o files) are retained, which dramatically reduces repeated compilation times when there are many source files in the project. There is some shortcut syntax in this `Makefile`. For example, `$<` is the name of the first prerequisite (`hello.o` in its first use), and `$@` is the name of the target (`hello` in its first use). The project can now be built using the following steps:

```
pi@erpi ~/exploringrpi/chp10/makefiles2 $ ls
hello.cpp  Makefile  test.cpp
pi@erpi ~/exploringrpi/chp10/makefiles2 $ make
g++ -c -o3 -Wall hello.cpp -o hello.o
g++ hello.o -o hello
g++ -c -o3 -Wall test.cpp -o test.o
g++  test.o -o test
pi@erpi ~/exploringrpi/chp10/makefiles2 $ ls
hello  hello.cpp  hello.o  Makefile  test  test.cpp  test.o
pi@erpi ~/exploringrpi/chp10/makefiles2 $ make clean
rm -rf *.o hello test
pi@erpi ~/exploringrpi/chp10/makefiles2 $ ls
hello.cpp  Makefile  test.cpp
```

This description only scratches the surface of the capability of make and makefiles. You can find a full GNU guide at `tiny.cc/erpi1012`.

CMake

Unfortunately, makefiles can become overly complex for tasks such as building projects that have multiple subdirectories, or projects that are to be deployed to multiple platforms. Building complex projects is where *CMake* really shines; CMake is a cross-platform makefile generator. Simply put, CMake automatically generates the makefiles for your project. It can do much more than that too (e.g., build MS Visual Studio solutions), but this discussion focuses on the compilation of library code. The first step is to install CMake on the RPi:

```
pi@erpi ~/exploringrpi/chp10/cmake $ sudo apt install cmake
pi@erpi ~/exploringrpi/chp10/cmake $ cmake -version
cmake version 3.0.2
```

A Hello World Example

The first project to test CMake is available in the `/chp10/cmake/` directory. It consists of the `hello.cpp` file and a text file called `CMakeLists.txt`, as provided in Listing 10-11.

Listing 10-11: /chp10/cmake/CMakeLists.txt

```
cmake_minimum_required(VERSION 3.0.2)
project (hello)
add_executable(hello hello.cpp)
```

The `CMakeLists.txt` file in Listing 10-11 consists of three lines:

- The first line sets the minimum version of CMake for this project, which is major version 3, minor version 0, and patch version 2 in this example. This version is somewhat arbitrary, but providing a version number allows for future support for your build environment. Therefore, you should use the current version of CMake on your system.

- The second line is the `project()` command that sets the project name.

- The third line is the `add_executable()` command, which requests that an executable is to be built using the `hello.cpp` source file. The first argument to the `add_executable()` function is the name of the executable to be built, and the second argument is the source file from which to build the executable.

The Hello World project can now be built by executing the `cmake` utility, and by passing to it the directory that contains the source code and the `CMakeLists.txt` file. In this case, ". " refers to the current directory:

```
pi@erpi ~/exploringrpi/chp10/cmake $ ls
CMakeLists.txt  hello.cpp
```

```
pi@erpi ~/exploringrpi/chp10/cmake $ cmake .
-- The C compiler identification is GNU 4.6.3
-- The CXX compiler identification is GNU 4.6.3
-- Check for working C compiler: /usr/bin/cc
-- Check for working C compiler: /usr/bin/cc -- works
...
pi@erpi ~/exploringrpi/chp10/cmake $ ls
CMakeCache.txt  cmake_install.cmake  hello.cpp
CMakeFiles      CMakeLists.txt       Makefile
```

CMake identified the environment settings for the RPi Linux device and created the `Makefile` for this project. You can view the content of this file, but do not make edits to it, because any edits will be overwritten the next time that the cmake utility is executed. You can now use the make command to build the project:

```
pi@erpi ~/exploringrpi/chp10/cmake $ make
Scanning dependencies of target hello
[100%] Building CXX object CMakeFiles/hello.dir/hello.cpp.o
Linking CXX executable hello
[100%] Built target hello
pi@erpi ~/exploringrpi/chp10/cmake $ ls -l hello
-rwxr-xr-x 1 pi pi 7832 Sep 26 05:19 hello
pi@erpi ~/exploringrpi/chp10/cmake $ ./hello
Hello from the RPi!
```

This is a lot of additional effort to build a simple Hello World example, but as your project scales, this approach can be invaluable.

Building a C/C++ Library

The code that is utilized throughout this book can be grouped together and organized into a single directory structure so that you can use it within your project as a library of code. For example, selected code is organized in the library directory within the repository, as follows:

```
pi@erpi ~/exploringrpi/library $ tree .
.
├── bus
│   ├── BusDevice.cpp
│   ├── BusDevice.h
│   ├── I2CDevice.cpp
│   ├── I2CDevice.h
│   ├── SPIDevice.cpp
│   └── SPIDevice.h
├── CMakeLists.txt
├── display
│   ├── LCDCharacterDisplay.cpp
│   ├── LCDCharacterDisplay.h
│   ├── SevenSegmentDisplay.cpp
│   └── SevenSegmentDisplay.h
...
```

A build directory (which is currently empty) is used to contain the final binary library and any temporary files that are required for the build. The CMakeLists .txt file is created in the library root, as in Listing 10-12.

Listing 10-12: /library/CMakeLists.txt

```
cmake_minimum_required(VERSION 3.0.2)
project(ExploringRPi)
find_package(Threads)
set(CMAKE_BUILD_TYPE Release)

# Only available from version 2.8.9 on
set(CMAKE_POSITION_INDEPENDENT_CODE TRUE)

# Bring the headers, such as BusDevice.h into the project
include_directories(bus display gpio motor network sensor)

# The file(GLOB...) allows for wildcard additions:
file(GLOB_RECURSE SOURCES "./*.cpp")

# Can build statically to ExploringRPi.a using the next line
#add_library(ExploringRPi STATIC ${SOURCES})

# Building shared library to ExploringRPi.so using the next line
add_library(ExploringRPi SHARED ${SOURCES})

# Specify the use of the pthread library when linking the target
target_link_libraries(ExploringRPi ${CMAKE_THREAD_LIBS_INIT})

install (TARGETS ExploringRPi DESTINATION /usr/lib)
```

The important features of the CMakeLists.txt file in Listing 10-12 are as follows:

- The find_package(Threads) adds pthread support to the build.

- The set(CMAKE_BUILD_TYPE Release) function is used to set the build type. A Release build will have slightly improved execution performance. The next call to set() adds the -fPIC compile flag to the build, so that the machine code is not dependent on being located at a specific memory address, which makes it suitable for inclusion in a library.

- The include_directories() function is used to bring the header files into the build environment.

- The file() command is used to add the source files to the project. GLOB (or GLOB_RECURSE) is used to create a list of all the files that meet the globbing expression (i.e., "src/*.cpp") and add them to a variable SOURCES.

- This example uses the add_library() function. The library is built as a shared library using the SHARED flag (other options are: STATIC or MODULE), and ExploringRPi is used as the name of the shared library.

■ The last line uses the `install()` function to define an installation location for the library (in this case it is the `/usr/lib/` directory). Deployment is invoked using a call to `sudo make install` in this case.

A STATICALLY LINKED LIBRARY (.A)

A statically linked library is created at compile time to contain all the code that relates to the library; essentially, the compiler makes copies of any dependency code, including that in other libraries. This results in a library that is typically larger in size than the equivalent shared library, but because all the dependencies are determined at compile time, there are fewer runtime loading costs, and the library may be more platform independent. Unless you are certain that you require a static library, you should use a shared library, because there will be fewer code duplications and the shared library can be updated (e.g., for bug fix releases) without recompilation.

To build a static library using CMake, the steps are almost exactly the same as in Listing 10-12; however, you must use the `add_library()` line entry that uses `STATIC`, rather than the line entry that uses `SHARED`. The steps that follow will then result in the creation of a static library with a `.a` extension:

```
pi@erpi ~/exploringrpi/library/build $ ls -l *.a
-rw-r--r-- 1 pi pi 141672 Sep 26 05:50 libExploringRPi.a
pi@erpi ~/exploringrpi/library/build $ ar -t libExploringRPi.a
Servo.cpp.o
DCMotor.cpp.o
...
```

Once the `CMakeLists.txt` file has been created, the library can be built as follows:

```
pi@erpi ~/exploringrpi/library $ mkdir build
pi@erpi ~/exploringrpi/library $ cd build
pi@erpi ~/exploringrpi/library/build $ cmake ..
-- The C compiler identification is GNU 4.6.3
-- The CXX compiler identification is GNU 4.6.3
pi@erpi ~/exploringrpi/library/build $ make
Scanning dependencies of target ExploringRPi
[  5%] Building CXX object CMakeFiles/ExploringRPi.dir/motor/Servo.cpp.o
...
Linking CXX shared library libExploringRPi.so
[100%] Built target ExploringRPi
pi@erpi ~/exploringrpi/library/build $ ls -l *.so
-rwxr-xr-x 1 pi pi 103944 Sep 26 05:42 libExploringRPi.so
```

NOTE   Ensure that you have removed the libi2c-dev package before building this library code by using `sudo apt remove libi2c-dev`.

The CMakeLists.txt file also includes a deployment step, which allows you to install the library in a suitably accessible location. Shared library locations can be added to the path, or if you want to make the libraries available for all users then you can deploy them to the /usr/lib/ directory. For example, the libExploringRPi.so library can be installed for all users as follows:

```
pi@erpi ~/exploringrpi/library/build $ sudo make install
[100%] Built target ExploringRPi
Install the project...
-- Install configuration: "Release"
-- Installing: /usr/lib/libExploringRPi.so
pi@erpi ~/exploringrpi/library/build $ ls -l /usr/lib/libExploringRPi.so
-rw-r--r-- 1 root root 103944 Sep 26 05:42 /usr/lib/libExploringRPi.so
```

This step has to be performed with root access to write to the /usr/lib/ directory. You will also find a file in the build directory, called install_manifest.txt that describes the locations at which the make install command applied changes.

Using a Shared (.so) or Static (.a) Library

Once a library has been developed, the next question is how you use the library in your projects. To simplify this process, CMake can once again be used to generate the makefiles for your project.

Listing 10-13 provides the source code for a CMakeLists.txt file that can be used to build a program which links to your project library (either dynamically or statically). The libExploringRPi.so shared library is used for this example. A short C++ program is available in Listing 10-14 that utilizes the functionality of the shared library, in this case to display a message on an LCD character display. This code is provided in the directory /chp10/libexample/.

Listing 10-13: /chp10/libexample/CMakeLists.txt

```
cmake_minimum_required(VERSION 3.0.2)
project (TestERPiLibrary)

#For the shared library:
set ( PROJECT_LINK_LIBS libExploringRPi.so )
link_directories( ~/exploringrpi/library/build )

#For the static library:
#set ( PROJECT_LINK_LIBS libExploringRPi.a )
#link_directories( ~/exploringrpi/library/build )

include_directories(~/exploringrpi/library/)
add_executable(libtest libtest.cpp)
target_link_libraries(libtest ${PROJECT_LINK_LIBS} )
```

Listing 10-14: /chp10/libexample/libtest.cpp

```cpp
#include <iostream>
#include <sstream>
#include "display/LCDCharacterDisplay.h"
using namespace exploringRPi;
using namespace std;

int main() {
   cout << "Testing the ERPi library" << endl;
   SPIDevice *busDevice = new SPIDevice(0,0);
   busDevice->setSpeed(1000000);       // access to SPI Device object
   ostringstream s;                    // using to combine text and ints
   LCDCharacterDisplay display(busDevice, 20, 4); // a 20x4 display
   display.clear();                    // Clear the character LCD module
   display.home();                     // Move to the (0,0) position
   display.print("   Exploring RPi");
   cout << "End of the ERPi library test" << endl;
   return 0;
}
```

There are only two files in the project (Listing 10-13 and Listing 10-14). The library of code (libExploringRPi.so) and associated header files are assumed to be in the ~/exploringrpi/library/ directory. The following steps can be used to build the executable.

```
pi@erpi ~/exploringrpi/chp10/libexample $ ls
CMakeLists.txt   libtest.cpp
pi@erpi ~/exploringrpi/chp10/libexample $ mkdir build
pi@erpi ~/exploringrpi/chp10/libexample $ cd build
pi@erpi ~/exploringrpi/chp10/libexample/build $ cmake ..
-- The C compiler identification is GNU 4.6.3
...
pi@erpi ~/exploringrpi/chp10/libexample/build $ make
[100%] Building CXX object CMakeFiles/libtest.dir/libtest.cpp.o
Linking CXX executable libtest
[100%] Built target libtest
pi@erpi ~/exploringrpi/chp10/libexample/build $ ls -l libtest
-rwxr-xr-x 1 pi pi 10840 Sep 26 14:48 libtest
pi@erpi ~/exploringrpi/chp10/libexample/build $ ./libtest
Testing the ERPi library
End of the ERPi library test
```

It is important to note that any changes to the libtest.cpp program in Listing 10-14 will not require re-compilation of the library. Indeed, that is also true of other C/C++ files in the same project. For further information on CMake, see the www.cmake.org website. In particular, the CMake Documentation Index provides a very useful list of available commands.

Summary

After completing this chapter, you should be able to do the following:

- Interface to actuators, such as DC motors, stepper motors, and relays.
- Condition a sensor signal so that it can be interfaced to an SPI ADC, which is attached to the RPi.
- Correctly interface analog sensors such as distance sensors, temperature sensors, and accelerometers to the RPi.
- Interface to low-cost display modules such as seven-segment displays, character LCD displays, and OLED dot-matrix displays.
- Utilize makefiles and CMake to build libraries of code that can be used to build highly scalable C/C++ projects.

# CHAPTER 11

Real-Time Interfacing Using the Arduino

A key strength of Linux on embedded systems is the vast amount of software and device drivers that is freely available. Unfortunately, the overhead of running Linux is problematic for the performance of high-speed interfacing tasks—for example, generating or sampling bit patterns on general-purpose inputs/outputs (GPIOs) at high speeds. One solution to this problem is to use dedicated real-time slave processors and to communicate with them using high-level protocols. There are many suitable slave processors available, but this chapter is focused on just one platform: the Arduino. This chapter describes how the Raspberry Pi (RPi) can interface effectively to the Arduino using UART serial, I²C, and Serial Peripheral Interface (SPI) communication. Examples are provided of the Arduino in use as an input/output extender and as a dedicated high-speed slave processor.

Equipment Required for This Chapter:

- Raspberry Pi (any model)
- An Arduino Uno or equivalent[1] (with a logic-level translator) and/or an Arduino Pro Mini with 3.3V or 5V logic levels

---

[1] The majority of examples in this chapter also work on the ARM-based Arduino Due. However, AVR-based low-level calls do not work correctly (e.g., accessing the TWBR register in Listing

- Sensors: TMP36 analog temperature sensor and an HC-SR04 distance sensor

Further details on this chapter are available at `www.exploringrpi.com/chapter11/`.

The Arduino

The *Arduino* (`www.arduino.cc`) is a popular, low-cost, and powerful microcontroller that can be used as a very capable companion controller for the RPi. The Arduino platform was designed as an introductory platform for embedded systems. It is programmed using the Arduino programming language, in the Arduino development environment, which are both designed to be as user friendly as possible.

An in-depth introduction to the Arduino is beyond the scope of this book; instead, this chapter focuses on possible interactions between the Arduino and the RPi platforms. In particular, the Arduino is used to develop a framework for RPi applications that distributes high-speed embedded systems workload to slave processors, while still maintaining high-level control.

NOTE There are videos on getting started with the Arduino on the web page associated with this chapter: `www.exploringrpi.com/chapter11/`.

In addition, a comprehensive book on the Arduino is available in this Wiley miniseries, called *Exploring Arduino*, by Jeremy Blum. See `www.exploringarduino.com` for more details.

Figure 11-1 illustrates to relative scale two Arduino models. The Arduino UNO in Figure 11-1(a) is a popular version of the Arduino that contains a replaceable ATmega IC in a DIP format. The Arduino Pro Mini in Figure 11-1(b) is a smaller, lower-cost version of the same platform; however, the ATmega IC is surface mounted and cannot be easily replaced should it be accidentally damaged.

Because the Arduino is open source hardware, it is available in many different forms. However, an open hardware Arduino Pro Mini (ATmega168 or ATmega328) is chosen as the focus of this chapter for three reasons:

- A 3.3V version is available, which simplifies communication with the RPi, because no logic-level translation circuitry is required. The more commonplace 5V version is also used throughout this chapter.

- It is a low-cost, open hardware device ($5–$10) that is only 1.3"× 0.7" (33mm × 18mm) in size; therefore, you can connect several boards to a single RPi while still maintaining a modest footprint.

11-6 and 11-7). The I²C examples will work correctly if you use the default I²C baud rate of 100KHz and comment out such low-level calls. The SPI example does not work correctly with the Due, as it is dependent upon low-level AVR register access.

- There is no USB input on the board (reducing size and cost), but it can be programmed using the USB-to-Serial TTL devices that are described in Chapter 1 and Chapter 9.

- The principles described for this board can be easily adapted for any Arduino model.

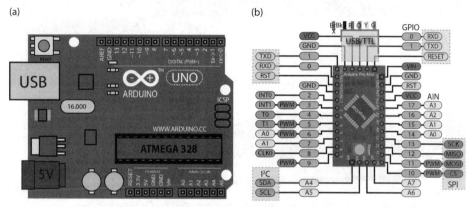

Figure 11-1: Arduino boards (to relative scale): (a) the Arduino UNO, and (b) the Arduino Pro Mini (3.3V or 5V)

WARNING   Pay special attention to voltage levels in this chapter. As discussed in Chapter 8, you have to be very careful when connecting 5V microcontrollers to the RPi inputs and outputs. Read the section in Chapter 8 on logic-level translation carefully before building the interfacing circuits in this chapter. Arduino board models can look similar but have quite different input/output configurations. If you have any doubts, measure the voltage levels on an output line before connecting it to the RPi.

Figure 11-2 illustrates the Arduino programming environment as it is used to develop a program to flash the onboard LED that is attached to Pin 13 on most Arduino boards (see Listing 11-1). The program sends the string "Hello from the Arduino" to the desktop machine when the program begins. An Arduino sketch has the extension .INO (previous versions used .PDE), but it is essentially a C++ program that is parsed by the Arduino preprocessor.

The Arduino Pro Mini can be programmed from a desktop machine by attaching a USB-to-Serial TTL cable/device as illustrated in Figure 11-2. Check the connections for your board; different models vary slightly. The same cable can be used to provide serial monitoring capabilities, which is extremely useful in debugging program code. The low-cost USB-to-Serial TTL devices described in Chapter 9 can also be used to program the Arduino from the desktop machine. In addition, several have selectable 5V/3.3V levels using

either a jumper connection or an onboard switch. Use a USB-to-Serial cable/
device that matches the logic-level voltages of your chosen Arduino.

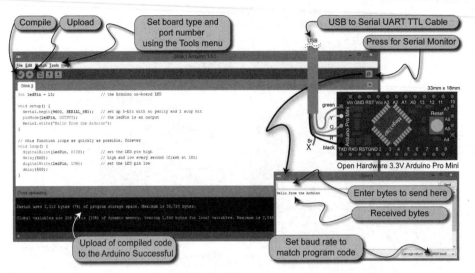

Figure 11-2: The Arduino platform "Hello World" example and the Arduino Pro Mini
programming configuration

Listing 11-1: `/chp11/hello/hello.ino`

```
int ledPin = 13;                      // the Arduino onboard LED

void setup() {                        // this function runs once on start up
  Serial.begin(9600, SERIAL_8N1);     // 8-bit, no parity and 1 stop bit
  pinMode(ledPin, OUTPUT);            // the ledPin is an output
  Serial.write("Hello from the Arduino");   // send the message once
}

void loop() {                         // function loops forever (each 1s)
  digitalWrite(ledPin, HIGH);         // set the LED pin high (LED on)
  delay(500);                         // high/low every second (1Hz flash)
  digitalWrite(ledPin, LOW);          // set the LED pin low (LED off)
  delay(500);                         // sleep for 500ms
}
```

The `setup()` function in Listing 11-1 is called once when the program is
started. It configures the serial port to use 9,600 baud (8N1 form). The program
flashes the onboard LED (attached to Pin 13) forever at a rate of 1Hz. It does this
using the `loop()` function, which repeats as fast as it possibly can. In this case,
it is programmed to sleep for 500ms when the LED is on and 500ms when the
LED is off, so each loop executes in approximately 1 second.

NOTE It is very important that you choose the correct Arduino board in the Tools menu, especially when using the Pro Mini board. If an incorrect board or frequency is chosen, the code may compile and upload correctly to the board, but the serial communication channel may appear to be corrupt.

You can open the Serial Monitor window in the Arduino development environment by pressing the button in the upper-right corner. Choose the baud rate that corresponds to that in the program code. When a string is entered in the text field and the Send button is pressed, the string is sent to the Arduino, and any response is displayed in the text area.

One method of overcoming the real-time limitations of the RPi that are discussed in earlier chapters is to outsource some of the workload to other embedded controllers, such as those provided by the Arduino, PIC, and TI Stellaris platforms. These embedded microcontrollers share common communication interfaces with the RPi that could be used for this task, including UART devices, I²C, and SPI. The following sections describe how the Arduino can be used as a slave processor to control different types of circuits and devices, and how it can be interfaced using these communications protocols. The same approaches can be used for other microcontroller families.

An Arduino Serial Slave

Using a UART connection between the RPi and an Arduino is probably the most straightforward method of establishing a slave-processor framework. As discussed in Chapter 8, UART communication has the advantage that there can be some degree of physical distance between the two devices.

WARNING   Do *not* connect a 5V Arduino to the RPi using the UART connection or you will damage your RPi. The Arduino Pro 3.3V can be connected directly to the RPi, but if you are connecting a 5V device, then be sure to use a logic-level translator or a simple voltage divider technique.

The RPi typically only has a single UART device available, but more can be added using USB-to-TTL devices (see Chapter 9). The following examples can use either the onboard UART device or a USB-to-TTL adapter. However, to use the onboard UART device you *must* stop the `serial-getty` service for the `ttyAMA0` device (or `ttyS0` for the RPi3), as described in the UART section in Chapter 8.

A UART Echo Test Example

The Arduino Pro Mini is used to test the UART communication capability of the RPi, first by using the `minicom` program and then by writing a C program to echo information to/from the Arduino. This approach is further developed to create a serial client/server command control framework.

Echoing minicom (with LED Flash)

Listing 11-2 provides an Arduino program that waits until serial data is available on the RXD pin. When it is, the LED is turned on, and a character is read in from the pin. The character is then written to the Arduino TXD pin. The program sleeps for 100ms to ensure that the LED flash is visible. The program then loops in preparation for the next character to be received on the RXD pin.

Listing 11-2: /chp11/uart/echo/echo.ino

```
int ledPin = 11;    // LED that flashes when a key is pressed

void setup() {                      // called once on start up
   // A baud rate of 115200 (8-bit with no parity and 1 stop bit)
   Serial.begin(115200, SERIAL_8N1);
   pinMode(ledPin, OUTPUT);         // the LED is an output
}

void loop() {                       // loops forever
   byte charIn;
   digitalWrite(ledPin, LOW);       // set the LED to be off
   if(Serial.available()){          // a byte has been received
      charIn = Serial.read();       // read the character in from the RPi
      Serial.write(charIn);         // send the character back to the RPi
      digitalWrite(ledPin, HIGH);   // light the LED
      delay(100);                   // delay so the LED is visible
   }
}
```

This program should be uploaded to the Arduino, where it will then execute, awaiting communication on its RXD pin. This program is stored in the EEPROM of the Arduino and will begin to execute as soon as power is applied.

WARNING The Arduino Pro Mini is a very useful board but there are many variants available. You need to manually check the voltages on the *Vin* and *Vcc* pins to verify the logic levels. For example, some 5V boards take a raw *Vin* of 5V but that level is regulated to a *Vcc* of 3.3V, and logic levels are set at 3.3V.

The next step is to disconnect the USB-to-Serial TTL cable/device and connect the Arduino to the RPi as illustrated in Figure 11-3, ensuring that the TXD pin on the RPi is connected to the RXD pin on the Arduino, and that the RXD pin on the RPi is connected to the TXD pin on the Arduino.

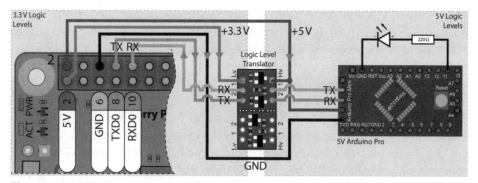

Figure 11-3: UART communication between the RPi and the Arduino UNO/Pro Mini 5V with a PWM LED example

When you are modifying the Arduino source code and uploading it to the Arduino, you should disconnect the UART connection to the RPi each time; otherwise, the process of programming the Arduino will likely fail.[2]

> **NOTE** If you are having communication problems, check carefully that you have selected the correct Arduino board type. Having the incorrect board type (e.g., wrong clock frequency) can result in consistent errors on only some character transmissions.

Once the Arduino is attached to the RPi, the next step is to open the minicom program and test the connection. The baud rate is set at 115,200 in the Arduino code, so the same setting must be passed to the minicom command. If the connection is displaying incorrect data, reduce the baud rate in the Arduino code and minicom arguments to a lower rate, such as 57,600, 19,200, or 9,600:

```
pi@erpi ~ $ minicom -b 115200 -o -D /dev/ttyAMA0
Welcome to minicom 2.7
OPTIONS: I18n
Compiled on Jan 12 2014, 05:42:53.
Port /dev/ttyAMA0, 01:09:36
Press CTRL-A Z for help on special keys
HHeelllloo  AArrdduuiinnoo
```

The characters appear twice when the minicom local echo feature is enabled—once as a result of the local key press and then again after the transmitted character is echoed by the Arduino. In addition, the LED that is connected to Arduino Pin 11 in Figure 11-3 flashes briefly each time a key is pressed.

---

[2] You can typically leave the USB-to-Serial TTL cable attached to the Arduino if you do not connect the (red) power pin from the desktop machine, but you still have to disconnect the RPi RX/TX pins before programming. There is a discussion at the end of this chapter on programming the Arduino directly from an RPi terminal.

The Analog Discovery Logic Analyzer can be connected in parallel to the TXD and RXD lines to analyze the transfer of data from the RPi to the Arduino. An example of the resulting signals is displayed in Figure 11-4(a) when only the letter H is being transmitted. The start and stop bits can be observed, along with the 8-bit data as it is sent, LSB first, from the RPi to the Arduino, at a sample bit-period of 8.7 μs. At a baud rate of 115,200, the effective byte rate will be somewhat lower due to the overhead of transmitting start, stop, and parity bits. The Arduino response delay is the time it takes for the Arduino to read the character from its RXD input and transmit it back to its TXD output. Test the voltage levels on the receive line from the Arduino before connecting it to the RPi directly, as illustrated in Figure 11-4(b).

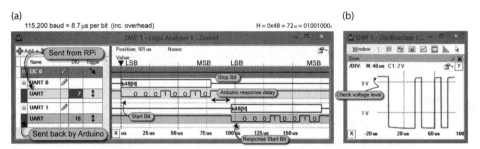

Figure 11-4: Analysis of the UART communication between the RPi and the Arduino Pro Mini: (a) the logic analyzer, and (b) the same letter H on the oscilloscope

UART Echo Example in C

The next step is to write C code on the RPi that can communicate with the Arduino program. The Arduino code in Listing 11-2 must be adapted slightly to remove the LED flash, because this slows down communication.

The C program in Listing 11-3 sends a string to the Arduino and reads the responding echo. It uses the Linux termios library (see Chapter 8), which provides a general terminal interface for the control of asynchronous communication ports. This example uses the `ttyAMA0` UART device. Adapt the source code accordingly for your chosen device (e.g., `ttyUSB0`, `ttyS0`).

Listing 11-3: /chp11/uart/echoC/echo.c

```
#include<stdio.h>
#include<fcntl.h>
#include<unistd.h>
#include<termios.h>    // using the termios.h library

int main(){
```

```
int file, count;
if ((file = open("/dev/ttyAMA0", O_RDWR | O_NOCTTY | O_NDELAY))<0) {
  perror("UART: Failed to open the file.\n");
  return -1;
}
struct termios options;        // the termios structure is vital
tcgetattr(file, &options);     // sets the parameters for the file

// Set up the communications options:
// 115200 baud, 8-bit, enable receiver, no modem control lines
options.c_cflag = B115200 | CS8 | CREAD | CLOCAL;
options.c_iflag = IGNPAR | ICRNL;   // ignore parity errors
tcflush(file, TCIFLUSH);            // discard file information
tcsetattr(file, TCSANOW, &options); // changes occur immmediately
unsigned char transmit[20] = "Hello Raspberry Pi!";  // send string
if ((count = write(file, &transmit, 20))<0){         // transmit
  perror("Failed to write to the output\n");
  return -1;
}
usleep(100000);                // give the Arduino a chance to respond
unsigned char receive[100]; // declare a buffer for receiving data
if ((count = read(file, (void*)receive, 100))<0){   //receive data
  perror("Failed to read from the input\n");
  return -1;
}
if (count==0) printf("There was no data available to read!\n");
else printf("The following was read in [%d]: %s\n",count,receive);
close(file);
return 0;
}
```

This program can be built and executed as follows, where the circuit is wired as in Figure 11-3:

```
pi@erpi ~/exploringrpi/chp11/uart/echoC $ gcc echo.c -o echo
pi@erpi ~/exploringrpi/chp11/uart/echoC $ ./echo
The following was read in [20]: Hello Raspberry Pi!
```

UART Command Control of an Arduino

The Arduino code in Listing 11-2 is adapted as shown in Listing 11-4 to create a simple LED brightness controller on the Arduino slave. The program on the Arduino expects to receive string commands from a master that have the format "LED" followed by a space, and then an integer value between 0 and 255. The integer value defines the brightness of an LED that is attached to the PWM output (Pin 11) on the Arduino. The program checks that the value is within range and issues an error if it is not. If the command string is not recognized, the Arduino program echoes it back to the sender. This program will continue to run on the Arduino forever.

Listing 11-4: /chp11/uart/command/command.ino

```
int ledPin = 11;            // LED with PWM brightness control

void setup() {              // called once on start up
   // A baud rate of 115200 (8-bit with no parity and 1 stop bit)
   Serial.begin(115200, SERIAL_8N1);
   pinMode(ledPin, OUTPUT);          // the LED is an output
}

void loop() {               // loops forever
   String command;
   char buffer[100];        // stores the return buffer on each loop
   if (Serial.available()>0){                   // bytes received
      command = Serial.readStringUntil('\0'); // C strings end with \0
      if(command.substring(0,4) == "LED "){   // begins with "LED "?
         String intString = command.substring(4, command.length());
         int level = intString.toInt();       // extract the int
         if(level>=0 && level<=255){          // is it in range?
            analogWrite(ledPin, level);       // yes, write out
            sprintf(buffer, "Set brightness to %d", level);
         }
         else{                                // no, error message back
            sprintf(buffer, "Error: %d is out of range", level);
         }
      }                                        // otherwise, unknown cmd
      else{ sprintf(buffer, "Unknown command: %s", command.c_str()); }
      Serial.print(buffer);            // send the buffer to the RPi
   }
}
```

The C program that is provided in Listing 11-5 is a general test program that sends its command-line argument over the UART connection to the Arduino. It has the same syntax as the echo example in the previous section.

Listing 11-5: /chp11/uart/command/command.c

```
#include<stdio.h>
#include<fcntl.h>
#include<unistd.h>
#include<termios.h>
#include<string.h>

int main(int argc, char *argv[]){
   int file, count;
   if(argc!=2){
      printf("Invalid number of arguments, exiting!\n");
      return -2;
   }
   if ((file = open("/dev/ttyAMA0", O_RDWR | O_NOCTTY | O_NDELAY))<0){
      perror("UART: Failed to open the file.\n");
      return -1;
   }
   struct termios options;
```

```
tcgetattr(file, &options);
options.c_cflag = B115200 | CS8 | CREAD | CLOCAL;
options.c_iflag = IGNPAR | ICRNL;
tcflush(file, TCIFLUSH);
tcsetattr(file, TCSANOW, &options);
// send the string plus the null character
if ((count = write(file, argv[1], strlen(argv[1])+1))<0){
   perror("Failed to write to the output\n");
   return -1;
}
usleep(100000);
unsigned char receive[100];
if ((count = read(file, (void*)receive, 100))<0){
   perror("Failed to read from the input\n");
   return -1;
}
if (count==0) printf("There was no data available to read!\n");
else {
   receive[count]=0;  //There is no null character sent by the Arduino
   printf("The following was read in [%d]: %s\n",count,receive);
}
close(file);
return 0;
}
```

This program can be built and executed as follows, whereupon the LED changes brightness according to the integer value supplied. In addition, the transfer of data can be observed on the logic analyzer, as in Figure 11-5:

```
pi@erpi ~/exploringrpi/chp11/uart/command $ gcc command.c -o command
pi@erpi ~/exploringrpi/chp11/uart/command $ ./command "LED 255"
The following was read in [21]: Set brightness to 255
pi@erpi ~/exploringrpi/chp11/uart/command $ ./command "LED 50"
The following was read in [20]: Set brightness to 50
pi@erpi ~/exploringrpi/chp11/uart/command $ ./command "LED 0"
The following was read in [19]: Set brightness to 0
pi@erpi ~/exploringrpi/chp11/uart/command $ ./command "LED 400"
The following was read in [26]: Error: 400 is out of range
pi@erpi ~/exploringrpi/chp11/uart/command $ ./command "rubbish"
The following was read in [24]: Unknown command: rubbish
```

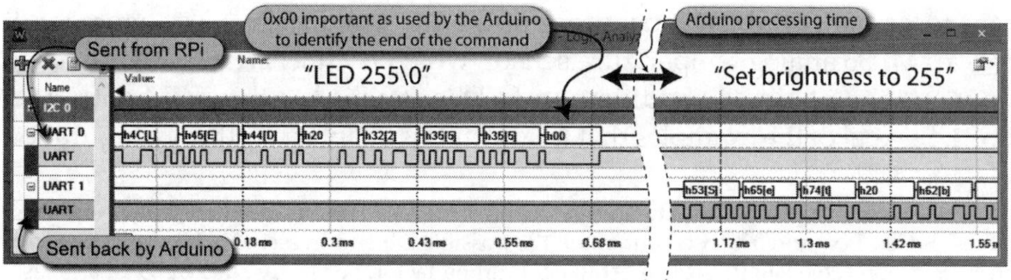

Figure 11-5: Sending the command "LED 255\0" to the Arduino and receiving the response string "Set brightness to 255"

The performance of this code could be improved by defining a list of single-byte commands and responses, to minimize data transfer time. This framework could be used to create a simple distributed embedded controller platform, and it is only limited by the number of available UART devices on the RPi.

An Arduino I²C Slave

Chapter 8 describes how digital devices, such as the ADXL345 accelerometer and a real-time clock, can be attached to the RPi using the I²C bus. It describes how you can use the bus to control these devices by reading from and writing to device registers. The Arduino can be configured as an I²C slave, which effectively allows you to create your own I²C digital sensors and controllers. This architecture is very useful for a number of reasons:

- A large number of Arduino microcontrollers can be connected to a single RPi using each of its two I²C buses.[3]
- The Arduino can be intermixed with other I²C devices on the same bus. Each Arduino can be assigned any address.
- As described in Chapter 8, there is a good framework in place for reading from and writing to I²C devices by using registers.
- Using the two-wire interface (TWI) on the Arduino allows it to perform other functions without having to explicitly check for incoming communications.

Relative to SPI or UART serial communications, one disadvantage of I²C is the maximum data rate; however, a master/slave arrangement typically performs the high-speed interfacing work on the slave device and only management commands and status information are passed between the master and the slave devices. Given these considerations, I²C communication is a strong choice for a master/slave arrangement, and is therefore the primary focus of this chapter.

An I²C Test Circuit

Figure 11-6 illustrates a test circuit that is used in several of the following sections to demonstrate the capabilities of the I²C master/slave arrangement. It uses a TMP36 analog temperature sensor, which is attached to a 10-bit analog input on the Arduino. In addition, an LED is attached to the PWM output on Pin 11. Several of the examples that follow in this chapter use this configuration

---

[3] You can connect up to 112 Arduino microcontrollers per I²C bus, as there are 16 reserved addresses (111 1xxx and 000 0xxx) out of the 128 possible 7-bit addresses (2^7). However, the total interconnection cable length is the most likely limiting factor. See tiny.cc/erpi1101. Also, remember that the second I²C bus on the RPi does not have onboard pull-up resistors, so add them as described in Chapter 8.

to demonstrate how you can read data from the temperature sensor and write a value to control the LED brightness.

NOTE   Despite warnings on logic voltage levels at the beginning of this chapter, it may be possible to connect a 5V Arduino to the I²C bus on the RPi. That is because the RPi has onboard pull-up resistors and the Arduino typically does not. This means that the high-level voltage that is used during communication is determined by the RPi, not the Arduino. However, if the Arduino (or other device) has onboard pull-up resistors, you cannot use it without bidirectional logic-level translation hardware, or the physical removal of the slave device's pull-up resistors.

A desktop PC (or the RPi itself) can be used to program the Arduino using a USB-to-TTL cable or one of the USB-to-TTL adapters described in Chapter 9. Do not connect the voltage supply pin (red) to the TTL adapter, as this configuration uses the RPi to power the Arduino. In this example, a 5V Arduino Pro Mini is utilized, but you will notice that there is no logic-level translation circuitry employed. As previously discussed, there are pull-up resistors on the first RPi I²C bus, and there are no pull-up resistors on this particular Arduino. Therefore, the Arduino can be safely attached to the RPi because the SDA and SCL lines can only be pulled high to a maximum of 3.3V. However, if the Arduino model you are using has onboard pull-up resistors, this configuration would damage your RPi; if in doubt, use a logic-level translator that is compatible with bidirectional data transfer, such as one of those described at the end of Chapter 8.

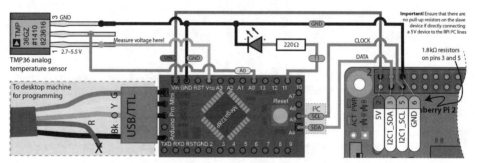

Figure 11-6: The Arduino I²C slave test circuit with a TMP36 analog temperature sensor

I²C Register Echo Example

The first example does not require the temperature sensor or LED circuit; instead, it is a test of I²C communication itself. This section uses Linux i2c-tools on the RPi to ensure that communication is taking place with the Arduino before examining a C code example.

Listing 11-6 is an Arduino sketch that configures the Arduino as a slave device using the Arduino Wire library and the two-wire interface (TWI) of the ATmega.[4] In this example, the `setup()` function explicitly sets a clock frequency that aligns with the I²C baud rate of the RPi. You can identify the RPi I²C baud rate using the following call:

```
pi@erpi ~ $ sudo cat /sys/module/i2c_bcm2708/parameters/baudrate
100000
```

The `setup()` function configures the Arduino to have the arbitrary I²C bus address of 0x44. It then registers two communication listener functions: `receiveRegister()`, which is called whenever data is written to the device using the I²C bus; and `respondData()`, which is called whenever data is read from the device. Importantly, you do not need to call these functions directly from the `loop()` function; instead, they are called automatically.

Listing 11-6: /chp11/i2c/echo/echo.ino

```
#include <Wire.h>                     // Uses the Two-Wire Interface (TWI)
const byte slaveAddr = 0x44;          // the slave address of the Arduino
int registerAddr;                     // the shared register addr variable

void setup() {                        // the setup function -- called once
  TWBR=100000L;                       // the i2c clk freq: 100000L = 100kHz
  Wire.begin(slaveAddr);              // set Arduino as an I2C slave device
  Wire.onReceive(receiveRegister);    // register receive listener below
  Wire.onRequest(respondData);        // register respond listener below
}

void loop() {
  delay(1000);                        // loop each second
}

void receiveRegister(int x){          // handler called when data available
  registerAddr = Wire.read();         // read in one-byte address from RPi
}

void respondData(){                   // handler that is called on response
  Wire.write(registerAddr);           // i.e., send the data back to the RPi
}
```

In this example, the Arduino code reads the request byte that comes from the RPi master (into the `registerAddr` variable) and writes it back as the response. This means that the Arduino echoes the address value that is requested as the response data, which is a useful first test application.

---

[4] There is a detailed description of the Arduino Wire library at `tiny.cc/erpi1102`.

When the Arduino is attached to the RPi as described in Figure 11-6 (even without the LED and temperature sensor), a call to the `i2cdump` command results in the following output:

```
pi@erpi ~ $ i2cdetect -y 1
     0  1  2  3  4  5  6  7  8  9  a  b  c  d  e  f
...
40: -- -- -- -- 44 -- -- -- -- -- -- -- -- -- -- --
...
pi@erpi ~ $ i2cdump -y 1 0x44 b
     0  1  2  3  4  5  6  7  8  9  a  b  c  d  e  f    0123456789abcdef
00: 00 01 02 03 04 05 06 07 08 09 0a 0b XX 0d 0e 0f   .??????????X???
10: 10 11 12 13 14 15 16 17 18 19 1a 1b 1c 1d 1e 1f   ????????????????
20: 20 21 22 23 24 25 26 27 28 29 2a 2b 2c 2d 2e 2f    !"#$%&'()*+,-./
30: 30 31 32 33 34 35 36 37 38 39 3a 3b 3c 3d 3e 3f   0123456789:;<=>?
40: 40 41 42 43 44 45 46 47 48 49 4a 4b 4c 4d 4e 4f   @ABCDEFGHIJKLMNO
...
f0: f0 f1 f2 f3 f4 f5 f6 f7 f8 f9 fa fb fc fd fe ff   ?????????????????.
```

You can see from this output that the Arduino program is designed to simply respond with the address that is requested. So, when the RPi requests the data at address 0x0A, the Arduino returns the data value 0x0A. This is a useful test to perform before continuing to the next section.

I²C Temperature Sensor Example

The next example uses the Arduino as an I²C slave device that wraps the TMP36 analog temperature sensor with a digital interface.

In this example, the Arduino uses its 10-bit ADC to read the analog output of the TMP36 sensor, and then calculates the temperature in degrees Celsius by using the formula that is provided in the TMP36 datasheet. The temperature is then stored in two byte values: one for the whole value part, and one for the fractional part of the temperature.

This example is similar to the TMP36 example in Chapter 10, except that all the processing is performed on the Arduino slave processor, rather than on the RPi. In fact, the Arduino also performs the conversion from degrees Celsius to degrees Fahrenheit and makes the converted value available at two further register addresses. The importance of this example is that the same approach can be applied to any analog sensor attached to the Arduino, facilitating you in building your own digital sensors.

Listing 11-7 provides the Arduino sketch that interfaces to the TMP36 analog temperature sensor that is attached to pin A0 (analog input 0) as illustrated in Figure 11-6. The Arduino calculates the temperature every 5 seconds and stores the Celsius value in bytes `data[0]` and `data[1]`, and the Fahrenheit value in bytes `data[2]` and `data[3]`. The indexes of these `data[]` values align with the register values that are requested by the RPi and returned by the `respondData()` listener function.

Listing 11-7: /chp11/i2c/i2cTMP36/i2cTMP36.ino

```
#include <Wire.h>                    // uses the Two-Wire Interface (TWI)
const byte slaveAddr = 0x44;         // the slave address of the Arduino
int registerAddr;                    // the shared register addr variable
const int analogInPin = A0;          // analog input for the TMP36
int data[4];                         // the data registers 0x00 to 0x03

void setup(){
  TWBR=100000L;                      // set the i2c clk freq e.g. 100000L
  Wire.begin(slaveAddr);             // set up the Arduino as an I2C slave
  Wire.onReceive(receiveRegister);   // register receive listener below
  Wire.onRequest(respondData);       // register respond listener below
}

void loop(){                         // update registers every five seconds
  int adcValue = analogRead(analogInPin);       // using a 10-bit ADC
  float curVoltage = adcValue * (5.0f/1024.0f);  // Vcc = 5.0V, 10-bit
  float tempC = 25.0 + ((curVoltage-0.75f)/0.01f); // from datasheet
  float tempF = 32.0 + ((tempC * 9)/5);          // deg. C to F
  data[0] = (int) tempC;                         // whole deg C (0x00)
  data[1] = (int) ((tempC - data[0])*100);       // fract C     (0x01)
  data[2] = (int) tempF;                         // whole deg F (0x02)
  data[3] = (int) ((tempF - data[2])*100);       // fract F     (0x03)
  delay(5000);                                   // delay 5 seconds
}

void receiveRegister(int x){         // passes the number of bytes
  registerAddr = Wire.read();        // read in the one-byte address
}

void respondData(){                  // respond function
  byte dataValue = 0x00;             // default response value is 0x00
  if ((registerAddr >= 0x00) && (registerAddr <0x04)){
    dataValue = data[registerAddr];
  }
  Wire.write(dataValue);             // send the data back to the RPi
}
```

Note that the two listener functions act independently of the `loop()` function, only called upon when the RPi makes a request. In other words, the `loop()` function does not need to explicitly check for a data request on each iteration, which was necessary in the UART example.

Once the code is compiled and deployed to the Arduino, you can then use the `i2cdump` command to view the register values:

```
pi@erpi ~ $ i2cdump -y 1 0x44 b
     0  1  2  3  4  5  6  7  8  9  a  b  c  d  e  f    0123456789abcdef
00: 17 49 4a 47 00 00 00 00 00 00 00 00 00 00 00 00    ?IJG............
```

```
10: 00 00 00 00 00 00 00 00 00 00 00 00 00 00 00 00      ................
...
pi@erpi ~ $ i2cget -y 1 0x44 0x00 b
0x17
pi@erpi ~ $ i2cget -y 1 0x44 0x01 b
0x49
```

The values are in hexadecimal form; therefore, the temperature value in this example is $23.73°C_{10}$ (i.e., $17.49°C_{16}$), which is $74.71°F_{10}$ (i.e., $4A.47°F_{16}$) as displayed in the i2cdump output at addresses 0×02 and 0×03.

I²C Temperature Sensor with a Warning LED

The next example builds on the previous example with the addition of a warning LED that lights when the room temperature exceeds a user-defined threshold. The importance of this example is that it demonstrates how you can send data to the Arduino from the RPi—in effect, by writing a value to a register on the I²C device. Figure 11-6 illustrates the warning LED circuit for this example.

From the perspective of the RPi, the whole-number alert threshold value is stored at address 0x04 on the Arduino. For example, if the value 0x20 is written to the address 0x04, then the warning LED will remain off unless the temperature exceeds 0x20 = 32°C. This value is appropriate for testing, as you can achieve this temperature by holding the TMP36 sensor with your fingers.

Listing 11-8 is the Arduino sketch required to read the alert threshold value from the RPi and to store it in the byte data[4]. The receiveRegister(int x) listener function checks to see if the RPi is accessing register 0x04 and if exactly two bytes of data have been passed (i.e., the address and value). If so, then the second byte (the value) that is passed is stored in data[4]. The example also contains some commented-out code to write to the Arduino serial console. You can enable these lines of code to help you in debugging any changes.

Listing 11-8: /chp11/i2c/i2cTMP36warn/i2cTMP36warn.ino

```
#include <Wire.h>                // uses the Two-Wire Interface (TWI)
const byte slaveAddr = 0x44;     // the slave address of the Arduino
int registerAddr;                // the shared register address variable
const int analogInPin = A0;      // analog input pin for the TMP36
int data[5];                     // the data registers 0x00 to 0x04
int alertTemp = 0xFF;            // alert temperature not set by default
int ledPin = 11;                 // the warning light LED

void setup(){
  pinMode(ledPin, OUTPUT);       // LED provides a visible temp alert
  TWBR=100000L;                  // set the i2c clk freq e.g. 400000L
  Wire.begin(slaveAddr);         // set up the Arduino as an I2C slave
  Wire.onReceive(receiveRegister); // register receive listener below
  Wire.onRequest(respondData);   // register respond listener below
  //Serial.begin(115200, SERIAL_8N1);  // remove for debug
}
```

```
void loop(){                                // update registers every five seconds
  int adcValue = analogRead(analogInPin);   // using a 10-bit ADC
  //Serial.print("\nThe ADC value is: ");   // remove for debug
  //Serial.print(adcValue);                 // remove for debug
  float curVoltage = adcValue * (3.3f/1024.0f);   // Vcc = 3.3V, 10-bit
  float tempC = 25.0 + ((curVoltage-0.75f)/0.01f);   // from datasheet
  float tempF = 32.0 + ((tempC * 9)/5);     // deg. C to deg. F
  data[0] = (int) tempC;                    // whole deg C (0x00)
  data[1] = (int) ((tempC - data[0])*100);  // fract deg C (0x01)
  data[2] = (int) tempF;                    // whole deg F (0x02)
  data[3] = (int) ((tempF - data[2])*100);  // fract deg F (0x03)
  data[4] = alertTemp;                      // alert tmp C (0x04)
  if (tempC > alertTemp) {                  // test alert?
     digitalWrite(ledPin, HIGH);            // yes, set LED on
  }
  else {
     digitalWrite(ledPin, LOW);             // else LED off
  }
  delay(5000);
}

void receiveRegister(int x){      // passes the number of bytes
  registerAddr = Wire.read();     // read in the one-byte address
  if(registerAddr==0x04 && x==2){ // if writing the alert value
    alertTemp = Wire.read();      // read in the alert temperature
  }
}

void respondData(){               // respond function
  byte dataValue = 0x00;          // default response value is 0x00
  if ((registerAddr >= 0x00) && (registerAddr <= 0x04)){
    dataValue = data[registerAddr];
  }
  Wire.write(dataValue);          // send the data back to the RPi
}
```

Once this program is uploaded to the Arduino the Linux i2c-tools can be used to query the registers. You can see a fifth register at 0x04, which has the initial value of 0xFF:

```
pi@erpi ~ $ i2cdump -y 1 0x44 b
    0  1  2  3  4  5  6  7  8  9  a  b  c  d  e  f    0123456789abcdef
00: 1b 3f 51 4a ff 00 00 00 00 00 00 00 00 00 00 00    ??QJ?..........
...
```

You can alter this value using the i2cset command, as follows:

```
pi@erpi ~ $ i2cget -y 1 0x44 0x04
0xff
pi@erpi ~ $ i2cset -y 1 0x44 0x04 0x20
pi@erpi ~ $ i2cget -y 1 0x44 0x04
0x20
```

These transactions are captured by the logic analyzer in Figure 11-7. In my case, the LED is currently off because the room temperature is approximately

27°C; however, once the sensor is pinched between my fingers, the temperature quickly rises above 32°C (0x20) and the warning LED turns on.

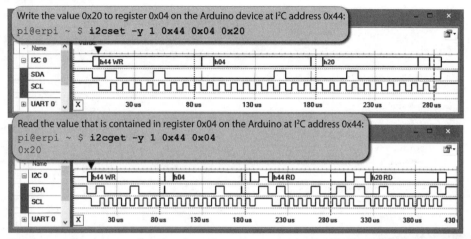

Figure 11-7: Writing to and reading from the 0x04 register that has been created on the Arduino

Importantly, the code in the `loop()` function continues completely independently of the RPi. For example, it can take a few seconds for the LED to turn on or off after a new temperature threshold is set. That is because the main loop in the Arduino code has a 5-second delay between readings, and the threshold comparison takes place at the end of the loop. It is important that you keep the listener functions (i.e., `receiveRegister()` and `respondData()`) as short as possible, because otherwise I²C communication may be somewhat unresponsive.

Arduino Slave Communication Using C/C++

C/C++ code examples for reading from and writing to I²C devices are presented in Chapter 8, but another example is provided here for completeness. Listing 11-9 is a C program for reading from and/or writing to the Arduino slave device.

Listing 11-9: chp11/i2c/i2cTMP36/i2cTMP36.c

```c
#include<stdio.h>
#include<fcntl.h>
#include<sys/ioctl.h>
#include<linux/i2c.h>
#include<linux/i2c-dev.h>
#define BUFFER_SIZE 5        //0x00 to 0x04

int main(int argc, char **argv){
    int file, i, alert=0xFF;
    // check if alert temperature argument passed
    if(argc==2){            // convert argument string to int value
```

```c
        if (sscanf(argv[1],"%i",&alert)!=1) {
            perror("Failed to read the alert temperature\n");
            return 1;
        }
        if (alert>255 || alert<0) {
            perror("Alert temperature is outside of range\n");
            return 1;
        }
    }
    if((file=open("/dev/i2c-1", O_RDWR)) < 0){
        perror("failed to open the bus\n");
        return 1;
    }
    if(ioctl(file, I2C_SLAVE, 0x44) < 0){
        perror("Failed to connect to the Arduino\n");
        return 1;
    }
    char rec[BUFFER_SIZE], send;
    for(i=0; i<BUFFER_SIZE; i++){          // sending char by char
      send = (char) i;
      if(write(file, &send, 1)!=1){
          perror("Failed to request a register\n");
          return 1;
      }
      if(read(file, &rec[i], 1)!=1){
          perror("Failed to read in the data\n");
          return 1;
      }
    }
    printf("The temperature is %d.%d°C", rec[0], rec[1]);
    printf(" which is %d.%d°F\n", rec[2], rec[3]);
    printf("The alert temperature is %d°C\n", rec[4]);

    if(alert!=0xFF) {
      char alertbuf[] = {0x04, 0};        // writing alert to 0x04
      alertbuf[1] = (char) alert;         // value read as argument
      printf("Setting alert temperature to %d°C\n", alert);
      if(write(file, alertbuf, 2)!=2){
          perror("Failed to set the alert temperature!\n");
          return 1;
      }
    }
    close(file);
    return 0;
}
```

This program can be built and executed as follows:

```
pi@erpi ~/exploringrpi/chp11/i2c/i2cTMP36warn $ gcc i2cTMP36.c -o i2cTMP36
pi@erpi ~/exploringrpi/chp11/i2c/i2cTMP36warn $ ./i2cTMP36
The temperature is 17.67°C which is 63.81°F
The alert temperature is 30°C
```

```
pi@erpi ~/exploringrpi/chp11/i2c/i2cTMP36warn $ ./i2cTMP36 40
The temperature is 17.67°C which is 63.81°F
The alert temperature is 30°C
Setting alert temperature to 40°C
pi@erpi ~/exploringrpi/chp11/i2c/i2cTMP36warn $ ./i2cTMP36
The temperature is 17.67°C which is 63.81°F
The alert temperature is 40°C
```

When an argument is provided, the program converts the value from a string to an integer and writes it to the register 0x04 on the Arduino using the I²C bus. This value then becomes the alert threshold temperature that triggers the LED to light should it be exceeded. If no argument is provided, the program displays the properly formatted current state of the Arduino slave device.

An I²C Ultrasonic Sensor Application

The HC-SR04 is a very low-cost ($2) ultrasonic sensor that you can use to determine the distance to an obstacle using the speed of sound. The sensor has a range of approximately 1″ (2.5cm) to 13′ (4m). Unlike the IR distance sensor that is used in Chapter 10, it is not affected by sunlight, but it does not perform well with soft materials that do not reflect sound well (e.g., clothing and soft furnishings). Figure 11-8 illustrates how this sensor can be connected to the RPi via an Arduino UNO. The use of the Arduino UNO is purely illustrative, and a 5V Arduino PRO mini can equivalently be used.

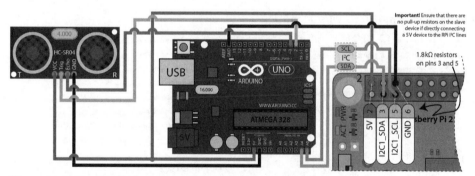

Figure 11-8: The HC-SR04 ultrasonic distance sensor circuit

Figure 11-9 illustrates how interaction takes place with this sensor. A 10µs trigger pulse is sent to the Trig input of the sensor; the sensor then responds on its Echo output with a pulse that has a width that corresponds to the distance of an obstacle (approximately 150µs to 25ms, or 38ms if no obstacle is in range). The maximum number of samples per second is approximately 20 for a single sensor.

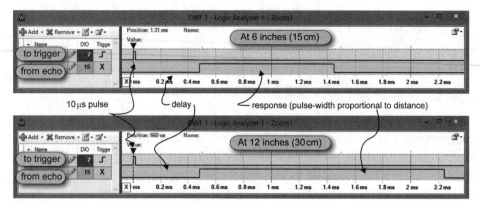

Figure 11-9: The signal response of the HC-SR04

It is possible, but difficult to get accurate results directly from Linux user space using regular GPIOs with this sensor. There are UART versions of this sensor that contain a microcontroller, but they are much more expensive. The solution that is presented here is fast enough to allow you to connect several such sensors to a single Arduino—a single trigger signal could be sent to many sensors simultaneously, and different Arduino GPIOs could be used to measure the response signals from each sensor. Listing 11-10 is the Arduino code for this example. The code builds on Listing 11-8 with code to generate the trigger pulse and read the width of the echo pulse response.

Listing 11-10: /chp11/i2c/sr04/sr04.ino

```
#include <Wire.h>                       // uses the Two-Wire Interface (TWI)
const byte slaveAddr = 0x55;            // the slave address of the Arduino
int registerAddr;                       // the shared register addr variable
int triggerPin = 2;                     // connected to trig
int echoPin = 3;                        // connected to echo
int ledPin = 13;                        // the onboard LED
byte data[4];                           // the data registers 0x00 to 0x03

void setup() {
    // Serial.begin(115200);            // for debugging
    pinMode(triggerPin, OUTPUT);        // the pin to send a 10us pulse
    pinMode(echoPin, INPUT);            // the response pin to measure
    pinMode(ledPin, OUTPUT);            // the onboard LED indicator
    TWBR=100000L;                       // set the i2c clk freq e.g., 100000L
    Wire.begin(slaveAddr);              // set up the Arduino as an I2C slave
    Wire.onReceive(receiveRegister);    // register receive listener below
    Wire.onRequest(respondData);        // register respond listener below
}

void loop() {                           // loop 20 times per second
    int duration;                       // the response pulse width
    float distancecm, distancein;       // the converted value
```

```
    digitalWrite(triggerPin, HIGH);     // send the 10us pulse
    delayMicroseconds(10);
    digitalWrite(triggerPin, LOW);
    duration = pulseIn(echoPin, HIGH);  // measure response pulse (in us)

    distancecm = (float) duration / 58.0;   // time converted to cm
    data[0] = (int) distancecm;              // whole part (0x00)
    data[1] = (int) ((distancecm - data[0])*100); // fract part (0x01)
    distancein = (float) duration / 148.0;   // time converted to in
    data[2] = (int) distancein;              // whole part (0x02)
    data[3] = (int) ((distancein - data[2])*100); // fract part (0x03)

    // code that can be added for debugging the program
    // Serial.print(distancecm);  Serial.println(" cm");
    // Serial.print(distancein);  Serial.println(" inches");
    digitalWrite(ledPin, LOW);          // LED off
    delay(50);                          // 20 samples per second
    digitalWrite(ledPin, HIGH);         // give a slight flash
}

void receiveRegister(int x){        // passes the number of bytes
    registerAddr = Wire.read();     // read in the one-byte address
}

void respondData(){                 // respond function
    byte dataValue = 0x00;          // default response value is 0x00
    if ((registerAddr >= 0x00) && (registerAddr <0x04)){
        dataValue = data[registerAddr];
    }
    Wire.write(dataValue);          // send the data back to the RPi
}
```

Once this program is built and uploaded to the Arduino, it can be tested from the RPi using the following calls:

```
pi@erpi ~ $ i2cdetect -y 1
     0  1  2  3  4  5  6  7  8  9  a  b  c  d  e  f
...
50: -- -- -- -- -- 55 -- -- -- -- -- -- -- -- -- --
...
pi@erpi ~ $ i2cdump -y 1 0x55 b
     0  1  2  3  4  5  6  7  8  9  a  b  c  d  e  f    0123456789abcdef
00: 0a 1b 04 02 00 00 00 00 00 00 00 00 00 00 00 00    ????............
...
```

With a one-line script you can find the decimal value represented by these registers using the following calls. (Ensure that you use a ` rather than a ' in wrapping the i2cget call; it is often on the keyboard directly below Esc.)

```
pi@erpi ~ $ printf "Distance is %d.%02d cm\n" `i2cget -y 1 0x55 0x00` →
 `i2cget -y 1 0x55 0x01`
Distance is 10.27 cm
pi@erpi ~ $ printf "Distance is %d.%02d inches\n" `i2cget -y 1 0x55 0x02` →
 `i2cget -y 1 0x55 0x03`
Distance is 4.02 inches
```

The C program in Listing 11-9 can be adapted to read the register values for the HC-SR04 Arduino program. Such a program would easily be able to communicate with the RPi over I^{2}C and read the calculated register values at the maximum rate possible for the sensor (a rate of ~20Hz).

An Arduino SPI Slave

A third way of interfacing the RPi with the Arduino is by using it as an SPI slave. This method of interfacing can be used for applications that require very fast high-level interaction between the RPi and the Arduino, as communication is only limited by the clock frequency of the Arduino (e.g., typically 8MHz or 16MHz). A 3.3V Arduino can be connected to the RPi as illustrated in Figure 11-10. Note that logic-level translation hardware is required if you are interfacing to a 5V Arduino using SPI.

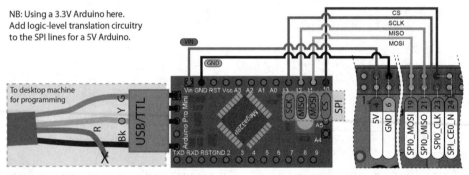

Figure 11-10: The Arduino as an SPI slave

The Arduino has strong support for applications in which it is the SPI master, but it does not have the same level of support for applications in which it acts as an SPI slave. Low-level operations are required, and therefore this approach is best avoided, particularly if an I^{2}C approach will suffice. For completeness, a code example is provided in Listing 11-11 that establishes the Arduino as an SPI slave device.

Listing 11-11: /chp11/spi/spi.ino

```
// Based on example code that is provided by Nick Gammon
// See: http://www.gammon.com.au/ for further details
#include <SPI.h>
#define MISO 12
volatile int count, lastcount;

void setup () {
   Serial.begin (115200);       // for serial output debug
```

```
    SPCR |= _BV(SPE);              // turn on SPI in slave mode
    pinMode(MISO, OUTPUT);        // Send on the MISO line
    SPI.setClockDivider(SPI_CLOCK_DIV16);   // A 1 MHz clock
    SPI.attachInterrupt();        // now turn on interrupts
    Serial.println("Setup complete");   // debug message
}

void loop() {
  if (count>lastcount) {         // demonstrate data sharing
    Serial.print("Count is now: ");
    Serial.println(count);       // use the serial console for debug
    //SPI.transfer(count);       // only if reading back values
    lastcount=count;             // get ready for the next increment loop
  }
}

ISR (SPI_STC_vect) {             // The SPI interrupt routine
  Serial.print("ISR invoked: Received (int)");
  byte c = SPDR;                 // get a byte from the SPI Data Register
  Serial.println((int)c);        // print out the integer equivalent value
  count++;
  Serial.println("End of ISR");
}
```

Once the code has been uploaded to the Arduino and the circuit constructed as in Figure 11-10, the connection can be tested using the following calls:

```
pi@erpi ~ $ echo -ne "\x41\x01" > /dev/spidev0.0
pi@erpi ~ $ echo -ne "\x41\x02" > /dev/spidev0.0
pi@erpi ~ $ echo -ne "\x41\x03" > /dev/spidev0.0
```

Where the Arduino Serial Console displays the following output:

```
Setup complete
ISR invoked: Received (int)1
End of ISR
Count is now: 1
ISR invoked: Received (int)2
End of ISR
Count is now: 2
ISR invoked: Received (int)3
End of ISR
Count is now: 3
```

This output demonstrates that data values are being passed from the RPi terminal shell to the Arduino SPI slave. Note that the leading byte is simply ignored in this code example.

Finally, Listing 11-12 is a short C example program that demonstrates how you can send data to the Arduino SPI slave using the wiringPi library.

Listing 11-12: /chp11/spi/spi.c

```
#include <stdio.h>
#include <wiringPiSPI.h>
```

```
int main() {
    char data[2] = {0, 99};
    wiringPiSPISetupMode(0, 1000000, 0);
    wiringPiSPIDataRW (0, data, 2) ;
    printf("Transaction complete...\n");
    return 0;
}
```

The code can be built and executed on the RPi using the following:

```
pi@erpi ~/exploringrpi/chp11/spi $ gcc spi.c -o spi -lwiringPi
pi@erpi ~/exploringrpi/chp11/spi $ ./spi
Transaction complete...
```

Execution results in the following display on the Arduino Serial Console:

```
Setup complete
ISR invoked: Received (int)99
End of ISR
Count is now: 1
```

The integer value 99 is passed successfully from the C program to the Arduino SPI slave device.

Programming the Arduino from the RPi Command Line

The Arduino can be programmed directly from the RPi with the Arduino development environment (illustrated in Figure 11-2) by using an attached display or a virtual network connection (see Chapter 14). However, it would also be useful to be able to build Arduino programs at the shell terminal and deploy them directly to the Arduino. For example, this facility would allow you to do the following:

- Remotely connect to the RPi using only a Secure Shell (SSH) terminal and remotely alter the behavior of an Arduino that is attached to the RPi via a UART connection
- Dynamically change the behavior of an Arduino during the day. For example, the Arduino might have one dedicated task in the morning and could be programmed dynamically to take on another task in the evening (see cron jobs in Chapter 12).

It is indeed possible to program an Arduino that is attached to the RPi by using a command-line interface (CLI) with the following steps:

1. First install the full suite of Arduino tools on the RPi:

```
pi@erpi ~ $ sudo apt install gcc-avr avr-libc avrdude arduino
Reading package lists... Done
```

2. You can then install a make script that has been written by Tim Marston (www.ed.am/about), which you can download from his website:

```
pi@erpi ~ $ mkdir arduino
pi@erpi ~ $ cd arduino/
pi@erpi ~/arduino $ wget http://ed.am/dev/make/arduino-mk/arduino.mk
...
pi@erpi ~/arduino $ ls -l
-rw-r--r-- 1 pi pi 16835 Mar  4  2013 arduino.mk
```

3. You need to rename the script to be a Makefile and you can use the `blink` `.ino` example from the code repository. The example blinks the onboard LED at 10Hz to make it obvious that these steps have worked correctly:

```
pi@erpi ~/arduino $ ln -s arduino.mk Makefile
pi@erpi ~/arduino $ cp ~/exploringrpi/chp11/cli/blink.ino .
pi@erpi ~/arduino $ ls -l
total 24
-rw-r--r-- 1 pi pi 16835 Mar  4  2013 arduino.mk
-rw-r--r-- 1 pi pi   401 Oct  6 01:24 blink.ino
lrwxrwxrwx 1 pi pi    10 Oct  6 01:23 Makefile -> arduino.mk
```

4. Identify the set of available boards:

```
pi@erpi ~/arduino $ make boards
Available values for BOARD:
uno          Arduino Uno
...
pro5v328     Arduino Pro or Pro Mini (5V, 16 MHz) w/ ATmega328
pro5v        Arduino Pro or Pro Mini (5V, 16 MHz) w/ ATmega168
pro328       Arduino Pro or Pro Mini (3.3V, 8 MHz) w/ ATmega328
pro          Arduino Pro or Pro Mini (3.3V, 8 MHz) w/ ATmega168
```

5. Set the environment variables for the build and then invoke the `make` command:

```
pi@erpi ~/arduino $ export BOARD=pro5v
pi@erpi ~/arduino $ export ARDUINODIR=/usr/share/arduino
pi@erpi ~/arduino $ export SERIALDEV=/dev/ttyUSB0
pi@erpi ~/arduino $ make
...
pi@erpi ~/arduino $ ls
arduino.mk  blink.hex  blink.ino  blink.o  Makefile
```

6. You can then upload the Arduino binary code in the `blink.hex` file to the Arduino as follows:[5]

```
pi@erpi ~/arduino $ make upload
Uploading to board...
stty -F /dev/ttyUSB0 hupcl
/usr/bin/avrdude  -DV -p atmega168 -P /dev/ttyUSB0 -c arduino -b 19200 -U
flash:w:blink.hex:i
```

---

[5] You may have to press the reset button to place the device in programming mode. This step could be automated by gating the reset input (see Figure 11-1) on the Arduino using a FET that is attached to an RPi GPIO.

```
avrdude: AVR device initialized and ready to accept instructions
Reading | ############################################### | 100% 0.01s
avrdude: Device signature = 0x1e9406
avrdude: reading input file "blink.hex"
avrdude: writing flash (1018 bytes):
Writing | ############################################### | 100% 0.69s
avrdude: 1018 bytes of flash written
avrdude: safemode: Fuses OK (E:00, H:00, L:00)
avrdude done.  Thank you.
```

For full details on the make script, see `www.ed.am/dev/make/arduino-mk`.

Summary

After completing this chapter, you should be able to do the following:

- Interface the RPi to the Arduino using a UART serial connection to create a master/slave communications framework.

- Interface the RPi to the Arduino using the I²C bus and use a register-based framework to read and write values to/from the Arduino.

- Build high-speed, real-time interfacing application examples that utilize the I²C register-based framework.

- Use SPI to create a simple communications framework between the RPi and a slave Arduino.

- Program an Arduino using an RPi command-line interface.

Part
III

Advanced Interfacing and Interaction

In This Part

The Internet of Things

This chapter describes how the Raspberry Pi can be used as a core building block of the Internet of Things (IoT). In this chapter, you are introduced to the concepts of network programming, the IoT, and the connection of sensors to the Internet. Several different communications architectures are described: The first architecture configures the RPi to be a web server that uses various server-side scripting techniques to display sensor data. Next, custom C/C++ code is described that can push sensor data to the Internet and to platform as a service (PaaS) offerings, such as ThingSpeak and the IBM Bluemix IoT service (using MQTT). Finally, a client/server pair for high-speed Transmission Control Protocol (TCP) socket communication is described. The latter part of the chapter introduces some techniques for managing distributed RPi sensors, and physical networking topics: setting the RPi to have a static IP address; and using Power over Ethernet (PoE) with the RPi. By the end of this chapter, you should be able to build your own full-stack IoT devices.

Equipment Required for This Chapter:

- Raspberry Pi (any model with an Internet connection)
- Sensors: temperature sensor (optional)

Further details on this chapter are available at www.exploringrpi.com/chapter12/.

The Internet of Things (IoT)

The terms *Internet of Things* (IoT) and *cyber-physical systems* (CPS) are broadly used to describe the extension of the web and the Internet into the physical realm, by the connection of distributed embedded devices. Presently, the Internet is largely an internet of people; the IoT concept envisions that if physical sensors and actuators can be linked to the Internet, then a whole new range of applications and services are possible. For example, if sensors in a home environment could communicate with each other and the Internet, they could be "smart" about how they function—a home heating system that could retrieve the weather forecast may be more efficient and could provide a more comfortable environment. Within smart homes, IoT devices should be able to automate laborious tasks; manage security; and improve energy efficiency, accessibility, and convenience. However, the IoT also has broad application to many large-scale industries, such as energy management, healthcare, transport, and logistics.

In Chapter 10, interaction with the physical environment is discussed in detail. When the physical world can be acted upon by devices that are attached to the Internet, such as actuators, the devices are often called CPS. The terms IoT and CPS are often used interchangeably, with certain industries such as smart manufacturing favoring the term CPS. However, it is not unreasonable to consider a CPS to be a constituent building block, which when combined with web sensors and large-scale communications frameworks forms the IoT.

In this chapter, the implementation of several software communication architectures that can be used to realize IoT or CPS is described. Figure 12-1 illustrates a summary of the different communication architectures that are implemented in this chapter.

Each of the architectures in Figure 12-1 has a different structure, and each can be applied to different communications applications:

1. **The RPi web server:** An RPi that is connected to a sensor and running a web server can be used to present information to the web when it is requested to do so by a web browser. Communications take place using the Hypertext Transfer Protocol (HTTP).

2. **The RPi web client:** An RPi can initiate contact with a web server using HTTP requests to send and receive data. A C/C++ program is written that uses TCP sockets to build a basic web browser, which can communicate over HTTP, or if necessary, securely over secure HTTP (HTTPS).

3. **The RPi TCP client/server:** A custom C++ client and server are presented that can intercommunicate at high speeds with a user-defined communications protocol.

4. **The RPi web sensor using a PaaS:** Code is written to enable the RPi to use HTTP and MQTT to send data to, and receive data from, web services

such as ThingSpeak and IBM Bluemix IoT. This code enables you to build large arrays of sensors that can intercommunicate and store data on remote servers. In addition, these web services can be used to visualize the data that is stored.

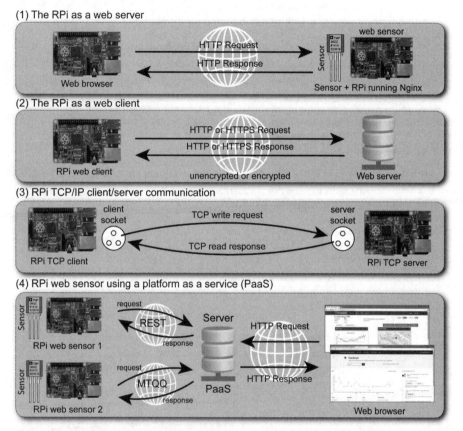

Figure 12-1: Different software communication architectures implemented in this chapter

Before examining these communication architectures, you need a *thing* to connect to the Internet, for which you can use any sensor from earlier in the book, and/or the RPi itself.

The RPi as an IoT Sensor

This book is filled with examples of sensors and actuators that you can use to create *things*. For example, the RPi can be turned into a *thing* by attaching a TMP36 temperature sensor (see Chapter 9) or the DHT temperature and humidity sensor (see Chapter 6). However, for simplicity the CPU temperature sensor on board the RPi is used primarily as the IoT sensor in this chapter.

You can read the current RPi CPU temperature and GPU temperature as follows:

```
pi@erpi ~ $ cat /sys/class/thermal/thermal_zone0/temp
35780
pi@erpi ~ $ /opt/vc/bin/vcgencmd measure_temp
temp=35.2'C
```

The CPU temperature value is a floating-point value that is scaled by 1000 and returned as an integer value; the value above is actually 35.78°C (96.4°F). Out of interest, you can format this value correctly, directly at the Linux shell prompt, using the awk command:

```
pi@erpi ~ $ awk '{printf("CPU temperature: %2.2f Celsius\n", $1/1000)}' →
 /sys/class/thermal/thermal_zone0/temp
CPU temperature: 35.78 Celsius
```

The Linux device driver for the CPU temperature sensor on the RPi also includes a trip point that can detect a critical over-temperature condition. You can see the properties of the device as follows:

```
pi@erpi ~ $ cd /sys/class/thermal/thermal_zone0
pi@erpi /sys/class/thermal/thermal_zone0 $ ls
mode     policy      temp                  trip_point_0_type   uevent
passive  subsystem  trip_point_0_temp  type
pi@erpi /sys/class/thermal/thermal_zone0 $ cat trip_point_0_type
hot
pi@erpi /sys/class/thermal/thermal_zone0 $ cat trip_point_0_temp
85000
```

It is unlikely that this point will be reached under normal operating condition as, in line with most modern microprocessors, the CPU frequency is lowered automatically should the temperature rise excessively.

ARE LOW-COST RPI CPU HEATSINKS USEFUL?

There are many low-cost RPi CPU heatsinks available, and several use unbranded thermal bonding adhesives. A test was performed to evaluate the benefits of adding a heatsink such as the one in Figure 12-2(a), which uses high-quality 3M bonding adhesive. A short script is used for the test (the gnuplot script is also provided in the same directory):

```
pi@erpi ~/exploringrpi/chp12/thermal $ more record_temp.sh
#!/bin/bash
TEMPERATURE="/sys/class/thermal/thermal_zone0/temp"
```

```
COUNT=0
echo "#Temperature Recordings" > data
# bash while loop
while [ $COUNT -lt 40 ]; do
    echo $COUNT " " `cat $TEMPERATURE` >> data
    let COUNT=COUNT+1
    sleep 10
done
```

The test was performed at a room temperature of approximately 24°C (75°F) and an RPi 2 that is overclocked at 1 GHz is used (with a performance governor). A single CPU load is provided by running the software performance test in Chapter 5, using the /chp05/performance/run script. The temperature sensor readings are captured over 400 seconds and displayed in Figure 12-2(b). It is clear that the heatsink reduces the CPU temperature by approximately 2°C, whether the RPi 2 is, or is not, under load. The thermal trip point is 85°C, so it is hardly worth the effort of attaching the heatsink. However, if the RPi is placed in a case then this temperature rises rapidly. For example, the case configuration in Figure 1-10(a) (with a heatsink) causes the unburdened CPU temperature to rise to 40°C; a well-ventilated case is likely more important than a heatsink!

(a)   (b)

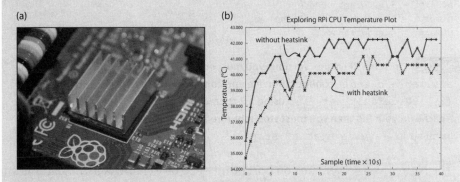

Figure 12-2: (a) A low-cost heatsink, and (b) the temperature plot from a CPU load test with and without a heatsink attached

The RPi as a Sensor Web Server

One significant advantage of an embedded Linux device over more traditional embedded systems is the vast amount of open source software that is available. In this section, a web server is installed and configured on the RPi. It is a straightforward process compared to the steps involved for a typical non-Linux embedded platform. In fact, one of the more difficult challenges is choosing which Linux web server to use! There are low-overhead servers available such as lighttpd, Boa, Monkey, and Nginx, and there are full-featured web servers such as the popular Apache server.

The Nginx web server is a lightweight server that has an overhead that is suitable for running on the RPi. Running a web server on the RPi provides you with a number of application possibilities, including the following:

- Present general web content to the world.
- Integrate sensors and display their values to the world.
- Integrate sensors and use it to intercommunicate between devices.
- Provide web-based interfaces to tools that are running on the RPi.

Nginx

The Nginx server is currently available through the Raspbian distribution. You can use the following commands to install it:

```
pi@erpi ~ $ sudo apt update
pi@erpi ~ $ sudo apt install nginx
pi@erpi ~ $ sudo reboot
```

> **NOTE** On some RPi Nginx versions you must edit the `/etc/nginx/sites-available/default` configuration file and comment out the entry `"listen [::]:80 default_server;"` using a # character. Also, if you have installed Apache on your RPi then you must stop it before installing Nginx; for example, by using `sudo service apache2 stop`.

The Nginx web server runs on port number 80 by default. A *port number* is an identifier that can be combined with an IP address to provide an endpoint for a communications session. It is effectively used to identify the software service that is required by a client. For example, you can find out the IP address of your RPi, and the list of services that are listening to ports on the RPi by using the network statistics (netstat) command:

```
pi@erpi ~ $ hostname -I
192.168.1.116
pi@erpi ~ $ sudo netstat -tlpn
Active Internet connections (only servers)
Proto Recv-Q Send-Q Local Address Foreign Addr  State   PID/Program name
tcp   0      0      0.0.0.0:80    0.0.0.0:*     LISTEN  2299/nginx
tcp   0      0      0.0.0.0:22    0.0.0.0:*     LISTEN  2253/sshd
```

Therefore, when a network request is received for port 80, it is directed to the Nginx web server application. The usual port number for unsecured web traffic is 80; this is assumed when you enter a URL in your web browser. You can also see that traffic for port 22 is directed to the Secure Shell (SSH) server. You can test the configuration of your Nginx server using the following:

```
pi@erpi ~ $ sudo nginx -t
nginx: the configuration file /etc/nginx/nginx.conf syntax is ok
nginx: configuration file /etc/nginx/nginx.conf test is successful
```

You can also get information about changes that you make to the server configuration before you perform a server restart, as follows:

```
pi@erpi ~ $ sudo service nginx configtest
[ ok ] Testing nginx configuration:.
pi@erpi ~ $ sudo service nginx restart
[ ok ] Restarting nginx: nginx.
```

Both of these tests are particularly useful in identifying configuration problems.

Configuring an Nginx Web Server

Nginx can be configured using the files in /etc/nginx/ where the core configuration files are as follows:

- nginx.conf is the main configuration file for the server.
- The sites-available directory contains the configuration files for any virtual sites, and the sites-enabled directory should contain a symbolic link to a configuration file in the sites-available directory, to activate a site. Most of the configuration changes are performed on the default file entry in the sites-available directory.

In addition to the configuration files, the functionality of Nginx can be further extended (e.g., to provide Python support) with the use of modules. You can identify the current modules that have been compiled into Nginx using the following:

```
pi@erpi ~ $ nginx -V
nginx version: nginx/1.6.2
TLS SNI support enabled ...
```

Creating Web Pages and Web Scripts

To create a simple web page for the RPi web server, you can use the nano editor and some basic HTML syntax as follows:

```
pi@erpi /var/www/html $ sudo nano index.html
pi@erpi /var/www/html $ more index.html
<HTML><TITLE>RPi First Web Page</TITLE>
<BODY><H1>RPi First Page</H1>
The Raspberry Pi test web page.
</BODY></HTML>
```

Now when you connect to the web server on the RPi using a web browser, you will see the output displayed as in Figure 12-3. You can use the local IP address of the RPi, or the Zeroconf name (e.g., `raspberrypi.local`).

Figure 12-3: The first web page from the Nginx server

Web pages are ideal for the presentation of static web content, and by using an editor like KompoZer, CoffeeCup, or Notepad++ you can quickly build HTML content for a personal web server. You could then use the port forwarding functionality of your home router, and a dynamic DNS service, to share your static web content with the world.

More advanced dynamic web content can also be developed for the RPi that interfaces to the physical environment for such tasks as reading sensor data or actuating motors. One relatively straightforward method of doing this is to use Common Gateway Interface (CGI) scripts. Unlike Apache, Nginx does not have support for simple CGI scripts by default. Therefore, to install them, use the following steps:

1. Install `fcgiwrap` and a sample configuration file:

```
pi@erpi ~ $ sudo apt install fcgiwrap
pi@erpi ~ $ sudo cp ./usr/share/doc/fcgiwrap/examples/nginx.conf →
/etc/nginx/fcgiwrap.conf
pi@erpi ~ $ cd /etc/nginx/sites-available
pi@erpi /etc/nginx/sites-available $ sudo nano default
```

2. Add the following highlighted line to the Nginx `default` file (note the use of a semicolon to delimit lines):

```
server {
        listen 80 default_server;
        include /etc/nginx/fcgiwrap.conf;
...
```

3. Then restart the server (should errors arise, use `sudo nginx -t`):

```
pi@erpi /etc/nginx/sites-available $ sudo service nginx configtest
[ ok ] Testing nginx configuration:.
pi@erpi /etc/nginx/sites-available $ sudo service nginx restart
[ ok ] Restarting nginx: nginx.
```

4 The `/etc/nginx/fcgiwrap.conf` file places the CGI root at the default
directory location of `/usr/lib/cgi-bin/`. A simple script can be created
at that location (see `/chp12/cgi-bin/test.cgi`):

```
pi@erpi ~/exploringrpi/chp12/cgi-bin $ sudo mkdir /usr/lib/cgi-bin/
pi@erpi ~/exploringrpi/chp12/cgi-bin $ sudo cp test.cgi /usr/lib/cgi-bin/
pi@erpi ~/exploringrpi/chp12/cgi-bin $ cd /usr/lib/cgi-bin/
pi@erpi /usr/lib/cgi-bin $ more test.cgi
#!/bin/bash
echo "Content-type: text/html"
echo ""
echo '<html><head>'
echo '<meta charset="UTF-8">'
echo '<title>Hello Raspberry Pi</title></head>'
echo '<body><h1>Hello Raspberry Pi</h1><para>'
hostname
echo ' has been up '
uptime
echo '</para></html>'
```

5. The script must then be made executable, and it can be tested as follows:

```
pi@erpi /usr/lib/cgi-bin $ sudo chmod a+x test.cgi
pi@erpi /usr/lib/cgi-bin $ ./test.cgi
Content-type: text/html

<html><head>
<meta charset="UTF-8">
<title>Hello Raspberry Pi</title></head>
<body><h1>Hello Raspberry Pi</h1><para>
erpi
 has been up
 05:51:30 up  2:30,  2 users,  load average: 0.00, 0.01, 0.05
</para></html>
```

The script is quite verbose, but you can see that it is very easy to call system
commands (e.g., `hostname` and `uptime`) from within it directly. When the script is
tested in the terminal window, its output displays HTML source code. However,
when this output is viewed using a web browser, as in Figure 12-4, the HTML
is rendered correctly.

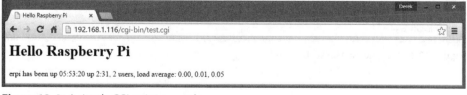

Figure 12-4: A simple CGI script example

As well as calling Linux system commands, you can also execute programs that have been written in C/C++. To demonstrate this capability, the AM2301/2302 (DHT) one-wire sensor circuit can be connected to the RPi as in Figure 6-19. The dht.cpp program in Listing 6-14 is adapted for this chapter so that it only outputs the temperature and humidity values in an HTML format when it is executed:

```
pi@erpi ~/exploringrpi/chp12/dht $ sudo ./dht
<div><h3>The temperature is 25.1°C</h3></div>
<div><h3>The humidity is 42.3%</h3></div>
```

This new dht binary executable can then be copied to the /usr/local/bin directory so that it is "permanently" installed on the RPi:

```
pi@erpi ~/exploringrpi/chp12/dht $ sudo cp dht /usr/local/bin
pi@erpi ~/exploringrpi/chp12/dht $ cd /usr/local/bin/
pi@erpi /usr/local/bin $ sudo chown root:root dht
pi@erpi /usr/local/bin $ sudo chmod ugo+s dht
pi@erpi /usr/local/bin $ ls -l dht
-rwsr-sr-x 1 root root 9360 Oct 11 15:36 dht
```

The CGI script can then be modified to output the temperature value directly from the sensor as follows (see chp12/cgi-bin/temperature.cgi):

```
pi@erpi /usr/lib/cgi-bin $ more temperature.cgi
#!/bin/bash
echo "Content-type: text/html"
echo ""
echo '<html><head>'
echo '<meta charset="UTF-8">'
echo '<title>Pi Weather Sensor</title></head>'
echo '<body><h1>Pi Weather Sensor</h1><para>'
/usr/local/bin/dht
echo '</para></html>'
```

This script results in the output displayed in Figure 12-5. If you are experiencing difficulties with your CGI scripts, the Nginx log files that can help you diagnose problems are stored in /var/log/nginx/.

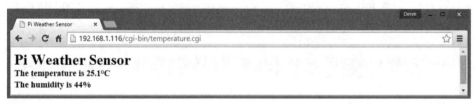

Figure 12-5: Weather sensor web page

WARNING   CGI scripts can be structured to accept data from the web by using form fields. To do so, you must filter the input to avoid potentially damaging cross-site scripting. In particular, you should filter out the characters <>&*?./ from form field entry.

PHP on the RPi

CGI scripts work very well for the short scripts used in the last section; they are lightweight and easy to edit. However, as well as security concerns (e.g., attacks via URL manipulations), they do not scale very well (e.g., for interfacing with databases). One alternative is to use the PHP server-side scripting language. PHP is a reasonably lightweight open source scripting language with a C-like syntax that can be written directly within HTML pages. It can be installed within Nginx as follows:

```
pi@erpi ~ $ sudo apt install php5-common php5-cli php5-fpm
```

Also, you should ensure that you have the following entries in the `default` site configuration file (in `/etc/nginx/sites-available/`):

```
location ~ \.php$ {
    fastcgi_pass unix:/var/run/php5-fpm.sock;
    fastcgi_index index.php;
    include fastcgi_params;
    fastcgi_param SCRIPT_FILENAME $document_root/$fastcgi_script_name;
}
```

Then restart the server:

```
pi@erpi /etc/nginx/sites-available $ sudo service nginx configtest
[ ok ] Testing nginx configuration:.
pi@erpi /etc/nginx/sites-available $ sudo service nginx restart
[ ok ] Restarting nginx: nginx.
```

A PHP program can then be written as shown in Listing 12-1 and placed in the `/var/www/html/` directory. Similarly to the CGI script, it interfaces to the DHT sensors by executing the `dht` program, resulting in the output shown in Figure 12-6 (see `chp12/php/hello.php`).

Listing 12-1: /var/www/html/hello.php

```
<?php $temperature = shell_exec('/usr/local/bin/dht'); ?>
<?php $cpu_temp = (float)
            file_get_contents('/sys/class/thermal/thermal_zone0/temp'); ?>
<html><head><title>RPi PHP Test</title></head>
 <body>
 <h1>Hello from the Raspberry Pi</h1>
 <div>Your IP address is: <?php echo $_SERVER['REMOTE_ADDR']; ?></div>
 <div><?php echo $temperature ?></div>
 <div><h3>The CPU temperature is: <?php echo $cpu_temp/1000 ?>°C</h3></div>
 </body>
</html>
```

NOTE To enter a Unicode symbol using nano you can press Ctrl-Shift-u and then type the Unicode value, e.g., 00b0 for degrees (°). Then press Enter and the symbol will appear. Also, 00a9=©, 00b1=±, 00b5=µ, 00d7=×, and 00f7=÷.

Figure 12-6: A PHP web-based weather sensor

GNU Cgicc Applications (Advanced)

The Common Gateway Interface (CGI) allows a web browser to pass environment and application information to a script/program using HTTP POST or GET requests. Almost all programming languages can be used to build CGI applications, because their only role in the transaction is to parse the input that is sent to them by the server, and to construct a suitable HTML output response.

The GNU Cgicc is a C++ library for building CGI applications. It is powerful and it greatly simplifies the process of building applications that allow you to interact with the RPi over the Internet using a HTML form-based interface. It could be argued that this is a "dated approach" to solving the problem of having an embedded system web server interact with a web browser client—it has been around since the 1990s. To some extent that is true. There are powerful alternatives available such as Java servlets, Node.js, Dart, and PHP; however, this approach:

- Has a low overhead on the RPi, as the code is compiled rather than interpreted
- Permits direct access to system calls
- Can interface readily with hardware using code libraries such as wiringPi

The downside is that it is not really suitable for novice programmers, the output format syntax can be verbose, and session management is complex. Even with that, it is worth pointing out that some large-scale web applications, including those by Google and Amazon, do use C++ on their servers for performance-critical systems. The RPi is not a high-end server, so any performance optimizations are always welcome, perhaps even at the cost of added complexity.

Cgicc can be downloaded and installed using the following steps:

```
pi@erpi ~ $ mkdir cgicc
pi@erpi ~ $ cd cgicc
pi@erpi ~/cgicc $ wget ftp://ftp.gnu.org/gnu/cgicc/cgicc-3.2.16.tar.gz
pi@erpi ~/cgicc $ tar xvf cgicc-3.2.16.tar.gz
pi@erpi ~/cgicc $ cd cgicc-3.2.16/
pi@erpi ~/cgicc/cgicc-3.2.16 $ ./configure --prefix=/usr
```

```
pi@erpi ~/cgicc/cgicc-3.2.16 $ make
pi@erpi ~/cgicc/cgicc-3.2.16 $ sudo make install
pi@erpi ~/cgicc/cgicc-3.2.16 $ ls /usr/lib/libcgi*
/usr/lib/libcgicc.a    /usr/lib/libcgicc.so     /usr/lib/libcgicc.so.3.2.10
/usr/lib/libcgicc.la   /usr/lib/libcgicc.so.3
```

As an example application, Cgicc can be used to control an LED that is attached to a GPIO on the RPi. Using the circuit from Figure 6-2, the LED can be attached to the RPi on GPIO 17 and a web interface can be developed, as illustrated in Figure 12-7 to control the LED using only a web browser; the interface can be used from anywhere in the world!

Figure 12-7: The LED Cgicc form post example

Listing 12-2 provides a form POST example. The form can contain elements such as check boxes, radio components, buttons, and text fields. The code dynamically generates the HTML web form in Figure 12-7 and updates the page output to display the current state of the LED by selecting the appropriate radio component.

The listing uses Cgicc functions such as HTTPHTMLHeader(), html(), and body() to generate the HTML content for the output. In addition, the example demonstrates how to interact with radio buttons, within HTML forms. It is important that the form data is parsed at the beginning of the program code, as the form data that was previously submitted needs to be propagated into the new output. Clearly, the first time this form is requested there is no data present and the code at the beginning of the program assigns a default value (e.g., cmd="off"). If this is not performed then the program will result in a segmentation fault. From that point onward, the form output needs to maintain the state and that is why these values appear in the HTML generation code.

Listing 12-2: /chp12/cgicc/led.cpp

```cpp
#include <iostream>          // for the input/output
#include <stdlib.h>          // for the getenv call
#include <sys/sysinfo.h>     // for the system uptime call
#include <cgicc/Cgicc.h>     // the Cgicc headers
#include <cgicc/CgiDefs.h>
#include <cgicc/HTTPHTMLHeader.h>
#include <cgicc/HTMLClasses.h>
#include <wiringPi.h>
#define LED_GPIO 17
```

```
using namespace std;
using namespace cgicc;

int main(){
    Cgicc form;                         // the CGI form object
    wiringPiSetupGpio();                // uses wiringPi - see Chp.6.
    pinMode(LED_GPIO, OUTPUT);          // GPIO17 is used as an output
    string cmd;                         // the Set LED command

    // get the state of the form that was submitted - script calls itself
    bool isStatus = form.queryCheckbox("status");
    form_iterator it = form.getElement("cmd");  // the radio command
    if (it == form.getElements().end() || it->getValue()==""){
        cmd = "off";                    // if it is invalid use "off"
    }
    else { cmd = it->getValue(); }      // otherwise use submitted value
    char *value = getenv("REMOTE_ADDR");    // The remote IP address

    // generate the form but use states that are set in the submitted form
    cout << HTTPHTMLHeader() << endl;       // Generate the HTML form
    cout << html() << head() << title("LED Example") << head() << endl;
    cout << body() << h1("Exploring RPi POST LED Example") << endl;;
    cout << "<form action=\"/cgi-bin/led.cgi\" method=\"POST\">\n";
    cout << "<div>Set LED: <input type=\"radio\" name=\"cmd\" value=\"on\""
        << ( cmd=="on" ? "checked":"") << "/> On ";
    cout << "<input type=\"radio\" name=\"cmd\" value=\"off\""
        << ( cmd=="off" ? "checked":"") << "/> Off ";
    cout << "<input type=\"submit\" value=\"Set LED\" />";
    cout << "</div></form>";

    // process the form data to change the LED state
    if (cmd=="on") digitalWrite(LED_GPIO, HIGH);        // turn on
    else if (cmd=="off") digitalWrite(LED_GPIO, LOW);   // turn off
    else cout << "<div> Invalid command! </div>";       // not possible
    cout << "<div> The CGI REMOTE_ADDR value is " << value << "</div>";
    cout << body() << html();
    return 0;
}
```

You can build and deploy this application as follows:

```
pi@erpi .../chp12/cgicc $ g++ led.cpp -o led.cgi -lcgicc -lwiringPi
pi@erpi .../chp12/cgicc $ sudo cp led.cgi /usr/lib/cgi-bin/
pi@erpi .../chp12/cgicc $ sudo chmod +s /usr/lib/cgi-bin/led.cgi
```

As described at the end of Chapter 6, you must enable the setuid bit on programs that utilize wiringPi to control GPIOs.

This example just scratches the surface of what can be performed using CGI and C++ on the RPi. For complex applications, you may be better placed to examine other frameworks, but for simple high-performance web interfaces, the GNU Cgicc library provides a perfectly appropriate solution.

It is worth noting that there is one important limitation with the current example. It is a single session solution—if two users access the led.cgi script at the same time, the LED state that is displayed will be inconsistent. For more complex applications, session management is very important.

For more information on the Cgicc library, see the GNU Cgicc library documentation at `tiny.cc/erpi1201`. By browsing the Class List, you will see that the library is capable of handling cookies, file transfers, and much more.

LAMP AND MEAN

In addition to web servers, it is possible to install a database such as MySQL onto the RPi, forming a LAMP (Linux, Apache/Nginx, MySQL, PHP) server. This allows you to further install content management systems (CMSs) such as WordPress or Drupal, allowing you to create advanced web content that can even include hardware interaction.

MEAN is a full-stack JavaScript framework for web application development that consists of MongoDB, Express, AngularJS, and Node.js. Essentially, MEAN is a more modern version of LAMP. MEAN is lightweight enough to be deployed on the RPi and provide a full framework for application development; however, developing software for a full MEAN framework is beyond what is possible in this text. A simple Node.js with Express example is presented here to get you started.

Node.js is first introduced in Chapter 5. Express (`expressjs.com`) is a fast, minimalist web framework for Node.js that can be used to build feature-rich web applications. To install Express using the following steps, you must first ensure that Node.js is up-to-date:

```
pi@erpi:~ $ sudo su
root@erpi:/home/pi# curl -sL https://deb.nodesource.com/setup_5.x | bash -
root@erpi:/home/pi# apt install -y nodejs
root@erpi:/home/pi# exit
exit
pi@erpi:~ $ node -v
v5.9.0
pi@erpi ~ $ mkdir express
pi@erpi ~ $ cd express/
pi@erpi ~/express $ sudo npm install express --save
pi@erpi ~/express $ cp ~/exploringrpi/chp12/express/* .
pi@erpi ~/express $ ls -l
total 8
-rw-r--r-- 1 pi pi  322 Oct 14 03:31 hello.js
drwxr-xr-x 3 pi pi 4096 Oct 14 03:21 node_modules
pi@erpi ~/express $ more hello.js
var express = require('express');
var app = express();

app.get('/', function (req, res) {
  res.send('Hello from the RPi!');
});
```

Continues

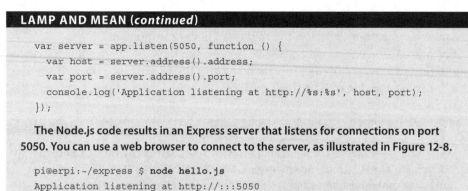

LAMP AND MEAN (*continued*)

```
var server = app.listen(5050, function () {
  var host = server.address().address;
  var port = server.address().port;
  console.log('Application listening at http://%s:%s', host, port);
});
```

The Node.js code results in an Express server that listens for connections on port 5050. You can use a web browser to connect to the server, as illustrated in Figure 12-8.

```
pi@erpi:~/express $ node hello.js
Application listening at http://:::5050
```

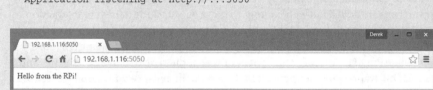

Figure 12-8: Express hello world example

To really appreciate the power of this framework you need to investigate the use of express-generator, AngularJS, and MongoDB. See www.mean.io for further information.

A C/C++ Web Client

Installing a web server on an RPi provides it with a simple, intuitive way to present information to a client web browser application. It is important to understand that the distinction between a client and a server is nothing to do with the hardware capability of the interconnected devices; rather, it relates to the role of each device at that particular point in time. For example, when retrieving a web page from the RPi using its Nginx web server, a desktop computer's web browser is a client of the RPi's web server. Table 12-1 provides a summary of the characteristics of the two types of application, which when used together is termed the client/server model.

Table 12-1: Characteristics of Server Versus Client Applications

SERVER APPLICATIONS	CLIENT APPLICATIONS
Special-purpose applications that are typically dedicated to one service	Typically become a client temporarily, but perform other computation locally
Typically invoked on system startup and they attempt to run forever	Typically invoked by a user for a single session

SERVER APPLICATIONS	CLIENT APPLICATIONS
Wait passively, and potentially forever, for contact from client applications	Actively initiate contact with the server. The client must know the address of the server.
Accept contact from client applications	Can access several servers simultaneously
Typically run on a shared machine	Typically run on a local machine

When the RPi acts as a server, it waits passively for a connection from a client machine, but there are many cases when the RPi might need to actively contact a server on another machine. In such cases, the RPi must act as a client of that server. At this point in the book you have already used many such client network applications on the RPi, such as `ping`, `wget`, `ssh`, `sftp`, and so on, and these applications can be used within shell scripts. However, it would also be useful if you could generate client requests from within C/C++ code, and for this you can use network sockets.

Network Communications Primer

A socket is a network endpoint that is defined using an IP address and a port number. An IP address (version 4) is simply a 32-bit number, which is represented as four eight-bit values (e.g., 192.168.1.116), and a port number is a 16-bit unsigned integer (0–65,535) that can be used to enable multiple simultaneous communications to a single IP address. Ports under 1,024 are generally restricted to root access in order to prevent users from hijacking core services (e.g., 80 for HTTP, 20/21 for FTP, 22 for SSH, 443 for HTTPS).

The description of a socket must also define the socket type, indicating whether it is a stream socket or a datagram socket. Stream sockets use the Transmission Control Protocol (TCP), which provides for reliable transfer of data where the time of transmission is not a critical factor. Its reliability means that it is used for services such as HTTP, e-mail (SMTP), and FTP, where data must be reliably and correctly transferred. The second type of socket is a datagram socket that uses the *User Datagram Protocol* (UDP), which is less reliable but much faster than TCP, as there is no error checking for packets. Time-critical applications such as Voice over IP (VoIP) use UDP, as errors in the data will be presented in the output as noise, but the conversation will not be paused awaiting lost data to be re-sent.

When communication is established between two network sockets, it is called a connection. Data can then be sent and received on this connection using write and read functions. It is important to note that a connection could also be created between two processes (programs) that are running on a single machine and thus used for interprocess communication.

A C/C++ Web Client

Full C/C++ support for socket communication can be added to your program by including the sys/socket.h header file. In addition, the sys/types.h header file contains the data types that are used in system calls, and the netint/in.h header file contains the structures needed for working with Internet domain addresses.

Listing 12-3 is the C source code for a basic web browser application that can be used to connect to a HTTP web server, retrieve a web page, and display it in raw HTML form—like a regular web browser, but without the pretty rendering. The code performs the following steps:

1. The server name is passed to the program as a string argument. The program converts this string into an IP address (stored in the hostent structure) using the gethostbyname() function.

2. The client creates a TCP socket using the socket() system call.

3. The hostent structure and a port number (80) are used to create a sock-addr_in structure that specifies the endpoint address to which to connect the socket. This structure also sets the address family to be IP-based (AF_INET) and the network byte order.

4. The TCP socket is connected to the server using the connect() system call; the communications channel is now open.

5. An HTTP request is sent to the server using the write() system call and a fixed-length response is read from the server using the read() system call. The HTML response is displayed.

6. The client disconnects and the socket is closed using close().

Listing 12-3: /chp12/webbrowser/webbrowser.c

```c
#include <stdio.h>
#include <sys/socket.h>
#include <sys/types.h>
#include <netinet/in.h>
#include <netdb.h>
#include <strings.h>

int main(int argc, char *argv[]) {
    int     socketfd, portNumber, length;
    char    readBuffer[2000], message[255];
    struct sockaddr_in serverAddress; // describes endpoint to connect socket
    struct hostent *server;           // stores information about host name

    // The command string for a HTTP request to get / (often index.html)
    sprintf(message, "GET / HTTP/1.1\r\nHost: %s\r\nConnection: close\r\n\r\n",
            argv[1]);
    printf("Sending the message: %s", message);
```

```
  if (argc<=1) {   // must pass the hostname
     printf("Incorrect usage, use: ./webbrowser hostname\n");
     return 2;
  }
  // gethostbyname accepts a string name and returns a host name structure
  server = gethostbyname(argv[1]);
  if (server == NULL) {
     perror("Socket Client: error - unable to resolve host name.\n");
     return 1;
  }
  // create the socket of IP address type, SOCK_STREAM for TCP connections
  socketfd = socket(AF_INET, SOCK_STREAM, 0);
  if (socketfd < 0) {
     perror("Socket Client: error opening TCP IP-based socket.\n");
     return 1;
  }
  // clear the data in the serverAddress sockaddr_in struct
  bzero((char *) &serverAddress, sizeof(serverAddress));
  portNumber = 80;
  serverAddress.sin_family = AF_INET; //set the address family to be IP
  serverAddress.sin_port = htons(portNumber);    //set port number to 80
  bcopy((char *)server->h_addr,(char *)&serverAddress.sin_addr.s_addr,
     server->h_length);   //set address to the resolved hostname address
  // try to connect to the server
  if (connect(socketfd, (struct sockaddr *) &serverAddress,
     sizeof(serverAddress)) < 0) {
     perror("Socket Client: error connecting to the server.\n");
     return 1;
  }
  // send the HTTP request string
  if (write(socketfd, message, sizeof(message)) < 0){
     perror("Socket Client: error writing to socket");
     return 1;
  }
  // read the HTTP response to a maximum of 2000 characters
  if (read(socketfd, readBuffer, sizeof(readBuffer)) < 0){
     perror("Socket Client: error reading from socket");
     return 1;
  }
  printf("**START**\n%s\n**END**\n", readBuffer); // display response
  close(socketfd);                                // close the socket
  return 0;
}
```

This code can be built and executed as follows. In this example, the simple web page from the local RPi Nginx web server is requested, by using localhost, which essentially means "this device" and it uses the Linux loopback virtual network interface (lo) which has the IP address 127.0.0.1:

```
pi@erpi ~/exploringrpi/chp12/webbrowser $ gcc webbrowser.c -o webbrowser
pi@erpi ~/exploringrpi/chp12/webbrowser $ ./webbrowser localhost
Sending the message: GET / HTTP/1.1
Host: localhost
Connection: close
```

```
**START**
HTTP/1.1 200 OK
Server: nginx/1.6.2
Date: Sun, 11 Oct 2015 23:16:09 GMT
Content-Type: text/html
Content-Length: 118
Last-Modified: Sun, 11 Oct 2015 03:27:20 GMT
Connection: close
ETag: "5619d718-76"
Accept-Ranges: bytes

<HTML><TITLE>RPi First Web Page</TITLE>
<BODY><H1>RPi First Page</H1>
The Raspberry Pi test web page.
</BODY></HTML>
**END**
```

The example works correctly, returning the `index.html` file from `/var/www/`. It can also connect to other web servers (e.g., call `./webbrowser www.google.com`).

Secure Communication Using OpenSSL

One of the limitations of the TCP socket application in the previous section is that all communications are sent "in the clear" across IP networks. This may not be of concern for home networks, but if your client and server are on different physical networks, the data that is transferred can be easily viewed on intermediary networks. Sometimes it is necessary to communicate securely between a client and a server (for example, if you are sending a username and password to an online service). In addition, particular care should be taken in applications where the RPi can actuate motors or relays; a malicious attack could cause physical destruction. One way to implement secure communications is to use the OpenSSL toolkit.

OpenSSL (`www.openssl.org`) is a toolkit that implements the Secure Sockets Layer (SSL), Transport Layer Security (TLS) protocols, and a cryptography library. This library can be installed using the following:

```
pi@erpi ~ $ sudo apt install openssl libssl-dev
```

OpenSSL is a complex and comprehensive toolkit that can be used to encrypt all types of communications. This section presents one example application to illustrate its use. For this example, the C/C++ web client code is modified to support SSL communications as shown in Listing 12-4. The code involved in this example is the same as in Listing 12-3, except for the following:

1. The TCP socket connection is formed to the HTTP secure (i.e., HTTPS) port, which is port 443 by default.

2. The SSL library is initialized using the `SSL_Library_init()` function.

3. An SSL context object is used to establish the TLS/SSL connection. The security and certificate options can be set in this object.

4. The network connection is assigned to an SSL object and a handshake is performed using the `SSL_connect()` function.

5. The `SSL_read()` and `SSL_write()` functions are used.

6. The `SSL_free()` function is used to shut down the TLS/SSL connection, freeing the socket and SSL context objects.

Listing 12-4: / chp12/webbrowserSSL/webbrowserSSL.c (segment)

```
/*** After the connection to the server is formed:  ***/
// Register the SSL/TLS ciphers and digests
SSL_library_init();
// Create an SSL context object to establish TLS/SSL enabled connections
SSL_CTX *ssl_ctx = SSL_CTX_new(SSLv23_client_method());
// Attach an SSL Connection to the socket
SSL *conn = SSL_new(ssl_ctx); // create an SSL structure for an SSL session
SSL_set_fd(conn, socketfd);   // Assign a socket to an SSL structure
SSL_connect(conn);            // Start an SSL session with a remote server
// send data across a SSL session
if (SSL_write(conn, message, sizeof(message)) < 0){ ... }
// read data scross a SSL session
if (SSL_read(conn, readBuffer, sizeof(readBuffer)) < 0){ ... }
printf("**START**\n%s\n**END**\n", readBuffer);  //display the response
SSL_free(conn);                                  //free the connection
close(socketfd);                                 //close the socket
SSL_CTX_free(ssl_ctx);                           //free the SSL context
```

The full source code is in the `/chp12/webbrowserSSL/` directory. It can be compiled and tested using the following commands:

```
.../chp12/webbrowserSSL $ gcc webbrowserSSL.c -o webbrowserSSL -lcrypto -lssl
.../chp12/webbrowserSSL $ ./webbrowserSSL www.google.ie
```

The application can successfully communicate with the SSL port (443) on secured web servers (e.g., `www.google.com`). The current code does not verify the authenticity of the server owner, but it does encrypt communications.

The RPi as a "Thing"

Earlier in this chapter a web server is configured on the RPi so that it can present weather information to the Internet. This mechanism is very useful, as it provides a snapshot in time of sensor outputs. In order to provide trend data, it would be possible to store the data in flat files or to install a lightweight database on the RPi (e.g., MongoDB). PHP charting tools such as *phpChart* and *pChart* could be used to visually represent the data.

An alternative way of performing the collection and visualization of web sensor information is to connect the RPi to online data aggregation services, which enable you to push sensor data to the cloud, directly from the RPi. In this section, online services are utilized directly from within C/C++ programs that are executing on the RPi. This enables you to develop very lightweight operations that can leverage Internet services in order to intercommunicate between several different RPi boards on different networks. It also enables the collection of sensor data from many RPi "web sensors" at the same time on different physical networks.

ThingSpeak

ThingSpeak is an open source IoT application and API that can be used to store data from web sensors (*things*). Using HTTP, the sensors can push numeric or alphanumeric data to the server, where it can be processed and visualized. The ThingSpeak application can be installed on a server that is running the *Ruby on Rails* web application framework and an SQL database.

In this example, the RPi pushes CPU temperature data to a hosted free service at www.thingspeak.com, where data can also be visualized as shown in Figure 12-9. Once you set up an account, you can then create a new channel, which provides you with read and write API keys for your channel. To upload data to your ThingSpeak channel, you must replace the API key highlighted in the C++ code example in Listing 12-6 with your own write API key. This can be found under the API Keys tab in your account settings.

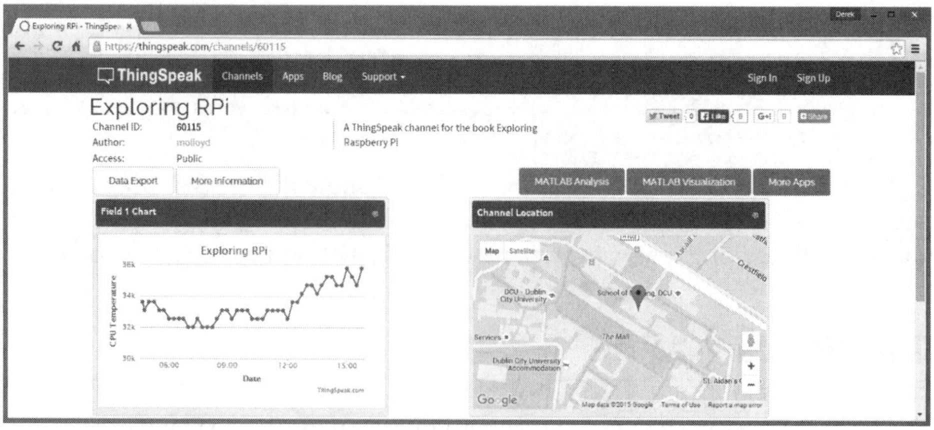

Figure 12-9: A ThingSpeak web sensor example

A C++ SocketClient class is available for this example. This class simply wraps the C code that is used for the C/C++ web browser application in Listing 12-3. The class interface definition is provided in Listing 12-5.

Listing 12-5: /chp12/thingSpeak/network/SocketClient.h

```
class SocketClient {
private:
    int         socketfd;
    struct      sockaddr_in    serverAddress;
    struct      hostent        *server;
    std::string serverName;
    int         portNumber;
    bool        isConnected;
public:
    SocketClient(std::string serverName, int portNumber);
    virtual int connectToServer();
    virtual int disconnectFromServer();
    virtual int send(std::string message);
    virtual std::string receive(int size);
    bool isClientConnected() { return this->isConnected; }
    virtual ~SocketClient();
};
```

The code example in Listing 12-6 uses this `SocketClient` class. The example reads the temperature sensor and pushes it to the hosted ThingSpeak server using an HTTP POST request.

Listing 12-6: /chp12/thingSpeak/thingSpeak.cpp

```
#include <iostream>
#include <sstream>
#include <fstream>
#include <stdlib.h>
#include "network/SocketClient.h"
#define CPU_TEMP "/sys/class/thermal/thermal_zone0/temp"
using namespace std;
using namespace exploringRPi;

int getCPUTemperature() {
    int cpuTemp;
    fstream fs;
    fs.open(CPU_TEMP, fstream::in);
    fs >> cpuTemp;
    fs.close();
    return cpuTemp;
}

int main(){
    ostringstream head, data;
    cout << "Starting ThingSpeak Example" << endl;
    SocketClient sc("thingspeak.com",80);
    data << "field1=" << getCPUTemperature() << endl;
    sc.connectToServer();
    head << "POST /update HTTP/1.1\n"
```

```
                << "Host: api.thingspeak.com\n"
                << "Connection: close\n"
                << "X-THINGSPEAKAPIKEY: ZHBQFC97APOXERPI\n"
                << "Content-Type: application/x-www-form-urlencoded\n"
                << "Content-Length:" << string(data.str()).length() << "\n\n";
        sc.send(string(head.str()));
        sc.send(string(data.str()));
        string rec = sc.receive(1024);
        cout << "[" << rec << "]" << endl;
        cout << "End of ThingSpeak Example" << endl;
        return 0;
}
```

To send data to the server at regular time intervals, POSIX threads and `sleep()` calls can be added to the code in Listing 12-6. However, an easier alternative is to use the Linux cron time-based job scheduler.

The Linux Cron Scheduler

The Linux *cron* daemon (named after Chronos, the Greek god of time) is a highly configurable utility for scheduling tasks to be performed at specific times and dates. It is typically used for system administration tasks, such as backing up data, clearing temporary files, rotating log files, updating package repositories, or building software packages during off-peak times.

When sensors or actuators are interfaced to the RPi, cron can also be very useful for applications such as logging data from these sensors at fixed intervals over long periods of time. On the RPi, you could use the scheduler for tasks such as collecting sensor data, building a stepper-motor clock, time-lapse photography, setting security alarms, and so on.

System crontab

Cron wakes once every minute and checks its configuration files, called *crontabs*, to see if any commands are scheduled to be executed. It can be used to schedule tasks to run with a maximum frequency of once per minute down to a minimum frequency of once per year. Configuration files for cron can be found in the `/etc` directory:

```
pi@erpi /etc $ cd cron.<Tab><Tab>
cron.d/        cron.daily/    cron.hourly/   cron.monthly/  cron.weekly/
```

The `crontab` file contains scheduling instructions for the cron daemon, according to the crontab fields that are listed in Table 12-2. Each line of the `crontab` file specifies the time at which the command field should execute. A wildcard value (*) is available. For example, if it is placed in the hour field, the command should execute at each and every hour of the day.

Table 12-2: Crontab Fields

FIELD	RANGE	DESCRIPTION
m	0–59	The minute field
h	0–23	The hour field
dom	1–31	Day of the month field
mon	1–12 or name	Month of the year (first three letters can be used)
dow	0–7 or name	0 or 7 is Sunday (first three letters can be used)
user		Can specify the user that executes the command
command		The command to be executed at this point in time

Ranges are permitted (e.g., 1-5 for Monday to Friday) and so are lists of times (e.g., 1, 3, 5). In addition, strings can be used in place of the first five fields: @reboot, @yearly, @annually, @monthly, @weekly, @daily, @midnight, and @hourly. The following custom crontab file in Listing 12-7 provides some examples. There are comments in the file to explain the functionality of the entries.

Listing 12-7: /etc/crontab

```
# /etc/crontab: system-wide crontab
SHELL=/bin/sh
PATH=/usr/local/sbin:/usr/local/bin:/sbin:/bin:/usr/sbin:/usr/bin

# m h dom mon dow user command
# Go to bed message, every night at 1am, sent to all users using wall
0  1    * * *    root    echo Go to bed! | wall
# Extra reminder, every work day night (i.e. 1:05am Monday-Friday)
5  1    * * 1-5 root    echo You have work in the morning! | wall
# Perform a task each day (same as 0 0  * * *). Clear the /tmp directory
@daily          root    rm -r /tmp/*

# The following are present in the default Debian crontab file:
17 *    * * *    root    cd / && run-parts --report /etc/cron.hourly
25 6    * * *    root    test -x /usr/sbin/anacron || ( cd / && run-parts ➜
--report /etc/cron.daily ) ...
```

Examples are added to the crontab file to send messages and to clear the /tmp directory (see the comments). You can also specify that a command should be executed every 10 minutes by using */10 in the minutes field.

You may have also noticed other entries in the crontab file that refer to an anacron command. *Anacron* (anachronistic cron) is a specialized cron utility for devices, such as laptop computers, that are not expected to be running 24/7. If regular cron were configured to back up files every week but the RPi happened to be powered off at that exact moment, the backup would never be performed.

However, with anacron the backup will be performed when the RPi next boots (i.e., jobs are queued). You can install anacron using the following:

```
pi@erpi ~ $ sudo apt install anacron
```

Now there will be a new /etc/anacrontab file that performs the same role as crontab does for cron. The configuration file for anacron can be found in /etc/init/anacron.conf.

One problem with having both cron and anacron installed on one system is that it is possible for cron to run a job that anacron has already run, or vice versa. That is the reason for the crontab entries at the end of Listing 12-7. These entries ensure that run-parts is executed only if anacron is not installed on the RPi. This is tested by the call to test -x /usr/sbin/anacron, which returns 0 if the anacron command is present, and 1 if it is not. Calling echo $? displays the output value.

An alternative to adding an entry directly to the crontab file is to add a script to one of the directories: cron.daily, cron.hourly, cron.monthly, or cron .weekly in the /etc directory. Any scripts in these directories are executed by cron. For example, you could create a script in the cron.hourly directory to update the temperature on ThingSpeak as follows:

```
pi@erpi .../chp12/thingSpeak $ sudo cp thingSpeak /usr/local/bin
pi@erpi .../chp12/thingSpeak $ cd /etc/cron.hourly/
pi@erpi /etc/cron.hourly $ sudo nano thingSpeakCPU
pi@erpi /etc/cron.hourly $ more thingSpeakCPU
#!/bin/bash
/usr/local/bin/thingSpeak
pi@erpi /etc/cron.hourly $ sudo chmod a+x thingSpeakCPU
```

An alternative to this is to execute the binary directly within the user account using *user crontab,* which is described in the next section.

User crontab

Each user account can have its own crontab. These files are placed in the /var/ spool/cron/crontabs directory, but they should not be edited in this location. The following creates a crontab for the pi user:

```
pi@erpi ~ $ crontab -e
no crontab for pi - using an empty one
crontab: installing new crontab
```

You can edit the user crontab file to upload the RPi CPU temperature to ThingSpeak every 15 minutes by adding the following line:

```
# m   h   dom mon dow   command
*/15 *   *   *   *     /usr/local/bin/thingSpeak > /dev/null 2>&1
```

The end of this command redirects the standard output to `/dev/null`. The call `2>&1` redirects the standard error to the standard output, and therefore also to `/dev/null`. If this were not present, then by default the output of the `thingSpeak` command would be e-mailed to the system administrator (if mail is configured on the RPi). You can back up your crontab file as follows:

```
pi@erpi ~ $ crontab -l > crontab-backup
pi@erpi ~ $ ls -l crontab-backup
-rw-r--r-- 1 pi pi 952 Oct 12 04:37 crontab-backup
```

To reinstate this backup file with crontab use the following:

```
pi@erpi ~ $ crontab crontab-backup
```

The administrator account can control which users have access to cron by placing either a `cron.allow` or a `cron.deny` file in the `/etc` directory. Under Debian/Raspbian all users can have their own crontab by default. Use the following to remove this capability:

```
pi@erpi /etc$ more cron.deny
pi
pi@erpi ~ $ crontab -e
You (pi) are not allowed to use this program (crontab)
```

With the crontab entry above, the `thingSpeak` program uploads CPU temperature data to the ThingSpeak server every 15 minutes, as illustrated in the plot in Figure 12-9. ThingSpeak also supports MATLAB server-side code execution. For example, Figure 12-10 illustrates a short MATLAB program to convert the most recent temperature from degrees Celsius to degrees Fahrenheit. The example is structured to populate the converted result into another ThingSpeak data channel.

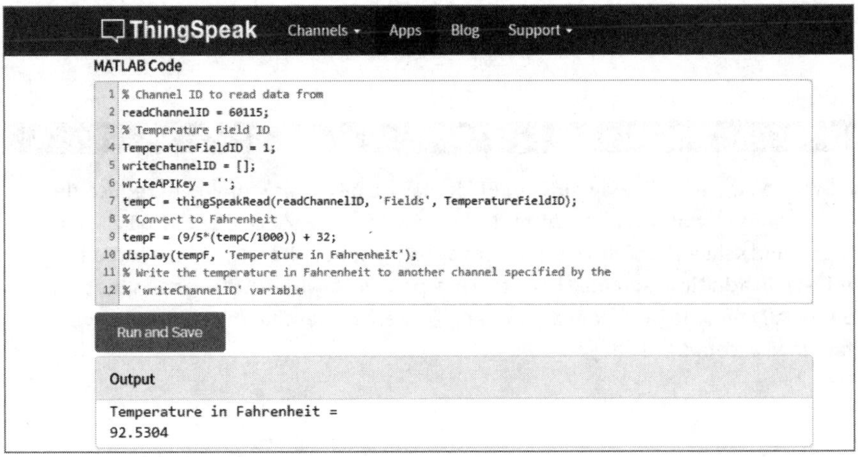

Figure 12-10: A ThingSpeak MATLAB example

Sending E-mail from the RPi

It can be very useful to send e-mail directly from the RPi so that detected system problems are relayed to a potentially remote administrator. In addition, it is useful for an e-mail to be sent when a sensor event occurs—for example, an e-mail could be sent if the room temperature exceeds 30°C. There are many mail client applications, but if you are using a secure *Simple Mail Transfer Protocol* (SMTP) server, like Gmail, the `ssmtp` program works well. Install `ssmtp` using the following command:

```
pi@erpi ~ $ sudo apt install ssmtp mailutils
```

Configure the e-mail settings in the file `/etc/ssmtp/ssmtp.conf`. For example, to configure your RPi to send e-mail through a Gmail account, replace the account name and password fields in the following:

```
pi@erpi /etc/ssmtp$ more ssmtp.conf
# Config file for sSMTP sendmail
root=myaccountname@gmail.com
mailhub=smtp.gmail.com:587
AuthUser=myaccountname@gmail.com
AuthPass=mysecretpassword
UseTLS=YES
UseSTARTTLS=YES
rewriteDomain=gmail.com
hostname= myaccountname@gmail.com
```

You should be aware that the default permissions for this file will allow any user on the RPi to read your password. You should therefore adjust the file attributes as follows:

```
pi@erpi:/etc/ssmtp $ sudo chmod o-r ssmtp.conf
pi@erpi:/etc/ssmtp $ ls -l ssmtp.conf
-rw-r----- 1 root root 698 Mar 26 19:16 ssmtp.conf
```

GMAIL SECURITY SETTINGS

To use Gmail as the e-mail relay for your RPi it may be necessary for you to reduce the security settings of your Gmail account. To do this, go to `myaccount.google.com/security` and select the "Allow less secure apps" option to be ON, as illustrated in Figure 12-11. In addition, you may have to use a password without characters that would typically need to be escaped (e.g., # or ""). Remember that it is easy to set up a specific Gmail account just for your RPi.

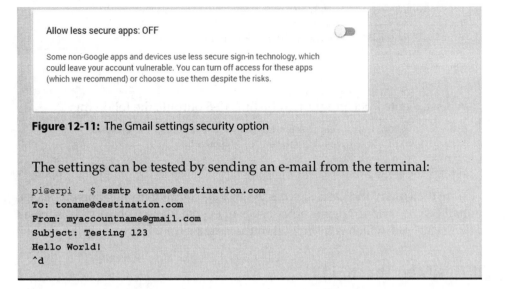

Figure 12-11: The Gmail settings security option

The settings can be tested by sending an e-mail from the terminal:

```
pi@erpi ~ $ ssmtp toname@destination.com
To: toname@destination.com
From: myaccountname@gmail.com
Subject: Testing 123
Hello World!
^d
```

Typing Ctrl+D at the end of the message sends the e-mail. An alternative to this is to place the message text, which is the same as that just shown (including the To/From/Subject lines), in a file (e.g., ~/.message) and then send it using the following call:

```
pi@erpi ~ $ ssmtp toname@destination.com < ~/.message
```

Or you can use the `mail` tool directly (from the `mailutils` package):

```
pi@erpi ~ $ echo "Test Body" | mail -s "Test Subject" toname@destination.com
```

All messages are sent using the user Gmail account. This command can be added to scripts or encapsulated within a C++ program that uses a `system()` call, as in Listing 12-8. C or C++ could be used for this example, but C++ strings make this task more straightforward.

Listing 12-8: /chp12/cppMail/cppMail.cpp

```cpp
#include <iostream>
#include <sstream>
#include <stdlib.h>
using namespace std;

int main(){
    string to("xxx@yyy.com");
    string subject("Hello Derek");
    string body("Test Message body...");
    stringstream command;
```

```
command << "echo \""<< body <<"\" | mail -s \""<< subject <<"\" "<< to;
int result = system(command.str().c_str());
cout << "Command: " << command.str() << endl;
cout << "The return value was " << result << endl;
return result;
}
```

When executed, the program in Listing 12-8 outputs the following:

```
pi@erpi ~/exploringrpi/chp12/cppMail $ g++ cppMail.cpp -o cppMail
pi@erpi ~/exploringrpi/chp12/cppMail $ ./cppMail
Command: echo "Test Message body..." | mail -s "Hello Derek" xxx@yyy.com
The return value was 0
```

Here the value 0 indicates success. As well as sending notification messages, e-mail can be used to trigger other types of events using web services such as www.ifttt.com, which is discussed in the next section.

If This Then That (IFTTT)

If This Then That (IFTTT) is a web service that enables you to create connections between online channels, such as Twitter, LinkedIn, Google Calendar, iPhone/Android Integration, YouTube, and many more. It works by connecting triggers and actions using the simple statement: "If *this* then *that*," where the trigger is the *this*, and the action is the *that*. For example, "If *it is night time* then *mute my phone ringer*," or "If *the weather forecast is for rain tomorrow* then *send me an Android or iOS notification*." These statements are called recipes and they can be activated in an IFTTT account and even shared with other users.

IFTTT has many triggers, but it does not have web triggers; however, it can be triggered using an e-mail message that is sent to trigger@recipe.ifttt .com from a linked Gmail account. Hashtags (e.g., #ERPi) can be used to differentiate events, and the subject and body of the e-mail message can be used as ingredients for the recipe. For example, the recipe in Figure 12-12 states that: "If *a message is sent to trigger@recipe.ifttt.com from X@gmail.com with #ERPi in the subject* then *send me an SMS message*." The body of the e-mail can be passed as an ingredient to the SMS message, which enables personalized messages to be sent from the RPi via SMS messaging (in many cases at no cost).

```
If send trigger7@recipe.ifttt.com an email tagged #ERPi from X@gmail.com,
then send me an SMS at 00353xxxxxxxx
```

The recipe should have the body text:

```
RPi Sent: {{Body}} {{AttachmentUrl}}
```

The recipe can then be triggered by sending an e-mail from the RPi:

```
pi@erpi ~ $ ssmtp trigger@recipe.ifttt.com
To: trigger@recipe.ifttt.com
From: xxxxxx@gmail.com
Subject: #ERPi
Hello Derek!
```

This results in a text message being received that contains the recipe message and the e-mail body (i.e., `"RPi Sent: Hello Derek!"`).

IFTTT enables you to construct quite sophisticated interactions by simply sending e-mails from the RPi when certain events occur. For example, if a motion sensor is triggered, then you can message someone. Certain physical devices can also be triggered using IFTTT, such as Nest devices, smart phones, Automatic/Dash car OBD sensors, WeMo switches, Fitbit Flex healthcare devices, Lifx RGB smart lighting, SmartThings devices, Ubi voice control, and the Quirky+GE Aros smart air conditioner.

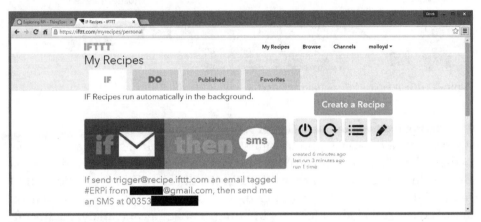

Figure 12-12: Example IFTTT recipe

Some example recipes for the IoT include the following:

- Receive an emergency call if motion is detected
- At sunrise, turn the security lights off
- Remotely set your Nest thermostat to …
- Delay watering your garden if it is going to rain tomorrow
- Every day at … turn the lights on

Large-Scale IoT Frameworks

The ThinkSpeak solution that is presented in this chapter is a useful introduction to hosted platform as a service (PaaS) offerings, and it demonstrates some underlying communication technologies that are required to connect the RPi to the IoT. However, connecting single devices to the Internet to log data does not solve all IoT challenges. In fact, it is only the starting point of the IoT.

Figure 12-13 illustrates some of the large-scale interactions required to more fully realize an IoT.

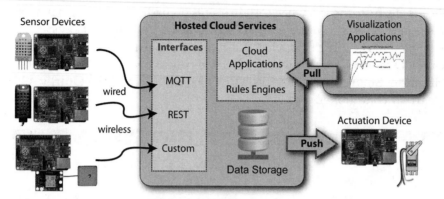

Figure 12-13: A typical IoT solution architecture

In the not too distant future, the IoT will involve billions of devices interchanging trillions of messages, and this must be performed in a secure and scalable manner. The challenges involved are immense and some of the world's largest cloud solutions providers are involved in the development of solutions. IBM released the Bluemix IoT service in August 2015, and in October 2015 Amazon launched the AWS IoT platform for building, managing, and analyzing the IoT. These are both enterprise-level solutions with price plans that scale according to usage. For example, Amazon charges $5–$8 per million messages (512 byte blocks) that are interchanged by IoT devices, which are using its PaaS.

In this section, an enterprise-level IoT PaaS is investigated that uses open source MQTT messaging APIs to ensure vendor portability.

MQ Telemetry Transport (MQTT)

Message Queueing Telemetry Transport (MQTT) is a lightweight connectivity protocol for *machine-to-machine (M2M)* communications. It was conceived in 1999 and has been used by industry since then; however, its applicability to the emerging IoT domain has placed it firmly in the spotlight, and in 2014 MQTT (version 3.1.1) became an OASIS standard. The lightweight nature of MQTT means that it can be used with low-level embedded devices and that it makes efficient use of network resources, while still providing reliable transactions. TCP/IP port 1883 is reserved for the MQTT protocol and 8883 is reserved for the protocol over SSL. In addition to SSL, MQTT supports username/password transactions.

With MQTT a client sends a connect message to a broker (never to another client) and the broker responds with an acknowledgment message and a status code (e.g., 0 for success, and 1–5 for different levels of failure). The connection then persists until the client disconnects. The client sends an MQTT packet that must contain a client ID, a clean session flag that indicates if a persistent session is to be created, and a *keepalive* time interval. The MQTT packet may also contain a username, password, and a *last will* message. The last will message can be used to notify other clients should this client be abruptly disconnected.

The Eclipse Paho project (`www.eclipse.org/paho/`) provides open source implementations of MQTT in C/C++, Java, Python, JavaScript, and other languages that can be used to build small footprint reliable MQTT client applications. In addition, the Eclipse IoT Working Group (`iot.eclipse.org`) provides strong support documentation and tools for developing open source IoT solutions.

To download, build, and install the Paho libraries on the RPi, use the following steps:

```
pi@erpi ~ $ sudo apt install libssl-dev
pi@erpi ~ $ git clone http://git.eclipse.org/gitroot/paho/org.ecli →
pse.paho.mqtt.c.git
pi@erpi ~ $ cd org.eclipse.paho.mqtt.c/
pi@erpi ~/org.eclipse.paho.mqtt.c $ make
mkdir -p build/output/samples
mkdir -p build/output/test
echo OSTYPE is Linux ...
pi@erpi ~/org.eclipse.paho.mqtt.c $ sudo make install
pi@erpi ~/org.eclipse.paho.mqtt.c $ ls /usr/local/lib/libpaho*
/usr/local/lib/libpaho-mqtt3a.so        /usr/local/lib/libpaho-mqtt3c.so
/usr/local/lib/libpaho-mqtt3a.so.1      /usr/local/lib/libpaho-mqtt3c.so.1
/usr/local/lib/libpaho-mqtt3a.so.1.0    /usr/local/lib/libpaho-mqtt3c.so.1.0
/usr/local/lib/libpaho-mqtt3as.so       /usr/local/lib/libpaho-mqtt3cs.so
/usr/local/lib/libpaho-mqtt3as.so.1     /usr/local/lib/libpaho-mqtt3cs.so.1
/usr/local/lib/libpaho-mqtt3as.so.1.0   /usr/local/lib/libpaho-mqtt3cs.so.1.0
```

IBM Bluemix Internet of Things

IBM Bluemix is an enterprise-grade *platform as a service* (*PaaS*) that allows the development of services on the Cloud using a variety of programming languages. One such service is the IBM Internet of Things that was released in August 2015. It facilitates the development of applications on the RPi that can connect to the PaaS to publish or to consume collected data. This is a commercial service with a price that scales according to the number of connected devices and the quantity of transaction traffic; however, the service is currently free for investigative usage levels.[1] The IBM IoT PaaS supports the MQTT protocol and REST API for communication.

---

[1] The service is currently free for fewer than 20 active devices, 100 MB of data transfer, and 1 GB of online data storage per month (October 2015). See: `tiny.cc/erpi1202`.

> **NOTE** Several steps are required in setting up an IBM IoT PaaS, and they are likely subject to change. However, the main steps and concepts should not change significantly, so it is useful to present them here. Also, if you do not wish to sign up for an IBM account, please jump to the section on "Visualize Data Using IBM Quickstart," as an account is not required and it will also give you a live demonstration of the service using your own RPi device.

Begin by registering for an IBM ID at: `tiny.cc/erpi1203`. The ID that you are allocated is your e-mail address. Once you have the IBM ID, you can sign up for the IBM Bluemix free trial[2] at `tiny.cc/erpi1204` by indicating that you already have an IBM ID. Complete the e-mail validation, and then log in to the service, which appears as in Figure 12-14.

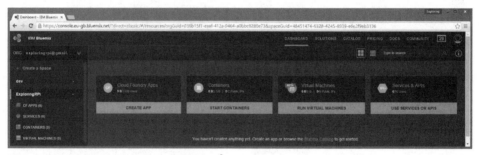

Figure 12-14: IBM Bluemix console window[3]

Use the Create a Space option as in Figure 12-14 to create a space such as ExploringRPi. Then click the Bluemix Catalog link at the bottom of the page to create an IoT application, as highlighted in Figure 12-15.

Figure 12-15: The Bluemix application catalog

---

[2] Unlike several other such services, a credit card is not currently required until 30 days have elapsed (March 2016).

[3] For the purpose of developing the content for this book, a temporary Google account exploringRPi@gmail.com was created. Note that this account is not monitored.

Set the service name to be erpi, select the free plan, and press Create. When the welcome window appears, click Launch Dashboard to connect your devices, which appears as in Figure 12-16. Here you can see your Organization ID, which is 4wyix6 in this case.

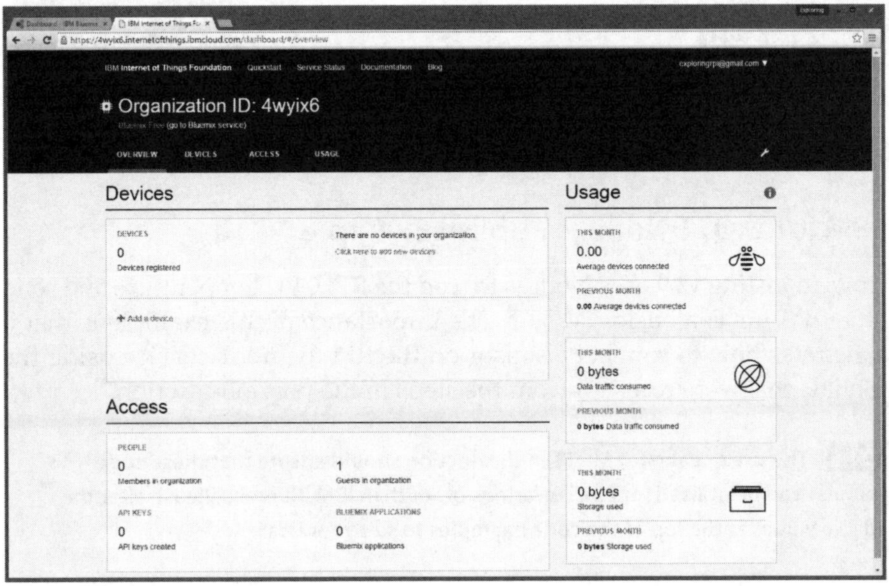

Figure 12-16: IBM IoT dashboard window

Connect a device by selecting the Add a Device link in Figure 12-16. You must first create a device type, which you can call RaspberryPi, and enter a short description. You can leave the remaining template information and optional Metadata blank. Choose the RaspberryPi device type and press Next. You can then choose a device ID of erpi01, which is used to identify a specific RPi board. Press Next for the remainder of the options, allowing the service to generate tokens automatically. Finally, you are presented with a window, as in Figure 12-17, which lists the device ID and the authentication token. It is very important that you note this token down as you will not see this value again! You can create new keys under the ACCESS ➪ API Keys menu option.

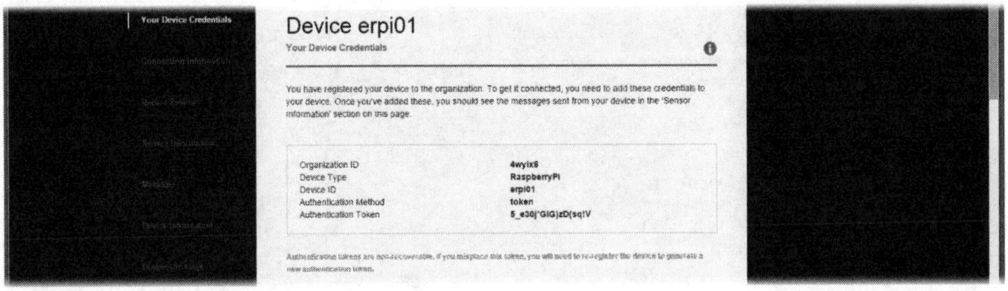

Figure 12-17: IoT device configuration

You now have everything that you need configured so that you can write code for your RPi device that connects to the IoT PaaS. You can see that the Connection Log is currently empty, as illustrated in Figure 12-18.

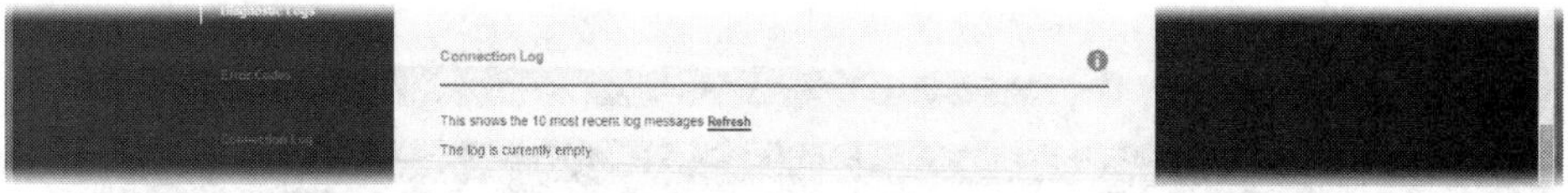

Figure 12-18: Connection Log

An IBM IoT MQTT Node.js Publish Example

The code in Listing 12-9 uses Node.js to read the RPi CPU temperature and send it to the IBM IoT PaaS using MQTT. The importance of this example is that it demonstrates how to connect a sensor on the RPi to an IoT service using the credentials that were received from the steps in the previous section.

> **NOTE** The use of Paho for MQTT in this section should ensure that these code examples can be utilized for PaaS offerings other than IBM Bluemix. Please alter the variable values at the top of the code examples to suit your PaaS.

Listing 12-9: chp12/paho/paho.js

```
// This example uses mqtt.js to upload the CPU temperature to IBM IoT
var mqtt      = require('mqtt');   // required module
var fs        = require('fs')

var ORG       = '4wyix6';          // the organization ID
var TYPE      = 'RaspberryPi';     // the device type
var DEVID     = 'erpi01';          // the individual device id
var AUTHTOKEN = '5_e30j*GlG)zD(sq!V';  // the private auth token
var PORT      = 1883;              // reserved MQTT port
var BROKER    = ORG + '.messaging.internetofthings.ibmcloud.com';
var URL       = 'mqtt://' + BROKER + ':' + PORT;
var CLIENTID  = 'd:' + ORG + ':' + TYPE + ':' + DEVID;
var AUTHMETH  = 'use-token-auth';  // using token authentication
var client    = mqtt.connect(URL, { clientId: CLIENTID,
                username: AUTHMETH, password: AUTHTOKEN });
var TOPIC     = 'iot-2/evt/status/fmt/json';   // sending JSON payload
var CPUTEMP   = '/sys/class/thermal/thermal_zone0/temp'
console.log(URL);

client.on('connect', function() {
    setInterval(function(){
```

```
    var tempStr = 'invalid';
    try {
        tempStr = fs.readFileSync(CPUTEMP, 'utf8');
    }
    catch (err){
        console.log('Failed to Read the CPU Temperature.');
    }
    var temp = parseFloat(tempStr) / 1000;
    console.log('Sending Temp: ' + temp.toString() + '°C to IBM IoT');
    client.publish(TOPIC, '{"d":{"Temp":' + temp.toString() + '}}');
}, 10000);  // publish data every ten seconds
});
```

To use this code example, you must first install the Node.js MQTT module. The code can then be executed, whereupon it connects to the IoT PaaS using the MQTT URL that is displayed by the program. The program reads the CPU temperature from the RPi sysfs entry and publishes it to the service. At this point you should be able to see activity on the IoT Console web interface, as illustrated in Figure 12-19. The data is sent in JavaScript Object Notation (JSON) format (e.g., {"d": {"Temp" : 32.552}}), and you can see the most recent data reading at the bottom of Figure 12-19. The d value identifies the client as a device. When the paho.js script is executed, the data points appear in the PaaS device configuration window, as illustrated in Figure 12-19.

```
pi@erpi ~/exploringrpi/chp12/paho $ npm install mqtt --save
pi@erpi ~/exploringrpi/chp12/paho $ node paho.js
mqtt://4wyix6.messaging.internetofthings.ibmcloud.com:1883
Sending Temp: 32.552°C to IBM IoT
Sending Temp: 32.552°C to IBM IoT
...
```

Figure 12-19: IoT PaaS receiving CPU temperature data samples in JSON format

An IBM IoT MQTT C++ Publish Example

Listing 12-10 is a C++ MQTT application that publishes the CPU temperature to the IoT PaaS. The code has the same structure as the Node.js code in Listing 12-9 and performs a very similar function.

Listing 12-10: /chp12/paho/paho.cpp

```cpp
// Based on the Paho C code example from www.eclipse.org/paho/
#include <iostream>
#include <sstream>
#include <fstream>
#include <string.h>
#include "MQTTClient.h"
#define  CPU_TEMP "/sys/class/thermal/thermal_zone0/temp"
using namespace std;

#define ADDRESS "tcp://4wyix6.messaging.internetofthings.ibmcloud.com:1883"
#define CLIENTID    "d:4wyix6:RaspberryPi:erpi01"
#define AUTHMETHOD "use-token-auth"
#define AUTHTOKEN   "5_e30j*GlG)zD(sq!V"
#define TOPIC       "iot-2/evt/status/fmt/json"
#define QOS         1
#define TIMEOUT     10000L

float getCPUTemperature() {        // get the CPU temperature
   int cpuTemp;                    // store as an int
   fstream fs;
   fs.open(CPU_TEMP, fstream::in); // read from the file
   fs >> cpuTemp;
   fs.close();
   return (((float)cpuTemp)/1000);
}

int main(int argc, char* argv[]) {
   MQTTClient client;
   MQTTClient_connectOptions opts = MQTTClient_connectOptions_initializer;
   MQTTClient_message pubmsg = MQTTClient_message_initializer;
   MQTTClient_deliveryToken token;
   MQTTClient_create(&client, ADDRESS, CLIENTID,
                     MQTTCLIENT_PERSISTENCE_NONE, NULL);
   opts.keepAliveInterval = 20;
   opts.cleansession = 1;
   opts.username = AUTHMETHOD;
   opts.password = AUTHTOKEN;
   int rc;
   if ((rc = MQTTClient_connect(client, &opts)) != MQTTCLIENT_SUCCESS){
      cout << "Failed to connect, return code " << rc << endl;
      return -1;
```

```
    }
    stringstream message;
    message << "{\"d\":{\"Temp\":" << getCPUTemperature() << "}}";
    pubmsg.payload = (char*) message.str().c_str();
    pubmsg.payloadlen = message.str().length();
    pubmsg.qos = QOS;
    pubmsg.retained = 0;
    MQTTClient_publishMessage(client, TOPIC, &pubmsg, &token);
    cout << "Waiting for up to " << (int)(TIMEOUT/1000) <<
         " seconds for publication of " << message.str() <<
         " \non topic " << TOPIC << " for ClientID: " << CLIENTID << endl;
    rc = MQTTClient_waitForCompletion(client, token, TIMEOUT);
    cout << "Message with token " << (int)token << " delivered." << endl;
    MQTTClient_disconnect(client, 10000);
    MQTTClient_destroy(&client);
    return rc;
}
```

You can build and execute this code example as follows:

```
pi@erpi ~/exploringrpi/chp12/paho $ g++ paho.cpp -o paho -lpaho-mqtt3c
pi@erpi ~/exploringrpi/chp12/paho $ ./paho
Waiting for up to 10 seconds for publication of {"d":{"Temp":33.628}}
on topic iot-2/evt/status/fmt/json for ClientID: d:4wyix6:RaspberryPi:erpi01
Message with token 1 delivered.
```

Execution results in a new data point appearing, as in Figure 12-19.

Visualize Data Using IBM Quickstart

You can use the IBM Quickstart services to visualize the live data that is being transmitted from your RPi sensor device. The Quickstart services require public access to your data; therefore, you must change the Organization ID for your data services to "quickstart" (i.e., from 4wyix6 in my case). In this example, the Topic string is set to iot-2/evt/temperature/fmt/json to indicate that the event name is temperature and that a JSON format payload is being transmitted. When the Paho client is executed it sends temperature samples to the IBM Watson IoT PaaS:

```
pi@erpi ~/exploringrpi/chp12/paho $ node paho.js
mqtt://quickstart.messaging.internetofthings.ibmcloud.com:1883
Sending Temp: 32.552°C to IBM IoT
Sending Temp: 32.552°C to IBM IoT
...
```

When you open internetofthings.ibmcloud.com, press on Quickstart, and enter the device ID (e.g., erpi01). A live visualization of the sample data is visible, as illustrated in Figure 12-20.

Figure 12-20: IBM Quickstart receiving CPU temperature data samples in JSON format

It is possible to write client code that subscribes directly to this data stream. For IBM Quickstart, subscribers connect as an *application*, rather than a *device*, so the client ID begins with an a rather than a d. The second client ID can be of the form a:quickstart:RaspberryPi:erpi02. For an application to send a command to a registered device, the topic has the format:

```
iot-2/type/<type-id>/id/<device-id>/cmd/<command>/fmt/<format>
```

- <type-id> is the type of the device to which you want to send the message (e.g., RaspberryPi).
- <device-id> is the specific device ID to which you want to send the message (e.g., erpi01).
- <command> is the command string.
- <format> is json in these examples.

To subscribe to the temperature data stream of the erpi01 device, a topic of the form iot-2/type/RaspberryPi/id/erpi01/evt/temperature/fmt/json can be used. To be clear, the devices can be virtual and both the device and application can be tested using a single RPi. For more information on the connectivity protocol, see tiny.cc/erpi1206.

The Node.js publisher client can be executed (with the Organization ID set to quickstart) and simultaneously, the subscribe application (in a separate terminal window) will receive the data stream messages as below:

```
pi@erpi ~/exploringrpi/chp12/paho $ node paho.js
mqtt://quickstart.messaging.internetofthings.ibmcloud.com:1883
Sending Temp: 32.552°C to IBM IoT
```

```
Sending Temp: 32.552°C to IBM IoT
...

pi@erpi ~/exploringrpi/chp12/paho $ ./subscribe
Subscribing to topic iot-2/type/RaspberryPi/id/erpi01/evt/temperature/fmt/json
 for client a:quickstart:RaspberryPi:erpi02 using QoS 1
 Press Q<Enter> to quit
Message arrived
   topic: iot-2/type/RaspberryPi/id/erpi01/evt/temperature/fmt/json
   message: {"d":{"Temp":32.552}}
Message arrived
   topic: iot-2/type/RaspberryPi/id/erpi01/evt/temperature/fmt/json
   message: {"d":{"Temp":32.552}}
...
```

This discussion only scratches the surface of what is possible with IoT PaaS such as IBM Bluemix. Along with brokered intercommunication between devices, there is support for the actuation of devices using commands. There is also full support for the deployment of enterprise-level applications on service such as the IBM Bluemix cloud to process, consume, and visualize the data that is generated.

The C++ Client/Server

The C/C++ client application described earlier in this chapter uses HTTP and HTTPS to connect to a web server and retrieve a web page. In this section a TCP server is described, to which a TCP client can connect in order to exchange information, which does not have to be in HTTP form. The same SocketClient class that is used earlier in the chapter is reused in this section, and a new class called SocketServer is described. Figure 12-21 illustrates the steps that take place during communication in this client/server example:

1. In Step 1, a TCP server that is running on the RPi at IP address 192.168.1.116 begins listening to a user-defined TCP port (54321). The *server socket* will listen to this port forever, awaiting contact from a client.

2. In Step 2, a TCP client application is executed. The client application must know the IP address and port number of the server to which it is to connect. The client application opens a *client socket*, using the next available Linux port allocation. The server, which can be running on a different RPi (or the same RPi in a different terminal window), accepts a connection request from the client. It then retrieves a reference to the client IP address and port number. A connection is formed, and the client writes a message to this connection, which is "Hello from the client."

3. In Step 3, the server reads the message from the connection and sends back a new message to the client, which is "The Server says thanks!" The

client reads the response message and displays it to the terminal. Then the client and server both close the network sockets. The programs run asynchronously—in this case running to completion.

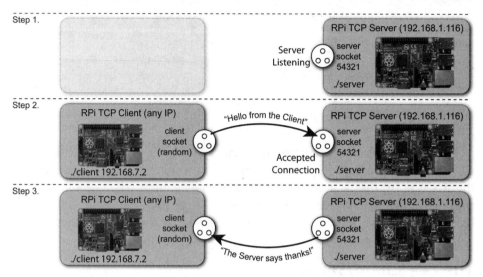

Figure 12-21: Client/server example

The full example is provided in the /chp12/clientserver/ directory. The client.cpp program in Listing 12-11 uses the SocketClient class from the network subdirectory (see Listing 12-5).

Listing 12-11: /chp12/clientserver/client.cpp

```cpp
#include <iostream>
#include "network/SocketClient.h"
using namespace std;
using namespace exploringRPi;

int main(int argc, char *argv[]){
    if(argc!=2){
        cout << "Incorrect usage: " << endl;
        cout << "   client server_name" << endl;
        return 2;
    }
    cout << "Starting RPi Client Example" << endl;
    SocketClient sc(argv[1], 54321);
    sc.connectToServer();
    string message("Hello from the Client");
    cout << "Sending [" << message << "]" << endl;
    sc.send(message);
    string rec = sc.receive(1024);
```

```
    cout << "Received [" << rec << "]" << endl;
    cout << "End of RPi Client Example" << endl;
    return 0;
}
```

The `SocketServer` class in Listing 12-12 is new, and it behaves in a quite different manner than the `SocketClient` class. An object of the class is created by passing the port number to the constructor. When the `listen()` method is called, the program counter will not return from this method call until a connection has been accepted by the server.

Listing 12-12: /chp12/clientserver/network/SocketServer.h

```
class SocketServer {
private:
    int      portNumber;
    int      socketfd, clientSocketfd;
    struct   sockaddr_in   serverAddress;
    struct   sockaddr_in   clientAddress;
    bool     clientConnected;
public:
    SocketServer(int portNumber);
    virtual int listen();
    virtual int send(std::string message);
    virtual std::string receive(int size);
    virtual ~SocketServer();
};
```

The `server.cpp` code example in Listing 12-13 creates an object of the `ServerSocket` class and awaits a client connection.

Listing 12-13: /chp12/clientserver/server.cpp

```
#include <iostream>
#include "network/SocketServer.h"
using namespace std;
using namespace exploringRPi;

int main(int argc, char *argv[]){
    cout << "Starting RPi Server Example" << endl;
    SocketServer server(54321);
    cout << "Listening for a connection..." << endl;
    server.listen();
    string rec = server.receive(1024);
    cout << "Received from the client [" << rec << "]" << endl;
    string message("The Server says thanks!");
    cout << "Sending back [" << message << "]" << endl;
    server.send(message);
    cout << "End of RPi Server Example" << endl;
    return 0;
}
```

The code for this example can be built using the `build` script in the `chp12/clientserver` directory. The server can then be executed:

```
pi@erpi ~/exploringrpi/chp12/clientserver $ ./server
Starting RPi Server Example
Listening for a connection...
```

The server will wait at this point until a client request has been received. In order to execute the client application, a separate terminal session on the same RPi, another RPi, or a Linux desktop machine can be used.[4] The client application can be executed by passing the IP address of the server. The port number (54321) is defined within the client program code:

```
pi@erpi ~/exploringrpi/chp12/clientserver $ ./client localhost
Starting RPi Client Example
Sending [Hello from the Client]
Received [The Server says thanks!]
End of RPi Client Example
```

When the client connects to the server, both the client and server execute simultaneously, resulting in the preceding and following output:

```
pi@erpi ~/exploringrpi/chp12/clientserver $ ./server
Starting RPi Server Example
Listening for a connection...
Received from the client [Hello from the Client]
Sending back [The Server says thanks!]
End of RPi Server Example
```

This code is further improved later in the book to add threading support, and to enable it to communicate with a better structure than simple strings. However, it should be clear that this code enables you to intercommunicate between Linux client/servers that are located anywhere in the world. The client/server pair communicates by sending and receiving bytes; therefore, communication can take place at very high data rates and is only limited by the physical network infrastructure.

IoT Device Management

One of the difficulties with remote web sensors is that they may be in physically inaccessible and/or distant locations. In addition, a period of system downtime may lead to a considerable loss of sensing data. If the problem becomes apparent you can SSH into the RPi and restart the application or perform a system reboot.

---

[4] When the server terminates it can take a short period of time for the Linux kernel to free the server socket and TCP port for re-use. This TIME-WAIT state in TCP prevents delayed packets from one connection being accepted by a later connection. As a result, you may have to wait a few seconds before the server application will restart, as you will receive an "Address already in use" error message.

In this section, two quite different management approaches are described: the first is manual web-based monitoring; the second is automatic, through the use of Linux watchdog timers.

Remote Monitoring of the RPi

One advantage of installing a web server in this chapter is that it supports a number of additional open source services. One such example is a remote monitoring service called *Linux-dash*. For simplicity, the following steps use Node.js as the server:

```
pi@erpi ~ $ sudo apt install php5 curl php5-curl php5-json
pi@erpi ~ $ sudo git clone https://github.com/afaqurk/linux-dash.git
pi@erpi ~ $ cd linux-dash/
pi@erpi ~/linux-dash $ sudo npm install
```

Then edit the `index.js` file `server.listen()` entry to choose a suitable port number (e.g., 81 in this case) that does not conflict with the port number chosen for the Nginx server:

```
pi@erpi:~/linux-dash $ sudo nano server/index.js
pi@erpi ~/linux-dash $ more server/index.js |grep server.listen
server.listen(81);
pi@erpi ~/linux-dash $ sudo node server
Linux Dash Server Started!
```

These steps result in a service running on the RPi using the chosen port number that you can view with a web browser at the address of the RPi: e.g., `http://192.168.1.116:81/` or `http://raspberrypi.local:81/`, as shown in Figure 12-22. This approach can help you quickly identify system problems, such as unusual loads, network traffic, and so on, but it still requires that you manually check the web page.

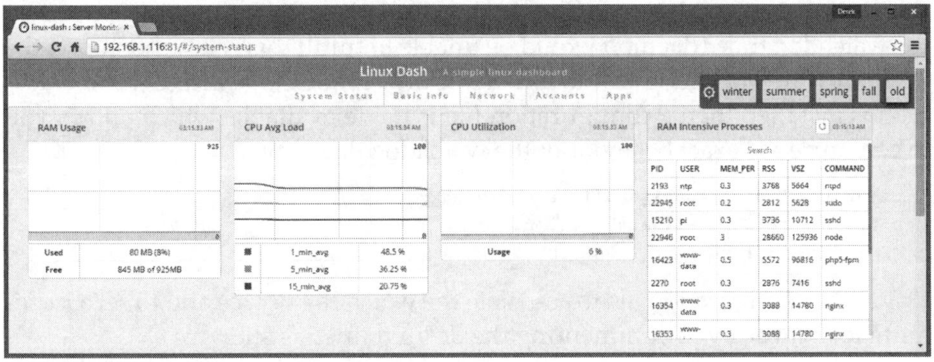

Figure 12-22: RPi remote monitoring using Linux Dash

RPi Watchdog Timers

One solution to automatically determine if there has been a significant problem with your application is to use a watchdog timer. Impressively, the RPi has full support for a hardware watchdog timer, which can be used to automatically reset the RPi should it lock up. Having a watchdog timer can be very important in IoT applications if the RPi is inaccessible or performing an important role that should not be halted (e.g., an RPi intruder alarm).

You can enable the hardware watchdog functionality by creating a new file in the `/etc/modeprobe.d/` directory and by then loading the `bcm2708_wdog` LKM. (The `nowayout=1` option prevents the watchdog from being stopped once it is started, and the heartbeat time is set to be 10 seconds in this configuration.):

```
pi@erpi /etc/modprobe.d $ more watchdog.conf
options bcm2708_wdog nowayout=1 heartbeat=10
pi@erpi /etc $ sudo modprobe bcm2708_wdog
pi@erpi /etc $ lsmod|grep wdog
bcm2708_wdog             2980  0
```

This LKM creates a new device entry in `/dev`:

```
pi@erpi /dev $ ls -l watchdog
crw------- 1 root root 10, 130 Oct 17 12:53 watchdog
```

You should enable this module on boot by adding an entry to the `/etc/modules` file and you can test that it loads by rebooting the RPi:

```
pi@erpi /etc $ more modules|grep bcm2708_wdog
bcm2708_wdog
pi@erpi ~ $ sudo reboot
pi@erpi ~ $ dmesg|grep watchdog
[    6.880679] bcm2708 watchdog, heartbeat=10 sec (nowayout=1)
```

Once the hardware module is enabled you can install the watchdog timer daemon under Raspbian. The daemon sends a message (*heartbeat*) to the watchdog device at a fixed interval. Should the Linux OS become unresponsive, then the watchdog timer daemon would be unable to fulfill this role, whereupon the RPi hardware watchdog would automatically reboot the board. Once the daemon is installed then a configuration file is made available, which allows you to configure the exact behavior of the watchdog daemon:

```
pi@erpi ~ $ sudo apt install watchdog chkconfig
pi@erpi /etc $ ls -l watchdog.conf
-rw-r--r-- 1 root root 1126 Oct 17  2014 watchdog.conf
```

Edit the configuration file to associate the watchdog device and to set a maximum load level, by uncommenting the desired lines as shown:

```
pi@erpi /etc $ sudo nano watchdog.conf
pi@erpi /etc $ more watchdog.conf | grep /dev/watchdog
```

```
watchdog-device = /dev/watchdog
pi@erpi /etc $ more watchdog.conf |grep max-load-1
max-load-1 = 24
```

Then it can be started under either SysV init or systemd as follows:

```
pi@erpi /dev $ sudo chkconfig watchdog on
pi@erpi /dev $ sudo update-rc.d watchdog enable
pi@erpi /etc $ /etc/init.d/watchdog status
[ ok ] watchdog is running.

pi@erpi /dev $ sudo systemctl start watchdog
pi@erpi /dev $ sudo systemctl enable watchdog
```

The watchdog service should then run as a process on the RPi:

```
pi@erpi ~ $ ps aux|grep watchdog
root   2498 0.0 0.1 1828 1736 ?  SLs  13:11   0:00 /usr/sbin/watchdog
```

To test that the watchdog timer is working correctly you can kill the watchdog daemon. This simulates a real-world condition in which the daemon is prevented from performing its duties as a result of system problems:

```
pi@erpi ~ $ sudo kill -9 2498
```

One alternative to using the watchdog daemon is developing a custom watchdog service that is tied specifically to your application. An example of such an application is provided in /chp12/watchdog/watchdog.c. If you build the principles of this code into an application, then you should "kick the dog" (i.e., reset the timer) each time an important block of code executes. For example, if a sensor value were read every 15 seconds in your code example, then you would also "kick the dog" each time you read the sensor value. That way, if the application is unable to connect to the sensor, then the RPi would reboot automatically. This is probably unnecessary, as a communications failure would likely be caused by a system-wide issue that would typically result in the Linux watchdog daemon rebooting the board.

Static IP Addresses

The RPi is configured by default to use the *Dynamic Host Configuration Protocol* (*DHCP*) for the allocation of its wired and wireless IP address. Network routers typically run a DHCP server that allocates a pool of addresses to devices attached to the network. While DHCP works well for most devices on a local network, it can cause difficulties if you want to make the RPi visible outside a home firewall via port forwarding. This is because DHCP devices may receive a different IP address each time they boot (depending on the router's lease time). *Port forwarding* (a.k.a. *port mapping*) means that a particular port on the RPi (e.g., port 80) can be mapped to a port that is visible outside your firewall, thus making a service on the RPi visible to the world. Many router/firewalls require the RPi to have a static IP address to set up a port forward to it.

To allocate a static IP address to a network adapter, you can alter the /etc/network/interfaces configuration file to manually specify the address (e.g., 192.168.1.33), the network mask, and the network gateway, with the following format:

```
pi@erpi /etc/network $ more interfaces
# The primary network interface
auto eth0
allow-hotplug eth0
iface eth0 inet static
    address 192.168.1.33
    netmask 255.255.255.0
    gateway 192.168.1.1
```

The RPi then has a static IP address after reboot:

```
molloyd@desktop:~$ ssh pi@192.168.1.33
pi@erpi ~ $
```

The same procedure applies to other adapter entries, such as the wlan0 wireless Ethernet adapter. Do not pick an address that is within the DHCP address pool range or assigned to another device, or it will result in IP conflicts on the network.

Power over Ethernet (PoE)

One common difficulty in using the RPi as a web sensor is related to the provision of power. It is possible to power the RPi using batteries, and there are many *USB battery pack* solutions available that can perform this role. For example, the *IntoCircuit Power Castle 11.2 Ah* (~$40) is a popular choice that could in theory power the RPi for ~50 hrs at an average load (this duration will fall dramatically if Wi-Fi is used). For example, such a battery configuration could be used for an RPi mobile robot platform.

When a fixed installation is required in a remote location (e.g., in a garden, gate/entrance) where power sockets are not readily available, then *Power over Ethernet (PoE)* is a good option. Regular Ethernet cables (Cat 5e or Cat 6) contain four pairs of wires that are twisted together in order to cancel out electromagnetic interference from external power sources. Low-cost *unshielded twisted-pair (UTP)* cables can therefore transmit data (and power) over long distances of up to 100 m/328 ft.

For standard Ethernet (100BASE-T), only two of the twisted pair wires are actually used for data transfer; therefore, the other two pairs are available to carry power. However, it is also possible to inject a *common-mode voltage* onto the pair of wires that carry the data signals. This is possible because Ethernet over twisted pair (similar to CAN bus, USB, and HDMI) uses *differential signaling*, which means that the receiver reads the difference between the two signals, rather than their voltage level with respect to ground. External interference affects both of the paired wires in the same way, so its impact is effectively canceled out by the differential signaling. PoE can therefore use the network cable to deliver power to attached devices. This structure is commonly used by VoIP phones and IP cameras so that they do not need a separate mains power point.

The RPi does not support PoE internally, so two main external options are available:

1. **Use a pseudo-PoE cabling structure:** Adafruit sells a *Passive PoE Injector Cable Set* (~$6), illustrated in Figure 12-23, for which you can use a regular 5 V mains supply to inject power into the unused twisted pair wires, and then draw that power at the other end of the cable. You can use the crimp tool that is described in Chapter 4 to terminate the DC power connector with a DuPont connector so that it can be attached to the RPi GPIO header (e.g., pins 4 and 6). **Do not connect such cables to a true PoE switch!**

2. **Use a true PoE (IEEE 802.3af) switch:** In order to send power over long distances, PoE switches provide a 48 V DC supply. Therefore, a *PoE power extraction module* is required to *step down* this voltage to a level that is acceptable by the RPi.

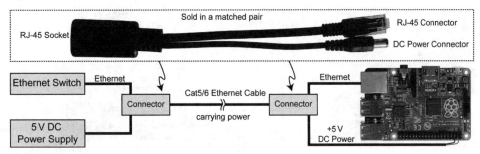

Figure 12-23: AdaFruit pseudo-PoE cable

PoE Power Extraction Modules (PEMs) (Advanced Topic)

One problem with the arrangement in Figure 12-23 is that the 5 V supply voltage will drop as the cable length increases due to the impact of cable resistance. Recently, low-cost network switches have become available that offer PoE functionality. *Power extraction modules* (PEMs) can be purchased to step down the 48 V DC voltage that is supplied by these switches to lower, fixed DC levels (e.g., 3.3 V, 5 V, 12 V). The low-cost ($10–$15) PEM that is used in this section is the PEM1305 (`tiny.cc/erpi1205`), which can be used to supply 5 V to the RPi. PoE

(802.3af) switches can provide up to 15.4 W of power per attached device. The IEEE 802.3af standard (IEEE Standards Association, 2012) requires that true-PoE devices support two types of PoE:

- **Type-A PoE:** Uses a common-mode DC voltage on the data wires to carry power. The spare pairs are unused.

- **Type-B PoE:** Uses the spare pair of wires to carry power. The data pairs are untouched.

Gigabit Ethernet uses all four pairs of wires to transmit data, so it is likely that Type-A PoE will be dominant in future PoE network switches.

Figure 12-24 illustrates a circuit that can be used to power the RPi using a PoE (IEEE 802.3af) supply. The PEM1305 can extract power from type-A and type-B PoE configurations. However, you must connect the module to DC isolation transformers in order to extract the power from the data wires. To do this, you can use a *MagJack* (a jack with integrated magnetics) with center-tapped outputs (e.g., the Belfuse 0826-1X1T-GJ-F). The MagJack contains the isolation transformers that are required to provide the 48 V supply to the PoE PEM, and to deliver the data pair safely to the RPi Ethernet jack at Ethernet signal voltage levels.

The resistor that is placed on the input side of the PEM1305 is used to select the power output level of the PoE switch—accurately selecting the power output level results in a more power-efficient implementation. The output voltage adjustment resistor can further refine the PEM output voltage level. The PEM pin outputs can be connected directly to 5 V Pins (Pin 2 or Pin 4) and the GND pins (Pin 6) of the RPi GPIO header.

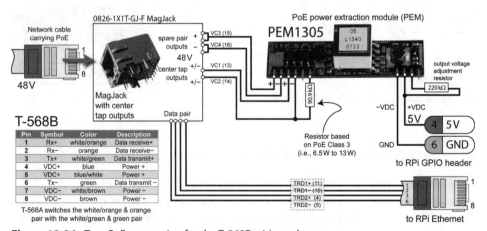

Figure 12-24: True PoE connection for the T-568B wiring scheme

NOTE Be careful in your choice of PoE power extraction module and MagJack. For example, the PEM1205 module appears to be very similar to the PEM1305, but it does not have rectifier bridges on the input, so you would need to add them yourself (otherwise, the circuit could not handle true Ethernet cross-over cables). Also, many Ethernet MagJacks do not have center-tap outputs from the isolation transformers and so are unsuitable for use with PoE PEMs, as the center-tap outputs deliver the 48 V DC power supply to the PEM.

Summary

After completing this chapter, you should be able to do the following:

- Install and configure a web server on the RPi and use it to display static HTML content.
- Enhance the web server to send dynamic web content that uses CGI scripts and PHP scripts to interface to RPi sensors.
- Write the code for a C/C++ client application that can communicate using either HTTP or HTTPS.
- Interface to platform as a service (PaaS) offerings, such as ThingSpeak and IBM Bluemix IoT, using HTTP and MQTT.
- Use the Linux cron scheduler to structure workflow on the RPi.
- Send e-mail messages directly from the RPi and utilize them as a trigger for web services such as IFTTT.
- Build a C++ client/server application that can communicate at a high speed and a low overhead between any two TCP devices.
- Manage remote RPi devices, using monitoring software and watchdog code, to ensure that deployed services are robust.
- Configure the RPi to use Wi-Fi adapters and static IP addresses, and wire the RPi to utilize Power over Ethernet (PoE).

# CHAPTER 13

Wireless Communication and Control

This chapter describes how the Raspberry Pi can be configured to wirelessly communicate to the Internet, and to wirelessly interface to devices and sensors using different communication standards. The chapter begins with a description of how Bluetooth communications can be used to develop a wireless RPi remote-control framework using mobile apps. Next, a description is provided on how the RPi can be configured to connect to the Internet using USB Wi-Fi adapters. The discussion on Wi-Fi continues with a description of how the low-cost NodeMCU (ESP8266) Wi-Fi microcontroller can be used to build a local network of wireless things, which can communicate sensor values to the RPi and to an IoT PaaS. The ZigBee protocol is then used to build peer-to-peer wireless networks that use the popular XBee ZigBee devices. Finally, NFC/RFID is used to build a simple security access control system. By the end of this chapter you should be able to choose an appropriate wireless communication standard to suit your needs and you should be able to build sophisticated wireless IoT applications.

Equipment Required for this Chapter:

- Raspberry Pi (any model)
- RPi 3 or USB Bluetooth adapter (e.g., Kinivo BTD-400)
- Access to an Android mobile device
- RPi 3 or USB Wi-Fi adapter (e.g., Wi-Pi)

- NodeMCU microprocessor (version 2)
- ZigBee modules (ideally the Digi XBee Series 2 ZigBee model)
- An XBee USB Explorer and two XBee-to-breadboard adapters
- An RFID card reader (ideally PN532 NFC compatible)
- TMP36 temperature sensor (or other analog sensors)

Further details on this chapter are available at `www.exploringrpi.com/chapter13/`.

Introduction to Wireless Communications

The addition of wireless capabilities to the RPi further enhances its application possibilities in areas such as robotics, environmental sensing, and remote imaging. Impressively, the RPi 3 has onboard wireless capabilities, and by using USB devices and interfacing communication modules, many different communication types can be realized on all RPi models. For example, low-cost USB Wi-Fi and Bluetooth adapters are widely available, many of which have Linux driver support. In addition, other communication standards such as *ZigBee* and *near field communication* (*NFC*) can be realized by interfacing modules that have serial-UART connections.

There is no single best solution for all projects; rather, each of the wireless communication standards has different advantages and disadvantages:

- *Bluetooth* is a popular standard for interfacing to computer peripherals, audio devices, *personal area networks* (*PANs*), and mobile devices—all applications where the data rate is not a critical factor. It has a low cost and low power consumption profile, which makes it particularly suitable for battery-powered devices. Recently, Bluetooth *low energy* (*LE*) was introduced, which aims to support very low-power applications while maintaining comparable communication ranges.

- *Wi-Fi* communication is more suitable than Bluetooth for full-scale networking applications in which a high data rate is critical; therefore, it is popular with media-rich Internet-attached devices and laptop computers. Unfortunately, Wi-Fi has heavy power consumption costs—as much as 40 times the power consumption of Bluetooth for comparable communication tasks.[1]

- The *ZigBee* communication standard can also be utilized by the RPi, usually by interfacing via a UART device to *XBee modules*. XBee devices are designed to have a low power profile and they can communicate over

[1] Rahul Balani, "Energy Consumption Analysis for Bluetooth, WiFi and Cellular Networks," Networked and Embedded Systems Laboratory, University of California, Los Angeles, Technical Report, 2007.

significant distances, forming mesh network arrangements to further extend the network range. Unfortunately, the maximum data rates are quite limited in comparison to Bluetooth and Wi-Fi; however, the low communications latency means that the standard is suitable for real-time control.

■ NFC is a short-range radio communication standard that builds on *radio frequency identification* (*RFID*) communications. It supports a communication range of up to 8 inches and enables very high data rates when the devices are almost touching (i.e., less than 2 inches). NFC supports communication with unpowered devices using *inductive coupling*.

The general characteristics of different wireless standards are summarized in Table 13-1. Clearly the data rate and communications range are very important factors in the choice of module. In this chapter each of these technologies is interfaced to the RPi so that you have a starting point from which to work.

Table 13-1: Summary Comparison of Different Wireless Standards

	BLUETOOTH	**WI-FI**	**ZIGBEE**	**NFC/RFID**
Standard	IEEE 802.15.1	IEEE 802.11	IEEE 802.15.4	ISO/IEC
Range	10m to 100m	50m to 100m	30m to 100m+	<20cm
Power	Low	High	Very Low	Very Low
Data Rate	<2.1Mb/s	10 to 300Mb/s	<250kb/s	Up to 20Mb/s
Topology	Star	Star	Mesh/Star	Point-to-point
Organization	Bluetooth SIG	Wi-Fi Alliance	ZigBee Alliance	NFC Forum

Bluetooth Communications

Bluetooth is a popular wireless communication system that was created by Ericsson and is now managed by the Bluetooth *Special Interest Group* (*SIG*). Bluetooth was designed as an open standard to enable very different device types to communicate wirelessly over short distances. It is often used for the digital transfer of data for audio headsets, keyboards, computer mice, medical devices, and many more applications. Only the RPi 3 has support for onboard Bluetooth, but support can be added to other RPi models using low-cost USB Bluetooth adapters.

Installing a Bluetooth Adapter

For models other than the RPi 3, the choice of USB Bluetooth adapter is very important; not every adapter has Linux driver support. Ideally, you should determine in advance of purchase that there is Linux support and that the device works with the RPi. Unfortunately, that is not always possible; furthermore, as Linux device driver support is usually chipset-dependent, it may even be the case that two devices with the same model number and ostensibly the same functionality have different chipsets, leaving one supported by Linux and the other not. The USB Bluetooth adapter used in this section is the Kinivo BTD-400 Bluetooth 4.0 USB adapter (~$15), shown in Figure 13-1. It is commonly available, and the current version uses a Broadcom chipset that has good Linux support.

The first step is to install the packages that are required for Bluetooth connectivity on all RPi models:

```
pi@erpi ~ $ sudo apt update
pi@erpi ~ $ sudo apt install bluetooth bluez
```

After installation, the USB adapter can be "hot plugged" into the RPi USB socket. You can list the USB modules that are currently connected to the RPi using the following command, where the Broadcom Corp. listing indicates that the USB adapter has been detected:

```
pi@erpi ~ $ lsusb
Bus 001 Device 004: ID 0a5c:2198 Broadcom Corp. Bluetooth Device
```

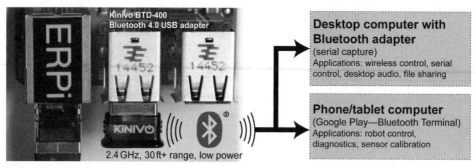

Figure 13-1: Bluetooth-connected RPi

Checking the LKM

As discussed in Chapter 8, a Linux *loadable kernel module* (*LKM*) is a mechanism for adding code to the Linux kernel at run time. They are ideal for device drivers, enabling the kernel to communicate with the hardware without it having to know how the hardware works. The alternative to LKMs would be to build the code for each and every driver into the Linux kernel, which would lead to an impractical kernel size and constant kernel recompilations. LKMs are loaded at run time, but they do not exist in user space—they are essentially part of the kernel. When the Bluetooth adapter is plugged into the RPi (or onboard Bluetooth is enabled on the RPi 3), you can use the lsmod command to find out which modules are loaded. For example, with a USB Bluetooth adapter, you can see the `btusb` module is loaded:

```
pi@erpi ~ $ lsmod
Module               Size  Used by
btusb               29247  0
btbcm                4430  1 btusb
btintel              1381  1 btusb
bluetooth          327442  23 bnep,btbcm,btusb,btintel ...
```

With onboard Bluetooth on the RPi 3, an `hci_uart` module is loaded, as the Bluetooth device is connected to an onboard UART device:

```
pi@erpi:~ $ lsmod
Module               Size  Used by
hci_uart            13533  1
btbcm                4196  1 hci_uart
bluetooth          317981  23 bnep,hidp,btbcm,hci_uart ...
```

The `modprobe` command enables you to add or remove an LKM to or from the Linux kernel at run time. However, if everything has worked correctly, the module should have loaded automatically. You can check `dmesg` for errors that may have arisen. Using `cat /proc/modules` provides similar information about the modules that are loaded, but it is in a less readable form. You can then test the status of the Bluetooth service under either SysV init *or* systemd as follows:

```
pi@erpi ~ $ /etc/init.d/bluetooth status
[ ok ] bluetooth is running.

pi@erpi ~ $ systemctl status bluetooth
• bluetooth.service - Bluetooth service
   Loaded: loaded (/lib/systemd/system/bluetooth.service; enabled)
   Active: active (running) since Fri 2015-10-30 03:40:38 UTC; 36s ago
     Docs: man:bluetoothd(8)
 Main PID: 12307 (bluetoothd)
   Status: "Running"
   CGroup: /system.slice/bluetooth.service
           └─12307 /usr/lib/bluetooth/bluetoothd
```

Configuring a Bluetooth Adapter

The `hcitool` command is used to configure Bluetooth connections, and if the `dev` argument is passed it provides information about the local Bluetooth device:

```
pi@erpi ~ $ hcitool dev
Devices:   hci0    00:02:72:CB:C3:53
```

This is the hardware device address of the adapter that was connected to my board. Using this command you can scan for devices, display connections, display power levels, and perform many more functions—check `man hcitool` for more details.

At this point, you should be able to scan for Bluetooth devices in the vicinity. Ensure that the devices are *discoverable*—that they can be found when a scan takes place. For example, under Windows you have to explicitly make an adapter discoverable, by using Windows taskbar ⇨ (Bluetooth logo) ⇨ right-click ⇨ Open Settings, and enabling "Allow Bluetooth devices to find this computer." You can scan for Bluetooth devices in the vicinity of the RPi, and test communication by sending an echo request using the BlueZ l2ping tool (use CTRL+C to quit):

```
pi@erpi ~ $ hcitool scan
Scanning          40:E2:30:13:CA:09        HOMEOFFICE-PC
pi@erpi ~ $ sudo l2ping 40:E2:30:13:CA:09
Ping: 40:E2:30:13:CA:09 from 00:02:72:CB:C3:53 (data size 44) ...
0 bytes from 40:E2:30:13:CA:09 id 0 time 4.27ms
0 bytes from 40:E2:30:13:CA:09 id 1 time 17.09ms ...
```

This means that the adapter on the RPi has discovered my desktop computer, HOMEOFFICE-PC (the hcitool scan command may activate Bluetooth devices in nearby rooms that use Bluetooth remote controls—smart televisions may magically activate!). The RPi can interrogate the available services on the desktop computer using the following:

```
pi@erpi ~ $ sdptool browse 40:E2:30:13:CA:09
Browsing 40:E2:30:13:CA:09 ...
Service Name: Service Discovery
Service Description: Publishes services to remote devices
Service Provider: Microsoft ...
```

This output is followed by a long list of available services, such as an audio source, audio sink, FTP server, printing service, and so on, each having its own unique channel number. Chapter 14 examines how you can pair a user-interface device to the RPi; however, this discussion focuses on how you can send commands to the RPi from a desktop machine, tablet computer, or mobile phone. Such a framework is suitable for localized wireless remote control of the RPi for applications such as robotic control or home automation.

Making the RPi Discoverable

If the RPi is to act as a wireless server, it is vital that it is discoverable by the client machines. The hciconfig command can configure the Bluetooth device (hci0) to enable page and inquiry scans, as follows:

```
pi@erpi ~ $ hciconfig
hci0:   Type: BR/EDR  Bus: USB
        BD Address: 00:02:72:CB:C3:53  ACL MTU: 1021:8  SCO MTU: 64:1
        UP RUNNING PSCAN ISCAN
        RX bytes:5520 acl:45 sco:0 events:106 errors:0
        TX bytes:2413 acl:42 sco:0 commands:45 errors:0
pi@erpi ~ $ sudo hciconfig hci0 piscan
pi@erpi ~ $ sudo hciconfig hci0 name RaspberryPi
pi@erpi ~ $ sudo hciconfig hci0 name
hci0:   Type: BR/EDR  Bus: USB
```

```
BD Address: 00:02:72:CB:C3:53   ACL MTU: 1021:8   SCO MTU: 64:1
Name: 'RaspberryPi'
```

A *Serial Port Profile* (*SPP*) is required on the RPi to define how virtual serial ports are connected via Bluetooth connections. The `sdptool` can be used to configure a profile for a *serial port* (*SP*) on Bluetooth channel 22, and find details about available services using the following:

```
pi@erpi ~ $ sudo sdptool add --channel=22 SP
Serial Port service registered
```

> **NOTE** To get the next step to work correctly, I had to start the `bluetoothd` process with a `--compat` option for my adapter. This should be resolved over time.
>
> ```
> pi@erpi /lib/systemd/system $ more bluetooth.service
> ...
> ExecStart=/usr/lib/bluetooth/bluetoothd --compat
> ```
> You must restart the Bluetooth service after making this file edit.

```
pi@erpi ~ $ sudo sdptool browse local
...
Service Name: Serial Port
Service Description: COM Port
Service Provider: BlueZ
Service RecHandle: 0x10005
Service Class ID List: "Serial Port" (0x1101)
Protocol Descriptor List:
  "L2CAP" (0x0100)   "RFCOMM" (0x0003)   Channel: 22  ...
```

At this point, a desktop computer or a tablet/phone device can be used to scan for devices, as illustrated in Figure 13-2(a) (using an Android mobile phone). The RPi should be detected with the hostname defined earlier in this section (i.e., `RaspberryPi`). However, in order to allow for communication between the RPi and the desktop PC or mobile device, a serial connection needs to be established to channel 22. The RPi must run a service that can listen for incoming connections on that specific Bluetooth channel, for example, by using the `rfcomm` tool:

```
pi@erpi ~ $ sudo rfcomm listen /dev/rfcomm0 22
Waiting for connection on channel 22
```

You can then use a serial terminal on the desktop machine with the associated COM port, or you can use a Bluetooth Terminal App (e.g., the app by Qwerty), as illustrated in Figure 13-2(b), to connect to the RPi `rfcomm` device (i.e., `/dev/rfcomm0`).

A serial terminal can then be opened from the phone or tablet computer, as illustrated in Figure 13-2(c). When a connection is formed to the RPi, the SSH window displays the following:

```
pi@erpi ~ $ sudo rfcomm listen /dev/rfcomm0 22
Waiting for connection on channel 22
Connection from C4:3A:BE:00:D9:9A to /dev/rfcomm0
Press CTRL-C for hangup
```

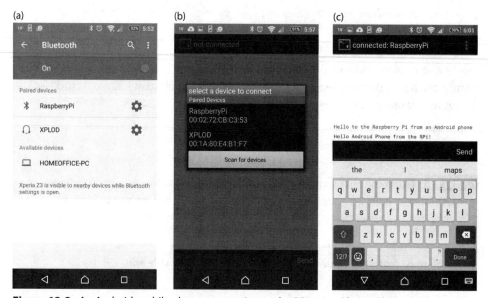

Figure 13-2: An Android mobile phone connecting to the RPi using Bluetooth: (a) device pairing, (b) a Bluetooth terminal application setup, and (c) terminal communication

Do *not* stop this service. While the service is listening, open a second SSH terminal to the RPi. In the second SSH terminal you can `cat` and `echo` to the device associated with the Bluetooth serial connection `rfcomm0`:

```
pi@erpi ~ $ cat /dev/rfcomm0
Hello to the Raspberry Pi from an Android phone^C
pi@erpi ~ $ echo "Hello Android Phone from the RPi!" > /dev/rfcomm0
```

Figure 13-2(c) captures the resulting communication from the mobile device's perspective. At this point it is clear that the device is working, and you can connect a `minicom` terminal to the mobile app or Windows terminal as follows:

```
pi@erpi ~ $ minicom -b 115200 -o -D /dev/rfcomm0
Welcome to minicom 2.7
OPTIONS: I18n
Port /dev/rfcomm0, 06:01:34
Hello from the Android device
Hello from the RPi
```

The resulting conversation is bidirectional and a message is sent whenever the Enter key is pressed. Once you have established serial communication between two devices, there is no limit to the number of possible applications. One such application is the command control of the RPi using a graphical user interface (GUI) that is running on an Android mobile device—this is the topic of the next section.

Android App Development with Bluetooth

There are many resources available for Bluetooth mobile application development with both Android and iOS. Mobile apps could be used for projects such as the remote control of an RPi robotic platform. For example, the app graphical user interface could have forward, backward, left, and right buttons that send string messages to a custom serial server that is running on the RPi. Code for such a server is provided in Chapter 8 in the section titled "RPi LED Serial Server."

A great place to start with mobile application development is the MIT App Inventor (`appinventor.mit.edu/`). It consists of a very innovative web-based graphical programming language (similar to MIT Scratch) for mobile application development. You can pair an Android tablet or phone with the App Inventor environment and view your code developments live on your mobile device. The App Inventor API has Bluetooth client and server libraries that can be integrated with your program code. Figure 13-3 illustrates a full Bluetooth application running on my mobile phone that was built with App Inventor 2. It is communicating to a `minicom` session that is executing on the RPi, while the `rfcomm` service is started in a second terminal window. The (real) phone can communicate directly with the RPi via Bluetooth using the custom-developed mobile application.

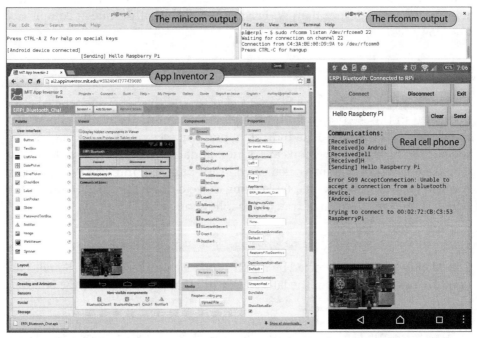

Figure 13-3: An example App Inventor Android application that uses the Bluetooth code library to communicate to the RPi

This application was based on the *Pura Vida Apps* code example, which is available at `tiny.cc/erpi1301`. The code for the example in Figure 13-3 has not been made available in the GitHub repository, as it is strongly based on the code described at that URL. Such a code example can be useful as the basis of an Android application that is capable of sending commands and receiving data from the RPi using Bluetooth communication. The receive function is on a 2.5-second timer, so if the timer triggers halfway through a string being entered, then the string is received in multiple parts. Applications that are developed with App Inventor 2 can be distributed like regular applications (e.g., using `.apk` files to be side-loaded on Android devices). The `ERPi_Bluetooth_Chat.apk` example application is available in the `/chp13/Android/` directory.

Wi-Fi Communications

Bluetooth is perfectly suited to local wireless remote control of the RPi, but Wi-Fi is more suitable for high data rate wireless applications. Wi-Fi can also be used for wireless remote control of the RPi but it requires a complex controller such as a mobile phone/tablet. There are low-cost Bluetooth remote control devices available that can be paired with the RPi and used for remote control applications, as discussed in Chapter 14. However, if you want to connect the RPi wirelessly to the Internet, then Wi-Fi is the clear solution, despite its complexity and power consumption cost.

Installing a Wi-Fi Adapter

Various popular low-profile USB *Wi-Fi adapters* and the RPi 3 onboard adapter are tested in this section, with the adapters and summary results illustrated in Figure 13-4. The table lists indicative performance results that may not be repeatable, as product revisions and Linux updates may affect the outcomes.

Once a USB Wi-Fi adapter is inserted (hot plugged) into the RPi, you can confirm that the network adapter is being detected using the `lsusb` command, which should result in an output of the following form:

```
pi@erpi ~ $ lsusb
Bus 001 Device 004: ID 148f:5370 Ralink Tech, Corp. RT5370 Wireless Adapter
```

The adapter should be detected by the RPi and its chipset identified. Sometimes you may need to search for the latest firmware that is available for the adapter:

```
pi@erpi ~ $ sudo apt update
pi@erpi ~ $ apt-cache search RTL8188
firmware-realtek - Binary firmware for Realtek wired and wireless adapters
pi@erpi ~ $ sudo apt install firmware-realtek
```

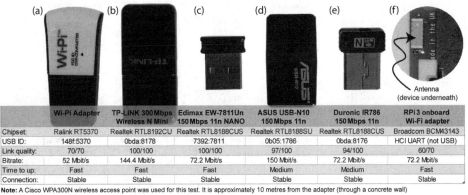

	Wi-Pi Adapter	TP-LINK 300 Mbps Wireless N Mini	Edimax EW-7811Un 150 Mbps 11n NANO	ASUS USB-N10 150 Mbps 11n	Duronic IR786 150 Mbps 11n	RPi3 onboard Wi-Fi adapter
Chipset:	Ralink RT5370	Realtek RTL8192CU	Realtek RTL8188CUS	Realtek RTL8188SU	Realtek RTL8188CUS	Broadcom BCM43143
USB ID:	148f:5370	0bda:8178	7392:7811	0b05:1786	0bda:8176	HCI UART (not USB)
Link quality:	70/70	100/100	100/100	97/100	94/100	60/70
Bitrate:	52 Mbit/s	144.4 Mbit/s	72.2 Mbit/s	150 Mbit/s	72.2 Mbit/s	72.2 Mbit/s
Time to up:	Fast	Fast	Fast	Medium	Medium	Fast
Connection:	Stable	Stable	Stable	Stable	Stable	Stable

Note: A Cisco WPA300N wireless access point was used for this test. It is approximately 10 metres from the adapter (through a concrete wall)
The RPi is running: Linux erpi 4.1.7-v7+ #817 SMP PREEMPT Sat Sep 19 15:32:00 BST 2015 armv7l GNU/Linux

Figure 13-4: A selection of Wi-Fi adapters and test results when they are connected to the RPi

If all goes well, the adapter should appear as `wlanX` in a call to `ifconfig`:

```
pi@erpi ~ $ ifconfig
wlan0     Link encap:Ethernet  HWaddr 00:c1:41:39:0b:f2
          UP BROADCAST MULTICAST  MTU:1500  Metric:1
          RX packets:0 errors:0 dropped:0 overruns:0 frame:0
          TX packets:0 errors:0 dropped:0 overruns:0 carrier:0
          collisions:0 txqueuelen:1000
          RX bytes:0 (0.0 B)  TX bytes:0 (0.0 B)
```

The adapter can then be configured in the `/etc/network/interfaces` configuration file. The default entry under Raspbian is as follows:

```
auto wlan0
allow-hotplug wlan0
iface wlan0 inet manual
wpa-conf /etc/wpa_supplicant/wpa_supplicant.conf
```

Because the network connection is likely encrypted, these settings are not sufficient, but they will allow you to determine your network settings. By default, the network adapter should already be active (or "up"):

```
pi@erpi ~ $ sudo ifup wlan0
ifup: interface wlan0 already configured
```

You can scan for wireless network access points, which will provide you with the settings that are required for the next step:

```
pi@erpi ~ $ sudo iwlist wlan0 scan
wlan0     Scan completed :
          Cell 02 - Address: 98:FC:11:B5:32:96
                    Channel:11           Frequency:2.462 GHz (Channel 11)
                    Quality=70/70        Signal level=-37 dBm
                    Encryption key:on    ESSID:"DereksSSID"
```

```
         Bit Rates:1 Mb/s; 2 Mb/s; 5.5 Mb/s; 11 Mb/s; 9 Mb/s
                   18 Mb/s; 36 Mb/s; 54 Mb/s ...
     IE: IEEE 802.11i/WPA2 Version 1
         Group Cipher : TKIP
         Pairwise Ciphers (2) : TKIP CCMP
         Authentication Suites (1) : PSK
```

Using these settings, you can generate a *WPA passphrase* using the wireless access point name (*SSID*) and network password, as follows:

```
pi@erpi ~ $ sudo sh -c "wpa_passphrase DereksSSID DereksPrivatePassword →
 >> /etc/wpa_supplicant/wpa_supplicant.conf"

pi@erpi ~ $ sudo more /etc/wpa_supplicant/wpa_supplicant.conf
ctrl_interface=DIR=/var/run/wpa_supplicant GROUP=netdev
update_config=1
network={
    ssid="DereksSSID"
    #psk="DereksPrivatePassword"
    psk=427bd5463a8ad022a6de77c8fbdcecb4d6d9d4b96f982fbc57dbfe97c0a12345
}
```

You can then add other settings to the generated configuration file (this step is usually not required). For example:

```
pi@erpi ~ $ sudo more /etc/wpa_supplicant/wpa_supplicant.conf
ctrl_interface=DIR=/var/run/wpa_supplicant GROUP=netdev
update_config=1
network={
    ssid="DereksSSID"
    key_mgmt=WPA-PSK
    pairwise=CCMP TKIP
    group=CCMP TKIP
    psk=427bd5463a8ad022a6de77c8fbdcecb4d6d9d4b96f982fbc57dbfe97c0a12345
}
```

The /etc/network/interfaces configuration file settings identify the location of the wpa_supplicant.conf file. If you are testing multiple Wi-Fi adapters (e.g., wlan0, wlan1), then they can all be configured to use the same wpa_supplicant.conf file. The network adapter interface can be restarted, the configuration checked, and then you can activate the wireless network adapter (wlan0), as follows:

```
pi@erpi ~ $ sudo systemctl restart networking
pi@erpi ~ $ ifconfig -a
wlan0     Link encap:Ethernet   HWaddr 00:c1:41:39:0b:f2
          inet addr:192.168.1.108  Bcast:192.168.1.255  Mask:255.255.255.0
          ...
          RX bytes:496576 (484.9 KiB)  TX bytes:11275 (11.0 KiB)
pi@erpi ~ $ hostname -I
192.168.1.116    192.168.1.108
```

The wireless adapter should now have been allocated an IP address via the wireless access point and the network DHCP service. The auto wlan0 line in the `/etc/network/interfaces` file causes the wireless interface to start on boot. You can disable this option until the adapter is fully working.

If these commands fail, then you should use `dmesg` to check for problems (e.g., `dmesg|grep wlan0|more`). If you receive the message "wpasupplicant daemon failed to start," then check the file `/etc/wpa_supplicant/wpa_supplicant.conf` for any errors, and check that the power supply is sufficient. If the adapter still fails to function correctly, then you may need to build drivers for the board. For example, for Realtek adapters you can download custom driver source code from `www.realtek.com.tw/downloads/` and build them on the RPi. If required, you can bring the adapter down using `ifdown wlan0`.

You can get more useful information about your adapter configuration using `iwconfig`:

```
pi@erpi ~ $ iwconfig wlan0
wlan0     IEEE 802.11bgn  ESSID:"DereksSSID"
          Mode:Managed  Frequency:2.462 GHz  Access Point: 98:FC:11:B5:32:96
          Bit Rate=52 Mb/s   Tx-Power=20 dBm   ...
```

Similarly, you can use the following command to present a display of the signal strength properties, which updates the display every second:

```
pi@erpi ~ $ watch -n 1 cat /proc/net/wireless
Inter-| sta-|  Quality         |Discarded packets           |Missed| WE
 face | tus |link level noise |nwid crypt   frag retry misc|beacon| 22
 wlan0: 0000  70.  -37.  -256   0      0      0    4    41    0
```

Alternatively, you can use the `wavemon` application (`sudo apt install wavemon`) to format that data appropriately for a Linux terminal.

One key advantage of Linux on an embedded device is the ease with which a device can be connected to the Internet using the vast choice of low-cost Wi-Fi adapters. Clearly the web server code, IoT code, and high-speed client/server code examples from Chapter 12 are all directly applicable to a wireless RPi device. Using Wi-Fi you can build untethered IoT devices and robots, typically for indoor applications, that connect directly to the Internet.

The NodeMCU Wi-Fi Slave Processor

In Chapter 11, the Arduino is used as a slave processor for the RPi, where the RPi can take control of its GPIOs and read analog values from its ADCs. The Arduino can be extended with a Wi-Fi shield ($30+), or the Arduino Yún ($75) can be used to build a wireless slave processor. However, there is a cheaper option with a small footprint that can be interfaced directly to the RPi as a slave processor: the NodeMCU.

The NodeMCU (`nodemcu.com`) uses the low-cost ESP8266 Wi-Fi microcontroller module ($2–$3) to create a low-cost Lua-based development platform for IoT applications. The NodeMCU version 2 ($5–$10) is breadboard ready and can be programmed over micro USB, which makes it a suitable prototyping platform for the development of wireless slave devices. Figure 13-5 illustrates the bottom and top of the NodeMCU processor along with its various input/output capabilities, including ADC, GPIO, PWM, SPI, software-based I²C, and serial UART.

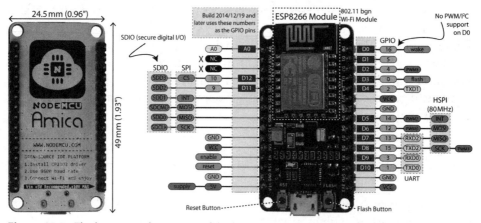

Figure 13-5: The bottom and top views of the low-cost NodeMCU (version 2) Wi-Fi slave processor

The ESP8266 module itself contains the microcontroller and it is affixed on top of the NodeMCU prototyping platform as a tiny daughterboard. It is possible to use the ESP8266 without the NodeMCU, but the ESP8266 module must be affixed to a breakout board to make it breadboard compatible. The documentation for the NodeMCU is available at `tiny.cc/erpi1302`, and the datasheet for the ESP8266 is available at `tiny.cc/erpi1303`.

Flashing with the Latest Firmware

The NodeMCU implements internal USB-to-UART conversion using the same CP2102 chipset that appears in Chapter 9. As discussed, there is typically built-in driver support for this chipset in Linux and Windows.[2]

The most straightforward method of upgrading the firmware on the NodeMCU is to download the open-source NodeMCU firmware programmer from `github.com/nodemcu/nodemcu-flasher` and to download the latest firmware from `github.com/nodemcu/nodemcu-firmware/releases`. You can choose a firmware release with and without floating-point support. The "integer" version without floating-point support is used in this section because it has a much lower resource footprint, and it is useful to investigate the limitations of not having floating-point operation support.

---

[2] If device support is not available or requires an update, then see `tiny.cc/erpi1310`.

The NodeMCU should appear as a device on your host OS, as illustrated for Windows in Figure 13-6(a). Figure 13-6(b) illustrates the NodeMCU firmware programmer in action. Note that you may have to press the reset button on the NodeMCU to begin the firmware update.

(a)   (b)

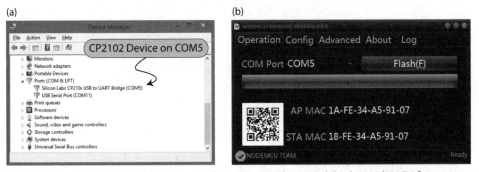

Figure 13-6: (a) The NodeMCU device profile under Windows, and (b) the NodeMCU firmware programmer

Connecting the NodeMCU to Wi-Fi

Once the NodeMCU has been flashed with the latest firmware, you can use PuTTY or the RPi minicom tool to connect to the device at 9,600 baud. For the remaining steps in this section, the NodeMCU is attached to the RPi using a USB-to-micro USB cable. Press the reset button on the NodeMCU after connecting it via USB; you should see the following output:

```
pi@erpi ~ $ lsusb
Bus 001 Device 009: ID 10c4:ea60 Cygnal Integrated Products, Inc.
CP210x UART Bridge / myAVR mySmartUSB light
pi@erpi ~ $ ls -l /dev/ttyUSB*
crw-rw---- 1 root dialout 188, 0 Oct 24 16:56 /dev/ttyUSB0
pi@erpi ~ $ sudo apt install minicom
pi@erpi ~ $ minicom -b 9600 -o -D /dev/ttyUSB0 -s
```

Press the reset button on the NodeMCU; a few strange characters may appear. Do *not* enable local echo in minicom, and be sure that you disable hardware flow control:

NOTE You must disable hardware flow control in minicom to connect to the NodeMCU device directly from the RPi via USB. You do this by pressing Ctrl+A Z O ⇨ Serial port setup ⇨ F (to set Hardware Flow Control to No). The -s option can be used when executing minicom to place you directly in this menu. If the NodeMCU displays the reset message but remains unresponsive, it is a symptom of incorrect hardware flow control settings.

If all goes well, you are now able to issue commands to the NodeMCU using Lua scripting, which is discussed in Chapter 5. Lua has a very low overhead, which makes it suitable for use on this device. The first step you should take is to configure the NodeMCU so that it can connect to your Wi-Fi network:

```
NodeMCU 0.9.6 build 20150704   powered by Lua 5.1.4
lua: cannot open init.lua
> =wifi.sta.getip()
nil
> wifi.setmode(wifi.STATION)
> wifi.sta.config("DereksSSID","DereksPrivatePassword")
> =wifi.sta.getip()
192.168.1.120   255.255.255.0   192.168.1.1
> =wifi.sta.getmac()
18:fe:34:a5:91:91
> =wifi.sta.status()
5
```

A value of 5 indicates that the NodeMCU "station" now has an IP address. These settings persist on the NodeMCU, even after it has been power cycled.

Programming the NodeMCU

To upload Lua programs to the NodeMCU from the RPi, you can use the `luatool`, which can be downloaded and installed as follows:

```
pi@erpi ~ $ git clone https://github.com/4refr0nt/luatool
Cloning into 'luatool'...
pi@erpi ~ $ cd luatool/luatool/
pi@erpi ~/luatool/luatool $ ls
init.lua   luatool.py   main.luav
```

You can install the tool for all users on the RPi by placing it in the /usr/local/bin/ directory:

```
pi@erpi ~/luatool/luatool $ sudo cp luatool.py /usr/local/bin
```

An example program is provided in /chp13/nodemcu/test/ and in Listing 13-1 that establishes a simple web server on the NodeMCU. The simple web server listens for TCP socket connections on port 80, and returns an HTML "hello world" message to the web client.

Listing 13-1: /chp13/nodemcu/test/main.lua

```
-- a simple http server
srv=net.createServer(net.TCP)
gpio.mode(1,gpio.INPUT)
srv:listen(80,function(conn)
    conn:on("receive",function(conn,payload) print(payload)
        conn:send("HTTP/1.1 200 OK\n\n")
        conn:send("<html><body><h1> Hello from the NodeMCU.</h1>")
        conn:send("<h2> GPIO 1 = ")
```

```
        conn:send(gpio.read(1))
        conn:send("</h2></body></html>")
        conn:on("sent",function(conn) conn:close() end)
    end)
end)
```

You must disconnect the `minicom` communications session in order to use the `luatool` to upload the program to the NodeMCU device—the two programs cannot share the same UART device connection. Because the `luatool` is installed in the `/usr/local/bin/` directory, you can execute it directly from the book's repository directory, as follows:

```
pi@erpi .../chp13/nodemcu/test $ ls
main.lua
pi@erpi .../chp13/nodemcu/test $ luatool.py -p /dev/ttyUSB0 -b 9600
->file.open("main.lua", "w") -> ok
->file.close() -> ok
->file.remove("main.lua") -> ok
->file.open("main.lua", "w+") -> ok
->file.writeline([==[-- a simple http server]==]) -> ok
->file.writeline([==[srv=net.createServer(net.TCP)]==]) -> ok  ...
--->>> All done <<<---
```

After a successful upload, you can once again connect to the NodeMCU using `minicom`. The program is named `main.lua` on the NodeMCU, so the warning message remains in relation to the absence of `init.lua`. This is perfectly fine—you should only write an `init.lua` script that automatically invokes `main.lua` on startup when you are certain that it is functioning correctly. For the moment it is best to manually call the `main.lua` script as follows so that you can observe any output errors within the `minicom` session:

```
pi@erpi ~ $ minicom -b 9600 -o -D /dev/ttyUSB0 -s
NodeMCU 0.9.6 build 20150704  powered by Lua 5.1.4
lua: cannot open init.lua
> node.restart()
...
NodeMCU 0.9.6 build 20150704  powered by Lua 5.1.4
lua: cannot open init.lua
> =node.info()
0    9    6    10850705    1458415 4096    2    40000000
> =wifi.sta.getip()
192.168.1.120    255.255.255.0    192.168.1.1
```

You can then execute the program as follows:

```
> dofile("main.lua")
```

Once the program has started, you can open a web browser on your desktop machine and direct it at the IP address of the NodeMCU device (`http://192.168.1.120/` in the example). In addition to the hello message, the Lua program displays the state of the D1 pin (GPIO 5). If you tie this pin high (to 3.3 V) or low (to GND), you will see that the web page changes to display the current GPIO state when the reload button is clicked on the web browser.

The NodeMCU Web Server Interface

The NodeMCU can be used as a wireless slave processor for the RPi, whereby communication takes place over TCP/IP, using the socket-based techniques that are described in Chapter 12. A circuit is illustrated in Figure 13-7(a) that can be used to read from a GPIO, write to a GPIO, and read from the 10-bit ADC on the NodeMCU. The NodeMCU uses 3.3 V logic levels, despite being powered at 5 V using the Vin pin. However, while the NodeMCU is tethered to the RPi using the USB cable, no external power supply is required. Remember though that communication, such as that illustrated in Figure 13-7(b), is taking place over Wi-Fi, not via the USB cable. Once development is complete, the USB cable can be removed and the NodeMCU can be powered by an external supply, such as a 5 V battery, using the Vin and GND pins.

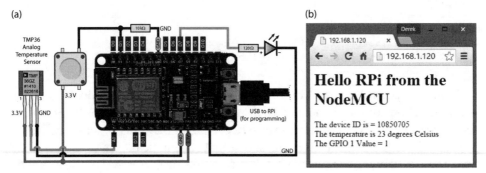

Figure 13-7: NodeMCU Wi-Fi slave test: (a) the test circuit, and (b) the web page output

The code for this example is provided in Listing 13-2. The program converts the ADC value presented by the TMP36 sensor into a temperature value; however, it does this using integer-based calculation only. As discussed, the firmware without floating-point support has a lower footprint and better performance. Should you need floating-point support, you can download and flash the NodeMCU with the floating-point firmware, as described previously in this chapter.

The LED flashes each time a request is received. Note that it flashes twice when the Chrome browser in Figure 13-7(b) sends a request, as the browser actually sends two requests: one for the HTML page, and another for the website icon.

Listing 13-2: /chp13/nodemcu/web/main.lua

```
srv=net.createServer(net.TCP)
gpio.mode(1,gpio.INPUT)                      -- the button
gpio.mode(7,gpio.OUTPUT)                     -- the LED
srv:listen(80,function(conn)
    conn:on("receive",function(conn,payload) print(payload)
        gpio.write(7, gpio.HIGH)
```

```
conn:send("HTTP/1.1 200 OK\n\n")
conn:send("<html><body><h1> Hello RPi from the NodeMCU</h1>")
conn:send("<div> The device ID is = ")
conn:send(node.chipid())
-- using integers only! float version uses more memory
raw_voltage = adc.read(0) - 233     -- 233 is 25C
diff_degC   = raw_voltage / 6       -- 6 steps is 1C
temperature = diff_degC + 25        -- add/sub from 25
conn:send("<div> The temperature is ")
conn:send(temperature)
conn:send(" degrees Celsius</div>")
conn:send("<div> The GPIO 1 Value = ")
conn:send(gpio.read(1))
conn:send("</div></body></html>")
gpio.write(7, gpio.LOW)
conn:on("sent",function(conn) conn:close() end)
    end)
end)
```

You can upload this program, start it, and test it using the steps described in the previous section. You can also test the output directly from the RPi using the web browser code described in Chapter 12. For example:

```
pi@erpi ~/exploringrpi/chp12/webbrowser $ ./webbrowser 192.168.1.120
Sending the message: GET / HTTP/1.1
Host: 192.168.1.120
Connection: close
**START**
HTTP/1.1 200 OK

<html><body><h1> Hello RPi from the NodeMCU</h1><div> The device ID is
= 10850705<div> The temperature is 23 degrees Celsius</div><div> The
GPIO 1 Value = 0</div></body></html>
**END**
```

This provides you with a method of writing code on the RPi that can communicate to the NodeMCU slave processor in order to retrieve information over TCP/IP. However, it would be a better solution if the data was easier to parse than the HTML output in this example—for this you can use JSON.

JSON

JSON is a lightweight data-interchange format that supports serialization and deserialization of data values from strings. It is described briefly in Chapter 12 where a data sample is transmitted from the RPi to the IBM Bluemix IoT service using MQ Telemetry Transport (MQTT). It is relatively straightforward to format a message for transmission, but it is more difficult to parse the received message. In this example, the NodeMCU transmits a JSON message to the RPi and the RPi must parse the message. *JsonCpp* is a lightweight C++ library that can be used for this task, but first it must be built and deployed on the RPi. It is useful to note that the library also has Python bindings. You can install the JsonCpp library on the RPi as follows:

```
pi@erpi ~ $ git clone https://github.com/open-source-parsers/jsoncpp.git
pi@erpi ~ $ cd jsoncpp/
pi@erpi ~/jsoncpp $ sudo apt install cmake
pi@erpi ~/jsoncpp $ mkdir -p build/debug
pi@erpi ~/jsoncpp $ cd build/debug
pi@erpi ~/jsoncpp/build/debug $ cmake -DCMAKE_BUILD_TYPE=debug →
-DBUILD_STATIC_LIBS=ON -DBUILD_SHARED_LIBS=OFF -DARCHIVE_INSTALL_DIR=. →
-G "Unix Makefiles" ../..
pi@erpi ~/jsoncpp/build/debug $ make
pi@erpi ~/jsoncpp/build/debug $ sudo make install
```

Listing 13-3 is a short JSON data file that can be used to test the JsonCpp library on the RPi. The file contains two fields: a floating-point temperature value, and a Boolean value that describes the state of a button.

Listing 13-3: /chp13/json/data.json

```
{
    "temperature" : 28.5,
    "button" : true
}
```

Listing 13-4 is a C++ example program that uses the JsonCpp library to parse the data.json file in Listing 13-3.

Listing 13-4: /chp13/json/json_test.cpp

```
#include "json/json.h"
#include<iostream>
#include<fstream>
using namespace std;

int main(){
    Json::Value root;          // the parsed data is at the root
    Json::Reader reader;       // read from the data.json file
    ifstream data("data.json", ifstream::binary);
    bool success = reader.parse(data, root, false);
    if(!success){              // has the parsing failed?
        cout << "Failed: " <<  reader.getFormattedErrorMessages() << endl;
    }
    // the deserialized data can be converted to a float and a bool
    float temperature = root.get("temperature", "UTF-8").asFloat();
    bool button = root.get("button", "UTF-8").asBool();
    cout << "The temperature is " << temperature << "°C" << endl;
    cout << "The button is " << (button ? "pressed":"not pressed") << endl;
    return 0;
}
```

Once the data file is open, the call `root.get("temperature", "UTF-8")`. `asFloat()` is used to get the `temperature` field value. It is important to note that the deserialized return value is of the type `float`. The JSON library has performed all of the work involved in parsing the file, identifying the temperature field, and deserializing the data. The program can be built and executed as follows:

```
pi@erpi .../chp13/json $ g++ json_test.cpp libjsoncpp.a -o test
pi@erpi .../chp13/json $ ./test
The temperature is 28.5°C
The button is pressed
```

Communicating Using JSON Messages

JSON can be used for all types of data interchange and it is not limited to use with NodeMCU devices; however, it is useful to develop a client/server socket example so that the RPi can communicate with the NodeMCU over Wi-Fi and then easily parse the communications response. Listing 13-5 is a Lua program that executes on the NodeMCU. It is very similar to Listing 13-2, with the exception that the return data is constructed as a JSON string of the form: `{ "temperature" : X, "button" : Y }`, where X and Y are the temperature and button press states.

Listing 13-5: /chp13/jsonNodeMCU/main.lua

```lua
-- a simple http server
srv=net.createServer(net.TCP)
gpio.mode(1,gpio.INPUT)
gpio.mode(7,gpio.OUTPUT)
srv:listen(80,function(conn)
    conn:on("receive",function(conn,payload) print(payload)
        gpio.write(7, gpio.HIGH)
        conn:send("{\n")
        raw_voltage = adc.read(0) - 233    -- 233 is 25C
        diff_degC   = raw_voltage / 6      -- 6 steps is 1C
        temperature = diff_degC + 25       -- add/sub from 25
        conn:send("   \"temperature\" : ")
        conn:send(temperature)
        conn:send(",\n")
        conn:send("   \"button\" : ")
        if gpio.read(1)==1 then
            conn:send("true\n")
        else
            conn:send("false\n")
        end
        conn:send("}\n")
        gpio.write(7, gpio.LOW)
        conn:on("sent",function(conn) conn:close() end)
    end)
end)
```

The code can be uploaded to the NodeMCU and executed as before:

```
pi@erpi .../chp13/jsonNodeMCU $ luatool.py -p /dev/ttyUSB0 -b 9600
pi@erpi .../chp13/jsonNodeMCU $ minicom -b 9600 -o -D /dev/ttyUSB0 -s
NodeMCU 0.9.6 build 20150704  powered by Lua 5.1.4
lua: cannot open init.lua
> node.restart()
> dofile("main.lua")
```

You can test that the script is working correctly by opening the NodeMCU web page, whereupon you should see an output of the following form:

```
{
    "temperature" : 22,
    "button" : true
}
```

The C++ socket code from Chapter 12 and the JsonCpp code from Listing 13-4 can be merged to create a program that can communicate to the NodeMCU using TCP sockets and parse the JSON response. An example is shown in Listing 13-6.

Listing 13-6: /chp13/jsonNodeMCU/jsonNodeMCU.cpp

```
#include <iostream>
#include "json/json.h"
#include "network/SocketClient.h"
using namespace std;
using namespace exploringRPi;

int main(int argc, char *argv[]){
   Json::Value root;
   Json::Reader reader;
   if(argc!=2){
      cout << "Usage is: jsonNodeMCU nodeMCU_IP" << endl;
      return 2;
   }
   SocketClient sc(argv[1], 80);
   sc.connectToServer();
   string message("GET / HTTP/1.1");
   sc.send(message);
   string rec = sc.receive(1024);
   bool success = reader.parse(rec, root, false);
   if(!success){                 // has the parsing failed?
      cout << "Failed: " <<  reader.getFormattedErrorMessages() << endl;
   }
   float temperature = root.get("temperature", "UTF-8").asFloat();
   bool button = root.get("button", "UTF-8").asBool();
   cout << "The temperature is " << temperature << "°C" << endl;
   cout << "The button is " << (button ? "pressed":"not pressed") << endl;
   return 0;
}
```

Listing 13-6 gives the following output when it is executed:

```
pi@erpi ~/exploringrpi/chp13/jsonNodeMCU $ ./build
pi@erpi ~/exploringrpi/chp13/jsonNodeMCU $ ./jsonNodeMCU 192.168.1.120
The temperature is 21°C
```

```
The button is not pressed
pi@erpi ~/exploringrpi/chp13/jsonNodeMCU $ ./jsonNodeMCU 192.168.1.120
The temperature is 20°C
The button is pressed
```

Note that the LED attached to the NodeMCU only flashes once in this example, as only a single HTTP request is received—there is no request for a website icon.

This approach to device messaging can be applied to other applications. For example, it could also be used to facilitate two RPi boards in communicating over TCP/IP.

The NodeMCU and MQTT

The NodeMCU firmware has full built-in support for MQTT. Therefore, the MQTT frameworks that are described in Chapter 12 can be used for brokered communication between the NodeMCU and the RPi. For example, the NodeMCU could publish sensor data to an IoT Platform as a Service (PaaS) and the RPi could subscribe to the same data stream. Listing 13-7 provides an MQTT example that runs directly on the NodeMCU. To use this example, you must create a device on the MQTT PaaS using the instructions in Chapter 12. For example, I created a NodeMCU device on IBM Bluemix IoT with the following settings:

```
Organization ID        4wyix6
Device Type            NodeMCU
Device ID              node01
Authentication Method  token
Authentication Token   &hnss1h+1i_*qKvMBH
```

The Lua code in Listing 13-7 uses these properties to connect the NodeMCU to the PaaS. The program opens an MQTT connection and publishes ten samples from the temperature sensor at ten-second intervals. Once ten samples have been sent, the program closes the connection to the PaaS. The program uses the same circuit that is illustrated in Figure 13-7(a).

Listing 13-7: /chp13/nodemcu/mqtt/main.lua

```lua
-- a simple NodeMCU MQTT publish example for IBM Bluemix IoT
BROKER = "4wyix6.messaging.internetofthings.ibmcloud.com"
BRPORT = 1883
BRUSER = "use-token-auth"
BRPWD  = "&hnss1h+1i_*qKvMBH"
DEVID  = "d:4wyix6:NodeMCU:node01"
TOPIC  = "iot-2/evt/status/fmt/json"
count  = 0              -- used to count the number of samples sent

gpio.mode(7, gpio.OUTPUT)
gpio.write(7, gpio.HIGH)
print("Starting the NodeMCU MQTT client test")
print("Current heap is: " .. node.heap())   -- .. appends strings
m = mqtt.Client(DEVID, 120, BRUSER, BRPWD)  -- keep alive time 120s
m:connect(BROKER, BRPORT, 0, function(conn) -- secure off
    print("Connected to MQTT Broker: " .. BROKER)
```

```
        tmr.alarm(0, 10000, 1, function()          -- repeat is on
            publish_sample()
            print("Time for another sample")
            count = count + 1
        end)
end)

function publish_sample()
    raw_voltage = adc.read(0) - 233      -- 233 is 25C
    diff_degC   = raw_voltage / 6        -- 6 steps is 1C
    temp        = diff_degC + 25         -- add/sub from 25
    msg = string.format("{\"d\":{\"Temp\": %d }}", temp)
    m:publish(TOPIC, msg, 0, 0, function(conn)
        print("Published a message: " .. msg)
        print("Value of count is: " .. count)
        if count>=10 then
            close()
            timer.cancel(0)
        end
    end)
end

function close()
    m:close()
    print("End of the NodeMCU MQTT Example")
    gpio.write(7, gpio.LOW)
end
```

This program can be uploaded from the RPi and executed on the NodeMCU as follows:

```
pi@erpi .../chp13/nodemcu/mqtt $ luatool.py -p /dev/ttyUSB0 -b 9600
NodeMCU 0.9.6 build 20150704  powered by Lua 5.1.4
lua: cannot open init.lua
> node.restart()
> dofile("main.lua")
Starting the NodeMCU MQTT client test
Current heap is: 29072
Connected to MQTT Broker: 4wyix6.messaging.internetofthings.ibmcloud.com
Time for another sample
Published a message: {"d":{"Temp": 23 }}
Value of count is: 1
...
Published a message: {"d":{"Temp": 22 }}
Value of count is: 10
End of the NodeMCU MQTT Example
```

The LED attached to the NodeMCU turns on when the program begins and turns off when the communication transaction has completed.

This final application of the NodeMCU demonstrates the numerous possibilities of IoT frameworks—it is possible to have many low-cost devices such as the NodeMCU wirelessly publishing sensor data to a cloud platform, whereupon the cloud platform can execute programs to analyze the data and trigger events on other such devices that are subscribed to data streams. The computationally powerful nature of the RPi means that it can aggregate data locally and/or perform advanced interactions (e.g., using computer vision techniques to recognize a face) for IoT applications. Finally, the example also confirms the low-overhead nature of MQTT, as it can clearly be used on a low-cost microcontroller such as the ESP8266 for persistent data communications.

ZigBee Communications

ZigBee is a global standard for power-efficient, low data rate, embedded wireless communication. It supports the concept of wireless mesh networking, in which nodes cooperate to relay data. This allows the range of the network to be extended far beyond what is possible with the single access point model. In addition, the mesh network can heal itself should a node in the network be lost. The ZigBee standard is maintained by the *ZigBee Alliance* (`zigbee.org`), a non-profit association of approximately 450 members, who promote the use of ZigBee.

Introduction to XBee Devices

Digi (`digi.com`) *XBee* devices, such as those illustrated in Figure 13-8(a), are possibly the best known hardware realization of the ZigBee standard. However, not all XBee devices are actually ZigBee compatible. In fact, Digi also manufactures devices that use a proprietary *DigiMesh* protocol for mesh networking, which is not compatible with ZigBee.[3] Care must be taken in choosing your devices. The ZigBee protocol defines three types of nodes:

1. *Coordinators*. There is one coordinator in each network that is used to establish the network and to distribute security keys. For RPi applications, the coordinator is usually connected directly to the RPi via a UART connection.

2. *Routers*. These nodes relay data from device to device and are not permitted to sleep.

3. *End Devices*. These devices are the leaf nodes in the network. They take information from sensor devices, and transmit it to routers and coordinators. They cannot relay data from other nodes, but are permitted to sleep.

In contrast, the DigiMesh protocol simplifies the mesh structure by using only one type of node that can take on any of the ZigBee roles. Unfortunately, it is not compatible with the ZigBee protocol or other vendor solutions. A separate *XBee 802.15.4* standard version is also available, but it only supports point-to-point or point-to-multipoint networking—it does not support mesh networking. The model numbering scheme used by Digi is confusing, but once you understand the

---

[3] A white paper is available at `tiny.cc/erpi1309` that describes the differences between ZigBee and DigiMesh in detail.

difference between ZigBee and DigiMesh you can choose a module accordingly. Table 13-2 summarizes these differences and lists the current naming convention for devices, which all operate at 2.4 GHz and are in a through-hole package.

(a)　　　　　　　　　　　　　　　　　　　　　　　　(b)

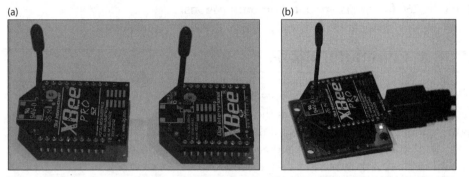

Figure 13-8: (a) The XBee Pro S2 and XBee S2 devices with wire antennas, and (b) the SparkFun XBee USB Explorer

Table 13-2: Comparison of XBee Models

XBEE NAME	PROTOCOL/ TOPOLOGY	DESCRIPTION
Series 2 ZigBee	ZigBee/Mesh	Standardized and interoperable with other vendor solutions. This model supports AT and API modes. There must be one coordinator in each network. Coordinators and routers cannot sleep.
Series 1 802.15.4	802.15.4/ Multipoint	Good point-to-point and point-to-multipoint support.
Series 1 DigiMesh	DigiMesh/Mesh	Uses firmware to implement proprietary mesh networking on Series 1 modules. Only one type of node is required.

www.digi.com/lp/xbee

The XBee Pro S2 and XBee S2 devices[4] are shown side by side in Figure 13-8(a). They have compatible pin layouts, but the XBee Pro S2 is physically longer. The Pro version is somewhat more expensive (~$29 versus ~$19) and uses greater power levels (63mW versus 2mW), but it is capable of free-space communication distances of up to 1 mile, whereas the non-Pro version is limited to approximately 400 feet. The versions in Figure 13-8(a) include an on-board wire antenna, which is a delicate but convenient option. Alternative configurations

---

[4] The precise Digi modules used in this section are the *XBee PRO ZB with a wire antenna* (XBP24-Z7WIT-004) and The *XBee ZB with a wire antenna* (XB24-Z7WIT-004).

include PCB trace antennas or external u.FL/RP-SMA antennas. The latter are particularly useful if you intend to place your project inside a metal and/or weather-sealed box. Most XBee devices, like Wi-Fi devices, operate at 2.4GHz. This band of frequencies does not need a license, as transmissions in this band do not interfere with licensed frequency bands, such as those used for radio broadcast and cellular phones.

Note that the 2 mm pin spacing on XBee modules is not compatible with 0.1-inch (2.5 mm) breadboard spacing, which means that an adapter board ($2–$3) is required for prototyping work. Also, remember to purchase at least two XBee modules—they are not much use on their own!

AT versus API Mode

XBee devices can be used in two modes, and it is important that you understand the distinction:

- *AT command mode. AT*tention commands are instructions that are used to control serial devices such as modems. These devices relay data precisely, but when a certain string of characters is sent to the device, it enters a special AT mode. This is the default mode of operation on XBee devices and it hides much of the underlying communications complexity. In effect, two XBee devices configured in this mode behave somewhat like a wireless serial UART connection. However, in this mode XBee devices enter AT command mode when the characters +++ are sent to the device. Subsequent AT commands, which are prefixed by the characters AT, can then be issued. For example, ATID returns the network ID (PAN ID). This topic is discussed in more detail shortly.

- *API mode.* The Digi XBee devices can also be used in API mode, which is used to transmit structured frames of data. The frames of data can be addressed and sent to an individual module without having to reprogram the device. In addition, API mode facilitates interaction with the input/output (I/O) capabilities of an XBee module, and it provides support for the receipt of data transfer acknowledgements.

API mode is much more capable than AT mode, but it is more complex to program. In the following sections an application is developed in both modes.

XBee Configuration

Once you have XBee devices, the first step is to configure them using your desktop computer and a device such as the SparkFun XBee USB Explorer, which is illustrated in Figure 13-8(b). The most intuitive way to configure an XBee device is to use the *XCTU* software platform from Digi.

XCTU

XCTU is a full-featured GUI-based configuration platform for XBee devices that is provided by Digi. It can discover modules that are attached to your desktop computer using the XBee USB Explorer, as illustrated in Figure 13-9(a), and configure the network properties, such as the PAN ID, as illustrated in Figure 13-9(b). XCTU is available for free on Windows, MacOS X, and Linux. You can download it from www.digi.com/xctu.

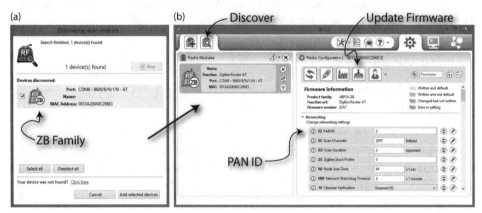

Figure 13-9: The Digi XCTU software: (a) device discovery using an XBee USB adapter, and (b) the device configuration window

Configuring an XBee Network Using XCTU

The first thing you should do with XCTU is to update the XBee modules to the latest firmware. Click the Update Firmware button (see Figure 13-9b) and then choose the product family, function set, and firmware version. There are different firmware versions depending on whether you are using AT or API mode, and whether you are setting up a coordinator, router, or end device. These options are described throughout this section.

To configure an AT or API-based network, you must set a *PAN ID*. The *personal area network ID* is a 16-bit address that allows you to configure a set of XBee devices to be on the same network. This network ID facility allows you to create multiple networks of devices that are independent from each other, even at the same physical location. To establish a network, ensure that all of the devices have the same PAN ID.

The two examples that follow provide step-by-step instructions on configuring XBee devices in AT and API mode. Each example identifies and utilizes different firmware versions, which necessitates the use of XCTU in reprogramming the firmware of the devices.

RESETTING OLDER/GENERIC XBEE USB EXPLORERS

You may have a SparkFun XBee USB Explorer from an older project or you may have purchased a generic XBee USB Explorer that does not have a reset button. If so, you may see a message such as the one in Figure 13-10(a) when you use it to update the firmware. You can add a pushbutton to the RST and GND pins on your XBee USB Explorer, as illustrated in Figure 13-10(b). The reset button that is illustrated in Figure 1-5(a) is ideal for this application.

(a)   (b)

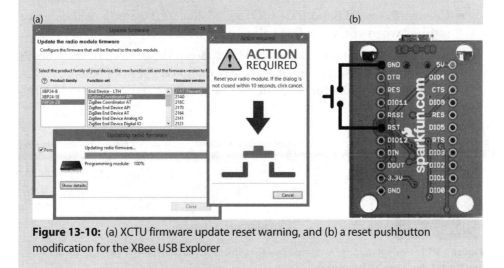

Figure 13-10: (a) XCTU firmware update reset warning, and (b) a reset pushbutton modification for the XBee USB Explorer

An XBee AT Mode Example

In this example, an Arduino is configured to be a wireless temperature sensor for the RPi. The Arduino takes an analog reading from the TMP36 temperature sensor and converts the voltage value into degrees Celsius (or Fahrenheit). One XBee router module in AT mode is connected to the Arduino (termed XBeeA). A second XBee coordinator module in AT mode is connected to the RPi (termed XBeePi). To be clear, both modules are physically identical but they will have different roles as a result of the firmware that is written to them. The final circuit is illustrated in Figure 13-12, but you should not connect it at this point, as the modules must be configured. In AT mode the XBee modules behave like a wireless UART connection, but you must first pair the devices to establish communication. Each device must be configured with the destination address set to that of the other XBee module.

Setting Up the Arduino XBee Device (XBeeA)

Place the XBeeA module in the XBee USB Explorer and attach it to your desktop machine—ensure that you align the pin numbers on the XBee module and the XBee USB Explorer. Click the Discover button in XCTU (as indicated in Figure 13-9(b)); the device appears in the list of available modules. In my case, XBeeA has the MAC address 0013 A200 40C8B460.

In XCTU, perform the following configuration steps:

- Update to the latest firmware for a ZigBee Router AT (version 22A7 at the time of writing).

- Change the PAN ID to 5432. Both XBee devices will use this address.

- Change the serial Baud Rate (BD) to 115,200. XCTU updates the device settings when you write this value to the XBee.

- Read the Destination Address (DH/DL) from the bottom of the XBeePi (see Figure 13-11a) and enter it as the destination address for XBeeA: DH as 0013A200 and DL as 40E8E355 in my case, as illustrated in Figure 13-11(b).

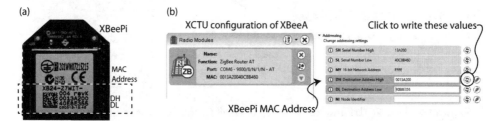

Figure 13-11: Configuring the Arduino XBee to connect to the RPi XBee Device: (a) the RPi XBee, and (b) Arduino XBee XCTU settings

Connect XBeeA to the Arduino as illustrated in Figure 13-12(a) but do not connect the RX and TX lines at this point. Listing 13-8 is an Arduino sketch that interfaces to analog input pin A0, reads in the current voltage, and converts it to degrees Celsius (as described in Chapter 11). The code then sends a JSON string out on the serial connection. You can change `tempC` to `tempF` to transmit the temperature in degrees Fahrenheit.

NOTE You must disconnect the TX and RX lines from the Arduino to the XBee device when you are programming the Arduino or you will have communication problems. If you are doing this regularly, then it might be worth adding two slider switches to your breadboard circuit.

Listing 13-8: chp13/xbee/at/xbee.ino

```
const int analogInPin = A0;          // analog input for the TMP36

void setup(){
    pinMode(13, OUTPUT);
    Serial.begin(115200, SERIAL_8N1);
}

void loop(){                          // update registers every five secs
```

```
digitalWrite(13, HIGH);                          // LED briefly on
delay(100);                                       // 100ms + processing
int adcValue = analogRead(analogInPin);           // using a 10-bit ADC
float curVoltage = adcValue * (3.3f/1024.0f);     // Vcc = 5.0V, 10-bit
float tempC = 25.0 + ((curVoltage-0.75f)/0.01f);  // from datasheet
float tempF = 32.0 + ((tempC * 9)/5);             // deg. C to F
Serial.print("{ \"Temperature\" : ");             // Send as JSON msg
Serial.print(tempC);                              // The temperature
Serial.println(" }");                             // close JSON message
digitalWrite(13, LOW);                            // LED off
delay(4900);                                       // delay ~5 secs total
}
```

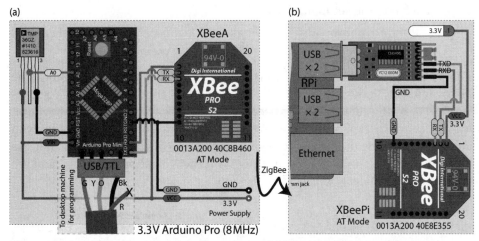

Figure 13-12: (a) The XBeeA circuit configuration, and (b) the XBeePi circuit configuration

Write the program to the Arduino using a USB-to-UART cable as described in Chapter 11. Then open the serial console on the Arduino programming environment (use a baud rate of 115,200); you should see the following JSON format messages every five seconds. If you hold the TMP36 sensor, then the temperature should change.

```
{ "Temperature" : 22.19 }
{ "Temperature" : 22.19 }
{ "Temperature" : 24.44 }
```

You can now connect the RX/TX pins from the Arduino to the XBee as illustrated in Figure 13-12(a). You can leave the Arduino Serial Console open. The on-board LED acts as a status indicator, flashing briefly each time a reading is transmitted. The Arduino XBee configuration is complete.

NOTE Several of the examples in this chapter use a USB-to-UART adapter. These adapters are described in Chapter 9 as a convenient alternative to the on-board UART device (`/dev/ttyAMA0` or `/dev/ttyS0`), which is described in Chapter 8. If you use the on-board UART device, remember to disable the `serial-getty` service that runs by default—see Chapter 8 for instructions.

Setting Up the RPi XBee Device (XBeePi)

The second XBee module, XBeePi, must be configured to have XBeeA as the communications destination. Place the XBeePi module in the XBee USB Explorer and attach it to your desktop machine. Click the Discover button in XCTU; in my case, the module appears with the MAC address 0013A200 40E8E355 as expected. Then perform the following steps using XCTU:

■ Update the firmware on the device to "ZigBee Coordinator AT." Note that this module should be set to be a *coordinator*, unlike the XBeeA *router*.

■ Change the PAN ID to 5432 and set the baud rate to 115,200 in order to conform to the settings of XBeeA.

■ Set the destination address DH and DL values according to the MAC address of XBeeA (0013A200 40C8B460 in my case).

With the XBeePi module still in the XBee USB Explorer, you can click the Discover Radio Nodes button and the XBeeA should appear in the list. You cannot view or configure the settings because the devices are in AT mode; however, you can switch to the Console working mode and click Connect, whereupon you should see an output similar to Figure 13-13. The output indicates that the Arduino is successfully communicating with the XBeePi module and you are now ready to connect it to the RPi.

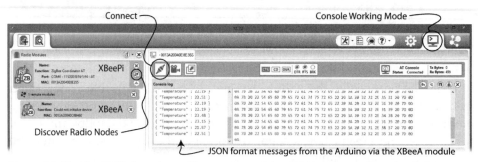

Figure 13-13: The XCTU Console working mode receiving JSON messages from the Arduino XBee device

The XBeePi can be removed from the XBee USB Explorer and attached to the RPi as described in Figure 13-12(b). The connection can be tested by using `minicom` as follows:

```
pi@erpi ~ $ minicom -b 115200 -o -D /dev/ttyUSB0
{ "Temperature" : 21.87 }
{ "Temperature" : 22.19 } ...
```

A new JSON format temperature reading appears after each five-second interval. The Arduino UART code from Chapter 11 can be used to read these values in C/C++, and the JSON code earlier in this chapter can be used to parse the data strings.

Remember, this circuit is a bi-directional communication channel—the UART Command Control code can also be used to control the Arduino, as described in Chapter 11.

XBEE AT COMMANDS

A useful exercise at this point is to become familiar with AT commands. Leave the `minicom` session running, but disconnect the power to the XBeeA module in order to halt the incoming data stream to the RPi. Then, using the `minicom` terminal, enter some AT commands:

- To turn on AT mode, type +++ (don't press Enter); OK will appear as the response.

- Then display the network ID (PAN ID) by typing ATID (i.e., ID prefixed by AT) and pressing Enter.

For example, following is an AT conversation to read the settings for the network ID, serial number (high and low parts), and destination address (high and low parts). Ensure that local echo is enabled in `minicom`, and note that AT mode ends ten seconds after you type the last valid AT command—you have to be quick!

```
pi@erpi ~ $ minicom -b 115200 -o -D /dev/ttyUSB0
+++OK
ATID
5432
ATSH
13A200
ATSL
40E8E355
ATDH
13A200
ATDL
40C8B460
```

To change a setting, you should append the new value to the command. For example, to set a new network ID 1234 (and then set it back to 5432), type the following:

```
ATID1234
OK
ATID
1234
ATID5432
OK
ATID
5432
```

A full list of AT commands is visible in the configuration entries of XCTU (see Figure 13-9b) and in the *XBee Command Reference Tables* at `tiny.cc/erpi1304`.

An XBee API Mode Example

Unfortunately, XBee AT mode does not provide access to the advanced features that are available on a ZigBee device. In the last example, the source and destination points are manually configured for the two devices. XBee API mode uses data frames, each with a software-configurable address that allows other modules in API mode to selectively receive the data.

Setting Up the RPi XBee Device (XBee1)

In this section two identical XBee S2 ZigBee devices are configured into API mode by writing new firmware to them. As illustrated in Figure 13-14, XBee1 is configured as a ZigBee Coordinator (API mode), and XBee2 is configured as a ZigBee Router (API mode). In this example, the coordinator is attached to the RPi, but the XBee router is utilized as a standalone microcontroller, as illustrated in Figure 13-15.

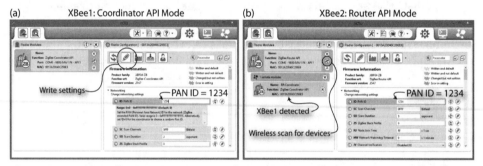

Figure 13-14: (a) Configuring XBee1 as a coordinator with PAN ID 1234, and (b) configuring XBee2 as a router with PAN ID 1234

The PAN ID is set to 1234 for both devices. Once the PAN ID is set for XBee1, it can be disconnected from the XBee USB Explorer and attached to the RPi, as illustrated in Figure 13-15(a).

Setting Up the Standalone XBee Device (XBee2)

The XBee2 can be placed in the XBee USB Explorer and programmed with ZigBee router firmware. A scan can then be performed by clicking the Wireless Scan for Devices button (as identified in Figure 13-14(b)). The XBee1 coordinator device that is attached to the RPi should be detected, and because the devices are both in API mode, it is possible to wirelessly change the settings on the XBee1 device.

In this example, the XBee2 router device is not attached to an Arduino; rather, it is used as a standalone microcontroller, as illustrated in Figure 13-15(b). The full list of input/outputs is illustrated in Figure 13-16(a), and the settings used to configure them in XCTU are illustrated in Figure 13-16(b).

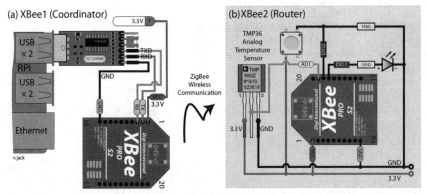

Figure 13-15: (a) The XBee1 RPi coordinator circuit, and (b) the standalone XBee2 router circuit with sample I/O connections

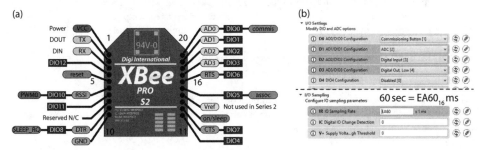

Figure 13-16: (a) The XBee S2 pinout, and (b) the XCTU I/O settings for an XBee S2 module

At this point you might try to use `minicom` to connect to the XBee1 device on the RPi—unfortunately, it will not work, as the XBee device is configured in API mode and therefore expects data frames. However, it is possible to interact with the XBee module using code that is written in several different languages, including Node.js and C/C++.

XBee API Mode and Node.js

The `xbee-api` Node.js module (`tiny.cc/erpi1305`) is a quick and effective way of writing applications that utilize the XBee devices in API mode. The module fully supports the XBee Series 2 (ZigBee) devices that are used in this section. To utilize the Node.js module, you must begin by ensuring that you have a recent version of Node.js. (See the "LAMP and MEAN" feature in Chapter 12 for instructions on updating Node.js.)

Listing 13-9 is a Node.js program that displays the Node Identifier (NI) information and any data frames that are sent on PAN ID 1234.

Listing 13-9: /chp13/xbee/nodejs/test.js

```
// From the example code at www.npmjs.com/package/xbee-api
var util        = require('util');
var SerialPort  = require('serialport').SerialPort;
var xbee_api    = require('xbee-api');
var C           = xbee_api.constants;

var xbeeAPI = new xbee_api.XBeeAPI({ // two API modes are available
  api_mode: 1
});

var serialport = new SerialPort("/dev/ttyUSB0", {
  baudrate: 9600,                    // default baud rate
  parser: xbeeAPI.rawParser()        // parsing raw frames
});

serialport.on("open", function() {   // uses the serialport module
  var frame_obj = {                  // AT Request to be sent...
    type: C.FRAME_TYPE.AT_COMMAND,   // Prepare for an AT command
    command: "NI",                   // Node identifer command
    commandParameter: [],            // No parameters needed
  };
  serialport.write(xbeeAPI.buildFrame(frame_obj));
});


// The data frames received are outputted by this function
xbeeAPI.on("frame_object", function(frame) {
    console.log(">>", frame);
});
```

To execute this code, you must first use the Node package manager (npm) to install the required `xbee-api` and `serialport` modules as follows:

```
pi@erpi ~/exploringrpi/chp13/xbee/nodejs $ npm install serialport
pi@erpi ~/exploringrpi/chp13/xbee/nodejs $ npm install xbee-api
pi@erpi ~/exploringrpi/chp13/xbee/nodejs $ sudo node test.js
>> { type: 136,
  id: 1,
  command: 'NI',
  commandStatus: 0,
  commandData: <Buffer 20 52 50 69 43 6f 6f 72 64 69 6e 61 74 6f 72> }
>> { type: 146,
  remote64: ,
  remote16: '885e',
  receiveOptions: 1,
  digitalSamples: { DIO2: 1, DIO3: 0 },
  analogSamples: { AD1: 617 },
  numSamples: 1 }
```

The program outputs the Node Identifier information, and then every 60 seconds (as configured in Figure 13-16(b)) the XBee2 router device reads its ADC input and transmits the value to the XBee1 coordinator node. You can see that the value received here is 617 (i.e., from a 10-bit ADC) and that the button (DIO2) is pressed.

Each time a new frame of data is received, the `xbeeAPI.on()` function is called and is passed that frame. The frame describes the following:

- `type` refers to the frame type. In this case it is 146 (0x92), which is an "IO Data Sample Rx Indicator."

- `remote64` is the address of the node that transmitted the data, which corresponds to the address of the XBee2 in Figure 13-15(b).

- `remote16` is the network address of the device that transmitted the data, which is 0x885E in this example.

The interactive *XBee API Frame generator* utility is available in the Tools menu of XCTU. It describes the contents of such a frame in detail.

You can see that the Node.js output is in JSON format. JSON support is built in to Node.js and the `JSON.parse()` method can be used to transform the string into useable data values.

XBee and C/C++

A C/C++ library called libxbee is available to support the use of XBee API mode devices. It is not as straightforward to use as the Node.js module, but it has full support for API mode transmissions. To get started with the library, you can download and build it using the following steps:

```
pi@erpi ~ $ git clone https://github.com/attie/libxbee3
pi@erpi ~ $ cd libxbee3/
```

Running `make configure` will copy a generic configuration file into the main build directory. You should disable RTS/CTS support before building on the RPi by uncommenting the `XBEE_NO_RTSCTS` line as follows:

```
pi@erpi ~/libxbee3 $ make configure
pi@erpi ~/libxbee3 $ nano config.mk
pi@erpi ~/libxbee3 $ more config.mk |grep RTSCTS
OPTIONS+=       XBEE_NO_RTSCTS
pi@erpi ~/libxbee3 $ make
pi@erpi ~/libxbee3 $ sudo make install
```

Using the same circuit configuration as in Figure 13-15, you can execute the `simple.c` program in `/chp13/xbee/cpp/` to test the library (remember to set the XBee UART device in the `simple.c` file):

```
pi@erpi ~/exploringrpi/chp13/xbee/cpp $ gcc simple.c -o simple -lxbee
pi@erpi ~/exploringrpi/chp13/xbee/cpp $ XBEE_LOG_LEVEL=100 ./simple
...
12#[rx.c:202] xbee_rxHandler() 0x143c128: received 'I/O' type packet...
 5#[rx.c:211] xbee_rxHandler() 0x143c128: connectionless 'I/O' packet...
10#[conn.c:181] xbee_conLogAddress() 0x143c128:address @ 0x76578cc4...
```

```
10#[conn.c:182] xbee_conLogAddress() 0x143c128: broadcast: No
10#[conn.c:184] xbee_conLogAddress() 0x143c128: 16-bit addr: 0x885E
10#[conn.c:191] xbee_conLogAddress() 0x143c128: 64-bit: 0x13A200 0x40C296E6
10#[conn.c:198] xbee_conLogAddress() 0x143c128: endpoints: --
10#[conn.c:203] xbee_conLogAddress() 0x143c128: profile ID: ----
10#[conn.c:208] xbee_conLogAddress() 0x143c128: cluster ID: ----
```

The libxbee C/C++ library requires detailed study in order to understand how to parse the resulting data frames. A guide to getting started is available at `tiny.cc/erpi1307` and the full documentation for the library is available at `github.com/attie/libxbee3/`.

Near Field Communication

Near field communication (*NFC*) is a wireless technology that allows two devices that are physically close to each other to communicate bi-directionally. NFC is a specialized high-frequency version of *radio frequency identification* (*RFID*) that supports secure communication and peer-to-peer communication. For example, NFC is the core technology involved in contactless payments using mobile devices, and is also used for phone-to-phone information sharing (e.g., by tapping two devices together). NFC devices operate at the same frequency as high-frequency RFID (13.56 MHz), which means that many NFC devices can also interface to passive or actively-powered RFID devices. Commonly available RFID cards do not have a power supply; rather, they contain a wire coil. The NFC device uses a magnetic field to generate power in the wire coils in order to initiate communication.

One of the difficulties of developing software for NFC/RFID is the complexity and large number of proprietary solutions. The open-source libnfc (`nfc-tools.org`) is a platform-independent, low-level software development kit for NFC/RFID, and it can be installed on the RPi. However, you also need NFC/RFID hardware. The circuit that is illustrated in Figure 13-17 can be used for this task—it uses the Philips PN532 NFC controller.

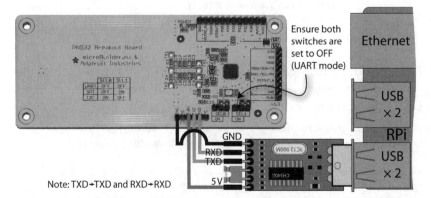

Figure 13-17: The Adafruit NFC/RFID interface for the RPi along with passive RFID tags

The Philips PN532 NFC controller (`tiny.cc/erpi1308`) supports contactless communication at 13.56 MHz using the ISO14443A/MIFARE and FeliCa communication schemes. It supports SPI, I²C, and serial UART interfaces; however, it is only available in a surface mount package and must be attached to an external antenna. Thankfully, Adafruit and others have developed breakout boards that simplify development with this technology. There is an Arduino shield and a standalone interface board, both retailing at approximately $40. There are other very low-cost PN532 controllers available—ensure that you purchase one that makes a UART connection available, such as those illustrated in Figure 13-18(a). In addition, passively-powered 13.56 MHz RFID/NFC stickers, cards, keyrings, buttons, plastic nails, bracelets, and laundry tags are also available at low cost, which opens up the application possibilities—see Figure 13-18(b).

(a)   (b)

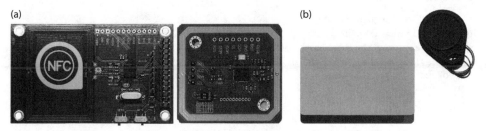

Figure 13-18: (a) Low-cost PN532 NFC breakout boards ($5–$16); (b) RFID cards and key chain tags

The latest version of libnfc can be downloaded and configured as follows:

```
pi@erpi ~ $ git clone https://github.com/nfc-tools/libnfc
pi@erpi ~ $ cd libnfc/
pi@erpi ~/libnfc $ sudo apt install libusb-dev
pi@erpi ~/libnfc $ sudo mkdir /etc/nfc/
pi@erpi ~/libnfc $ sudo cp libnfc.conf.sample /etc/nfc/libnfc.conf
```

The last step in this example copies a sample configuration file onto the RPi that can be used to identify the NFC device configuration. In Figure 13-17, a USB-to-UART device (see Chapter 9) is used to interface to the RPi, so this must be specified in the configuration file as follows:

```
pi@erpi /etc/nfc $ more libnfc.conf
allow_autoscan = true
device.name = "microBuilder.eu"
device.connstring = "pn532_uart:/dev/ttyUSB0"
```

Once the configuration file is in place, you can build libnfc for the RPi as follows. The `ldconfig` step is used to update the shared library cache:

```
pi@erpi ~/libnfc $ cmake .
pi@erpi ~/libnfc $ make
pi@erpi ~/libnfc $ sudo make install
pi@erpi ~/libnfc $ sudo ldconfig -v
pi@erpi ~/libnfc $ ls /usr/local/lib/libnfc*
```

```
libnfc.so          libnfc.so.5.0.1      libnfc.so.5
pi@erpi ~/libnfc $ ls /usr/local/bin/nfc*
nfc-scan-device   nfc-list      ...
```

If the interface board is now attached as in Figure 13-17, then you can test your configuration using the binary tools that are provided with libnfc:

```
pi@erpi ~ $ sudo nfc-list
nfc-list uses libnfc 1.7.1
NFC device: pn532_uart:/dev/ttyUSB0 opened
```

If you get a shared library error, then check the ldconfig step. (You can use the ldd tool that is described in Chapter 5 in the section on "Static and Dynamic Compilation" to test shared library dependencies.) Now, when two individual RFID cards are used with the circuit, you will see different but consistent IDs presented:

```
pi@erpi ~ $ sudo nfc-poll
nfc-poll uses libnfc 1.7.1
NFC reader: pn532_uart:/dev/ttyUSB0 opened
NFC device will poll during 30000 ms (20 pollings of 300 ms for 5 modulations)
ISO/IEC 14443A (106 kbps) target:
    ATQA (SENS_RES): 00  44
       UID (NFCID1): 04  60  28  4a  fe  32  80
      SAK (SEL_RES): 00
nfc_initiator_target_is_present: Target Released
Waiting for card removing...done.

pi@erpi ~ $ sudo nfc-poll
...   ATQA (SENS_RES): 00  04
       UID (NFCID1): 8e  3f  34  03
      SAK (SEL_RES): 08  ...
```

A sample C program is available in /chp13/libnfc/nfc_test.c that can be used to build your own NFC access control program in C. The program stores a UID as an array of characters (char secretCode[] = {0x8e, 0x3f, 0x34, 0x03};), which is compared against the individual RFID values that are read from different RFID cards. The program grants notional access when the correct card with that "secret" ID is presented, as can be observed in the following test example:

```
pi@erpi ~/exploringrpi/chp13/nfc $ ./build
pi@erpi ~/exploringrpi/chp13/nfc $ ./nfc_test
ERPi NFC reader: pn532_uart:/dev/ttyUSB0 opened
 Waiting for you to use an RFID card or tag....
The following tag was found:
   UID (NFCID1): 04  60  28  4a  fe  32  80
 *** ERPi Access NOT allowed! ***

pi@erpi ~/exploringrpi/chp13/nfc $ ./nfc_test
ERPi NFC reader: pn532_uart:/dev/ttyUSB0 opened
```

```
Waiting for you to use an RFID card or tag....
The following tag was found:
  UID (NFCID1): 8e  3f  34  03
*** ERPi Access allowed! ***
```

Summary

After completing this chapter, you should be able to do the following:

- Choose an appropriate wireless communication protocol and associated hardware for your projects.
- Configure a USB Bluetooth adapter for the RPi and connect to it from a mobile device for the purpose of building a basic remote-control application.
- Install a USB Wi-Fi adapter on the RPi and configure the RPi to connect to a secured Wi-Fi network.
- Use the NodeMCU device to build a distributed wireless network of things that is controlled by the RPi.
- Build on skills developed in Chapter 12 to create IoT devices that can be wireless.
- Use the ZigBee protocol with XBee adapters in AT mode to establish a wireless serial data link.
- Investigate ZigBee using XBee devices that are configured in API mode, which allows for the use of advanced ZigBee features.
- Use NFC/RFID devices to build a basic access control system.

# CHAPTER 14

Raspberry Pi with a Rich User Interface

In this chapter, you are introduced to rich user interface (UI) architectures and application development on the Raspberry Pi (RPi). Rich UIs allow for a depth of interaction with an application that is not possible with command-line interfaces (CLIs)—in particular, the addition of graphical display elements can result in easier-to-use applications. Also introduced are different RPi architectures that can support rich UIs, such as general-purpose computing, touchscreen display modules, and virtual network computing (VNC). Different software application frameworks are examined for rich UI development, such as GTK+ and Qt. The Qt framework is the focus of the discussion, largely due to its comprehensive libraries of code. An example rich UI application is developed for the RPi that uses the DHT temperature and humidity sensor from Chapter 6. Finally, a feature-rich remote fat-client TCP application framework is developed, along with an example that uses the same sensor.

Equipment Required for This Chapter:

- Raspberry Pi (any model)
- Aosong AM230x humidity and temperature sensor (DHT)
- USB/HDMI accessories from Chapter 1 (optional)

Further resources for this chapter are available at www.exploringrpi.com/chapter14/.

Rich UI RPi Architectures

In Chapters 9 and 10, low-cost LED displays and character LCD displays are introduced. They can be coupled with sensors, switches, or keyboard modules to form simple, low-cost UI architectures that are sufficient for many applications, such as for configuration or interaction with hardware devices (e.g., vending machines, printer control interfaces). However, the RPi has a powerful processor, which when coupled with the Linux OS is capable of providing very sophisticated user interfaces—similar to those to which you are accustomed on your desktop machine and/or mobile devices.

The RPi can be connected directly to a physical display (e.g., monitor, television, or LCD touchscreen) to create a sophisticated self-contained physical UI device. This is one application of the RPi that demonstrates the strength of embedded Linux in particular, as it supports open source UI development frameworks such as GTK+ and Qt. These frameworks provide libraries of visual components (a.k.a. *widgets*) that you can combine to create applications with considerable depth of interaction.

Before examining software development frameworks, this section first introduces four different RPi UI hardware architectures:

- **General-purpose computing:** By connecting the RPi to a monitor/television by HDMI, and a keyboard and mouse by USB, it can be used as a general-purpose computer. The RPi 3 is the best model for this architecture type.

- **LCD touchscreen display:** By attaching an LCD touchscreen to the GPIO headers, it can be used as a stand-alone UI device. Any RPi model can be used in this way.

- **Virtual network computing (VNC):** By using remote access and control software on a network-attached RPi, it can control UIs on a virtual display. This architecture is best suited to a wired network RPi model.

- **Remote fat-client applications:** By using custom client/server programming with a network-attached RPi, it can interact with remote UIs by sending and receiving messages. Any RPi model can be used in this way.

These architectures are described in detail in this section, but to give the discussion some context, Table 14-1 summarizes the strengths and weaknesses of each approach when used with the RPi.

Table 14-1: Strengths and Weaknesses of Different RPi UI Architectures

APPROACH	STRENGTHS	WEAKNESSES
RPi as a general-purpose computer	Low-cost computing platform with low power consumption. Ideal for a network-attached information display point application, by connecting it to a TV/monitor. Can interact with it using a USB keyboard and mouse.	Requires a dedicated monitor/TV. RPi models lack the processing power to replace a modern desktop computer; however, the RPi 3 is a capable general-purpose device.
RPi with an LCD touchscreen	Very portable interactive display that can be battery powered. Ideal for custom UI process controls. A range of display sizes are available.	Expensive and modest resolution. Cheaper options are typically resistive touch, rather than capacitive touch.
VNC	No display required on the RPi. RPi could be battery powered and wireless, but wired connections are preferable.	Requires a desktop computer/tablet device and network connection. Display update over the network connection can be sluggish.
Fat-client applications	No display is required on the RPi. RPi could be battery powered and wireless (e.g., RPi Zero based). Very low RPi processor overhead, as the display is updated by the desktop computer. Many simultaneous displays possible.	Requires custom application development (e.g., using TCP socket programming). Requires network connection and a device on which to run the fat-client applications.

The RPi as a General-Purpose Computer

The HDMI video output capability on the RPi platform means that it can be directly connected to a monitor/television, enabling it to be configured as a general-purpose desktop computer. For example, Figure 14-1(a) illustrates the use of an HDMI cable alongside the Kinivo Bluetooth adapter, together providing support for video output and keyboard/mouse input. Figure 14-1(b) displays a low-cost Bluetooth keyboard/touchpad that is used for this example; it is a compact device that is displayed to scale with the RPi.

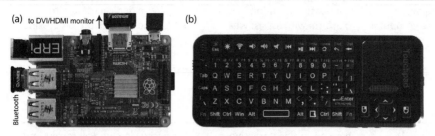

Figure 14-1: (a) Connection to an HDMI and a Bluetooth adapter, and (b) a Bluetooth keyboard/touchpad (to scale with RPi)

The Ethernet connector can be used to provide network support, and a powered USB hub can be connected to the RPi in order to provide support for more devices, such as Wi-Fi adapters or separate keyboard and mouse peripherals. Figure 14-2 displays a screen capture of the RPi display output when connected directly to a computer monitor using the HDMI interface.

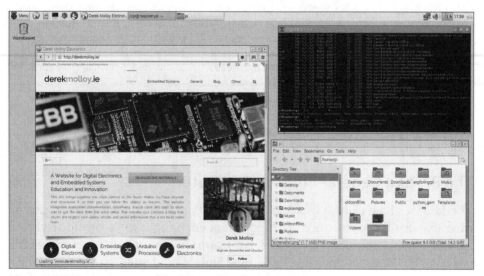

Figure 14-2: Screen capture of the RPi monitor display

To be clear, this display is running on a standalone monitor at a screen resolution of 1920 × 1200 pixels and the screen was captured on the RPi using a Linux tool called scrot that can be installed and executed from the CLI using the following call:

```
pi@erpi:~ $ sudo apt install scrot
pi@erpi ~ $ scrot screenshot.png
```

```
pi@erpi ~ $ ls -l screenshot.png
-rw-r--r-- 1 pi pi 1798498 Nov 14 17:53 screenshot.png
```

Connecting a Bluetooth Input Peripheral

A regular USB keyboard and mouse can be directly connected to the RPi for this architecture. Bluetooth keyboard/touchpads are also useful, as they can be reused in other applications, such as wireless robotic control and home automation. The RPi 3 onboard Bluetooth adapter and the Kinivo Bluetooth adapter (see Chapter 13) can directly interface to devices such as the handheld *iPazzPort Bluetooth keyboard and touchpad* (~$20). Bluetooth devices can be configured using the following steps so that they are always available to the RPi on reboot:

```
pi@erpi ~ $ sudo apt install bluez bluetooth
pi@erpi ~ $ sudo reboot
pi@erpi ~ $ sudo bluetoothctl
[NEW] Controller 00:02:72:CB:C3:53 raspberrypi [default]
[NEW] Device 40:E2:30:13:CA:09 HOMEOFFICE-PC
[NEW] Device 54:46:6B:01:E2:13 bluetooth iPazzport
[bluetooth]# agent KeyboardOnly
Agent registered
[bluetooth]# default-agent
Default agent request successful
[bluetooth]# scan on
Discovery started
[CHG] Controller 00:02:72:CB:C3:53 Discovering: yes
[CHG] Device 40:E2:30:13:CA:09 RSSI: -38
[CHG] Device 54:46:6B:01:E2:13 RSSI: -44
[bluetooth]# pair 54:46:6B:01:E2:13
Attempting to pair with 54:46:6B:01:E2:13
[CHG] Device 54:46:6B:01:E2:13 Connected: yes
[agent] PIN code: 798521
```

To pair the device, a pin code of 798521 is presented by the tool in the preceding instructions, so 798521 must also be keyed on the Bluetooth device (followed by Enter), which results in the following output:

```
[CHG] Device 54:46:6B:01:E2:13 Paired: yes
Pairing successful ...
[bluetooth]# trust 54:46:6B:01:E2:13
[CHG] Device 54:46:6B:01:E2:13 Trusted: yes
Changing 54:46:6B:01:E2:13 trust succeeded
[bluetooth]# connect 54:46:6B:01:E2:13
Attempting to connect to 54:46:6B:01:E2:13
Connection successful
[bluetooth]# info 54:46:6B:01:E2:13
Device 54:46:6B:01:E2:13
        Name: bluetooth iPazzport      Alias: bluetooth iPazzport
        Class: 0x000540                Icon: input-keyboard
        Paired: yes                    Trusted: yes
        Blocked: no                    Connected: yes  ...
```

The Bluetooth keyboard/touchpad is now attached to the RPi and it will automatically connect from then on. It can control the general-purpose computing environment that is displayed in Figure 14-2.

NOTE Linux allows virtual consoles (a.k.a. virtual terminals) to be opened while an X Window System (windowing display) is executing. Use Ctrl+Alt+F1 to open a virtual console—there are six virtual text-based consoles (F1 to F6). Use Ctrl+Alt+F7 to return to the X Window System. Using Alt+Left arrow and Alt+Right arrow switches in order between the consoles.

Also, you can kill a frozen SSH session by typing Enter ~ . in sequence (i.e., the Enter key followed by the tilde followed by a period). Use Enter ~ ? to display a list of the escape sequences that are available within an SSH session.

RPi with an LCD Touchscreen

The RPi can be connected directly to LCD HATs that support Linux desktop display. This allows you to develop sophisticated Linux GUI displays for embedded controller applications (e.g., smart light switches, robotic controls, 3D printer controls), but such displays are typically expensive or alternatively quite limited in resolution. Two such examples are:

- The 4Dpi-24-HAT: A 2.4″ LCD display (~$35) with a resolution of 240 × 320 pixels and integrated 4-wire resistive touch panel. It supports a frame rate of 17 frames per second (FPS). It utilizes the RPi SPI bus to drive the display, and requires a custom kernel to be utilized (under Raspbian only). See `tiny.cc/erpi1401`.

- The RPi 7″ Touchscreen Display: An impressive 800 × 480 pixel display with ten finger capacitive multi-touch sensing (~$70). This display uses the DSI port on the RPi (not available on the RPi Zero) to drive the display, which means that most of the GPIO pins are available for interfacing. This display also requires a recent version of Raspbian. See `tiny.cc/erpi1402`.

The second option is expensive; however, capacitive touch displays are flexible in comparison to resistive touch displays, which typically require a stylus for their use. Most low-cost options utilize resistive touch displays and require custom Linux kernels.

Other display types are available, such as the high-contrast PaPiRus ePaper/eInk Display HATs, which are supplied with SPI source code examples. The display sizes currently range from 1.44″ (~$45) with a resolution of 128 × 96, to 2.7″ (~$85) with a resolution of 264 × 176. Usefully, the display image persists after it has been powered down. See `tiny.cc/erpi1406`.

Virtual Network Computing (VNC)

Virtual network computing (VNC) enables desktop applications on one computer (the server) to be shared and remotely controlled from another computer (the client). Keystrokes and mouse interactions on the VNC client are transmitted to the VNC server over the network. The VNC server determines the impact of these interactions and then updates the remote frame buffer (RAM containing bitmap image data) on the VNC client machine. VNC uses the remote frame buffer protocol, which is similar to the Remote Desktop Protocol (RDP) that is tightly coupled to the Windows OS, but because VNC works at the frame buffer level, it is available for many OSs. The RPi does not require a physical display in order to act as a VNC server. Importantly, with VNC the Linux applications are executing on the RPi using its processor, but the frame buffer display is being updated on the remote machine.

VNC Using VNC Viewer

Many VNC client applications are available that can be installed on your desktop machine, but VNC Viewer is described here because it is available for Windows, Mac OS X, and Linux platforms. It can be downloaded and installed free from www.realvnc.com. Once it is executed on your desktop machine, a login screen appears that requests the VNC server address. However, for this configuration you must ensure that your RPi is running a VNC server before you can log in. The VNC server allows the VNC client application to remotely connect to and control the RPi.

The *tightvncserver* is available under the Raspbian distribution by default. The first time you execute the server you will be prompted to define a password for remote access, as follows:

```
pi@erpi ~ $ sudo apt install tightvncserver
pi@erpi ~ $ tightvncserver
You will require a password to access your desktops.
Password:
Verify:
Would you like to enter a view-only password (y/n)? n
New 'X' desktop is erpi:1
```

Once the server is running, you can check the process description to determine the port number; here it is running on port 5901:

```
pi@erpi ~ $ ps aux | grep vnc
pi       1538  2.0  1.2  19684 11688 pts/0    S    22:53   0:02 Xtightvnc
 :1 -desktop X -auth /home/pi/.Xauthority -geometry 1024x768 -depth 24
 -rfbwait 120000 -rfbauth /home/pi/.vnc/passwd -rfbport 5901 ...
```

The VNC Viewer session can then be started on your desktop machine using the server address and its port number (e.g., `erpi.local:5901`). The RPi desktop is contained within a window frame, as displayed in Figure 14-3. Note that the tightvncserver session in Figure 14-3 was started by the root user so that the RPi Weather Application could be executed.

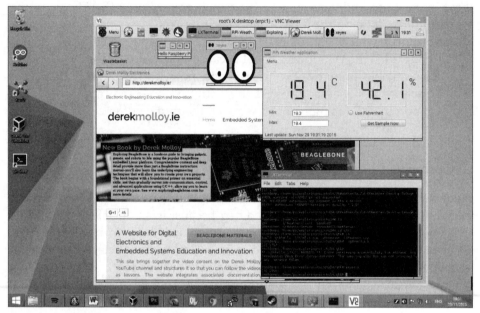

Figure 14-3: VNC Viewer on Windows

VNC with Xming and PuTTY

The Xming X Server (`tiny.cc/erpi1403`)[1] for Windows, in combination with PuTTY, is a different approach to the same task; however, it does not require that a VNC server is running on the RPi. Once Xming is installed and executed, it appears only in the Windows taskbar with an X icon. The PuTTY RPi session can be configured using Connection ➪ SSH ➪ X11 to "Enable SSH X11 forwarding" to the local X display location and to set the X display location to be `:0.0`.

When an SSH session is opened to the RPi, you can simply perform the following instructions, which result in the display of an xterm and xeyes display. The xterm window is the standard terminal emulator for the X Window System and the "magical" xeyes follow your mouse cursor around the desktop

---

[1] Note that there is a "website release" and a "public domain release" version available at this link. The website release version requires a donation but the older version (Xming v6.9) is currently available for free. You must also install the Xming-fonts release.

computer. Remember that the xeyes display is being updated by the RPi, not the desktop computer:

```
pi@erpi ~ $ sudo apt install x11-apps xterm
pi@erpi ~ $ xeyes &
pi@erpi ~ $ xterm &
```

One advantage of this approach is that you can seamlessly integrate RPi applications and Windows applications on the display. You can also start the RPi's LXDE (Lightweight X11 Desktop Environment) standard panel by calling lxpanel or lxsession, which results in a bottom-bar menu display.

VNC with a Linux Desktop Computer

If you are running Linux as your desktop OS (e.g., Debian x64 on a VM), you can usually start a VNC session using the following steps, where -x enables X11 forwarding and -c requests that compression is used in the transmission of frame buffer data:

```
molloyd@desktop:~$ ssh -XC pi@erpi.local
pi@erpi ~ $ sudo apt install x11-apps xterm
pi@erpi ~ $ xeyes &
pi@erpi ~ $ xterm &
```

Fat-Client Applications

At the beginning of Chapter 12, the RPi is configured as a web server; essentially, the RPi is serving data to a thin-client web browser that is executing on a client machine. The weather sensor application executes on the RPi and the data is served to the client's web browser using the Nginx web server and CGI/PHP scripts. With thin-client applications, most of the processing takes place on the server machine (server side). In contrast, fat-client (a.k.a. thick-client) applications execute on the client machine (client side), and send and receive data messages to and from the server.

Recent computing architecture design trends have moved away from fat-client architectures and toward thin-client (and cloud) browser-based frameworks. However, the latter frameworks are usually implemented on a powerful cluster of server machines and are unsuitable for deployment on embedded devices. When working with the RPi, it is likely that the client desktop machine is the more computationally powerful device.

A fat-client application is typically more complex to develop and deploy than a thin-client application, but it reduces the demands on the server while allowing for advanced functionality and user interaction on the client machine. Later in this chapter, a fat-client UI application is developed that executes on a desktop computer and communicates to the RPi via TCP sockets. Importantly, the fat-client applications use the resources of the desktop computer for graphical display, and therefore there is a minimal computational cost on the RPi. As such, it is possible for many fat-client applications on different desktop computers to simultaneously communicate with a single RPi.

Rich UI Application Development

Once a display framework is available to the RPi, a likely next step is to write rich UI applications that can utilize its benefits. Such applications are termed *graphical user interface (GUI)* applications; if you have used desktop computers, tablet computers, or smartphones, you are familiar with their use. There are many different ways to implement GUI applications on the RPi. For example, Java has comprehensive built-in support for GUI development with its *Abstract Windowing Toolkit (AWT)* libraries, and Python has libraries such as pyGTK, wxPython, and Tkinter.

To develop GUI applications under C/C++ for the RPi, there are two clear options: the *GIMP Toolkit (GTK+)* and the *Qt* cross-platform development framework. This section describes how you can get started with both of these options. It is important to note that the applications in this section will function regardless of whether they are used directly on the RPi (i.e., general-purpose computer or touchscreen form) or through VNC. GTK+ and Qt can also be used as the basis for building fat-client applications, which is covered later in this chapter.

Introduction to GTK+ on the RPi

GTK+ (www.gtk.org) is a cross-platform toolkit for creating GUI applications. It is most well known for its use in the Linux GNOME desktop and the GNU Image Manipulation Program (GIMP). Figure 14-4 illustrates a sample GTK+ application running on the RPi using VNC. The same application also works perfectly if the application is running on the RPi directly (e.g., refer to Figure 14-3).

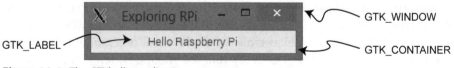

Figure 14-4: The GTKhello application

The "Hello World" GTK+ Application

The code for the application shown in Figure 14-4 is provided in Listing 14-1. The application consists of a single label, which contains the text "Hello Raspberry

Pi" that has been added to a GTK+ window. Each line of the code has been commented in the listing to explain the important steps.

Listing 14-1: /chp14/gtk/GTKhello.cpp

```
#include<gtk/gtk.h>

int main(int argc, char *argv[]){
    // This application will have a window and a single label
    GtkWidget *window, *label;
    // Initialize the toolkit, pass the command line arguments
    gtk_init(&argc, &argv);
    // Create the top-level window (not yet visible)
    window = gtk_window_new(GTK_WINDOW_TOPLEVEL);
    // Set the title of the window to Exploring RPi
    gtk_window_set_title ( GTK_WINDOW (window), "Exploring RPi");
    // Create a label
    label = gtk_label_new ("Hello Raspberry Pi");
    // Add the label to the window
    gtk_container_add(GTK_CONTAINER (window), label);
    // Make the label visible (must be done for every widget)
    gtk_widget_show(label);
    // Make the window visible
    gtk_widget_show(window);
    // Runs the main loop until gtk_main_quit() is called  (hit Ctrl C)
    gtk_main();
    return 0;
}
```

The application can be compiled using the following call, which is also captured in the Git repository build script (use the grave accent character `, not the single opening quotation mark character '):

```
pi@erpi .../chp14/gtk $ sudo apt install libgtk-3-dev
pi@erpi .../chp14/gtk $ g++ `pkg-config --libs --cflags gtk+-3.0` →
 GTKhello.cpp -o gtkhello
```

This call uses `pkg-config`, a tool that is useful when building applications and libraries under Linux, as it inserts the correct system-dependent options. It does this by collecting metadata about the libraries that are installed on the Linux system. For example, to get information about the current GTK+ library, you can use the following:

```
pi@erpi .../chp14/gtk $ pkg-config --modversion gtk+-3.0
3.14.5
```

The application in Figure 14-4 does not quit when the X button (top right-hand corner) is clicked; the window itself disappears, but the program continues to execute. This is because the preceding code has not defined that something should happen when the X button is clicked; you need to associate a "close" function with the signal that is generated when the button is clicked.

The Event-Driven Programming Model

GUI applications typically use an event-driven programming model. Under this model, the application waits in its main loop until an event (e.g., the user action of clicking a button) is detected, which triggers a callback function to be performed. In GTK+, a user action causes the main loop to deliver an event to GTK+, which is initialized by the call to `gtk_init()`. GTK+ then delivers this event to the graphical widgets, which in turn emit signals. These signals can be attached to callback functions of your own design or to windowing functions. For example, the following GTK+ code quits the application if the window X button is clicked:

```
g_signal_connect(window, "destroy", G_CALLBACK (gtk_main_quit), NULL);
```

The signal is attached to the `window` handle, so that when a signal named `destroy` is received, the `gtk_main_quit()` function is called, which causes the application to exit. The last argument is `NULL` because no data is required to be passed to the `gtk_main_quit()` function.

The GTK+ Temperature and Humidity Application

Listing 14-2 provides a segment of code for a more complete GTK+ application, which executes on the RPi as shown in Figure 14-5. It uses the same one-wire DHT temperature and humidity sensor used in Chapter 6 (i.e., in Listing 6-14). This example is a GUI application that reads the RPi GPIO input when a button is clicked, and then displays the temperature and humidity readings in two label widgets. In this example, a signal is connected to the `button` object, so when it is clicked the callback function `getReading()` is called.

Figure 14-5: The GTKsensor application

Listing 14-2: /chp14/gtk/GTKsensor.cpp (segment)

```
// Same as code in Chapter 6 to read DHT sensor (see Listing 6-14)
int readDHTSensor() { ... }

// The callback function associated with the button. It passes a ptr
// to the label, so that it can be changed when the button is pressed
static void getReadings(GtkWidget *widget, gpointer read_label) {
    // cast the generic gpointer into a GtkWidget label
```

```
   GtkWidget *reading_label = (GtkWidget *) read_label;
   while (readDHTSensor()==-1){
      usleep(2000000);                  // sleep for 2 seconds
   };
   stringstream ss;
   ss << "Reading: Temperature="  << temperature
      << "°C  Humidity=" << humidity << "%";
   // set the text in the label
   gtk_label_set_text( GTK_LABEL(reading_label), ss.str().c_str());
   ss << endl;  // add a \n to the string for the standard output
   g_print(ss.str().c_str());    // output to the terminal (std out)
}

int main(int argc, char *argv[]) {
   GtkWidget *window, *reading_label, *button, *button_label;
   gtk_init(&argc, &argv);
   window = gtk_window_new(GTK_WINDOW_TOPLEVEL);
   gtk_window_set_title(GTK_WINDOW (window), "Exploring RPi");

   // Fix the size of the window so that it cannot be resized
   gtk_widget_set_size_request(window, 220, 50);
   gtk_window_set_resizable(GTK_WINDOW(window), FALSE);
   // Place a border of 5 pixels around the inner window edge
   gtk_container_set_border_width (GTK_CONTAINER (window), 5);

   // Quit application if X button is pressed
   g_signal_connect(window, "destroy", G_CALLBACK (gtk_main_quit), NULL);

   // set window to contain two vertically stacked widgets using a box
   GtkWidget *box = gtk_box_new(GTK_ORIENTATION_VERTICAL, 5);
   gtk_container_add (GTK_CONTAINER (window), box); // add box to window
   gtk_widget_show (box);                           // set visible

   // this is the label in which to display the weather data
   reading_label = gtk_label_new ("Reading is Undefined");
   gtk_widget_show(reading_label);                  // make it visible
   gtk_label_set_justify( GTK_LABEL(reading_label), GTK_JUSTIFY_LEFT);
   // Add the label to the vbox
   gtk_box_pack_start (GTK_BOX (box), reading_label, FALSE, FALSE, 0);

   // create a button and connect it to the getReadings() callback fn
   button = gtk_button_new();
   button_label = gtk_label_new ("Get Reading"); // label button text
   gtk_widget_show(button_label);               // show label
   gtk_widget_show(button);                     // show button
   gtk_container_add(GTK_CONTAINER (button), button_label); // add label
   // Connect the callback function getReadings() to the button press
   g_signal_connect(button, "clicked", G_CALLBACK (getReadings),
                    (gpointer) reading_label);
   // Add the button to the box
```

```
    gtk_box_pack_start (GTK_BOX (box), button, FALSE, FALSE, 0);
    gtk_widget_show(window);
    gtk_main();
    return 0;
}
```

To execute this program, you must have superuser permissions in order to use the wiringPi library. This means that you also need to authorize the root user to use VNC:

```
pi@erpi .../chp14/gtk $ sudo cp ~/.Xauthority /root
pi@erpi .../chp14/gtk $ sudo ./gtksensor
```

The application then appears as in Figure 14-5.

Introduction to Qt on the RPi

Qt (pronounced "cute") is a powerful cross-platform development framework that uses standard C++. It provides libraries of C++ code for GUI application development and for database access, thread management, networking, and more. Importantly, code developed under this framework can be executed under Windows, Linux, Mac OS X, Android, iOS, and on embedded platforms, such as the RPi. Qt can be used under open source or commercial terms and it is supported by freely available development tools, such as qmake and Qt Creator. The capability and flexibility of this framework make it an ideal candidate for GUI applications that are to run directly on the RPi, or on devices that control the RPi.

Qt is described in greater detail in the next section, but it is useful to get started using a simple "hello world" example, as illustrated in Figure 14-6, which can be compiled and executed on the RPi either directly or using VNC.

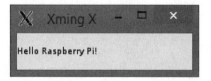

Figure 14-6: Qt "hello world" RPi example executing using VNC

Installing Qt Development Tools on the RPi

The first step is to install the Qt development tools on the RPi. The last command in the following code snippet installs a full suite of tools (60 MB to 200 MB of additional storage required):

```
pi@erpi ~ $ apt-cache search qt5
pi@erpi ~ $ sudo apt install qt5-default
```

You can then test the version of the installation using the following:

```
pi@erpi ~ $ qmake -version
QMake version 3.0
Using Qt version 5.3.2 in /usr/lib/arm-linux-gnueabihf
```

The Hello World Qt Application

Listing 14-3 is a very concise Qt application that can be used as a test—it does not represent good Qt programming practice! It uses an object of the QLabel class, which is a subclass of the QWidget class, to display a message in the application. A widget is the primary UI element that is used for creating GUIs with Qt. The parent QWidget class provides the code required to render (draw) the subclass object on the screen display.

Listing 14-3: /chp14/simpleQt/simpleQt.cpp

```cpp
#include <QApplication>
#include <QLabel>
int main(int argc, char *argv[ ]){
    QApplication app(argc, argv);
    QLabel label("Hello Raspberry Pi!");
    label.resize(200, 100);
    label.show();
    return app.exec();
}
```

The simpleQt.cpp file in Listing 14-3 is the only file required in a directory before the following steps take place. The qmake cross-platform Makefile generator can then be used to create a default project:

```
pi@erpi ~/exploringrpi/chp14/simpleQt $ ls
simpleQt.cpp
pi@erpi ~/exploringrpi/chp14/simpleQt $ qmake -project
pi@erpi ~/exploringrpi/chp14/simpleQt $ ls
simpleQt.cpp  simpleQt.pro
pi@erpi ~/exploringrpi/chp14/simpleQt $ more simpleQt.pro
######################################################################
# Automatically generated by qmake (3.0) Mon Nov 16 04:02:43 2015
######################################################################
TEMPLATE = app
TARGET = simpleQt
INCLUDEPATH += .
# Input
SOURCES += simpleQt.cpp
```

This project .pro file describes the project settings and, if required, it can be edited manually to add additional dependencies. In this case the line:

```
QT += widgets
```

must be added to the `.pro` file (e.g., between the TEMPLATE and TARGET lines), as otherwise the libraries required for the GUI display widgets will not be linked correctly. The qmake `Makefile` generator can then be executed again, this time with no `-project` argument:

```
pi@erpi ~/exploringrpi/chp14/simpleQt $ qmake
pi@erpi ~/exploringrpi/chp14/simpleQt $ ls
Makefile  simpleQt.cpp  simpleQt.pro
```

This step results in a `Makefile` file being created in the current directory that allows the executable to be built using a call to the `make` program, which in turn uses g++ to build the final application:

```
pi@erpi ~/exploringrpi/chp14/simpleQt $ make
g++ -c -pipe -O2 -Wall -W -D_REENTRANT -fPIE -DQT_NO_DEBUG ...
```

The executable is now present in the directory and can be executed as follows, which results in the visual display shown earlier in Figure 14-6:

```
pi@erpi ~/exploringrpi/chp14/simpleQt $ ls
Makefile  simpleQt  simpleQt.cpp  simpleQt.o  simpleQt.pro
pi@erpi ~/exploringrpi/chp14/simpleQt $ ./simpleQt
```

Clearly, there are additional steps involved in using qmake to build a Qt application, but these are necessary to take advantage of the cross-platform nature of Qt. For example, you can perform similar steps on your desktop machine to build the same application, regardless of its OS.

Qt Primer

Qt is a full cross-platform development framework that is written in C/C++. It is used in the preceding section for UI programming, but it also provides support for databases, threads, timers, networking, multimedia, XML processing, and more. Qt extends C++ by adding macros and introspection, code that examines the type and properties of an object at run time, which is not natively available in C++. It is important to note that *all the code is still just plain C++!*

Qt Concepts

Qt is built in modules, each of which can be added to your project by including the requisite header files in your C++ program and by identifying that the module is used in the project `.pro` file. For example, to include the classes in the QtNetwork module, you add `#include<QtNetwork>` to your program code and link against the module by adding `QT += network` to the qmake `.pro` file. A list of important Qt modules is provided in Table 14-2.

Table 14-2: Summary of the Important Qt Modules

NAME	DESCRIPTION
QtCore	Contains the core non-GUI classes, such as `QString`, `QChar`, `QDate`, `QTimer`, and `QVector`. It is included by default in Qt projects, as all other Qt modules rely on this module.
QtGui	Core module that adds GUI support to the QtCore module, with classes such as `QDialog`, `QWidget`, `QToolbar`, `QLabel`, `QTextEdit`, and `QFont`. This module is included by default. If your application has no GUI, you can add `Qt -= gui` to your `.pro` file.
QtMultimedia	Contains classes for low-level multimedia functionality, such as `QVideoFrame`, `QAudioInput`, and `QAudioOutput`. To use this module, add `#include <QtMultimedia>` to your source file and `QT += multimedia` to your `.pro` file.
QtNetwork	Contains classes for network communication over TCP and UDP, including SSL communications, with classes such as `QTcpSocket`, `QFtp`, `QLocalServer`, `QSslSocket`, and `QUdpSocket`. As above, use `#include <QtNetwork>` and `QT += network`.
QtOpenGL	The Open Graphics Library (OpenGL) is a cross-platform application programming interface (API) for 3-D computer graphics, which is widely used in industrial visualization and computer gaming applications. This module makes it straightforward to contain OpenGL in your application with classes such as `QGLBuffer`, `QGLWidget`, `QGLContext`, and `QGLShader`. As above, use `#include <QtOpenGL>` and `QT += opengl`.
QtScript	Enables you to make your Qt application scriptable. Scripts are used in applications such as Microsoft Excel and Adobe Photoshop to enable users to automate repetitive tasks. QtScript includes a JavaScript engine, which you can use within the core application to interlink functionality in scripts. It can also be used to expose the internal functionality of your application to users, enabling them to add new functionality without the need for C++ compilation. As above, use `#include <QtScript>` and `QT += script`.
QtSql	Contains classes for interfacing to databases using the SQL programming language, such as `QSqlDriver`, `QSqlQuery`, and `QSqlResult`. As above, use `#include <QtSql>` and `QT += sql`.
QtSvg	Contains classes for creating and displaying scalar vector graphics (SVG) files, such as `QSvgWidget`, `QSvgGenerator`, and `QSvgRenderer`. As above, use `#include <QtSvg>` and `QT += svg`.

Continues

Table 14-2 (*continued*)

NAME	DESCRIPTION
QtTest	Contains classes for unit testing Qt applications using the QTestLib tool, such as `QSignalSpy` and `QTestEventList`. As above, use `#include <QtTest>` and `QT += testlib`.
QtWebKit	Provides a web browser engine and classes for rendering and interacting with web content, such as `QWebView`, `QWebPage`, and `QWebHistory`. As above, use `#include <QtWebKit>` and `QT += webkit`.
QtXml	Extensible markup language (XML) is a human-readable document format that can be used to transport and store data. The QtXml module provides a stream reader and writer for XML data, with classes such as `QXmlReader`, `QDomDocument`, and `QXmlAttributes`. As above, use `#include <QtXml>` and `QT += xml`.

The QObject Class

The `QObject` class is the base class of almost all the Qt classes and all the widgets.[2] This means that most Qt classes share common functionality for handling memory management, properties, and event-driven programming.

Qt implements introspection by storing information about every class that is derived from `QObject` using a `QMetaObject` object within its Meta-Object System. When you build projects using Qt you will see that new `.cpp` files appear in the build directory; these are created by the Meta-Object Compiler (moc).[3] The C++ compiler will then compile these files into a regular C/C++ object file (`.o`), which is ultimately linked to create an executable application.

Signals and Slots

Similar to GTK+, Qt has an event-driven programming model that enables events and state changes to be interconnected with reactions using a mechanism termed signals and slots. For example, a Qt button widget can be configured so that when it is clicked, it generates a signal, which has been connected to a slot. The slot, which is somewhat like a callback function, performs a user-defined function when it receives a signal. Importantly, the signals and slots mechanism can be applied to non-GUI objects; it can be used for intercommunication between

---

[2] Java programmers will notice that this is similar to the Object class in Java; however, in Qt, classes requiring object instances that can be copied do not subclass `QObject` (e.g., `QString`, `QChar`).

[3] At compile time, the moc uses information from the class header files (e.g., if the class is a descendent of `QObject`) to generate a "marked-up" version of the `.cpp` file. For example, if you have a class X that is defined in the files `X.h` and `X.cpp`, the moc will generate a new file called `moc-X.cpp`, which contains the meta-object code for the class X.

any object that is in any way derived from the QObject class. Signals and slots provide a powerful mechanism that is possibly the most unique feature of the Qt framework.

A full-featured Qt sensor application is developed shortly that makes extensive use of signals and slots. For example, the application updates the display every 5 seconds by reading the sensor value; Figure 14-7 illustrates how this takes place. In this example, the QTimer class has a signal called timeout() that is emitted whenever an object called timer "times out" (which it does after five seconds). This signal is connected to the on_timerUpdate() slot on an object of the QMainWindow class called mainWindow. The connection is made by a call of the form

```
QObject::connect(source,SIGNAL(signature),destination,SLOT(signature));
```

where source and destination are objects of classes that are derived from the QObject class. The signature is the function name and argument types (without the variable names).

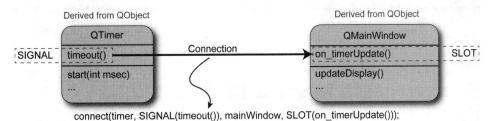

Figure 14-7: QTimer signals and slots example

The website www.qt.io provides an excellent detailed description of the behavior of signals and slots, but here are some further summary points on signals, slots, and connections that will get you started:

- Signals can be connected to any number of slots.
- Signals are defined in the signals section of the code (under a signals: label, which is usually in the class header file).
- Signal "methods" must return void and may not have any implementation.
- A signal can be explicitly emitted using the emit keyword.
- Slots can be connected to any number of signals.
- Slots are defined in the slots section of the code (under a slots: label that can be public, private, or protected).
- Slots are regular methods with a full implementation.
- Connections can be explicitly formed (as in the timer example) or automatically created when using the Qt graphical design tools in the next section.

Qt Development Tools

The Qt framework also has associated development tools. As well as the qmake tool, there is a full-featured IDE called Qt Creator, which is similar in nature to Eclipse, except that it is specifically tailored for Qt development. The IDE, which is illustrated in Figure 14-8, is available for Linux, Windows, and Mac OS X, and can execute on the RPi directly. Qt Creator can be used to build native applications, or it can be used to cross-compile applications for the RPi, by installing a cross-platform toolchain (similar to Eclipse in Chapter 7). To install and execute Qt Creator on the RPi (e.g., via VNC) use the following steps, whereupon the IDE appears as in Figure 14-8.

```
pi@erpi ~ $ sudo apt install qtcreator
pi@erpi ~ $ qtcreator &
```

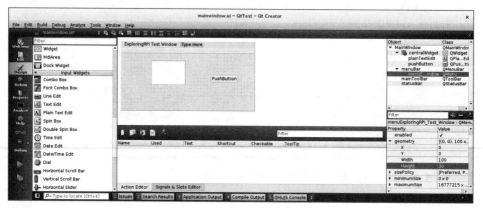

Figure 14-8: Qt Creator IDE visual design editor running directly on the RPi (via VNC)

One of the key features that Qt Creator provides is its visual design editor, which enables you to interactively drag-and-drop widgets onto window designs, called forms. The interface enables the properties of the widgets to be configured easily, and it provides a straightforward way of enabling signals and associating slots against the UI components. For example, to write code that executes when the pushbutton is clicked (refer to Figure 14-8), you can simply right-click the button and choose "Go to slot," which provides a dialog with a list of available signals (such as `clicked()`, `pressed()`, and `released()`).[4] Once a signal is chosen, the IDE will automatically enable the signal, provide a slot code template, and associate the signal with the slot. The form UI's properties are stored in an XML file and associated with the project (e.g., `mainwindow.ui`).

---

[4] A click is a press and a release. Code can be associated with the complete click action and/or the constituent actions.

NOTE When using Qt Creator, unusual problems can arise (e.g., changes to the code not appearing in the application build), particularly when switching projects. In such cases, go to the Build menu and choose Clean All.

In addition, "unresolved external" link errors (e.g., when adding new classes) can often be resolved by selecting Run qmake from the Build menu.

A First Qt Creator Example

You can create a simple Qt GUI application on the RPi using Qt Creator by following these steps:

- Using VNC or by developing on the RPi directly, start Qt Creator with the following call:

  ```
  pi@erpi ~ $ qtcreator &
  ```

- Create a new project of type Qt Widgets Application. Call it QtTest and create it in the /home/pi/ directory.

- Select the Desktop kit and choose the default class information. This results in a new project being created within Qt Creator, which appears as in Figure 14-8 when you double click the mainwindow.ui form entry.

- In this window view, add a Push Button and a Text Edit (QTextEdit) component, as illustrated in Figure 14-8.

- Right-click on the text edit box and choose Change objectName. Change the object name to be output.

- Right-click on the button and use the Change text option to retitle the button to "Press Me." Right-click the button again and choose Go to Slot and then pick a signal (for example clicked()). This creates a new function in the mainwindow.cpp file called on_pushButton_clicked(). See Figure 14-9.

- You can then add a line of code to this method that sets the text of the output QTextEdit component, which is accessed via the ui main window:

  ```
  void MainWindow::on_pushButton_clicked() {
      ui->output->setText("Hello from the RPi");
  }
  ```

The application can be executed by clicking the play button on the bottom-left side of Figure 14-9.[5] The application window appears as in Figure 14-9. When the Press Me button is clicked, the text "Hello from the RPi" appears in the output QTextEdit component.

---

[5] In some cases you may have to manually add the g++ compiler to the kit. Go to Tools ⇨ Options ⇨ Build & Run ⇨ Compilers and add it under the Manual category.

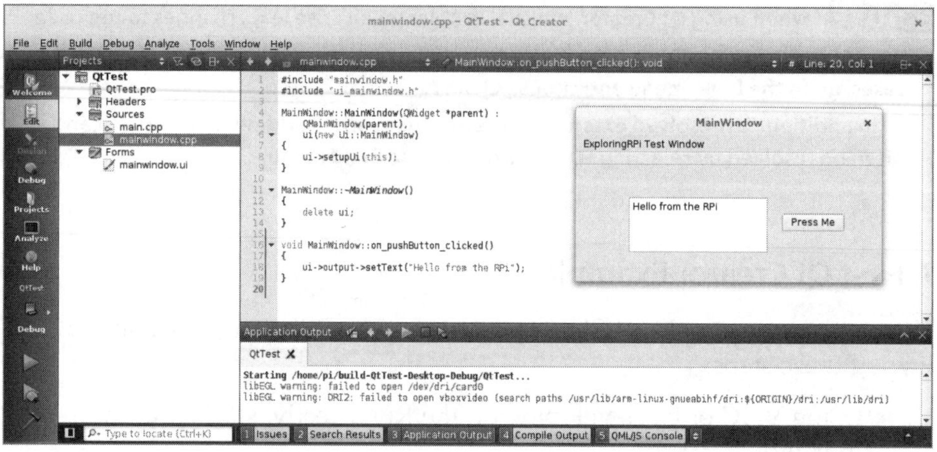

Figure 14-9: Qt Creator IDE test application

A Qt Weather GUI Application

In this section, the Qt Creator IDE is used on the RPi to build a full-featured GUI weather sensor application, as illustrated in Figures 14-10 and 14-11. This application executes directly on the RPi, regardless of the UI architecture used. In fact, if you look back at Figure 14-3, you will see that it makes a guest appearance. This application demonstrates some of the capabilities of Qt on the RPi, while being cognizant of the volume of code to be studied. It could be greatly extended; for example, it could also provide historical charting or fancy display dials. This example application supports the following features:

- A timer thread takes a reading every five seconds from the RPi GPIO using the one-wire interface to the DHT sensor.

- An LCD-style floating-point temperature and humidity displays are used.

- A display of the minimum and maximum temperature is provided.

- A mechanism is provided to convert the main display from a Celsius scale to a Fahrenheit scale by clicking the Use Fahrenheit radio widget.

- A status display is used at the very bottom of the window.

The full source code and executable for this application are available in the Git repository /chp14/QtWeather/ directory.

There are four important source files to describe for this application, the first of which is in Listing 14-4. It provides the `main()` starting point for the application in which an instance of the `QApplication` and `MainWindow` classes are created. The `QApplication` class manages the GUI application control flow (the main loop).

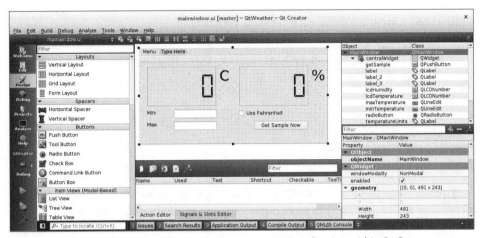

Figure 14-10: Development of the Qt weather sensor GUI application within Qt Creator

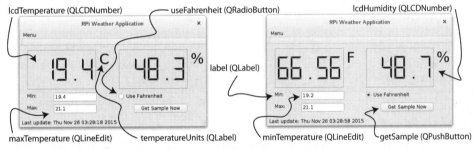

Figure 14-11: The Qt weather sensor GUI application components

Listing 14-4: /chp14/QtWeather/QtWeather/main.cpp

```cpp
# #include "mainwindow.h"
#include <QApplication>

int main(int argc, char *argv[])
{
    QApplication a(argc, argv);
    MainWindow w;
    w.show();
    return a.exec();
}// it is the main loop that processes events
```

Listing 14-5 is the Qt project file. To use the wiringPi library from within Qt, the LIBS line must be manually added to the .pro file.

Listing 14-5: /chp14/QtWeather/QtWeather/QtWeather.pro

```
QT          += core gui
greaterThan(QT_MAJOR_VERSION, 4): QT += widgets
TARGET      =  QtWeather
TEMPLATE    =  app
LIBS        += -lwiringPi
SOURCES     += main.cpp\
               mainwindow.cpp
HEADERS     += mainwindow.h
FORMS       += mainwindow.ui
```

The MainWindow class is defined in Listings 14-6 and 14-7. The MainWindow class is a child of the QMainWindow class (which is child of QWidget and ultimately QObject). That means that any methods that are available in the parent classes are also available in the MainWindow class itself.

Listing 14-6: /chp14/QtWeather/QtWeather/mainwindow.h

```
#include <QMainWindow>
#include <QTimer>

#define USING_DHT11     false   // The DHT11 uses only 8 bits
#define DHT_GPIO        22      // Using GPIO 22 for this example
#define LH_THRESHOLD    26      // Low=~14, High=~38 - pick avg.

namespace Ui {
class MainWindow;
}

class MainWindow : public QMainWindow {
    Q_OBJECT
public:
    explicit MainWindow(QWidget *parent = 0);
    ~MainWindow();
private slots:
    void on_getSample_clicked();                // when button is pressed
    void on_radioButton_toggled(bool checked);  // when radio clicked
    void on_timerUpdate();                       // when timer times out
private:
    float temperature, humidity;                // states
    float maxTemperature, minTemperature;
    bool isFahrenheit;
    QTimer *timer;                              // pointer to timer
    void updateDisplay();                       // sets the UI values
    int readDHTSensor();                        // read DHT sensor
```

```cpp
    float celsiusToFahrenheit(float valueCelsius);
    Ui::MainWindow *ui;
};
```

Listing 14-7: /chp14/QtWeather/QtWeather/mainwindow.cpp

```cpp
#include "mainwindow.h"
#include "ui_mainwindow.h"
#include <QDateTime>
#include <wiringPi.h>
#include <unistd.h>
using namespace std;

MainWindow::MainWindow(QWidget *parent) :
    QMainWindow(parent),
    ui(new Ui::MainWindow) {
    ui->setupUi(this);
    this->isFahrenheit = false;
    statusBar()->showMessage("Sensor Application Started");
    this->maxTemperature = -100.0f;        // initial values
    this->minTemperature = 100.0f;
    this->updateDisplay();                 // refresh UI values (below)
    this->timer = new QTimer(this);        // create the timer
    //when the timer times out, call the on_timerUpdate() function
    connect(timer, SIGNAL(timeout()), this, SLOT(on_timerUpdate()));
    this->timer->start(5000);              // time out after 5 sec
}

float MainWindow::celsiusToFahrenheit(float valueCelsius) {
    return ((valueCelsius * (9.0f/5.0f)) + 32.0f);
}

void MainWindow::on_getSample_clicked() {  // called when button pressed
    QDateTime local(QDateTime::currentDateTime()); // display sample time
    statusBar()->showMessage(QString("Update: ").append(local.toString()));
    this->readDHTSensor();
    if(temperature<minTemperature) minTemperature = temperature;  // min?
    if(temperature>maxTemperature) maxTemperature = temperature;  // max?
    this->updateDisplay();
}

void MainWindow::on_timerUpdate() {
    this->on_getSample_clicked();
    this->updateDisplay();
}

void MainWindow::updateDisplay() {
    if(this->isFahrenheit) {                    // in Fahrenheit mode?
        ui->lcdTemperature->display(celsiusToFahrenheit(temperature));
        ui->temperatureUnits->setText("F");  // set the label to F
    }
    else {
```

```
        ui->lcdTemperature->display((double)temperature);
        ui->temperatureUnits->setText("C");
    }
    ui->lcdHumidity->display((double)humidity);
    ui->minTemperature->setText(QString::number(minTemperature));
    ui->maxTemperature->setText(QString::number(maxTemperature));
}

void MainWindow::on_radioButton_toggled(bool checked) {
    this->isFahrenheit = checked;
    this->updateDisplay();
}

MainWindow::~MainWindow() { delete ui; }

int MainWindow::readDHTSensor(){ // same as before in Chapter 6 }
```

Figure 14-12 illustrates the relationship between the UI components and the slots that are declared in Listing 14-6 and defined in Listing 14-7. The timer code is also summarized; it is not a GUI component, but it does generate a `timeout()` signal, which is connected to the `on_timerUpdate()` slot. The exact nature of the code in Listings 14-6 and 14-7 is described by the comments. However, the clearest way to fully understand the code is to edit it and see what impact your edits have.

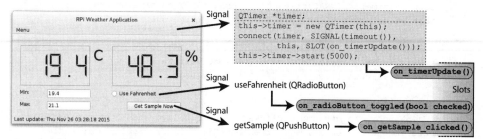

Figure 14-12: The UI component signals and associated slots

The code can be executed on the RPi from within a root session, which is required due to the use of the wiringPi library:

```
molloyd@desktop:~$ ssh -XC pi@erpi.local
pi@erpi ~ $ cd ~/exploringrpi/chp14/QtWeather/
pi@erpi ~/exploringrpi/chp14/QtWeather/ $ sudo bash
root@erpi:.../chp14/QtWeather# cd build-QtWeather-Desktop-Debug/
root@erpi:.../chp14/QtWeather/build-QtWeather-Desktop-Debug# ./QtWeather
```

Remote UI Application Development

In Chapter 12, a C++ client/server application is introduced that can be used for direct intercommunication between two processes that are running on two different machines (or the same machine) using TCP sockets. The machines could be situated on the same physical/wireless network, or could even be on different continents. Direct socket communication requires programmers to frame their own intercommunication protocol. That results in programming overhead, but it also leads to very efficient communication, which is only really limited by the speed of the network.

In this section, the functionality of the Qt weather sensor GUI application and the C++ client/server application (from Chapter 12) are combined. This enables the creation of a fat-client GUI Weather application that can intercommunicate with a weather service, which is running on the RPi. The weather service server code is enhanced from that presented in Chapter 12, by making it multithreaded. This change enables many client applications to attach to the server at the same time. The architecture is illustrated in Figure 14-13.

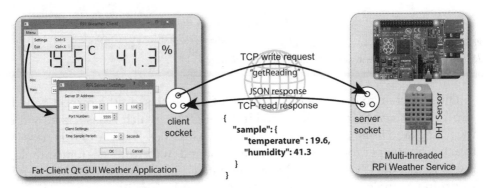

Figure 14-13: The Qt fat-client GUI weather application client/server architecture

The full source code for the Qt GUI application is available in the /chp14/ QtWeatherClient directory, and the server source code is available in the /chp14/QtWeatherServer directory.

Fat-Client Qt GUI Application

In this section, the Qt weather GUI application from earlier in this chapter is modified so that it becomes "Internet enabled." This change means that the application does not have to execute on the RPi; rather, the GUI application can run on a desktop machine and communicate to the RPi sensor using TCP sockets. To achieve this outcome, the following changes are made to the GUI application code (The server application is described in the next section.):

1. A new dialog window is added to the application that can be used to enter the server IP address, the service port number, and the reading refresh frequency. This dialog is illustrated in Figure 14-14.

2. Rather than read from the RPi one-wire GPIO interface, the GUI application must open a TCP socket and communicate to the RPi server application.

The client application sends the string command "getReading" to the server. The server is programmed to respond with the temperature and humidity values, which are read from the DHT sensor. Clearly, many different commands could be introduced.

3. A menu is enabled on the application UI that can be used to open the Server Settings dialog or to quit the application. The respective key sequences Ctrl+S or Ctrl+X can also be used.

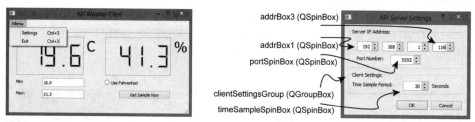

Figure 14-14: The menu and the Server Settings dialog

The first change involves the addition of a new class to the project called `ServerSettingsDialog`, as described in Listing 14-8, which is associated with the dialog (and its `serversettingsdialog.ui` XML file). The role of this class is to act as a wrapper for the values that are entered in the dialog—for example, it will return the IPv4 address that a user entered in the `QSpinBox` widgets, by returning a single 32-bit `unsigned int` (`quint32`) when its `getIPAddress()` method is called.

Listing 14-8: /chp14/QtWeatherClient/serversettingsdialog.h

```
class ServerSettingsDialog : public QDialog {
    Q_OBJECT                              // the required Qt macro
public:
    explicit ServerSettingsDialog(QWidget *parent = 0);  // pass reference
    ~ServerSettingsDialog();
    quint32 virtual getIPAddress();     // return IP address as a 32-bit int
    int virtual getTimeDelay()  { return timeDelay; }       // sample time
    int virtual getServerPort() { return serverPortNumber; } // port number
private slots:
    void on_buttonBox_accepted();        // OK button is pressed
    void on_buttonBox_rejected();        // Cancel button is pressed
private:
    Ui::ServerSettingsDialog *ui;        // pointer to the UI components
    int serverPortNumber;                // port number (default 5555)
    int timeDelay;                       // time delay sec (default 30)
    int address[4];                      // IP address (default 192.168.1.1)
};
```

The second change involves the addition of socket code to the `getSensor-Reading()` method, as provided in Listing 14-9. This code uses the QtNetwork module, which requires that you add

```
QT        += core gui network
```

to the `QWeatherClient.pro` project file so that the project links to that module. The `QTcpSocket` class is used to create a client connection to the RPi TCP Weather server. Regular TCP sockets are used on the RPi, which does not cause any difficulty in the transaction of string data. Interestingly, you could equivalently use Java socket code on either end of a connection. Just be careful to ensure that the byte order is preserved.

Listing 14-9: /chp14/QtWeatherClient/mainwindow.cpp (segment)

```cpp
void MainWindow::createActions() {                      // set up the menu
    QAction *exit = new QAction("&Exit", this);
    exit->setShortcut(QKeySequence(tr("Ctrl+X")));
    QAction *settings = new QAction("&Settings", this);
    settings->setShortcut(QKeySequence(tr("Ctrl+S")));
    QMenu *menu = menuBar()->addMenu("&Menu");
    menu->addAction(settings);
    menu->addAction(exit);
    connect(exit, SIGNAL(triggered()), qApp, SLOT(quit()));  //quit
    connect(settings, SIGNAL(triggered()), this, SLOT(on_openSettings()));
}

void MainWindow::on_openSettings() {
    this->dialog->exec();                               // display the dialog box
    this->timer->start(1000*this->dialog->getTimeDelay());  //update delay
}

int MainWindow::getSensorReading() {
    // Get the server address and port from the settings dialog box
    int serverPort = this->dialog->getServerPort();   // from dialog box
    quint32 serverAddr = this->dialog->getIPAddress();
    QTcpSocket *tcpSocket = new QTcpSocket(this);     // create socket
    tcpSocket->connectToHost(QHostAddress(serverAddr), serverPort);
    if(!tcpSocket->waitForConnected(1000)){  // up  to 1s for connection
        statusBar()->showMessage("Failed to connect to server...");
        return 1;
    }
    // Send the message "getReading" to the server
    tcpSocket->write("getReading");
    if(!tcpSocket->waitForReadyRead(3000)){    // up to 3s for the server
        statusBar()->showMessage("Server did not respond...");
        return 1;
    }
    // If the server has sent bytes back to the client
```

```
if(tcpSocket->bytesAvailable()>0){
    int size = tcpSocket->bytesAvailable(); // how many bytes ready?
    char data[200];                         // upper limit of 200 chars
    tcpSocket->read(&data[0],(qint64)size); // read number of bytes rec.
    data[size]='\0';                        // terminate the string
    cout << "Received the data [" << data << "]" << endl;
    this->parseJSONData(QString(data));
    if(temperature<=minTemperature) minTemperature = temperature;
    if(temperature>=maxTemperature) maxTemperature = temperature;
}
else{
    statusBar()->showMessage("No data available...");
}
return 0;
}

int MainWindow::parseJSONData(QString str){
    QJsonDocument doc = QJsonDocument::fromJson(str.toUtf8());
    QJsonObject obj = doc.object();
    QJsonObject sample = obj["sample"].toObject();
    this->temperature = (float) sample["temperature"].toDouble();
    this->humidity = (float) sample["humidity"].toDouble();
    cout << "The temperature is " << temperature << " and humidity is "
        << humidity << endl;
    return 0;
}
```

The third change is implemented by the createActions() method in Listing 14-9, which creates the GUI menu when it is called by the class constructor. It adds two actions to the menu: The Exit item quits the application, and the Settings item triggers the execution of the on_openSettings() slot, which opens the Server Settings dialog.

The RPi does not have to update the client-side GUI of the application in this architecture. Instead, it manages TCP socket connections, processes strings, and reads values from the DHT sensor. Such operations have a very low overhead on the RPi, and therefore it is capable of simultaneously handling many client requests. Unfortunately, the server code that is presented in Chapter 12 is not capable of handling multiple *simultaneous* requests; rather, it processes requests in sequence, and would reject a connection if it is presently occupied.

Multithreaded Server Applications

For many server applications it is important that the server can handle multiple simultaneous requests—for example, if the Google search engine web page could only handle requests sequentially, there might be a long queue and/or many rejected connections! Figure 14-15 illustrates the steps that must take place for a multithreaded server application to communicate simultaneously with two individual client applications. The steps are as follows:

1. TCP Client 1 requests a connection to the RPi TCP Server. It must know the server's IP address (or name) and the port number.

2. The RPi TCP Server creates a new thread (Connection Handler 1) and passes the TCP Client's IP address and port number to it. The RPi TCP Server immediately begins listening for new connections (on port 5555). The Connection Handler 1 thread then forms a connection to the TCP Client 1 and begins communicating.

3. TCP Client 2 requests a connection to the RPi TCP Server. The Connection Handler 1 thread is currently communicating to TCP Client 1, but the RPi TCP Server is also listening for connections.

4. The RPi TCP Server creates a new thread (Connection Handler 2) and passes the second TCP Client's IP address and port number to it. The RPi TCP Server immediately begins listening for new connections. The Connection Handler 2 thread then forms a connection to the TCP Client 2 and begins communication.

At this point, communication is simultaneously taking place between both client/connection handler pairs, and the server main thread is listening for new connections. The client/connection handler communication session could persist for a long time—for example, for video streaming Internet services such as YouTube or Netflix.

If the connection handler objects were not implemented as threads, the server would have to wait until the client/connection handler communication is complete before it could listen again for new connections. With the structure described, the server is only unavailable while it is constructing a new connection handler threaded object. Once the object is created, the server returns to a listening state. Client socket connections have a configurable time-out limit (typically on the order of seconds), so a short processing delay by the server should not result in rejected connections.

A C++ multithreaded client/server example is available in the /chp14/ threadedclientserver directory. An artificial 5-second delay is present in the ConnectionHandler class to prove conclusively that simultaneous communication is taking place. For example, you can open three terminal sessions on the RPi and start the server:

```
pi@erpi ~/exploringrpi/chp14/threadedClientServer $ ls
build  client  client.cpp  network  server  server.cpp
pi@erpi ~/exploringrpi/chp14/threadedClientServer $ ./server
Starting RPi Server Example
Listening for a connection...
```

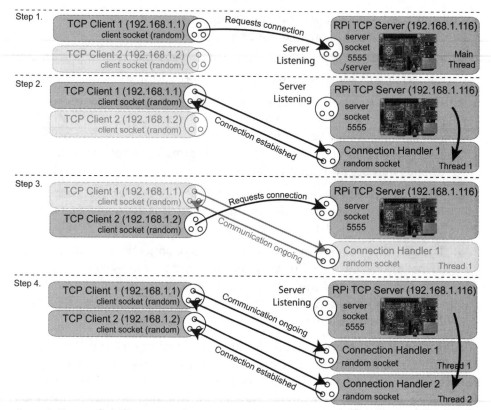

Figure 14-15: A multithreaded server

Then start TCP Client 1 in the next terminal:

```
pi@erpi ~/exploringrpi/chp14/threadedClientServer $ ./client localhost
Starting RPi Client Example
Sending [Hello from the Client]
```

Then start TCP Client 2 in the last terminal (quickly—the delay is 5 seconds!):

```
pi@erpi ~/exploringrpi/chp14/threadedClientServer $ ./client localhost
Starting RPi Client Example
Sending [Hello from the Client]
```

The fact that the second client is able to connect while the first client is awaiting a (artificially delayed) response means that the server must be multithreaded. The final output of the server is as follows:

```
pi@erpi ~/exploringrpi/chp14/threadedClientServer $ ./server
Starting RPi Server Example
Listening for a connection...
Received from the client [Hello from the Client]
Sending back [The Server says thanks!]
  but going asleep for 5 seconds first....
```

```
Received from the client [Hello from the Client]
Sending back [The Server says thanks!]
  but going asleep for 5 seconds first....
```

Both clients will display the same final output:

```
pi@erpi ~/exploringrpi/chp14/threadedClientServer $ ./client localhost
Starting RPi Client Example
Sending [Hello from the Client]
Received [The Server says thanks!]
End of RPi Client Example
```

The class definition for the ConnectionHandler class is provided in Listing 14-10. This class has a slightly complex structure so that a thread is created and started when an object of the class is created. This code can be used as a template—just rewrite the threadLoop() implementation.

Listing 14-10: /chp14/threadedclientserver/network/ConnectionHandler.h

```cpp
class SocketServer;   // class declaration, due to circular ref problem
                      // and C/C++ single definition rule.
class ConnectionHandler {
public:
   // Constructor expects a reference to the server that called it and
   // the incoming socket and file descriptor
   ConnectionHandler(SocketServer *server, sockaddr_in *in, int fd);
   virtual ~ConnectionHandler();
   int   start();
   void wait();
   void stop() { this->running = false; }  // stop the thread loop
   virtual int send(std::string message);  // send message to the client
   virtual std::string receive(int size);   // receive a message
protected:
   virtual void threadLoop();       // the user-defined thread loop
private:
   sockaddr_in  *client;          // a handle to the client socket
   int          clientSocketfd;    // the client socket file desc.
   pthread_t    thread;            // the thread
   SocketServer *parent;           // a handle to the server object
   bool         running;           // is thread running? (default true)

   // static method to set the thread running when an object is created
   static void * threadHelper(void * handler){
         ((ConnectionHandler *)handler)->threadLoop();
         return NULL;
   }
};
```

The Multithreaded Weather Server

The code in the previous section is modified in this section to create the Multithreaded Weather Service in Listing 14-11, which is available in the

/chp14/QtWeatherServer directory. It is unlikely that you will need to check the room temperature every fraction of a second. Therefore, a multithreaded approach is overkill in this example. However, this structure is very important for applications that stream data, so it is useful to be exposed to it.

Listing 14-11: /chp14/QtWeatherServer/network/ConnectionHandler.cpp

```
#define USING_DHT11     false   // The DHT11 uses only 8 bits
#define DHT_GPIO        22      // Using GPIO 22 for this example
#define LH_THRESHOLD    26      // Low=~14, High=~38 - pick avg.

int ConnectionHandler::readDHTSensor() { ... // same as before }

void ConnectionHandler::threadLoop() {
   cout << "*** Created a Connection Handler threaded Function" << endl;
   string rec = this->receive(1024);
   if (rec == "getReading"){
      cout << "Received from the client [" << rec << "]" << endl;
      if (this->readDHTSensor()<0) {
         cout << "Failed to make a reading from the DHT sensor" << endl;
      }
      stringstream ss;
      ss << " { \"sample\": { \"temperature\" : " << temperature;
      ss << ", \"humidity\": " << humidity << " } } ";
      this->send(ss.str());
      cout << "Sent [" << ss.str() << "]" << endl;
   }
   else {
      cout << "Received from the client [" << rec << "]" << endl;
      this->send(string("Unknown Command"));
   }
   cout << "*** End of the Connection Handler Function" << endl;
   this->parent->notifyHandlerDeath(this);
}
```

The Weather Server code can be tested by using the clientTest CLI test application, which is in the same directory as the server, by using the following:

```
pi@erpi ~/exploringrpi/chp14/QtWeatherServer $ sudo ./server
Starting RPi Server Example
Listening for a connection...
```

Then execute the test client in a different terminal:

```
pi@erpi ~/exploringrpi/chp14/QtWeatherServer $ ./clientTest localhost
Starting RPi Client Test
Sending [getReading]
Received [ { "sample": { "temperature" : 19, "humidity": 49.5 } } ]
End of RPi Client Test
```

The final output of the server is then as follows:

```
pi@erpi ~/exploringrpi/chp14/QtWeatherServer $ sudo ./server
Starting RPi Server Example
Listening for a connection...
```

```
Starting the Connection Handler thread
*** Created a Connection Handler threaded Function
Received from the client [getReading]
Sent [ { "sample": { "temperature" : 19, "humidity": 49.5 } } ]
*** End of the Connection Handler Function
Server: Found and deleted the connection reference...
Destroyed a Connection Handler
```

The `localhost` host name is resolved to the loopback address 127.0.0.1, which enables the RPi to communicate with itself. If the client application outputs a temperature and humidity value (e.g., 19°C and 49.5%), this test is successful and the Qt fat-client GUI application should also connect to the server, as illustrated in Figure 14-14.

Parsing Stream Data

The obvious approach to sending data between a server and a client is to use byte data and to marshall and unmarshall the data values. This can be performed by manually converting numeric data into string values; however, manual conversion is prone to parsing errors, particularly as the complexity of communication increases. One solution to this problem is to use an XML format to communicate between the client and the server. For example the sample data could be structured as a simple XML message format:

```
<sample><temperature>18.2</temperature><humidity>45.4</humidity></sample>
```

The Qt framework has full support for XML parsing in the `QtXml` module by using the `QXmlStreamReader` class.

An alternative solution is to use JavaScript Object Notation (JSON), which is also a human-readable format and is commonly used to transmit data between server and web applications. As you will have noticed, the sample data in the QtWeather client/server application is transmitted in the JSON format as follows:

```
{
    "sample": {
       "temperature" : 18.2,
       "humidity": 45.4
    }
}
```

The Qt framework also has full support for parsing JSON data using the `QJsonDocument` class. Listing 14-12 is a segment of code from the Qt Weather Client application that parses the JSON data format and retrieves the floating-point temperature and humidity values. By converting the byte data into a `sample` object of the `QJsonObject` class, the data values can be retrieved by calling `sample["name"].toDouble()`, where `name` is the string name of the value to be retrieved. There are similar functions for other data types, for example `toInt()`, `toString()`, `toBool()`, and `toArray()`.

Listing 14-12: /chp14/QtWeatherClient/mainwindow.cpp (segment)

```
int MainWindow::parseJSONData(QString str){
    QJsonDocument doc = QJsonDocument::fromJson(str.toUtf8());
    QJsonObject obj = doc.object();
    QJsonObject sample = obj["sample"].toObject();
    this->temperature = (float) sample["temperature"].toDouble();
    this->humidity = (float) sample["humidity"].toDouble();
    cout << "The temperature is " << temperature << " and humidity is "
        << humidity << endl;
    return 0;
}
```

This framework is flexible and can be applied to many client/server applications on the RPi. In fact, it can even be reversed so that the RPi is the client and a desktop/server machine acts as the TCP server. Regardless, the same multithreading and data interchange principles can be applied.

Summary

After completing this chapter, you should be able to do the following:

- Configure the RPi as a general-purpose computing device and use Bluetooth peripherals to control it.
- Acquire hardware for LCD touchscreen display applications.
- Use virtual network computing (VNC) to remotely execute graphical user interface (GUI) applications on the RPi.
- Build rich user interface (UI) applications that execute directly on the RPi using the GTK+ and Qt frameworks.
- Build Qt applications with advanced interfaces that connect to hardware sensors on the RPi.
- Build fat-client remote Qt applications that communicate using TCP sockets to a server that is executing on the RPi.
- Enhance TCP server code to be multithreaded, in order to allow multiple simultaneous connections from TCP client applications.
- Build remote Qt GUI server applications that communicate, using TCP sockets and JSON messages, to a client application on the RPi.

Further Reading

The following additional links provide further information on the topics in this chapter:

- **Chapter web page:** www.exploringrpi.com/chapter14
- **Core documentation on GTK+3.0:** tiny.cc/erpi1404
- **Qt Signals and Slots:** tiny.cc/erpi1405

# CHAPTER 15

Images, Video, and Audio

In this chapter, peripherals are attached to the RPi so that it can be used for capturing image, video, and audio data using low-level Linux drivers and application programming interfaces (APIs). It describes Linux applications and tools that can be used to stream captured video and audio data to the Internet. Open Source Computer Vision (OpenCV) image processing and computer vision approaches are investigated that enable the Raspberry Pi (RPi) to draw inferences from the information content of the captured image data. Capture and playback of audio streams is described, along with the use of Bluetooth A2DP audio. The chapter also covers some applications of audio on the RPi, including streaming audio, Internet radio, and text-to-speech (TTS).

Equipment Required for This Chapter:

- Raspberry Pi (any model, but ideally an RPi3)
- Raspberry Pi camera or a USB webcam
- USB audio, audio HAT, and/or Bluetooth adapter

Further resources for this chapter are available at www.exploringrpi.com/chapter15/.

Capturing Images and Video

In this section, the RPi is used as a platform for capturing image and video data and saving the data on the RPi file system. This is useful for RPi applications such as robotics, home security, home automation, and aeronautics, when networked image streaming is not an available option—for example, if the application is untethered and distant from a wireless network. With suitable peripherals, the RPi can be used to capture very high-quality video streams, which can be viewed asynchronously. The durations of the video streams are limited only by the available storage on the RPi and any attached USB memory devices. Alternatively, the video can be streamed to the network, which is discussed in the next section of this chapter.

The RPi Camera

The RPi camera ($30), illustrated in Figure 15-1(a), is a small (25mm × 24mm) camera module that is attached to the RPi *camera serial interface* (*CSI*) connector via a 15cm ribbon cable (15core, 1mm pitch). The CSI connector is on all RPi models, except the RPi Zero. The fixed-focus camera uses an Omnivision 5647 sensor that has still picture resolution of 2592 × 1944 pixels (5MP) and supports full HD video recording (1920 × 1080) at various frame rates (including 640 × 480 at 90FPS!). The camera is also available with and without an infrared filter; the latter is called the NoIR model, and it is useful for night-vision applications (with the use of active IR illumination), but daylight image colors are badly affected. The RPi NoIR is currently produced on a black PCB, whereas the regular model is produced on a green PCB.

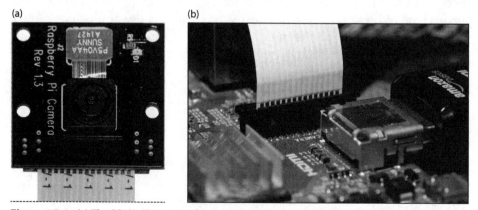

Figure 15-1: (a) The RPi NoIR camera; (b) correct attachment of the ribbon cable to the RPi CSI connector

The camera is attached to the RPi as illustrated in Figure 15-1(b) using the following steps:

- Power down the RPi and avoid touching the metal contacts at the end of the ribbon cable to avoid damage due to static discharge.
- Remove the plastic protector from the lens.
- Gently pull up the housing clip (typically black or white) on the CSI connector (next to the Ethernet connector).
- Point the metal contacts on the ribbon cable away from the Ethernet port and insert the ribbon cable evenly into the connector slot.
- Push the plastic housing clip down. The cable should appear as in Figure 15-1(b).

After the RPi has been powered, you can use the `raspi-config` tool to enable the camera, and reboot:

```
pi@erpi ~ $ sudo raspi-config
```

You will see that the `/boot/config.txt` file is updated to allocate memory to the graphical processor unit (GPU) in order for the camera to work (by default `gpu_mem=128`). The camera requires a minimum of 32MB, but 128MB is recommended. You can disable the camera LED from lighting when the camera is recording by adding the following line to the same configuration file:

```
disable_camera_led=1
```

NOTE The examples that follow in this chapter are written with the assumption that you have configured a display for your RPi, as described in Chapter 14. For example, a VNC client/server (e.g., Xming or VNC Viewer) allows the output images to be displayed on your desktop machine. An alternative approach is to `sftp` image files back and forth between the desktop machine and the RPi.

Capturing Still Images

After the RPi camera has been installed, you can test it using the `raspistill` and `raspivid` applications, which respectively facilitate the capture of still images and video to the file system. For example, to capture a 5 megapixel (2592 × 1944) JPEG-format image, you can use the following steps:

```
pi@erpi ~ $ raspistill -o image.jpg
pi@erpi ~ $ ls -l image.jpg
-rw-r--r-- 1 pi pi 2706220 Dec  1 02:21 image.jpg
pi@erpi ~ $ gpicview image.jpg
```

The last line displays the image using the `gpicview` utility; this requires that you have a display attached to the RPi, or that you are using VNC. The resolution can be adjusted, and a time delay of 1 second can be added by using command-line options such as (type `raspistill` with no arguments to get the full list):

```
pi@erpi ~ $ raspistill -t 1000 -o test.jpg -w 1280 -h 960
pi@erpi ~ $ ls -l test.jpg
-rw-r--r-- 1 pi pi 660387 Dec  1 03:05 test.jpg
```

If you have a TV/monitor attached to the video output of the RPi, you can get a live view of the camera on it using the same tool. For example, to display the camera preview output for 30 seconds on the attached TV/monitor (5 seconds is the default time):

```
pi@erpi ~ $ raspistill -v -t 30000
raspistill Camera App v1.3.8
```

Recording Video

The `raspivid` application can be used to capture video from the camera at very impressive resolutions and frame rates. For example, to record 5 seconds of full-HD video to the SD card, you can use the following:

```
pi@erpi ~ $ raspivid -t 5000 -o video.h264
pi@erpi ~ $ ls -l video.h264
-rw-r--r-- 1 pi pi 10106227 Dec  1 03:08 video.h264
```

You can see that this video is captured at a rate of approximately 2MB (16Mb) per second; therefore, 1 hour of video would require approximately 7.2GB of storage. You can adjust the bitrate using the `-b` option. For example, to record 1 minute of video at 8Mb/sec (1MB/sec) to a USB key that is attached to the RPi, use the following call:

```
pi@erpi ~ $ raspivid -t 60000 -b 8000000 -o - > /media/pi/key/video.h264
pi@erpi ~ $ cd /media/pi/key/
pi@erpi /media/pi/key $ ls -l video.h264
-rw------- 1 pi pi 59849757 Dec  5 02:09 video.h264
```

The resulting file is approximately 60MB in size; however, to play this video on media players such as VLC, it may have to be converted from a raw H.264 format into a "packaged" MP4 format:

```
pi@erpi /media/pi/key $ sudo apt install gpac
pi@erpi /media/pi/key $ MP4Box -add video.h264 video.mp4
```

The RPi camera can capture video at high frame rates; for example, 60FPS at 720p (i.e., 1280 × 720) and 90FPS at 640 × 480. The latter allows for impressive slow-motion effects by capturing at 90FPS and replaying the video at lower frame rates (e.g., 30FPS):

```
pi@erpi ~ $ raspivid -t 20000 -w 640 -h 480 -fps 90 -o - >        →
  /media/pi/key/v90fps.h264
```

```
pi@erpi ~ $ cd /media/pi/key/
pi@erpi /media/pi/key $ MP4Box -add v90fps.h264:rescale=30000 v30fps.mp4
pi@erpi /media/pi/key $ ls -l v*fps.*
-rw------- 1 pi pi 28957257 Dec  5 03:43 v30fps.mp4
-rw------- 1 pi pi 25299257 Dec  5 03:42 v90fps.h264
```

Another utility, raspiyuv, has the same option set as raspivid, but captures uncompressed *YUV* (*YCbCr*) video, which is an image color space that is commonly used in place of RGB (red, green, blue) by video devices, largely for historical compatibility as the *Y* channel (luma or brightness) is all that is required for output to "black and white" displays.

Using the RPi Camera in Linux User Space

The tools described for the RPi camera use the Broadcom multimedia abstraction layer (MMAL), which is specifically written for the Videocore 4 system on the RPi. MMAL provides high-performance video, but it means that the camera is not compatible with many user space Linux applications. Video4Linux2 is shortly described, and the RPi MMAL camera can be used as a Linux user space device by loading the bcm2835-v4l2 LKM, which results in the appearance of a video device (for example, /dev/video0):

```
pi@erpi ~ $ sudo modprobe bcm2835-v4l2
pi@erpi ~ $ lsmod | grep v4l2
bcm2835_v4l2           37223  0
videobuf2_vmalloc       5397  1 bcm2835_v4l2
videobuf2_core         33918  1 bcm2835_v4l2
v4l2_common             3766  2 bcm2835_v4l2,videobuf2_core
videodev              124119  3 bcm2835_v4l2,v4l2_common,videobuf2_core
pi@erpi ~ $ ls -l /dev/vid*
crw-rw----+ 1 root video 81, 0 Dec  2 02:07 /dev/video0
```

Remember to add an entry to the /etc/modules file should you want this change to persist after a reboot.

> **WARNING**   Problems with USB webcams and the RPi camera (typically requires 200mA–250mA) can be caused by low power. The camera LED may indicate that the camera is working, but the lack of power may result in data transmission problems. If you are combining a USB webcam with a Wi-Fi adapter, you should use a powered USB hub, such as the PiHut 7 Port USB Hub for the RPi (tiny.cc/erpi1501).

USB Webcams

USB webcams are widely available and can be reused as a general-purpose desktop peripheral. The Logitech HD C270 ($26), HD C310 ($30), and HD Pro C920 ($70), shown in Figure 15-2, are chosen, as they are commonly available HD cameras that are known to function under Linux.

(a) (b) (c)

Figure 15-2: Logitech USB HD webcams (a) C270, (b) C310, and (c) C920

When one of the USB cameras is connected to the RPi, the "list USB devices" utility provides the following output:

```
pi@erpi ~ $ lsusb
Bus 001 Device 005: ID 046d:082d Logitech, Inc. HD Pro Webcam C920
Bus 001 Device 004: ID 0a5c:2198 Broadcom Corp. Bluetooth 3.0 Device
...
```

The output lists the device ID for the camera and a USB Bluetooth adapter. The fact that "Logitech" is listed against the device ID indicates that some level of Linux support is already present on the RPi for such a device. If this is not the case, you will have to source proprietary Linux drivers from the webcam manufacturer. Typically, such drivers would have to be built and deployed on the RPi before the webcam could be used.

Full information about the modes that are available on a USB camera can be displayed using the following:

```
pi@erpi ~ $ lsusb -v | less
```

This command results in detailed and verbose output. In addition, the LKMs that are currently loaded can be listed using the `lsmod` command:

```
pi@erpi ~ $ lsmod | grep video
uvcvideo                72838  0
videobuf2_vmalloc        5397  1 uvcvideo
videobuf2_memops         1564  1 videobuf2_vmalloc
videobuf2_core          33918  1 uvcvideo
v4l2_common              3766  1 videobuf2_core
videodev               124119  3 uvcvideo,v4l2_common,videobuf2_core
media                   11633  2 uvcvideo,videodev
```

The `uvcvideo` LKM supports UVC (USB video class) compliant devices, such as the webcams in Figure 15-2. The `videobuf2_vmalloc` LKM is the memory allocator for the Video4Linux video buffer. If everything is working as expected, there should be new video (and audio devices) available, which can be listed using the following:

```
pi@erpi ~ $ ls /dev/vid*
/dev/video0   /dev/video1
pi@erpi ~ $ ls /dev/snd/controlC*
/dev/snd/controlC0   /dev/snd/controlC1
```

In this example, the RPi camera and USB camera are attached to the RPi. The audio device related to the USB webcam is mapped to `/dev/snd/controlC1` in this example.

Video4Linux2 (V4L2)

Video4Linux2 (V4L2) is a video capture driver framework tightly integrated with the Linux kernel and supported by the `uvcvideo` LKM. It provides drivers for video devices, such as webcams, PCI video capture cards, and TV (DVB-T/S) tuner cards/peripherals. V4L2 primarily supports video (and audio) devices through the following types of interfaces:

- **Video capture interface:** Used to capture video from capture devices, such as webcams, TV tuners, or video capture devices
- **Video output interface:** For video output devices (e.g., video transmission devices or video streaming devices)
- **Video overlay interface:** Enables the direct display of the video data without requiring the data to be processed by the CPU
- **Video blanking interval (VBI) interface:** Provides access to legacy data that is transmitted during the VBI of an analog video signal (e.g., teletext)
- **Radio interface:** Provides access to AM/FM tuner audio streams

V4L2 provides support for many types of devices, and simply put, it is complex! In addition to supporting video input/output, the V4L2 API also has stubs for codec and video effect devices, which enable manipulation of the video stream data. The focus in this section is on the capture of video data from webcam devices using V4L2 by performing the following steps (not necessarily in this order):

- Opening the V4L2 device
- Changing the device properties (e.g., camera brightness)
- Agreeing on a data format and input/output method
- Performing the transfer of data
- Closing the V4L2 device

The main source of documentation on V4L2 is available from `www.kernel` `.org` at `tiny.cc/erpi1502`, and the V4L2 API specification is available at `tiny` `.cc/erpi1503`.

Image Capture Utility

The first step is to install the V4L2 development libraries, abstraction layer, utilities, and a simple webcam application for V4L2-compatible devices.

Always update the package lists, to get information about the newest packages and their dependencies, before installing a system library:

```
pi@erpi ~ $ apt-cache search v4l2
fswebcam - Tiny and flexible webcam program
...
pi@erpi ~ $ sudo apt install fswebcam libv4l-dev v4l-utils view libav-tools
```

The fswebcam application can then be used to test that the attached web camera is working correctly. It is a surprisingly powerful and easy-to-use application that is best used by writing a configuration file, as shown in Listing 15-1, which contains settings for choosing the device, capture resolution, output file type, and the addition of a title banner. It can even be used on a continuous loop by adding a loop entry that specifies the time in seconds between frame captures.

Listing 15-1: /exploringrpi/chp15/fswebcam/fswebcam.conf

```
device /dev/video0
input 0
resolution 1280x720
bottom-banner
font /usr/share/fonts/truetype/ttf-dejavu/DejaVuSans.ttf
title "Exploring Raspberry Pi"
timestamp "%H:%M:%S %d/%m/%Y (%Z)"
png 0
save exploringRPi.png
```

The fswebcam application can be configured with these settings by passing it the configuration filename on execution:

```
pi@erpi ~/exploringrpi/chp15/fswebcam $ ls
fswebcam.conf
pi@erpi ~/exploringrpi/chp15/fswebcam $ fswebcam -c fswebcam.conf
--- Opening /dev/video0...
Trying source module v4l2...
/dev/video0 opened.
--- Capturing frame... ...
pi@erpi ~/exploringrpi/chp15/fswebcam $ ls
exploringRPi.png  fswebcam.conf
```

The image can then be viewed using gpicview, which requires that you have attached a display to the RPi, such as a VNC connection:

```
.../chp15/fswebcam$ gpicview exploringRPi.png
```

This will result in output like that in Figure 15-3. The image data has been modified to include a formatted bottom text banner, which contains a title, and the date and time of image capture.

NOTE   You can output a live view of the webcam by using the command mplayer tv:// or by installing Cheese (sudo apt install cheese) and executing it using cheese.

(a)

(b)

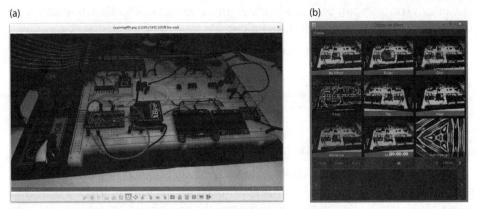

Figure 15-3: (a) The fswebcam webcam capture (1280 × 720) displayed using gpicview via VNC, and (b) the Cheese application displaying some available image filters

Interestingly, the fswebcam application could be executed on a loop and combined with the Nginx web server (as described in Chapter 12) to create a simple web camera, which uses a web page that links to the captured image file present on the RPi file system that is updating over time.

Video4Linux2 Utilities

V4L2 provides a set of user space utilities that can be used for obtaining information about connected V4L2-compatible devices. It is also possible to use the user space utilities to change camera settings; however, it is possible that executed applications will be programmed to override such changes. The most important role of these tools is to verify that connected V4L2 devices are functioning correctly. You can list the available V4L2 devices using the following:

```
pi@erpi ~ $ v4l2-ctl --list-devices
mmal service 16.1 (platform:bcm2835-v4l2): /dev/video0
HD Pro Webcam C920 (usb-3f980000.usb-1.4): /dev/video1
```

The devices appear in the order in which they are attached to the USB hub. You can get information about a particular device by listing its modes (where -d 0 refers to the RPi MMAL camera in this instance):

```
pi@erpi ~ $ v4l2-ctl --all -d 0
Driver Info (not using libv4l2):
        Driver name    : bm2835 mmal
        Card type      : mmal service 16.1
        Bus info       : platform:bcm2835-v4l2
        Driver version: 4.1.13
        Capabilities   : 0x85200005   Video Capture
```

Certain controls can be used to configure a camera, which can be accessed using the `--list-ctrls` option, as follows:

```
pi@erpi ~ $ v4l2-ctl --list-ctrls -d 0
    brightness (int)       : min=0 max=100 step=1 default=50 value=50
    contrast (int)         : min=-100 max=100 step=1 default=0 value=0
    saturation (int)       : min=-100 max=100 step=1 default=0 value=0
    red_balance (int)      : min=1 max=7999 step=1 default=1000 value=1000
    blue_balance (int)     : min=1 max=7999 step=1 default=1000 value=1000
    horizontal_flip (bool): default=0 value=0
    vertical_flip (bool)   : default=0 value=0 ...
```

For the RPi camera, other controls include white balance, color temperature, sharpness, backlight compensation, exposure (auto or absolute), focus, zoom, and support for pan/tilt. For example, to change the brightness on device `video0` to 100 (currently 50 as shown in the preceding snippet), you can use the following:

```
pi@erpi ~ $ v4l2-ctl --set-ctrl=brightness=100 -d 0
pi@erpi ~ $ v4l2-ctl --list-ctrls -d 0 | grep brightness
    brightness (int)       : min=0 max=100 step=1 default=50 value=100
    brightness (int)       : min=0 max=100 step=1 default=50 value=100
```

You can also list the modes of the cameras. In the case of the RPi MMAL camera there are thirteen different video capture pixel formats; the Logitech C920 has three. Examples of fourcc color space video include codes such as `'YUYV'` (a common broadcast format with one luminance and two chrominance channels), `'H264'` (a common modern interframe video compression format), and `'MJPG'` (a common, but older, intraframe-only motion JPEG video compression format). The listing is obtained using the following:

```
pi@erpi ~ $ v4l2-ctl --list-formats -d 0
ioctl: VIDIOC_ENUM_FMT ...
    Index       : 1                    Type      : Video Capture
    Pixel Format: 'YUYV'               Name      : 4:2:2, packed, YUYV
    Index       : 4                    Type      : Video Capture
    Pixel Format: 'H264' (compressed)  Name      : H264 ...
pi@erpi ~ $ v4l2-ctl --list-formats -d 1
ioctl: VIDIOC_ENUM_FMT
    Index       : 0                    Type      : Video Capture
    Pixel Format: 'YUYV'               Name      : YUV 4:2:2 (YUYV)
    Index       : 1                    Type      : Video Capture
    Pixel Format: 'H264' (compressed)  Name      : H.264
    Index       : 2                    Type      : Video Capture
    Pixel Format: 'MJPG' (compressed)  Name      : MJPEG
```

The C270 and C310 cameras do not have a H.264 mode, but they both have `'YUYV'` and `'MJPG'` compressed pixel formats at indices 0 and 1 respectively. It is possible to explicitly set the resolution and pixel format of a camera as follows:

```
pi@erpi ~ $ v4l2-ctl --set-fmt-video=width=1920,height=1080,pixelformat=4 -d
0
pi@erpi ~ $ v4l2-ctl --all -d 0
Driver Info (not using libv4l2):
```

```
    Driver name    : bm2835 mmal ...
Format Video Capture:
    Width/Height   : 1920/1080      Pixel Format   : 'H264'
    Field          : None           Bytes per Line: 0
    Size Image     : 2088960
    Colorspace     : Broadcast NTSC/PAL (SMPTE170M/ITU601) ...
```

This output provides very useful state information, such as the resolution, video frame image size, frame rate, and so on.

Writing Video4Linux2 Programs

As with other devices in Linux (e.g., SPI in Chapter 8), it is possible to send data to and receive data from a video device by opening its /dev/videoX file system entry by using a call to open(). Unfortunately, such an approach would not provide the level of control or the performance level that is required for video devices. Instead, low-level input/output control (ioctl()) calls are required to configure the settings of the device, and memory map (mmap()) calls are used to perform image frame memory copy, rather than using a byte-by-byte serial transfer.

The Git repository contains programs in the /chp15/v4l2/ directory that use V4L2 and its low-level ioctl() calls to perform video frame capture and video capture tasks:

- grabber.c: Grabs raw image frame data from a webcam into memory using libv4l2. The images can be written to the file system.

- capture.c: Grabs raw video data to a stream or file. It does this quickly enough to be used for real-time video capture.

These code examples are almost entirely based on the examples that are provided by the V4L2 project team. The code is too long to display here, but you can view it in the Git repository. To build and execute the code examples, use the following steps:

```
.../chp15/v4l2$ ls *.c
capture.c  grabber.c
.../chp15/v4l2$ gcc -O2 -Wall `pkg-config --cflags --libs libv4l2` →
  grabber.c -o grabber
.../chp15/v4l2$ gcc -O2 -Wall `pkg-config --cflags --libs libv4l2` →
  capture.c -o capture
.../chp15/v4l2$ ./grabber
.../chp15/v4l2$ ls *.ppm
grabber000.ppm  grabber005.ppm  grabber010.ppm  grabber015.ppm ...
.../chp15/v4l2$ gpicview grabber000.ppm
```

The .ppm file format describes an uncompressed color image format, which gpicview will display. You can use the "forward" button on gpicview to step through the 20 image frames. To capture data using the capture.c program, use a selection of the following options:

```
.../chp15/v4l2$ ./capture -h
Usage: ./capture [options]
Version 1.3    Options:
-d | --device name    Video device name [/dev/video0] ...
-f | --format         Force format to 640x480 YUYV
-F | --formatH264     Force format to 1920x1080 H264
-c | --count          Number of frames to grab [100] - use 0 for infinite
Example usage: capture -F -o -c 300 > output.raw
Captures 300 frames of H264 at 1920x1080. Use raw2mpg4 script to convert to
mpg4
```

If you have the C920 or RPi camera, you can capture 100 frames of H.264 data using the first of the following commands. A second command then converts the .raw file to a .mp4 file format, which can be played on a desktop machine:

```
.../chp15/v4l2 $ ./capture -d /dev/video0 -F -o -c 100 > output.raw
Force Format 2
.......................................................................
.../chp15/v4l2 $ avconv -f h264 -i output.raw -vcodec copy output.mp4
.../chp15/v4l2 $ ls -l output*
-rw-r--r-- 1 pi pi 2494753 Dec  5 07:07 output.mp4
-rw-r--r-- 1 pi pi 2493142 Dec  5 07:07 output.raw
```

The file sizes are almost identical because the video data is actually captured in a raw H.264 format. The conversion is performed using the avconv (Libav) utility, which is a fork of the FFmpeg project that is better supported by the Raspbian/Debian Linux distribution. The -vcodec copy option enables the video to be copied without transcoding the video data format. This will work for the USB C920 or the RPi MMAL cameras, but not cameras that do not have H.264 format capabilities.

However, the capture.c program can also be used with cameras such as the C270 and C310, which do not have hardware H.264 functionality; however, the capabilities are more limited:

```
...$ v4l2-ctl --set-fmt-video=width=1280,height=720,pixelformat=1 -d 1
...$ v4l2-ctl --all -d 1
Format Video Capture: Width/Height:1280/720   Pixel Format:'MJPG'
.../chp15/v4l2$ ./capture -d /dev/video2 -o -c 100 > output.raw
Force Format 0 ...................................................
.../chp15/v4l2$ ls -l output.raw
-rw-r--r-- 1 pi pi 4496449 Dec  5 01:51 output.raw
.../chp15/v4l2$ avconv -f mjpeg -i output.raw output.mp4
.../chp15/v4l2$ ls -l output.mp4
-rw-r--r-- 1 pi pi 1466046 Dec  5 02:00 output.mp4
```

The video conversion using avconv can take quite some time on the RPi. In this example you can see that the H.264 video file requires significantly less space than the MJPEG file, as it is a more efficient interframe video encoding format.

NOTE   A common problem arises when using the `capture.c` program: The camera returns a "select timeout" error. If this happens, you need to change the time-out properties of the `uvcvideo` LKM as follows:

```
pi@erpi ~ $ sudo rmmod uvcvideo
pi@erpi ~ $ sudo modprobe uvcvideo nodrop=1 timeout=5000
pi@erpi ~ $ lsmod | grep uvcvideo
uvcvideo               72838  0
videobuf2_vmalloc       5397  2 uvcvideo,bcm2835_v4l2
videobuf2_core         33918  2 uvcvideo,bcm2835_v4l2 ...
```

Please note that you should usually call `modprobe  -r` instead of `rmmod`, as it performs dependency checking and removes any unused LKMs. In this example the `uvcvideo` LKM is reloaded immediately, so dependency checking is not required.

Streaming Video

It is possible to use the RPi to capture and stream live video. The RPi MMAL or Logitech C920 cameras are particularly useful for this purpose, as they have built-in H.264 hardware support. The raw 1080p H.264 data can be passed directly from the camera stream to the network without transcoding, which means that the computational load on the RPi is reasonably low. Streaming scripts are available in the `/chp15/v4l2/` repository directory. For example, Listing 15-2 provides a script for sending H.264 video data over UDP to port 12345 on a desktop PC at IP address 192.168.1.4 using the C920 webcam.

Listing 15-2: /chp15/v4l2/streamVideoUDP_C920

```
#!/bin/bash
echo "Video Streaming for the Raspberry Pi - Exploring Raspberry Pi"
v4l2-ctl --set-fmt-video=width=1920,height=1080,pixelformat=1
./capture -d /dev/video0 -F -o -c0|avconv -re -i - -vcodec copy -f mpegts →
udp://192.168.1.4:12345
```

This script pipes the raw video output from the capture program to the `avconv` application, which "copies" the raw data to the network stream using UDP. You can open this stream on the desktop machine (at address 192.168.1.4) in VLC by using the option Media ⇨ Open Network Stream ⇨ and entering the network URL `UDP://@:12345`. The RPi can stream full-HD video to the desktop PC with a slight delay that is caused by encoding/decoding.

There are various methods of streaming full-HD video from the RPi MMAL camera. One of the most stable approaches appears to be through the use of VideoLAN VLC (`www.videolan.org`), albeit it suffers from slight latency problems.

Do not enable the user space driver for the RPi camera. Disable the user space driver for the RPi camera (e.g., using sudo rmmod bcm2835-v4l2) and pipe the output of the raspivid program directly to VLC as follows:

```
pi@erpi ~ $ sudo apt install vlc
pi@erpi ~ $ raspivid -o - -t 0 -hf -w 1920 -h 1080 -fps 30 | cvlc -vvv stre →
am:///dev/stdin --sout '#standard{access=http,mux=ts,dst=:12345}' :demux=h264
```

This stream can be opened within VLC using the URL http://erpi .local:12345, where erpi.local is the IP address of your RPi.

There is an additional script outline to multicast the video stream to multiple network points (streamVideoMulti) using the broadcast network address 226.0.0.1 and to stream the video using the Real-time Transport Protocol (RTP) (streamVideoRTP).

A second RPi can be used to receive the network video stream and display it using a video player that takes advantage of the Raspberry Pi's H.264 hardware decoder. For example, the OMXplayer supports hardware decoding, and it can be used to open the network broadcast stream using the following:

```
pi@erpi2 ~ $ omxplayer -o hdmi udp://226.0.0.1:12345
```

The RPi can decode the video stream and display it live on a monitor, albeit with a varying degree of latency.

Image Processing and Computer Vision

Once a USB or RPi camera is attached to the RPi, it is possible to capture images and process them using a comprehensive high-level library called Open Source Computer Vision (OpenCV). OpenCV (www.opencv.org) provides a cross-platform library of functions for computer vision, such as gesture recognition, motion understanding, motion tracking, augmented reality, and structure-from-motion. It also provides supporting libraries for applications such as artificial neural networks, support vector machines, classification, and decision tree learning. OpenCV is written in C/C++ and is optimized for real-time applications, including support for multicore programming. The OpenCV libraries can be installed using the following:

```
pi@erpi ~ $ sudo apt install libopencv-dev
```

Image Processing with OpenCV

OpenCV supports V4L2 and provides a high-level interface for capturing image data, which can be used instead of the grabber.c program. Listing 15-3 is an OpenCV application that captures data from a webcam and filters it using some simple image processing techniques. The steps that it performs are as follows:

1. Capture of the image from the webcam.

2. Conversion of the image into grayscale form.

3. Blurring of the image to remove high-frequency noise.

4. Detecting regions in the image where the image brightness changes sharply. This is achieved using an image processing operator known as an edge detector—the Canny edge detector in this example.

5. Storage of the image files to the RPi file system.

OpenCV uses a file-naming convention whereby an .hpp file extension is used for header files that contain C++ code. This convention enables a C version of a header file (e.g., opencv.h) to coexist alongside a C++ header file (e.g., opencv .hpp). Because OpenCV mixes both C and C++ code, this is an appropriate way to distinguish one form from the other.

Listing 15-3: /chp15/openCV/filter.cpp

```
#include<iostream>
#include<opencv2/opencv.hpp>    // C++ OpenCV include file
using namespace std;
using namespace cv;             // using the cv namespace too

int main() {
    VideoCapture capture(0);    // capturing from /dev/video0
    cout << "Started Processing - Capturing Image" << endl;
    // set any  properties in the VideoCapture object
    capture.set(CV_CAP_PROP_FRAME_WIDTH,1280);   // width in pixels
    capture.set(CV_CAP_PROP_FRAME_HEIGHT,720);   // height in pixels
    capture.set(CV_CAP_PROP_GAIN, 0);            // enable auto gain
    if(!capture.isOpened()){    // connect to the camera
       cout << "Failed to connect to the camera." << endl;
    }
    Mat frame, gray, edges;     // original, grayscale and edge image
    capture >> frame;           // capture the image to the frame
    if(frame.empty()){          // did the capture succeed?
       cout << "Failed to capture an image" << endl;
       return -1;
    }
    cout << "Processing - Performing Image Processing" << endl;
    cvtColor(frame, gray, CV_BGR2GRAY);       // convert to grayscale
    blur(gray, edges, Size(3,3));             // blur image using a 3x3 kernel
    // use Canny edge detector that outputs to the same image
    // low threshold = 10, high threshold = 30, kernel size = 3
    Canny(edges, edges, 10, 30, 3);           // run Canny edge detector
    cout << "Finished Processing - Saving images" << endl;

    imwrite("capture.png", frame);     // store the original image
    imwrite("grayscale.png", gray);    // store the grayscale image
    imwrite("edges.png", edges);       // store the processed edge image
    return 0;
}
```

The RPi MMAL camera should be placed in user space mode as described earlier in this chapter. The camera device must also be chosen on the first line of the `main()` function; use 0 for `/dev/video0` and 1 for `/dev/video1`. This example can be built and executed as follows (in the `/chp15/openCV` directory), which results in the output displayed in Figure 15-4(a):

```
.../openCV $ g++ -O2 `pkg-config --cflags --libs opencv` filter.cpp -o filter
.../openCV $ ./filter
Started Processing - Capturing Image
Processing - Performing Image Processing
Finished Processing - Saving images
.../openCV $ ls *.png
capture.png  edges.png  grayscale.png
.../openCV $ gpicview capture.png
```

(a)   (b)

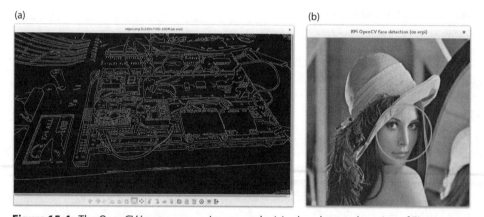

Figure 15-4: The OpenCV image processing example: (a) edge-detected version of Figure 15-3(a), and (b) face detection on the Lenna image

A second example application in the same directory can be used to test the performance of using OpenCV for image processing. In each iteration, it performs an image capture at a 640 × 480 resolution, converts the image to grayscale form, and performs an edge detection operation. The program performs 100 iterations, after which the execution time is measured on the RPi2 at 1GHz:

```
pi@erpi ~/exploringrpi/chp15/openCV $ ./timing
It took 6.95347 seconds to process 100 frames
Capturing and processing 14.3813 frames per second
```

And on the RPi3 at 1.2GHz:

```
pi@erpi ~/exploringrpi/chp15/openCV$ ./timing
It took 4.07931 seconds to process 100 frames
Capturing and processing 24.5139 frames per second
```

During this test, the application uses 99% of CPU and 4% of memory capacity.

NOTE The RPi2/3 has a NEON SIMD (single instruction multiple data) engine that allows you to perform certain instructions in parallel on multiple data values. The engine is capable of greatly accelerating image processing operations; however, utilizing the engine may require that inline assembly language code is written in your C/C++ programs.

Computer Vision with OpenCV

Image processing involves manipulating images by filters (e.g., smoothing, contrast enhancement) or transformations (e.g., scaling, rotation, stretching) for purposes such as enhancing or even reducing the information content of digital images. Image processing is one tool that is used in *computer vision*, which often has the goal of "understanding" the information content within digital images.

Computer vision applications often try to replicate the capabilities of human vision by drawing inferences, making decisions, and taking actions based on visual data. For example, the OpenCV application described in this section uses the RPi to process image data and apply computer vision techniques to determine whether a human face is present in a webcam image frame or an image file. Importantly, the approach is designed for face detection, not face recognition. Face detection can be used for applications such as security and photography; however, the processing required has a significant computational overhead and is not suitable for high frame rates on the RPi.

Listing 15-4 provides an example computer vision application that uses OpenCV for face detection. It uses a Harr feature-based cascade classifier, which uses a characterization of adjacent rectangular image regions to identify regions of interest. For example, in human faces, the region near the eyes has a darker intensity than the region containing the cheeks. Human faces can be detected using such observations. Usefully, OpenCV provides some codified rules for detecting human faces, which have been used in this example.

Computer vision is an entire research domain, and it requires a significant time investment before you will be able to perform some of its more complex operations. The "Further Reading" section at the end of this chapter provides links to resources to get you started.

Listing 15-4: /chp15/openCV/face.cpp

```cpp
#include <iostream>
#include <opencv2/highgui/highgui.hpp>
#include <opencv2/objdetect/objdetect.hpp>
#include <opencv2/imgproc/imgproc.hpp>
```

```cpp
using namespace std;
using namespace cv;

int main(int argc, char *args[]) {
    Mat frame;
    VideoCapture *capture;  // capture needs full scope of main()
    cout << "Starting face detection application" << endl;
    if(argc==2){  // loading image from a file
        cout << "Loading the image " << args[1] << endl;
        frame = imread(args[1], CV_LOAD_IMAGE_COLOR);
    }
    else {
        cout << "Capturing from the webcam" << endl;
        capture = new VideoCapture(0);
        // set any  properties in the VideoCapture object
        capture->set(CV_CAP_PROP_FRAME_WIDTH,1280);    // width pixels
        capture->set(CV_CAP_PROP_FRAME_HEIGHT,720);    // height pixels
        if(!capture->isOpened()){    // connect to the camera
            cout << "Failed to connect to the camera." << endl;
            return 1;
        }
        *capture >> frame;    // populate the frame with captured image
        cout << "Successfully captured a frame." << endl;
    }
    if (!frame.data){
        cout << "Invalid image data... exiting!" << endl;
        return 1;
    }
    // loading the face classifier from a file (standard OpenCV example)
    CascadeClassifier faceCascade;
    faceCascade.load("haarcascade_frontalface.xml");

    // faces is a STL vector of faces - will store the detected faces
    std::vector<Rect> faces;
    // detect objects in the scene using the classifier above (frame,
    // faces, scale factor, min neighbors, flags, min size, max size)
    faceCascade.detectMultiScale(frame, faces, 1.1, 3,
                    0 | CV_HAAR_SCALE_IMAGE, Size(50,50));
    if(faces.size()==0){
        cout << "No faces detected!" << endl;    // display the image
    }
    // draw oval around the detected faces in the faces vector
    for(int i=0; i<faces.size(); i++)
    {
        // Using the center point and a rectangle to create an ellipse
        Point cent(faces[i].x+faces[i].width*0.5,
                    faces[i].y+faces[i].height*0.5);
        RotatedRect rect(cent, Size(faces[i].width,faces[i].width),0);
        // image, rectangle, color=green, thickness=3, linetype=8
```

```
        ellipse(frame, rect, Scalar(0,255,0), 3, 8);
        cout << "Face at: (" << faces[i].x << "," <<faces[i].y << ")" << endl;
    }
    imshow("RPi OpenCV face detection", frame);  // display image results
    imwrite("faceOutput.png", frame);    // save image too
    waitKey(0);                          // dislay image until key press
    return 0;
}
```

The face detection example can be built and executed using the following commands:

```
.../openCV $ g++ -O2 `pkg-config --cflags --libs opencv` face.cpp -o face
.../openCV $ ./face Lenna.png
Starting face detection application
Loading the image Lenna.png
Face at: (217,201)
```

When executed, it results in displaying image in Figure 15-4(b) (if an X Window session is configured), with ellipses identifying any faces that are detected in the image.

Boost

Similar to OpenCV, Boost (www.boost.org) provides a comprehensive free library of C++ source code that can be used for many applications on the RPi. There are libraries for multithreading, data structures, algorithms, regular expressions, memory management, mathematics, and more. The range of libraries available is too exhaustive to detail here, but a full listing is available at www.boost.org/doc/libs/. Boost can be installed on the RPi using the following:

```
pi@erpi ~ $ sudo apt install libboost-dev
...  libboost1.55-dev
```

Listing 15-5 provides an example of usage of the Boost library for calculating the geometric distance between two 2D points.

Listing 15-5: /chp15/boost/test.cpp

```
#include <boost/geometry.hpp>
#include <boost/geometry/geometries/point_xy.hpp>
using namespace boost::geometry::model::d2;
#include <iostream>

int main() {
    point_xy<float> p1(1.0,2.0), p2(3.0,4.0);
    float d = boost::geometry::distance(p1,p2);
    std::cout << "The distance between points is: " << d << std::endl;
    return 0;
}
```

Similarly to OpenCV, it utilizes an `.hpp` extension form. It also makes extensive use of C++ namespaces. The preceding code can be built and executed using the following:

```
pi@erpi ~/exploringrpi/chp15/boost $ g++ test.cpp -o test
pi@erpi ~/exploringrpi/chp15/boost $ ./test
The distance between points is: 2.82843
```

Raspberry Pi Audio

There are several approaches to utilizing audio inputs and outputs with the RPi, including the following:

- **HDMI and onboard audio:** These outputs are enabled by default on the RPi and allow audio signals to be sent to a television via HDMI (not DVI) or to a four-pole audio/video connector on newer RPi models.

- **USB audio:** Low-cost USB adapters can be attached to the RPi that have Linux driver support for the input/output of audio. In addition, USB webcams can be used as audio input devices.

- **Bluetooth audio:** A Linux-compatible Bluetooth adapter (or the RPi3 onboard Bluetooth) can be used to input from, or output to, external Bluetooth recorder/speaker devices.

- **RPi HATs:** HATs can be attached to the RPi that provide advanced audio capabilities. Figure 15-5 illustrates the popular HiFiBerry Digi+ board ($35), which is available in different versions for older and newer RPi models. This board supports high-quality S/PDIF output at up to 192kHz, with 24-bit resolution.

It is also possible to use an electret microphone such as the Sparkfun breakout board (BOB-09964) that can be connected via an op-amp circuit to an SPI ADC circuit (with a 10kΩ potentiometer on the GND line) and used for tasks such as impact detection (e.g., a door knock). The MCP3008 circuit in Chapter 9 could be used to sample such a sensor.

(a) (b)

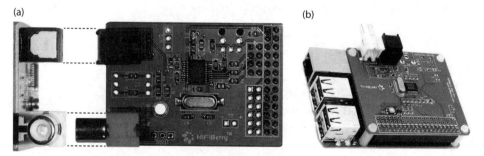

Figure 15-5: The HiFiBerry audio HAT: (a) for the RPiA/B, and (b) for the RPiA+/B+/2

In this section, the most common approaches are examined, as is software that enables you to perform basic audio input/output tasks.

Core Audio Software Tools

The following tools are used in this section of the book:

- **MPlayer:** A movie player for Linux that has optimized built-in support for audio devices. It works very well as an MP3 audio stream player on the RPi.

- **ALSA utilities:** Contains tools for configuring and using ALSA (advanced Linux sound architecture) devices. It includes the `aplay`/`arecord` utilities for the playback and recording of audio streams; the `amixer` tool for controlling volume levels; and the `speaker-test` utility.

- **Libav:** Contains libraries and programs for handling multimedia data. In particular, `avconv` is a fast video and audio conversion tool that can also be used to capture audio data from devices or to stream data to the network (see `libav.org/avconv.html`).

To install these tools, ensure that your packages lists are up-to-date and install the tools as follows:

```
pi@erpi ~ $ sudo apt update
pi@erpi ~ $ sudo apt install mplayer alsa-utils libav-tools
```

Audio Devices for the RPi

After you have the core software installed, the next step is to utilize an audio device that is connected to the RPi. In this section, an example is used in which multiple audio devices are attached simultaneously to the RPi: the HDMI audio interface, a webcam, and two USB audio adapters.

HDMI and USB Audio Playback Devices

Figure 15-6(a) illustrates the USB hub with three USB devices attached—the two USB audio adapters and the Bluetooth adapter. When a webcam is also attached to the Velleman USB hub, a call to `lsusb` results in the following:

```
pi@erpi ~ $ lsusb
Bus 001 Device 008: ID 0d8c:013c C-Media Electronics CM108 Audio Controller
Bus 001 Device 009: ID 046d:082d Logitech, Inc. HD Pro Webcam C920
Bus 001 Device 007: ID 041e:30d3 Creative Technology, Ltd Sound Blaster Play!
Bus 001 Device 006: ID 1a40:0201 Terminus Technology Inc. FE 2.1 7-port Hub
Bus 001 Device 004: ID 0a5c:2198 Broadcom Corp. Bluetooth 3.0 Device
...
```

(a)   (b)   (c)

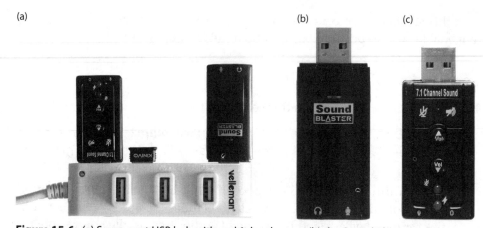

Figure 15-6: (a) Seven-port USB hub with multiple adapters, (b) the Sound Blaster audio adapter, and (c) the Dynamode USB audio adapter

The USB hub in Figure 15-6(a) is not a powered hub, which limits the number of devices that can be attached simultaneously. The Sound Blaster ($20) and Dynamode ($5) USB adapters are illustrated in Figure 15-6(b) and (c), respectively. These adapters can be hot-plugged into the RPi, where their LKMs can be dynamically loaded and unloaded.

When the various adapters are connected to the RPi, you can obtain information about them as follows:

```
pi@erpi ~ $ cat /proc/asound/pcm
00-00: bcm2835 ALSA : bcm2835 ALSA : playback 8
00-01: bcm2835 ALSA : bcm2835 IEC958/HDMI : playback 1
01-00: USB Audio : USB Audio : playback 1 : capture 1
02-00: USB Audio : USB Audio : playback 1 : capture 1
03-00: USB Audio : USB Audio : capture 1
```

In this case, the HDMI adapter is capable of playback only, the two USB adapters are capable of playback and capture, and the USB webcam is only capable of capture. An alternative approach is to use the `aplay` utility to list the available playback devices:

```
pi@erpi ~ $ aplay -l
**** List of PLAYBACK Hardware Devices ****
card 0: ALSA [bcm2835 ALSA], device 0: bcm2835 ALSA [bcm2835 ALSA]
  Subdevices: 8/8  Subdevice #0: subdevice #0 ...
card 0: ALSA [bcm2835 ALSA], device 1: bcm2835 ALSA [bcm2835 IEC958/HDMI]
  Subdevices: 1/1  Subdevice #0: subdevice #0
card 1: U0x41e0x30d3 [USB Device 0x41e:0x30d3], device 0: USB Audio [USB Audio]
  Subdevices: 1/1  Subdevice #0: subdevice #0
card 2: Device [USB PnP Sound Device], device 0: USB Audio [USB Audio]
  Subdevices: 1/1  Subdevice #0: subdevice #0
```

After you have identified the devices, you can play back an audio file on the Creative Sound Blaster and Dynamode USB adapters, respectively, using the `mplayer` and `aplay` utilities, as follows:

```
.../chp15/audio$ mplayer -ao alsa:device=hw=1 320sample.mp3
.../chp15/audio$ mplayer -ao alsa:device=hw=2 320sample.mp3
.../chp15/audio$ aplay -D plughw:1,0 cheering.wav
.../chp15/audio$ aplay -D plughw:2,0 cheering.wav
```

The sound quality is audibly richer on the Sound Blaster adapter (card 1) than the Dynamode adapter (card 2). However, the quality of the Dynamode adapter is good for its price, and its manual volume control feature is useful.

The HDMI device adapter can also be used, either by connecting the RPi directly to an HDMI receiver or HDMI television (or a monitor with built-in speakers), or by using a HDMI-to-VGA adapter to extract the HDMI audio channel to a 3.5mm stereo audio jack. The quality of the audio that is extracted from the latter devices can be quite variable, and can suffer from auto-gain line noise when no audio stream is being played back.

To test an output device, you can use the `speaker-test` utility (where `-c2` indicates two channels are to be tested):

```
.../chp15/audio$ speaker-test -D plughw:2,0 -c2
```

The ALSA utilities also provide you with detailed information about the capabilities of a USB device. For example, `amixer` can be used to get and set an adapter's available properties. Using `amixer` on the Sound Blaster device provides its current state information:

```
pi@erpi ~/exploringrpi/chp15/audio $ amixer -c 1
Simple mixer control 'Speaker',0
  Capabilities: pvolume pswitch pswitch-joined
  Playback channels: Front Left - Front Right
  Limits: Playback 0 - 151
  Mono:  Front Left: Playback 44 [29%] [-20.13dB] [on]
         Front Right: Playback 44 [29%] [-20.13dB] [on]
Simple mixer control 'Mic',0
  Capabilities: pvolume pvolume-joined cvolume cvolume-joined pswitch
               pswitch-joined cswitch cswitch-joined
  Playback channels: Mono      Capture channels: Mono
  Limits: Playback 0 - 32 Capture 0 - 16
  Mono: Playback 23 [72%] [34.36dB] [off] Capture 0 [0%] [0.00dB] [on]
Simple mixer control 'Auto Gain Control',0
  Capabilities: pswitch pswitch-joined
  Playback channels: Mono      Mono: Playback [on]
```

To get its available control settings, use the following:

```
pi@erpi ~/exploringrpi/chp15/audio $ amixer -c 1 controls
numid=3,iface=MIXER,name='Mic Playback Switch'
numid=4,iface=MIXER,name='Mic Playback Volume'
```

```
numid=7,iface=MIXER,name='Mic Capture Switch'
numid=8,iface=MIXER,name='Mic Capture Volume'
numid=9,iface=MIXER,name='Auto Gain Control'
numid=5,iface=MIXER,name='Speaker Playback Switch'
numid=6,iface=MIXER,name='Speaker Playback Volume'
numid=2,iface=PCM,name='Capture Channel Map'
numid=1,iface=PCM,name='Playback Channel Map'
```

Therefore, to control the Speaker Playback Volume setting, you can use this:

```
.../audio $ amixer -c 1 cset iface=MIXER,name='Speaker Playback Volume' 10,10
numid=6,iface=MIXER,name='Speaker Playback Volume'
  ; type=INTEGER,access=rw---R--,values=2,min=0,max=151,step=0
  : values=10,10  |  dBminmax-min=-28.37dB,max=-0.06dB
```

This adjusts the volume on the speaker output of the Sound Blaster USB card—the `10,10` values are the left and right volume percentage settings, so `0,30` would turn off the left channel and set the volume level at 30% for the right channel.

Internet Radio Playback

You can play Internet radio channels using the same `mplayer` application. For example, by using www.xatworld.com/radio-search/, you can search for a radio station of your preference to determine its IP address. You can then stream the audio to your USB adapter using the following:

```
.../audio $ mplayer -ao alsa:device=hw=1 http://178.18.137.246:80
MPlayer2 2.0-728-g2c378c7-4+b1 (C) 2000-2012 MPlayer Team
Playing http://178.18.137.246:80.
Resolving 178.18.137.246 for AF_INET6...
Couldn't resolve name for AF_INET6: 178.18.137.246
Connecting to server 178.18.137.246[178.18.137.246]: 80...
Name    : Pinguin Radio
Genre   : Alternative
Website: http://www.pinguinradio.com
Public : yes
Bitrate: 320kbit/s
Cache size set to 320 KiB
Cache fill:  0.00% (0 bytes)
ICY Info: StreamTitle='Talk Talk  - It's My Life ';
```

This stream runs at 4% of CPU and 3.5% memory usage on the RPi2 with good sound quality (regardless of what you might think of the music itself!). In fact, with multiple sound output devices, there is no difficulty in configuring the RPi to connect to multiple Internet radio streams simultaneously and streaming audio to separate audio adapters.

TURNING THE RASPBERRY PI INTO AN FM TRANSMITTER

It is possible to use the RPi as an FM transmitter by connecting a 70cm length of wire to GPIO4 on the RPi to act as an antenna, and by using code by Oliver Mattos and Oskar Weigl to transmit a signal at 103.3MHz. See `tiny.cc/erpi1504`.

Recording Audio

The USB adapters and the USB webcams can be used to capture audio directly to the RPi file system. You can use the `arecord` utility to provide a list of the available devices—for example, with one webcam and the two USB audio adapters connected:

```
pi@erpi ~ $ arecord -l
**** List of CAPTURE Hardware Devices ****
card 1: U0x41e0x30d3 [USB Device 0x41e:0x30d3], device 0: USB Audio [USB Audio]
  Subdevices: 1/1  Subdevice #0: subdevice #0
card 2: Device [USB PnP Sound Device], device 0: USB Audio [USB Audio]
  Subdevices: 1/1  Subdevice #0: subdevice #0
card 3: C920 [HD Pro Webcam C920], device 0: USB Audio [USB Audio]
  Subdevices: 1/1  Subdevice #0: subdevice #0
```

These devices are also indexed at the following `/proc` location:

```
pi@erpi ~ $ cat /proc/asound/cards
 0 [ALSA        ]:bcm2835 - bcm2835 ALSA
        bcm2835 ALSA
 1 [U0x41e0x30d3]:USB-Audio - USB Device 0x41e:0x30d3
        USB Device 0x41e:0x30d3 at usb-3f980000.usb-1.4.2, full speed
 2 [Device      ]:USB-Audio - USB PnP Sound Device
        USB PnP Sound Device at usb-3f980000.usb-1.4.5, full speed
 3 [C920        ]:USB-Audio - HD Pro Webcam C920
        HD Pro Webcam C920 at usb-3f980000.usb-1.4.4, high speed
```

You can record audio from each of the audio capture devices using the `arecord` utility[1] and the device's address. Interestingly, the LED does not light on the webcams described when they are recording only audio:

```
pi@erpi ~/tmp $ arecord -f cd -D plughw:1,0 -d 10 test1.wav
Recording WAVE 'test1.wav' : Signed 16 bit Little Endian, Rate 44.1kHz, Stereo
pi@erpi ~/tmp $ arecrd -f cd -D plughw:2,0 -d 10 test2.wav
```

---

[1] There is a known issue in `arecord` version 1.0.28, which means that the recording does not stop after the duration has elapsed and Ctrl-C must be pressed. This is resolved in version 1.0.29.

```
Recording WAVE 'test2.wav' : Signed 16 bit Little Endian, Rate 44.1kHz Hz, Stereo
pi@erpi ~/tmp $ aplay -D plughw:1,0 test1.wav
pi@erpi ~/tmp $ aplay -D plughw:2,0 test2.wav
```

The waveform audio file format (WAV) stores uncompressed audio data, which will quickly consume your RPi file storage free space. To avoid this, you can compress WAV files into the popular MP3 compressed format using the LAME MP3 encoder, as follows:

```
pi@erpi ~/tmp $ sudo apt install lame
pi@erpi ~/tmp $ lame test2.wav output.mp3
LAME 3.99.5 32bits (http://lame.sf.net)
Using polyphase lowpass filter, transition band: 16538 Hz - 17071 Hz
Encoding test2.wav to output.mp3
Encoding as 44.1 kHz j-stereo MPEG-1 Layer III (11x) 128 kbps qval=3 ...
pi@erpi ~/tmp $ mplayer -ao alsa:device=hw=2 output.mp3
```

NOTE AlsaMixer is a very useful tool for setting the volume levels for each of the attached sound devices. Execute it by calling `alsamixer`.

Audio Network Streaming

Earlier in this chapter, a description is provided of video streaming to the network using `avconv`. It is also possible to use the same application to stream audio, as it is captured by an audio device, live to the network. For example, here is the command required to stream audio from a device attached to the address `2,0` using UDP to a desktop computer (port 12345 at IP address 192.168.1.4):

```
pi@erpi ~/tmp $ avconv -ac 1 -f alsa -i hw:2,0 -acodec libmp3lame -ab  →
32k -ac 1 -f mp3 udp://192.168.1.4:12345
avconv version 11.4-6:11.4-1~deb8u1+rpi1,(c)2000/14 the Libav developers
   built on Jun 16 2015 05:32:34 with gcc 4.9.2 (Raspbian 4.9.2-10)
[alsa @ 0x39b1e0] Estimating duration from bitrate, may be inaccurate
Guessed Channel Layout for  Input Stream #0.0 : mono
Input #0, alsa, from 'hw:2,0':
  Duration: N/A, start: 77656.998974, bitrate: N/A
    Stream #0.0: Audio: pcm_s16le, 48000 Hz, 1 channels, s16, 768 kb/s
Output #0, mp3, to 'udp://192.168.1.4:12345' ...
```

A desktop player such as VLC can be used to open the network UDP stream. For example, in VLC use Media ➪ Open Network Stream, and set the network URL to be `udp://@:1234`. Streaming audio from the RPi in this form has a 30% CPU load (2% memory) in this instance and has a latency of approximately 1 second.

NOTE Wireshark (`www.wireshark.org`) is a great tool for debugging network connection and communication problems that might occur in audio/video streaming and network socket programming (as in Chapters 12 and 13).

Bluetooth A2DP Audio

The use of a Bluetooth adapter (or onboard Bluetooth on the RPi3) is first introduced in Chapter 13 for general-purpose serial communication. It is used again in Chapter 14 to attach peripherals to the RPi. Here again, Bluetooth can be used with the RPi—this time to communicate with audio devices.

One of the most common uses of the Bluetooth wireless communication system is for the connection of smartphones to in-car audio systems, or to home entertainment centers. For this purpose, the Bluetooth Advanced Audio Distribution Profile (A2DP) can be used to stream high-quality stereo audio from a media source to a media sink. The source device (SRC) acts as the source of a digital audio stream (e.g., Bluetooth headset, smartphone media player), which is sent in a compressed format to a sink device (SNK) (e.g., Bluetooth headphones, stereo receiver, in-car receiver).

When connected to a Bluetooth adapter, the RPi can be configured to act as an A2DP SRC or SNK. In this example, the RPi is configured as a SRC that is connected to a Hi-Fi system. There are many low-cost A2DP audio receivers available that provide audio output on a 3.5mm stereo jack, which can be used to retrospectively add A2DP capability to Hi-Fi systems. However, the Hi-Fi system that is used as the test platform has built-in A2DP support.

NOTE It is recommended that you go through the process of connecting a smartphone to a Bluetooth A2DP SNK before attempting to connect the RPi. This will help you to verify that a connection is possible and help you to become familiar with the steps that are required to pair A2DP devices.

After a Bluetooth adapter is attached to the RPi, the first step is to install the necessary packages, configure the RPi to support A2DP, and test that the Bluetooth audio SNKs are visible:

```
pi@erpi ~ $ hcitool scan
Scanning ...    00:1D:BA:2E:BC:36    CMT-HX90BTR
                40:E2:30:13:CA:09    HOMEOFFICE-PC
```

The RPi has detected the desktop PC and the Sony Hi-Fi system (CMT-HX90BTR). An additional Linux service called PulseAudio, a background process that reroutes all audio streams, is required for recent A2DP services. It aims to support legacy devices, as well as to provide support for network audio (e.g., for VNC). PulseAudio is complex and should be avoided unless you have a specific need to use it on the RPi. It does provide useful user interface tools, such as pavucontrol, and can be installed using the following:

```
pi@erpi ~ $ sudo apt install pulseaudio pavucontrol →
pulseaudio-module-bluetooth
```

PulseAudio can be configured as follows:

```
pi@erpi /etc/pulse $ sudo nano default.pa
```

The service can be started and stopped using the following (note: no sudo):

```
.../chp15/audio$ pulseaudio --kill
.../chp15/audio$ pulseaudio --start
```

One of the best ways to debug problems with PulseAudio is to kill the service and start the service using pulseaudio -v to get a verbose output. Once you have ensured that PulseAudio is working correctly, you can execute it in daemon mode (-D) and begin the process of pairing the RPi with the Bluetooth device:

```
pi@erpi ~ $ pulseaudio -D
pi@erpi ~ $ sudo bluetoothctl
[bluetooth]# scan on
Discovery started
[CHG] Controller 00:02:72:CB:C3:53 Discovering: yes
[NEW] Device 40:E2:30:13:CA:09 HOMEOFFICE-PC
[CHG] Device 00:1D:BA:2E:BC:36 Name: CMT-HX90BTR
[CHG] Device 00:1D:BA:2E:BC:36 Alias: CMT-HX90BTR
[CHG] Device 00:1D:BA:2E:BC:36 LegacyPairing: yes
```

You can then connect to the SNKs using the following commands. (You will likely have to enter a code [e.g., 0000] on both devices in order to pair the devices in the first step.)

```
[bluetooth]# pair 00:1D:BA:2E:BC:36
Attempting to pair with 00:1D:BA:2E:BC:36
[CHG] Device 00:1D:BA:2E:BC:36 Connected: yes
[CHG] Device 00:1D:BA:2E:BC:36 Paired: yes
[bluetooth]# trust 00:1D:BA:2E:BC:36
[CHG] Device 00:1D:BA:2E:BC:36 Trusted: yes
Changing 00:1D:BA:2E:BC:36 trust succeeded
[bluetooth]# paired-devices
Device 00:1D:BA:2E:BC:36 CMT-HX90BTR
[bluetooth]# info 00:1D:BA:2E:BC:36
Device 00:1D:BA:2E:BC:36
        Name: CMT-HX90BTR        Alias: CMT-HX90BTR
        Class: 0x240428          Icon: audio-card
        Paired: yes              Trusted: yes
        Blocked: no              Connected: no
        LegacyPairing: yes
        UUID: Audio Sink         ...
```

```
[bluetooth]# connect 00:1D:BA:2E:BC:36
Attempting to connect to 00:1D:BA:2E:BC:36
[CHG] Device 00:1D:BA:2E:BC:36 Connected: yes
Connection successful
```

Now, if you use the PulseAudio sound configuration tool, pacmd, you can see that the Bluetooth device is now available as a sound sink:

```
pi@erpi ~ $ pacmd
Welcome to PulseAudio 5.0! Use "help" for usage information.
>>> list-sinks
3 sink(s) available ...
index: 2
      name: <bluez_sink.00_1D_BA_2E_BC_36>
      driver: <module-bluez5-device.c> ...
>>> set-default-sink 2
```

You can then play audio files to the Bluetooth device by using PulseAudio as the device:

```
pi@erpi ~/exploringrpi/chp15/audio $ aplay -D pulse cheering.wav
Playing WAVE 'cheering.wav' : Unsigned 8 bit, Rate 11025 Hz, Mono
```

Text-to-Speech

Once you have a working playback adapter connected to the RPi, you can then utilize Linux tools and online services to perform some interesting audio applications. One such application is text-to-speech (TTS); it is possible to generate audio from text using tools such as eSpeak, FestVox Festival, and pico2wave. Presently, pico2wave must be built from source, but eSpeak and Festival are available in binary form under the Raspbian distribution.

You can install and use eSpeak to output audio to the aplay application as follows:

```
pi@erpi ~ $ sudo apt install espeak
pi@erpi ~ $ espeak "Hello Raspberry Pi" --stdout | aplay -D plughw:1,0
Playing WAVE 'stdin' : Signed 16 bit Little Endian, Rate 22050 Hz, Mono
```

You can install Festival and use it to output a text file to a WAV format file as follows:

```
pi@erpi ~ $ sudo apt install festival festival-freebsoft-utils
pi@erpi ~ $ more hello.txt
Hello Raspberry Pi
pi@erpi ~ $ text2wave hello.txt -o hello.wav
pi@erpi ~ $ ls -l hello.wav
-rw-r--r-- 1 pi pi 56048 Dec  7 05:15 hello.wav
pi@erpi ~ $ aplay -D plughw:1,0 hello.wav
Playing WAVE 'hello.wav' : Signed 16 bit Little Endian, Rate 16000 Hz, Mono
```

Also, text can be piped into the `text2wave` application as follows:

```
pi@erpi ~ $ echo 'Hello' | text2wave -o test.wav
pi@erpi ~ $ aplay -D plughw:1,0 test.wav
Playing WAVE 'test.wav' : Signed 16 bit Little Endian, Rate 16000 Hz, Mono
```

TTS engines can be integrated into your own applications. For example, you can use the output from a binary application as follows (for the `date` application) to provide dynamic speech output:

```
pi@erpi ~ $ echo $(date +"It is %M minutes past %l %p") | text2wave -o →
   test.wav
pi@erpi ~ $ aplay -D plughw:1,0 test.wav
Playing WAVE 'test.wav' : Signed 16 bit Little Endian, Rate 16000 Hz, Mono
pi@erpi ~ $ lame test.wav test.mp3
pi@erpi ~ $ mplayer -ao alsa:device=hw=1 test.mp3
```

Finally, it is also possible to install the CMU Sphinx Speech Recognition Toolkit on the RPi. Open source speech recognition tools are notoriously difficult to train when compared to commercial offerings such as Nuance's Dragon NaturallySpeaking. However, with some time investment, PocketSphinx can be trained to provide good results. To install it on the RPi, you must manually download and build two repositories: `sphinxbase` and `pocketsphinx`. You can use SourceForge (`sourceforge.net`) to find the latest versions of both repositories. Build them directly on the RPi using steps such as `./configure --enable-fixed`, followed by `make`, and `sudo make install`.

Summary

After completing this chapter, you should be able to do the following:

- Capture image and video data on the RPi using the RPi MMAL camera or USB webcams combined with Linux Video4Linux2 drivers and APIs.
- Use Video4Linux2 utilities to get information from and adjust the properties of video capture devices.
- Stream video data to the Internet using Linux applications and UDP, multicast, and RTP streams.
- Use OpenCV to perform basic image processing on the RPi.
- Use OpenCV to perform a computer vision face-detection task.
- Utilize the Boost C++ libraries on the RPi.
- Play audio data on the RPi using HDMI audio and USB audio adapters. The audio data can be raw waveform data or compressed MP3 data from the RPi file system or from Internet radio streams.
- Record audio data using USB audio adapters or webcams.

- Stream audio data to the Internet using UDP.
- Play audio to Bluetooth A2DP audio devices, such as Hi-Fi systems.
- Use text-to-speech (TTS) approaches to verbalize the text output of commands that are executed on the RPi.

Further Reading

Many links to websites and documents are provided throughout this chapter. Additional links and further information on the topics are provided at www .exploringrpi.com/chapter15/ and the following:

- Video4Linux2 core documentation: tiny.cc/erpi1502
- V4L2 API Specification: tiny.cc/erpi1503
- The Boost C++ Libraries, Boris Schäling: theboostcpplibraries.com
- Computer Vision Cascaded Classification: tiny.cc/erpi1505
- CVonline: The Evolving, Distributed, Non-Proprietary, On-Line Compendium of Computer Vision, at tiny.cc/erpi1506

# CHAPTER 16

Kernel Programming

In this chapter, you are introduced to Linux kernel programming on an embedded device such as the Raspberry Pi (RPi). Kernel programming is an advanced topic that requires in-depth study of the source code for the Linux kernel; however, this chapter is structured as a practical step-by-step guide to the focused task of writing Linux loadable kernel modules (LKMs) that interface to general-purpose inputs/outputs (GPIOs). The first example is a straightforward "Hello World" module that can be used to establish a configuration for LKM development on the RPi. The second LKM example introduces interrupt service routines (ISRs), and interfaces a simple GPIO button and LED circuit to Linux kernel space. Two further examples are provided that introduce the kobject interface and the use of kernel threads to build kernel-space sysfs devices for the RPi. By the end of this chapter, you should be familiar with the steps required to write kernel code, and appreciate the programming constraints that such development entails.

Equipment Required for This Chapter:

- Raspberry Pi (any model)

Further details on this chapter are available at www.exploringrpi.com/chapter16/.

Introduction

As introduced in Chapter 3, a loadable kernel module (LKM) is a mechanism for adding code to, or removing code from, the Linux kernel at run time. They are ideal for device drivers, enabling the kernel to communicate with the hardware without it having to know how the hardware works. Without this modular capability, the Linux kernel would be very large, because it would have to support every driver that would ever be needed on the RPi. You would also have to rebuild the kernel every time you want to add new hardware or update a device driver. The downside of LKMs is that driver files have to be maintained for each device. LKMs are loaded at run time, but they do not execute in user space; they are essentially part of the kernel.

Kernel modules run in kernel space and applications run in user space, as illustrated in Figure 16-1. Both kernel space and user space have their own unique memory address spaces that do not overlap. This approach ensures that applications running in user space have a consistent view of the hardware, regardless of the hardware platform. The kernel services are then made available to the user space in a controlled way through the use of system calls. The kernel also prevents individual user space applications from conflicting with each other or from accessing restricted resources through the use of protection levels (e.g., superuser versus regular user permissions).

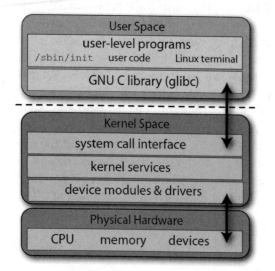

Figure 16-1: The Linux kernel and user space architecture

Why Write Kernel Modules?

When interfacing to electronics circuits under embedded Linux, you are exposed to sysfs and the use of low-level file operations for interfacing to electronics circuits. This approach can appear to be inefficient (especially if you have experience of traditional embedded systems); however, these file entries are memory mapped and the performance is sufficient for many applications. As discussed in Chapter 6, it is possible to achieve response times of about one eighth of a millisecond, with negligible CPU overhead, from within Linux user space by using pthreads, callback functions, and sys/poll.h.

Also described in Chapter 6 is an approach for bypassing the Linux kernel on the RPi, using direct memory manipulation to take control of the SoC inputs and outputs. Unfortunately, this approach means that your programs will not be portable to other embedded Linux platforms. In addition, because the Linux kernel is unaware of such direct memory manipulations, you could potentially generate resource conflicts.

An alternative approach is to use kernel code, which has support for interrupts. However, kernel code is difficult to write and debug. My advice is that you should always try to accomplish your task in Linux user space unless you are certain that there is no other possible way!

Loadable Kernel Module (LKM) Basics

The runtime lifecycle of a typical computer program is reasonably straightforward: A loader allocates memory for the program, and loads the program with any required shared libraries. Instruction execution then begins at some entry point (typically identified by the main() point in C/C++ programs), statements are executed, exceptions are thrown, dynamic memory is allocated and deallocated, and the program eventually runs to completion. On program exit, the operating system frees the memory that was allocated to the program back to the heap memory pool.

Kernel modules are written in C, but they are not programs; for a start, there is no main() function! Some of the key differences are that kernel modules:

- Do not execute sequentially: A kernel module registers itself to handle requests using its initialization function, which runs and then terminates. The type of requests that it can handle are defined within the module code. This is quite similar to the event-driven programming model that is commonly utilized in graphical user interface (GUI) applications.

- Do not clean up automatically: Any resources that are allocated to the module must be manually released when the module is unloaded, or they may be unavailable until a system reboots.

- Do not have printf() functions: Kernel code cannot access libraries of code that is written for the Linux user space. The kernel module lives and runs in kernel space, which has its own memory address space. The interface between kernel space and user space is clearly defined and controlled. However, a printk() function is available that can be used to output information, which can be viewed from within user space.

- Can be interrupted: One conceptually difficult aspect of kernel modules is that they can be used by several different programs/processes at the same time. Modules must be constructed so that they have a consistent and valid behavior when they are interrupted. The RPi2/3 has a multicore processor, which means that you also have to consider the issues involved in simultaneous access from multiple processes.

- Have a higher level of execution privilege: Typically, more CPU cycles are allocated to kernel modules than to user space programs. This sounds like an advantage; however, you have to be very careful that your module does not adversely affect the overall performance of your system.

- Do not have floating-point support: It is kernel code that uses traps to transition from integer to floating-point mode for your user space applications. However, it is very difficult to perform these traps in kernel space. The alternative is to manually save and restore floating-point operations—a task that is best avoided and left to user space code.

A First LKM Example

The concepts just described are a lot to digest, and it is important that they are all addressed, but not all in the first example! Listing 16-1 provides the code for a first example LKM. When no kernel argument is provided, the code uses the printk() function to display "Hello world!" in the kernel logs. If the argument "Derek" is provided, then the logs display "Hello Derek!" The comments in Listing 16-1, which are written using a Doxygen format (see Chapter 7), describe the role of each statement. Further description is available after the code listing.

> **WARNING**   It is very easy to crash the system when you are writing and testing LKMs. It is always possible that such a system crash could corrupt your file system; it is unlikely, but it is possible. Performing a sudo reboot, or pressing the reset button on the RPi (see Chapter 1) will usually put everything back in order. Should something go wrong, the RPi can easily be reflashed, which makes it a good practice platform for LKM development. For your information, I have yet to corrupt any embedded Linux device file system as a result of a system crash, despite my being the cause of many!

Listing 16-1: /exploringrpi/chp16/hello/hello.c

```
/**
 * @file    hello.c
 * @author  Derek Molloy
 * @date    6 November 2015
 * @version 0.1
 * @brief   An introductory "Hello World!" loadable kernel module (LKM)
 * that can display a message in the /var/log/kern.log file when the
```

```
 * module is loaded and removed. The module can accept an argument when
 * it is loaded -- the name, which appears in the kernel log files.
 */

#include <linux/init.h>        // macros for marking up functions e.g. __init
#include <linux/module.h>      // core header for loading LKMs
#include <linux/kernel.h>      // contains kernel types, macros, functions

MODULE_LICENSE("GPL");         // the license type (affects behavior)
MODULE_AUTHOR("Derek Molloy");  // The author visible with modinfo
MODULE_DESCRIPTION("A simple Linux LKM for the RPi."); // desc.
MODULE_VERSION("0.1");         // the version of the module

static char *name = "world"; // example LKM argument default is "world"
// param description charp = char pointer, defaults to "world"
module_param(name, charp, S_IRUGO); // S_IRUGO can be read/not changed
MODULE_PARM_DESC(name, "The name to display in /var/log/kern.log");

/** @brief The LKM initialization function
 * The static keyword restricts the visibility of the function to within
 * this C file. The __init macro means that for a built-in driver (not
 * an LKM) the function is only used at initialization time and that it
 * can be discarded and its memory freed up after that point.
 * @return returns 0 if successful
 */
static int __init helloERPi_init(void) {
    printk(KERN_INFO "ERPi: Hello %s from the RPi LKM!\n", name);
    return 0;
}

/** @brief The LKM cleanup function
 * Similar to the initialization function, it is static. The __exit
 * macro establishes that if this code is used for a built-in driver (not
 * an LKM) that this function is not required.
 */
static void __exit helloERPi_exit(void) {
    printk(KERN_INFO "ERPi: Goodbye %s from the RPi LKM!\n", name);
}

/** @brief A module must use the module_init() module_exit() macros from
 * linux/init.h, which identify the initialization function at insertion
 * time and the cleanup function (as listed above).
 */
module_init(helloERPi_init);
module_exit(helloERPi_exit);
```

In addition to the points described by the comments in Listing 16-1, there are some additional points worth noting:

- The statement MODULE_LICENSE("GPL") provides information (via modinfo) about the licensing terms of the module that you have developed, thus allowing users of your LKM to ensure that they are using free software.

Because the kernel is released under the GPL, your license choice impacts upon the way that the kernel treats your module. You can choose `"Proprietary"` for non-GPL code, but the kernel will be marked as "tainted," and a warning will appear. There are nontainted alternatives to GPL, such as `"GPL v2"`, `"GPL and additional rights"`, `"Dual BSD/GPL"`, `"Dual MIT/GPL"`, and `"Dual MPL/GPL"`. See `linux/module.h` for more information.

■ The `name` (`char *`) is declared as static and is initialized to contain the string "world". You should avoid using global variables in kernel modules; it is even more important than in application programming, because global variables are shared kernel wide. You should use the `static` keyword to restrict a variable's scope to within the module. If you must use a global variable, add a prefix that is unique to the module that you are writing.

■ The `module_param(name, type, permissions)` macro has three parameters: `name` (the parameter name displayed to the user and the variable name in the module), `type` (the type of the parameter—i.e., one of `byte`, `int`, `uint`, `long`, `ulong`, `short`, `ushort`, `bool`, an inverse Boolean `invbool`, or a char pointer `charp`), and permissions (this is the access permissions to the parameter when using sysfs and is covered later). A value of `0` disables the entry, but `S_IRUGO` allows read access for user/group/others; see the *Mode Bits for Access Permissions Guide* at `tiny.cc/erpi1601`.

■ The functions in the module can have whatever names you like (e.g., `helloERPi_init()` and `helloERPi_exit()`); however, the same names must be passed to the special macros `module_init()` and `module_exit()` at the very end of Listing 16-1.

■ The `printk()` is very similar in usage to the familiar `printf()` function, and you can call it from anywhere within the kernel module code. The only significant difference is that you should specify a log level when you call the function. The log levels are defined in `linux/kern_levels.h` as one of `KERN_EMERG`, `KERN_ALERT`, `KERN_CRIT`, `KERN_ERR`, `KERN_WARNING`, `KERN_NOTICE`, `KERN_INFO`, `KERN_DEBUG`, and `KERN_DEFAULT`. This header is included via the `linux/kernel.h` header file, which includes it via `linux/printk.h`.

Essentially, when this module is loaded, the `helloERPi_init()` function executes, and when the module is unloaded, the `helloERPi_exit()` function executes.

The LKM Makefile

A Makefile is required to build the kernel module; in fact, it is a special kbuild Makefile. The kbuild Makefile required to build the kernel module can be viewed in Listing 16-2. (Remember that there must be a Tab character in front of the calls to `make` in the `Makefile` file.)

Listing 16-2: /exploringrpi/chp16/hello/Makefile

```
obj-m+=hello.o

all:
        make -C /lib/modules/$(shell uname -r)/build/ M=$(PWD) modules
clean:
        make -C /lib/modules/$(shell uname -r)/build/ M=$(PWD) clean
```

The first line of the Makefile is called a goal definition, and it defines the module to be built (`hello.o`). The syntax is surprisingly intricate. For example, `obj-m` defines a loadable module goal, whereas `obj-y` indicates a built-in object goal. The syntax becomes more complex when a module is to be built from multiple objects, but Listing 16-2 is sufficient to build this example LKM.

The remainder of the Makefile is similar to a regular Makefile. The `$(shell uname -r)` is a useful call to return the current kernel build version; this ensures a degree of portability for the Makefile. The `-C` option switches the directory to the kernel directory before performing any make tasks. The `M=$(PWD)` variable assignment tells the `make` command where the actual project files exist. The modules target is the default target for external kernel modules. An alternative target is `modules_install`, which would install the module. (The `make` command would have to be executed with superuser permissions, and the module installation path is required.)

Building the LKM on a Linux Desktop Machine

Unfortunately, the process of building the LKM on the RPi is typically more complex than might be expected, as quite specific and detailed steps are required to install the Linux kernel headers. This is typically a trivial step for a desktop Linux installation, so it is useful to first build a module on the desktop machine for two reasons: First, it will give you an understanding of what to expect. Second, it is likely that the Raspbian distribution will be improved over time to provide similar ease of installation.

The Linux kernel headers are C header files that define the interfaces between the different kernel modules, and the kernel and user space. These header files are required in order to build external LKMs, and they must be the exact same version as the kernel for which you want to build a module.

The first thing to do is to install Linux kernel header files that perfectly align with the Linux kernel distribution on your device or machine. The `uname` command provides a long description (`-a` for all), and a kernel release output (`-r` for release) as follows:

```
molloyd@desktop:~$ uname -a
Linux desktop 3.16.0-4-amd64 #1 SMP Debian 3.16.7-ckt11-1+deb8u2 GNU/Linux
molloyd@desktop:~$ uname -r
3.16.0-4-amd64
```

The kernel release output can be used to search for the appropriate Linux header files:

```
molloyd@desktop:~$ apt-cache search linux-headers-$(uname -r)
linux-headers-3.16.0-4-amd64 - Header files for Linux 3.16.0-4-amd64
molloyd@desktop:~$ sudo apt install linux-headers-$(uname -r)
```

At this point, the headers should be installed in /lib/modules/$(uname -r)/build/, which should likely be a symbolic link to the location /usr/src/linux/$(uname -r)/. For historical reasons, an additional symbolic link is usually available at /usr/src/linux:

```
molloyd@desktop:/usr/src$ ls -l
lrwxrwxrwx 1 root root   28 Aug  1 11:55 linux -> linux-headers-3.16.0-
4-amd64
drwxr-xr-x 4 root root 4096 Nov  4 21:07 linux-headers-3.16.0-4-amd64
...
molloyd@desktop:/lib/modules/3.16.0-4-amd64$ ls -l build
lrwxrwxrwx 1 ... 20:17 build -> /usr/src/linux-headers-3.16.0-4-amd64
```

Once the Linux kernel headers are in place, you can build the hello LKM using the Makefile from Listing 16-2. For example:

```
molloyd@desktop:~/exploringrpi/chp16/hello$ make
make -C /lib/modules/3.16.0-4-amd64/build/ →
 M=/home/molloyd/exploringrpi/chp16/hello modules
make[1]: Entering directory `/usr/src/linux-headers-3.16.0-4-amd64'
  CC [M]  /home/molloyd/exploringrpi/chp16/hello/hello.o
  Building modules, stage 2.
  MODPOST 1 modules
  CC      /home/molloyd/exploringrpi/chp16/hello/hello.mod.o
  LD [M]  /home/molloyd/exploringrpi/chp16/hello/hello.ko
make[1]: Leaving directory '/usr/src/linux-headers-3.16.0-4-amd64'
```

At this point, the LKM has been created with the name hello.ko in the current directory. Note that this LKM can only be executed on your desktop machine and is applicable only to the current kernel version. The instructions for how to use this module are provided after a discussion on building the LKM on the RPi:

```
molloyd@desktop:~/exploringrpi/chp16/hello$ ls -l
-rw-r--r-- 1 molloyd molloyd   2430 Nov  4 21:11 hello.c
-rw-r--r-- 1 molloyd molloyd 116352 Nov  4 21:11 hello.ko
-rw-r--r-- 1 molloyd molloyd    769 Nov  4 21:11 hello.mod.c
-rw-r--r-- 1 molloyd molloyd  64248 Nov  4 21:11 hello.mod.o
-rw-r--r-- 1 molloyd molloyd  53592 Nov  4 21:11 hello.o
-rw-r--r-- 1 molloyd molloyd    154 Nov  4 21:03 Makefile
-rw-r--r-- 1 molloyd molloyd     55 Nov  4 21:11 modules.order
-rw-r--r-- 1 molloyd molloyd      0 Nov  4 21:11 Module.symvers
```

Building the LKM on the RPi

If you are planning to use a recent kernel, you should first update the RPi so as to ensure that the kernel release aligns with the kernel release that is present in the source repository. If you are planning to use an older kernel release, you should skip this step and adapt the steps that follow accordingly:

```
pi@erpi ~ $ sudo apt update
pi@erpi ~ $ sudo apt upgrade
pi@erpi ~ $ sudo rpi-update
 *** Raspberry Pi firmware updater by Hexxeh, enhanced by AndrewS and Dom
 *** Performing self-update
  % Total    % Received % Xferd  Average Speed   Time    Time     Time  Current
                                 Dload  Upload   Total   Spent    Left  Speed
100 10206  100 10206    0     0  36936      0 --:--:-- --:--:-- --:--:-- 37112
This update bumps to rpi-4.1.y linux tree
...
 *** depmod 4.1.12-v7+
 *** Updating VideoCore libraries
 *** Using HardFP libraries
 *** Updating SDK
pi@erpi ~ $ sudo reboot
pi@erpi ~ $ uname -a
Linux erpi 4.1.12-v7+ #824 SMP PREEMPT ... GMT 2015 armv7l GNU/Linux
```

In theory, you should be able to install the Linux kernel headers using the following two steps (as described for the desktop machine):

```
pi@erpi ~ $ apt-cache search linux-headers-$(uname -r)
pi@erpi ~ $ sudo apt install linux-headers-$(uname -r)
```

Or you can use the Linux virtual headers package. Unfortunately, though, the headers are not available for the current kernel version:

```
pi@erpi ~ $ sudo apt-get install linux-headers
Reading package lists... Done
Building dependency tree
Reading state information... Done
Package linux-headers is a virtual package provided by:
  linux-headers-3.6-trunk-rpi 3.6.9-1~experimental.1+rpi7
  linux-headers-3.10-3-rpi 3.10.11-1+rpi7
You should explicitly select one to install.
pi@erpi:~ $ apt-cache search linux-headers
...
linux-headers-3.18.0-trunk-common - Common header files for Linux
3.18.0-trunk
linux-headers-3.18.0-trunk-rpi - Header files for Linux 3.18.0-trunk-rpi
linux-headers-3.18.0-trunk-rpi2 - Header files for Linux 3.18.0-trunk-rpi2 ...
```

Therefore, it is necessary to manually download and build the Linux kernel headers for the current image. There are prepackaged headers available from some sites, such as `tiny.cc/erpi1602`, but I recommend that you follow a manual process to ensure that you can always obtain the headers directly from Raspbian source.

Because all the following steps require superuser permissions, it is preferable to execute them from within a root shell:

1. Begin by downloading the kernel source to the `/usr/src/` directory. The version that you download must align with the current kernel version. See Chapter 7 for instructions on how to choose a specific kernel release:

```
pi@erpi /usr/src $ sudo bash
root@erpi:/usr/src# wget →
  https://github.com/raspberrypi/linux/tarball/rpi-4.1.y
root@erpi:/usr/src# tar zxf rpi-4.1.y
root@erpi:/usr/src# ls -l
drwxrwxr-x 23 root root     4096 Nov  5 12:01 raspberrypi-linux-503f879
-rw-r--r--  1 root root 128436889 Nov  6 02:40 rpi-4.1.y
drwxr-xr-x  3 root root     4096 Sep 24 14:44 sense-hat
```

2. Overwrite the build configuration file with the configuration file for the current RPi image. The configuration file for your current image is typically available in compressed form at `/proc/config.gz`. If the file is missing, type the command `modprobe configs`:

```
root@erpi:/usr/src# cd raspberrypi-linux-503f879/
root@erpi:/usr/src/raspberrypi-linux-503f879# zcat /proc/config.gz > →
  .config
```

3. Check that there are no user options in the current kernel configuration file that are not present in the `.config` file, and then ensure that the kernel contains the information required for building external modules using the following steps, which take a few minutes to execute:

```
root@erpi:/usr/src/raspberrypi-linux-503f879# make oldconfig
root@erpi:/usr/src/raspberrypi-linux-503f879# make modules_prepare
```

4. Next you need a file called `Module.symvers`. This is a file that defines the exported symbols that are not defined in the kernel. You can take this file from a kernel that you built in Chapter 7, or you can download it directly from the RPi source repository. The RPi2/3 has a different `Module.symvers` than other models, so it is best if you visit the repository site first at `https://github.com/raspberrypi/firmware/raw/master/extra/` before downloading the file. For non-RPi2 models, use the following:

```
root@erpi:/usr/src/raspberrypi-linux-503f879# wget →
  https://github.com/raspberrypi/firmware/raw/master/extra/Module.symvers
```

Or, use `Module7.symvers` for the RPi2/3:

```
root@erpi:/usr/src/raspberrypi-linux-503f879# wget →
  https://github.com/raspberrypi/firmware/raw/master/extra/Module7.symvers
pi@erpi /usr/src/linux # cp Module7.symvers Module.symvers
```

5. Finally, symbolic links must be set up so that the Makefile can find the Linux kernel header files (use `4.x.x-v7+` for the RPi2/3, and `4.x.x+` for other RPi models):

```
root@erpi:/usr/src/raspberrypi-linux-503f879# KHEADER=`pwd`
root@erpi:/usr/src/raspberrypi-linux-503f879# echo $KHEADER
/usr/src/raspberrypi-linux-503f879
root@erpi:/usr/src/raspberrypi-linux-503f879# cd /lib/modules/4.1.12-v7+/
```

```
root@erpi:/lib/modules/4.1.12-v7+# ln -s $KHEADER source
root@erpi:/lib/modules/4.1.12-v7+# ln -s $KHEADER build
root@erpi:/lib/modules/4.1.12-v7+# ls -l build source
... 34 Nov 12 04:12 build -> /usr/src/raspberrypi-linux-503f879
... 34 Nov 12 04:12 source -> /usr/src/raspberrypi-linux-503f879
root@erpi:/lib/modules/4.1.12-v7+# cd /usr/src
root@erpi:/usr/src# ls
raspberrypi-linux-503f879  rpi-4.1.y  sense-hat
root@erpi:/usr/src# ln -s $KHEADER linux-`uname -r`
root@erpi:/usr/src# ln -s $KHEADER linux
root@erpi:/usr/src# ls
linux  linux-4.1.12+  raspberrypi-linux-503f879  rpi-4.1.y  sense-hat
```

The Linux kernel headers are now installed on the RPi.

Finally, you can build the LKM with a call to `make`. Do not use `sudo make`; otherwise, it will cause the Linux kernel headers to be rebuilt:

```
pi@erpi ~/exploringrpi/chp16/hello $ make
make -C /lib/modules/4.1.12-v7+/build/ M= modules
make[1]: Entering directory '/usr/src/raspberrypi-linux-503f879'
...
pi@erpi ~/exploringrpi/chp16/hello $ ls -l
-rw-r--r-- 1 pi pi 2199 Nov  7 01:12 hello.c
-rw-r--r-- 1 pi pi 4348 Nov  6 22:45 hello.ko
-rw-r--r-- 1 pi pi  154 Nov  5 00:20 Makefile
...
```

Testing the First LKM Example

The "Hello World!" LKM can then be tested on the desktop machine or the RPi by loading it into the kernel. Once again, these steps require superuser permissions:

```
pi@erpi ~/exploringrpi/chp16/hello $ sudo bash
root@erpi:/home/pi/exploringrpi/chp16/hello# ls
hello.c    hello.mod.c  hello.o    modules.order
hello.ko   hello.mod.o  Makefile   Module.symvers
root@erpi:/home/pi/exploringrpi/chp16/hello# ls -l *.ko
-rw-r--r-- 1 pi pi 4348 Nov  6 22:45 hello.ko
```

The LKM can be loaded using the `insmod` program to insert a module into the Linux kernel:

```
root@erpi:/home/pi/exploringrpi/chp16/hello# insmod hello.ko
root@erpi:/home/pi/exploringrpi/chp16/hello# lsmod
Module                  Size  Used by
hello                    737  0           ...
```

You can get information about the loaded LKM using the `modinfo` command, which identifies the description, author, and any module parameters that are defined by the LKM source code:

```
root@erpi:/home/pi/exploringrpi/chp16/hello# modinfo hello.ko
filename:       /home/pi/exploringrpi/chp16/hello/hello.ko
```

```
version:          0.1
description:      A simple Linux driver for the RPi.
author:           Derek Molloy
license:          GPL
srcversion:       92E5000BB5C10D0021FF527
depends:
vermagic:         4.1.12-v7 SMP preempt mod_unload modversions ARMv7
parm:             name: The name to display in /var/log/kern.log (charp)
```

You can see that the kernel version is compiled into the module and any module parameters are visible, such as name in this instance.

The module can be removed from the Linux kernel using the rmmod program:

```
root@erpi:/home/pi/exploringrpi/chp16/hello# rmmod hello.ko
```

You can repeat these steps and view the output live in the kernel log as a result of the use of the printk() function in Listing 16-1. I recommend that you use a second terminal window and view the live output as your LKM is loaded and unloaded, as follows:

```
pi@erpi ~ $ sudo bash
root@erpi:/home/pi# cd /var/log
root@erpi:/var/log# tail -f kern.log
... erpi kernel: [275408.309510] ERPi: Hello world from the RPi LKM!
... erpi kernel: [275562.544255] ERPi: Goodbye world from the RPi LKM!
... erpi kernel: [276435.032469] ERPi: Hello world from the RPi LKM!
... erpi kernel: [276450.192676] ERPi: Goodbye world from the RPi LKM!
```

Testing the LKM Parameter

The code in Listing 16-1 contains a custom LKM parameter that can be set when the module is being loaded. For example:

```
root@erpi:/home/pi/exploringrpi/chp16/hello# insmod hello.ko name=Derek
```

If you view /var/log/kern.log at this point, the message "Hello Derek" appears in place of "Hello world":

```
root@erpi:/var/log# tail -f kern.log
... erpi kernel: [279690.417709] ERPi: Hello Derek from the RPi LKM!
```

However, you can also see information about the kernel module that is loaded, as follows:

```
root@erpi:/home/pi/exploringrpi/chp16/hello# cd /proc
root@erpi:/proc# cat modules|grep hello
hello 737 0 - Live 0x7f3d4000 (O)
```

This is the same information that is provided by the lsmod command, but it also provides the current kernel memory offset for the loaded module, which is useful for debugging.

The LKM also has an entry under `/sys/module/`, which provides you with direct access to the custom parameter state. For example:

```
root@erpi:/proc# cd /sys/module
root@erpi:/sys/module# ls -l | grep hello
drwxr-xr-x 6 root root 0 Nov  8 06:37 hello
root@erpi:/sys/module# cd hello
root@erpi:/sys/module/hello# ls
coresize   initsize   notes       refcnt    srcversion  uevent
holders    initstate  parameters  sections  taint       version
root@erpi:/sys/module/hello# cat version
0.1
root@erpi:/sys/module/hello# cat taint
0
```

The version value is 0.1 as per the `MODULE_VERSION("0.1")` entry in Listing 16-1 and the taint value is 0 as per the license that has been chosen, which is `MODULE_LICENSE("GPL")`.

The custom parameter value can be viewed as follows:

```
root@erpi:/sys/module/hello# cd parameters/
root@erpi:/sys/module/hello/parameters# ls -l
total 0
-r--r--r-- 1 root root 4096 Nov  8 06:45 name
root@erpi:/sys/module/hello/parameters# cat name
Derek
```

Using this directory structure, you can see that the state of the name variable is displayed. Superuser permissions are not required to read the value, due to the `s_IRUGO` argument that is used in defining the module parameter. It is possible to configure this value for write access, but your module code will need to detect such a state change and act accordingly. Finally, you can remove the module and observe the output:

```
root@erpi:/sys/module/hello/parameters# cd ~/
root@erpi:~# rmmod hello.ko
root@erpi:~# tail /var/log/kern.log
... erpi kernel: [279690.417709] ERPi: Hello Derek from the RPi LKM!
... erpi kernel: [280373.162268] ERPi: Goodbye Derek from the RPi LKM!
```

It is important that you leave any directory associated with the LKM before you unload it, because otherwise you can cause a kernel panic with something as simple as a call to `ls`.

An Embedded LKM Example

Now that you have built a first LKM, more sophisticated device drivers can be developed. For example, see the chapter web page on how to build a character device. However, the remaining examples in this chapter focus on interfacing LKM code to simple hardware circuits using kernel-based GPIO code. A single circuit is used for this chapter, as illustrated in Figure 16-2(a). The hardware configuration is similar to the user space GPIO circuits that are described in Chapter 6.

(a)   (b)

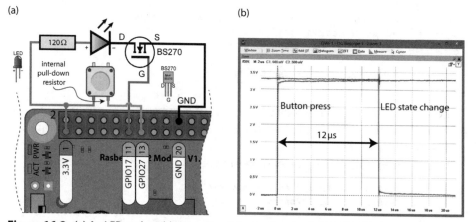

Figure 16-2: (a) An LED and pushbutton circuit for testing the GPIO LKM; (b) the LKM performance results (with debouncing disabled)

Unlike Linux user space, the Linux kernel space has full support for interrupts. The first example in this section demonstrates how you can write an LKM that uses GPIOs and interrupts to achieve a faster response time than is possible in user space. I am not suggesting that you write all of your GPIO code in kernel space, but these examples may provide inspiration for discrete tasks that you can perform in kernel space; the higher-level code can still be written in Linux user space.

First test that your circuit is working correctly by setting up GPIO17 as an output and testing the LED, and by setting up GPIO27 as an input and testing that the button works correctly:

```
pi@erpi /sys/class/gpio $ echo 17 > export
pi@erpi /sys/class/gpio $ cd gpio17
pi@erpi /sys/class/gpio/gpio17 $ echo out > direction
pi@erpi /sys/class/gpio/gpio17 $ echo 1 > value
pi@erpi /sys/class/gpio/gpio17 $ echo 0 > value
pi@erpi /sys/class/gpio/gpio17 $ cd ..
pi@erpi /sys/class/gpio $ echo 27 > export
pi@erpi /sys/class/gpio $ cd gpio27
pi@erpi /sys/class/gpio/gpio27 $ echo in > direction
pi@erpi /sys/class/gpio/gpio27 $ cat value
0
pi@erpi /sys/class/gpio/gpio27 $ cat value
1
pi@erpi /sys/class/gpio/gpio27 $ cd ..
```

```
pi@erpi /sys/class/gpio $ echo 17 > unexport
pi@erpi /sys/class/gpio $ echo 27 > unexport
```

Interestingly, the steps to control the GPIOs in Linux kernel space are very similar to the steps above. Linux GPIOs can easily be accessed and controlled from kernel space using the functions that are described in linux/gpio.h. Here are some of the most important functions that are available through the inclusion of this kernel header file:

```
static inline bool gpio_is_valid(int number)
static inline int  gpio_request(unsigned gpio, const char *label)
static inline int  gpio_export(unsigned gpio, bool direction_may_change)
static inline int  gpio_direction_input(unsigned gpio)
static inline int  gpio_get_value(unsigned gpio)
static inline int  gpio_direction_output(unsigned gpio, int value)
static inline int  gpio_set_debounce(unsigned gpio, unsigned debounce)
static inline int  gpio_sysfs_set_active_low(unsigned gpio, int value)
static inline void gpio_unexport(unsigned gpio)
static inline void gpio_free(unsigned gpio)
static inline int  gpio_to_irq(unsigned gpio)
```

Importantly, you can associate an interrupt request (IRQ) with a GPIO using the last function in the list above. IRQs enable you to build efficient, high-performance code that detects a change in the input state

Interrupt Service Routines (ISRs)

An *interrupt* is a signal that is sent to a microprocessor from an attached hardware device, software application, or circuit to indicate that an event has occurred which requires attention. Interrupts are high-priority conditions; the term essentially implies "interrupt what you are currently doing and do something instead." The processor suspends its current activities, saves the current state, and executes an interrupt handler function, which is also known as an *interrupt service routine (ISR)*. Once the handler function has run to completion, the processor reloads its previous state and continues with its previous activities.

The LKM driver must register a handler function for the interrupt, which defines the actions that the interrupt should perform. In this example the handler function is called erpi_gpio_irq_handler() and it has the following form:

```
static irq_handler_t erpi_gpio_irq_handler(unsigned int irq, void *dev_id,
                                           struct pt_regs *regs) {
    // the actions that the interrupt should perform
    ... }
```

This handler function is then registered with an *interrupt request (IRQ)* using the request_irq() function as follows:

```
result = request_irq(irqNumber,                      // the interrupt number
        (irq_handler_t) erpi_gpio_irq_handler,// pointer to the handler
        IRQF_TRIGGER_RISING,                  // interrupt on rising edge
        "erpi_gpio_handler",                  // used to identify the owner
        NULL);                     // *dev_id for shared interrupt lines, NULL
```

The `irqNumber` is determined automatically in the code example in Listing 16-3 by using the interrupt number that is associated with the respective GPIO number. Importantly, the GPIO number is not the interrupt number; however, there is a direct one-to-one mapping.

To undo the IRQ request, there is also a `free_irq()` function. In this first example, the `free_irq()` function is called from within the `erpi_gpio_exit()` function, which is invoked when the LKM is unloaded.

In this example, a simple momentary push button (as illustrated in Figure 16-2(a)) is used to generate an interrupt on the rising edge of a button press. It is also possible to generate the interrupt on the falling edge. (A full set of interrupt definitions is available in `/include/linux/interrupt.h`.) These flags can be combined using the bitwise OR operator to provide precise control over interrupt configuration.

The full source code for the first GPIO LKM is provided in Listing 16-3. The comments in the listing provide a description of the role of each function.

> **NOTE** Listing 16-3 uses a `gpio_set_bounce()` function call to ignore repeated edge transitions for a time period (typically of the order of 100ms to 200ms), once a single transition is detected. You should remove the `gpio_set_debounce()` function call if you want to use this code to detect multiple edge transitions on a "clean" digital signal, because software debouncing severely limits detection performance.

Listing 16-3: /chp16/gpio/gpio_test.c

```c
#include <linux/init.h>
#include <linux/module.h>
#include <linux/kernel.h>
#include <linux/gpio.h>                  // for the GPIO functions
#include <linux/interrupt.h>             // for the IRQ code

MODULE_LICENSE("GPL");
MODULE_AUTHOR("Derek Molloy");
MODULE_DESCRIPTION("A Button/LED test driver for the RPi");
MODULE_VERSION("0.1");

static unsigned int gpioLED = 17;        // pin 11 (GPIO17)
static unsigned int gpioButton = 27;     // pin 13 (GPIO27)
static unsigned int irqNumber;           // share IRQ num within file
static unsigned int numberPresses = 0;   // store number of presses
static bool         ledOn = 0;           // used to invert state of LED

// prototype for the custom IRQ handler function, function below
static irq_handler_t  erpi_gpio_irq_handler(unsigned int irq, void
                                *dev_id, struct pt_regs *regs);

/** @brief The LKM initialization function */
static int __init erpi_gpio_init(void) {
```

```
        int result = 0;
        printk(KERN_INFO "GPIO_TEST: Initializing the GPIO_TEST LKM\n");
        if (!gpio_is_valid(gpioLED)) {
            printk(KERN_INFO "GPIO_TEST: invalid LED GPIO\n");
            return -ENODEV;
        }
        ledOn = true;
        gpio_request(gpioLED, "sysfs");         // request LED GPIO
        gpio_direction_output(gpioLED, ledOn);  // set in output mode and on
//      gpio_set_value(gpioLED, ledOn);         // not reqd - see line above
        gpio_export(gpioLED, false);            // appears in /sys/class/gpio
                                                // false prevents in/out change

        gpio_request(gpioButton, "sysfs");      // set up gpioButton
        gpio_direction_input(gpioButton);       // set up as input
        gpio_set_debounce(gpioButton, 200);     // debounce delay of 200ms
        gpio_export(gpioButton, false);         // appears in /sys/class/gpio

        printk(KERN_INFO "GPIO_TEST: button value is currently: %d\n",
                gpio_get_value(gpioButton));
        irqNumber = gpio_to_irq(gpioButton);    // map GPIO to IRQ number
        printk(KERN_INFO "GPIO_TEST: button mapped to IRQ: %d\n", irqNumber);

        // This next call requests an interrupt line
        result = request_irq(irqNumber,             // interrupt number requested
                (irq_handler_t) erpi_gpio_irq_handler,   // handler function
                IRQF_TRIGGER_RISING,     // on rising edge (press, not release)
                "erpi_gpio_handler",     // used in /proc/interrupts
                NULL);                   // *dev_id for shared interrupt lines
        printk(KERN_INFO "GPIO_TEST: IRQ request result is: %d\n", result);
        return result;
}

/** @brief The LKM cleanup function  */
static void __exit erpi_gpio_exit(void) {
        printk(KERN_INFO "GPIO_TEST: button value is currently: %d\n",
                gpio_get_value(gpioButton));
        printk(KERN_INFO "GPIO_TEST: pressed %d times\n", numberPresses);
        gpio_set_value(gpioLED, 0);         // turn the LED off
        gpio_unexport(gpioLED);             // unexport the LED GPIO
        free_irq(irqNumber, NULL);          // free the IRQ number, no *dev_id
        gpio_unexport(gpioButton);          // unexport the Button GPIO
        gpio_free(gpioLED);                 // free the LED GPIO
        gpio_free(gpioButton);              // free the Button GPIO
        printk(KERN_INFO "GPIO_TEST: Goodbye from the LKM!\n");
}

/** @brief The GPIO IRQ Handler function
 * A custom interrupt handler that is attached to the GPIO. The same
 * interrupt handler cannot be invoked concurrently as the line is
 * masked out until the function is complete. This function is static
 * as it should not be invoked directly from outside of this file.
 * @param irq    the IRQ number associated with the GPIO
 * @param dev_id the *dev_id that is provided - used to identify
```

```
 * which device caused the interrupt. Not used here.
 * @param regs    h/w specific register values - used for debugging.
 * return returns IRQ_HANDLED if successful - return IRQ_NONE otherwise.
 */
static irq_handler_t erpi_gpio_irq_handler(unsigned int irq, void *dev_id,
                                  struct pt_regs *regs) {
   ledOn = !ledOn;                             // invert the LED state
   gpio_set_value(gpioLED, ledOn);             // set LED accordingly
   printk(KERN_INFO "GPIO_TEST: Interrupt! (button is %d)\n",
          gpio_get_value(gpioButton));
   numberPresses++;                            // global counter
   return (irq_handler_t) IRQ_HANDLED;         // announce IRQ handled
}


module_init(erpi_gpio_init);
module_exit(erpi_gpio_exit);
```

> **NOTE**   If you see the message in the kernel logs "no symbol version for module_lay-out," you should perform a make clean in the project directory, and then down-load the Module.symvers file again (Step 4). Finally, perform a make in the project directory. This issue can occur if you should type sudo make instead of make in the example directories.

The LKM that is described in Listing 16-3 can be built and loaded using the same steps as for the first LKM example:

```
pi@erpi ~/exploringrpi/chp16/gpio $ make
pi@erpi ~/exploringrpi/chp16/gpio $ ls
gpio_test.c   gpio_test.mod.c   gpio_test.o   modules.order
gpio_test.ko  gpio_test.mod.o   Makefile      Module.symvers
pi@erpi ~/exploringrpi/chp16/gpio $ sudo insmod gpio_test.ko
```

Then when the physical momentary push button that is wired as in Figure 16-2(a) is pressed, the kernel log reacts as follows:

```
root@erpi:/var/log# tail -f kern.log
... erpi kernel: [318326.665496] GPIO_TEST: Initializing the GPIO_TEST LKM
... erpi kernel: [318326.665753] GPIO_TEST: button value is currently: 0
... erpi kernel: [318326.665765] GPIO_TEST: button mapped to IRQ: 507
... erpi kernel: [318326.665834] GPIO_TEST: IRQ request result is: 0
... erpi kernel: [320001.467957] GPIO_TEST: Interrupt! (button is 1)
... erpi kernel: [320002.104784] GPIO_TEST: Interrupt! (button is 1)
...
```

At this point, you can view the /proc/interrupts entry, and you can see that the name of the interrupt handler is listed as erpi_gpio_handler, as configured in the code in Listing 16-3. You can also see that the interrupt associated with the GPIO has number 507, which aligns with the value that is outputted in the preceding kernel logs:

```
pi@erpi /proc $ cat interrupts | grep erpi
507:   8    0    0    0 pinctrl-bcm2835  27 Edge   erpi_gpio_handler
```

Again, it is important to note that the interrupt number is not the GPIO number, which is GPIO27 for the button. In fact, you can see the number 27 in the interrupts line above, because it is associated with the `pinctrl-bcm2835` module. You can also see that this GPIO number is exported for use by the GPIO functions in Listing 16-3 (the GPIOs are automatically unexported when the LKM is unloaded):

```
pi@erpi /sys/class/gpio $ ls -l gpio*
lrwxrwxrwx 1 root gpio 0 Nov  8 17:21 gpio17 -> ...
lrwxrwxrwx 1 root gpio 0 Nov  8 17:21 gpio27 -> ...
```

When the module is unloaded, the log output becomes the following:

```
pi@erpi ~/exploringrpi/chp16/gpio $ sudo rmmod gpio_test
pi@erpi ~/exploringrpi/chp16/gpio $ sudo tail /var/log/kern.log
... erpi kernel: [321054.037902] GPIO_TEST: button value is currently: 0
... erpi kernel: [321054.037968] GPIO_TEST: pressed 8 times
... erpi kernel: [321054.042150] GPIO_TEST: Goodbye from the LKM!
```

Performance

One useful feature of this LKM is that it allows you to evaluate the response time (interrupt latency time) of the system as a whole. A press of the momentary push button results in the inversion of the state of the LED; if the LED is on, it turns off when the button is pressed. To measure this delay, an oscilloscope is used, which is configured to trigger on the rising edge of the button signal. The oscilloscope provides an independent time measurement, and its output is displayed in Figure 16-2(b). The latency is approximately 12µs. On repeated testing this delay varies between a minimum of 10µs to a maximum of 20µs approximately.

Enhanced Button GPIO Driver LKM

The third example builds on the second example to create an enhanced GPIO driver, which permits a user to configure and interact with a GPIO button using sysfs. This module allows a GPIO button to be mapped to Linux user space where it can be utilized directly. The best way to explain the capability of this module is with a use case example. In this example, the button is attached to GPIO27, and once the LKM is loaded, it can be accessed and manipulated as follows:

```
root@erpi:/sys/erpi/gpio27# lsmod | grep button
button                  2931  0
root@erpi:/sys/erpi/gpio27# ls -l
total 0
-r--r--r-- 1 root root 4096 Nov  9 01:04 diffTime
-rw-rw---- 1 root root 4096 Nov  9 01:04 isDebounce
-r--r--r-- 1 root root 4096 Nov  9 01:04 lastTime
```

```
-r--r--r-- 1 root root 4096 Nov  9 01:04 ledOn
-rw-rw---- 1 root root 4096 Nov  9 01:04 numberPresses
root@erpi:/sys/erpi/gpio27# cat numberPresses
0
root@erpi:/sys/erpi/gpio27# cat numberPresses
5
root@erpi:/sys/erpi/gpio27# cat ledOn
0
root@erpi:/sys/erpi/gpio27# cat lastTime
01:04:59:304524323
root@erpi:/sys/erpi/gpio27# cat diffTime
0.340584664
root@erpi:/sys/erpi/gpio27# echo 0 > isDebounce
root@erpi:/sys/erpi/gpio27# cat isDebounce
0
root@erpi:/sys/erpi/gpio27# echo 1 > isDebounce
root@erpi:/sys/erpi/gpio27# cat isDebounce
1
```

Despite the complexity involved in creating this LKM, the user space interface is very straightforward and can be utilized by an executable program on your embedded system that can be written in any programming language. Sysfs is a memory-based file system that provides a mechanism to export kernel data structures, attributes, and linkages to Linux user space. The infrastructure that enables sysfs to function is heavily based on the kobject interface.

The kobject Interface

The driver model in Linux uses a kobject abstraction. To understand this model, you must first appreciate the following important concepts:[1]

- kobject: A kobject is a struct that consists of a name, a reference count, a type, a sysfs representation, and a pointer to a parent object (see Listing 16-4). Importantly, kobjects are not useful on their own; instead, they are embedded within other data structures and used to control access. This is similar to the object-oriented concept of generalized top-level parent classes (e.g., the Object class in Java, or the QObject class in Qt).

- ktype: A ktype is the type of the object that the kobject is embedded within. It controls what happens when the object is created and destroyed.

- kset: A kset is a group of kobjects that can be of different ktypes. A kset of kobjects can be thought of as a sysfs directory that contains a collection of subdirectories (kobjects).

---

[1] From "Everything you never wanted to know about kobjects, ksets, and ktypes," Greg Kroah-Hartman, https://www.kernel.org/doc/Documentation/kobject.txt.

Listing 16-4: The kobject Structure

```
#define KOBJ_NAME_LEN    20

struct kobject {
    char             *k_name;    // kobject name pointer (not NULL)
    char             name[KOBJ_NAME_LEN];  // short internal name
    struct kref      kref;       // the reference count
    struct list_head entry;      // linked list to members of the kset
    struct kobject   *parent;    // the parent kobject
    struct kset      *kset;      // kobject can be a member of a set
    struct kobj_type *ktype;     // kobj_type describes object type
    struct dentry    *dentry;    // the sysfs directory entry
};
```

For this example LKM, a single kobject is required, which is mapped to /sys/erpi/ on the file system. This single kobject contains all the attributes required for the interaction that is demonstrated above (e.g., viewing the numberPresses entry). This is achieved in Listing 16-5 through the use of the kobject_create_and_add() function, as follows:

```
static struct kobject *erpi_kobj;
erpi_kobj = kobject_create_and_add("erpi", kernel_kobj->parent);
```

The kernel_kobj pointer provides a reference to /sys/kernel/. If you remove the call to ->parent, the erpi entry will be placed at /sys/kernel/erpi/, but for clarity, I have placed it at /sys/erpi/; this is not best practice! (Also, sysfs_create_dir() performs the same role.) For this example LKM, a set of subsystem-specific callback functions must be implemented to expose its attributes via sysfs using functions of the form:

```
static ssize_t dev_attribute_show(struct kobject *kobj,
                struct kobj_attribute *attr, char *buf);
static ssize_t dev_attribute_store(struct kobject *kobj,
                struct kobj_attribute *attr, char *buf);
```

When a sysfs attribute is read from or written to, the _show and _store functions are called respectively. The sysfs.h header file defines the following helper macros that make defining the attributes more straightforward:

- __ATTR(_name,_mode,_show,_store): Long-hand version. You must pass the attribute variable name _name, the access mode _mode (e.g., 0664 for read/write access, except for *others*), the pointer to the show function _show, and the pointer to the store function _store.

- __ATTR_RO(_name): Short-hand read-only attribute macro. You must pass the attribute variable name _name, and the macro sets the _mode to be 0444 (read-only) and the _show function to be _name_show.

- __ATTR_WO(_name) and __ATTR_RW(_name): Write-only and read/write. Not available in Linux 3.8.x, but added in 3.11.x.

Listing 16-5 provides the full source code for the enhanced GPIO button LKM. It may appear to be quite lengthy, but you will see that this is because there is a lot of comment, and additional `printk()` calls so that you can see exactly what is happening as the code is executing. This example builds on the work in Listing 16-3; it also includes an LED so that you can observe interaction at the circuit itself.

Listing 16-5: /exploringrpi/chp16/button/button.c

```c
#include <linux/init.h>
#include <linux/module.h>
#include <linux/kernel.h>
#include <linux/gpio.h>          // Required for the GPIO functions
#include <linux/interrupt.h>     // Required for the IRQ code
#include <linux/kobject.h>       // Using kobjects for the sysfs bindings
#include <linux/time.h>          // Using clock to measure button press times
#define   DEBOUNCE_TIME 200      // The default bounce time -- 200ms

MODULE_LICENSE("GPL");
MODULE_AUTHOR("Derek Molloy");
MODULE_DESCRIPTION("A simple Linux GPIO Button LKM for the RPi");
MODULE_VERSION("0.1");

static bool isRising = 1;               // rising edge default IRQ property
module_param(isRising, bool, S_IRUGO);  // S_IRUGO read/not changed
MODULE_PARM_DESC(isRising, " Rising edge = 1 (default), Falling edge = 0");

static unsigned int gpioButton = 27;    // default GPIO is 27
module_param(gpioButton, uint, S_IRUGO);  // S_IRUGO can be read/not changed
MODULE_PARM_DESC(gpioButton, " GPIO Button number (default=27)");

static unsigned int gpioLED = 17;       // default GPIO is 17
module_param(gpioLED, uint, S_IRUGO);   // S_IRUGO can be read/not changed
MODULE_PARM_DESC(gpioLED, " GPIO LED number (default=17)");

static char    gpioName[8] = "gpioXXX"; // null terminated default string
static int     irqNumber;               // used to share the IRQ number
static int     numberPresses = 0;       // store number of button presses
static bool    ledOn = 0;               // used to invert the LED state
static bool    isDebounce = 1;          // use to store debounce state
static struct timespec ts_last, ts_current, ts_diff;  // nano precision

// Function prototype for the custom IRQ handler function
static irq_handler_t  erpi_gpio_irq_handler(unsigned int irq,
                            void *dev_id, struct pt_regs *regs);

/** @brief A callback function to output the numberPresses variable
 *  @param kobj a kernel object device that appears in the sysfs filesystem
 *  @param attr the pointer to the kobj_attribute struct
 *  @param buf the buffer to which to write the number of presses
 *  @return return the total number of characters written to the buffer
 */
```

```c
static ssize_t numberPresses_show(struct kobject *kobj,
                             struct kobj_attribute *attr, char *buf) {
   return sprintf(buf, "%d\n", numberPresses);
}

/** @brief A callback function to read in the numberPresses variable */
static ssize_t numberPresses_store(struct kobject *kobj, struct
                    kobj_attribute *attr, const char *buf, size_t count) {
   sscanf(buf, "%du", &numberPresses);
   return count;
}

/** @brief Displays if the LED is on or off */
static ssize_t ledOn_show(struct kobject *kobj, struct kobj_attribute *attr,
                    char *buf) {
   return sprintf(buf, "%d\n", ledOn);
}

/** @brief Displays the last time the button was pressed - manually output*/
static ssize_t lastTime_show(struct kobject *kobj,
                          struct kobj_attribute *attr, char *buf){
   return sprintf(buf, "%.2lu:%.2lu:%.2lu:%.9lu \n", (ts_last.tv_sec/3600)%24,
         (ts_last.tv_sec/60) % 60, ts_last.tv_sec % 60, ts_last.tv_nsec );
}

/** @brief Display the time diff in the form secs.nanosecs to 9 places */
static ssize_t diffTime_show(struct kobject *kobj,
                          struct kobj_attribute *attr, char *buf){
   return sprintf(buf, "%lu.%.9lu\n", ts_diff.tv_sec, ts_diff.tv_nsec);
}

/** @brief Displays if button debouncing is on or off */
static ssize_t isDebounce_show(struct kobject *kobj,
                          struct kobj_attribute *attr, char *buf){
   return sprintf(buf, "%d\n", isDebounce);
}

/** @brief Stores and sets the debounce state */
static ssize_t isDebounce_store(struct kobject *kobj, struct kobj_attribute
                          *attr, const char *buf, size_t count){
   unsigned int temp;
   sscanf(buf, "%du", &temp);        // use temp var for correct int->bool
   gpio_set_debounce(gpioButton,0);
   isDebounce = temp;
   if(isDebounce) { gpio_set_debounce(gpioButton, DEBOUNCE_TIME);
      printk(KERN_INFO "ERPi Button: Debounce on\n");
   }
   else { gpio_set_debounce(gpioButton, 0);  // set the debounce time to 0
      printk(KERN_INFO "ERPi Button: Debounce off\n");
   }
   return count;
}
```

```
/**  Use these helper macros to define the name and access levels of the
 *  kobj_attributes. The kobj_attribute has an attribute attr (name and mode),
 *  show and store function pointers. The count variable is associated with
 *  the numberPresses variable and it is to be exposed with mode 0664 using
 *  the numberPresses_show and numberPresses_store functions above. Using mode
 *  0664 gives user and group read/write access, but others only read access.
 *  Recent kernel versions do not like write permission settings for "others".
 */
static struct kobj_attribute count_attr = __ATTR(numberPresses, 0664,
            numberPresses_show, numberPresses_store);
static struct kobj_attribute debounce_attr = __ATTR(isDebounce, 0664,
            isDebounce_show, isDebounce_store);

/**  The __ATTR_RO macro defines a read-only attribute. There is no need to
 *  identify that the function is called _show, but it must be present.
 *  __ATTR_WO can be  used for a write-only attribute but only Linux 3.11.x+
 */
static struct kobj_attribute ledon_attr = __ATTR_RO(ledOn);
static struct kobj_attribute time_attr  = __ATTR_RO(lastTime);
static struct kobj_attribute diff_attr  = __ATTR_RO(diffTime);

/**  The erpi_attrs[] is an array of attributes that is used to create the
 *  attribute group below. The attr property of the kobj_attribute is used
 *  to extract the attribute struct
 */
static struct attribute *erpi_attrs[] = {
      &count_attr.attr,         // the number of button presses
      &ledon_attr.attr,         // is the LED on or off?
      &time_attr.attr,          // button press time in HH:MM:SS:NNNNNNNNN
      &diff_attr.attr,          // time difference between last two presses
      &debounce_attr.attr,      // is debounce state true or false
      NULL,
};

/**  The attribute group uses the attribute array and a name, which is
 *  exposed on sysfs -- in this case it is gpio27, which is automatically
 *  defined in the erpi_button_init() function below using the custom kernel
 *  parameter that can be passed when the module is loaded.
 */
static struct attribute_group attr_group = {
      .name  = gpioName,       // the name generated in erpi_button_init()
      .attrs = erpi_attrs,     // the attributes array defined just above
};

static struct kobject *erpi_kobj;

/** @brief The LKM initialization function */
static int __init erpi_button_init(void){
   int result = 0;
   unsigned long IRQflags = IRQF_TRIGGER_RISING;
   printk(KERN_INFO "ERPi Button: Initializing the button LKM\n");
   sprintf(gpioName, "gpio%d", gpioButton);   // create /sys/erpi/gpio27
```

```
   // create the kobject sysfs entry at /sys/erpi
   erpi_kobj = kobject_create_and_add("erpi", kernel_kobj->parent);
   if(!erpi_kobj){
      printk(KERN_ALERT "ERPi Button: failed to create kobject mapping\n");
      return -ENOMEM;
   }
   // add the attributes to /sys/erpi/ e.g., /sys/erpi/gpio27/numberPresses
   result = sysfs_create_group(erpi_kobj, &attr_group);
   if(result) {
      printk(KERN_ALERT "ERPi Button: failed to create sysfs group\n");
      kobject_put(erpi_kobj);               // clean up remove entry
      return result;
   }
   getnstimeofday(&ts_last);                 // set last time to current time
   ts_diff = timespec_sub(ts_last, ts_last); // set the initial time diff=0

   // set up the LED. It is a GPIO in output mode and will be on by default
   ledOn = true;
   gpio_request(gpioLED, "sysfs");           // gpioLED is hardcoded to 17
   gpio_direction_output(gpioLED, ledOn);    // set in output mode
   gpio_export(gpioLED, false);              // appears in /sys/class/gpio/
   gpio_request(gpioButton, "sysfs");        // set up the gpioButton
   gpio_direction_input(gpioButton);         // set up as an input
   gpio_set_debounce(gpioButton, DEBOUNCE_TIME); // ddebounce the button
   gpio_export(gpioButton, false);           // appears in /sys/class/gpio/
   printk(KERN_INFO "ERPi Button: button state: %d\n",
           gpio_get_value(gpioButton));
   irqNumber = gpio_to_irq(gpioButton);
   printk(KERN_INFO "ERPi Button: button mapped to IRQ: %d\n", irqNumber);
   if(!isRising){                            // if kernel param isRising=0
      IRQflags = IRQF_TRIGGER_FALLING;       // set on falling edge
   }
   // This next call requests an interrupt line
   result = request_irq(irqNumber,                  // the interrupt number
                        (irq_handler_t) erpi_gpio_irq_handler,
                        IRQflags,             // use custom kernel param
                        "erpi_button_handler", // used in /proc/interrupts
                        NULL);                // the *dev_id for shared
lines
   return result;
}

static void __exit erpi_button_exit(void){
   printk(KERN_INFO "ERPi Button: The button was pressed %d times\n",
           numberPresses);
   kobject_put(erpi_kobj);           // clean up, remove kobject sysfs entry
   gpio_set_value(gpioLED, 0);       // turn the LED off, device was unloaded
   gpio_unexport(gpioLED);           // unexport the LED GPIO
   free_irq(irqNumber, NULL);        // free the IRQ number, no *dev_id reqd
   gpio_unexport(gpioButton);        // unexport the Button GPIO
   gpio_free(gpioLED);               // free the LED GPIO
   gpio_free(gpioButton);            // free the Button GPIO
   printk(KERN_INFO "ERPi Button: Goodbye from the ERPi Button LKM!\n");
}
```

```
/** @brief The GPIO IRQ Handler function
 *  This function is a custom interrupt handler that is attached to the GPIO
 *  above. The same interrupt handler cannot be invoked concurrently as the
 *  interrupt line is masked out until the function is complete. This function
 *  is static as it should not be invoked directly from outside of this file.
 *  @param irq    the IRQ number that is associated with the GPIO
 *  @param dev_id the *dev_id that is provided -- used to identify device.
 *  Not used in this example as NULL is passed.
 *  @param regs   h/w specific register values -- used for debugging.
 *  return returns IRQ_HANDLED if successful -- return IRQ_NONE otherwise.
 */
static irq_handler_t erpi_gpio_irq_handler(unsigned int irq,
                          void *dev_id, struct pt_regs *regs){
   ledOn = !ledOn;                      // invert LED on each button press
   gpio_set_value(gpioLED, ledOn);   // set the physical LED accordingly
   getnstimeofday(&ts_current);      // get the current time as ts_current
   ts_diff = timespec_sub(ts_current, ts_last);   // determine the time diff
   ts_last = ts_current;             // store current time as ts_last
   printk(KERN_INFO "ERPi Button: The button state is currently: %d\n",
                gpio_get_value(gpioButton));
   numberPresses++;                  // count number of presses
   return (irq_handler_t) IRQ_HANDLED;  // announce IRQ was handled correctly
}

// This next calls are  mandatory -- they identify the initialization function
// and the cleanup function (as above).
module_init(erpi_button_init);
module_exit(erpi_button_exit);
```

The code in Listing 16-5 is described by the comments throughout; however, there are a few more points that are worth mentioning:

- Three module parameters are made available to be configured as the LKM is loaded (isRising, gpioButton, and gpioLED). The use of LKM parameters is described in the first LKM example. This allows you to define different GPIOs for the button input and LED output; their sysfs mount names are automatically adjusted. The code also allows for a falling-edge interrupt in place of the default rising-edge interrupt.

- There are five attributes associated with the kobject entry (erpi). These are diffTime, isDebounce, lastTime, ledOn, and numberPresses. They are all read-only, with the exception of isDebounce and numberPresses (i.e., can be set to any value, e.g., reset to 0).

- The erpi_gpio_irq_handler() function performs the majority of the timing. The clock time is stored and the inter-press time is determined each time that the interrupt is handled.

The module can be loaded in falling-edge mode and tested using the following:

```
pi@erpi ~/exploringrpi/chp16/button $ make
pi@erpi ~/exploringrpi/chp16/button $ sudo insmod button.ko
pi@erpi ~/exploringrpi/chp16/button $ cd /sys/erpi/gpio27/
pi@erpi /sys/erpi/gpio27 $ ls -l
total 0
-r--r--r-- 1 root root 4096 Nov  9 01:37 diffTime
-rw-rw-r-- 1 root root 4096 Nov  9 01:37 isDebounce
-r--r--r-- 1 root root 4096 Nov  9 01:37 lastTime
-r--r--r-- 1 root root 4096 Nov  9 01:37 ledOn
-rw-rw-r-- 1 root root 4096 Nov  9 01:37 numberPresses
pi@erpi /sys/erpi/gpio27 $ cat numberPresses
0
pi@erpi /sys/erpi/gpio27 $ cat numberPresses
3
pi@erpi /sys/erpi/gpio27 $ cat diffTime
15.074734332
pi@erpi /sys/erpi/gpio27 $ cat lastTime
01:46:36:030219769
pi@erpi /sys/erpi/gpio27 $ sudo sh -c "echo 0 > numberPresses"
pi@erpi /sys/erpi/gpio27 $ cat numberPresses
0
pi@erpi /sys/erpi/gpio27 $ cd ~/exploringrpi/chp16/button/
pi@erpi ~/exploringrpi/chp16/button $ sudo rmmod button
```

Note the permissions (0664) on the isDebounce and numberPresses entries, which correlate directly with the program code in Listing 16-5. Ensure that you exit the /sys/erpi/ directory before unloading the module; otherwise, you will cause a kernel panic if you perform an operation such as ls.

The simultaneous output in the kernel logs (/var/log/kern.log) is as follows:

```
... erpi kernel: [337494.885001] ERPi Button: Initializing the button LKM
... erpi kernel: [337494.885473] ERPi Button: button state: 0
... erpi kernel: [337494.885490] ERPi Button: button mapped to IRQ: 507
... erpi kernel: [337598.271292] ERPi Button: The button state is currently: 1
... erpi kernel: [337598.979912] ERPi Button: The button state is currently: 1
... erpi kernel: [337599.559666] ERPi Button: The button state is currently: 1
... erpi kernel: [337710.564613] ERPi Button: The button was pressed 3 times
... erpi kernel: [337710.564963] ERPi Button: Goodbye from the ERPi Button LKM!
```

Enhanced LED GPIO Driver LKM

The final example in this chapter is a driver for controlling an LED using an LKM. This example is designed to introduce the use of kernel threads, kthreads, which can be started in response to an event that occurs in our LKM. In this example, kthreads are used to flash the LED at a user-defined interval.

Kernel Threads

The general structure of the code in this example is provided in Listing 16-6. This is a reasonably unusual thread in the Linux kernel, as we require a specific sleep time to get a consistent flash period. The return of resources to the kthread scheduler is usually performed with a call to `schedule()`.

The call to `kthread_run()` is quite similar to the user space pthread function `pthread_create()`. (See the section on POSIX threads in Chapter 6.) The `kthread_run()` call expects a pointer to the thread function (`flash()` in this case), the data to be sent to the thread (NULL in this case), and the name of the thread, which is displayed in the output from a call to `top` or `ps`. The `kthread_run()` function returns a `task_struct`, which is shared between the various functions within this C file as `*task`.

Listing 16-6: An Outline of the kthread Implementation

```c
#include <linux/kthread.h>
static struct task_struct *task;         // pointer to the thread task

static int flash(void *arg) {
    while(!kthread_should_stop()){        // kthread_stop() call returns true
        set_current_state(TASK_RUNNING);  // prevent sleeps temporarily
        ...                               // state change instructions (flash)
        set_current_state(TASK_INTERRUPTIBLE);    // sleep but can be awoken
        msleep(...);                               // millisecond sleep
    }
}

static int __init erpi_LED_init(void) {
    task = kthread_run(flash, NULL, "LED_flash_thread");    // start kthread
    ...
}

static void __exit erpi_LED_exit(void) {
    kthread_stop(task);                  // Stop the LED flashing kthread
    ...
}
```

The final source code is not presented here because it is lengthy and very similar to Listing 16-5, but with the addition of the thread code. It is available at `/chp16/LED/led.c`, and the comments therein provide a full description of the integration of all the tasks. However, there are a few additional points worth noting:

- An enumeration, called modes, is used to define the three possible running states. When you are passing commands to a LKM, you have to very carefully parse the data to ensure it is valid and within range. In this example, the string command can only be one of three values ("on", "off", or "flash"), and the period value must be between 2 and 10000 (ms).

- The `kthread_should_stop()` evaluates to a `bool`. When a function such as `kthread_stop()` is called on the kthread, this function will wake and return true. This causes the kthread to run to completion, after which the return value from the kthread will be returned by the `kthread_stop()` function.

This example can be built and executed as follows, where you can increase the frequency of the flash by reducing the sleep period to be 2ms so that we can observe the CPU loading, using the following call:

```
pi@erpi ~/exploringrpi/chp16/LED $ make
pi@erpi ~/exploringrpi/chp16/LED $ sudo insmod led.ko
pi@erpi ~/exploringrpi/chp16/LED $ cd /sys/erpi/led17/
pi@erpi /sys/erpi/led17 $ ls -l
total 0
-rw-rw-r-- 1 root root 4096 Nov  9 02:25 blinkPeriod
-rw-rw-r-- 1 root root 4096 Nov  9 02:25 mode
pi@erpi /sys/erpi/led17 $ cat blinkPeriod
1000
pi@erpi /sys/erpi/led17 $ sudo sh -c "echo 100 > blinkPeriod"
pi@erpi /sys/erpi/led17 $ cat blinkPeriod
100
```

The CPU loading of this LKM is quite low at ~0.0% of CPU when it is flashing with a sleep duration of 2ms:

```
pi@erpi /sys/erpi/led17 $ sudo sh -c "echo 2 > blinkPeriod"
pi@erpi /sys/erpi/led17 $ ps aux|grep LED
root 27618 0.0 0.0   0 0 ?   D  02:57  0:00   [LED_flash_threa]
pi@erpi /sys/erpi/led17 $ sudo sh -c "echo off > mode"
pi@erpi /sys/erpi/led17 $ sudo sh -c "echo on > mode"
pi@erpi /sys/erpi/led17 $ sudo sh -c "echo flash > mode"
pi@erpi /sys/erpi/led17 $ cd ~/exploringrpi/chp16/LED
pi@erpi ~/exploringrpi/chp16/LED $ sudo rmmod led
```

The kernel logs give the following output:

```
... erpi kernel: [350999.939466] ERPi LED: Initializing the ERPi LED LKM
... erpi kernel: [350999.940003] ERPi LED: Thread has started running
... erpi kernel: [351159.656388] ERPi LED: Thread has run to completion
... erpi kernel: [351159.656656] ERPi LED: Goodbye from the ERPi LED LKM!
```

The results for this approach are quite impressive when compared to similar tests in Linux user space. The results have a consistent ~50% duty cycle, and the range of frequency values is quite consistent.

Conclusions

Remember that the kernel is essentially a program—a big and complex program, but a program nevertheless. It is possible to make changes to the kernel code, recompile, redeploy, and then reboot, which is quite a lengthy process.

This chapter has exposed you to writing your own Linux loadable kernel modules (LKMs), which allow you to create binary code that can be loaded and unloaded from the kernel at run time.

The examples that are presented in this chapter are for the purpose of learning. It is unlikely that you would ever need to write a LKM to control pushbuttons or LEDs directly. For example, there are GPIO-keys and GPIO-LEDs drivers available in Linux to provide sophisticated kernel support for such circuits. However, these examples should provide a strong basis for other embedded LKM development tasks.

For further information on GPIO kernel programming under Linux, see:

- The GPIO Sysfs Interface for User Space: `tiny.cc/erpi1603`

- GPIO Interfaces (in Kernel Space): `tiny.cc/erpi1604`

- *Linux Kernel Development*, Robert Love, Addison-Wesley Professional, Third edition (July 2, 2010), 978-0672329463

Summary

After completing this chapter, you should be able to do the following:

- Write a basic Linux loadable kernel module (LKM) that can receive a kernel argument.

- Build, load, and unload a custom LKM on a desktop machine and/or the RPi.

- Undertake the steps required to build a module for embedded devices that can control GPIOs.

- Appreciate some of the concepts required to build LKMs on an embedded Linux device, such as interrupts, kobjects, and kernel threads.

Index